WITHDRAWN

British
Columbia
& the Canadian Rockies

**Yukon
Territory**
p244

**British
Columbia**
p106

Alberta
p40

THIS EDITION WRITTEN AND RESEARCHED BY

John Lee, Korina Miller, Ryan Ver Berkmoes

Contents

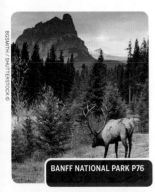

BGSMITH / SHUTTERSTOCK ©

BANFF NATIONAL PARK P76

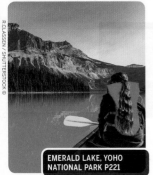

R.CLASSEN / SHUTTERSTOCK ©

EMERALD LAKE, YOHO
NATIONAL PARK P221

Contents

Welcome to BC & the Canadian Rockies

Sigh-inducing mountains, mist-shrouded forests and epic tooth-and-claw wildlife: this is Canada's legendary outdoor wonderland. And it's served alongside a full menu of distinctive, ever-inviting communities.

Grand Outdoors

A large, lung-filling intake of breath is the usual response upon encountering this region's sparkling diorama of sawtooth peaks, dense forests, ethereally colored lakes and crenulated coastlines ever-whipped by dramatic ocean waves. It's the vast scale of this seemingly infinite wilderness that strikes most visitors, triggering a humble response in the face of nature's grand scheme. There has never been a more persuasive argument for blissful tree-hugging – but of course when it comes to the area's astonishing wildlife, from whales and grizzlies to wolves and moose, it's best to keep the hugging to a minimum.

Epic Adrenaline Rushes

Steely calved West Coasters have been discovering ways to interact with the outdoors for decades, and there are hundreds of operators here that can help you do the same. From skiing or mountain biking on Whistler's spectacular slopes, to hiking the flower-studded alpine meadows in Banff National Park or surfing with the beach nuts in Tofino, there are more ways to work up a sweat here than you can swing a paddle at. Which reminds us: these are prime kayaking waters, with tree-lined lakes and rough-and-tumble ocean routes that will call your name like a siren song.

Urban Adventures

It's easy to be seduced by the outdoors but this region also offers sparkling city action. Urbanites will enjoy the Edmonton arts scene and Calgary's contemporary cowboy vibe, but it's British Columbia that offers the best city-based shenanigans, with two very different approaches. Provincial capital Victoria frames its cool scene with a backdrop of historic buildings, while Vancouver, Western Canada's largest city, provides a full menu of tasty neighborhoods that are ripe for exploration. From slick Yaletown to hipster-haven Main St and from cool Gastown to the 'gayborhood' of West End, you'll never run out of places to explore on foot.

Foodie Explorations

Discovering its local foodie mojo in recent years, this region serves up a full menu of juicy seafood, ranchland steaks, and fruit and vegies piled high at an ever-expanding array of seasonal farmers markets. Restaurants fall over themselves to showcase these delicious local ingredients, but it's Vancouver, possibly Canada's top dining city, that leads the way. Alongside the Okanagan Valley and its wine-producing satellite regions, and a surge in regional artisan distilleries, there's been a tidal wave of new microbreweries, making BC the country's top destination for traveling beer fans.

Why I Love BC & the Canadian Rockies

By John Lee, Writer

My first Western Canada visit included spine-tingling sightings of deer, bears and a hulking moose that eyed me quizzically from the edge of a Rocky Mountains forest. Coming from the UK, I was deeply and instantly smitten. But although I've now lived here for 25 years, I'm still enthralled. Whether you're gliding along the mountain-framed coastline on a ferry, watching eagles whirling en masse overhead, or simply sipping a hoppy ale in a tiny Vancouver micro-brewery tasting room, it's easy to believe this is the best place on earth.

For more about our writers, see p320

Above: Moraine Lake (p86), Banff National Park

British Columbia & the Canadian Rockies

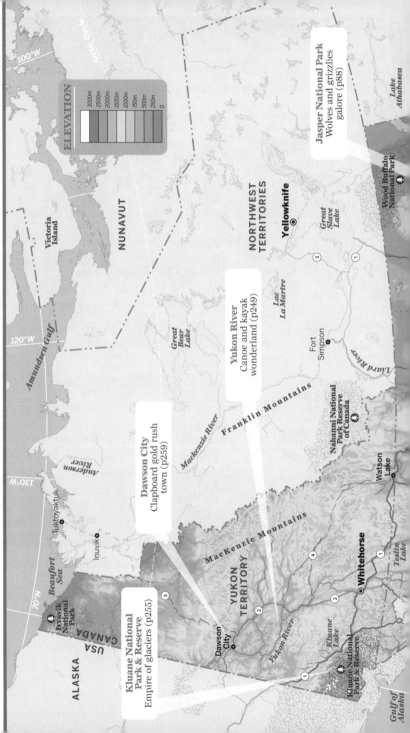

ELEVATION

3000m
2500m
2000m
1500m
1000m
750m
500m
250m
0

Jasper National Park
Wolves and grizzlies galore (p88)

Yukon River
Canoe and kayak wonderland (p249)

Dawson City
Clapboard gold rush town (p259)

Kluane National Park & Reserve
Empire of glaciers (p255)

NUNAVUT

Victoria Island

NORTHWEST TERRITORIES

Yellowknife ◉

Great Slave Lake

Wood Buffalo National Park

Lake Athabasca

Great Bear Lake

Lac La Martre

Fort Simpson ◉

Liard River

Franklin Mountains

Nahanni National Park Reserve of Canada

Watson Lake ◉

Amundsen Gulf

Mackenzie River

MacKenzie Mountains

YUKON TERRITORY

Whitehorse ◉

Teslin Lake

Kluane Lake

Kluane National Park & Reserve

Yukon River

Beaufort Sea

Tuktoyaktuk ◉

Inuvik ◉

Anderson River

Ivvavik National Park

ALASKA

USA
CANADA

Dawson City ◇

Gulf of Alaska

Arctic Circle

100°W

120°W

130°W

70°N

400 km
200 miles

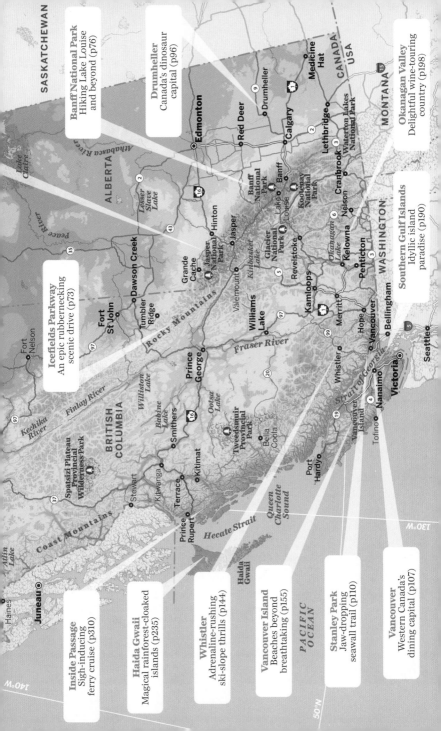

Banff National Park
Hiking Lake Louise
and beyond (p76)

Drumheller
Canada's dinosaur
capital (p96)

Okanagan Valley
Delightful wine-touring
country (p198)

Icefields Parkway
An epic rubbernecking
scenic drive (p73)

Southern Gulf Islands
Idyllic island
paradise (p190)

Inside Passage
Sigh-inducing
ferry cruise (p310)

Haida Gwaii
Magical rainforest-cloaked
islands (p235)

Whistler
Adrenaline-rushing
ski-slope thrills (p144)

Vancouver Island
Beaches beyond
breathtaking (p155)

Stanley Park
Jaw-dropping
seawall trail (p110)

Vancouver
Western Canada's
dining capital (p107)

SASKATCHEWAN

ALBERTA

BRITISH COLUMBIA

MONTANA

WASHINGTON

CANADA
USA

Edmonton
Red Deer
Calgary
Medicine Hat
Lethbridge
Drumheller
Cranbrook
Nelson
Kelowna
Penticton
Banff National Park
Kootenay National Park
Lake Louise
Banff
Glacier National Park
Revelstoke
Kamloops
Merritt
Hope
Vancouver
Whistler
Victoria
Nanaimo
Bellingham
Seattle
Waterton Lakes National Park

Jasper National Park
Jasper
Hinton
Grande Cache
Valemount
Williams Lake
Prince George
Tumbler Ridge
Fort St John
Dawson Creek
Fort Nelson

Smithers
Terrace
Kitimat
Kitwanga
Stewart
Prince Rupert
Bella Coola
Port Hardy
Tofino

Spatsizi Plateau
Provincial Wilderness Park

Tweedsmuir Provincial Park

Juneau
Haines

Rocky Mountains
Coast Mountains

Peace River
Finlay River
Kechika River
Athabasca River
Fraser River
Lake Claire
Lesser Slave Lake
Williston Lake
Babine Lake
Ootsa Lake
Kinbasket Lake
Okanagan Lake
Atlin Lake

Queen Charlotte Sound
Hecate Strait
Strait of Georgia
Vancouver Island
Haida Gwaii

PACIFIC OCEAN

140°W
130°W
50°N

BC & the
Canadian Rockies'
Top 15

Wildlife-Spotting in Jasper

1 Elk nose their way around the town's edge, nervous deer dart between the trees and seemingly giant bald eagles swoop high overhead. The dramatic mountain setting of Jasper National Park (p88) is enough to keep most camera-wielding visitors content, but the surfeit of wandering wildlife makes you feel like you're part of a 3-D nature documentary. If you're lucky, you might even spot the show's stars: grizzly bears snuffling for berries alongside the highway or, across the other side of a river, wolves silently tracking their next fresh-catch ungulate.

Stanley Park's Seawall Promenade

2 It sometimes takes awestruck visitors to remind Vancouverites they have Canada's finest urban park (p110) on their doorstep. But when you grow up alongside a 404-hectare temperate rainforest swath that's lined with multitudinous hiking and biking trails, it's easy to think everyone is just as lucky. Stroll the park's 8.8km wave-licked, forest-backed seawall and you'll soon deplete your camera battery. But save some juice for the beady-eyed birdlife (especially the blue herons) around Lost Lagoon and a panoramic pyrotechnic sunset at Third Beach.

ALEKTE / SHUTTERSTOCK ©

KARAMYSH / SHUTTERSTOCK ©

Skiing the Slopes at Whistler

3 This scenic, alpine village is frosted with icicles and filled with excited visitors throughout the winter season; but it's the powder-hugging slopes (p144) that are the main adrenaline lure here. Whistler was the host mountain for the 2010 Winter Olympics, and you can emulate your Lycra-clad heroes on some of North America's most popular downhills. Then it's back to the village to compare your bruises, Tweet about your black-diamond abilities and imbibe a few Irish coffees. As the fireplace blazes nearby, watch the skiers outside and plan your next run.

Hiking in Lake Louise & Beyond

4 Alongside craggy mountains that are like nature's skyscrapers, the lakes of Banff National Park (p68) are so ethereally colored you begin to wonder if Mother Nature has Photoshop. And it's not just legendary Lake Louise (p84) that catches the eye; visitors can't help sighing at the visuals almost everywhere they turn. Head off the beaten path a little and you'll also find hidden waterfalls, alpine meadows teeming with flowers, and wildlife-packed valleys – all under blue skies ringed with majestic peaks.
Moraine Lake (p86)

Dawson City

5 You're bouncing around for hours on some rickety old bus on the Klondike Hwy in the height of summer, not knowing whether it's three o'clock in the morning or afternoon, and suddenly you arrive in Dawson City (p259). Women in frilled skirts, straight out of a gambling hall, chat on wooden sidewalks, and a buzz of stories about gold can be heard everywhere – it's like stumbling into another world. True adventurers will try the infamous Sourtoe cocktail, and all who encounter Dawson City will brag about their experience forevermore.

Sailing the Inside Passage

6 Relax in the sunlight on the deck of a BC Ferries' day-long sailing (p310) to Prince Rupert, a nautical odyssey guaranteed to slow heart rates to hibernation levels. With a gentle breeze on your face, you let the Inside Passage diorama roll past: sharp crags, tree-blanketed islands, red-capped lighthouses and tiny shoreline settlements with exotic names such as Namu and Dryad Point. Then the captain stirs you from your hypnotic relaxation with an announcement: grab your camera and try not to miss that pod of passing orcas.

7

8

Driving the Icefields Parkway

7 Canada's most rugged scenic driving route, the Icefields Parkway (p73), is handily located between Banff and Jasper. In an ideal world you'd have a designated driver so you could keep your eyes off the road: colossal peaks rise alongside, while the promise of spotting wildlife – especially bears and bighorn sheep – keeps things lively. There's even a celebrated attraction to lure you from your car: take a guided hike on the Athabasca Glacier for an appreciation of how this craggy region was shaped.

Dining in Vancouver

8 While a fancy dinner in Vancouver (p124) once meant rubbery steaks and baked potatoes, in recent years this metropolis has become one of Canada's foodie capitals. Start with Granville Island Public Market for inspiration; grab lunch at one of the city's 100-plus food carts; then enjoy dinner at your pick of numerous top-notch restaurants. From shimmering seafood to authentic taquerias, Canada's best Asian cuisine and farm-to-table joints, the choice is only limited by your straining belt buckle.
Granville Island Public Market (p113)

Wine Tasting in the Okanagan

9 Enjoying a winding trip around the bucolic, vine-striped hills of the Okanagan Valley (p198) region is the best way for any tipple-loving visitor to spend their time in Western Canada. There are dozens of wineries to tempt you, from legendary faves such as Mission Hill Family Estate and Quails' Gate Winery to Summerhill Pyramid Winery. One thing is certain: you won't go thirsty. Nominate a designated driver, and don't forget to dine: many winery tasting rooms are adjoined by excellent restaurants.

Paddling the Yukon River

10 Relive the days of craggy-faced frontier folk by canoeing (or kayaking) from Whitehorse to Dawson City. Not for the faint-hearted and certainly not for the uninitiated, the 16-day Yukon River paddle (p249) will glide you past rough-and-tumble rocky landscapes lined with critter-packed forests. Keep your eyes on the water: you might feel like panning for gold if you spot something glittery. For a less-intense taster, take a trip from Dawson City to Eagle City, Alaska: it's just three days.

RONNIE CHUA / SHUTTERSTOCK ©

CHRIS HOWEY / SHUTTERSTOCK ©

SARA WINTER / SHUTTERSTOCK ©

Dino Digging in Drumheller

11 For kids who are in that wide-eyed dinosaur phase, there's no better place on the planet than this desert-fringed Alberta town (p96). You'll find Canada's best dino museum here, which will indulge your child's insatiable need for facts, plus there's a chance to do a fossil dig and for photo ops with the world's biggest T rex – a 26m fiberglass fella who looms over the town like Godzilla. You're also in the heart of the Badlands here, an eerie, evocative landscape where it's frighteningly easy to imagine giant roaming reptiles.
World's Largest Dinosaur (p97)

Aboriginal Culture in Haida Gwaii

12 Taking the ferry from Prince Rupert to this dagger-shaped archipelago (p235) is like traveling to another country: perfect preparation for experiencing a place that is like no other in Canada. Visit the Haida Heritage Centre and immerse yourself in the rich artistic culture of the people who have called this area home for thousands of years. You'll find intricately carved artworks, and current practitioners illustrate the energetic resurgence of Haida culture. The magical Gwaii Haanas National Park Reserve offers mystical reminders of ancient communities. Totem pole

Beachcombing on Vancouver Island

13 The largest populated landmass off North America's west coast, Vancouver Island (p155) has a rich array of life-affirming beaches. There's the surf-whipped golden expanses around Tofino and the family-friendly bays around Parksville. But it's the remote north coast that wins our vote. Pushing though the dense, ferny undergrowth of Cape Scott, you'll emerge blinking in the sunlight on a white-sand beach that's studded with tide pools and rocky outcrops. The waves lap invitingly while the shorebirds swoop around as if they own the place. Cox Bay Beach (p177)

Kluane National Park & Reserve

14 From the Alaska Hwy you get just a glimpse of the beauty within the 22,015-sq-km Kluane National Park and Reserve (p255), one of the largest protected wilderness areas in the world. Hike for a day to the interior – or board a helicopter – and you'll witness an otherworldly landscape that has garnered Unesco World Heritage site recognition. Huge icebergs break off glaciers and the water at the shoreline freezes; this is nature in all its grand, terrifying beauty. Kluane Lake (p255)

Hopping the Southern Gulf Islands

15 The islands (p190) off BC's southern mainland wink invitingly whenever you get close to the coastline. But it's only when you take a short-hop ferry trip that you realize how different life is here. Your body clock will readjust to island time and you'll feel deeply tranquil. If you have time, visit more than one of these islands; each has a unique feel. Start with the Saturday Market on Salt Spring Island, then consider a delightful kayak excursion around Mayne or a cycling weave on Galiano.

Need to Know

For more information, see Survival Guide (p299)

Currency
Canadian dollar ($)

Language
English

Visas
Not required for visitors from the US, the Commonwealth and most of Western Europe for stays up to 180 days. Required by those from more than 130 other countries.

Money
ATMs widely available. Credit cards accepted in most hotels and restaurants.

Cell Phones
Local SIM cards can be used in unlocked European and Australian GSM cell (mobile) phones. Other phones must be set to roaming.

Time
Pacific Time in most of BC and the Yukon (GMT/UTC minus eight hours); Mountain Time in Alberta (GMT/UTC minus seven hours)

When to Go

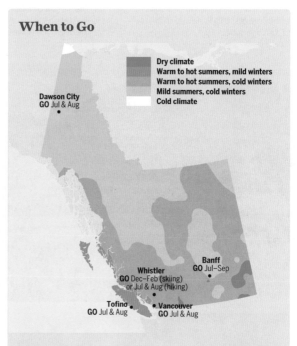

Dry climate
Warm to hot summers, mild winters
Warm to hot summers, cold winters
Mild summers, cold winters
Cold climate

Dawson City
GO Jul & Aug

Banff
GO Jul–Sep

Whistler
GO Dec–Feb (skiing)
or Jul & Aug (hiking)

Tofino
GO Jul & Aug

Vancouver
GO Jul & Aug

High Season
(Jul & Aug)

➡ Sunshine and warm weather prevail throughout the region.

➡ Accommodation prices reach a peak, sometimes 50% above low season.

➡ Festivals and farmers markets abound in communities large and small.

Shoulder
(Apr & May, Sep & Oct)

➡ Temperatures are cool but comfortable; rain is typical.

➡ Crowds and accommodation prices reduced.

➡ Attraction hours outside cities are often reduced.

Low Season
(Nov–Mar)

➡ Snow and cold (below freezing) temperatures, especially in the north.

➡ The year's best hotel rates, except in ski resorts.

➡ Outside resorts and cities, visitor attractions may be closed.

Useful Websites

Hello BC (www.hellobc.com) The province's official Destination BC visitor website profiles regions and attractions and has an accommodations booking service.

Tourism Alberta (www.travelalberta.com) Official visitor site for the province, with downloadable resources and accommodations listings.

Tourism Yukon (www.travelyukon.com) Official visitor site, packed with inspiring images and suggested experiences to help with planning a trip.

Lonely Planet (www.lonelyplanet.com/british-columbia) Destination information, hotel bookings, traveler forum and more.

Important Numbers

Dial all 10 digits when making local calls. Add 1 to the front of the number if the call is long-distance, even if it's within the same region (eg calling Whistler from Vancouver).

Country code	☏1
International access code	☏011
Emergency	☏911
Local directory assistance	☏411

Exchange Rates

Australia	A$1	$0.99
Euro zone	€1	$1.46
Japan	¥100	$1.29
NZ	NZ$1	$0.94
UK	UK£1	$1.74
US	US$1	$1.30

For current exchange rates, see www.xe.com.

Daily Costs

Budget: Less than $100

➡ Dorm bed: $30–45

➡ Campsite: $25–40

➡ Food court or street-food vendor lunch: $8-10

➡ Transit day pass: $5–10

Midrange: $100–300

➡ En suite standard hotel room: $150–200

➡ Meal in midrange local restaurant (excluding drinks): $15–25

➡ Admission to top local attraction: $15–30

➡ Two drinks in local pub: $15–20

Top End: More than $300

➡ Boutique hotel or posh B&B: $250

➡ Three-course meal in good restaurant (excluding drinks): $75

➡ Car hire: up to $75 per day

➡ Ski day pass: $60–100

Opening Hours

The following standard opening hours apply throughout the region. Note that many attractions have reduced hours in the low season.

Banks 9am or 10am to 5pm Monday to Friday; some open 9am to noon Saturday

Bars 11am to midnight or later; some only open from 5pm

Post offices 9am to 5pm Monday to Friday; some open on Saturday

Restaurants breakfast 7am to 11am, lunch 11:30am to 2pm, dinner 5pm to 9:30pm (8pm in rural areas)

Shops 10am to 5pm or 6pm Monday to Saturday; noon to 5pm Sunday; some (especially in malls) open to 8pm or 9pm Thurday and/or Friday

Arriving in BC & the Rockies

Vancouver International Airport (p136) SkyTrain's Canada Line runs to the city center every few minutes from 5.10am to 12.57am ($7.75 to $10.50). Travel time around 25 minutes. Taxis to city center hotels cost $35 to $45 (30 minutes).

Calgary International Airport (p67) Allied Airport Shuttles runs shuttle buses every 30 minutes from 8am to midnight ($15). Downtown-bound taxis cost around $40 (30 minutes).

Edmonton International Airport (p54) Sky Shuttle airport buses run to city hotels ($18), taking about 45 minutes to reach downtown. Taxis from the airport cost about $50.

Getting Around

BC is a vast region, and while there are many transportation options available, car travel is the most popular way to get around beyond the cities.

Train Efficient commuter rail transit is available in Vancouver, Calgary and Edmonton, with limited VIA Rail and luxurious Rocky Mountaineer scenic services in other regions.

Car A good intercity highway system encourages road trips. Vehicles are essential in many far-flung areas.

Bus Good public transit systems in big cities, with intercity services provided by Greyhound and smaller operators throughout the region.

Ferries Many short and long-haul routes provided by BC Ferries along the western coastline.

For much more on **getting around**, see p309

If You Like...

Wildlife-Watching

Jasper National Park Often stopping the traffic, the local elk – plus abundant deer, eagles and bears – make it perfectly clear who's in charge here. (p88)

Icefields Parkway Dramatic Rocky Mountains highway drive lined with jaw-dropping wildlife. (p73)

Telegraph Cove Whale-watching operators line the region but this Vancouver Island departure point is an evocative favorite. (p188)

Khutzeymateen Grizzly Bear Sanctuary Around 50 of the salmon-snaffling furballs call the area around Prince Rupert home. (p234)

Northern Lights Wolf Centre A Yoho National Park refuge for the lupine critters, this is a great spot to learn all about them. (p220)

Adrenaline Rushes

Whistler Canada's favorite ski resort is also packed with summer activities, from zip-lining to white-water rafting. (p144)

Tofino Idyllic beaches and a spectacular wave-whipped waterfront make this Canada's top surfing spot. (p178)

Canmore Perfect for Rockies-region rock fans, the climbing here – including winter waterfall climbs – is superb. (p71)

Athabasca Glacier Avoid the too-easy bus tour and take a breathtaking guided hike on the icy surface, crampons included. (p73)

Mt Washington Vancouver Island's ski resort transforms into a muscle-popping mountain-biking magnet in summer. (p184)

Breathtaking Views

Maligne Lake A picture-postcard, peak-ringed lake vista that may well be the Rockies' most famous view. (p89)

Lake Louise Gobsmackingly gorgeous colors at one of the Rockies' signature viewpoints. (p86)

Stanley Park seawall Shoreline promenade with views of shimmering, mountain-framed ocean. (p110)

Tombstone Territorial Park The Yukon's rugged splendor, lined with sawtooth crags. (p259)

Tofino's beaches Wave-whipped and eye-poppingly beautiful sandy swaths on Vancouver Island's wild west coast. (p178)

Historic Sites

Fort Langley National Historic Site The colonial outpost where BC was signed into existence offers a kid-friendly smorgasbord of activities and costumed 'residents.' (p138)

North Pacific Cannery National Historic Site You can feel the ghosts of canning workers past at this hulking, wood-built former plant near Prince Rupert. (p234)

Head-Smashed-In Buffalo Jump With the region's most eye-popping name, this fascinating aboriginal interpretive center in Alberta recalls the local heritage. (p98)

Klondike National Historic Sites The gritty gold-rush days are on every street corner in Dawson City, where frontier buildings stud the area like shiny nuggets. (p259)

Barkerville Historic Town Stroll the streets of a pioneer town that once housed thousands of grubby frontiersmen, plus the occasional woman. (p231)

Craigdarroch Castle Victoria's delightful stately home, complete with evocative, antique-lined rooms. (p155)

Lip-Smacking Eats

Vancouver restaurants
Canada's top dining scene is also its most diverse – from the best seafood to authentic Asian adventures. (p124)

Granville Island Public Market
A stroll-worthy buffet of deli and bakery goods, and fresh fruit and vegetable treats. (p113)

Cowboy cuisine Alberta beef is second to none and Calgary is the steak capital of Canada. (p63)

Salt Spring Saturday Market
The biggest and best of hundreds of alfresco farmers and craft markets around the region. (p190)

Cowichan Bay Idyllic waterfront spot to sample goods from artisan food producers and local wines. (p170)

Cornucopia Whistler's annual multiday party for food and wine fans. (p147)

PLAN YOUR TRIP IF YOU LIKE...

Top: Khutzeymateen Grizzly Bear Sanctuary (p234)
Bottom: Maligne Lake (p89), Jasper National Park

Month by Month

January

It's peak ski season, with winter-wonderland views and temperatures below freezing in Alberta, the Yukon and much of BC; the south coast is warmer, with rain likely.

Winter Okanagan Wine Festival

BC's gable-roofed Sun Peaks Resort warms up with the taste-tripping winter Okanagan Wine Festival (www.thewinefestivals.com) where ice wine is the major draw. Saturday night's progressive tasting crawl is essential.

Ice Magic Festival

Banff National Park's spectacular Lake Louise shoreline is the snow-swathed backdrop for this annual ice-carving event (www.banfflakelouise.com/area-events). Dress warmly and take lots of photos.

February

Spring may be in the air in southern BC but winter dominates much of the region. Dressing for rain on the coast is advised, with thick coats (and hip flasks) suggested elsewhere.

Yukon Quest

This legendary 1600km dog-sled race (www.yukonquest.com) zips from Whitehorse to Fairbanks, Alaska, through darkness and -50°C temperatures. It's a hardy celebration of the tough north.

Chinese New Year

This giant Vancouver celebration (www.vancouver-chinatown.com) takes place in January or February depending on the calendar each year, and it always includes plenty of color, great food and a large parade.

Vancouver International Wine Festival

The city's oldest and finest wine party (www.vanwinefest.ca) makes grape-fans out of everyone in late February with its jam-packed, slightly tipsy galas and tasting events. (p121)

March

The ski season is winding up, although there are still plenty of great slopes to barrel down. Southern coastal cities and Vancouver Island are rainy.

April

Spring is budding across the region, but it's also a good time to bag deals on accommodations and snow gear in all the shoulder-season ski resorts.

World Ski & Snowboard Festival

One of the biggest festivals in Whistler, this hugely popular nine-day celebration (www.wssf.com) includes daredevil demonstrations, outdoor concerts and a smile-triggering party atmosphere.

May

Blossoms (and farmers markets) open up across the region, while bears are stirring from hibernation. Expect warmish sun in the south, and rain and late-season snow elsewhere.

Vancouver Craft Beer Week

Celebrating the region's surging microbrewing scene, Vancouver's top booze event showcases BC's best beer makers with tastings, parties and dinners. Arrive parched and drink deep. (p121)

June

Even in colder BC and Alberta areas, the sun will be out, making this the time to consider donning your hiking boots and embracing the great outdoors.

☆ Bard on the Beach

This joyously West Coast approach to Shakespeare features up to four plays staged in a lovely tented complex on Vancouver's mountain-framed waterfront. Runs to September, but book ahead. (p283)

☆ Vancouver International Jazz Festival

Mammoth music celebration on stages around the city, including a generous helping of free outdoor shows. Book in advance for top-drawer acts. (p121)

Penticton Elvis Festival

Dozens of hip-swinging impersonators invade this small Okanagan town for a three-day celebration of all-things Elvis; it's a kitschtastic, eye-popping party. (p206)

July

It's summertime and the living is easy for visitors who enjoy warming their skin under sunny skies. It's also crowded, which means Banff and Jasper are super-busy.

Canada Day Celebrations

Canada's version of July 4 in the US is the country's flag-waving annual birthday party held on July 1. Expect celebrations across the region, with the biggest at downtown Vancouver's Canada Place.

Calgary Stampede

North America's biggest rodeo event is a rocking cavalcade of cowboy culture where everyone finds their inner wearer of Stetson cowboy hats. (p60)

August

Crowds (and hotel prices) are at their summer peak. Interior BC can be hot and humid, while the rest of the region is generally pleasantly warm and sunny.

☆ Edmonton International Fringe Theatre Festival

Canada's oldest and largest fringe fest lures thousands to Edmonton's Old Strathcona neighborhood for a multiday buffet of short but eclectic comic and dramatic performances. (p47)

Discovery Days

The pioneer-era streets of Dawson City are home to the Yukon's most popular annual event, a colorful week-long party of parades, games, races and movie shows recalling the region's gold-rush heyday. (p263)

Pride Week

Canada's biggest and boldest pride event, this Vancouver party includes a massive mardi-gras-style parade that draws thousands. Galas, fashion shows and saucy shenanigans keep things lively. (p121)

Crankworx

It's definitely summer in Whistler when the ski slopes become a bike park and this massive annual celebration of mountain-bike antics kicks off. (p147)

September

A great month to visit: the crowds have departed, there are still stretches of sunny weather, and the colors are turning to fall's golden hues.

☆ Rifflandia

Victoria's coolest music festival lures local and visiting hipsters with dozens of live-music happenings at venues throughout the city. (p159)

☆ Vancouver International Film Festival

Starting at the end of September, this is the city's favorite movie-watching event. Book ahead for indie, international and documentary flicks. (p121)

October

Fall foliage is in full blaze but temperatures are cooling, while rain is returning to coastal communities that have forgotten where they put their umbrellas.

Fall Okanagan Wine Festival

The Okanagan Valley's largest annual wine festival (www.thewinefestivals.com) sees more than 150 flavorful events spread throughout the region's autumnal-hued rolling hills.

November

The ski season kicks off for some resorts while southern cities are unpacking their waterproofs. Temperatures are just a taste of what's to come for winter, though.

🍷 Cornucopia

November in Whistler means this indulgent multiday showcase of great food and wine. It's also a chance to dress up and schmooze at decadent parties. (p147)

December

The region is in festive mood with a full advent calendar of Christmas events. Temperatures are dropping and the snow is back in many areas.

🎄 Santa Claus Parade

The best reason to stand outside in the Vancouver cold, this huge parade includes floats, marching bands as well as an appearance by the jolly old elf himself. (p122)

Itineraries

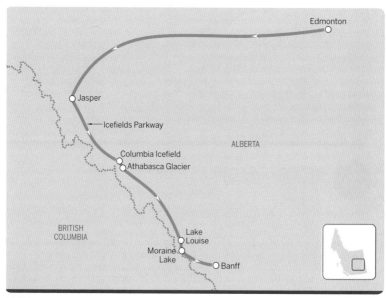

 Epic Rockies Roll

The Rockies are a must-see for any visitor to Canada. You can cover all the jaw-dropping highlights on this grand tour.

Start in gateway city **Edmonton**, spending a couple of days shopping, perusing museums and puttering around the Old Strathcona neighborhood. Then hit Hwy 16 westward for your first big drive: a half-day weave to **Jasper**. Check in for three nights, grab a beer at the Jasper Brewing Co and plan your wildlife-watching around the region's lakes and mountains. Next it's time to move on southwards via the **Icefields Parkway**, Canada's most scenic drive. It's shadowed by looming crags and studded with inquisitive bighorn sheep that peer at you from the clifftops. Stop en route at the **Columbia Icefield** and take a hike or truck tour on the **Athabasca Glacier**. After lunch at the nearby Columbia Icefield Discovery Centre, continue southwards to **Lake Louise**: take photos and wander the shoreline, saving time for a visit to the equally dazzling **Moraine Lake** a short drive away. Back in the car, you'll soon be in **Banff**. Treat yourself to a fancy hotel sleepover and spend the rest of your visit hiking flower-covered alpine trails and marveling at the epic Unesco-listed landscapes.

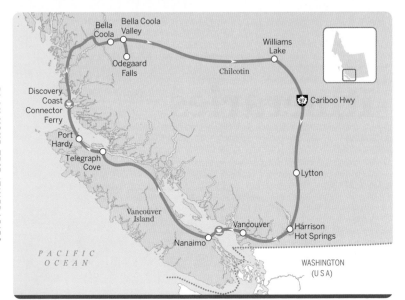

2 WEEKS BC's Grand Circle Tour

There's much more to BC than its cities; take your time and head off the beaten path via this trip-of-a-lifetime circle odyssey.

Start your journey of discovery in **Vancouver**. Catch the BC Ferries vessel from West Vancouver's Horseshoe Bay for the short ride to **Nanaimo**, where you can sink into 'island time' and start to enjoy Vancouver Island's laid-back culture – it's distinctly more independent and small-town than the mainland. After spending the night, head north on Hwy 19, taking an eastward detour to waterfront **Telegraph Cove**. Take a whale- or bear-watching tour here and check in for a night in one of the restored cottage buildings (book ahead in summer).

Continue north on Hwy 16 the next morning and check in to **Port Hardy** for the night: if it's still daylight, consider an oceanfront hike. You'll have an early start to catch the **Discovery Coast Connector Ferry** the next morning (summer only) but it's well worth it: a languid all-day odyssey of coastline gazing with the ever-present promise of spotting eagles, whales, seals and more from the sun-dappled deck.

Arriving in tiny **Bella Coola**, which sits at the end of a long fjord, find yourself a rustic retreat for a few nights in the **Bella Coola Valley**. Spend your days exploring trails alongside huge old cedars and make the hike to pounding **Odegaard Falls**. Go for a river float and lose count of the grizzlies wandering the shores. When you leave, tackle The Hill, a thrill-ride for drivers, and head east through the lonely **Chilcotin** area. Stop at the alpine waters of the little lakes along the way or just take any little tributary road and lose civilization – what little there is – altogether. At **Williams Lake** say yee-ha to cowboy country.

Turn south on the Cariboo Hwy (Hwy 97), otherwise known as the Gold Rush Trail. The road follows the route of the first pioneers and gold seekers who settled in BC's unforgiving interior. From **Lytton**, head out for white-water rafting on the Fraser and Thompson Rivers. After these chilly waters, warm up with a soak in **Harrison Hot Springs**. From here, it's an easy drive back to Vancouver on Hwy 1.

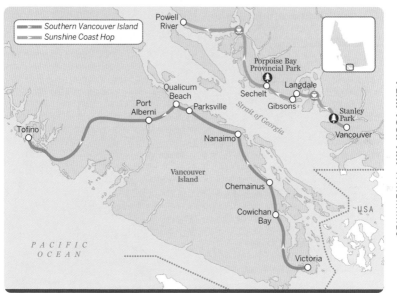

Southern Vancouver Island
1 WEEK

The BC capital is the perfect gateway for exploring the charms of Vancouver Island on a winding weave that links several inviting communities. Start with two nights in capital city **Victoria**, giving yourself plenty of time to explore museums, galleries and historic streets before departing northwards on day three via Hwy 1. Take your time weaving through the Malahat Mountain region but allow time for a long lunch in the idyllic waterfront community of **Cowichan Bay**. It'll be hard to tear yourself away (there are B&Bs in the area if you can't manage it) but worthwhile to continue north to **Chemainus**, a former logging town now adorned with dozens of murals. It's not far to your sleepover in **Nanaimo**, the island's second city, where there are some decent restaurants and a popular museum. Next morning, you'll be off to check out the friendly oceanfront communities of **Parksville** and **Qualicum Beach** – ideal for beachcombing fans – before veering inland via Hwy 4 towards the dramatic west coast. **Port Alberni** is a handy lunch stop, but you'll likely be eager to thread through the winding mountain roads to **Tofino**. Spend several nights here soaking up BC's wild Pacific Ocean coastline.

Sunshine Coast Hop
4 DAYS

It's hard to get lost on this easy escape from Vancouver; the area's only highway links all the main communities in a linear fashion. Drive on and enjoy a laid-back, island-like ambience. Head north from **Vancouver** on Hwy 99 through **Stanley Park** and make for West Van's Horseshoe Bay ferry terminal. Take the Sunshine Coast vessel to **Langdale** and roll off onto Hwy 101, the region's main artery. After a few minutes you'll be in artist-studded **Gibsons**, an ideal lunch stop – waterfront dining recommended. Check into a local B&B, then take an early-evening kayak tour on the glassy ocean. Rejoining Hwy 101 the next morning, continue on to **Sechelt** and consider a shoreline forest hike in **Porpoise Bay Provincial Park**. If you're lucky, you'll also catch the summertime Farmers & Artisans Market, a great way to meet the locals. Stay in a waterfront B&B here, then hit the road early the next morning. You'll have a short ferry hop before arriving in **Powell River**. The area's town town, it combines old-school heritage and a funky young population. Stick around for a day or two of hiking and mountain biking, and be sure to toast your trip at Townsite Brewing.

6 DAYS Due North

Southern BC lures the lion's share of visitors but the north will always be calling your name; dive in with this scenic weave. From downtown **Vancouver**, drive through Stanley Park on Hwy 1 then join Hwy 99 northwards to **Whistler**. Spend the afternoon hiking or mountain biking the summer trails and check into one of the resort's grand hotels. Next morning, continue north via Pemberton; keep your eyes peeled for towering Mt Currie. You're now in the heart of cowboy country but it's probably too late to swap your car for a horse. After a five-hour drive, stop for two nights in a **Williams Lake** motel. Time your visit for the rodeo and you'll have a blast, or book a local white-water rafting tour. Next, hit Hwy 97 towards Prince George; the heart of northern BC's logging country is about three hours away but stop off – via Hwy 26 – at **Barkerville**, an evocative re-creation of an old pioneer town. After a **Prince George** layover, start early on the four-hour Yellowhead Hwy drive to **Smithers**, an artsy little town with cool sleepover options. Your final four-hour drive the next day delivers you eastward to **Prince Rupert**, northern BC's loveliest town.

2 WEEKS Yukon Bound

The best way to experience the north is to hop in a car and immerse yourself in some rugged Yukon-flavored wilderness. Spend two days exploring **Prince Rupert** – the Museum of Northern BC and North Pacific Cannery are must-sees – before rolling onto an Alaska Marine Highway ferry to Haines, AK. It's a two-day odyssey that cruise ships charge a comparative arm and leg for. Back on dry land, spend a night in **Haines, AK**. From here, you'll be (almost) on the doorstep of one of the world's largest protected wildernesses. Accessed 249km away via the BC town of **Haines Junction**, **Kluane National Park & Reserve** is a vast Unesco-recognized realm of glaciers and mountains. Weave through the park and cross over again into Alaska briefly to access the **Top of the World Hwy**. Continue on your merry way to **Dawson City**, Yukon's coolest old-school town and center of gold-rush heritage. Stick around for two nights to enjoy the historic ambience, then head south on the Klondike Hwy for 538km to **Whitehorse**, the territory's capital. There are enough museums and galleries here to keep you occupied for another Yukon night.

Lake O'Hara (p222), Yoho National Park

Plan Your Trip
National & Regional Parks

Canada-bound visitors often imagine towering sawtooth peaks, huge mirrored lakes and wildlife-packed forests. But what they're really imagining is British Columbia, the Rockies and the Yukon, home of the country's most awe-inspiring landscapes. From Unesco World Heritage sites to breathtaking local gems, here's how to explore this region's awesome natural wonders.

Best of National & Regional Parks

Best for Hiking

Pacific Rim National Park Reserve; Banff, Jasper and Waterton Lakes National Parks.

Best for Skiing

Banff National Park; Strathcona, Mt Seymour and Cypress Provincial Parks.

Best for Rock Climbing

Kootenay National Park; Stawamus Chief Provincial Park, Horne Lake Caves Provincial Park.

Best for Wildlife-Watching

Jasper, Banff, Wood Buffalo and Yoho National Parks.

Best for Kayaking

Gwaii Haanas and Gulf Islands National Park Reserves; Bowron Lake Provincial Park.

Best Unesco World Heritage Sites

Banff, Jasper and Yoho National Parks; Dinosaur Provincial Park.

Best National Historic Sites

Banff Park Museum; Head-Smashed-In Buffalo Jump; Gulf of Georgia Cannery.

pared to its smaller sibling Jasper to the north. While Banff offers close proximity to dramatic mountains lapped by ethereally blue lakes, Jasper is the region's center for watching incredible wildlife in its natural setting. And by wildlife, we mean the epic kind: bears, wolves, moose et al. That's not to say there isn't great mountain scenery in Jasper or wildlife aplenty in Banff, of course, but knowing this difference may help you choose between the two, if you have to.

High alpine adventure awaits around Rogers Pass in BC's Glacier National Park, while among the highlights of craggy and uncrowded Yoho National Park are spectacular glacier-fed lakes such as O'Hara and Emerald.

In BC's Kootenays region, a multitude of microclimates are crammed into the comparatively tiny Kootenay National Park, which straddles the border between BC and Alberta. Gateway town Radium Hot Springs is an ideal spot for a soak here. Alternatively, consider Mt Revelstoke National Park, where you can hike wildlife-studded trails to the summit for breathtaking views over the Selkirks.

Alberta is home to three other visually thrilling national parks: sublimely tranquil Waterton Lakes, with its off-the-beaten-path location and network of alpine day hikes; giant Wood Buffalo, where the world's last free-roaming herd of wood bison hang out; and Elk Island, a comparatively small park close to Edmonton that bristles with elk and plains bison.

The Yukon has two remote national parks: Vuntut and Ivvavik.

Where to Go

National Parks

These carefully protected parks of national and internationally recognized importance are the region's must-see attractions. They typically have excellent visitor centers and do all they can to maintain a successful balance between wilderness preservation and enabling tourist access.

Banff was designated Canada's first national park in 1885. It offers something for everyone, which is just as well given the number of visitors it draws. But its grand size means you can still escape into the backcountry and be wowed by its sheer-faced glacier-cut peaks. It is often com-

TOP FIVE PROVINCIAL PARKS

Try to weave in a visit to some of these parks. You won't regret it... and you'll have major bragging rights when you get back home.

➡ Bowron Lake Provincial Park (p231)

➡ Dinosaur Provincial Park (p98)

➡ Garibaldi Provincial Park (p142)

➡ Kokanee Glacier Provincial Park (p227)

➡ Strathcona Provincial Park (p186)

Top: Red Rock Canyon
(p102), Waterton Lakes
National Park

Bottom: Pacific Rim
National Park Reserve
(p177)

ELENA ELISSEEVA / SHUTTERSTOCK ©

These are also national park reserves in BC and the Yukon. These are areas that have been earmarked as national parks, pending the settlement of aboriginal land claims. They are managed in much the same way as national parks, with entry fees, visitor centers, and various environmental rules and regulations.

For more information on the region's national parks and national park reserves, visit the Parks Canada website (www.pc.gc. ca). And if you're Alberta-bound, pick-up Lonely Planet's *Banff, Jasper & Glacier National Parks* guide.

Provincial & Territorial Parks

Alberta has more than 500 provincial parks and protected areas (see www. albertaparks.ca for listings) while BC is home to almost double that number (visit www.bcparks.ca for information). Among the highlights are Alberta's fossil-rich Dinosaur Provincial Park, and Writing-on-Stone Provincial Park with its fascinating 3000-year-old aboriginal artworks.

The Yukon Territory's large parks (described in detail at www.env.gov. yk.ca) are called 'territorial parks.' These include the rugged, bird-studded Herschel

Island Territorial Park, also known as Qikiqtaruk to the native people who still hold it sacred, and Tombstone Territorial Park, a wild and windswept area of broad tundra-cloaked valleys and jaw-dropping hiking trails.

Alongside the region's provincial and territorial parks systems there are hundreds of city parks and some of them are among Western Canada's must-see highlights. These include Calgary's Prince's Island Park, and Vancouver's spectacular waterfront Stanley Park, one of North America's finest urban greenspaces.

Plan Ahead

When (& How) to Go

Summer is the most popular time to visit Western Canada's parks, but that can mean rubbing shoulders with waves of camera-wielding tour groups at hot spots such as Banff, Jasper and Lake Louise. There are three ways to deal with this and ensure the magic of your visit: when you arrive at the aforementioned must-see spots, head off the beaten path and onto a less-trafficked trail. Secondly, add some less-visited national park gems to your

PARK TOUR OPERATORS

OPERATOR	ACTIVITIES	WHERE?	MORE INFORMATION
Athabasca Glacier Icewalks	guided glacier hikes	Columbia Icefield	www.icewalks.com
Brewster Travel	bus tours	Banff, Jasper and Columbia Icefield	www.brewster.ca
Discover Banff Tours	guided tours of the region, including wildlife tours	Banff	www.banfftours.com
North Island Daytrippers	guided hikes to North Vancouver Island's remote parks	North Vancouver Island	www.islanddaytrippers.com
Maple Leaf Adventures	multiday tours around Haida Gwaii (& beyond) via vintage sailboat	Haida Gwaii	www.mapleleafadventures.com
Tonquin Valley Adventures	multiday horseback riding tours	Jasper	www.tonquinadventures.com
Up North Adventures	kayaking, guided bike trips & winter sports	Yukon	www.upnorthadventures.com
Yamnuska Mountain Adventures	guided rock climbing	Lake Louise	www.yamnuska.com

GREAT NATIONAL PARK HIKES

PARK	TRAIL	LENGTH (KM)	LEVEL
Banff	Lake Agnes	3.4	medium-hard
Jasper	Discovery Trail	8	easy
Pacific Rim	West Coast Trail	75	hard
Waterton Lakes	Carthew-Alderson Trail	19	medium
Yoho	Lake O'Hara Alpine Circuit	12	medium

visit: Yoho and Glacier, for example, are great Rockies parks with far fewer visitors. Thirdly, consider visiting outside the summer peak. Locals prefer late spring and early fall, at which times there are no crowds, the colors are even more vibrant and the wildlife-watching – from post-hibernation bears to rutting elk and bighorn sheep – is often spectacular.

Fees

National parks charge for entry, and you'll need to pay and display your pass in your car. In large parks such as Banff and Jasper passes are purchased at tollbooth-style barriers; in parks such as Vancouver Island's Pacific Rim National Park Reserve they're purchased at ticket machines or visitor centers. Daily fees go up to $9.80/4.90/19.60 per adult/child/family. If you're planning on visiting several parks over a number of days or weeks, the Parks Canada Discovery Pass is recommended. It costs $67.70/33.30/136.40 per adult/child/family and covers unlimited entry for 12 months to national parks and historic sites. The family passes include entry for groups of up to seven people (two adults only).

The BC Parks system does not charge admission. In addition, parking fees – which were first levied in 2002 – have since been scrapped at most BC parks.

The Yukon Parks system does not charge for entry to its parks.

When You're There

Bears & Bugs

Wildlife attacks on humans in Canada's parks are rare but you need to be aware that you are going to be encroaching on areas that some scarily large critters call home. While animals such as elk and deer may seem perfectly at ease with the cameras pointing their way in busy parks such as Banff and Jasper, Parks Canada works very hard to keep animals and humans from becoming too used to each other.

During spring and summer, black flies and mosquitoes blight the interior and northern reaches of BC, Alberta and the Yukon. The cumulative effect of scores of irritated, swollen bites can wreck your park trip. Bringing a liquid insect repellent is a necessity, as is camping in a tent with a zippered screen. In clearings, along shorelines or anywhere there's a breeze you'll be safe from most bugs.

Driving Tips

Weather and driving conditions can change rapidly in the parks and wilderness areas of Western Canada. If you're driving in winter, expect snow. In addition, when you see an animal by the side of the road, the etiquette is to slow down and alert other drivers by using your hazard lights.

Plan Your Trip

Outdoor Activities

There's no shortage of world-class hiking, mountain biking, skiing, kayaking, rafting and climbing in this region, and the experience will likely be one you'll brag about for years. Alternatively, rub shoulders with the friendly locals and watch someone else do all the work by taking in some popular spectator sports.

Top Short Hikes

Discovery Trail, Jasper

An easy 8km circle around the town with a high possibility of elk and deer sightings.

Lake Louise, Banff

Stroll around the shoreline or hit the 1.6km uphill trail to the Big Beehive lookout for a grand panorama.

Stanley Park, Vancouver

A delightful tree-lined 8.8km seawall trail with ocean and mountain vistas.

Athabasca Glacier, Columbia Icefields

Uphill tramping on a crunchy glacier, complete with breathtaking views.

Hiking

Hiking in this region ranges from a leisurely wander around Vancouver's salt-sprayed Stanley Park seawall to tramping across glaciers under blue sky at the Columbia Icefield between Banff and Jasper. Whatever your level, a walk through nature is a must here.

On Vancouver Island, the spectacular Pacific Rim National Park Reserve offers some of nature's most dramatic vistas: swaying old-growth rainforest fringes white-sand beaches. The park's signature West Coast Trail (p178) is a challenge but it's one you'll never forget: rock-face ladders, stream crossings and wandering wildlife, plus the occasional passing whale, make it a rite of passage for serious hikers. It links to the lesser-known Juan de Fuca Marine Trail (p169) if you want to keep going. Atop Vancouver Island, the remote North Coast Trail (p189) is equally dramatic but far less crowded: it's ideal if you like hiking without having other people around. You'll have a similar crowd-free ramble on the mainland's hidden gem, the Sunshine Coast Trail (p154).

In contrast, the Okanagan's Kettle Valley Rail Trail (p212) meanders over towering wooden trestle bridges in Myra Canyon. It offers hikers the perfect chance to explore this beautiful valley without having to worry about traffic or steep hills. It's also a popular bike route.

In the Rockies, you'll find a hikers' paradise that even non-walkers will be blown away by. There are plenty of easy short walks at popular attractions such as the impossibly azure Lake Louise (p84). And turn your back on the tour-bus crowds, and you'll suddenly feel at one with the vastness of nature. Banff is the hot spot for Rockies hikers and its top routes include the Sawback Trail (p79) and the Hoodoos Trail (p77). Also consider a couple of lesser-known Alberta gems: Northover Ridge in Kananaskis Country and Banff's challenging but awesome Caldron Lake area.

Those who love challenges should check out the steep and difficult Chilkoot Trail (p258) in the northern Yukon region; it is still lined with the detritus of those who desperately tried to seek their fortune in the gold rush. Elsewhere in the territory, Kluane National Park and Reserve and Tombstone Territorial Park offer world-class challenges, and spectacles such as thousands of migrating caribou.

Cycling & Mountain Biking

Mountain biking is as huge as the mountains in BC and the Rockies. This is the birthplace of 'freeride,' which combines downhill and dirt-jumping.

Home to some of BC's best technical trails, Rossland and its West Kootenay surroundings is a pedal-tastic hot spot. Vying for the 'mountain biking capital of Canada' moniker, Squamish (see www.sorca.ca) also offers dozens of off-road trails twisting around the mountain-framed region; expect a freerider's fantasy, with narrow boards and logs spanning lush, wet ferns. You'll find a similar setup – and a burgeoning local scene – on Vancouver's North Shore: see www.nsmba.ca for more information on this area. The Sunshine Coast's Powell River is also worth checking out; see www.bikepowellriver.ca. Visit www.mountainbikingbc.ca for an introduction to the wider region.

Whistler has the province's best-organized mountain-bike park, with jumps, beams and bridges winding

PEDAL-TASTIC NELSON

Freeriding pedalheads have plenty of favorite spots in British Columbia and the Rockies, but many also enjoy the bikey ambience of just hanging out in a cool community. In the heart of the Kootenay Rockies region, Nelson – which many locals will tell you is the coolest small town in BC – fits the bill perfectly. The historic downtown area is lined with funky hangouts (an after-ride Nelson Brewing beer is recommended), while the surrounding area is striped with great trails, from the epic downhill of Mountain Station to the winding Svoboda Road Trails in West Arm Provincial Park.

through 200km of maintained downhill trails. In summer, the resort hosts the giant Crankworx festival (www.crankworx.com), a pedal-packed nirvana of contests, demos and live music.

Back in the urban sprawl, Victoria is one of Canada's best cycling cities, closely trailed by Vancouver, which has been carving out new citywide routes for cyclists in recent years. The city has also just introduced a public bike share scheme.

In the Rockies region, Canmore and Banff are biking hot spots, with the latter offering a good combination of road and off-road options and plenty of wildlife-spotting opportunities. And if you're in the Yukon, there are more than 800km of trails extending from Whitehorse.

Skiing & Snowboarding

If you're staying in Vancouver, you can be on the slopes within a 30-minute drive of downtown, and Whistler, one of North America's most popular ski resorts, is just another hour away.

But many would argue that there's even better skiing to be found in the east of BC, where vast swaths of mountains – especially in the Kootenays – are annually covered by 10m or more of snow. In fact, this region now boasts the 'Powder Hwy,' a marketing moniker for a series of roads linking the major ski resorts.

SKIING HOT SPOTS

Some of the region's best ski resorts:

Apex Mountain Resort (p205) Known for its plethora of double-black-diamond and technical runs (the drop is more than 600m), as well as gladed chutes and vast powdery bowls. Near Penticton.

Banff National Park ski resorts Three excellent mountain resorts, Ski Banff@ Norquay (p79), Sunshine Village (p77) and the Lake Louise Ski Area (p86), offer 250 runs of every description. Sunshine Village is the most popular of these resorts.

Big White Ski Resort (p213) BC's highest ski resort features 118 runs, and is excellent for downhill and back-country skiing. The drop is 777m and you can night ski. Near Kelowna.

Cypress Mountain (p120) The 2010 Winter Olympic snowboarding and freestyle skiing venue, with dozens of runs and 19km of cross-country runs. Near Vancouver.

Fernie Alpine Resort (p224) With 142 runs across five large bowls, there's plenty of virgin powder where you can leave your mark. Near the town of Fernie.

Grouse Mountain (p120) A 30-minute drive from Vancouver, Grouse is a favorite for night skiing and snowboarding.

Kicking Horse Mountain Resort (p220) Many of the runs here are rated advanced or expert. A gondola gives you a great vantage over the 1260m vertical of this relatively snow-heavy location. Near Golden.

Kimberley Alpine Resort (p226) A good all-round resort – especially if you like smaller ones with comparatively minimal nightlife. Near the town of Kimberley.

Mt Seymour (p119) Some 1000m up, this North Shore provincial resort offers popular runs including Brockton, Mystery Peak and Mushroom Junior Park. Also family-friendly tobogganing. Near North Vancouver.

Mt Washington Alpine Resort (p184) Vancouver Island's main ski resort; there are dozens of runs, plus cross-country trails and a snowshoe park. Near Comox.

Revelstoke Mountain Resort (p217) BC's newest major resort has 65 runs with a focus on intermediate and advanced runs. Heli-skiing operators can take you out to track-free bowls across the ranges. Near Revelstoke.

Silver Star Mountain Resort (p214) With 131 runs and a pioneer-town atmosphere, Silver Star has 12 lifts and a 760m vertical drop. Near Vernon.

Sun Peaks Resort (p198) BC's second-largest resort, with three mountains and more than 100 runs. Snowshoeing, dog sledding and Nordic skiing also available. Near Kamloops.

Whistler-Blackcomb (p145) This world-famous, dual-mountain paradise was the host resort for the 2010 Winter Olympic Games. Its lifts include the 4.4km-long gondola linking Mts Whistler and Blackcomb. Boasts 37 lifts and more than 200 runs to keep the international crowds happy.

Elsewhere in the province, the Okanagan has resorts such as Sun Peaks, Apex and Big White, boasting good snow year after year. Snowpack here ranges from 2m to 6m-plus, depending on how close the resort is to the Pacific Ocean.

You'll slide through stunning postcard-worthy landscapes in the Rockies, especially at Sunshine Village in Banff National Park. But for amazing cross-country skiing, head to Canmore: its popular trails were part of the Canadian Winter Olympics held in Calgary in 1988.

For insights and resources covering the region and beyond, check the website of the Canadian Ski Council (www.skicanada.org).

Rock Climbing & Mountaineering

All those inviting crags you've spotted on your trip are an indication that Western Canada is a major climbing capital, ideal for both short scales and multiday crampon-picking jaunts.

Near Banff, the Rocky Mountain resort town of Canmore is an ideal first stop, no matter what your skill level. Climbing stores, the Yamnuska Mountain Adventures climbing school (p71) and thousands of limestone sport climbs within a 30-minute radius make this a one-stop shop for rock fans.

Further west, BC's Squamish 'Chief' is the highlight – and one of the most challenging climbs – of a burgeoning local scene that includes dozens of area peaks. Tap the local scene via Squamish Rock Guides (p143).

If mountaineering is more your thing, the Rockies are, not surprisingly, a hot spot. On the border with BC, Mt Assiniboine is the Matterhorn of Canada. Other western classics include Alberta's Mt Edith Cavell, in Jasper; BC's Mt Robson; and Sir Donald in the Rockies. Closer to Vancouver, Garibaldi Peak, in Garibaldi Provincial Park, lures many city-based climbers for weekend jaunts.

If you need a guide, check in with the excellent Alpine Club of Canada (www.alpineclubofcanada.ca).

Diving

Justly famous for its superb, albeit chilly conditions, BC features three of the top-ranked ocean dive spots in the world: Vancouver Island, the Sunshine Coast and the Gulf Islands. It's best to go in winter, when the plankton has decreased and visibility is at its best.

The water temperature drops to between 7°C and 10°C in winter; in summer, it may reach 15°C. Expect to see a full range of marine life, including oodles of crabs, from tiny hermits to intimidating kings. If you're lucky you may also encounter seals and sea lions or bizarre creatures such as wolf eels and large Pacific octopuses.

Popular Vancouver Island dive areas include Port Hardy and Campbell River, but Nanaimo also lures many with its aquatic wildlife and its three sunk-to-order navy vessels that are now vibrant marine habitats.

For more information as well as operator listings for BC, see www.diveindustry association.com.

Water Sports

Inland

The 116km Bowron Lake canoe circuit in Bowron Lake Provincial Park is one of the world's great canoe trips, covering 10 lakes with easy portages between each. Slightly less fabled – and less crowded – is the 116km-long circuit in Wells Gray Provincial Park.

During the short Yukon summer, scores of paddlers from around the world paddle the famed Yukon River and its tributaries, the route of the Klondike gold rush. You can still experience the stunning raw wilderness that the prospectors encountered, but from a modern canoe or kayak rather

---

WINDSURFING & KITEBOARDING

The breeze-licked tidal flats around Vancouver are popular with windsurfers. On many a day you'll see scores of colorful sails darting around the shallows like flocks of birds – it's a signature photo from the Kitsilano coastline. But further north, Squamish is the real center of the region's kiteboarding and windsurfing frenzy: an hour from Vancouver, its wind-whipped Squamish Spit area is often studded with adrenaline-fueled locals. Stand-up paddleboarding is also taking off in the region: consider Deep Cove, on Vancouver's North Shore, for an introduction.

than a raft of lashed-together logs. White-horse is the center for guides and gear.

For the ultimate adrenaline rush, try white-water rafting. Rugged canyons and seasonal melting snow make BC's rivers great for white-water action. You don't need to be experienced to have a go, as licensed commercial rafting operators offer guided tours for all abilities. Trips can last from three hours (average cost $100) up to a couple of weeks. Popular areas include the Thompson River near Lytton and the Kootenays – many consider the Kicking Horse River near Golden as one of province's best raft trips. In the Yukon, Haines Junction is also a good base, while in the Rockies the Jasper region has several popular operators.

Coastal

Although some people swear by their ocean-going canoes, the BC coast is truly the domain of kayaks. Since people first stretched skin over a frame and deployed a double paddle some 4000 years ago, these little crafts have been an excellent marriage of human and mode.

Options are as numerous as BC's endlessly crenulated coast and islands. The greatest concentration of outfitters is on Vancouver Island, which is one big paddling playground. The Broken Group Islands offer BC's best wilderness kayaking; they're revered for remoteness and rugged natural beauty, and give the opportunity to kayak to the little islands and camp overnight.

It's always safest to kayak with other people. Someone in the group should know how to plot a course by navigational chart and compass, pilot in fog, read weather patterns, assess water hazards, interpret tide tables, handle boats in adverse conditions, and perform group- and self-rescues. Always check weather forecasts before setting out, and don't expect your cell (mobile) phone to work.

If you have only a short time, you can rent a kayak for a few hours or take an introductory lesson in pretty much any of the island's coastal towns.

Urban paddlers can take in Vancouver's cityscape from the waters of False Creek (rentals available on Granville Island) while in the Rockies, Banff has several operators if you'd like to paddle the region's glassy, mountain-backed lakes.

Horseback Riding

Surveying the region's spectacular scenery from between the perky ears of a trusty steed is highly recommended: feel free to bring a costume and release your inner Mountie. BC's Cariboo and Chilcotin regions have long been horseback-riding areas: you can stay on a ranch there or climb into the saddle for a tour. Alternatively, in the midst of the Great Bear Rainforest, there are plenty of trails to explore in the Bella Coola Valley. Saddling up in Banff or Jasper is one of the best ways to feel at one with the region, while Calgary is the home of the cowboy: drop by in summer for the spectacular Calgary Stampede rodeo fest or check out your options on the region's cool Cowboy Trail (www.thecowboytrail.com).

Regions at a Glance

This region encompasses three diverse areas: the adjoining provinces of British Columbia and Alberta – which straddle the Rocky Mountains – plus the Yukon Territory, a remote northern wilderness next to Alaska. Each offers spectacular outdoor vistas and once-in-a-lifetime experiences. But they also have distinctions that you'll want to know about before you plan your trip.

Southern coastal BC and the Rockies region attract the lion's share of visitors. Their biggest draws are Vancouver – cosmopolitan metropolis and gateway to Whistler, Victoria and wider Vancouver Island – and the iconic national parks of Banff and Jasper, which lure with picture-postcard, wildlife-packed mountains. But if your idea of communing with nature means leaving the crowds behind, the vast and unremitting Yukon may be your nirvana: you'll certainly never forget your visit.

Alberta

Wildlife-Watching
Scenic Drives
Breathtaking Hiking

Jasper Tooth & Claw

There's wildlife throughout the Rockies but in Jasper you'll be closer than ever to a menagerie of elk, moose, bighorn sheep and, of course, bears (of the black as well as grizzly varieties). But it's a wolf sighting that will tingle your spine like nothing else.

Rocky Roads

A drive-through diorama of towering peaks, mammoth forests and glacier-fed lakes, the Rockies are idyllic car country. Among the wide, wildlife-lined highway highlights is the Icefields Parkway, a smooth, leisurely ribbon linking Banff and Jasper.

Life-Affirming Hikes

There's no better way to temporarily abandon your digitally overloaded life than a soul-stirring hike through the mountains. Look out for alpine flowers, sawtooth crags and a snuffling critter or two.

p40

British Columbia

Coastline
Food & Drink
Activities

Ocean Vistas

The vast, multi-fjorded BC coastline defines a visit to this region, whether you're strolling the Stanley Park seawall, hiking Vancouver Island's rugged West Coast Trail or reclining on a BC Ferries deck and watching for passing orcas.

Locavores United

From Vancouver's top restaurant tables to produce-packed farmers markets throughout the province, BC's local bounty is a foodie's delight. Seafood is the way to go, preferably coupled with regional wine or craft beer.

Adrenaline Rush

From ski resorts large and small to life-enhancing hiking, mountain biking, kayaking and beyond, visitors will never run out of ways to challenge themselves in the great outdoors. Start small with a forest stroll, and you'll be zip-lining through the valleys in no time.

p106

Yukon Territory

History
Raw Nature
Outdoor Activities

Gold Rush

The imprint of the 1898 Klondike gold rush is indelible here, especially on the clapboard streets of old Dawson City. You wouldn't be surprised to see a wily-faced geezer run down the main drag proclaiming his discovery – although if you do, it's probably time to stop drinking.

Spectacular Beauty

You won't have to jostle with the kind of crowds that flock to the Rockies at remote Kluane National Park and Reserve. And you'll be rewarded for your persistence with a vast, Unesco-recognized wonderland of glacier-sliced mountains. Humbling is the word.

Frontier Kayaking

Re-create the early days of gritty pioneer exploration by traveling the way they used to: via canoe or kayak along the Yukon River. Gold panning along the way is optional.

p244

On the Road

Alberta

Best Places to Eat

➡ Packrat Louie Kitchen & Bar (p50)

➡ Market (p64)

➡ 49° North Pizza (p103)

➡ Trough (p72)

➡ Other Paw Bakery (p94)

➡ Al Forno Cafe & Bakery (p63)

Best Places to Sleep

➡ Deer Lodge (p87)

➡ Tekarra Lodge (p93)

➡ Mt Engadine Lodge (p70)

➡ Varscona (p48)

➡ Heartwood Inn & Spa (p97)

➡ Prince of Wales Hotel (p103)

Why Go?

Alberta does lakes and mountains like Rome does cathedrals and chapels, but without the penance. For proof head west to Jasper and Banff, two of the world's oldest national parks; despite their wild and rugged terrain, they remain untrammeled and easily accessible. No one should leave this mortal coil without first laying eyes on Lake Louise and the Columbia Icefield – and think twice about dying before you've traveled east to the dinosaur-encrusted badlands around Drumheller, south to the Crypt Lake trail in Waterton Lakes National Park, and north to spot bison in the vast northern parklands.

In the center of the province, the wheat blows and the cattle roam; here you'll find historic ranches, sacred native sights and the eerie landscape of the hoodoos. What Alberta's cities lack in history they make up for with their spirit: Calgary has become unexpectedly cool, with top museums and cocktail bars, while Edmonton's fringe theater festival is the world's second largest.

When to Go
Edmonton

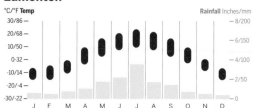

Jul Prime time for festivals, with Edmonton's Street Performers and the Calgary Stampede.

Jul–Sep Banff and Jasper's trails are snow-free, making a full range of hikes available.

Dec–Feb Winter-sports season in the Rocky Mountains.

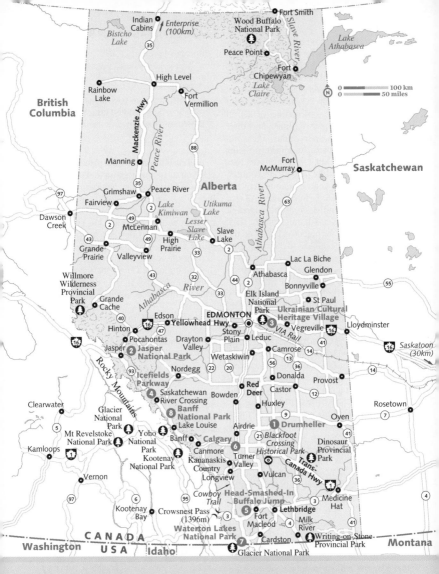

Alberta Highlights

1 **Royal Tyrrell Museum of Palaeontology** (p96) Exploring the Jurassic remnants of Drumheller.

2 **Miette Hot Springs** (p88) Soaking beaneath the mountain peaks of Jasper National Park.

3 **Ukrainian Cultural Heritage Village** (p53) Stepping back in time to

experience new immigrant life at the turn of the century.

4 **Icefields Parkway** (p73) Driving between towering mountains, a bevy of bears and scenic viewpoints.

5 **Head-Smashed-In Buffalo Jump** (p98) Delving into the fascinating history of First Nations culture.

6 **National Music Centre** (p57) Living out your rock-and-roll fantasies at Calgary's newest and coolest museum.

7 **Waterton Lakes National Park** (p101) Kayaking surrounded by fairy-tale scenery.

8 **Lake Agnes Teahouse** (p87) Enjoying glacial-water tea high above Lake Louise.

History

Things may have started off slowly in Alberta, but it's making up for lost time. Human habitation in the province dates back 7500 years: the Aboriginal peoples of the Blackfoot, Kainaiwa (Blood), Siksika, Peigan, Atsina (also called Gros Ventre), Cree, Tsuu T'ina (Sarcee) and Assiniboine tribes all settled here in prehistoric times, and their descendants still live here today. These nomadic peoples roamed the southern plains of the province in relative peace and harmony until the middle of the 17th century, when the first Europeans began to arrive.

With the arrival of Europeans, Alberta began to change and evolve – the impact of these new arrivals was felt immediately. Trading cheap whiskey for buffalo skins set off the decline of both the buffalo and the traditional ways of the indigenous people. Within a generation, the Aboriginal peoples were restricted to reserves and the buffalo all but extinct.

In the 1820s, the Hudson's Bay Company set up shop in the area, and European settlers continued to trickle in. By 1870 the North West Mounted Police (NWMP) – the predecessor of the Royal Canadian Mounted Police (RCMP) – had built forts within the province to control the whiskey trade and maintain order. It was a good thing they did, because 10 years later the railroad reached Alberta and the trickle of settlers turned into a gush.

These new residents were mostly farmers, and farming became the basis of the economy for the next century. Vast reserves of oil and gas were discovered in the early 20th century, but it took time to develop them. At the conclusion of WWII there were 500 oil wells; by 1960, there were 10,000, by which time the petroleum business was the biggest in town. Nevertheless, in the 1980s and again in 2016, a serious dip in oil prices brought heavy recession – a stark reminder that natural resources can offer both boom and bust.

Albertans have strong civic pride, as shown by the rallying support following the 2013 floods in Calgary and the 2016 wildfires in Fort McMurray. With their can-do attitude, there's little doubt they'll pull through.

Land & Climate

The prairies that cover the eastern and southern parts of Alberta give way to the towering Rocky Mountains that form the western edge of the province. That mountainous spine forms the iconic scenery for which Alberta is known.

Alberta is a sunny sort of place; any time of year you can expect the sun to be out. Winters can be cold, when the temperature can plummet to a bone-chilling -20°C (-4°F). Climate change has started to influence snowfall, with the cities receiving less and less every year.

Chinook winds often kick up in the winter months. These warm westerly winds blow in from the coast, deposit their moisture on the mountains and give Albertans a reprieve from the winter chill, sometimes increasing temperatures by as much as 20°C (36°F) in one day!

Summers tend to be hot and dry; the warmest months are July and August, when the temperature sits at a comfortable 25°C (77°F). The 'June Monsoon' is often rain-filled, while the cooler temperatures and fall colors of September are spectacular.

❶ Information

Travel Alberta (☑ 800-252-3782; www.travelalberta.com) Links to info on parks and visitor centers across the province.

❶ Getting There & Away

Alberta is easily accessible by bus, car, train and air. The province shares an international border with Montana, USA, and provincial borders with the Northwest Territories (NWT), British Columbia (BC) and Saskatchewan.

AIR

The two major airports are in Edmonton and Calgary, and there are daily flights to both from major hubs across the world. Carriers serving the province include Air Canada, American Airlines, British Airways, Delta, Horizon Air, KLM, United Airlines and WestJet.

BUS

Greyhound Canada (☑ customer service 877-463-6446, fares & schedules 800-661-8747; www.greyhound.ca) has bus services to Alberta from neighboring provinces, and Greyhound has services from the USA. Times can vary greatly, based upon connections, and fares can be reduced by booking in advance.

Useful destinations, with one-way fares, from Edmonton:

Prince George ($100, 10 hours, daily)
Vancouver ($150, 17 hours, five daily)
Whitehorse ($240, 29 hours, one daily)
Winnipeg ($170, 20 hours, three daily)

Destinations from Calgary:

Kamloops ($95, 10 hours, four daily)
Regina ($85, 10 hours, two daily)
Saskatoon ($78, nine hours, four daily)
Vancouver ($99, 15 hours, five daily)
Winnipeg ($175, 20 hours, daily)

Moose Travel Network (☑ 604-297-0255; www.moosenetwork.com) runs a variety of trips in western Canada. Tours start in Vancouver or Banff and along the way hit the highlights of the mountain parks and other Alberta must-sees. In winter it operates ski-focused tours that are a great option for car-less ski bums. Trips depart daily during the summer months and a few times per week in the winter season.

CAR & MOTORCYCLE

Alberta was designed with the car (and an unlimited supply of oil) in mind. There are high-quality, well-maintained highways and a network of back roads to explore. Towns will for the most part have services, regardless of the population.

Be aware that in more remote areas, especially in the north, those services could be a large distance apart. Fill up your gas tank wherever possible and be prepared for possible emergencies with things like warm clothes and water.

TRAIN

Despite years of hard labor, countless work-related deaths and a reputation for being one of the great feats of 19th-century engineering, Alberta's contemporary rail network has been whittled down to just two regular passenger train services. **VIA Rail** (☑ 888-842-7245; www.via.ca) runs the *Canadian* from Vancouver to Toronto two or three times per week, passing through Jasper and Edmonton in both directions. Edmonton to Vancouver costs $225 and takes 27 hours; Edmonton to Toronto costs $405 and takes 55 hours. The Toronto-bound train stops in Saskatoon, Saskatchewan; Winnipeg, Manitoba; and Sudbury Junction, Ontario. VIA Rail also operates the train from Jasper to Prince Rupert, BC ($117, 32 hours, three weekly).

ALBERTA ITINERARIES

One Week

Spend the day in **Calgary** exploring the **Glenbow Museum** (p57) and the **National Music Centre** (p57), then grab a meal on trendy 17th Ave or wander through the artsy neighborhoods of Kensington and Inglewood. The next day, get into dino mode by taking a day trip to **Drumheller** and visiting the **Royal Tyrrell Museum of Palaeontology** (p96). Back in Calgary, head east to spot wild bison at **Elk Island National Park** (p55) and step back in time at the authentic **Ukrainian Cultural Heritage Village** (p53).

Wake early and head west. Have fresh bagels for breakfast in **Canmore** and then carry on to into **Banff National Park** and check out the **Whyte Museum of the Canadian Rockies** (p76).

After a stay in Banff, follow the scenic Bow Valley Pkwy to **Lake Louise**, finding time for the short, steep hike to the **Lake Agnes Teahouse** (p87) and a trip up the **Lake Louise Gondola** (p86) to spot grizzly bears. Head out on the spectacular **Icefields Parkway** to the **Columbia Icefield** (p74).

Roll into **Jasper** and check into **Tekarra Lodge** (p93) for some much-needed R & R. Drive out to **Maligne Lake** (p89), where a short hike might let you spot a bear or a moose. Carry on north to **Miette Hot Springs** (p88) for a fabulous soak amid mountain scenery. Escape the mountains and head to **Edmonton**, diving into the Old Strathcona neighborhood, and finishing your Alberta adventure with a gourmet meal at **Packrat Louie Kitchen & Bar** (p50).

The Complete Rockies

Follow the One Week itinerary, but before reaching Canmore, head south down Hwy 5, known as the **Cowboy Trail**, to take in **Bar U Ranch** (p99). Continue south to **Waterton Lakes National Park** (p101), experiencing this less-visited mountain paradise. Return north through Kananaskis Country, stopping for tea or an overnight stay at **Mt Engadine Lodge** (p70). Then carry on north to **Canmore**.

Rocky Mountaineer (☑ 604-606-7245; www.rockymountaineer.com; 5 days from $2650; ☺ May-Oct) tours chug east from Vancouver through the Rockies via Kamloops to Jasper or Banff, or north from Vancouver to Jasper via Whistler and northern BC. These luxury trains have been transporting tourists on multiday journeys for a quarter century.

EDMONTON

POP 899, 447

Modern, spread out and frigidly cold for much of the year, Alberta's second-largest city and capital is a government town that you're more likely to read about in the business pages than the travel supplements. Edmonton is often a stopover en route to Jasper National Park, which is four hours' drive west, or for explorations into the vast and empty landscape to the north.

Downtown is for the moneyed and the down-and-out. There's hope that the much-lauded Rogers Place will breathe life into it, but this seems like a tall order. For the soul of the city, head south of the river to the university district and happy-go-lucky Whyte Ave, home to small theaters, diners and a spirited Friday-night mood. Edmonton also has a few decent museums, an annual fringe festival second only to Edinburgh's, and some top nearby sights like the Ukrainian Cultural Village and Elk Island National Park.

History

The Cree and Blackfoot tribes can trace their ancestry to the Edmonton area for 5000 years. It wasn't until the late 18th century that Europeans first arrived in the area. A trade outpost was built by the Hudson's Bay Company in 1795, which was dubbed Fort Edmonton.

Trappers, traders and adventurers frequented the fort, but it wasn't until 1870, when the government purchased Fort Ed and opened up the area to pioneers, that Edmonton saw its first real growth in population. When the railway arrived in Calgary in 1891, growth really started to speed up.

Meanwhile, the Aboriginal tribes had been severely weakened by disease and the near extinction of their primary food source, the bison. Increasingly vulnerable, they signed away most of their land rights to the Canadian government in a series of treaties between 1871 and 1921 in return for money, reservation lands and hunting rights.

Gold was the first big boom for the area – not gold found in Alberta, but gold in the Yukon. Edmonton was the last stop in civilization before dreamers headed north to the Klondike. Some made their fortunes, most did not; some settled in Edmonton, and the town grew.

In the 1940s, WWII precipitated the construction of the Alaska Hwy, and the influx of workers further increased the population. Ukrainians and other Eastern European immigrants came to Edmonton in search of work and enriched the city.

Edmonton is again the hub for those looking to earn their fortune in the north. But it isn't gold or roads this time – it's oil.

◎ Sights & Activities

★ Art Gallery of Alberta   GALLERY

(Map p48; ☑ 780-422-6223; www.youraga.ca; 2 Sir Winston Churchill Sq; adult/child $12.50/8.50; ☺ 11am-5pm Tue-Sun, to 9pm Wed) With the opening of this maverick art gallery in 2010, Edmonton at last gained a modern signature building to counter the ubiquitous boxy skyscrapers with a giant glass-and-metal space helmet. Its collection comprises 6000 pieces of historical and contemporary art, many of which have strong Canadian bias, that rotate through eight galleries. Numerous worthwhile temporary shows also pass through, and you'll find a shop, theater and restaurant on-site.

★ Fort Edmonton Park   HISTORIC SITE

(☑ 780-496-8787; www.fortedmontonpark.ca; cnr Fox & Whitemud Drs; adult/child/family $26.20/20.90/95; ☺ 10am-5pm Jul & Aug, 10am-3pm Mon-Fri, 10am-5pm Sat & Sun May-Jun, 11am-5pm Sat & Sun Sep & holidays; ⊞) The riverside reconstruction of Hudson's Bay Company's log fort gives you a glimpse into life in a trading post in the 1840s, right down to the smell of tanned hides. To reach it, pass by a 1920s midway and farm, and a few blocks of Edmonton in the 1920s, 1905 and 1885. Hop on a street car or horse carriage, chat with 'locals' (employees dressed up from the relevant era), do some yesteryear shopping or try the penny arcade.

Muttart Conservatory   GARDENS

(Map p46; ☑ 780-496-8755; www.muttart conservatory.ca; 9626 96A St; adult/child/family $12.50/6.50/37; ☺ 10am-5pm Fri-Wed, to 9pm Thu) Looking like some sort of pyramid-shaped, glass bomb shelter, the Muttart Conservatory is actually a botanical garden that sits south of the river off James MacDonald Bridge. Each of the four pyramids holds a different climate region and corresponding foliage. It's an interesting place to wander about, especially for gardeners, plant fans and those in the mood for something low-key. The excellent on-site cafe uses locally sourced ingredients and fresh greens from the greenhouse.

Royal Alberta Museum   MUSEUM
(Map p46;   📞780-453-9100; www.royalalberta museum.ca; ⊙9am-5pm) Since getting its 'royal' prefix in 2005 when Queen Liz II dropped by, Edmonton's leading museum has successfully received funding – a cool $340 million – for a new downtown home, which should be complete by late 2017. The new museum (103A Ave) will be the largest in western Canada, with an enormous collection of Alberta's natural and cultural history. Until then, the museum is closed.

Alberta Railway Museum   MUSEUM
(📞780-472-6229; www.albertarailwaymuseum.com; 24215 34th St; adult/child $7/3.50; ⊙10am-5pm Sat & Sun May-Aug) This museum, on the northeast edge of the city, has a collection of more than 75 railcars, including steam and diesel locomotives and rolling stock, built and used between 1877 and 1950. On weekends, volunteers fire up some of the old engines, and you can hop on the diesel locomotives on Sundays or the 1913 steam locomotive on holiday weekends.

Ukrainian Museum of Canada   MUSEUM
(www.umcalberta.org; 10611 110th Ave; by donation; ⊙10am-4pm May-Aug) FREE With a huge Ukrainian population and a long history of immigration, this museum is surprisingly small. While it continues to search for bigger digs, it shows a tiny collection of traditional costumes, toys and artwork. The cultural center in the same building hosts pierogi suppers on the last of Friday of each month ($15). Check its website (www.uocc-stjohn.ca) for details.

Telus World of Science   MUSEUM
(📞780-451-3344; www.edmontonscience.com; 11211 142nd St; adult/child $28/20; ⊙9am-6pm Sun-Wed, to 10pm Thu, to 8pm Fri & Sat; 🚼) With an emphasis on interactive displays, this science museum has a million things to do, all under one roof. Fight crime with the latest technology, see what living on a spacecraft is all about, go on a dinosaur dig and

explore what makes the human body tick. The center also includes an IMAX theater (extra cost) and an observatory with telescopes (no extra cost).

Valley Zoo   ZOO
(Map p46;   📞780-496-8787; www.valleyzoo.ca; 13315 Buena Vista Rd; adult/child/family $14/8.75/45.50; ⊙9am-6pm; 🚼) The Valley Zoo has more than 100 exotic, endangered and native animals. Kids will enjoy the petting zoo, camel and pony rides, miniature train, carousel and paddleboats. If you want to brave the zoo in the frigid winter, admission costs are reduced.

North Saskatchewan River Valley   PARK
Edmonton has more designated urban parkland than any other city in North America, most of it contained within an interconnected riverside green belt that effectively cuts the metropolis in half. The green zone is flecked with lakes, bridges, wild areas, golf courses, ravines, and approximately 160km worth of cycling and walking trails. It is easily accessed from downtown.

Sir Winston Churchill Square   SQUARE
(Map p48) With huge umbrellas, a splashing fountain, and tables and chairs, this public square is a good place to catch your breath in the summer. A giant chess board on the ground, Ping-Pong tables and daily classes in everything from Zumba to lightsaber training are all here. It's also worth checking out the awesome gift shop in Tix on the square, with work from local artists.

**Alberta
Government House**   HISTORIC BUILDING
(Map p46;   📞780-427-2281; 12845 102nd Ave; ⊙11am-4:30pm Sun & holidays mid-Feb–Nov) FREE This opulent mansion was the former residence of the lieutenant governor but is now used for government conferences and receptions. It is steeped in history and immaculately preserved – you'd never guess it's over 100 years old. The artwork alone is worth visiting: the walls are lined with stunning works by Canadian artists.

👉 Tours

Quirky free walking tours of downtown are offered in the summer months by students on vacation and employed by the Downtown Business Association. They leave weekdays at 1pm from the corner of 104th St and 101st Ave.

ALBERTA EDMONTON

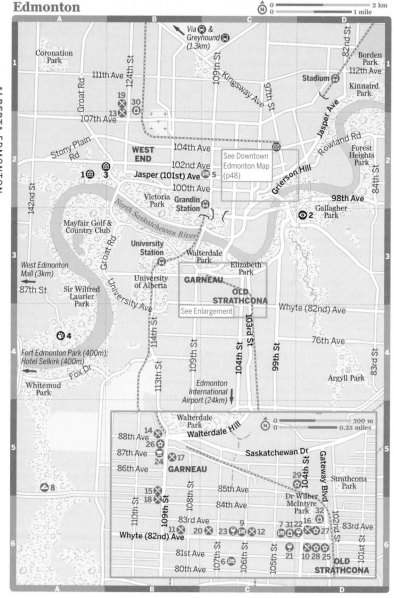

★**Cobblestone Freeway** CULTURAL
(☏780-436-7482; cobblestonefreeway.ca; day tours
from C$89) With knowledgeable guides who
have strong links to the local Ukrainian community, on these tours you can experience
traditional dance performances, authentic
Ukrainian food and heritage sights, as well
neighboring Ukrainian communities. They
can also get you to the city's must-see sights
or as far afield as Jasper. Especially great at
tailoring tours to traveler's interests, service
is both personable and professional.

Edmonton

Edmonton Ghost Tours WALKING
(www.edmontonghosttours.com; tours per person $10; ☺9pm Mon-Thu Jul & Aug) Spooky walking tours led by storytellers recounting the ghostly history of Edmonton. Tours cover various neighborhoods; check the website to see where to meet. No booking is required, just turn up 15 minutes early. Cash only.

★ Festivals & Events

International Street
Performers Festival THEATER
(www.edmontonstreetfest.com; ☺2nd week Jul) Sometimes the best theater is outside. International performers perform alfresco in this busker bonanza. Performers are curated and most strut their stuff in Sir Winston Churchill Sq.

K-Days CARNIVAL
(www.k-days.com; ☺late Jul) For years, Capital Ex (Klondike Days) was the big summer festival in Edmonton. Since 2012, it has been known as K-Days, with less focus on goldrush history and more on contemporary fun. Big names in music grace two stages, the midway has adrenaline charged rides and you'll still find a nugget's worth of olden-days fun.

Edmonton International
Fringe Festival THEATER
(www.fringetheatre.ca; tickets $13; ☺mid-Aug) The ultimate Edmonton experience is an 11-day program of live alternative theater on outdoor stages, in the parks, and in small theaters and venues. It's second in size only to the Edinburgh Fringe Festival. Many shows are free and no ticket costs more than $15. There's no booking – you choose a theater and stand in line. The festival draws half a million people each year to Old Strathcona.

🛏 Sleeping

While many hotels in the city are banking on visitors traveling on an expense account, Edmonton has a decent range of independent accommodations, including some with some character. If you are in town mainly to visit the West Edmonton Mall, then staying in or near it is feasible, but the digs there are definitely leaning toward the touristy side of the spectrum.

HI-Edmonton Hostel HOSTEL **$**
(Map p46; ☏780-988-6836; www.hihostels. ca; 10647 81st Ave; d $85, dm/d with shared bath $31/69; P @ ☞) Situated in the heart of Old Strathcona, this busy hostel is a safe bet. Many of the rooms are a bit jam-packed with bunks and it feels somewhat like a converted old people's home (it used to be a convent), but recent renovations have brightened things up and produced a fantastic outdoor patio. The location and price are hard to beat.

Downtown Edmonton

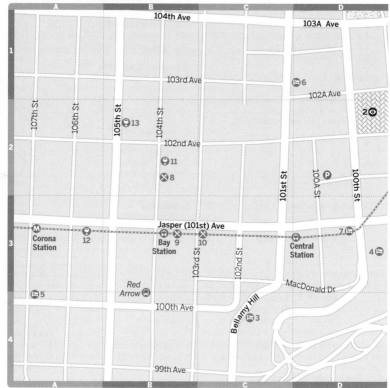

Rainbow Valley Campground & RV Park
CAMPGROUND **$**

(Map p46; ☑ 780-434-5531; www.rainbow-valley.com; 13204 45th Ave; tent/RV sites $37/42; ☉ Apr-Oct; Ⓟ) For an inner-city camping spot, this one is pretty good. It's in a good location to get to 'The Mall' and keep some distance from it at the same time. There are lots of trees, a playground, cookhouse, showers and wood-burning stoves. Rates are reduced out of peak season (late May to early September).

★ Matrix
BOUTIQUE HOTEL **$$**

(Map p48; ☑ 780-429-2861; www.matrixedmonton.com; 10001 107th St; r from $150; Ⓟ@🛜) Modern and slick, the lobby here could be James Bond's living room, complete with low leather furniture and a large glassed-in fireplace. Rooms are similarly stylish with plenty of up-to-date gadgets. Service is stellar and genuine, breakfasts are mammoth,

there's free wine and cheese in the evening, and a shuttle downtown.

★ Varscona
BOUTIQUE HOTEL **$$**

(Map p46; ☑ 780-434-6111; www.varscona.com; 8208 106th St, cnr Whyte Ave; r incl breakfast from $140; Ⓟ@🛜) This charming hotel is elegant but not too hoity-toity, suggesting you can roll up in a tracksuit or a business suit – or some kind of combination of the two. Recently renovated rooms have splashes of color and lots of comfort, and Edmonton's coolest neighborhood is on the doorstep. Parking, and evening wine and cheese sweeten the deal.

Metterra Hotel on Whyte
BOUTIQUE HOTEL **$$**

(Map p46; ☑ 780-465-8150; www.metterra.com; 10454 Whyte Ave; r from $150; Ⓟ@🛜) Sleek and regularly updated, this small hotel has a prime location on Whyte Ave. Earthy tones, cloud-like beds and splashes of Indonesian art give rooms a luxurious feel. The friendly

tors. This riverside behemoth has 24 floors, wonderful views and a revolving restaurant. It's not exactly swish but with an opulent lobby, fitness center and club-ish bar, it remains regally plush – and now at a bargain price!

Canterra Suites Hotel　　　　　HOTEL **$$**
(Map p46; ☎780-421-1212; www.canterrasuites.com; 11010 Jasper Ave; ste from $199; ✳🛜) Catering to traveling businesspeople, the Canterra has large, comfortable suites equipped with modern kitchenettes. It's close to downtown and right next to a supermarket. Ideal for long- or short-term stays.

★Union Bank Inn　　　　BOUTIQUE HOTEL **$$$**
(Map p48; ☎780-423-3600; www.unionbankinn.com; 10053 Jasper Ave; r from $220; P✳@🛜) This posh boutique hotel on Jasper Ave, in a former bank building dating from 1910, is an upmarket masterpiece. With just 34 rooms, the staff will be at your beck and call, and the in-room fireplaces make even Edmonton's frigid winters almost bearable. There's an equally fancy restaurant – Madison's Grill (p51) – on the ground floor.

Fairmont Hotel Macdonald　　　HOTEL **$$$**
(Map p48; ☎780-424-5181; www.fairmont.com; 10065 100th St; r from $210; P@🛜🏊) Stealing

staff can fill you in on what's happening in the neighborhood.

Hotel Selkirk　　　　　　　　HOTEL **$$**
(☎780-496-7227; www.fortedmontonpark.ca/hotel-selkirk/; 7000 143rd St, Fort Edmonton Park; r/ste from $149/169; P✳🛜) If you're into the idea of visiting the past at Fort Edmonton, why not take it to the next level and spend the night? This historic hotel has simple period-decorated rooms from the roaring 1920s, and staying here gives you free entry into the fort and its surrounds. There's an on-site restaurant and English high tea ($20) on offer during the summer. Once the park closes, it's quiet – very, very quiet.

Chateau Lacombe　　　　　　HOTEL **$$**
(Map p48; ☎780-428-6611; www.chateaulacombe.com; 10111 Bellamy Hill; r from $120; P✳@🛜) Going defiantly against the grain, the spectacular Chateau was a chain hotel that, in 2013, was bought out by local private inves-

the best nook in town (as Fairmont always does), Edmonton's historic Fairmont Hotel exhibits the usual array of intricate stucco, Italian marble, ornate chandeliers and lush carpets. In the early 20th century it was one in a luxurious chain of railway hotels that dotted the cross-continental line from east to west.

Sutton Place Hotel
HOTEL **$$$**

(Map p48; ☎780-428-7111; www.suttonplace. com; 10235 101st St; r from $230; P@☎☒) Silk papered walls, thick carpets and plush linen are some of the luxuries you'll enjoy at the Sutton. You may not get the intimacy you find in smaller hotels but there's a beautiful pool, great restaurants and a cocktail lounge that's full of glitz and glamour. Look out for room-rate specials.

✖ Eating

Edmonton's food scene reflects its multiculturalism and if you're willing to hunt around, you can get a quality meal at any price. The most varied and economical place to eat is on or around Whyte Ave, while the best downtown nexus is Jasper Ave or the rejuvenated warehouse district north of Jasper Ave on 104th St.

★ Duchess Bake Shop
BAKERY, CAFE **$**

(Map p46; ☎780-488-4999; www.duchessbake shop.com; 10720 124th St; baked goods from $2, breakfast & lunch $6-13; ☺9am-8pm Tue-Fri, 10am-6pm Sat, to 5pm Sun) Duchess is a destination. You'd cross town to eat here – barefoot in snow if necessary. Feeling like it dropped straight from France, complete with Louis XV–style chairs, the Duchess' French-press coffee and huge array of fresh baking leave you spoiled for choice. Mocha meringues, cream-cheese-and-leek croissants, and cherry basil eclairs are just the tip of the iceberg.

★ Block 1912
CAFE **$**

(Map p46; www.block1912.com; 10361 Whyte Ave; snacks $5-12; ☺9am-midnight Mon-Sat, 10am-11pm Sun) A regal attempt at a genuine Torinese coffee bar, this inviting place allows you to recline on European-style sofas and armchairs and enjoy your coffee, beer or wine beneath twinkly lights. Grab a snack or something more substantial like coffee-crusted steak or Thai chicken. Gelato comes in fab flavors like root-beer float or crème caramel and desserts are drool worthy.

Remedy Cafe
INDIAN **$**

(Map p48; ☎780-433-3096; www.remedycafe.ca; 10279 Jasper Ave; mains $8-10; ☺8am-midnight; ☎)

The 'remedy' here is cheap, authentic Indian food served in a casual cafe setting – meaning you can use wi-fi with one hand and dip your naan in curry sauce with the other. Everyone raves about the chai and the butter chicken, but you can also get good cakes (vegans are catered for) and excellent *masala dosas* (curried vegetables inside a crisp pancake).

The larger, original **branch** (Map p46; 8631 109th St) is in Garneau on the south side of the river.

Café Mosaics
VEGETARIAN **$**

(Map p46; ☎780-433-9702; www.cafemosaics. com; 10844 Whyte Ave; mains $6-12; ☺9am-9pm Mon-Sat, 11am-2:30pm Sun; ☒☑) ✔ A Strathcona institution, this artsy, cool vegetarian-vegan haunt is a meat-free zone that has taken a page out of San Francisco's book: it makes vegetable dishes both interesting and tasty. Think earthy and clean, rather than hippy and crusty. As a litmus test, check the number of carnivores who take a day off meat to come here.

Tokyo Noodle Shop
JAPANESE **$**

(Map p46; ☎780-430-0838; www.tokyonoodle shop.com; 10736 Whyte Ave; mains $10-22; ☺11:30am-9:30pm Mon-Thu, to 10:30pm Fri & Sat, noon-9pm Sun) Great sushi and noodles by the gallon, plush bento boxes, rice bowls and all the tasty appetizers you'd expect in an authentic Japanese restaurant. Nothing fancy, but that's the point.

High Level Diner
DINER **$**

(Map p46; ☎780-433-1317; www.highleveldiner. com; 10912 88th Ave; mains $6-15; ☺8am-10pm Mon-Thu, to 11pm Fri & Sat, 9am-9pm Sun; ☒) Popular for its weekend brunch and sticky cinnamon buns, this cheerful diner is frequented by students, neighbors in the know and the odd hipster. Specials like Ukrainian Thursdays and Short Rib Saturdays keep things lively, and there are some great vegetarian options like black bean chili and spinach pie. And the ketchup is made in-house!

★ Packrat Louie Kitchen & Bar
CANADIAN **$$**

(Map p46; ☎780-433-0123; www.packratlouie. com; 10335 83rd Ave NW; lunch $14-18, dinner $17-35; ☺11.30am-10pm Mon-Sat) Tucked off Whyte Ave in a converted brick building, Louie's is truly gourmet. Mains like black-olive-crusted cod, housemade chorizo fritters, or pork tenderloin with spätzle and wild mushroom wine sauce have graced the ever-changing menu that's always impressive. Pizzas are taken to a new level and even the lunchtime sandwiches are orgasmic. Reservations recommended.

Three Boars Eatery
TAPAS $$

(Map p46; ☑780-757-2600; www.threeboars.ca; 8424 109th St; small plates $13-21; ⊙4pm-late) ✒

Three Boars is part of the burgeoning farm-to-table food movement, using local suppliers to create gourmet food. It specializes in small plates, fine Edmonton microbrews on draught and divinely crafted cocktails. If you have an appetite for a large Alberta steak, this isn't your bag. If you're up for tasting pork terrine and smoked quail, it definitely is.

Tiramisu Bistro
ITALIAN $$

(Map p46; ☑780-452-3393; www.cafetiramisu.ca; 10750 124th St; pastas $12-15; ⊙9am-8pm Mon, to 9pm Tue-Thu, to 10pm Fri & Sat; ☝) This bistro serves fresh salads, wraps, panini and pasta, but its risottos are the coup – try saffron with duck confit, or beet, lime, goat's cheese and Pinot Grigio. Mornings bring breakfast pizzas and crepes with fillings like elk cherry sausage. It also has an awesome kids menu that assumes children like food beyond chicken strips.

Blue Plate Diner
VEGETARIAN $$

(Map p48; ☑780-429-0740; www.blueplatediner.ca; 10145 104th St; mains $12-18; ⊙7:30am-9pm Mon-Thur, to 10pm Fri, 9am-10pm Sat, 9am-9pm Sun; ☝) ✒ In one of the redbrick buildings in Edmonton's warehouse district, this vegetarian-biased diner serves healthy food in hearty portions. And there's style too. Cool colored lighting and exposed brickwork mean you can eat locally grown veggies without feeling as if you've joined a hippy commune. The creative menu is well executed, there's an excellent kids menu, and the desserts? Mmm...

Da-De-O
CAJUN $$

(Map p46; ☑780-433-0930; www.dadeo.ca; 10548a Whyte Ave; mains $15-26; ⊙11:30am-10pm Mon, Tue & Thu, to 11pm Fri & Sat, noon-10pm Sun) An unexpected summoning up of the Big Easy in the frozen north, this retro diner – complete with red vinyl chairs, chrome kitchen tables and a jukebox – whips up Cajun calamari, oysters, jambalaya and southern fried chicken. Plucked straight out of Louisiana legend are the spice-dusted sweet-potato fries and the ginormous po'boys (especially the blackened catfish). No minors allowed.

Noorish
VEGETARIAN $$

(Map p46; ☑780-756-6880; www.noorish.ca; 8440 109th St; mains $10-20; ⊙11am-10pm Tue-Sun; ☝) Noorish takes healthy eating to a whole new level. Walnut-zucchini meat and

EDMONTON'S WEST END

While Edmonton's downtown struggles to forge a collective personality, a small neighborhood 3km to the west, centered on 124th St, exhibits enough charisma to be referred to as the 'West End.' Acting as a kind of quirky antidote to West Edmonton Mall, 124th St between Jasper Ave and 111th Ave is home to an abundance of small art galleries linked by occasional art walks, along with some interesting locally owned restaurants, the cutting-edge Roxy Theatre and two of the best European bakery-cafes this side of Winnipeg: Duchess Bake Shop (p50) and Tiramisu Bistro (p51). A small street market has also taken root: 124 Grand Market (p54) plies organic wares sold by local producers. It's a classic case of local businesses and businesspeople claiming back their community.

coconut bacon might sound odd, but it packs in the diners. Dig into full-flavored pad Thai or truffle mac 'n' cheese and you'll see why. Raw food, gluten-free and vegan options are available, and you can head downstairs to the yoga room to feed your soul afterwards.

Corso 32
ITALIAN $$$

(Map p48; ☑780-421-4622; www.corso32.com; 10345 Jasper Ave; mains $24-40; ⊙5-11pm Tue-Sun) Chef and owner, Daniel Costa, delivers the best of Italy. Classy, small and candlelit, with a narrow interior and minimalist decor, the evolving menu features dishes with ingredients like homemade goat ricotta, rabbit and pancetta ragu or black truffle honey. The pasta is all handmade and the wine list is the best in Edmonton (if you're Italian).

Madison's Grill
FUSION $$$

(Map p48; ☑780-401-2222; www.unionbankinn.com; 10053 Jasper Ave; mains $34-45; ⊙8am-10pm Mon-Thu, to 11pm Fri & Sat, to 8pm Sun) Located in the posh Union Bank Inn, Madison's has no problem keeping up with its high standards of service and quality. Its delicate dishes are beautifully presented; try pork-cheek pierogi with saskatoon berries, seared halibut with basil gnocchi, or fig- and brie-stuffed chicken roulade wrapped in prosciutto. The three-course meal with wine pairing for $100 is well worth it.

ALBERTA EDMONTON

🍷 Drinking & Nightlife

The best nightlife scene has traditionally centered on or around Whyte Ave in Old Strathcona. Clubs open and close in a blink; bars tend to stay longer.

Transcend Coffee COFFEE
(Map p46; www.transcendcoffee.ca/garneau; 8708 109th St; ⊙7:30am-9pm Mon-Sat, to 5pm Sun; 🛜) ✦ In a city where cafes producing their own microroasted coffee beans are few, Transcend should be treated like gold dust. Expert baristas on first-name terms with their Guatemalan farmer-producers concoct cups of their own roasted coffee with enough precision to satisfy a severely decaffeinated Seattleite. In a renovated theater, this spot is hip but not remotely pretentious.

Yellowhead Brewery BREWERY
(Map p48; www.yellowheadbrewery.com; 10229 105th St NW; ⊙11am-6pm Mon-Fri) First things first. This isn't a pub. It's a tasting room next door to a brewery where you can sup on Yellowhead's one and only offering: Yellowhead amber ale – a light, not unpleasant lager, brewed in the big vats visible through a glass partition. It also serves small snacks and offers brewery tours if you book in advance.

Cavern WINE BAR
(Map p48; ☑780-455-1336; www.thecavern.ca; 10169 104th St NW; ⊙7am-8pm Mon-Thu, to 11pm Fri, 8am-11pm Sat, 10am-5pm Sun) ✦ Once a commerical warehouse, this industrial and candlelit small cafe is an underground bastion of good taste in vogue 104th St, particularly in the deli department (plates $6 to $16). You can browse the glass cabinet filled with divine cheese before you choose and wash it down with a glass of wine.

Next Act PUB
(Map p46; www.nextactpub.com; 8224 104th St NW; ⊙11am-1am Sun-Thu, to 2am Fri & Sat) Theater-district pub just off Whyte Ave with a good quotient of arty types. There are well-selected ales, including local stalwarts Yellowhead and Alley Kat, plus a long list of imports. Decent burgers and mac 'n' cheese are here to soak up the beer.

Black Dog Freehouse PUB
(Map p46; ☑780-439-1089; www.blackdog.ca; 10425 Whyte Ave; ⊙2pm-2am) Insanely popular with all types, the Black Dog is essentially a pub with a couple of hidden extras: a rooftop patio, known as the 'wooftop patio,' a traditional ground-floor bar (normally packed cheek to jowl on weekday nights), and a basement that features live music, DJs and occasional parties. The sum of the three parts has become a rollicking Edmonton institution.

O'Byrne's PUB
(Map p46; ☑780-414-6766; www.obyrnes.com; 10616 Whyte Ave; ⊙11:30am-2am) Get lost in the labyrinth of rooms in this popular Irish pub – Edmonton's oldest. There's a variety of beers on tap, including the obligatory stout. Live music (from 8:30pm) keeps the place lively and the big patio is most often packed.

Pub 1905 PUB
(Map p48; ☑780-428-4711; 10525 Jasper Ave; ⊙11am-midnight) A popular local watering hole with a happening happy hour, billiards and plates of smoked chicken drumsticks or riblets to snack on. The plethora of TVs is usually tuned in to the latest Oilers game.

☆ Entertainment

Theater! Don't leave Edmonton without trying some. *See* and *Vue* are free local alternative weekly papers with extensive arts and entertainment listings. For daily listings, see the *Edmonton Journal* newspaper.

Roxy Theatre THEATER
(Map p46; ☑780-453-2440; www.theatre network.ca; 8529 Gateway Blvd) This theatre opened after Theatre Network's beloved 1940's Roxy theater burned down. Nevertheless, it keeps things eclectic, showing burlesque, live bands and comedy.

Garneau Theatre CINEMA
(Map p46; www.metrocinema.org; 8712 109th St NW) Edmonton's only surviving art-deco-era cinema has operated under various guises since 1940, changing hands most recently in 2011. It's affectionately described as 'vintage,' meaning the seats could be more comfortable, but who cares when you roll in for a *Trainspotting* matinee and the concession stand is open for beer?

New Varscona Theatre THEATER
(Map p46; www.varsconatheatre.com; 10329 83rd Ave; tickets from $14) There are only 176 precious seats at the Varscona, a cornerstone of the Old Strathcona theater district that puts on 350 performances annually of edgy plays, late-night comedy and morning kids' shows.

Princess Theatre CINEMA
(Map p46; ☑780-433-0728; www.princesstheatre .ca; 10337 Whyte Ave; tickets adult/student & child

EDMONTON'S UKRAINIAN COMMUNITIES

If you've been in Edmonton for any length of time, you may well be wondering, 'Why all the perogies?' Between the 19th and early 20th century, around 250,000 Ukrainians immigrated to Canada, settling in farming communities on the prairies where the landscape reminded them of the snowy steppes of home. Today the Ukrainian population in Canada is second only to that in Russia and Ukraine itself, and many famous Canadians trace their roots back to the Ukraine, including Wayne Gretzky and Randy Bachman. The largest number of Ukrainian-Canadians live in and around Edmonton and, with 16% of the city's population claiming Ukrainian heritage, the cultural influence extends far beyond perogies.

Vincent Rees has a Masters in Ukrainian Culture, is a professional Ukrainian dancer, and runs cultural tours in both Edmonton and Ukraine. A resident of Edmonton for more than two decades, if anyone knows where to experience Ukrainian culture in the region, it's him.

'I think you would find it difficult not to feel the presence of Ukrainians in Edmonton. There are stores and restaurants, dance groups and choirs, and domes decorating the skyline. The culture is very alive and very present. One of the most interesting ways to experience it is to explore the **Ukrainian Cultural Heritage Village** (☑780-662-3640; www.history.alberta.ca/ukrainianvillage; adult/child/family $15/10/40; ⊘10am-5pm May-Sep) with its character role players acting out what life in a rural Ukrainian-Canadian community would have been like.' He also suggests checking out the small Ukrainian towns east of the city, including Vegreville, with the world's largest Easter egg; Mundare, with a giant Ukrainian sausage; and Glendon, with the biggest – you guessed it – perogy.

But today's Ukrainian-Canadian culture isn't just grandmas pushing perogies; many young Edmontonians are full of Ukrainian pride. 'The Ukrainian bilingual school program is popular and there are over a dozen Ukrainian dance groups within the city alone and a Ukrainian studies program at the University of Alberta.' Nevertheless, those grannies are pretty persuasive. 'There are many Ukrainian specialty restaurants and the churches often have special perogy nights and sell bulk perogies to take home for emergencies. In Edmonton, you're never very far from a perogy.'

To experience Ukrainian culture firsthand, check out Cobblestone Freeway (p46), which runs both city and regional tours.

$10/8) The Princess is a grand old theater that defiantly sticks her finger up at the multiplexes that are dominant elsewhere. Dating from the pre-talkie days (1915), it screens first-run, art-house and cult classics. Tickets for Mondays and weekend matinees are reduced.

Blues on Whyte　　　　　　LIVE MUSIC
(Map p46; ☑780-439-981; www.bluesonwhyte. ca; 10329 Whyte Ave) This is the sort of place your mother warned you about: dirty, rough, but still somehow cool. It's a great place to check out some live music; blues and rock are the standards.

Edmonton Eskimos　　　SPECTATOR SPORT
(www.esks.com; adult/child from $43/21.50) The Eskimos take part in the Canadian Football League (CFL) from July to October at **Commonwealth Stadium** (11000 Stadium Rd).

Edmonton Oilers　　　SPECTATOR SPORT
(www.edmontonoilers.com; tickets from $38.50) To avoid any embarrassing situations, wise up on the Oilers before you arrive in Edmonton. The local National Hockey League (NHL) team dominated the game in the 1980s thanks to a certain player named Wayne Gretzky – aka 'The Great One' – but haven't won much since. The season runs from October to April.

The team will likely have moved downtown to the new Rogers Place by the time you read this.

Edmonton Opera　　　　　　OPERA
(☑780-424-4040; www.edmontonopera.com; tickets from $24; ⊘Oct-Apr) Since its beginning in 1963, Edmonton Opera has been getting rave reviews from opera lovers, and breathing new life into classics like *Carmen* and *The Barber of Seville*. Performances are infrequent but worth seeing if you're in town.

Citadel Theatre　　　　　　THEATER
(Map p48; www.citadeltheatre.com; 9828 101A Ave; tickets from $45; ⊘Sep-May) Edmonton's foremost company is based in downtown's Winston Churchill Sq. Expect glowing performances of Shakespeare and Stoppard, Dickens adaptations and the odd Sondheim musical.

🛍 Shopping

Old Strathcona is the best area for unique independent stores – vintage magazines, old vinyl, retro furnishings and the like. If you're in search of the opposite – ie big chains selling familiar brands – sift through the 800-plus stores in West Edmonton Mall.

★ Old Strathcona Farmers Market FOOD
(Map p46; ☎780-439-1844; osfm.ca; 10310 83rd Ave, at 103rd St; ☺noon-5pm Tue, 8am-3pm Sat Jul & Aug) 🍴 Since it began in 1983, the market's motto has been 'We Make it! We Bake it! We Grow it! We Sell it!' Inside the city's old bus garage, it offers everything from organic food to arts and crafts, and hosts some 130 vendors. Everyone comes here on Saturday morning. You'd be wise to do the same.

124 Grand Market MARKET
(Map p46; www.124grandmarket.com; 108th Ave, btwn 123rd & 124th Sts; ☺4-8pm Thu) 🍴 Plenty of food trucks, artisans and produce to keep your belly and your shopping bag well satiated.

Junque Cellar FASHION & ACCESSORIES
(Map p46; 10442 Whyte Ave; ☺10am-9pm Mon-Sat, to 6pm Sun) What is plain old junk to some is retro-cool to others. Sift through the typewriters, lava lamps, old phones, comics, clothes and other flashbacks of erstwhile pop culture.

West Edmonton Mall SHOPPING MALL
(www.westedmontonmall.com; 170th St; ☺10am-9pm Mon-Fri, to 6pm Sat, noon-6pm Sun; 🅿) Kitsch-lovers who can't afford the trip to Vegas might just be enchanted with West Edmonton Mall, while those less enamored by plastic plants and phony re-creations of 15th-century galleons will hate it. Edmonton's urban behemoth has waterslides, an indoor wave pool, an amusement park, a skating rink, minigolf courses, a fake reef with a real seal lion and a penguin swimming around, a petting zoo, a hotel and 800 retail stores thrown in as a bonus.

ℹ Information

Custom House Global Foreign Exchange
(10104 103rd Ave) Foreign currency exchange.
Edmonton Tourism (Map p48; exploreedmonton.com/visitor-centre; 9797 Jasper Ave; ☺8am-5pm) Friendly place with tons of flyers and brochures.
Main post office (Map p46; 9808 103A Ave; ☺8am-5:45pm Mon-Fri)

Royal Alexandra Hospital (☎780-477-4111; 10240 Kingsway Ave) Has a 24-hour trauma center. Located 1km north of the downtown core.

ℹ Getting There & Away

AIR
Edmonton International Airport (YEG; www.flyeia.com) is about 30km south of the city along the Calgary Trail, about a 45-minute drive from downtown.

BUS
The large **Greyhound bus station** (12360 121st St) has services to numerous destinations, including Jasper ($74, 4½ hours, four daily) and Calgary ($50, from 3½ hours, from 10 daily).
Red Arrow (Map p48; www.redarrow.ca) buses stop downtown at the Holiday Inn Express and serve Calgary ($70, 3½ hours, six daily) and Fort McMurray ($87, six hours, three daily). The buses are a step up, with wi-fi, sockets for your laptop, single or double seats, a free minibar and hot coffee.

CAR & MOTORCYLE
All the major car-rental firms have offices at the airport and around town. **Driving Force** (www.thedrivingforce.com; 11025 184th St) will rent, lease or sell you a car. Check the website; it often has some good deals.

TRAIN
The small **VIA Rail station** (www.viarail.ca; 12360 121st St) is rather inconveniently situated 5km northwest of the city center near Edmonton City Centre Airport. The *Canadian* travels three times a week east to Saskatoon ($105, eight hours), Winnipeg ($220, 20 hours) and Toronto ($480, 55 hours), and west to Jasper ($143, 5½ hours), Kamloops ($207, 16½ hours) and Vancouver ($268, 27 hours). At Jasper, you can connect to Prince George and Prince Rupert.

ℹ Getting Around

TO/FROM THE AIRPORT
Bus 747 leaves from outside the arrivals hall every 30 to 60 minutes and goes to Century Park ($5), the southernmost stop on Edmonton's Light Rail. From here regular trains connect to Strathcona and downtown.
Sky Shuttle Airport Service (☎780-465-8515; www.edmontonskyshuttle.com; adult/child $18/10) runs three different routes that service hotels in most areas of town, including downtown and the Strathcona area. The office is by carousel 12. Journey time is approximately 45 minutes. If you're looking for a lift to the airport, reserve at least 24 hours in advance.
Cab fare from the airport to downtown costs about $50.

CAR & MOTORCYCLE

There is metered parking throughout the city. Most hotels in Old Strathcona offer complimentary parking to guests. Visitors can park their car for the day and explore the neighborhood easily on foot. Edmonton also has public parking lots, which cost about $12 per day or $1.50 per half-hour; after 6pm you can park for a flat fee of about $2.

PUBLIC TRANSPORTATION

City buses and a 16-stop Light Rail Transit (LRT) system cover most of the city. The fare is $3.20. Buses operate at 30-minute intervals between 5:30am and 1:30am. Check out the excellent transit planning resources at www.edmonton.ca. Daytime travel between Churchill and Grandin stations on the LRT is free.

Between mid-May and early September you can cross the High Level Bridge on a streetcar ($5 round-trip, every 30 minutes between 11am and 10pm). The vintage streetcars are a great way to travel to the Old Strathcona Market (103rd St at 94th Ave), where the line stops. Or go from Old Strathcona to the downtown stop, next to the Grandin LRT Station (109th St between 98th and 99th Aves).

TAXI

Two of the many taxi companies are **Yellow Cab** (☑ 780-462-3456) and **Alberta Co-Op Taxi** (☑ 780-425-2525; co-optaxi.com). The fare from downtown to the West Edmonton Mall is about $25. Flag fall is $3.60, then it's 20¢ for every 150m. Most cab companies offer a flat rate to the airport calculated from your destination.

AROUND EDMONTON

West of Edmonton

Heading west from Edmonton toward Jasper, Hwy 16 is a long and fairly monotonous drive through rolling wooded hills and past ranches with what appear to be a bazillion cows. **Hinton** is a small, rough-around-the-edges town carved from the bush. It's here that you'll get your first true view of the Rockies. The pervasive logging industry keeps the majority of the town's population gainfully employed.

Just northwest of Hinton lies the settlement of **Grande Cache**. There's little of interest in this small industry town – only a few over-priced hotels aimed at expense-account-wielding natural-resources workers. However, the drive along **Highway 40** between Hinton and Grande Cache is spectacular, with rolling forested foothills, lakes and wildlife.

 Activities

There's some good **mountain biking** to be found here; the **visitor info center** (☑ 780-865-2777; Hwy 16, Hinton; ⊙ 9am-7pm) has information on trails, including the 3km bike park and longer routes of varying difficulty beyond the park. You can rent your ride from **Vicious Bikes** (☑ 780-865-7787; www.vicious canada.com; 106 Park St, Hinton; bikes per day from $35; ⊙ 10am-6pm Mon-Sat, 11am-5pm Sun).

WORTH A TRIP

ELK ISLAND NATIONAL PARK

In case you hadn't noticed, there are five national parks in Alberta, and three of them *aren't* Jasper or Banff. Overshadowed by the Gothic Rockies, tiny **Elk Island National Park** (www.pc.gc.ca/elkisland; adult/6-16yr/senior $7.80/3.90/6.80, campsites & RV sites $25.50, campfire permits $8.80; ⊙ dawn-dusk) attracts just 5% of Banff's annual visitor count despite its location only 50km east of Edmonton. Not that this detracts from its attractions. The park – the only one in Canada that is entirely fenced – contains the highest density of wild hoofed animals in the world after the Serengeti. If you come here, plan on seeing the 'big six' – plains bison, wood bison, mule deer, white-tailed deer, elk and the more elusive moose. The wood bison live entirely in the quieter southern portion of the park (which is cut in two by Hwy 16), while the plains bison inhabit the north. Most of the infrastructure lies in the north, too, around **Astotin Lake**. Here you'll find a campground, a nine-hole golf course (with a clubhouse containing a restaurant), a beach and a boat launch. Four of the park's 11 trails lead out from the lakeshore through trademark northern Albertan aspen parkland – a kind of natural intermingling of the prairies and the boreal forests.

Public transportation to the park is nonexistent. Either hire a car or join a guided tour from Edmonton with **Watchable Wildlife Tours Group** (☑ 780-405-4880; www.bird sandbackcountry.com; per person $95), led by wildlife expert Wayne Millar. It's a lovely way to watch the sunset surrounded by animals on a long summer evening.

While you're in Hinton, it's also worth heading out to the **Beaver Boardwalk** at nearby Maxwell Lake. There are 5kms of lovely trails here and – you guessed it – beavers!

Athabasca Lookout Nordic Centre SKIING, CYCLING

(www.hintonnordic.ca; William A Switzer Park, Hwy 40; day pass $10) When there's snow on the ground, the Athabasca Lookout Nordic Centre offers winter visitors beautifully groomed cross-country ski trails up to 25km long. There's also illuminated night skiing on a 1.5km trail, plus a 1km luge run. In summer you can cycle here, too. For more information, contact the Hinton Visitor Information Centre (p55), off Hwy 16.

ℹ️ Getting There & Away

Greyhound (p42) has a daily service from Edmonton to Hinton (three hours and 40 minutes, $57) and on to Jasper Town (five hours, $71). **Sundog** (Map p92; www.sundogtours.com; 414 Connaught Dr, Jasper Town; ☺ 8am-8pm) also services this route between Edmonton airport and Jasper Town ($99), with stops along the way.

CALGARY

POP 1,097,000

Calgary will surprise you with its beauty, cool eateries, nightlife beyond honky-tonk and long, worthwhile to-do list. Calgarians aren't known for their modesty; it's their self-love and can-do attitude that got them through disastrous flooding in 2013 and, in 2016, saw them helping residents of wildfire-stricken Fort McMurray with unquestioning generosity. We mustn't forget – Calgary also hosted the highly successful 1988 Winter Olympics, elected North America's first Muslim mayor, and throws one of Canada's biggest parties, the Calgary Stampede.

Calgary was once known to forsake quality for quantity, but this trend is changing with fantastic results. Community activists in emerging neighborhoods like Inglewood and Kensington are finally waking up and smelling the single-origin home-roasted coffee, with new bars, boutiques, restaurants and entertainment venues exhibiting more color and experimentation. The city that to non-Calgarians long served as a somewhat bland business center or a functional springboard has actually become – ahem – cool.

History

From humble and relatively recent beginnings, Calgary has been transformed into a cosmopolitan modern city that has hosted an Olympics and continues to wield huge economic clout. Before the growth explosion, the Blackfoot people called the area home for centuries. Eventually they were joined by the Sarcee and Stoney tribes on the banks of the Bow and Elbow Rivers.

In 1875, the North-West Mounted Police (NWMP) built a fort and called it Fort Calgary after Calgary Bay on Scotland's Isle of Mull. The railroad followed a few years later and, buoyed by the promise of free land, settlers started the trek west to make Calgary their home. The Blackfoot, Sarcee and Stoney Aboriginals signed Treaty 7 with the British Crown in 1877 that ushered them into designated tribal reservations and took away their wider land rights.

Long a center for ranching, the cowboy culture was set to become forever intertwined with the city. In the early 20th century, Calgary simmered along, growing slowly. Then, in the 1960s, everything changed. Overnight, ranching was seen as a thing of the past, and oil was the new favorite child. With the 'black gold' seeming to bubble up from the ground nearly everywhere in Alberta, Calgary became the natural choice of place to set up headquarters.

The population exploded, and the city began to grow at an alarming rate. As the price of oil continued to skyrocket, it was good times for the people of Cowtown. The 1970s boom stopped dead at the '80s bust. Things slowed and the city diversified.

The 21st century began with an even bigger boom. House prices have gone through the roof, there is almost zero unemployment and the economy is growing 40% faster than the rest of Canada. Not bad for a bunch of cowboys.

👁 Sights

Calgary's downtown has the Glenbow Museum and the new National Music Centre, but it's the surrounding neighborhoods that hold more allure. **Uptown 17th Avenue** has some of the top restaurants and bars and is a hive of activity in the evening. **Inglewood**, just east of downtown, is the city's hippest neighborhood, with antique shops, indie boutiques and some esoteric eating options. **Kensington**, north of the Bow River, has some good coffee bars and a tangible community spirit.

★ **National Music Centre** MUSEUM
(Map p58; ☑ 403-543-5115; http://studiobell.ca; 850 4 St SE; adult/child $18/11; ◉ 10am-5pm Wed-Sun) Looking like a whimsical copper castle, this fabulous new museum is entirely entertaining, taking you on a ride through Canada's musical history with cool artifacts (like the guitar Guess Who used to record 'American Woman') and interactive displays. Test your skill at the drums, electric guitar or in a sound-recording room and even create your own instruments. Don't miss the Body Phonic room or the solar-powered Skywalk with its repurposed pianos destroyed in the 2013 flood.

★ **Glenbow Museum** MUSEUM
(Map p58; ☑ 403-777-5506; www.glenbow.org; 130 9th Ave SE; adult/child/family $16/10/40; ◉ 9am-5pm Mon-Sat, noon-5pm Sun, closed Mon Oct-Jun) With an extensive permanent collection and an ever-changing array of traveling exhibitions, the impressive Glenbow has plenty for the history buff, art lover and pop-culture fiend to ponder. Temporary exhibits are often daring, covering contemporary art and culture. Permanent exhibits bring the past to life with strong historic personalities and lots of voice recordings. Hang out in a tipi, visit a trading post and walk through the rail car of a train.

Bow Habitat Station AQUARIUM
(☑ 403-297-6561; aep.alberta.ca; 1440 17A St SE; adult/child $10/6; ◉ 10am-4pm Tue-Sat, tours noon & 2pm) Raising and releasing up to 1.5 million trout each year, this working hatchery is a favorite with kids for its aquariums, hands-on exhibits and chance to fish in the pond (May to October). Look down over the hatchery pools or get up close and feed the juvenile fish on a tour.

Esker Foundation Contemporary Art Gallery MUSEUM
(eskerfoundation.com; 1011 9th Ave SE, Inglewood; ◉ 10am-6pm Tue-Sun) FREE This small, private art gallery hosts fabulous temporary exhibitions in its beautiful 4th-floor location. Past exhibitions have considered everything from immigration to the Northwest Passage. Check the website for workshops and be sure to check out the very cool boardroom nest.

Prince's Island Park PARK
(Map p58) For a little slice of Central Park in the heart of Cowtown, take the bridge over to this island, with grassy fields made for tossing Frisbees, bike paths and ample space to stretch out. During the summer months, you can catch a Shakespeare production in the park's natural grass amphitheater or check out the Folk Music Festival in July. You'll also find the upscale River Island restaurant here.

Heritage Park Historical Village HISTORIC SITE
(☑ 403-259-1900; www.heritagepark.ab.ca; 1900 Heritage Dr SW, at 14th St SW; adult/child $26.25/13.50; ◉ 9.30am-5pm daily May-Aug, Sat & Sun Sep & Oct) Want to see what Calgary used to look like? Head down to this historical park where all the buildings are from 1915 or earlier. There are 10 hectares of re-created town to explore, with a fort, grain mill, church and school. Go for a hay ride, visit the antique midway or hop on a train. Costumed interpreters are on hand to answer any questions.

Calgary Tower NOTABLE BUILDING
(Map p58; ☑ 403-266-7171; www.calgarytower.com; 101 9th Ave SW; adult/youth $18/9; ◉ observation gallery 9am-9pm Sep-Jun, to 10pm Jul-Aug) This 1968 landmark tower is an iconic feature of the Calgary skyline, though it has now been usurped by numerous taller buildings and is in danger of being lost in a forest of skyscrapers. There is little doubt that the aesthetics of this once-proud concrete structure have passed into the realm of kitsch, but, love it or hate it, the slightly phallic 191m structure is a fixture of the downtown area.

Contemporary Calgary GALLERY
(Map p58; ☑ 403-770-1350; www.contemporarycalgary.com; 117 8th Ave SW; ◉ noon-6pm Wed-Sun) FREE This small, inspiring modern-art gallery has four floors of temporary exhibits that change every four months. The gallery has plans to move to the former Centennial Planetarium in the southwest; renovations are due to be completed in 2018. With much more exhibition space, great things are expected.

Calgary Zoo ZOO
(☑ 403-232-9300; www.calgaryzoo.com; 1300 Zoo Rd NE; adult/child $25/17; ◉ 9am-5pm; ♿) More than 1000 animals from around the world, many in enclosures simulating their natural habitats, make Calgary's zoo one of the top rated in North America. The zoo's well-regarded conservation team study, reintroduce and protect endangered animals in Canada.

Calgary

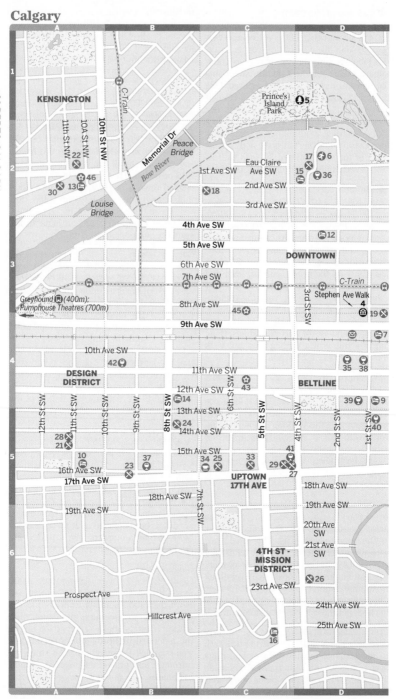

KENSINGTON

Prince's Island Park

5

11th St NW
10A St NW
10th St NW

C-Train

Memorial Dr

Peace Bridge

Bow River

22

46
30 13

Louise Bridge

1st Ave SW
Eau Claire Ave SW
2nd Ave SW
3rd Ave SW

17 6
15 36

18

4th Ave SW
5th Ave SW
6th Ave SW
7th Ave SW
8th Ave SW
9th Ave SW

DOWNTOWN

12

C-Train
Stephen Ave Walk
3rd St SW
4
19

Greyhound (400m);
Pumphouse Theatres (700m)

45

10th Ave SW

42

DESIGN DISTRICT

11th Ave SW
12th Ave SW
13th Ave SW
14th Ave SW
15th Ave SW
16th Ave SW
17th Ave SW

43

BELTLINE

35 38

39 9

40

12th St SW
11th St SW
10th St SW
9th St SW
8th St SW
6th St SW
5th St SW
4th St SW
3rd St SW
2nd St SW
1st St SW

14
24

28
21

10

23 37

34 25 33

41
29 27

UPTOWN 17TH AVE

18th Ave SW
19th Ave SW

7th St SW

18th Ave SW
19th Ave SW
20th Ave SW
21st Ave SW

4TH ST - MISSION DISTRICT

23rd Ave SW

26

Prospect Ave

Hillcrest Ave

24th Ave SW
25th Ave SW

16

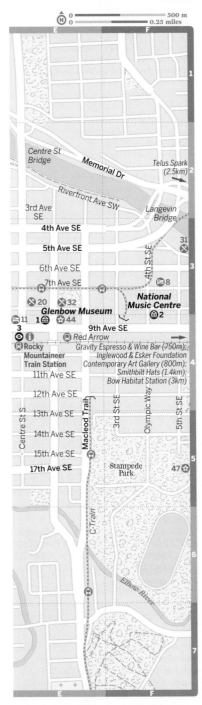

Telus Spark
SCIENCE CENTER

(☑403-817-6800; www.sparkscience.ca; 220 St George's Dr NE; adult/child $20/13; ⊙10am-5pm; 👪) You'll wish science class was as fun as the Telus World of Science. Kids get a big bang out of this user-friendly and very interactive science center. There is a giant dome, where light shows depicting the cosmos are projected.

Fish Creek Provincial Park
PARK

(☑403-297-5293; www.albertaparks.ca; ⊙8am-dusk) Cradling the southwest edge of Calgary, this huge park is a sanctuary of wilderness hidden within the city limits. Countless trails intertwine to form a labyrinth, to the delight of walkers, mountain bikers and the many animals who call the park home.

Calaway Park
AMUSEMENT PARK

(☑403-240-3822; www.calawaypark.com; adult/child/family $38/31/120; ⊙10am-7pm Jul-early Sep, 11am-6pm Sat & Sun early Sep-early Oct, 5-9pm Fri, 10am-7pm Sat & Sun late May-Jul) Children of all ages will enjoy Calaway Park, western Canada's largest outdoor family amusement park. It features 30 rides from wild to mild, live stage entertainment, 22 food vendors, 28 different carnival games, a trout-fishing pond and an interactive maze. The youngsters will love camping at the amusement park, close enough to town to be not too far to drive.

Inglewood Bird Sanctuary
NATURE RESERVE

(☑403-268-2489; 2425 9th Ave SE; sanctuary & interpretive center free, donations appreciated; ⊙dawn-dusk, interpretive center 10am-4pm) Get the flock over here. With more than 260 bird species calling the sanctuary home, you're assured of meeting some feathered friends. It's a peaceful place, with walking paths and benches to observe the residents.

🏃 Activities

Rapid Rent
CYCLING

(Map p58; www.outlawsports.ca; Barclay Pde SW; bikes/rollerblades/helmet per day from $30/15/5; ⊙10am-7pm Mon-Fri, to 6pm Sat, to 5pm Sun) Rents bikes, child trailers and rollerblades.

Olympic Oval
ICE SKATING

(☑403-220-7954; www.ucalgary.ca/oval; University of Calgary; adult/child/family $7/5/18.50; ⊙Jul–mid Mar) Get the Olympic spirit at the University of Calgary, where you can go for a skate on Olympic Oval. Used for the speed-skating events at the Olympics, it offers public skating on the long track and has skates available to rent, as well as mandatory helmets. See the website for current schedules.

Calgary

Canada Olympic Park   ADVENTURE SPORTS

(☑ 403-247-5452; www.canadaolympicpark.ca; 88 Canada Olympic Rd SW; mountain biking hill tickets/lessons $22/99; ⊙ 9am-9pm Mon-Fri, 10am-5pm Sat & Sun) In 1988 the Winter Olympics came to Canada for the first time. Calgary played host, and many of the events were contested at Canada Olympic Park. It's near the western edge of town along Hwy 1 – you can't miss the distinctive 70m and 90m ski jumps crowning the skyline.

Calgary Walking Tours   CULTURAL

(☑ 855-620-6520; www.calgarywalks.com; adult/youth/under 7yr $18/15/free) Join the two-hour Core City tour to learn about the architecture, history and culture of various buildings, sculptures, gardens and hidden nooks.

★☆ Festivals & Events

For a year-round list of the city's events, go to www.visitcalgary.com/things-to-do/events-calendar. The big festival in Calgary is the annual Calgary Stampede; however, there are many other smaller festivals, markets and exhibitions throughout the year.

Calgary Folk Music Festival   MUSIC

(www.calgaryfolkfest.com; ⊙ late Jul) Grassroots folk is celebrated at this annual four-day event featuring great live music on Prince's Island. Top-quality acts from around the globe make the trek to Cowtown. It's a mellow scene hanging out on the grass listening to the sounds of summer with what seems like 12,000 close friends. Tickets per day are around $85 or it's $195 for all four days.

Calgary International Children's Festival   FESTIVAL

(☑ 403-294-9494; calgarykidsfest.ca; Epcor Centre for the Performing Arts, 205 8th Ave SE; tickets $17; ⊙ late May) There's all sorts of kidding around at this annual festival. Taking to the stage are musicians, puppeteers and actors, and sometimes even a mad scientist or circus act. Big Canadian names like Fred Penner often join in.

Calgary Stampede   RODEO

(www.calgarystampede.com; ⊙ 2nd week Jul) Billed as the greatest outdoor show on earth, rodeos don't come much bigger than the Calgary Stampede. Daily shows feature bucking broncos, steer wrestling, chuckwagon races, a midway and a sensational grandstand show. Civic spirits soar, with free pancake breakfasts and a cowboy hat on every head in the city. All of this is strongly tempered by animal rights issues.

Each year, numerous animals are put down after suffering injuries at the stampede. Humane societies and animal rights activists strongly oppose endangering animals for entertainment and spotlight calf roping and chuckwagon races as two of the most dangerous activities at the Stampede.

🛏 Sleeping

Calgary has recently found its independent spirit and established a range of boutique hotels across different price ranges.

Downtown hotels are notoriously expensive, although many run frequent specials. Business-oriented hotels are often cheaper over weekends. Near the city's western edge (next to the Banff Trail C-Train station), you'll find every chain hotel you can think of.

During the Calgary Stampede (early July), rates rise and availability plummets. Book ahead.

Calgary West Campground   CAMPGROUND **$**
(✆403-288-0411; www.calgarycampground.com; Hwy 1; tent/RV sites $36/44; ☉mid-Apr–mid-Oct; P@🛜≊) Featuring terraced grounds with views across the city, this campground has 320 sites with great facilities, including a heated outdoor pool, nature trails, mini-golf and free wi-fi. Situated west of downtown Calgary on the Trans-Canada Hwy (Hwy 1), it's a quick trip into the city.

HI-Calgary   HOSTEL **$**
(Map p58; ✆403-269-8239; www.hostellingintl. ca/Alberta; 520 7th Ave SE; dm/d from $33/100; @🛜) Clean and comfortable, if not particularly homey, this pleasant hostel is one of the only options for budget-minded travelers in Calgary, with fairly standard bunk rooms and a few doubles. It has a kitchen, laundry, pool table and internet facilities, as well as a patio with a barbecue. It's a popular crossroads for travelers and a good place to organize rides and share recommendations.

★Kensington

Riverside Inn   BOUTIQUE HOTEL **$$**
(Map p58; ✆403-228-4442; www.kensington riversideinn.com; 1126 Memorial Dr NW; r from $199; P🛜) This small inn has impeccable service

and rooms to match. Soaker tubs, fireplaces, balconies, Geneva sound systems, French doors and fine linens are all to be found. It's a short trip over the bridge to downtown and the hotel restaurant is top-notch.

Hotel Alma   BOUTIQUE HOTEL **$$**
(✆403-220-3203; www.hotelalma.ca; 169 University Gate NW; r from $129, apt $180; 🛜) Cleverly tucked away on the university campus, this fashionable boutique establishment has a definite hip vibe. Super modern Euro-style rooms are small but cozy rather than cramped. The city suites have one bedroom and are lovely right down to their Piero Lissoni sofas and hand-embroidered cushions. Guests have access to on-campus facilities, including a fitness center, pool and fine lobby bistro.

Hotel Elan   BOUTIQUE HOTEL **$$**
(Map p58; ✆403-229-2040; www.hotelelan. ca; 1122 16th Ave SW; r weekday/weekend from $249/160; ❋🛜) Stylish and modern, Hotel Elan is popular with business travelers. The rooms are a splendid surprise after the more-functional-than-fancy lobby. Heated bathroom floors and pillow-top mattresses are among the creature comforts, along with rain shower heads and gourmet coffee pods. Away from downtown, it's an easy walk to the happening scene on 17th Ave.

Nuvo Hotel Suites   HOTEL **$$**
(Map p58; ✆403-452-6789; www.nuvohotel suites.com; 827 12th Ave SW; ste from $150; ❋🛜) Your hip home away from home, the Nuvo has large, stylish studio apartments with full kitchens, including washing machines, all for an excellent price in the Beltline neighborhood. Handy for downtown and Uptown 17th action.

Centro Motel   MOTEL **$$**
(✆403-288-6658; www.centromotel.com; 4540 16th Ave NW; r incl breakfast from $114; P❋@🛜) A 'boutique motel' sounds like an oxymoron until you descend on the misleadingly named Centro, an old motel building that has been transformed with modern features. The indie owners have left no detail missing, from light fittings to bathrobes, wooden floors and walk-in spa showers. You'll find it 7km northwest of downtown on the Trans-Canada Hwy (Hwy 1).

International Hotel   HOTEL **$$**
(Map p58; ✆403-265-9600; www.international hotel.ca; 220 4th Ave SW; d from $109; P@🛜≊) Even the standard rooms here are suites

LOCAL KNOWLEDGE

CARLESS IN CALGARY

As the main operations center for Canada's oil industry, Calgary has a reputation for big, unsubtle automobiles plying endless low-rise suburbs on a network of busy highways. But, hidden from the ubiquitous petrol heads is a parallel universe of urban parkways (712km of 'em!) dedicated to walkers, cyclists and skaters, and many of them hug the banks of the city's two mighty rivers, the Bow and the Elbow. Even better, this non-car-traffic network is propped up by a cheap, efficient light-rail system: the C-Train was significantly expanded in 2012 and carries a number of daily riders comparable to the Amsterdam metro. Yes, dear reader, Calgary without a car is not an impossible – or even unpleasant – experience.

Not surprisingly, the best trails hug the riverbanks. The Bow River through downtown and over into Prince's Island is eternally popular, with the new pedestrian-only Peace Bridge providing a vital link. If you're feeling strong, you can follow the river path 20km south to Fish Creek Provincial Park and plenty more roadless action. Nose Creek Parkway is the main pedestrian artery to and from the north of the city, while the leafy Elbow River Pathway runs from Inglewood to Mission in the south.

Abutting the downtown Bow River Pathway is Rapid Rent (p59), an outlet of Outlaw Sports located next to the Eau Claire shopping center.

The city publishes an official *Calgary Pathways and Bikeways* map available from any local leisure center or downloadable from the City of Calgary website (www.calgary.ca). There's also a mobile app at www.calgary.ca/mobileapps.

with great city views and cloud-comfy beds. Decor is fairly neutral but service is not. There's a level for women only and another for gentlemen with tailored (if slightly stereotypical) conveniences.

Carriage House Inn INN $$
(✆403-253-1101; www.carriagehouse.net; 9030 Macleod Trail S; r $159-189; P❄@☀) When you arrive here, the boxlike exterior is less than inspiring, but things brighten inside. Recently renovated rooms are classy with modern interiors. Feather beds are hard to get out of, but there are lots of eating and shopping options nearby. The inn is 8km south of downtown Calgary on the arterial MacLeod Trail.

Twin Gables B&B B&B $$
(Map p58; ✆403-271-7754; www.twingables.ca; 611 25th Ave SW; ste $99-175; P@) This could be your grandma's house – if you were visiting her in 1910. Featuring hardwood floors, stained-glass windows, Tiffany lamps and antique furnishings, this B&B is a little fussy but entirely comfortable. With just three rooms, it's located in a historic house across from the Elbow River, meaning walking trails are at the ready.

★**Hotel Le Germain** BOUTIQUE HOTEL $$$
(Map p58; ✆403-264-8990; www.germain calgary.com; 899 Centre St SW; d from $309; P❄@☃) ✈ A posh boutique hotel to counteract the bland assortment of franchise inns that service downtown Calgary. Part of a small French-Canadian chain, the style verges on opulent. Rooms are elegant, while the 24-hour gym, in-room massage, complimentary newspapers and Jetson-style lounge add luxury touches.

Hotel Arts BOUTIQUE HOTEL $$$
(Map p58; ✆403-266-4611; www.hotelarts.ca; 119 12th Ave SW; ste from $269; P❄@☃☀) This boutique hotel plays hard on the fact that it's not part of an international chain. Aimed at the traveler with an aesthetic eye, there are hardwood floors, thread counts Egyptians would be envious of and art on the walls that could be in a gallery. Standard king rooms are small but well designed with rain shower heads and blackout curtains.

Fairmont Palliser HOTEL $$$
(Map p58; ✆403-262-1234; www.fairmont.com/palliser; 133 9th Ave SW; r from $319; P@☃☀) All satin, velvet and crystal, with marble columns and golden ceiling domes, the Fairmont is palatial. Cut from the same elegant cloth as other Fairmont hotels, the Palliser has a deep regal feel to it, unlike anything else that lies within the city limits. All 407 rooms are newly renovated and elegant. Classic, beautiful and worth every penny.

Sheraton Suites Calgary Eau Claire HOTEL $$$

(Map p58; ☑ 403-266-7200; www.sheraton.com; 255 Barclay Pde SW; ste from $379; ⓟ❄@🛜🏊) With a great location and overflowing with amenities, this business-oriented all-suite hotel is comfortable without being plush. The staff go the extra mile, and valet parking and a pool top it all off.

✖ Eating

In Calgary, the restaurant scene isn't just fast-moving – it's supersonic, with ever-better quality and greater variety. Where solitary cows once roamed, vegetables and herbs now prosper, meaning that trusty old stalwart, Alberta beef, is no longer the only thing propping up the menu.

You'll find good eat streets in Kensington, Inglewood, Uptown 17th Ave and downtown on Stephen St.

★ Al Forno Cafe & Bakery CAFE $

(Map p58; ☑ 403-454-0308; alforno.ca; 222 7th St SW; mains $8-15; ⊙ 7am-9pm Mon-Fri, 8am-9pm Sat & Sun) This ultra-modern, super-comfortable cafe is the kind of place you'll want to hang out all day. Beer on tap, carafes of wine and excellent coffee won't discourage you from lingering, nor will magazines, comfy sofas or window seats. With pastas, flatbreads, salads, soups and panini, all homemade, it's difficult to leave room for the amazing cakes, tarts and biscuits.

★ 1886 Buffalo Cafe BREAKFAST $

(Map p58; 187 Barclay Pde SW; ⊙ 6am-3pm Mon-Fri, from 7am Sat & Sun) This is a true salt-of-the-earth diner in the high-rise-dominated city center. Built in 1911 and the only surviving building from the lumber yard once here, the interior feels fairly authentic with family photos and antique clocks. This is a ketchup on the table, unlimited coffee refills kind of place famous for its brunches and especially its huevos rancheros.

Myhre's Deli DELI $

(Map p58; 1411 11th St SW; mains $5-13; ⊙ 11am-4pm) Satisfying meat cravings for 15 years, this deli's mahogany interior and vintage signs are restored from the Palace of Eats, a Stephen Ave institution from 1918 to 1964. Well-filled smoked Montreal meat sandwiches are made fresh, and all beef hot dogs, including the steamed Ruben dog with sauerkraut, are embellished with your choice of seven mustards. Everything is topped with a pickle.

Janice Beaton Fine Cheese CHEESE $

(Map p58; ☑ 403-229-0900; janicebeaton.com/shop; 1017 16th Ave SW; cheese $3-15; ⊙ 10am-6pm Sat-Thu, to 7pm Fri) Selling cheeses to Calgarians for 15 years, this shop is a serious find for any cheese-lover. Eat your way from Switzerland to Salt Spring; whether you're into blue cheese or cheddar, there's something here to fill your belly. It all goes down perfectly with a bag of homemade flatbread. And Janice Beaton? This woman knows her cheeses.

Jelly Modern Doughnuts BAKERY $

(Map p58; ☑ 403-453-2053; www.jellymodern doughnuts.com; 1414 8th St SW; doughnuts from $2; ⊙ 7am-6pm Mon-Fri, 9am-6pm Sat, to 5pm Sun) Bright pink and sugary-smelling, Jelly Modern has grabbed the initiative on weird doughnut flavors. The maple and bacon or bourbon vanilla varieties won't help ward off any impending heart attacks, but they'll make every other doughnut you've ever tasted seem positively bland by comparison.

Gravity Espresso & Wine Bar CAFE $

(www.cafegravity.com; 909 10th St SE; light lunches $6-12; ⊙ 8am-6pm Sun & Mon, to 10pm Tue-Thu, to midnight Fri & Sat) 🖉 This hybrid cafe-bar, which alters its personality depending on the clientele and the time of day, is a thoughtful, community-led business. The crux of the operation is the locally roasted Phil & Sebastian coffee beans, but that's just an overture for loads of other stuff, including live acoustic music, curry nights, home-baked snacks and fund-raisers.

Galaxie Diner BREAKFAST $

(Map p58; ☑ 403-228-0001; www.galaxiediner. com; 1413 11th St SW; mains $9-15; ⊙ 7am-3pm Mon-Fri, to 4pm Sat & Sun) Looking more authentic than themed, this classic, no-nonsense 1950s diner serves all-day breakfasts, burgers and milkshakes. Squeeze into a booth, grab a pew at the bar or (more likely) join the queue at the door.

Higher Ground CAFE $

(Map p58; ☑ 403-270-3780; www.higher groundcafe.ca; 1126 Kensington Rd NW; snacks $5-8; ⊙ 7am-11pm Mon-Thu, 8am-midnight Fri-Sun) 🖉 Giving Calgary's indie coffee-bar scene the shot of home-roasted caffeine it needs, Higher Ground is a delicious mix of art gallery, gossip shop, public theater and community resource. It is also where you come for lunch-size panini and a damned fine cup of coffee.

Peter's Drive-In
BURGERS $

(☎ 403-277-2747; www.petersdrivein.com; 219 16th Ave NE; mains $2.50-5; ☺ 9am-midnight) In 1962 Peter's opened its doors and locals have been flocking here ever since to a largely unchanged menu of super thick shakes, burgers off the grill and fries that make no pretense of being healthy. It's a true drive-in, so either bring the car along or be happy to eat on the lawn out front.

★ Market
CANADIAN $$

(Map p58; ☎ 403-474-4414; marketcalgary.ca; 718 17th Ave SW; mains lunch $12-17, dinner $8-20; ☺ 11.30am-late) With an earthy yet futuristic feel, award-winning Market has gone a step further in the fresh-local trend. Not only does it bake its own bread, it butchers and cures meat, makes cheese and grows 16 varieties of heirloom seeds year-round. As if that weren't enough, it's then all whipped into meals that are scrumptious and entirely satisfying.

Simmons Mattress Factory
CANADIAN $$

(Map p58; www.evexperience.com/simmons; 618 Confluence Way SE; bakery $7-12, restaurant mains $12-25; ☺ bakery items 8am-6pm, restaurant 11.30am-10pm, cafe 7.30am-9pm) This old brick factory is breathing new life into Inglewood, where you can have all of your culinary cravings satisfied: Charbar's upstairs and rooftop restaurant serves incredible meals straight from the fire pit, Sidewalk Citizen Bakery can fill your belly with salads, sandwiches and yummy treats, and Phil & Sebastian Coffee Roasters makes a damn fine cup of joe.

Without Papers
PIZZA $$

(☎ 403-457-1154; wopizza.ca; 1216 9th Ave SE; pizzas $16-22; ☺ 11am-10pm Mon-Thu, to 11pm Fri & Sat, 4-9pm Sun) These authentic pizzas are baked in an Italian pizza oven that was lowered through the ceiling. The busy pizzeria's name is a nod to early Italian immigrants, while its pizzas and calzones are fresh and creative. The walls are covered in old movie posters and the tables are filled with happy pizza eaters.

Una
PIZZA $$

(Map p58; ☎ 403-453-1183; www.unapizzeria. com; 618 17th Ave SW; pizzas $17-22; ☺ 11.30am-1am) There's often a line out the door but nobody seems to mind waiting – that's how good these thin-crust pizzas are. Toppings like double smoked bacon and *fior di latte* mozzarella could quite possibly be addictive. There's plenty of good house wine, too.

Ox and Angela
TAPAS $$

(Map p58; ☎ 403-457-1432; www.oxandangela. com; 528 17th Ave SW; tapas $4-14; ☺ 11:30am-late) Re-creating Spain in modern Calgary isn't an obvious go-to but Ox and Angela has somehow managed it with colorful tiles and delicious tapas. Order piecemeal from a menu of Manchego cheese, tortilla (Spanish omelette) and cured *jamón serrano*.

Mercato
ITALIAN $$

(Map p58; ☎ 403-263-5535; www.mercato gourmet.com; 2224 4th St SW; mains $16-22; ☺ 11:30am-11pm) Attached to an open-plan Italian market-deli that sells everything from coffee to salami, Mercato is one of those local restaurants that gets everything right. Decor, service, atmosphere, food and price all hit the spot in a modern but authentic take on la dolce vita in the endearing Mission neighborhood.

Pulcinella
ITALIAN $$

(Map p58; ☎ 403-283-1166; www.pulcinella.ca; 1147 Kensington Cres NW; pizzas $15-20; ☺ 11:30am-11pm) With an authentic pizza oven, Pulcinella specializes in amazing thin crispy Neapolitan pizzas with purposefully simple toppings. You won't want to leave without trying the homemade gelato with flavors like black cherry and pistachio.

Blink
FUSION $$

(Map p58; ☎ 403-263-5330; www.blinkcalgary. com; 111 8th Ave SW; mains from $20; ☺ 11am-2pm Mon-Fri, 5-10pm Mon-Sat) 🌿 It's true, you could miss this small oasis tucked along a busy street and that would be a shame. Inside this trendy gastro haven, an acclaimed chef oversees an ever-evolving menu of fine dishes like smoked ricotta ravioli with walnuts and truffle vinaigrette or grilled striploin with caramelized shallots and red-wine sauce. Food is fresh and, wherever possible, locally sourced.

Catch
SEAFOOD $$

(Map p58; ☎ 403-206-0000; www.catchrestaurant. ca; 100 8th Ave SW; mains $17-27; ☺ 11:30am-2pm Mon-Fri, 5-10pm Mon-Sat) The problem for any saltwater fish restaurant in landlocked Calgary is that if you're calling it fresh, it can't be local. Overcoming the conundrum, the lively, ever-popular Catch, situated in an old bank building on Stephen Ave Walk, flies its 'fresh catch' in daily from both coasts (British Columbia and the Maritimes).

Teatro

ITALIAN $$$

(Map p58; ☑ 403-290-1012; www.teatro.ca; 200 8th Ave SE; mains lunch $18-20, dinner $28-50; ⊘noon-4pm Mon-Fri, 5-10pm daily) In a regal bank building next to the Epcor Centre of Performing Arts, Teatro has an art nouveau touch with its marble bar top, swirling metalwork and high-backed curved sofas. Dishes are works of art and fuse Italian influences, French nouvelle cuisine and a bit of traditional Alberta.

Model Milk

CANADIAN $$$

(Map p58; ☑ 403-265-7343; www.modelmilk.ca; 108 17th Ave SW; mains $19-32; ⊘5pm-1am) Model Milk's revolving menu changes before the ink's even dry, but your choices are always great at the former dairy turned hip restaurant. Look for favorites like grits and sausage or chicken with buttermilk waffles and peanut coleslaw. More certain is the excellent service and the cool ambience that comes with an open kitchen and communal seating.

Rouge

FUSION $$$

(☑403-531-2767; www.rougecalgary.com; 1240 8th Ave SE; mains lunch $16-20, dinner $30-46; ⊘11:30am-1:30pm Mon-Fri, 5-10pm Mon-Sat) One of the city's most celebrated restaurants, Rouge is located in a historic 1891 mansion in Inglewood. It's to hard to get a table, but once inside, enjoy the inspired, sustainable food and exceptional fit-for-a-king service. The menu evolves weekly but you'll find dishes like duck and pistachio terrine, beef bolognaise with hand-cut noodles or rockfish with curry coconut broth.

🍷 Drinking & Nightlife

Hit 17th Ave NW for a slew of martini lounges and crowded pubs, and 4th St SW for a lively after-work scene. Other notable areas include Kensington Rd NW and Stephen Ave. Evenings bring out stretch limos and noisy stag nights in corporate bars. For Calgary's gay and lesbian nightlife, pick up a copy of *Outlooks* (www.outlooks.ca).

★ Proof

COCKTAIL BAR

(Map p58; ☑ 403-246-2414; www.proofyyc.com; 1302 1st St SW; ⊘4pm-1am) This place might be small but the bar is big enough to require a library ladder. Big leather chairs and lots of metal and wood highlight craftsmanship – as do the expertly created cocktails. The menu itself is a beautiful thing to behold and the drinks look so stunning, you almost don't want to drink them. Almost.

Cru Juice

JUICE BAR

(Map p58; ☑ 403-452-2159; www.crujuice.com; 816 16th Ave SW; juice $7-12) Cold-pressed juice is the latest craze in Calgary. Like a meal in a bottle, it can be found in trendy cafes or at this flagship store. Some flavors are super tasty, like The Pixie (watermelon, pink grapefruit, strawberry, lime and mint), while others are a little more challenging – take the Dirty Lemonade (lemon, honey, clay and charcoal).

Analog Coffee

COFFEE

(Map p58; www.fratellocoffee.com; 740 17th Ave SW; coffees $2-5; ⊘7am-10pm) The third-wave coffee scene is stirring in Calgary, led by companies like Fratello, which runs this narrow, overflowing hipster-ish 17th Ave cafe, which displays the beans of the day on a clipboard and has rows of retro vinyl spread along the back wall.

Barley Mill

PUB

(Map p58; ☑403-290-1500; www.barleymillcalgary. com; 201 Barclay Pde SW; ⊘11am-late) Built in a 1900s style, with the original distillery's lumber used for the top floor and an actual waterwheel churning outside, the Barley Mill draws crowds for its pub grub, long lineup of draught beers and a well-stocked bar. Two patios for when it's warm and a big stone fireplace for when it's not keeps it busy in every season.

Back Lot

GAY

(Map p58; thebacklotbar.com; 209 10th Ave SW; ⊘9pm-2:30am) Calgary's oldest gay bar is West Hollywood–style – as in rough around the edges. Drinks are cheap and it often has live bands or karaoke.

Twisted Element

GAY & LESBIAN

(Map p58; www.twistedelement.ca; 1006 11th Ave SW; ⊘9pm-late Wed-Sun) Consistently voted the best gay dance venue by the local community, this club has weekly drag shows, karaoke nights and DJs spinning nightly. Its tagline reads: Coming out was hard enough; going out shouldn't be.

HiFi Club

CLUB

(Map p58; www.hificlub.ca; 219 10th Ave SW; ⊘9pm-2:30am Wed-Sun) The HiFi is a hybrid. Rap, soul, house, electro, funk – the dance floor swells nightly to the sounds of live DJs who specialize in making you sweat.

Rose & Crown

PUB

(Map p58; ☑ 403-244-7757; www.roseandcrown calgary.ca; 1503 4th St SW; ⊘11am-late) Originally a funeral home in the 1920s and believed by many to be haunted, this popular, multilevel British-style pub is a popular place for a pint. Upstairs you'll find vintage wallpaper and possibly a ghost or two.

Hop In Brew
PUB

(Map p58; ☏ 403-266-2595; 213 12th Ave SW; ☺4pm-late) Without the hand-printed Pub sign in the window, this would just look like the old arts-and-crafts-style house that it is, clinging on for dear life amid the spanking new condos. Downscale and snug, the Hop continues to be listed in Calgary's top pub lists with good tunes and plenty of beers on tap.

☆ Entertainment

For complete entertainment guides, pick up a copy of *ffwd* (www.ffwdweekly.com), the city's largest entertainment weekly. The paper is free and found in numerous coffee bars, restaurants and street boxes in Calgary, Banff and Canmore.

Ironwood Stage & Grill
LIVE MUSIC

(www.ironwoodstage.ca; 1229 9th Ave SE, Inglewood; ☺shows 8pm Sun-Thu, 9pm Fri & Sat) Cross over into the hip universe of Inglewood to find the grassroots of Calgary's music scene. Local bands alternate with bigger touring acts for nightly music in the welcoming, woody confines of Ironwood. Country and folk are the staples. Events are all ages.

Calgary Flames
SPECTATOR SPORT

(☏ 403-777-0000; flames.nhl.com) Archrival of the Edmonton Oilers, the Calgary Flames play ice hockey from October to April at the **Saddledome** (Map p58; Stampede Park). Make sure you wear red to the game and head down to 17th Ave afterwards, or the 'Red Mile,' as they call it during play-offs.

Loose Moose Theatre Company
THEATER

(☏ 403-265-5682; www.loosemoose.com; 1235 26th Ave SE) Guaranteed to be a fun night out, Loose Moose has digs near the Inglewood neighborhood. It specializes in improv comedy and, at times, audience participation. (You've been warned.) You'll also find kids' theater.

Epcor Centre for the Performing Arts
THEATER

(Map p58; www.epcorcentre.org; 205 8th Ave SE) This is the hub for live theater in Calgary. With four theaters and one of the best concert halls in North America, here you can see everything from ballet to Bollywood.

Globe Cinema
CINEMA

(Map p58; www.globecinema.ca; 617 8th Ave SW) This art-house theater specializes in foreign films and Canadian cinema – both often hard to find in mainstream movie houses. Look for discounts on Tuesdays and matinees on the weekend.

Plaza Theatre
CINEMA

(Map p58; ☏ 403-283-3636; 1113 Kensington Rd NW) Built in the 1920s as a garage but turned into a neighbourhood theatre during the 1930s depression, the Plaza is the last operating neighborhood theater in Calgary. Right in the heart of Kensington, it shows art-house flicks and cult classics. Call the 24-hour movie line for what's on.

Broken City
LIVE MUSIC

(Map p58; ☏ 403-262-9976; www.brokencity.ca; 613 11th Ave SW; ☺11am-2am) There's something on stage here most nights – everything from jazz jams to hip-hop, along with comedy and quiz nights. The rooftop patio is ace in the summer, and the small but well-curated menu keeps you happy whether you're after a steak sandwich or vegan cauliflower wings.

Calgary Stampeders
SPECTATOR SPORT

(☏ 403-289-0258; www.stampeders.com) The Calgary Stampeders, part of the CFL, play from July to September at **McMahon Stadium** (1817 Crowchild Trail NW) in the University District, located 6km northwest of downtown.

Pumphouse Theatres
THEATER

(www.pumphousetheatres.ca; 2140 Pumphouse Ave SW) Set in what used to be, you guessed it, the pumphouse, this theater company puts on avant-garde, edgy productions like *One Man Star Wars Trilogy*.

🛍 Shopping

Calgary has several hot shopping spots, but these districts are reasonably far apart. The Kensington area and 17th Ave SW have a good selection of interesting, fashionable clothing shops and funky trinket outlets. Stephen Ave Walk is a pedestrian mall with shops, bookstores and atmosphere. Inglewood is good for antiques, junk, apothocaries, and secondhand books and vinyl.

Tea Trader
TEA

(☏ 403-264-0728; www.teatrader.com; 1228a 9th Ave SE; ☺10am-5pm Tue-Sat, noon-4pm Sun) Canadians are Canadians and even in Calgary they drink tea. This little shop is up a set of stairs and very easy to miss but also worth searching out. Teas from all over the world line the shelves, as well as some local flavors: try Calgary Welsh Breakfast or the Alberta Clipper.

Smithbilt Hats CLOTHING
(☑ 403-244-9131; www.smithbilthats.com; 1103 12th St SE; ⊙ 9am-5pm Mon-Thu, 8am-4:30pm Fri) Ever wondered how a cowboy hat is made? Well, here is your chance to find out. Smithbilt has been shaping hats in the traditional way since you parked your horse out front. You can pick up one made of straw or beaver felt and priced accordingly.

Alberta Boot Co SHOES
(☑ 403-263-4605; www.albertaboot.com; 50 50th Ave SE; ⊙ 9am-6pm Mon-Sat) Visit the factory and store run by the province's only Western boot manufacturer and pick up a pair of your choice made of kangaroo, bullhide or boring old cowhide. Over 200 hours of labor go into each boot, which can be custom-designed. Prices range from $375 to $2100.

❶ Information

Main post office (Map p58; 207 9th Ave SW; ⊙ 8am-5:45pm Mon-Fri)
Tourism Calgary (Map p58; www.tourism calgary.com; 101 9th Ave SW; ⊙ 8am-5pm)

Has a visitor center in the base of the Calgary Tower. The staff will help you find accommodations. Information booths are also available at both the arrivals and departures levels of the airport.

❶ Getting There & Away

AIR
Calgary International Airport (YYC; www.ycc. com) is about 15km northeast of the center off Barlow Trail, a 25-minute drive away.

BUS
Greyhound Canada (☑ bus station 403-263-1234, ticket purchase 800-661-8747; www. greyhound.ca; 850 16th St SW) has services to Banff ($29, 1¾ hours), Edmonton ($52, 3½ hours), Drumheller ($38, 1¾ hours) and Lethbridge ($46, 2½ hours). Note that discounts are available online.

For a more comfortable experience, go with the super-luxurious **Red Arrow** (Map p58; www.redarrow.pwt.ca; 205 9th Ave SE) buses to Edmonton ($71, 3½ hours, six daily) and Lethbridge ($49, 2½ hours, one daily).

Canmore and Banff ($65, 2¼ hours, eight daily) are served by the legendary Brewster (www.brewster.ca).

Red Arrow picks up downtown on the corner of 9th Ave SE and 1st Ave SE. Brewster buses pick up at various downtown hotels. Inquire when booking.

WORTH A TRIP

TURNER VALLEY

As you head south on the Cowboy Trail (Hwy 22), you'll pass through Turner Valley. At first glance it looks like many of the small towns...until you put your nose to the air and get a waft of the aroma-imbued air. It's definitely worth stopping here to fill both your belly and your liquor cabinet.

Chuck Wagon Cafe (www.chuckwagoncafe.ca; 105 Sunset Blvd, Turner Valley; mains $15-30; ⊙ 8am-2:30pm Mon-Fri, to 3:30pm Sat & Sun) Housed in a tiny red barn, this legendary cafe feels much like the homestead kitchen it is – it draws hungry diners from miles around. The enormous, all-day breakfast of smoked hash, triple-A steak and eggs Benedict will have you shouting, "Yeehaw!" This is ranch cooking at its best.

Eau Claire Distillery (www.eauclairedistillery.ca; tasting $6.50, tasting & tour $12, cocktails $17-20; ⊙ 11am-6pm Mon-Thu, 10am-8pm Fri & Sat, 10am-6pm Sun, tours noon, 2pm & 4pm) Next door to the cafe, this is the province's first craft distillery, using Alberta grain and custom-crafted German stills. Having taken over the town's original movie theater and built on the site of the neighboring brothel, this award-winning place pours tastings of gin, vodka and EquineOx – a barley-based spirit – infused with natural flavors like prickly pear and lemon, as well as single-malt whiskey. Take a tour and sit yourself down at the bar for a cocktail.

CAR & MOTORCYCLE

All the major car-rental firms are represented at the airport and downtown.

TRAIN

Inexplicably, Calgary welcomes no passenger trains (which bypass the city in favor of Edmonton and Jasper). You have to find other transport from those destinations.

❶ Getting Around

TO/FROM THE AIRPORT

Sundog Tours (☑ 403-291-9617; www.sundog tours.com; adult/child one-way $15/8) runs every half-hour from around 8:30am to 9:45pm between all the major downtown hotels and the airport.

You can also go between the airport and downtown on public transportation. From the airport, take bus 57 to the Whitehorn stop (northeast of the city center) and transfer to the C-Train; reverse that process coming from downtown. You can also take bus 300 from the city center all the way to the airport. Either way, the trip costs only $3, and takes between 45 minutes and an hour.

A taxi to the airport costs about $35 from downtown.

CAR & MOTORCYCLE

Parking in downtown Calgary is an expensive nightmare – a policy designed to push people to use public transportation. Luckily, downtown hotels generally have garages. Private lots charge about $20 per day. There is also some metered parking. Outside the downtown core, parking is free and easy to find.

Calgary has the largest fleet of car2go smart cars (www.car2go.com), making it a super convenient way to get around town and even to the airport.

PUBLIC TRANSPORTATION

Calgary Transit (www.calgarytransit.com) is efficient and clean. You can choose from the Light Rapid Transit (LRT) rail system, aka the C-Train, and ordinary buses. One fare ($3) entitles you to transfer to other buses or C-Trains. The C-Train is free in the downtown area along 7th Ave between 10th St SW and 3rd St SE. If you're going further or need a transfer, buy your ticket from a machine on the C-Train platform. Most buses run at 15- to 30-minute intervals daily. There is no late-night service.

TAXI

For a cab, call **Checker Cabs** (☑ 403-299-9999; www.thecheckergroup.com) or **Calgary Cabs** (☑ 403-777-1111). Fares are $3 for the first 150m, then 20¢ for each additional 150m.

BANFF & JASPER NATIONAL PARKS

With the Rocky Mountains stretched across them, Banff and Jasper National Parks are filled with dramatic, untamed wilderness. Rugged mountaintops scrape the skyline while enormous glaciers cling to their precipices. Glassy lakes flash emerald, turquoise and sapphire, filled by waterfalls tumbling down cliff faces and thundering through bottomless canyons. Deep forests blanket wide valleys and lofty alpine meadows explode with vibrant flowers. It's the scenery that you only expect to see on postcards, right here at your fingertips. And through it wander a cast of elusive wildlife characters such as bears, elk, moose, wolves and bighorn sheep.

Of the thousands of national parks scattered around the world today, Banff, created in 1885, is the third oldest and Canada's first, while adjacent Jasper was only 22 years behind. Situated on the eastern side of the Canadian Rockies, the two bordering parks were designated Unesco World Heritage sites in 1984. In contrast to some of North America's more remote parks, they both support small towns that lure from two to five million visitors each year.

Despite the throngs who come for the parks' more famous sites, like Lake Louise and Miette Hot Springs, it's by no means difficult to escape to a more tranquil experience of this sublime wonderland. However you choose to experience the parks, be it through hiking, backcountry skiing, paddling or simply sitting at a lake's edge beneath towering, castle-like mountains, the intensity and scale of these parks will bowl over even the most seasoned traveler. The more you see, the more you'll come to appreciate these parks' magic – and the more you'll want to discover.

Kananaskis Country

Kananaskis, or K-Country as the locals call it, is a mountainous Shangri-la, with all the natural highlights of Banff National Park, but with almost no clamor. With less traffic and no fencing, you are very likely to encounter plenty of wildlife here. Kananaskis abuts Banff National Park in the southeast, and at an impressive 4000 sq km, it's a hefty tract of landscape to try and take in. Luckily, there's a network of hiking trails to get you into the backcountry and away from the roads. Hikers,

Banff National Park

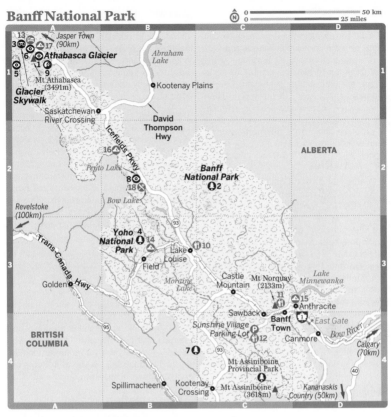

cross-country skiers, cyclists and climbers – mainly in-the-know Albertans – all lust over these hills, which are the perfect combination of wild, accessible, unspoiled and inviting. If you recognize anything, it's probably because you've seen it in one of a score of films made here, including *Brokeback Mountain*.

On the eastern edge of the mountains you can drive the scenic and sparsely trafficked Hwy 40 (south off Hwy 1, 20km east of Canmore) to the Kananaskis lakes, before turning down onto the unsealed Smith Dorrien Rd to complete the drive back to Canmore by a circuitous, picturesque route. Or if you can, continue along Hwy 40 – which will treat you to blankets of pine forest interspersed with craggy peaks and the odd moose in the verge – all the way to Highwood House. This scenic drive is definitely the road less traveled and well worth exploring (but be aware that this portion of the road is closed over winter).

🏃 Activities

K-Country is also C-Country. Cowboy-up and go for a trail ride with **Boundary Ranch** (☑ 403-591-7171; www.boundaryranch.com; Hwy 40; rides from $46; ☺ May-Oct), which could last anywhere from one hour to a few days.

Purpose-built to host the alpine skiing events in the 1988 Olympics, **Nakiska** (www.skinakiska.com; Hwy 40; day pass adult/youth $77/58), five minutes' drive south of the region's main service center Kananaskis Village, is a racer's dream. Top Canadian skiers still train here, in fact. K-Country's other ski resort, Fortress Mountain, has been closed on and off (mainly off) since 2004.

The Kananaskis River has class II and III rapids and is popular with white-water rafting companies operating out of Banff.

★ **Peter Lougheed Provincial Park**   HIKING
(www.albertaparks.ca/peter-lougheed) K-Country's quiet trails and backcountry offer superb hiking, especially around this 304-sq-km park on the west side of Kananaskis Valley, which includes the **Upper** and **Lower Kananaskis Lakes** and the **Highwood Pass**, the highest navigable road pass in Canada (2350m; usually open from June to October). It's an excellent area for wildlife-spotting: watch for foxes, wolves, bears, lynx and coyotes.

Kananaskis Outfitters   ADVENTURE SPORTS
(www.kananaskisoutfitters.com; Kananaskis Village; bike/ski rental per day $45/25; ☺ 10am-6pm) Outfitter in Kananaskis Village that rents bikes, cross-country skis and fat bikes for winter rides. It also runs canoe tours in the summer on Barrier Lake and winter bike tours over frozen waterfalls.

🛌 Sleeping

★ **Sundance Lodges**   CAMPGROUND $
(☑ 403-591-7122; www.sundancelodges.com; Kananaskis Trail; campsites $32, tipis $65-90, trappers' tents $90; ☺ mid-May–Oct) For that authentic Canadian experience, try the hand-painted tipis and old-timey trappers' tents at this privately run campground. As you'd expect, facilities are basic – sleeping platforms and a kerosene lantern are about all you'll find inside – so you'll need the usual camping gear, but kids are bound to lap up the John Muir vibe.

Delta Lodge at Kananaskis   HOTEL $$
(☑ 403-591-7711; www.deltahotels.com; 1 Centennial Dr, Kananaskis Village; r from $169; 🅿 ❄ @ 🛜 🏊) Kananaskis 'village' effectively consists of this sprawling lodge and its outbuildings, which include half a dozen restaurants and an outfitters store. The lodge gained international fame when it hosted the 2008 G8 summit (with GW Bush, Putin, Blair et al), an event that helped put K-Country on the map.

★ **Mt Engadine Lodge**   LODGE $$$
(☑ 403-678-4080; www.mountengadine.com; Mt Shark Rd; s/d/4-person chalets $220/500/795; 🅿 🛜) You can't get much more rural – or more peaceful – than this remote mountain lodge. The lodge has peaceful rooms and family suites (with balcony and sitting room) overlooking unspoiled meadows and a natural salt lick frequented by moose. The decor is lodge-style, with an antler chandelier and antique skis on the wall. Room are comfy without being fussy.

ℹ Information

Barrier Lake Information Centre (☑ 403-673-3985; www.albertaparks.ca; Hwy 40; ☺ 9am-5pm) Has info and sells backcountry camping permits ($12); located on Hwy 40, about 8km from Hwy 1.

Elbow Valley Visitor Centre (☑ 403-949-2461; www.albertaparks.ca; ☺ 10:30am-2pm & 3-6pm Fri, 9am-12:30pm & 1:30-4:30pm Sat & Sun May-Oct) Just west of Bragg Creek.

Peter Lougheed Information Centre (☑ 403-591-6322; www.albertaparks.ca/peter-lougheed; Kananaskis Lakes Rd; ☺ 9am-9pm Jul & Aug, 9:30am-4pm Apr-Jun, Sep & Oct, closed Nov-Mar) Near the junction with Hwy 742, north of Kananaskis Lakes.

ℹ Getting There & Away

Brewster (☑ 403-762-6750; www.brewster.ca; 100 Gopher St, Banff Town) runs two or three buses between the Delta Lodge in Kananaskis Village and Calgary's airport (adult/youth $60/30). You can also sometimes get a shuttle from the Delta to Nakoda Resort on Hwy 1, where you can meet up with Brewster buses to Banff or Jasper.

It's best to have your own wheels. Be sure to double-check your policy if you're driving a rental; the Smith Dorrien Rd is unsealed so not all rental insurance will cover it. Also be aware that there is virtually no cell-phone service along that route, and no gas stations.

Canmore

POP 12,288

A former coal-mining town, Canmore was once the quiet alternative to the mass tourism of Banff. But after one too many 'best-kept secret' travel articles, everybody started coming here for a little peace and quiet. Despite the commotion, the soul of the town has remained intact, and Canmore, although not national-park protected, has been developed sensibly and sustainably – so far. At just 26km from Banff and on the cusp of Kananaskis Country, it's at the crossroads of some of the most magnificent scenery you will ever see. For those seeking a mountain holiday with slightly less glitz – with more of a rugged feel and less pretension – Canmore can still cut it.

◉ Sights

Canmore Museum & Geoscience Centre   MUSEUM
(www.cmags.org; 907 7th Ave, Canmore; adult/youth/child $7/5/free; ⊙noon-5pm Mon-Fri, 11am-5pm Sat & Sun May-Sep, 1-4pm Fri-Mon Oct-Apr) Completely renovated in 2016 following flood damage from three years previous, this small but well-curated museum is worth a visit. Exhibits cover the region's coal-mining past and the community's survival following the mine closure in 1979. Check out the 160-million-year-old petrified cypress stump and the stunning images taken by local photographer Craig Richards.

North West Mounted Police Barracks   MUSEUM
(www.cmags.org; 601 8th St; ⊙1-4pm Mon & Tue, 10am-5pm Wed-Sun summer, 1-4pm Fri-Mon winter) **FREE** The oldest surviving barracks in western Canada was built in 1893 and used by the Royal Canadian Mounted Police (RCMP) until 1929. Today this itty-bitty wooden building is home to a small display of Mountie-themed memorabilia and a quaint tearoom.

🏃 Activities

Canmore excels in three mountain activities: cross-country skiing, mountain biking and rock climbing.

★**Canmore Nordic Centre**   MOUNTAIN BIKING, SKIING
(www.canmorenordiccentre.ca; Olympic Way) Nestled in the hills to the west of town on the way to the Spray Lakes Reservoir, this huge trail center was originally developed for the Nordic events of the 1988 Winter Olympics. It's now one of the best mountain-bike parks in western Canada, with over 65 km (40 miles) of groomed trails developed by some of the nation's top trail designers. In winter, trails are open to cross-country skiers (day pass $15), with 6.5km lit for night skiing.

Yamnuska Mountain Adventures   CLIMBING
(☑403-678-4164; www.yamnuska.com; Suite 200, Summit Centre, 50 Lincoln Park; ⊙9am-5pm Mon-Fri, to 4pm Sat) This well-regarded company offers instruction courses in both rock and ice climbing, for beginner, intermediate or advanced climbers. From Tuesday to Saturday in July and August there's a daily climb for $140 per person, including gear and transport. Just show up at Bow Falls (p76) in Banff at 8:30am.

Canmore Cave Tours   ADVENTURE
(☑403-678-8819; www.canmorecavetours.com) Buried deep beneath the Grotto Mountain near Canmore is a system of deep caves known as the **Rat's Nest**. Canmore Cave Tours runs guided trips into the maze of twisting passageways and claustrophobic caverns.

Snowy Owl Tours   DOG SLEDDING
(☑403-678-9588; www.snowyowltours.com; 829 10th St; 2hr tour adult/child $160/85) Dog sledding has been a traditional mode of travel in the Canadian Rockies for centuries, and it's a wonderful way to see the wilderness. Snowy Owl Tours offers sled trips on custom-built sleighs pulled by your own well-cared-for team of Siberian and Alaskan huskies.

🛏 Sleeping

Staying in Canmore is often seen as a cheaper, more relaxed alternative to Banff. Nevertheless, the good selection of hotels and B&Bs has made it popular in its own right so it's wise to book ahead.

Canmore Clubhouse   HOSTEL $
(☑403-678-3200; www.alpineclubofcanada.ca; Indian Flats Rd; dm from $40; ℗) 🌿 Steeped in climbing history and mountain mystique, the Alpine Club of Canada's beautiful hostel sits on a rise overlooking the valley,

LOCAL KNOWLEDGE

THE LEGACY TRAIL

It's not often that getting from point A to B involves dazzling scenery, the possibility of spotting a moose and a huge dose of mountain air. The Legacy Trail is a 26.8km paved route that connects cyclists, pedestrians and skaters with Canmore and Banff Town. Shadowing Hwy 1 and gaining 30m elevation, the trail takes most peddlers two or three hours round-trip. For those not up to cycling/walking in both directions, **Bike 'n' Hike Shuttle** (☏ 403-762-2282; www.bikeandhikeshuttle.com; $10-20; ☺ May-Oct) offer a handy bus service between the trailheads to get you back to your starting point.

Banff and Canmore are linked by two additional trails, the rugged **Rundle Riverside Trail** (for experienced off-road cyclists) and the easier **Goat Creek Trail**. Check with **Parks Canada** (www.pc.gc.ca) for current conditions.

with views through big picture windows. There's all of the usual hostel amenities here, along with a sauna. It's a great place to find climbing partners or just soak up the spirit of adventure. It is located 5km south of town.

Lady Macdonald Country Inn GUESTHOUSE $$
(☏ 800-567-3919; www.ladymacdonald.com; 1201 Bow Valley Trail; r $125-199, ste $200-250; P ☎) This quaint little inn wouldn't look out of place in small-town Connecticut, with its elegant verandahs, turrets and wooden cladding. Rooms are petite, with wrought-iron beds, cushions and some floral print for good measure. Each is unique so it's worth checking out a few.

Blackstone Mountain Lodge HOTEL $$
(☏ 888-830-8883; www.blackstonecanmore. ca; 170 Kananaskis Way; d/ste from $160/200; P ✳ ☎ ⌘) The pick of several Bellstar properties around Canmore, the Blackstone is located a quick drive out of town on the Bow Valley Trail. Traditional rooms have plush linens while suites come with their own fully equipped kitchen (complete with oven, dishwasher and washing machine), making them ideal for families. All in all, it's a bit of a steal.

Paintbox Lodge B&B $$
(☏ 403-609-0482; www.paintboxlodge.com; 629 10th St, Canmore; r $150-280; P ☎) Run by ex-Olympic skiers Thomas Grandi and Sarah Renner, this B&B takes Canadian decor to a new level, right down to the tartan carpet. Its five unique suites offer a mix of country chic and luxury comfort. For maximum space ask for the Loft Suite, which sleeps four people and features beamed ceilings, mountain-view balcony and sexy corner tub.

🍴 Eating

★ **Communitea** CAFE $
(www.thecommunitea.com; 1001 6th Ave; lunch mains $12-15; ☺ 9am-5pm; ☎ ⌘) 🍴 Locally run, ethically aware and all organic, this community cafe somehow manages to sidestep any crusty hippy vibe with a warm, relaxed feel and simple style. Food is ultra fresh and an explosion of flavor: think noodles, rice bowls, wraps, salads and burgers. Slurp fresh-pressed juices, well-executed coffee and, of course, every type of tea you can conceive of.

Rocky Mountain Bagel CAFE $
(☏ 403-678-9978; www.thebagel.ca; 829 8th St; bagels $6-8; ☺ 6am-6pm; ☎) 🍴 Is there anything better in life than sitting under the flower baskets at Rocky Mountain Bagel, studying the morning shadows on the Three Sisters peaks while enjoying a toasted maple bagel and a latte? Possibly not. Bagelwiches, pizza bagels, breakfast bagels or a bag of bagels to go. Rocky Mountain Bagels has got it covered.

Grizzly Paw PUB FOOD $$
(☏ 403-678-9983; www.thegrizzlypaw.com; 622 8th St; mains $13-20; ☺ 11am-midnight) 🍴 Alberta's best microbrewery (offering six year-round beers) is hiding in the mountains of Canmore. With beer and food pairings, big burgers, hand-crafted sodas and a view-filled patio, it's a popular spot. The veterans of Raspberry Ale and Grumpy Bear beer have a nearby brewery and microdistillery where tours and tasters are available.

★ **Trough** CANADIAN $$$
(☏ 403-678-2820; www.thetrough.ca; 725 9th St; mains $32-38; ☺ 5:30pm-late Tue-Sun) Canmore's slinkiest bistro is a bit tucked away on 9th St, but it's absolutely worth the effort

to find. It regularly features in the Rockies' top restaurant lists, and with good reason. The mother-son team here create amazing dishes like Prince Edward Island (PEI) mussels with house-smoked tomatoes, Moroccan-spiced Alberta lamb chops, and BC halibut with mango and sweet peppers. With just nine tables, it's wise to book ahead.

ⓘ Information

Alberta Visitor Information Centre (☑403-678-5277; www.travelalberta.com; 2801 Bow Valley Trail; ☺8am-8pm May-Oct, to 6pm Nov-Apr) Regional visitor center just off the Trans-Canada Hwy northwest of town.

Canmore Visitors Information Centre (www.tourismcanmore.com; 907a 7th Ave; ☺9am-5pm)

ⓘ Getting There & Away

Canmore is easily accessible from Banff Town and Calgary from Hwy 1. The **Banff Airporter** (☑403-762-3330; www.banffairporter.com) runs up to 10 buses a day to/from Calgary Airport ($59). **Brewster** (☑866-606-6700; www.brewster.ca) has connections with the airport and downtown Calgary for roughly the same price.

Greyhound (www.greyhound.ca) has multiple daily trips to Calgary ($27, 75 minutes) and Banff ($6, 25 minutes). **Roam** (☑403-762-0606; www.roamtransit.com; ☺6am-10pm) buses run every hour to Banff ($6, 20 minutes). Buses stop downtown on 9th St near 7th Ave.

Icefields Parkway

As the highest and most spectacular road in North America, the Icefields Parkway (www.icefieldsparkway.ca; Hwy 93) takes you about as close as you're going to get to the Rockies' craggy summits in your vehicle; if you get out and follow one of the many trailheads en route, you'll feel like you're on top of the world within a matter of hours. Numerous roadside stops give you the chance to take in the parkway's brilliantly colored glacial lakes, gushing waterfalls and exquisite viewpoints. While you can cover the 230km route between Lake Louise and Jasper within a few hours, it's worth spending a few days exploring the region.

Much of the route followed by the parkway was established in the 1800s by Aboriginal people and fur traders. An early road was built during the 1930s as part of a work project for the unemployed, and the present highway was opened in the early 1960s. These days it's used almost entirely by tourists, with the exception of the occasional elk,

coyote or bighorn sheep meandering along its perimeter. It can get busy in July and August, particularly with large recreational vehicles (RVs). Many also tackle it on a bike – the road is wide and sprinkled with plenty of strategically spaced campgrounds, hostels and hotels.

⦿ Sights & Activities

There are two types of sights here: static (lakes, glaciers and mountains) and moving (elk, bears, moose etc). If you don't see at least one wild animal (look out for the inevitable 'bear jams') you'll be very unlucky.

★**Athabasca Glacier**   GLACIER
(Map p69) The tongue of the Athabasca Glacier runs from the Columbia Icefield to within walking distance of the road opposite the Icefield Centre. It can be visited on foot or in a Snocoach bus. It has retreated about 2km since 1844, when it reached the rock moraine on the north side side of the road. To reach its toe (bottom edge), walk from the Icefield Centre along the 1.8km **Forefield Trail**, then join the 1km **Toe of the Athabasca Glacier Trail**.

You can also park at the start of the latter trail. While it is permitted to stand on a small roped section of the ice, do not attempt to cross the warning tape – many do, but the glacier is riddled with crevasses and there have been fatalities.

To walk safely on the Columbia Icefield, you'll need to enlist the help of **Athabasca Glacier Icewalks** (Map p69; ☑780-852-5595; www.icewalks.com; Icefield Centre, Icefields Pkwy; 3hr tour adult/child $95/50, 6hr tour adult/child $120/60; ☺Jun-Oct), which supplies all the gear you'll need and a guide to show you the ropes. Its basic tour is three hours; there's a six-hour option for those wanting to venture further out on the glacier. Hikers must be at least seven years of age.

The other, far easier (and more popular) way to get on the glacier is via a **Snocoach** (Map p69; www.columbiaicefield.com; Snocoach & Skywalk tour adult/child $85/43; ☺9am-6pm Apr-Oct) ice tour offered by Brewster in conjunction with its **Skywalk** (Map p69; www.brewster.ca; skywalk adult/child $32/16; ☺10am-5pm Apr-Oct) tour. For many people this is the defining experience of their Columbia Icefield visit. The large hybrid bus-truck grinds a track onto the ice, where it stops to allow you to go for a wander on the glacier. Dress warmly, wear good shoes and bring a water bottle to try some freshly melted glacial water. Tickets

CYCLING THE ICEFIELDS PARKWAY

With its ancient geology, landscape-altering glaciers, and lakes bluer than Picasso paintings from his blue period, the 230km-long Icefields Parkway is one of the world's most spectacular roads, and, by definition, one of the world's most spectacular bicycle rides – if your legs and lungs are up to it. Aside from the distance, there are several long uphill drags, occasional stiff headwinds and two major passes to contend with, namely Bow Summit (2088m) and Sunwapta Pass (2035m). Notwithstanding these issues, the route is highly popular in July and August (don't even think about doing it in the winter), with aspiring cyclists lapping up its bicycle-friendly features. No commercial trucks are allowed on the parkway, there's a generous shoulder throughout, two-wheeled company is virtually guaranteed, and accommodations along the route (both campgrounds and hostels/hotels) is plentiful and strategically placed. Some ply the parkway as part of an organized tour (with back-up vehicles), others do it solo over two to five days. There's a choice of six HI hostels and four lodge/motel accommodations en route. Book ahead. Basic provisions can be procured at Saskatchewan River Crossing, 83km north of Lake Louise.

It's considered slightly easier to cycle from north to south, starting in Jasper and finishing in Lake Louise, but the differences aren't great. Some people tack on the extra 60km between Banff and Lake Louise at the start or finish, proceeding along the quiet Bow Valley Parkway and avoiding the busy Trans-Canada (Hwy 1).

Sturdy road bikes can be rented from **Wilson Mountain Sports** (www.wmsll.com; Samson Mall, Lake Louise village; ⊙9am-7pm) in Lake Louise village. Brewster buses can sometimes transport bicycles, but always check ahead. **Backroads** (☑510-527-1555; www.backroads.com; 7-day tour from $2800) runs a Canadian Rockies Bike Tour, a six-day organized trip that incorporates cycling along the parkway.

can be bought at the Icefield Centre or online; tours depart every 15 to 30 minutes.

Weeping Wall   WATERFALL
(Map p69) This towering rock wall sits just above the east side of the highway. In the summer months it is a sea of waterfalls, with tears of liquid pouring from the top, creating a veil of moisture. Come winter, it's a whole different story: the water freezes up solid to form an enormous sheet of ice. The vertical ice field is a popular playground for ice climbers, who travel from around the globe to test their mettle here.

Mt Edith Cavell   MOUNTAIN
(Map p90) Rising like a snowy sentinel over Jasper Town, Mt Edith Cavell (3363m) is one of the park's most distinctive and physically arresting peaks. What it lacks in height it makes up for in stark, ethereal beauty. Accessed via a winding, precipitous road that branches off the Icefields Pkwy 6km south of Jasper, the mountain is famous for its flower meadows and its wing-shaped **Angel Glacier**.

Columbia Icefield   GLACIER
(Map p69) About halfway between Lake Louise village and Jasper Town, you'll glimpse the vast Columbia Icefield, covering an area the size of Vancouver and feeding eight gla-

ciers. This remnant of the last ice age is up to 350m thick in places and stretches across the plateau between **Mt Columbia** (3747m) and **Mt Athabasca** (3491m). For serious hikers and climbers, this is also the only accessible area of the icefield. For information and conditions, visit Parks Canada at the Columbia Icefield Discovery Centre (p74).

Peyto Lake   LAKE
(Map p69) You'll have already seen the indescribable blue of Peyto Lake in a thousand publicity shots, but there's nothing like gazing at the real thing – especially since the viewing point for this lake is from a lofty vantage point several hundred feet above the water. The lake is best visited in early morning, between the time the sun first illuminates the water and the first tour bus arrives.

Columbia Icefield
Discovery Centre   CENTER
(Map p69; www.brewster.ca; Icefields Pkwy; ⊙10am-5pm May-Oct) **FREE** Situated on the Icefields Pkwy, close to the toe of the Athabasca Glacier, the green-roofed Icefield Centre is a bit of a zoo in the summer, with tour coaches cramming the car park. Decamp here to purchase tickets and board buses for the Snocoaches and Glacier Skywalk. You'll

also find a hotel, cafeteria, restaurant, gift shop and Parks Canada information desk.

Athabasca Glacier to
Jasper Town   SCENIC DRIVE
As you snake your way through the mountains on your way to Jasper, there are a few places worth stopping at. **Sunwapta Falls** (Map p90) and **Athabasca Falls** (Map p90), closer to Jasper, are both worth a stop. The latter is the more voluminous and is at its most ferocious in the summer, when it's stoked with glacial meltwater.

A less visited spot is idyllic, blue-green Horseshoe Lake (p88), revered by ill-advised cliff divers. Don't be tempted to join them.

At Athabasca Falls, Hwy 93A quietly sneaks off to the left. Take it. Literally the road less traveled, this old route into Jasper offers a blissfully traffic-free experience as it slips serenely through deep, dark woods and past small, placid lakes and meadows.

🛏 Sleeping & Eating

The Icefields Parkway is punctuated by several well-camouflaged hostels. Most are close to the highway in scenic locations. More substantial hotels/lodges are available at Bow Lake, Saskatchewan Crossing, Columbia Icefield and Sunwapta Falls.

There are also numerous primitive campgrounds in the area. Good options are **Honeymoon Lake** (Map p90; Icefields Pkwy; tent & RV sites $16; ⊗Jun-Sep), **Jonas Creek** (Map p90; Icefields Pkwy; tent & RV sites $16; ⊗May-Sep), **Mt Kerkeslin** (Map p90; Icefields Pkwy; tent & RV sites $16; ⊗Jun-Sep), **Waterfowl Lakes** (Map p69; Icefields Pkwy; tent & RV sites $22; ⊗Jun-Sep) and **Wilcox Creek** (Map p69; Icefields Pkwy; tent & RV sites winter/summer $10/16) campgrounds. These campsites are nonreservable.

Mt Edith Cavell
International Hostel   HOSTEL $
(Map p90; ☑780-852-3215; www.hihostels.ca; Cavell Rd; dm $26; ⊗mid-May–mid-Oct) 🍴 Sitting in the foothills of one of the Rockies' most sublime mountain peaks, this hostel enjoys phenomenal views from the deck and outdoor firepit. The kitchen and common room have wooden beams and homey touches. There's solar electricity but no flush toilets, showers, phone or wi-fi. It's located directly across the road from the trailhead for the Tonquin Valley.

There's a manager here from June to October but the hostel is open for cross-country

skiers from February to May on a key-collect system. Guests have use of showers at the main hostel in Jasper (p93).

Athabasca Falls
International Hostel   HOSTEL $
(Map p90; ☑780-852-3215; www.hihostels.ca; Icefields Pkwy; dm/d $30/72; ⊗May-Sep) 🍴 A super-friendly hostel in the woods with an ingenious watering-can shower (summer only); a big, alpine-style kitchen–sitting area; table tennis; and heated dorms in separate wooden cabins. There's no running water (just an outdoor pump) and the toilets are in outhouses, earning the place a 'rustic' tag.

Sunwapta Falls Resort   HOTEL $$
(Map p90; ☑888-828-5777; www.sunwapta.com; Icefields Pkwy; r from $225; 🅿@) A handy Icefields rest stop 53km south of Jasper Town, Sunwapta offers a comfortable mix of suites and lodge rooms, each with a fireplace or wood-burning stove and cocooned in pleasant natural surroundings. Clean and comfortable but not fancy, it's close to the falls and plenty of hiking. There's also a home-style restaurant on-site that's popular with the tour-bus crowd.

Glacier View Inn   HOTEL $$$
(Map p69; ☑877-423-7433; Icefield Centre, Icefields Pkwy; r with mountain/glacier view $269/289; ⊗May-Oct; 🅿) Panoramic views of the glacier are unbelievable at this chalet, found in the same complex as the Icefield Centre. At times it can feel like staying in a shopping mall, but once the buses go away you're left in one of the most spectacular places around. Rooms aren't luxurious but are very comfortable.

★ Num-Ti-Jah Lodge   CANADIAN $$$
(Map p69; ☑403-522-2167; www.num-ti-jah.com; Icefields Pkwy; mains $32-45; ⊗5-10pm May-Oct) Rustic yet elegant, the Num-Ti-Jah's historic Elkhorn Dining Room lets you step back in time to a Simpson's 1940s hunting lodge, complete with stone fireplace and majestic views. Dine on braised bison short rib or mushroom pappardelle beneath the watchful eye of moose, wolverines and other hunting trophies. Guests get seating priority; if you're staying elsewhere make sure you reserve ahead.

ℹ Information

Columbia Icefield Discovery Centre (p74)
Parks Canada has a desk here where they dole out information about Jasper, Banff and the

Icefields Parkway. Check in here for current hiking conditions.

South Gate The entrance to the parkway north of Lake Louise, where you can purchase your park pass and pick up a map and brochures.

❶ Getting There & Away

Brewster (www.brewster.ca) has buses plying the parkway between Banff, Lake Louise and Jasper, with stops at Saskatchewan Crossing, Columbia Icefield Discovery Centre and Sunwapta Falls.

If you're driving, start out with a full tank of gas. It's fairly pricey to fill up at Saskatchewan Crossing, the only gas station on the parkway.

Banff Town

POP 7584

A resort town with boutique shops, nightclubs and fancy restaurants is not something any national-park purist would want to claim credit for. But Banff is no ordinary town. It developed not as a residential district, but as a service center for the park that surrounds it. Today it brings busloads of tourists keen to convene with shops as much as nature, as well as artists and writers who are drawn to Banff.

Nevertheless, wander 15 minutes in any direction and you're in wild country, a primeval food chain of bears, elk and wolves. Banff civilized? It's just a rumor.

◉ Sights

★**Banff National Park**   NATIONAL PARK
(Map p69; www.pc.gc.ca/banff; day pass adult/youth/family $9.80/4.90/19.60) Towering like giant castles in the sky, the mountains and valleys of Banff provide endless opportunities for wildlife-watching, hiking, boating, climbing, mountain biking, skiing or simply convening with nature. Lush canyons compete for your attention with lofty fields of alpine wildflowers, while tranquil waterways meander past and dense emerald forests bid you to delve inside. Created in 1885 and ranging over 6641 sq km, Banff is the world's third-oldest national park – and was Canada's first.

★**Whyte Museum of
the Canadian Rockies**   MUSEUM
(Map p78; www.whyte.org; 111 Bear St; adult/student/child $10/4/free; ⊙10am-5pm) Founded by local artists Catharine and Peter Whyte, the century-old Whyte Museum is more than just a rainy-day option. It boasts a beautiful, ever-changing gallery displaying art from 1800 to present, by both regional,

Canadian and international artists, many with a focus on the Rockies. Watch for work by the Group of Seven (aka the Algonquin School). There's also a permanent collection telling the story of Banff and the hardy men and women who forged a home among the mountains.

Banff Gondola   CABLE CAR
(✔403-762-2523; Mountain Ave; adult/child $45/23, after 6pm $37/16; ⊙8am-6pm May, 9am-9pm Jun, 8am-10pm Jul-Oct) In summer or winter, you can summit a peak near Banff thanks to the Banff Gondola, with four-person enclosed cars that glide up to the top of Sulphur Mountain in less than 10 minutes. Named for the thermal springs that emanate from its base, this peak is a perfect viewing point and a tick-box Banff attraction.

Upper Hot Springs Pool   HOT SPRINGS
(www.hotsprings.ca; Mountain Ave; adult/child/family $7.30/6.30/22.50; ⊙9am-11pm mid-May–mid-Oct, 10am-10pm Sun-Thu, to 11pm Fri & Sat mid-Oct–mid-May) Banff quite literally wouldn't be Banff if it weren't for its hot springs, which gush out from 2.5km beneath **Sulphur Mountain** at a constant temperature of between 32°C (90°F) and 46°C (116°F) – it was the springs that drew the first tourists to Banff. You can still sample the soothing mineral waters at the Upper Hot Springs Pool, near the Banff Gondola.

Vermilion Lakes   NATURE RESERVE
Northwest of town, this trio of tranquil lakes is a great place for **wildlife-spotting**: elk, beavers, bald eagles and ospreys can often be seen around the lakeshore, especially at dawn and dusk. A paved driveway – part of the **Legacy bike trail** – runs along the lake's southern side for 4.5km, but the proximity of the Trans-Canada Hwy means that it's not as peaceful as it could be.

Bow Falls   WATERFALL
About 500m south of town, just before the junction with Spray River, the Bow River plunges into a churning melee of white water at Bow Falls. Though the drop is relatively small – just 9m at its highest point – Bow Falls is a dramatic sight, especially in spring following heavy snowmelt.

Banff Park Museum   MUSEUM
(Map p78; ✔403-762-1558; 93 Banff Ave; adult/child $3.90/1.90; ⊙10am-5pm) Occupying an old wooden Canadian Pacific Railway building dating from 1903, this museum

is a national historic site. Its exhibits – a taxidermic collection of local animals, including grizzly and black bears, plus a tree carved with graffiti dating from 1841 – was curated by Norman Sanson, who ran the museum and Banff weather station until 1932. Much-needed restorations were done in the early 2000s.

Cave & Basin National Historic Site

HISTORIC SITE

(☑ 403-762-1557; Cave Ave; adult/child $3.90/1.90; ⊙ 10am-5pm mid-May–mid-Oct, noon-4pm Wed-Sun mid-Oct–mid-May) The Canadian National Park system was effectively born at these hot springs, discovered accidentally by three Canadian Pacific Railway employees on their day off in 1883 (though known to Aboriginals for 10,000 years). The springs quickly became a bun fight for private businesses offering facilities for bathers to enjoy the then-trendy thermal treatments.To avert an environmental catastrophe, the government stepped in, declaring Banff Canada's first national park in order to preserve the springs.

🏃 Activities

Canoeing & Kayaking

Despite a modern penchant for big cars, canoe travel is still very much a quintessential Canadian method of transportation. The best options near Banff Town are **Lake Minnewanka** and nearby **Two Jack Lake**, both to the northeast, or – closer to the town itself – the **Vermilion Lakes**. Unless you have your own canoe, you'll need to rent one; try **Banff Canoe Club** (Map p78; ☑ 403-762-5005; www.banffcanoeclub.com; cnr Wolf St & Bow Ave; canoe & kayak rental per first/additional hour $36/20; ⊙ 10am-6pm mid-May–mid-Sep).

Cycling

There are lots of riding options around Banff, both on the road and on selected trails. Popular routes around Banff Town include **Sundance** (7.4km round-trip) and **Spray River Loop** (12.5km); either is good for families. **Spray River & Goat Creek** (19km one way) and **Rundle Riverside** (14km one way) are both A-to-Bs with start/finish points near Canmore. The former is pretty straightforward; the latter is more challenging, with ups and downs and potential for thrills and spills.

Serious road cyclists should check out Hwy 1A between Banff and Lake Louise; the rolling hills and quiet road here are a roadie's dream. Parks Canada publishes the brochure *Mountain Biking & Cycling Guide – Banff National Park,* which describes trails and regulations. Pick it up at the Banff Visitor Centre (p84).

Snowtips/Bactrax (Map p78; ☑ 403-762-8177; www.snowtips-bactrax.com; 225 Bear St; bike rental per hour/day from $12/42; ⊙ 8am-8pm) has a barn full of town and trail bikes to rent (from $12/42 per hour/day) and will deliver them to your hotel. Ask about shuttles to trailheads.

Hiking

Hiking is Banff's tour de force and the main focus of many travelers' visit to the area. The trails are easy to find, well signposted and maintained enough to be comfortable to walk on, yet rugged enough to still get a wilderness experience.

In general, the closer to Banff Town you are, the more people you can expect to see and the more developed the trail will be. But regardless of where in the park you go walking, you are assured to be rewarded for your efforts.

Before you head out, check at the Banff Visitor Centre (p84) for trail conditions and possible closures. Keep in mind that trails are often snow-covered much later into the summer season than you might realize, and trail closures due to bears are a possibility, especially in berry season (June to September).

One of the best hikes from the town center is the **Bow River Falls & The Hoodoos Trail**, which starts by the Bow River Bridge and tracks past the falls to the Hoodoos – weird-looking rock spires caused by wind and water erosion. The trail plies its way around the back of Tunnel Mountain through forest and some river meadows (10.2km round-trip).

You can track the north shore of Lake Minnewanka for kilometers on a multi-use trail that is sometimes closed due to bear activity. The classic hike is to walk as far as the **Alymer Lookout**, just shy of 10km one way. Less taxing is the 5.6km round-trip hike to **Stewart Canyon**, where you can clamber down rocks and boulders to the Cascade River.

Some of the best multiday hikes start at the Sunshine Village parking lot (where skiers grab the gondola in winter). From here you can plan two- to four-day sorties up over **Healy Pass** and down to **Egypt Lake**, or else get a bus up to **Sunshine Village** (Map p69; www.skibanff.com; day ski pass adult/youth $95/73), where you can cross the border into

Banff Town

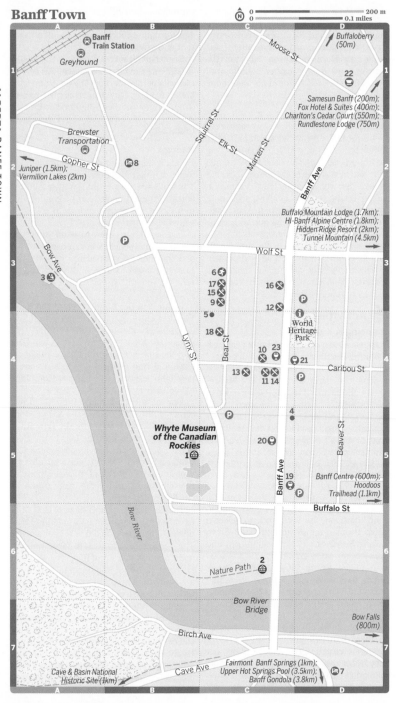

0   200 m
0   0.1 miles

Banff Train Station

Greyhound

Buffaloberry (50m)

Moose St

22

Samesun Banff (200m);
Fox Hotel & Suites (400m);
Charlton's Cedar Court (550m);
Rundlestone Lodge (750m)

Brewster Transportation

Squirrel St

Elk St

Marten St

Banff Ave

Gopher St   8

Juniper (1.5km);
Vermilion Lakes (2km)

Buffalo Mountain Lodge (1.7km);
HI-Banff Alpine Centre (1.8km);
Hidden Ridge Resort (2km);
Tunnel Mountain (4.5km)

Wolf St

Bow Ave

3

6
17
15   16
9
5   12
18
World
Heritage
Park
Lynx St

Bear St

10   23
13   21
11   14
Caribou St

Beaver St

Whyte Museum
of the Canadian
Rockies

1

20

4

Banff Ave

19   Banff Centre (600m);
Hoodoos
Trailhead (1.1km)

Buffalo St

Bow River

Nature Path   2

Bow River
Bridge

Bow Falls (800m)

Birch Ave

Cave & Basin National
Historic Site (1km)

Cave Ave

Fairmont Banff Springs (1km);
Upper Hot Springs Pool (3.5km);
Banff Gondola (3.8km)   7

Banff Town

ALBERTA BANFF TOWN

BC and head out across Sunshine Meadows and **Mt Assiniboine Provincial Park**.

The best backcountry experience is arguably the **Sawback Trail**, which travels from Banff up to Lake Louise the back way – it's over 74km, with six primitive campsites and three spectacular mountain passes.

Check out Lonely Planet's *Banff, Jasper & Glacier National Parks* guide for more details about more single-day and multiday hikes.

Horseback Riding

Banff's first European explorers – fur traders and railway engineers – penetrated the region primarily on horseback. You can re-create their pioneering spirit on guided rides with **Warner Guiding & Outfitting** (Map p78; ☑403-762-4551; www.horseback. com; 132 Banff Ave; guided rides per person $54-139; ☺9am-6pm), which will fit you out with a trusty steed and lead you along narrow trails for part of the day. Instruction and guiding are included; a sore backside is more or less mandatory for beginners. Grin and bear it.

If you're really into it, Warner's six-day Wildlife Monitoring Adventure Expeditions will take you out to limited-access areas, accompanied by a Parks Canada researcher.

Skiing & Snowboarding

Strange though it may seem, there are three ski areas in the national park, two of them located in the vicinity of Banff Town. Large, snowy Sunshine Village is consid-

ered world-class. Tiny Norquay, situated a mere 5km from the center, is your half-day, family-friendly option.

Sunshine Village (p77) straddles the Alberta–BC border. Though slightly smaller than Lake Louise in terms of skiable terrain it gets much bigger dumpings of snow, or 'Champagne powder' as Albertans like to call it (up to 9m annually). Aficionados laud Sunshine's advanced runs and lengthy ski season, which lingers until Victoria Day weekend in late May. A high-speed gondola whisks skiers up in 17 minutes to the village, which sports Banff's only ski-in hotel, the Sunshine Mountain Lodge.

Ski Banff@Norquay (Map p69; ☑403-762-4421; www.banffnorquay.com; Mt Norquay Rd; day ski pass adult/youth/child $65/50/25; ☒), just 6km north of downtown Banff, has a long history of entertaining Banff visitors. The smallest and least visited of the three local hills, this is a good place to body-swerve the major show-offs and hit the slopes for a succinct half-day.

Local buses shuttle riders from Banff hotels to both resorts (and Lake Louise) every 30 minutes during the season.

White-Water Rafting

The best rafting is outside the park (and province) on the **Kicking Horse River** in Yoho National Park, BC. There are class IV rapids here, meaning big waves, swirling holes and a guaranteed soaking. Lesser rapids are found on the **Kananaskis River** and the Horseshoe Canyon section of the **Bow**

River. The Bow River around Banff is better suited to mellower float trips.

Several rafting companies are located in the park. They offer tours starting at around $80. (Factor in $15 more for a Banff pickup.)

Tours

Hydra River Guides   RAFTING
(Map p78; 403-762-4554; www.raftbanff. com; 211 Bear St; 9am-7pm) This well-regarded company has been running rafting trips for three decades. The most popular is the 20km Kicking Horse Classic ($125), with varied rapids (up to class IV) and a BBQ lunch. Hardier rafters can try the full-day trip ($179); for novices and families there's a sedate float trip ($55). The Flast Blast ($90) is for those short on time.

Discover Banff Tours   TOURS
(Map p78; 403-760-5007; www.banfftours. com; Sundance Mall, 215 Banff Ave) Discover Banff has a great selection of tours to choose from, including three-hour Banff Town tours, sunrise and evening wildlife tours, Columbia Icefield day trips and even a 10-hour grizzly-bear tour, taking in a grizzly-bear refuge.

GyPSy Guide   DRIVING
(Map p78; 403-760-8200; www.gypsyguide. com/canada; per day $39) Offers downloadable tours of the area with lively running commentary about local highlights and history and recommending places to stop. Tours run from 1½ hours to three to five days and range from $3 to $15, covering Banff, Lake Louise, Columbia Icefield, Jasper and Calgary. Best of all, if you tire of the tour guide, just turn it off.

Sleeping

Compared with elsewhere in the province, accommodations in Banff Town are fairly costly and, in summer, often hard to find. The old adage of the early bird catching the worm really holds true here, and booking ahead is strongly recommended.

The Banff/Lake Louise Tourism Bureau tracks vacancies on a daily basis; check the listings at the Banff Visitor Centre (p84). You might also try **Enjoy Banff** (888-313-6161; www.enjoybanff.com), which books rooms for more than 75 different lodgings.

Camping in Banff National Park is popular and easily accessible. There are 13 campgrounds to choose from, most along the Bow Valley Parkway or near Banff Town.

Two Jack Lakeside   CAMPGROUND $
(Map p69; Minnewanka Loop Dr; tent & RV sites $28; May-Oct;) Right on Two Jack Lake, and the most scenic of the Banff-area campgrounds, Lakeside fills its 74 nonreservable sites quickly. You can now 'glamp' at Two Jack in one of 10 'oTENTiks' – fully serviced A-frame 'tents' with hot showers and electricity. They sleep up to six people and cost a thoroughly reasonable $120 per night.

HI-Banff Alpine Centre   HOSTEL $
(403-762-4122; www.hihostels.ca; 801 Hidden Ridge Way; dm from $32, d with shared/private bath from $85/104, private cabins from $124;) Near the top of Tunnel Mountain, Banff's best hostel is well away from the madness of Banff Ave. Buildings are classic mountain-lodge style without classic mountain-lodge prices. Rooms are spic-n-span; choose from dorms, private doubles and cabins. Common areas are open and comfortable, with fireplaces and good views. The public bus runs right by the front door; passes are complimentary.

Samesun Banff   HOSTEL $
(403-762-5521; www.banffhostel.com; 433 Banff Ave; dm incl breakfast from $60;) The Samesun is zanier, edgier and a little cheaper than other local budget digs, and features a large central courtyard with barbecue, an on-site bar, plenty of activities and 100 dorm beds spread across modern, compact six- to 14-person rooms with en suites (some with fireplaces); DIY breakfast included. The clientele is international, backpacker and young (at least at heart).

Banff Y Mountain Lodge   HOSTEL $
(Map p78; 403-762-3560; www.ymountain-lodge.com; 102 Spray Ave; s/d $109/129, with shared bath $99/109;) The YWCA is Banff's swankiest hostel option, offering dorm rooms along with private family-oriented accommodations down by the river. Spacious, wheelchair-accessible buildings with fireplaces and big decks create an alpine – if not exactly homey – atmosphere. There's a kitchen, sauna and family room and activities galore. Rates drop significantly in the winter.

Tunnel Mountain   CAMPGROUND $
(Tunnel Mountain Dr; tent & RV sites $28-39; kiosk 7am-midnight) Banff's massive campground is split over three separate 'villages' halfway up the slope of Tunnel Mountain, offering 1000 sites. It fills to capacity in summer thanks

SASQUATCH

In the untamed land between Banff and Jasper, you may well expect to encounter a little wildlife. However, if you're anticipating elk or even a grizzly, what lurks beyond that next bend might surprise you.

That's what happened to David Thompson. In 1811, as a young surveyor forging across the Rocky Mountains en route to Jasper, he became the first European to encounter was what known as the Monster Bear. He had stumbled upon tracks near the Athabasca River that measured a staggering 36cm x 20cm.

Around Saskatchewan River, the Stoney people had been catching glimpses of Monster Bears throughout the previous century. It was known to them as 'M-s-napeo' – today it's more commonly called Sasquatch or Bigfoot. Big, hairy and supposedly preceded by a foul smell, sightings continue to be reported by locals and visitors around Banff and Jasper National Parks right into the present decade. Keep your eyes – and nose – on the lookout!

to its convenient location just a quick drive from downtown Banff. With its many trees, it's not as grim as it sounds but if you're truly after tranquillity, you might want to look elsewhere.

Poplar Inn B&B $$
(Map p78; ☑ 403-760-8688; www.thepoplarinn. ca; 316 Lynx St; d $185; ℗) Two lovely rooms in a beautiful heritage home just steps from Banff Ave offer a home away from home. Both have luxury touches such as Egyptian cotton sheets and sliding doors onto private garden patios. Breakfast of muffins, croissants and homemade granola is served in one of the house's turrets.

Juniper HOTEL $$
(☑ 403-762-2281; www.thejuniper.com; 1 Juniper Way; r $229-460; ℗ ✴ 🛜 🛁) Perched beneath Mt Norquay, the modern, pet-friendly Juniper has comfortable rooms, and suites with Jacuzzis and fireplaces. Staff are friendly and welcome many hikers, skiers and cyclists. The bistro has a creative menu, awesome views and a big patio. Not far from the highway, the hotel gets some traffic noise.

Charlton's Cedar Court MOTEL $$
(☑ 403-762-4485; www.charltonsbanff.com; 513 Banff Ave; r from $219; ℗ ✴ 🛜 🛁) Yes, it's a bit old-fashioned, but this motel complex on Banff Ave has some of the most consistent rates in town. Cheaper rooms are dowdy, so better to opt for one of the larger, split-level suites, some of which have kitchenettes and mezzanine sleeping areas. Luxury it ain't, but it's a reasonable downtown base.

Rundlestone Lodge HOTEL $$
(☑ 403-762-2201; www.rundlestone.com; 537 Banff Ave; d/ste from $209/274; ℗ 🛜 🛁) This

place is filled with pseudo 'old English' charm, complete with *Masterpiece Theater*-style chairs in the lobby. The standard rooms are fairly, well…standard, but family and honeymoon suites come with a kitchen, fireplace and loft.

★ Buffalo Mountain Lodge HOTEL $$$
(☑ 800-661-1367; www.crmr.com/buffalo; 700 Tunnel Mountain Dr; r $339-379; 🛜) Three hectares of private forested grounds make this lodge on Tunnel Mountain one of Banff's most pleasant mountain retreats. Rooms have plush rustic charm, with timber beams, clawfoot tubs, fieldstone log fires and underfloor heating in the bathrooms. Dine at the in-house restaurant Cilantro or wander 15 minutes by foot into town.

★ Fox Hotel & Suites HOTEL $$$
(☑ 800-760-8500; www.bestofbanff.com; 461 Banff Ave; d from $329; ℗ @ 🛜 🛁) Aesthetically, the Fox is a step above its neighbors. Its forest-like lobby is instantly calming. Centered around a courtyard, rooms aren't overly plush but have a Canadian feel to them, right down to the wallpaper. The highlight is the Cave & Basin–inspired hot tub, with an opening in the roof that gives out to the sky. Service is attentive.

Buffaloberry B&B $$$
(☑ 403-762-3750; www.buffaloberry.com; 417 Marten St; r $385; ℗ ✴ 🛜) This purpose-built B&B makes a comfortable place to stay. The four bedrooms are each unique and heavy on homey charm, and the underfloor heating and nightly turn-down treats keep the pamper factor high. With an ever-changing menu (such as baked Camembert egg custard, homemade granola and buttermilk pancakes), the breakfast is divine.

Hidden Ridge Resort
RESORT $$$

(☑ 403-762-3544; www.bestofbanff.com; 901 Coyote Dr; condos $319-629; P ❋ 🛜 🐾) Half hotel, half self-catering resort, the Hidden Ridge is a great option for families, with modern condos and A-frame chalets. The basic chalets boast wood-burning stoves, galley kitchens and mountain-view porches; at the top end you can get Jacuzzis and cozy loft bedrooms for the kids. There's even a forest hot tub if you can brave the mountain air.

Fairmont Banff Springs
HOTEL $$$

(☑ 403-762-2211; www.fairmont.com/banffsprings; 405 Spray Ave; r from $559; P @ 🛜 🏊) Rising like a Gaelic Balmoral above the trees at the base of Sulphur Mountain and visible from miles away, the Banff Springs is a wonder of early 1920s revivalist architecture and one of Canada's most iconic buildings. Wandering through its grand lobby and elegant lounge, wine bar and restaurant, it's easy to forget that it's also a hotel.

🍴 Eating

Banff dining is more than just hiker food. Sushi and foie gras have long embellished the restaurants of Banff Ave, and some of the more elegant places will inspire grubby hikers to return to their hotel rooms and take a shower before pulling up a chair. Many of Banff's hotels also have their own excellent on-site restaurants, which welcome nonguests. AAA Alberta beef makes an appearance on even the most exotic à la carte menu.

Wild Flour
CAFE $

(Map p78; ☑ 403-760-5074; www.wildflourbakery.ca; 211 Bear St; mains $5-10; ⊙ 7am-7pm; 🛜 🔥) 🍴 If you're in a need of a relatively guilt-free treat, come here for cheesecake, dark-chocolate torte or – well, 'and' really – macaroons. These, along with breakfasts, well-stuffed sandwiches on homemade bread, and soups, are all organic. Not surprisingly, it's busy; so much so that a smaller version with the bare necessities (coffee and pastries) is opening on Banff Ave.

Evelyn's Coffee Bar
CAFE $

(Map p78; ☑ 403-762-0352; www.evelyns coffeebar.com; 215 Banff Ave; mains $6-10; ⊙ 6:30am-11pm; 🛜) Pushing Starbucks onto the periphery, Evelyn's parades two downtown locations, both on Banff Ave. Dive in to either one of them for wraps, pies and – best of all – its own selection of giant homemade

cookies, the saviour of many an exhausted hiker. The second branch is a block further south at 119 Banff Ave.

★ Saltlik
STEAK $$

(Map p78; ☑ 403-762-2467; www.saltlik.com; 221 Bear St; mains $18-29; ⊙ 11am-late Mon-Fri, 11:30am-late Sat & Sun) With rib eye in citrus-rosemary butter and peppercorn New York strip loin on the menu, Saltlik is clearly no plain-Jane steakhouse knocking out flavorless T-bones. No, this polished dining room abounds with rustic elegance and a list of steaks the length of many establishments' entire menu. In a town not short on steak providers, this could be number one.

★ Bear St Tavern
PUB FOOD $$

(Map p78; www.bearstreettavern.ca; 211 Bear St; mains $15-19; ⊙ 11:30am-late) This gastro-pub hits a double whammy: ingeniously flavored pizzas washed down with locally brewed pints. Banffites head here in droves for a plate of pulled-pork nachos or a bison-and-onion pizza, accompanied by pitchers of hoppy ale. The patio overlooking Bison Courtyard is the best place to linger if the weather cooperates.

Block Kitchen & Bar
TAPAS $$

(Map p78; ☑ 403-985-2887; www.banffblock.com; 201 Banff Ave; tapas $7-26; ⊙ 11am-1am; 🔥) This casual bar serves up tapas with heavy Asian and Mediterranean influences – or 'Mediterrasian,' as they call it. The small but creative tapas plates might not satisfy truly ravenous post-hiking appetites, but there are plenty of vegan and gluten-free options and it continues to serve until 1am. Decorated with bird cages and copper, it's got a quirky, welcoming edge.

Nourish
VEGETARIAN $$

(Map p78; ☑ 403-760-3933; www.nourishbistro.com; 215 Bear St; mains $12-29; ⊙ 11:30am-10pm; 🔥) Confronted by a huge and strangely beautiful papier-mâché tree when you walk in the door, you instantly know this vegetarian bistro is not average. With locally sourced dishes like bourbon-glazed stuffed mushrooms and gluten-free beer-batter onion rings, Nourish has carved out a gourmet following in Banff. Dinner is served as shareable platters (think giant tapas).

Eddie Burger & Bar
BURGERS $$

(Map p78; ☑ 403-762-2230; www.eddieburger bar.ca; 6/137 Banff Ave,; burgers $13-19; ⊙ 11am-

2am) Eddie's are not your average burgers. His love for the patty has inspired him to create large, crave-worthy burgers, from the usual classics to specialties like the elk burger with avocado and Gouda. Add to this a hearty helping of poutine and a shaken Caesar garnished with a chicken wing, and you're set – for the next week.

Magpie & Stump
MEXICAN $$
(Map p78; ☑ 403-762-4067; www.magpieandstump.ca; 203 Caribou St; mains $9-21; ⊙ 11:30am-2am) A classic, lively cantina full of Sol-swigging snowboarders. It has ramped up some of the classics, like the Three Pig Queso Quesadilla with pulled pork, smoky bacon *and* chorizo, or the Popcorn Shrimp Tacos with mango salsa. The Build-Your-Own nacho menu is just asking for trouble. It's difficult to save room for the key lime pie in a jar.

Park
MODERN AMERICAN $$$
(Map p78; ☑ 403-762-5114; www.parkdistillery.com; 219 Banff Ave; mains $17-44; ⊙ 11am-late) Banff gets hip with a microdistillery to complement its microbrewery, plying spirits (gin, vodka and whiskey) and beer made from Alberta's foothills' grain. It all goes down perfectly with a mesquite beef hoagie, fish tacos or anything off the excellent appetizer menu.

Bison Restaurant & Terrace
CANADIAN, FUSION $$$
(Map p78; ☑ 403-762-5550; www.thebison.ca; 211 Bear St; mains $16-45; ⊙ 5pm-late) Rustically elegant, the Bison is often full of trendy, well-off Calgarians dressed in expensive hiking gear, drawn by its regionally sourced, meat-heavy menu. Appetizers like seafood waffles and escargot in a bone, followed up with Peking-style duck or cider-braised pork belly, fill the creative, seasonal menu. You'll find the more casual Bear St Tavern (p82) on the terrace below.

Maple Leaf Grille
CANADIAN $$$
(Map p78; ☑ 403-762-7680; www.banffmapleleaf.com; 137 Banff Ave; mains $25-55; ⊙ 11am-10pm) With plenty of local and foreign plaudits, the classy Maple Leaf eschews all other pretensions in favor of one defining word: 'Canadian.' The menu is anchored by Albertan beef, along with BC salmon, East Coast cod and Okanagan Wine Country salad. Not surprisingly, the interior is all wood and stone, with local artwork.

🍸 Drinking & Nightlife

Throw a stone in Banff Ave and you're more likely to hit a gap-year traveller than a local. This makes for a lively, if rather young, drinking scene. Many of the local watering holes also have live music. Have a look through the listings in the 'Summit Up' section of the weekly newspaper *Banff Crag & Canyon*.

★ Wild Bill's Legendary Saloon
BAR
(Map p78; ☑ 403-762-0333; www.wildbillsbanff.com; 201 Banff Ave; ⊙ 11am-late) Forget swanky wine bars and cafes – you haven't really been to Banff if you miss Wild Bill's. Hang out with real live cowboys and get an eyeful of two-stepping, bull riding, karaoke and live music of the twangy Willie Nelson variety. The grub is exactly what you'd expect: big portions of barbecued pork rinds, crispy corn fritters, burgers and chili.

Elk & Oarsman
PUB
(Map p78; www.elkandoarsman.com; 119 Banff Ave; ⊙ 11am-1am) Located upstairs with a crow's-nest view of Banff Ave, this is the town's most refined sports pub, with a decent lineup of beers on tap and live music; the kitchen will fix you up with some good food if you so desire. The rooftop patio is prime real estate in the summer.

Whitebark Cafe
COFFEE
(Map p78; ☑ 403-760-7298; www.whitebarkcafe.com; 401 Banff Ave; ⊙ 6:30am-7pm) Coffee in Banff recently got a wake-up call thanks to this new cafe in the Aspen Lodge on Banff Ave. What it lacks in indoor seating space, the Whitebark makes up for in the excellence of its java, expertly confected by a team of friendly baristas. Snacks and sandwiches provide added fuel, but it's primarily about the high-quality brews.

Banff Ave Brewing Co
MICROBREWERY
(Map p78; www.banffavebrewingco.ca; 110 Banff Ave; ⊙ 11:30am-2am) Feeling like a prairie beer hall, this place has plenty of craft brews, created on the premises and infused with Saskatoon berries and the like. It also has soft pretzels, bratwurst, burgers and salads, although the service often gives you plenty of time to savor your drink before the food arrives.

Rose & Crown
PUB
(Map p78; ☑ 403-762-2121; www.roseandcrown.ca; 202 Banff Ave, Banff Town; ⊙ 11am-2am) Banff's oldest pub (since 1985!) is a fairly standard

British-style boozer with pool tables and a rooftop patio. Out of all of the town's drinking houses, it's best known for its live music, which raises the rafters seven nights a week – everything from communal sing-alongs to Seattle grunge.

ⓘ Information

Banff Visitor Centre (Map p78; ☑ 403-762-1550; www.pc.gc.ca/banff; 224 Banff Ave, Banff Town; ◷ 9am-7pm mid-Jun–Aug, to 5pm Sep–mid-Jun) The Parks Canada office doles out info and maps. This is where you can find current trail conditions and weather forecasts, and register for backcountry hiking and camping.

Friends of Banff (Map p78; ☑ 403-760-5331; www.friendsofbanff.com; 224 Banff Ave) Charitable organization that runs educational programs, including walking tours and junior naturalist workshops. It also runs Park Radio 101.1FM, offering weather and trail reports, local history and info. It runs a gift shop and has an info booth inside the Banff Visitor Centre.

Mineral Springs Hospital (☑ 403-762-2222; 305 Lynx St; ◷ 24hr) For emergency medical treatment.

ⓘ Getting There & Away

AIR

The nearest airport is **Calgary International Airport** (p67). Over 20 shuttle buses a day operate year-round between the airport and Banff. Buses are less frequent in the spring and fall. Companies include Brewster Transportation (p70) and **Banff Airporter** (☑ 403-762-3330; www.banffairporter.com). The adult fare for each is around $55 to $65 each way.

BUS

Greyhound Canada (Map p78; ☑ 800-661-8747; www.greyhound.ca; 327 Railway Ave) operates buses to Calgary ($28, one hour 40 minutes, four daily), Vancouver ($104, 13 hours, four daily) and points in between.

Brewster Transportation (p70) will pick you up from your hotel. It services Calgary ($65, one hour 15 minutes), Jasper ($100, five hours, daily) and Lake Louise ($30, one hour, several daily).

SunDog (www.sundogtours.com) also runs transport between Banff and Jasper (adult/child $69/39, five hours, daily) and Lake Louise ($20, one hour, daily).

CAR & MOTORCYCLE

All of the major car-rental companies (Avis, Budget, Enterprise) have branches in Banff Town. During summer all vehicles might be reserved in advance, so call ahead. If you're flying into Calgary, reserving a car at the airport (where the fleets are huge) may yield a better deal than waiting to pick up a car when you reach Banff Town.

ⓘ Getting Around

Banff Transit (☑ 403-762-1215; www.banff.ca) runs four hybrid 'Roam' buses on two main routes. Stops include Tunnel Mountain, the Rimrock Resort Hotel, Banff Upper Hot Springs, Fairmont Banff Springs and all the hotels along Banff Ave. Route maps are printed on all bus stops. Buses start running at 6:30am and finish at 11pm; the fare is adult/child $2/1 (or $5 for a day pass).

Taxis (which are metered) can easily be hailed on the street, especially on Banff Ave. Otherwise call **Banff Taxi** (☑ 403-762-4444).

Lake Louise

POP 1175

Lake Louise is what makes Banff National Park the phenomenon it is, an awe-inspiring natural feature that is impossible to describe without resorting to shameless clichés. Standing next to the serene, implausibly turquoise lake, the natural world feels (and is) tantalizingly close, with a surrounding amphitheater of finely chiseled mountains that hoist Victoria Glacier up for all to see. Famous for its teahouses, grizzly bears and hiking trails, it's also well-known for its much-commented-on 'crowds,' plus a strangely congruous (or incongruous – depending on your viewpoint) lump of towering concrete known as Chateau Lake Louise. But, frankly, who cares? You don't come to Lake Louise to dodge other tourists. You come to share in one of the most spectacular sights in the Rockies, one that has captured the imaginations of mountaineers, artists and visitors for more than a century.

When you're done with gawping on the shimmering lakeshore, try hiking up into the beckoning mountains beyond. Lake Louise also has a widely lauded ski resort and some equally enticing cross-country options. Thirteen kilometers to the southeast along a winding seasonal road is Moraine Lake, another spectacularly located body of water; it may not have the dazzling color of its famous sibling, but has an equally beguiling backdrop in the Valley of Ten Peaks and the jaw-dropping Tower of Babel, which ascends solidly skyward. In summer, this narrow road is sometimes shut to new visitors for short periods to empty out the traffic.

The village of Lake Louise, just off Hwy 1, is little more than an outdoor shopping mall, a gas station and a handful of hotels. The object of all your yearnings is 5km away by car or an equitable distance on foot along

Lake Louise Area

N

0 ——————— 4 km
0 ——————— 2 miles

Golden, BC
(75km)

Trans-Canada Hwy

93

South
Gate

Icefields
Pkwy

Bow River

Trail

Lake Louise
Ski Area (4km)

Gondola
Base
Terminal

Whitehorn
Rd

HI-Lake Louise
Alpine Centre

Lake Louise
Station Restaurant

Lake Louise
Inn

Trailhead
Cafe

**Lake Louise
Village**

Bow Valley Pkwy

Mt St Piran
(2649m)

Little
Beehive

Fairmount
Chateau
Lake Louise

Deer
Lodge

Louise
Creek Trail

Lake Louise Dr

Paradise
Lodge

Lake Louise
Tent & RV
Campground

Fairview Rd

1A

Banff
(54km)

Lake Agnes
Teahouse

Mirror
Lake

Mt Niblock
(2976m)

Lake
Agnes

Big
Beehive

Lake
Louise
Boathouse

Mt Whyte
(2983m)

Lake
Louise

Trans-Canada Hwy

Banff
(52km)

Plain of Six
Glaciers
Teahouse

Plain of Six Glaciers

Mt Fairview
(2744m)

Saddle
Mountain
(2433m)

Moraine Lake Rd
(closed Oct-Jun)

Paradise Creek

Mt Sheol
(2779m)

Mt Aberdeen
(3152m)

Paradise Valley

Banff
National
Park

Lake
Annette

Trail

The Mitre
(2886m)

Mt Lefroy
(3423m)

Ringrose
Peak
(3278m)

Mt Temple
(3453m)

Moraine Creek

Pinicle
Mountain
(3067m)

Sentinel
Pass

Mt Hungabee
(3490m)

Eiffel Peak
(3084m)

Larch
Valley
(2360m)

Moraine
Lake Lodge

Wenkchemna
Peaks (3170m)

Trail

Moraine
Lake
Boathouse

Mt Bell
(2910m)

Wenkchemna
Pass

Eiffel
Lake

Yoho
National
Park

Mt Neptuak
(3233m)

Valley of the Ten Peaks

Alberta

Moraine
Lake

Consolation
Lakes

Mt Babel
(3101m)

Mt Tuzo
(3245m)

Mt Bowlen
(3072m)

Mt Fay
(3235m)

Mt Deltaform
(3424m)

Mt Tonsa
(3054m)

Kootenay
National
Park

**British
Columbia**

Mt Allen
(3301m)

Mt Perren
(3051m)

Mt Little
(3088m)

the pleasantly wooded Louise Creek trail, if the bears aren't out on patrol (check at the visitor center).

The Bow Valley Parkway between Banff Town and Lake Louise is slightly slower, but much more scenic, than Hwy 1. As it isn't fenced, it's a great route for wildlife sightings.

💿 Sights

⭐ Lake Louise   LAKE

Named for Queen Victoria's otherwise anonymous fourth daughter (who also lent her name to the province), the gobsmackingly gorgeous Lake Louise is a place that requires multiple viewings. Aside from the standard picture-postcard shot (blue sky, even bluer lake, glistening glacier), try visiting at six in the morning, at dusk in August, in the October rain or after a heavy winter storm.

You can also rent a canoe from the **Lake Louise Boathouse** (📞403-522-3511; canoe rental per 30min/1hr $75/85; ⏱8am-8:30pm Jun-Sep, weather permitting) and go for a paddle around the lake. Don't fall overboard – the water is freezing.

Lake Louise Gondola   CABLE CAR

(📞403-522-3555; www.lakelouisegondola.com; off Hwy 1A; adult/child $33/16; ⏱9am-4pm May-Jun & Sep-Oct, 8am-5:30pm Jul & Aug; 🐕) For a bird's-eye view of the Lake Louise area – and a good chance of spotting grizzly bears on the avalanche slopes – climb aboard the Lake Louise Gondola, which crawls up the side of **Whitehorn Mountain** via an open ski lift or enclosed gondola to a dizzying viewpoint 2088m above the valley floor. Look out for the imposing fang of 3544m-high **Mt Temple** piercing the skyline on the opposite side of the valley.

Moraine Lake   LAKE

The scenery will dazzle you long before you reach the spectacular, deep teal waters of Moraine Lake. The lake is set in the **Valley of the Ten Peaks**, and the narrow winding road leading to it offers views of these distant imposing summits. With little hustle or bustle and lots of beauty, many people prefer the more rugged and remote setting of Moraine Lake to Lake Louise.

🏃 Activities

Hiking

In Lake Louise beauty isn't skin-deep: the hikes behind the stunning views are just as impressive. Most of the classic walks start from Lake Louise and Moraine Lake. Some are straightforward, while others will give even the most seasoned alpinist reason to huff and puff. Be sure to bring along bug spray and a bear bell.

From Chateau Lake Louise, two popular day walks head out to alpine-style teahouses perched above the lake. The shorter but slightly harder hike is the 3.4km grunt past **Mirror Lake**, up to the Lake Agnes Teahouse (p87) on its eponymous body of water. After tea made from glacier water and soup or thick-cut sandwiches (cash only), you can trek 1.6km further and higher to the view-embellished **Big Beehive** lookout and Canada's most unexpectedly sited gazebo. Continue on this path down to the **Highline Trail** to link up with the **Plain of Six Glaciers**, or approach it independently from Chateau Lake Louise along the lakeshore (5.6km one-way). Either way, be sure to get close enough for ice-crunching views of the **Victoria Glacier**. On this route is the Plain of Six Glaciers Teahouse (p87), which supplements its brews with thick-cut sandwiches and spirit-lifting mugs of hot chocolate with marshmallows.

From Moraine Lake, the walk to **Sentinel Pass**, via the stunning **Larch Valley**, is best in the fall, when the leaves are beginning to turn. A strenuous day walk with outstanding views of **Mt Temple** and the surrounding peaks, the hike involves a steep, scree-covered last push to the pass. If you're lucky you might spy some rock climbers scaling the **Grand Sentinel** – a 200m-tall rock spire nearby.

Shorter and easier, the 6km out-and-back **Consolation Lakes Trail** offers that typical Banff juxtaposition of crowded parking lot disappearing almost instantly into raw, untamed wilderness.

In recent years there has been a lot of bear activity in the Moraine Lake area. Because of this, a minimum group size of four has been imposed by the park on some hikes during berry-gathering season (June to September). If you're arriving solo, check on the noticeboard in the information center in Lake Louise village for other hikers looking to form groups.

Skiing & Snowboarding

The **Lake Louise Ski Area** (Map p69; www.skilouise.com; day pass adult/youth from $92/72; 🐕), 3km east of Lake Louise village and 60km northwest of Banff, is marginally larger than Sunshine Village but gets less natural snow. The ample runs, containing plenty of beginner and intermediate terrain, are on four separate mountains, so it's closer to a European ski experience than anything else on offer in Canada. The front side is a good place to get your ski legs back with a good selection of simpler stuff and fantastic views. On the far side there are some great challenges, from the knee-pulverizing moguls of Paradise Bowl to the high-speed cruising of the Larch area. Make sure you grab a deck burger at the Temple Lodge – it's part of the whole experience.

🛏 Sleeping

Other than a very popular hostel and a fantastic campground, Lake Louise doesn't have much in the way of budget accommodations options.

Lake Louise Tent & RV Campground
CAMPGROUND $

(www.reservation.parkscanada.gc.ca; Lake Louise village; tent/RV sites $28/33; ☺tent park May-Sep, RV park year-round) Near the village, this efficient, wooded campground is divided into two, with RVs on one side of the river and all tents and soft-sided vehicles on the other, protected from bears behind an electric fence. Many tent sites have fire pits ($9). Choose a site away from the railway tracks to enjoy views of Mt Temple in relative peace.

HI-Lake Louise Alpine Centre
HOSTEL $

(☑403-522-2201; www.hihostels.ca; Village Rd, Lake Louise village; dm/d from $42/115; P) This is what a hostel should be: clean, friendly, affordable and full of interesting travelers. With raw timber and stone, the rustic, comfortable building fits in well with Rockies architecture. Dorm rooms are fairly standard and the private rooms are small and a bit overpriced, but this as close as you'll get to budget in Lake Louise.

★ Deer Lodge
HOTEL $$$

(☑403-410-7417; www.crmr.com; 109 Lake Louise Dr; r from $250; P☎) Tucked demurely behind Chateau Lake Louise, historic Deer Lodge dates from the 1920s and has managed to keep its genuine alpine feel intact. The rustic exterior and maze of corridors can't have changed much since the days of bobbed hair and F Scott Fitzgerald. Lodge rooms are fairly tiny but quaint, while spacious Heritage rooms have smart, boutique-like furnishings.

★ Moraine Lake Lodge
HOTEL $$$

(☑800-522-2777; www.morainelakelodge.com; d $400-700; ☺Jun-Sep; P☎) 🚲 The experience here is intimate, personal and private, and the service is famously good. While billed as rustic (ie no TVs), the rooms and cabins offer mountain-inspired luxury with big picture windows, wood-burning or antique gas fireplaces, soaking tubs, feather comforters and balconies overlooking the lake. The fine-dining restaurant on-site wins equal plaudits. Canoe use is free for guests.

Paradise Lodge
CABIN $$$

(☑403-522-3595; www.paradiselodge.com; r $260-340; ☺May-Sep) Cozy and well restored, these 1930s log cabins are surrounded by woods and only moments from Lake Louise's shore. Each is unique, but look for huge comfy beds, cast-iron stoves and claw-foot soaking tubs. The newer lodge rooms are hotel-style, and the surrounding lawns provide plenty of lounging opportunities beneath the forest's trees.

Fairmont Chateau Lake Louise
HOTEL $$$

(☑403-522-3511; www.fairmont.com/lake-louise; Lake Louise Dr; d from $470; P@☎🏊) The opulent Fairmont enjoys one of the world's most enviable locations on the shores of Lake Louise. Built in the 1890s and added to in 1925 and 2004, the hotel and its plastered exterior does little to fit in with its surroundings. Nevertheless, the giant interloper's facilities, service and fork-dropping views are undeniably luxurious.

🍴 Eating

★ Lake Agnes Teahouse
CAFE $

(lunch $7-13; ☺9am-6pm Jun-Aug, 10am-5:30pm Sep & Oct) The 3.4km view-filled hike from Lake Louise to Lake Agnes is one of the area's most popular – surely because it ends here, at this fabulously rustic alpine teahouse that seems to hang in the clouds beside the ethereal lake and its adjacent waterfall. Homemade bread, soup, thick-cut sandwiches and lake-water tea offer fuel for the jaunt back down. Cash only.

Plain of Six Glaciers Teahouse
CAFE $

(snacks $6-14; ☺8am-6pm Jun–mid-Oct) Constructed in 1927 as a way station for Swiss mountaineering guides leading clients up to the summit of Mt Victoria, this twin-level log chalet looks like something out of the pages of *Heidi*. Nestled in a quiet glade, it dishes up homemade sandwiches, cakes,

ALBERTA LAKE LOUISE

gourmet teas and hot chocolates to a steady stream of puffed-out hikers.

Bill Peyto's Café
CAFE $

(✆403-522-2201; www.hihostels.ca; HI-Lake Louise Alpine Centre, Village Rd, Lake Louise village; mains $5-12; ☺7am-10pm May-Sep, to 9pm Oct-Apr) Lively Peyto's is a popular hangout, with live music and a decent bar. The menu's not fancy but the food is consistently good. Fill up on homemade granola or a burrito *huevo* for breakfast; try seafood chili or mac 'n' cheese at dinner. The patio is nice when the sun (or moon) is shining. Expect queues when the hostel's full.

★ Lake Louise Station Restaurant
CANADIAN $$

(✆403-522-2600; www.lakelouisestation.com; 200 Sentinel Rd; mains $20-45; ☺11am-4pm & 5-9pm) Dine in the station's great hall or one of the dining cars, which are nothing short of elegant. Details like stacks of turn-of-the-century luggage and the stationmaster's desk take you back to 1910, when the station was first built. Dig into the first-class Rocky Mountain sausage plate, maple salmon or bison burger and soak up the almost palpable atmosphere. Reservations recommended.

❶ Information

Lake Louise Visitors Centre (Samson Mall, Lake Louise village; ☺9am-7pm mid-Jun–Aug, to 5pm May–mid-Jun & Sep–mid-Oct, 9am-4:30pm Thu-Sun mid-Oct–Apr) Come here for Parks Canada info on Banff and Jasper and to register for backcountry hikes. You'll also find some good geological displays, a local tourist information desk and a small film theater.

❶ Getting There & Away

Brewster (p73) runs bus service here from Banff and Jasper; the bus terminal is a marked stop at Samson Mall.

The easiest way to get here from Banff is by car.

Jasper Town & Around

Take Banff, halve the annual visitor count, increase the total land area by 40% and multiply the number of bears, elk, moose and caribou by three. The result: Jasper, a larger, less trammeled, more wildlife-rich version of the other Rocky Mountains parks. Its rugged backcountry wins admiring plaudits for its deep river canyons, rampart-like mountain ranges and delicate ecosystems.

Most people enter Jasper Town from the south via the magnificently Gothic Icefields Parkway that meanders up from Lake Louise amid foaming waterfalls and glacier-sculpted mountains, including iconic Mt Edith Cavell, easily visible from the town. Another option is to take a legendary VIA Rail train (from either Edmonton or BC) through foothills imbued with fur-trading and Aboriginal history.

Stacked up against Canada's other national parks, Jasper scores high marks for its hiking, pioneering history, easy-to-view wildlife and hut-to-hut backcountry skiing possibilities. Similarly, bike enthusiasts consistently laud it as having one of the best single-track cycling networks in North America.

◉ Sights

★ Jasper National Park
NATIONAL PARK

(Map p90; www.pc.gc.ca/jasper; day pass adult/youth/family $9.80/4.90/19.60) Mountain lions, wolves, caribou, beaver and bear roam freely; glaciers stretch out between mountain peaks; waterfalls thunder over slopes; and valleys are wide and lush, with rivers charging turbulently through them – this is Jasper National Park, covering a diverse 10878sq km. Jasper is far from built up: while activities like hiking and mountain biking are well established and deservedly popular, it's still easy to experience the solitude and remoteness that abound in this park.

★ Miette Hot Springs
HOT SPRINGS

(Map p90; www.pc.gc.ca/hotsprings; Miette Rd; adult/child/family $6/5/18.50; ☺8:30am-10:30pm) More remote than Banff's historic springs, Miette Hot Springs ('discovered' in 1909) are 61km northeast of Jasper off Hwy 16, near the park boundary. The soothing waters, kept at a pleasant 40°C (104°F), are surrounded by peaks and are especially enjoyable when the fall snow is drifting down and steam envelops the crowd. Raining summer evenings also make for stunning, misty conditions.

Horseshoe Lake
LAKE

(Map p90) This idyllic, blue-green, horseshoe-shaped lake just off the Icefields Pkwy is missed by many visitors, making a stop-over here all the more alluring. A choice spot for a bracing summer swim or a short stroll around the perimeter, the lake is surrounded by steep cliffs and is frequented by cliff divers. It's probably safer to watch than join in.

Maligne Lake
LAKE

(Map p90) Almost 50km from Jasper at the end of a stunning road that bears its name, 22km-long Maligne Lake is the recipient of a lot of hype. It is billed as one of the most beautiful lakes within the park and there's no denying its appeal: the baby-blue water and a craning circle of rocky, photogenic peaks are a feast for the eyes.

Maligne Canyon
CANYON

(Map p90) A steep, narrow gorge shaped by a river flowing at its base, this canyon at its narrowest is only a few meters wide and drops a stomach-turning 50m beneath your feet. Crossed by six bridges, it has various **trails** leading out from the parking area on Maligne Lake Rd, where there's also a quaint, basic teahouse. In the winter, waterfalls freeze solid into sheets of white ice and are popular with ice climbers.

Jasper Skytram
CABLE CAR

(Map p90; ☑780-852-3093; www.jaspertramway.com; Whistlers Mountain Rd; adult/child/family $40/20/100; ☺9am-8pm Apr-Oct) If the average, boring views from Jasper just aren't blowing your hair back, go for a ride on this sightseeing gondola. The journey zips up through various mountain life zones to the high barren slopes of the Whistlers, where there's a small, pricey cafe. From the top of the gondola you can take the steep 1.5km hike to the mountain's true summit, where views stretch for 75km.

Medicine Lake
LAKE

(Map p90) A geological rarity, Medicine Lake is perhaps best described as a sinking lake that has holes in the bottom and functions rather like a bathtub without a plug. In summer, when the run-off is high, the lake fills more quickly than it can drain away, and the body of water appears deep and expansive. In winter, as the run-off slows, the water empties, causing the lake to shrink to the size of a small stream.

Lakes Annette & Edith
LAKE

(Map p90) On the opposite side of the highway to the town, Lakes Annette and Edith are popular for water activities in the summer; both have small beach areas and a number of picnic spots. If you're brave and it's very hot, Annette is good for a quick summer dip – just remember that the water was in a glacier not too long ago! Edith is frequented more by kayakers and boaters.

Patricia & Pyramid Lakes
LAKE

(Map p90) These two lakes, less than 10km (6.2 miles) from town, offer abundant water activities. Patricia Lake contains the wreck of a WWII ice-based aircraft carrier called *Habbakuk,* sunk after a secret wartime mission to create the unsinkable ship. Experienced divers can examine it close up with **Jasper Dive Adventures** (☑780-852-3560; www.jasperdiveadventures.com; dives $75; ☺May-Sep). Pyramid Lake, overlooked by a resort, is popular with canoers and kayakers in summer and ice-skaters in winter. It has a lovely island, popular with nighttime stargazers, that's accessible by a bridge.

🏃 Activities

Cycling

Jasper tops Banff for single-track mountain biking; in fact, it's one of the best places in Canada for the sport. Many routes are within striking distance of the town. Flatter, on-road options include the long-distance grunt along the Icefields Parkway. The holy grail for experienced off-road cyclists is the **Valley of the Five Lakes** – it's varied and scenic, with plenty of places where you can let rip. For more information, get a copy of *Mountain Biking Guide, Jasper National Park* from the Jasper Information Centre (p95).

Vicious Cycle (Map p92; ☑780-852-1111; www.viciouscanada.com; 630 Connaught Dr, Jasper Town; bike rental per hour/day from $8/32; ☺9am-6pm) can sort out bike rentals and offer additional trail tips.

Hiking

Even when judged against other Canadian national parks, Jasper's trail network is mighty, and with comparatively fewer people than its sister park to the south, you've a better chance of seeing more wildlife and fewer humans.

Initiate yourself on the interpretative **Discovery Trail**, an 8km easy hike that encircles the town and highlights its natural, historical and railway heritage.

Other short trails include the 3.2km **Mary Schäffer Loop** by Maligne Lake, named for one of the earliest European visitors to the area; the 3.5km **Old Fort Loop** to the site of an old fur-trading post; and the 9km **Mina and Riley Lakes Loop** that leads out directly from the town.

Further away and slightly harder, the famous 9.1km **Path of the Glacier Trail** runs below the impressive face of Mt Edith Cavell

Jasper National Park

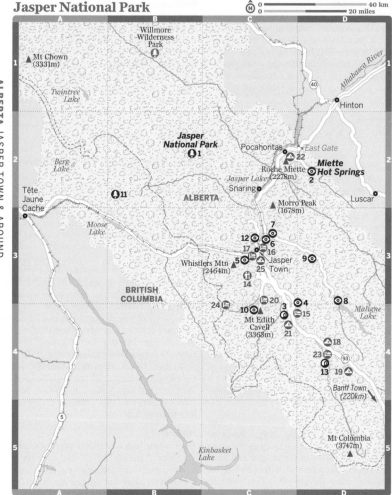

and takes you to the foot of the Angel Glacier through the flower-scattered Cavell meadows.

The blue-ribbon multiday hike is the **Skyline Trail** – unusual in that almost all of its 46km are on or above the tree line, affording amazing cross-park views. The hike is usually split over two days, starting at Maligne Lake and emerging near Maligne Canyon on Maligne Lake Rd. You can pitch your tent in a campground or stay in the historic Shovel Pass Lodge (p93).

The leaflet *Day-Hikers' Guide to Jasper National Park* has descriptions of most of the park's easy walks, while the backcountry visi-

tor guide *Jasper National Park* details longer trails and backcountry campsites, with suggested itineraries for hikes of two to 10 days. If you're hiking overnight, you must obtain a backcountry permit (per person per night $10; a season pass is $69) from Parks Canada in the Jasper Information Centre (p95).

Horseback Riding

Incredible, fully guided summer pack-trips head into the roadless **Tonquin Valley**, where you are bivouacked in the backcountry (but comfortable) Tonquin Amethyst Lake Lodge (p93). The trips are run by **Tonquin Valley**

Jasper National Park

Adventures (☏ 780-852-1188; www.tonquin adventures.com; 3-/4-day trips $895/1195) and include accommodations, meals and complimentary fishing trips on Amethyst Lake.

Skiing & Snowboarding

Jasper National Park's only downhill ski area is **Marmot Basin** (Map p90; www.skimarmot. com; Marmot Basin Rd; day pass adult/child $89/71), which lies 19km southwest of town off Hwy 93A. Though not legendary, the presence of 86 runs and the longest high-speed quad chairlift in the Rockies mean Marmot is no pushover – and its relative isolation compared to the trio of ski areas in Banff means shorter lift lines.

On-site are some cross-country trails and a predictably expensive day lodge, but no overnight accommodations. Regular shuttles link to Jasper Town in season. Seriously cold weather can drift in suddenly off the mountains, so dress appropriately.

White-Water Rafting

There's nothing like a glacial splashdown to fight the summer heat. The Jasper area has lots of good rafting opportunities, from raging to relaxed, on the **Maligne, Sunwapta** and **Athabasca Rivers**. The season runs from May to September.

🞆 Tours

Jasper Walks & Talks   HIKING
(Map p92; ☏ 780-852-4994; www.walksntalks. com; 626 Connaught Dr, Jasper Town; adult/child $90/50; ☺ Jun-Oct) A local resident and former Parks Canada guide leads small groups on breathtaking five- to six-hour tours that can take in Mt Edith Cavell Meadows, Maligne Canyon or the Valley of Five Lakes. Bring a picnic lunch, good walking shoes, your camera and lots of questions for your very knowledgeable guide. Tours depart at 9:30am from June to October.

Rockaboo Adventures   CLIMBING
(Map p92; ☏ 780-820-0092; www.rockaboo.ca; 807 Tonquin St, Jasper Town; 🚼) Jasper's most comprehensive year-round climbing guides offer everything from a four-hour Experience Rock Climbing course ($125), suitable for kids aged six and up, to strenuous ascents of lofty Mt Edith Cavell. They also arrange rappelling ($79).

🎉 Festivals & Events

Dark Sky Festival   SCIENCE
(tickets $45-100; ☺ late Oct) Two weeks are filled with events celebrating space and the night sky. Hear talks by astronauts and celebrities like Bill Nye, listen to the symphony under the stars, see the aurora borealis reflected in a glacial lake and gaze through a telescope into the great beyond. There are some free events but the big hitters sell out months in advance.

🛏 Sleeping

Despite its reputation as a quiet antidote to Banff, Jasper Town still gets busy in the summer. Book ahead or consider visiting in the less crowded late winter/early spring shoulder season, when the deserted mountainous landscapes (best accessed on cross-country skis) take on a whole new dimension. There are considerable winter discounts to be found.

Accommodations in Jasper are generally cheaper than Banff, but that's not really saying much. Several places outside the town proper offer bungalows (usually wooden

Jasper Town

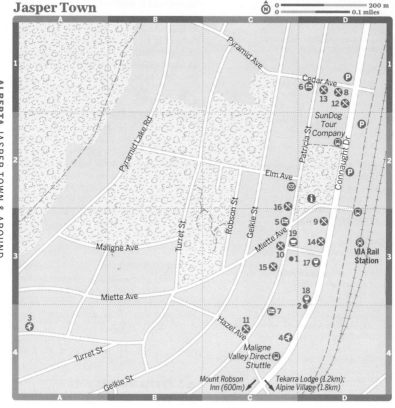

Jasper Town

cabins) that are open only in summer. Jasper's 10 park campgrounds are open from mid-May to September/October. One (Wapiti) is partly open year-round; four of them take reservations. For information, contact Parks Canada at the Jasper Information Centre (p95).

★ **Jasper Downtown Hostel** HOSTEL $
(Map p92; ☑780-852-2000; www.jasperdowntown hostel.ca; 400 Patricia St, Jasper Town; dm/d $40/126; ☎) Stay right downtown for a song? Yes! Rooms in this former residence have been remodeled to create simple, modern two- to eight-bed dorms, along with comfortable pri-

vate rooms for up to five. Upstairs rooms are brighter, with wooden floors, and many have private baths. There is no kitchen or common area, but town is on your doorstep.

Pocahontas Campground   CAMPGROUND $

(Map p90; www.reservation.parkscanada.gc. ca; Miette Hot Springs Rd; tent & RV sites $21.50; ⊙ May-Sep) As spacious and densely wooded as it is, you'd never know this place has 140 sites. Facilities are minimal, albeit with flush toilets and wheelchair-accessible sites, but it's very well maintained.

Wapiti Campground   CAMPGROUND $

(Map p90; www.reservation.parkscanada.gc.ca; Hwy 93; tent/RV sites $28/33) Jasper's second-biggest campground (362 sites) is located close to its largest (the Whistlers), with a handy bike/hike trail linking them and continuing on to Jasper Town (5km). Clean and well-maintained shower and toilet blocks are a given here, but Wapiti's main draw is its location on the banks of the Athabasca River.

HI-Jasper Hostel   HOSTEL $

(Map p90; ☑780-852-3215; www.hihostels.ca; Whistlers Mountain Rd; dm/d $30/80; ⓟ@🛜) 🏊 It would be easy to not like this hostel. With dorm rooms that sleep upward of 40 people, meaning you're pretty much guaranteed some midnight snoring, and a location just far enough from town that the walk is a killer, it's already two strikes down. Despite all of this, though, it's a great place to stay.

★Tekarra Lodge   HOTEL $$

(☑780-852-3058; www.tekarralodge.com; Hwy 93A; lodge/cabins from $199/240; ⊙ May-Oct; ⓟ🛜) The most atmospheric cabins in the park are set next to the Athabasca River amid tall trees and splendid tranquillity. Hardwood floors, wood-paneled walls plus stone fireplaces and kitchenettes inspire coziness. It's only 1km from town, but has a distinct backcountry feel. The on-site restaurant is fine dining by Jasper standards.

★Park Place Inn   BOUTIQUE HOTEL $$

(Map p92; ☑780-852-9970; www.parkplaceinn. com; 623 Patricia St, Jasper Town; r $229-269; @🛜) Its ordinary exterior among a parade of downtown shops gives nothing away, but the Park Place is a head-turner as soon as you ascend the stairs to its plush open lobby. Parks Canada offices until 2002, the 14 renovated heritage rooms are elegant, with gleaming wooden floors, claw-foot or Jacuzzi tubs and a general air of refinement and luxury.

Shovel Pass Lodge   LODGE $$

(☑780-852-4215; www.skylinetrail.com; r per person incl meals $199; ⊙ Jun-Sep) Built in 1921 and rebuilt in 1991, the Shovel Pass Lodge is situated halfway along the emblematic Skyline Trail. The seven guest cabins are basic, with log bed frames, fresh linen, propane lights and hot water delivered daily. Two hearty meals and a packed lunch are included, as are some of the most phenomenal views around.

Athabasca Hotel   HOTEL $$

(Map p92; ☑780-852-3386; www.athabasca hotel.com; 510 Patricia St, Jasper Town; r without/ with bath $139/199; ⓟ@🛜) A taxidermist's dream, the Atha-B (as it's known) has small, clean rooms with wooden and brass furnishings and thick, wine-colored carpets. Many of the rooms share a bathroom; there's no elevator. Dated but not worn, it feels like you're staying at Grandma's (if Grandma liked to hunt). Service is fickle and the bar downstairs can get noisy. Around since 1929, this is the best bargain in town. Expect significant discounts in winter.

Miette Hot Springs Resort   MOTEL, CABIN $$

(Map p90; ☑780-866-3750; www.mhresort.com; Miette Hot Springs Rd; r/chalets/cabins $99/127/187; ⓟ) This low-key 'resort' at the hot springs is a collection of old-fashioned but charming log cabins and motel rooms dating from 1938 and chalets from the 1970s. Cabins sleep up to six and have kitchenettes and stone fireplaces (some of the 17 motel rooms also have kitchenettes). The restaurant has reasonably priced standard meals. Bears regularly meander through the grounds.

Alpine Village   CABIN $$$

(☑780-852-3285; www.alpinevillagejasper.com; 2-/4-person cabins from $210/420; ⊙ May-Oct; ⓟ🛜) Characterful log cabins with modern, renovated bathrooms are a cut above the competition, with an ace location flush against the Athabasca River. Enjoy the tranquillity – you're just outside the hubbub of town, but close enough to walk. The cabins have plush, country-style decor, with mezzanine bedrooms and stone fireplaces. The nearest neighbors are usually elk.

Tonquin Amethyst Lake Lodge   LODGE $$$

(Map p90; ☑780-852-1188; www.tonquinadventures.com; r per person incl meals $195) Rustic accommodations in historic cabins with views of Amethyst Lake and the towering mountains of The Ramparts range, approximately

JASPER IN WINTER

Half of Jasper shuts down in the winter; the other half just adapts and metamorphoses into something just as good (if not better) than its summertime self. Lakes become skating rinks, hiking and biking routes (and some roads) become cross-country skiing trails, waterfalls become ice climbs, and – last but by no means least – prices become far more reasonable.

The best natural outdoor skating rink is on **Lac Beauvert** in front of the Fairmont Jasper Park Lodge, an area that is floodlit after dark. More skating can be found 6km northeast of the town on **Pyramid Lake**.

The park has an incredible 200km of cross-country skiing trails. Routes less prone to an early snow melt are the **Pyramid Lake Fire Road**, the **Meeting of the Waters** (along a closed section of Hwy 93A), the **Moab Lake Trail** and the **Mt Edith Cavell Road**. Relatively safe, but dramatic, backcountry skiing can be found in the **Tonquin Valley**; however, these routes are sometimes closed due to caribou conservation (see www.tonquinvalley.com for more details).

Slightly less athletic is the three-hour **Maligne Canyon Ice Walk** offered by **Jasper Adventure Centre** (Map p92; ☑780-852-5595; www.jasperadventurecentre.com; 611 Patricia St, Jasper Town; adult/child $65/29), a walk through frozen waterfalls viewable from December to April. Extremists tackle these slippery behemoths with rappels and ice axes.

24km from the nearest road. You can hike in on your own or join one of the lodge's multiday **horseback-riding treks** (three/four days $895/1195) in summer, while in winter you can arrive via cross-country skis. Reservations are required.

Mount Robson Inn   MOTEL $$$

(☑780-852-3327; www.mountrobsoninn.com; 902 Connaught Dr, Jasper Town; r incl breakfast from $260; P❋@☏) A plush and newly renovated place laid out motel-style on the edge of Jasper Town that offers hot tubs, an on-site restaurant and a substantial complimentary breakfast. With everything from sleek queen rooms to family and Jacuzzi suites, you'd be hard-pressed to find something you didn't like.

Fairmont Jasper Park Lodge   HOTEL $$$

(Map p90; ☑780-852-3301; www.fairmont.com/jasper; 1 Old Lodge Rd, Jasper Town; r from $480; P@☏) Sitting on the shore of Lac Beauvert and surrounded by manicured grounds and mountain peaks, this classic old lodge can't quite match the panache of the Banff and Lake Louise Fairmonts, although you'll bump into fewer afternoon-tea-seeking tourists. With a country-club-meets-1950s-holiday-camp air, the amenity-filled cabins and chalets are a throwback to a more opulent era.

✖ Eating

★ Other Paw Bakery   CAFE, BAKERY $

(Map p92; 610 Connaught Dr, Jasper Town; snacks $2-6; ☉7am-6pm) An offshoot of the Bear's Paw, a larger cafe around the cor-

ner, the Other Paw offers the same insanely addictive mix of breads, pastries, muffins and coffee, along with tasty soups and well-stuffed wraps. This one stays open later, too.

Patricia Street Deli   SANDWICHES $

(Map p92; 610 Patricia St, Jasper Town; sandwiches $7-9; ☉10am-5pm Mon-Fri, to 6pm Sat & Sun) Come to the Patricia Street Deli hungry – really hungry. Homemade bread is made into generously filled sandwiches by people who are just as generous with their hiking tips. Choose from a huge list of fillings, including various pestos, chutneys, veggies and meat cuts. Join the queue and satiate your ravenous backcountry appetite.

Bear's Paw Bakery   BAKERY, CAFE $

(Map p92; www.bearspawbakery.com; 4 Cedar Ave, Jasper Town; pastries $3-5; ☉6am-6pm) One of the best bakery-cafes west of Winnipeg. Thank your lucky stars the Bear Paw is situated here, just where you need it most at the end of an energy-sapping hike/bike/ski. Try any of the insanely addictive scones, cookies, muffins, focaccia-like breads and wraps. The coffee is equally gratifying.

Coco's Cafe   CAFE $

(Map p92; ☑780-852-4550; 608 Patricia St, Jasper Town; mains $5-12; ☉8am-4pm; ☑) ✿ If you're looking for breakfast, you can't go wrong at Coco's. There's not much room inside, but many are happy to cram in to plan hikes and trade bear sightings. There's plenty of locally sourced, vegan, veggie and celiac-friendly fare on the menu, while carnivores are kept happy with Montreal smoked meat, pulled pork and lox.

For lunch, try the grown-up grilled cheese sandwich with apple and onion chutney.

Olive Bistro
MEDITERRANEAN **$$**

(Map p92; ☑ 780-852-5222; www.olivebistro. ca; 401 Patricia St, Jasper Town; mains $16-25; ☺5-11pm; ☑) This casual restaurant with big booths has a classy menu. Choose from main dishes like whiskey barbecue ribs, bison lasagna or wild-mushroom risotto, or opt for sharing plates like white-truffle scallops or a charcuterie plate of local smoked meats. The cocktails are excellent and there's often mellow live music.

Cassio's Trattoria
ITALIAN **$$**

(Map p92; 602 Connaught Dr, Jasper Town; mains $14-30; ☺7:30am-11pm; ☑) In the long-standing Whistlers Inn, the Cassio family concentrates on presenting *real* Italian fare: gnocchi, meatballs, veal marsala, pasta marinara and a well-stuffed antipasto plate. There's not a lot of atmosphere, but you won't care once you dive in to the food.

Jasper Pizza Place
PIZZA **$$**

(Map p92; ☑ 780-852-3225; 402 Connaught Dr, Jasper Town; pizzas $13-20; ☺noon-10pm) Baked in a traditional wood-burning oven, the much-sought-after pizzas here are rather good. Build your own from a long list of toppings and sauces or choose one of their crafty creations. This place can get packed, with a long line out the door. Inside it's casual, with sports on the TVs and beer on tap.

Raven Bistro
MEDITERRANEAN **$$$**

(Map p92; ☑ 780-852-5151; www.theravenbistro. com; 504 Patricia St, Jasper Town; mains $24-32; ☺5-10pm; ☑) This small, tastefully designed bistro offers vegetarian dishes, encourages shared plates and wouldn't be out of place in a small Spanish city. Creative offerings like pomegranate-braised lamb shank and Kaffir lime–coconut seafood pot grace the menu. In summer, brunch is available on weekends from 9am to 1pm.

Evil Dave's Grill
CANADIAN, FUSION **$$$**

(Map p92; ☑ 780-852-3323; www.evildaves. com; 622 Patricia St, Jasper Town; mains $22-35; ☺5-11pm Mon-Fri, 4-11pm Sat & Sun) There's nothing evil about Dave's, other than its attempts to bury Jasper's image as a bastion of family-friendly, post-hiking grub that fills stomachs rather than excites taste buds. The excellent fusion food comes from all over the map, with Caribbean, Middle Eastern and Japanese influences lighting up the fish and beef. Save room for the deadly desserts.

Drinking & Nightlife

SnowDome Coffee Bar
COFFEE

(Map p92; www.607patricia.com; 607 Patricia St, Jasper Town; ☺7:45am-8pm) Some of the best damn coffee in Jasper is – no lie! – served out of a launderette. Patricia St's Coin Clean Laundry is no ordinary washing place – as well as being surgically clean, it also serves as an art gallery, shower facility, internet cafe and all-round community resource. Sanitize your dirty hiking socks and savor a latte.

Downstream Bar
BAR

(Map p92; 620 Connaught Dr, Jasper Town; ☺4pm-late) This is likely the most well-stocked bar in town, with a wide array of whiskeys, vodkas and other alcoholic indulgences – and a bar staff who know how to use them. There's some awesome food to keep your head above water and, often, live music.

Jasper Brewing Co
BREWERY

(Map p92; ☑ 780-852-4111; www.jasperbrewing co.ca; 624 Connaught Dr, Jasper Town; ☺11:30am-1am) ⊘ This brewpub was the first of its type in a Canadian national park, using glacial water to make its fine ales, including the signature Rockhopper IPA and the slightly more adventurous Rocket Ridge Raspberry Ale. It's a sit-down affair, with TVs and a good food menu.

ⓘ Information

Jasper Information Centre (Map p92; ☑ 780-852-6176; www.pc.gc.ca/jasper; 500 Connaught Dr, Jasper Town; ☺9am-7pm May-Oct, 10am-5pm Nov-Apr) This wonderful information center is housed in Jasper's oldest building, dating from 1913. You'll find a Parks Canada desk and the local tourist information stand, plus an excellent gift shop.

Post office (Map p92; 502 Patricia St; ☺9am-5pm Mon-Fri)

Seton General Hospital (☑ 780-852-3344; 518 Robson St)

ⓘ Getting There & Away

BUS

The **bus station** (Map p92; 607 Connaught Dr, Jasper Town) is at the train station. **Greyhound** (☑ 800-661-8747; www.greyhound.ca) buses have daily services to Edmonton ($70, from five hours), Prince George ($70, six hours),

ALBERTA JASPER TOWN & AROUND

Kamloops ($78, six hours) and Vancouver ($148, from 12 hours).

Brewster Transportation (☑ 403-762-6700; www.brewster.ca), departing from the same station, operates express buses to Lake Louise village ($75, four hours, at least one daily) and Banff Town ($100, five hours, at least one daily). SunDog (p56) also has daily services from May to October to Edmonton airport ($50), Lake Louise ($59), Banff ($69) and Calgary airport ($119).

TRAIN

VIA Rail (☑ 888-842-7245; www.viarail.ca) offers tri-weekly train services west to Vancouver ($242, 20 hours) and east to Toronto ($516, 62 hours). In addition, there is a tri-weekly service to Prince Rupert, BC ($205, 33 hours). Call or check in at the **train station** (607 Connaught Dr, Jasper Town) for exact schedule and fare details.

❶ Getting Around

Maligne Valley Shuttle (Map p92; ☑ 780-852-3331; www.maligneadventures.com; adult one-way/round-trip $30/60, youth one-way/round-trip $14/30) Runs a 9am daily shuttle from outside the Jasper Information Centre to Maligne Lake, with stops at trailheads along the way. Shuttles return from the lake at 10:15am, 2pm and 5pm.

Jasper Taxi (☑ 780-852-3600) Has metered cabs.

SOUTHERN ALBERTA

Alberta's national parks and cities grab most of the headlines, leaving the expansive south largely forgotten. This is true cowboy land, where the ghosts of herders like John Ware and the Sundance Kid are woven through the history of endless ranch land. It's often interrupted by deep, dramatic canyons carved in the last ice age, as well as towering hoodoos – funky, Dr Seuss–like rock sculptures. History abounds at Head-Smashed-In Buffalo Jump and Dinosaur Provincial Park, two Unesco World Heritage areas that preserve the region's past.

Picture-perfect landscapes are plentiful here. The dusty badlands around Drumheller open up into wide open prairies that stretch east all the way to the Cyprus Hills of western Saskatchewan. To the west lies Waterton Lakes National Park, with some of the most spectacular scenery in the Rockies – utterly different from Banff and Jasper yet still under the radar of most visitors.

Drumheller & Around

As you approach Drumheller, the road dips down dramatically into the Red Deer Valley, looking like a big layered cake. This community was founded on coal but now thrives on another subterranean resource – dinosaur bones. A small town set amid Alberta's enigmatic badlands, it acts as the nexus of the so-called **Dinosaur Trail**. Paleontology is a serious business here (the nearby fantastic Royal Tyrrell Museum is as much research center as tourist site), and downtown the cartoon dino statues on most street corners add some color and character to an otherwise average town (though the dino-related prefixes to business names is sometimes pushing it a little). And then there's the large matter of the 26m-high fiberglass *Tyrannosaurus rex* that haunts a large tract of downtown. But don't let the paleontological civic pride deter you: there's enough to do around here (dinosaur-related and otherwise) to keep you from dwelling on the kitsch. Add in the museums in nearby East Coulee and the ghosts of Wayne, and you've got a full itinerary.

The summers are hot, and the deep-cut river valley in which Drumheller sits provides a much-needed break to the monotony of the prairies. Hoodoos dominate this badlands landscape, which has featured in many a movie (mainly Westerns).

◉ Sights & Activities

★**Royal Tyrrell Museum of Palaeontology**   MUSEUM
(☑ 403-823-7707; www.tyrrellmuseum.com; 1500 North Dinosaur Trail, Midlands Provincial Park, Drumheller; adult/child $18/10; ☺ 9am-9pm mid-May–Aug, 10am-5pm Sep, 10am-5pm Tue-Sun Oct–mid-May; ❹) This fantastic museum is one of the preeminent dinosaur museums on the planet. Even if you have no interest in dinos, you'll come out feeling like you missed your calling as a paleontologist. The exhibits are nothing short of mind-blowing. Look for the skeleton of 'Hell-Boy', a new dinosaur discovered in 2005, and 'Black Beauty', a 67-million-year-old *T rex* rearing into the sky. You can learn how they're extracted and even peer into the fossil lab.

Rosedale Suspension Bridge   BRIDGE
(Hwy 56, Rosedale) This suspension bridge isn't very long or high, but it's definitely not for the faint of heart. Made of see-through wire

mesh, it sways like a river reed in the wind. The bridge was used by miners from 1931 to 1957; on the far side of the Red Deer river, you can see the now-closed mines. Despite previous use of rowboats and aerial cable cars, it was the bridge that was considered dangerous due to high winds and floods.

Horseshoe Canyon   CANYON
(Hwy 9) The baddest of the badlands can be seen at Horseshoe Canyon, a spectacular chasm cut into the otherwise flat prairie located 17km west of Drumheller on Hwy 9. A large sign in the parking lot explains the geology of the area; **hiking trails** lead down into the canyon, where striated colored rock reveals millions of years of geological history. (Beware: trails are very slippery when wet.)

World's Largest Dinosaur   LANDMARK
(60 1st Ave W, Drumheller; $3; ⊗10am-6pm; ♿) In a town filled with dinosaurs, this *T rex* is the king of them all. Standing 26m high above a parking lot, it dominates the Drumheller skyline (and is featured in the *Guinness Book of Records*). It's worth climbing the 106 steps to the top for the novelty of standing in the dino's toothy jaws – plus the views are mighty good. Ironically, the dinosaur isn't technically very accurate: at 46m long, it's about 4.5 times bigger than its extinct counterpart.

Dinosaur Trail & Hoodoo Drive   SCENIC DRIVE
Drumheller is on the Dinosaur Trail, a 48km loop that runs northwest from town and includes Hwys 837 and 838. The scenery is stunning and worth the drive – badlands and river views await you at every turn.

The loop takes you past **Midland Provincial Park** (no camping), where you can take a self-guided hike, and the past the vast **Horsethief Canyon** and its picturesque views. Glide peacefully across the Red Deer River on the free, cable-operated **Bleriot Ferry**, which has been running since 1913; watch for beavers, who have a dam here. This area is also frequented by moose, lynx and cougars. On the west side of the valley, pause at **Orkney Viewpoint**, which overlooks the area's impressive canyons.

The 25km Hoodoo Drive starts about 18km southeast of Drumheller on Hwy 10; the route is usually done as an out-and-back with Wayne as the turnaround point. Along this drive you'll find the best examples of **hoodoos** – weird, eroded, mushroom-like columns of sandstone rock – between Rose-

dale and Lehigh; there's also an interpretive trail.

This area was once the site of a prosperous coal-mining community; the historic **Atlas Coal Mine** (☑403-822-2220; www.atlascoalmine.ab.ca; East Coulee; $10, tours $20-25; ⊗9:45am-5pm Sep-Jun, to 7:30pm Jul-Aug) and **East Coulee School Museum** (☑403-822-3970; www.ecsmuseum.ca; 359 2nd Ave, East Coulee; ⊗10am-5pm) are both worth a stop. Take the side trip on Hwy 10X (which includes 11 bridges within 6km) from Rosedale to the small community of **Wayne** (population 27) with its famous and supposedly haunted saloon.

🛏 Sleeping

River Grove Campground & Cabins   CAMPGROUND $
(☑403-823-6655; www.campgrouprivergrove.com; 25 Poplar St, Drumheller; campsites/RV sites/tipis/cabins from $35/41/67/125; ⊗May-Sep; P ☀) Right in town and close to the big *T rex*, this shaded campground next to the river has lots of amenities. You can even rent a tipi for the night, although it's not an entirely faithful re-creation (the Stoney people likely didn't have concrete floors in theirs).

★**Heartwood Inn & Spa**   INN $$
(☑403-823-6495; www.innsatheartwood.com; 320 N Railway Ave E, Drumheller; d $155-190; @ 🛜) This lovely country inn is full of character and reason enough to visit Drumheller. The rooms are luxurious and each uniquely decorated; some have Jacuzzis and fireplaces and all have beautiful touches. There's a deck, a small garden and an on-site spa. The friendly owners are founts of local knowledge.

Taste the Past B&B   B&B $$
(☑403-823-5889; 281 2nd St W, Drumheller; s/d $115/140; P 🛜) This converted turn-of-the-century house has evolved into a cozy downtown B&B. All rooms have a private bathroom, and there is a communal living room that could have been airlifted straight from your Grandma's house. With only three rooms, a stay here feels more like visiting with friends.

🍴 Eating & Drinking

Ivy's Awesome Kitchen & Bistro   BISTRO $
(www.ivysawesomekitchen.com; 35 3rd Ave West, Drumheller; mains $8-12; ⊗8am-5pm; 🍴) With good, home-style cooking that won't clot your arteries, Ivy's offers breakfasts, panini, burgers, fresh soups and beautiful salads. You'll find dishes that cater to vegans,

vegetarians and gluten-free diets. Chilled and friendly, it's a great place to have lunch. Save room for the homemade desserts: the chocolate lava cake and sticky toffee pudding are difficult to resist.

Bernie and the Boys Bistro
DINER $

(☑ 403-823-3318; www.bernieandtheboys.com; 305 4th St W, Drumheller; burgers $6-8; ☺11am-8:30pm Tue-Sat) Bistro it isn't, but Bernie's is a small-town, family-run diner that replenishes appetites with hearty gourmet burgers and legendary milkshakes. Join the queue.

★Last Chance Saloon
BAR

(☑ 403-823-9189; www.visitlastchancesaloon.com; Hwy 10X, Wayne; ☺11am-11pm) Last Chance is the real thing – a Western saloon from 1913, complete with bear skins, old kerosene lamps, antique photos and bullet holes in the wall. Since its original heyday, Wayne's population has dwindled from 2500 to 33, many of whom you'll find in this lively, eclectic place. Meat pies, maple-bacon burgers and chicken dinners go well with the beer.

❶ Information

Tourist information center (☑ 403-823-1331; www.traveldrumheller.com; 60 1st Ave W, Drumheller; ☺9am-9pm) At the foot of the *T rex*. The entrance to the body of the beast is in the same building.

❶ Getting There & Away

Greyhound (p42) runs buses from the bus station (308 Centre St, Drumheller) to Calgary ($38, two hours, two daily) and Edmonton ($69, seven hours, two daily).

Hammerhead Tours (www.hammerheadtours.com) runs a full-day tour ($124) from Calgary to the Drumheller badlands and the Royal Tyrrell Museum.

Dinosaur Provincial Park

In no other place on earth has such a large number of dinosaur bones been found in such a small area – over 40 species and 400 skeletons. Set where *The Lost World* meets *Little House on the Prairie*, **Dinosaur Provincial Park** (☑ 403-378-4344; www.dinosaurpark.ca; off Hwy 544; ☺8:30am-5pm Sun-Thu, to 7pm Fri & Sat) FREE – a Unesco World Heritage site – comes at you by surprise, deep in a chasm that opens before your feet from the grassy plain. A dehydrated fantasy landscape, there are hoodoos, colorful rock formations and dinosaurs aplenty.

The 81-sq-km park begs to be explored, with wildflowers, the odd rattler in the rocks and, if you're lucky, maybe even a *T rex*. This isn't just a tourist attraction, but a hotbed for science: paleontologists have uncovered countless skeletons here, which now reside in many of the finest museums around the globe.

There are five short interpretive **hiking trails** to choose from and a driving loop runs through part of the park, giving you the chance to see a number of dinosaur skeletons in their death posts. To preserve the fossils, access to 70% of the park is restricted and may be seen only on guided hikes or **bus tours** (adult/child $15/8), which operate from late May to October. (The hikes and tours are popular, so be sure to reserve a place.)

The park's **Dinosaur Visitors Centre** (☑ 403-378-4342; www.albertaparks.ca; adult/child $6/3; ☺8:30am-5pm) is a field station of the Royal Tyrrell Museum (p96) in Drumheller and has a small, yet excellent, series of dino displays, as well as exhibits on the realities of paleontology.

In a hollow by a small creek sits the park's **Dinosaur Campground** (☑ 403-378-4342; www.albertaparks.ca; campsites/RV sites $28/35, comfort camping $105-130, reservations $12; ☺year-round; ℗). The ample tree cover is a welcome reprieve from the volcanic sun. Laundry facilities and hot showers are available, as are a small shop and cafe. This is a popular place, especially with the RV set, so phone ahead.

Though 75 million years ago dinosaurs cruised around a tropical landscape, it's now a hot and barren place – make sure you dress for the weather, with sunscreen and water at the ready. It's halfway between Calgary and Medicine Hat, and some 48km northeast of Brooks. From Hwy 1, take Secondary Hwy 873 to Hwy 544.

Head-Smashed-In Buffalo Jump

The story behind the place with the strangest name of any attraction in Alberta is one of ingenuity and resourcefulness – and is key to the First Nations' (and Canada's) cultural heritage. For thousands of years, the Blackfoot people used the cliffs near the town of Fort Macleod to hunt buffalo. **Head-Smashed-In Buffalo Jump** (☑ 403-553-2731; www.head-smashed-in.com; Secondary Hwy 785; adult/child $15/10; ☺9am-5pm mid-May–Sep, 10am-5pm Sep–mid-May)

WORTH A TRIP

BAR U RANCH & THE COWBOY TRAIL

Cowboy culture is woven into the cultural fabric of southern Alberta, but to experience it in its rustic purity you have to exit Calgary and its Stetson-wearing oil entrepreneurs and head south through the province's verdant rolling foothills on Hwy 22, aka the Cowboy Trail. What is today a smooth asphalt road frequented by shiny SUVs was once a dirt track used by dust-encrusted cow herders driving their cattle north to the Canadian Pacific Railway in Calgary. Unperturbed by the modern oil rush, these rolling foothills are still punctuated by giant ranches, one of which, **Bar U Ranch** (www.friendsofthebaru.ca; Hwy 22, Longview; adult/child/family $7.80/3.90/19.60; ⊙ 10am-5pm Jun-Oct), has been converted into a historic site by Parks Canada.

Founded in 1882, Bar U was once one of the largest commercial ranches in the world, covering 160,000 acres. John Ware, a freed African American slave and, allegedly, Alberta's first cowboy, was an early visitor. A decade later, the ranch's horses were trained by Harry Longabaugh (known to history and Hollywood as the Sundance Kid), a dapper cowboy who worked at the ranch in 1891 before taking up a more lucrative career holding up banks with the Wild Bunch. The next visitor was more regal but no less notorious: the Prince of Wales, later King Edward VIII, passed through in 1919 and was so taken with the place that he bought the EP Ranch next door. Edward visited the region five times, including twice after his abdication; the EP was managed in his name until 1962.

Wander back in time through the Bar U's two dozen buildings – including a cookhouse, post office, corral, smithy and slaughterhouse – which have been preserved in their Sundance Kid–era glory. Costumed interpreters demonstrate ranch skills while telling stories of the past. Visitors can hop on a wagon ride, saddle up horses, try to rope a steer and gather with the ranch hands beneath the cottonwood trees for a campfire and cowboy coffee. The on-site restaurant dishes up ranch-style food like hamburger soup and bison black-bean chili.

Bar U Ranch is just off Hwy 22, 13km south of the town of Longview.

was a marvel of simple ingenuity. The well-presented displays and films at the interpretive center built cleverly into the hillside are definitely worth the excursion from Calgary or Lethbridge.

You can walk along the cliff trail to the end of the drive land, the spot where the buffalo plummeted. The site, about 18km northwest of Fort Macleod and 16km west of Hwy 2, also has a cafe and a shop staffed by Blackfoot First Nations.

Lethbridge

Right in the heart of southern Alberta farming country sits the former coal-mining city of Lethbridge, divided by the distinctive coulees of the Oldman River. Though there isn't a lot to bring you to the city, copious parkland and a few good historical sites and museums will help you to easily fill a day. The downtown area, like many North American downtowns, has made a good stab at preserving its not-so-ancient history. To the east, less inspiring Mayor Magrath Dr (Hwy 5) is a chain-store-infested main drag that could be Anywhere, North America.

⊙ Sights & Acivities

There are ample hiking opportunities in the **Oldman River Valley**, a 100m-deep coulee bisected by the proverbial Eiffel Tower of steel railway bridges, and the largest of its kind in the world.

Galt Museum & Archives   MUSEUM
(www.galtmuseum.com; 320 Galt St; adult/child $6/3; ⊙ 10am-5pm Mon-Sat, to 9pm Thu, 1-5pm Sun) The story of Lethbridge is told at the Sir Alexander Galt Museum, encased in an old hospital building (1910) on the bluff high above the river. Interactive kid-oriented displays let you sit in a streetcar and watch historical footage, set print at the *Herald* newsroom and try to put out a (virtual) fire; a small gallery with contemporary and historical art will interest bigger kids. The view from the lobby out onto the coulee is great – and free.

Southern Alberta Art Gallery   MUSEUM
(☑ 403-327-8770; www.saag.ca; 601 3rd Ave S; adult/child $5/free, Sun free; ⊙ 10am-5pm Tue-Sat, to 7pm Thu, 1-5pm Sun) With new temporary exhibits every three months, this small gallery focuses on contemporary art. Past

exhibitions have included local artists as well as national and international ones, with everything from photography to installation art. The space itself is open and bright and the gift shop is ace.

Helen Schuler Nature Centre & Lethbridge Nature Reserve   NATURE RESERVE

(www.lethbridge.ca; Indian Battle Rd; by donation; ⊘10am-4pm Tue-Sun Apr-May & Sep-Nov, 10am-6pm Jun-Aug, 1-4pm Tue-Sun Dec-Mar) Permanent displays tell the story of the river valley and coulee, while temporary exhibits focus on bats, bees and the like. Check out Sophie the gopher snake and say hello to Taco Charlie, the tiger salamander. The surrounding trails give you the opportunity to see long-eared and great horned owls and plenty of porcupines sleeping in the trees.

Nikka Yuko Japanese Garden   GARDENS

(www.nikkayuko.com; cnr Mayor Magrath Dr & 9th Ave S; adult/child $9/4; ⊘9am-6pm mid-May–mid-Oct) The Nikka Yuko Japanese Garden is the perfect antidote to the stresses of the road. These immaculate grounds, interspersed with ponds, flowing water, bridges, bonsai trees and rock gardens, form an oasis of calm amid the bustle of everyday life.

Authentic Japanese structures sit among the grassy mounds.

Fort Whoop-Up   FORT, MUSEUM

(☑403-329-0444; www.fortwhoopup.ca; 200 Indian Battle Park Rd; ⊘May-Sep) Inside expansive Indian Battle Park, bizarrely named Fort Whoop-Up is a replica of Alberta's first and most notorious illegal-whiskey trading post. Around 25 of these outposts were set up in the province between 1869 and 1874 for trading whiskey, guns, ammunition and blankets for buffalo hides and furs from the Blackfoot tribes. At the time of writing, it was closed and new management was being sought. Check the website to see if it has reopened.

🛏 Sleeping & Eating

Lethbridge Lodge   HOTEL $$

(☑403-328-1123; www.lethbridgelodge.com; 320 Scenic Dr S; r from $99; ℗@🛜) Rooms here are clean and bright, if a little unmemorable; the atrium, on the other hand, is something else, making this a great deal. All of the rooms look down into the fake-foliage-filled tropical interior, complete with winding brick pathways, a kidney-shaped pool and water features.

WORTH A TRIP

VULCAN

Originally named by a railway surveyor after the Roman god of fire, the 1990s saw Vulcan boldly go where no Canadian town had gone before and proclaim itself Canada's *Star Trek* headquarters – an unlikely title for this tiny prairie town but one made official by the Canadian Broadcasting Corporation (CBC) in 2010.

Your first encounter will be the **Vulcan Tourism & Trek Station** (☑403-485-2994; www.vulcantourism.com; 115 Centre Street E; ⊘9am-6pm May-Sep, 10am-5pm Oct-Apr), built like a space station and crammed full of memorabilia. You can look up local info on the control center that's been signed by the *Star Trek: Next Generation* cast and dress up and snap photos with their cardboard counterparts. You can also stock up on Mr Spock T-shirts and other Trekker goodies.

Outside, a replica starship *Enterprise* is poised on the edge of town, a beacon to hundreds of *Star Trek* fans who flock here in costume from all corners of the world for the annual Spock Days and Vul-Con Conventions. Previous guests have included Leonard Nimoy and other stars from the show.

As you wander down the main street, passing busts of the crew, wall-sized murals and businesses with names like Latinum Loonie and Starfleet Supplies, it becomes clear that this town is in deep. While some Vulcans are tired of it – 'I'm not even a *Star Trek* fan,' one local whispered to us – there's no denying that this out-there bid for tourism has put an otherwise missable town on the map and added an unlikely but very welcome economic opportunity. It's certainly the only place in Canada where you can buy Vulcan ears in the grocery store and enter the local pub wielding a phaser without getting a second glance. It appears Vulcan won't go the way of its nearly-ghost-town neighbors but will, in fact, live long and prosper.

To reach Vulcan from Lethbridge, follow Hwy 23 north for 92km.

★ **Telegraph Tap House** PUB $
(☑ 403-942-4136; 310 6th Street S; mains $10-16;
⊙ 11:30am-late) So this is where cool Lethbridgians go. Park yourself at the bar with a craft brew and pulled-pork sliders or chili-cheese fries. Feeling brave? Take on the Dead Albertan burger, a 6oz beef patty between two grilled cheese sandwiches. Is the stack of antique suitcases left over from others who dared it and didn't make it out the door?

The walls are lined with B&W images of Letherbridge from yesteryear, and popular TV shows are often shown on the big screen.

Bread Milk & Honey CAFE $
(☑ 403-381-8605; www.breadmilkhoney.ca; 427 5th St S; menu items $6-12; ⊙ 7:30am-7pm Mon-Fri, 9am-3pm Sat; 🛜) With excellent coffee and everything from oatmeal loaded with banana, cinnamon and almond to a bacon burrito, this is *the* place to come for breakfast. The interior is all exposed brick and wood; if Lethbridge had hipsters, they'd hang out here, devouring a grilled turkey and Brie wrap or a freshly baked scone.

❶ Information

Chinook Country Tourist Association
(☑ 403-320-1222; www.chinookcountry.com; 2805 Scenic Dr S; ⊙ 9am-5pm)

❶ Getting There & Away

The **Lethbridge airport** (☑ 403-329-4474; www.lethbridgeairport.ca; 417 Stubb Ross Rd), a short drive south on Hwy 5, is served by commuter affiliates of Air Canada. Six or seven flights per day go to Calgary.

Greyhound Canada (☑ 403-327-1551; www.greyhound.ca; 411 5th St S) goes to Calgary ($46, three hours, five daily) and Regina ($117, 16½ hours, two daily). Luxurious **Red Arrow** (☑ 800-232-1958; www.redarrow.ca; 449 Mayor Magrath Dr S) buses connect once daily with Calgary ($55, three hours) and Fort MacLeod ($34, 45 minutes)

Writing-on-Stone Provincial Park

Perhaps the best thing about the **Writing-on-Stone Provincial Park** (☑ 403-647-2364; www.albertaparks.ca) FREE is that it really isn't on the way to anywhere. For those willing to get off the main thoroughfare, all efforts will be rewarded. It's named for the extensive carvings and paintings made by the Plains First Nations on the sandstone cliffs along the banks of Milk River – more than 3000 years ago. There is an excellent, self-guided **interpretive trail** that takes you to some of the more spectacular viewpoints and accessible pictographs.

You must stay on the trails to prevent damage to the hoodoos. Many visitors feel the need to add their own marks to the hoodoos – don't be one of them. Not only are you vandalizing a piece of history, you're also desecrating a sacred First Nations site.

The best art is found in a restricted area (to protect it from vandalism), which you can visit only on a **guided tour** (10am, 2pm and 6pm daily in summer; adult/youth/child $18/8/5) with the park ranger. Other activities possible here include **canoeing** and **swimming** in the river in summer and **cross-country skiing** in winter. Park wildlife is ample, and the visitor center, built in the shape of a traditional tipi, blends perfectly with the region's natural and cultural heritage. Beware: it can get exceedingly hot in the summer and you must have close-toed shoes. (This is rattlesnake country!)

The park's riverside campground has 64 sites, running water, showers and flush toilets. It's popular on weekends.

The park is southeast of Lethbridge and close to the US border; the Sweetgrass Hills of northern Montana are visible to the south. To get to the park, take Hwy 501 east for 42km from the town of Milk River, on Hwy 4.

Waterton Lakes National Park

Here flat prairies collide dramatically with the Rockies, with a sparkling lake and a hilltop castle that may make you wonder if you've fallen into a fairy tale. Sadly, **Waterton Lakes National Park** (www.pc.gc.ca/waterton; adult/child per day $7.80/3.90) is rarely known to outside visitors. While Banff and Jasper, its siblings to the north, hemorrhage with tourists and weekend warriors, Waterton is a pocket of sublime tranquillity.

Established in 1895 and now part of a Unesco World Heritage site, Unesco Biosphere Reserve and International Peace Park (with the USA's Glacier National Park), this 525-sq-km reserve lies in Alberta's southwestern corner. The park is a sanctuary for numerous iconic animals – grizzlies, elk, deer and cougar – along with 800-odd wildflower species.

WORTH A TRIP

BLACKFOOT CROSSING HISTORICAL PARK

Standing stoically in the center of a First Nations reserve, **Blackfoot Crossing Historical Park** (📱403-734-5171; www.blackfootcrossing.ca; Hwy 842; adult/child $12/8; ⊘9am-5pm Mon-Fri) celebrates and embraces authentic Siksika (Blackfoot) culture and is entirely worth exploring.

The history of southern Alberta pre-1880 belongs to the Blackfoot confederacy, an amalgamation of the Peigan, Blood and Montana-based Blackfeet tribes. Blackfoot Crossing, long an important tribal nexus, was unique in that it was the only place where nomadic First Nations tribes built a semi-permanent settlement. It was here that the notorious Treaty 7 was signed by Chief Crowfoot in 1877, ceding land to the British crown and establishing the Siksika reservation. After a visit from Prince Charles in 1977, the idea for a historical site was hatched; after 30 years of planning, the park finally opened in 2007.

It's anchored by an architecturally stunning, ecofriendly main building that incorporates elements of tipis and feathered headdresses into its creative design. Within its walls lie a 100-seat theater showcasing cultural dances, a set of exhibits chronicling Blackfoot history and guided tours with local Siksika interpreters and storytellers. Outside, you can enjoy various trails, prairie viewpoints, and a tipi village where traditional crafts are practiced and taught.

To get here, head 100km east of Calgary on Hwy 1 and then 7km south on Hwy 842. The historical park hasn't yet made it onto the mainstream tourist track and remains curiously light on visitors.

The town of **Waterton**, a charming alpine village with a winter population of about 40, provides a marked contrast to larger, flashier Banff. Its 1920s-era Prince of Wales Hotel stands regally above town on the lakefront.

◉ Sights

★**Red Rock Canyon**   CANYON
FREE The clear waters of Blakiston Creek rush through the startlingly crimson Red Rock Canyon. Follow a 0.7km interpretive **loop trail** along the cliffs to learn a little geology and see jaw-dropping scenery. Amazingly, half the beauty is in getting here: the 15km trip along **Red Rock Parkway** through Blakiston Valley offers spectacular views of grassy plains crashing into looming mountains, with bears and wildflowers aplenty.

Cameron Lake   LAKE
Backed by the sheer-sided slopes of Mt Custer, placid Cameron Lake is tucked tantalizingly beneath the Continental Divide at the three-way meeting point of Montana, Alberta and British Columbia. Poised at the end of the 16km (10-mile) **Akamina Parkway**, this is where day-trippers stop to picnic, hike and rent boats. From foam flowers to fireweed, copious wildflower species thrive here, while grizzly bears are known to frequent the lake's isolated southern shores.

Cameron Falls   WATERFALL
(Cameron Falls Dr) Located at the west end of Cameron Falls Dr (a short hop from the center of town) is this dramatically poised torrent of foaming water, notable among geologists for harboring the oldest exposed Precambrian rocks in the Canadian Rockies. Estimates suggest they are 1.5 billion years old, give or take the odd millennium. The lookout here is paved for wheelchair access and the falls are rather fetchingly lit up at night.

🏃 Activities

Hiking
Those looking to stretch their legs are in luck – Waterton is a hiker's haven. With over 225km of walking tracks, you'll run out of time before you run out of trails. The trails are shared with bikes and horses (where permitted); once the snow lands, cross-country skis will get you to the same places. The 17km walk to **Crypt Lake** is a standout: there's a 20m tunnel, a stream that materializes out of the ground and a ladder to negotiate. The only way to get to the trailhead is by boat. **Waterton Shoreline Cruises** (📱403-859-2362; www.watertoncruise.com; adult/youth/child $47/24/16; ⊘May-Oct) leave the town's marina in the morning and pick up the weary at the **Crypt Lake trailhead** in the afternoon (adult/child $24/12).

Another example of Waterton's 'small is beautiful' persona is the 19km **Carthew–Alderson Trail**, often listed as one of the best high-alpine day hikes in North America. **Tamarack Outdoor Outfitters** (✉ 403-859-2378; www.hikewaterton.com; 214 Mt View Rd; ⊙ 8am-8pm May-Sep) runs a shuttle every morning in summer to the trailhead by Cameron Lake (reservations recommended). From here you'll hike back over the mountains to town.

Tamarack also offers shuttles to many other trailheads, including free shuttles to all of the hikes on the Akamina Pkwy.

Lake Cruises

A highlight for many visitors here is a boat ride with Waterton Shoreline Cruises (p102) across the shimmering waters of Upper Waterton Lake to the far shore of Goat Haunt, Montana (USA). The two-hour trip is scenic, with a lively commentary as you go. Grab your passport before you jump on the (often rather full) boats, as they dock in the USA for about 30 minutes.

🛏 Sleeping

The park has three vehicle-accessible Parks Canada campgrounds, with one right in the town of Waterton. Regular campsites can be reserved online or by phone, but backcountry campsites are limited and should be reserved through the visitor center (p104).

Crandell Mountain Campground   CAMPGROUND $
(✉ 403-859-5133; Red Rock Pkwy; tent & RV sites $22; ⊙ June-early Sep; P) For big, wide-open views, head out to this secluded camping spot a few minutes' drive up Red Rock Pkwy. Some of the loops, especially H and L, offer beautiful mountain views and direct access to Blakiston Brook. Evening ranger talks are held in a charming amphitheater. There are no services, toilets but no showers, and no reservations.

★**Northland Lodge**   B&B $$
(✉ 403-859-2353; www.northlandlodgecanada. com; 408 Evergreen Ave; r $169-209; ⊙ mid-May–mid-Oct; 🕾) Located on the edge of town within earshot of gushing Cameron Falls is this cozy house that Louis Hill (the genius behind the Prince of Wales Hotel) built for himself. A B&B with a wide range of quaint rooms (some with shared bath) and a creaking staircase, it's steeped in character. The welcoming host's freshly baked breakfast is fabulous.

Crandell Mountain Lodge   HOTEL $$
(✉ 403-859-2288; www.crandellmountainlodge.com; 102 Mt View Rd; r from $130; 🕾) With home-made cookies in the lobby, this 1940s lodge is doing a good impersonation of a Tudor cottage plucked from a quiet English village. The Crandell has old-fashioned rooms with quilts like Grandma used to make, fireplaces and a front deck facing Emerald Bay across the street. Service is very welcoming.

Bear Mountain Motel   MOTEL $$
(✉ 403-859-2366; www.bearmountainmotel.com; 208 Mt View Rd; r $115-135; ⊙ mid-May–Sep; P 🐾) Upfront about its offerings, Bear Mountain is a standard, retro-style motel with immaculate rooms and friendly service. There are barbecues and picnic tables; some rooms are pet friendly and some have kitchenettes. This is about as 'budget' as you get in Waterton.

Aspen Village Inn   HOTEL $$
(✉ 403-859-2255; www.aspenvillageinn.com; 111 Windflower Ave; r $129-269; ⊙ May–mid-Oct; P 🕾) These standard, motel-style rooms are a favorite with families, with an on-site kids playground and resident deer finding shade in the grounds. Barbecues and picnic tables offer ambience on warm summer nights, while satellite TV can take the chill out of a damp autumn evening. Many rooms have kitchenettes.

★**Prince of Wales Hotel**   HISTORIC HOTEL $$$
(✉ 403-859-2231; www.princeofwaleswaterton. com; Prince of Wales Rd; r from $249; ⊙ May-Sep; P 🕾) With a Hogwarts-like setting on a bluff overlooking Upper Waterton Lake, the grand Prince of Wales blends Swiss-style architecture with the atmosphere of a Scottish castle. The old-world charms extend to serving staff in kilts and high tea in the main lounge – very civilized. The large lake-facing windows show the raw wilderness that awaits.

🍴 Eating & Drinking

★**49° North Pizza**   PIZZA $
(✉ 403-859-3000; www.49degreesnorthpizza. com; 303 Windflower Ave; pizzas $10-20; ⊙ noon-10pm May-Sep) Seriously satisfying pizza with all of the expected renditions, plus some creative gourmet options such as bison and Saskatoon berries. Service is top-notch and there's a good beer selection; if the handful of tables and patio are full, you can get takeout. Need we say more?

Wieners of Waterton HOT DOGS $

(www.wienersofwaterton.com; 301 Windflower Ave; hot dogs $6-8; ⊙11am-11pm; 🖉) Not all wieners are made equal and those served here approach the gourmet level, including locally smoked and breakfast-dog varieties. Get 'em with a side of sweet-potato fries. Rightfully popular, it commonly sees lines out the door in the summer months.

Waterton Bagel & Coffee Co CAFE $

(🖉403-859-2466; 309 Windflower Ave; bagels from $5; ⊙10am-10pm) A godsend if you've just staggered out of the wilderness, this tiny caffeine stop has a handful of window stools, life-saving peanut-butter-and-jam bagels and refreshing blended coffee drinks.

Thirsty Bear Saloon PUB

(🖉403-859-2211; 111 Waterton Ave; ⊙4pm-2am Mon-Sat mid-May–Sep) It may look like a dark, sketchy hall from the outside but it's worth crossing the threshold. Inside, this large, friendly, barnlike pub is where wild nights happen in the wilderness, aided by live music, pool tables and good beer.

❶ Information

My Waterton (www.mywaterton.ca) Waterton Lakes' Chamber of Commerce website with up-to-date visitor information, including a listing of monthly events.

Parks Canada Visitor Centre (🖉403-859-2378; www.pc.gc.ca/waterton; ⊙8am-7pm May-Sep) The central stop for information on everything from trail conditions to hotels. Across the street from the Prince of Wales Hotel.

❶ Getting There & Away

Waterton lies in Alberta's southwestern corner, 130km from Lethbridge and 156km from Calgary. The one road entrance into the park is in its northeastern corner, along Hwy 5. Most visitors coming from Glacier and the USA reach the junction with Hwy 5 via Hwy 6 (Chief Mountain International Hwy) from the southeast. From Calgary, to the north, Hwy 2 shoots south toward Hwy 5 into the park. From the east, Hwy 5, through Cardston, heads west and then south into the park.

There is no public transportation from Canadian cities outside the park. However, a shuttle service (adult/child US$50/25) operated by **Glacier Park Inc** (🖉reservations 866-435-1605; www.glacierparkinc.com) offers daily transport from the Prince of Wales Hotel to the Glacier Park Lodge in Montana (USA) from May to September. From here you can link up with the Amtrak train network for travel elsewhere in the US.

❶ Getting Around

Tamarack Outdoor Outfitters (p103) offers shuttles to many trailheads, including Chief Mountain ($20) and Tamarack ($30). It also offers free shuttles to all hikes on the Akamina Pkwy. Book your seat online or at the kiosk inside the shop.

Crowsnest Pass

West of Fort Macleod the Crowsnest Hwy (Hwy 3) heads through the prairies and into the Rocky Mountains to Crowsnest Pass (1396m) and the British Columbian border. The Pass, as it's known, is a string of small communities just to the east of the BC border. Of note is the story of the town of **Frank**. In 1903, Frank was almost completely buried when 30 million cubic meters (some 82 million tonnes' worth) of nearby Turtle Mountain collapsed and killed around 70 people. Some believe the coal mine dug into the base of the mountain was to blame. But the mining didn't stop; this black gold was the ticket to fortune for the entire region some hundred years ago. Eventually the demand for coal decreased, and after yet more cave-ins and fear of a second slide, the mines shut down for good.

★**Frank Slide**
Interpretive Centre MUSEUM

(www.frankslide.org; Hwy 3; adult/child $13/9; ⊙9am-6pm July-Aug, 10am-5pm Sep-Jun; ♿) This excellent museum overlooks the Crowsnest Valley and helps put a human face on the tragedy of the Frank landslide. Displays bring mining, the railroad and the early days of this area to life; kids will enjoy having things to pull, push and jump on, as well as puzzles and other interactive activities. There's also a fantastic film dramatizing the tragic events of 1903. Trails from the museum take you out over the slide site itself.

NORTHERN ALBERTA

Despite the presence of its increasingly infamous oil sands, the top half of Alberta is little visited and even less known. Once you travel north of Edmonton, the population drops off to Siberian levels. The sense of remoteness here is almost eerie.

If it's solitude you seek, then this is paradise found. Endless stretches of pine forests seem to go on forever, nighttime brings aurora borealis displays that are better than any chemical hallucinogens, and it's here you can still see herds of buffalo roaming.

The Cree, Slavey and Dene were the first peoples to inhabit the region, and many of them still depend on fishing, hunting and trapping for survival. The northeast has virtually no roads and is dominated by Wood Buffalo National Park, the Athabasca River and Lake Athabasca. The northwest is more accessible, with a network of highways connecting Alberta with northern BC and the NWT.

Peace River & Around

Heading northwest along Hwy 43 leads to the town of Dawson Creek, BC, and mile zero of the Alaska Hwy. Dawson is a whopping 590km from Edmonton, so it's a long way to go to check out this isolated section of northern Alberta. Along the way you'll pass through **Grande Prairie**, the base of operations for the local agricultural industry and home to chuckwagon-racing legend Kelly Sutherland.

Peace River is so named because the warring Cree and Beaver Indians made peace along its banks. The town of **Peace River** sits at the confluence of the Heart, Peace and Smoky Rivers. West out of town, Hwy 2 leads to the Mackenzie Hwy.

Mackenzie Highway

The small town of **Grimshaw** is the official starting point of the Mackenzie Hwy (Hwy 35) north to the NWT. There's not much here except the mile-zero sign and a few shops. The relatively flat and straight road is mostly paved, though there are stretches of loose gravel where the road is being reconstructed.

The mainly agricultural landscape between Grimshaw and Manning gives way to endless stretches of spruce and pine forest. Come prepared – this is frontier territory: services become fewer (and more expensive) as you head northward through the wilderness. Make sure you fill your tank any time you see a gas station from here on.

High Level, the last settlement of any size before the NWT border, is a timber-industry center. Workers often stay in its motels during the week. The only service station between High Level and Enterprise (in the NWT) is at Indian Cabins.

Lake District

From St Paul, more than 200km northeast of Edmonton, to the NWT border lies Alberta's immense lake district. As you cross over the North Saskatchewan River, the land turns to rolling forested hills, peppered with abandoned farms and eerily beautiful dilapidated houses and barns. Fishing is popular (even in winter, when there is ice fishing), but many of the lakes, especially further north, have no road access and you have to fly in.

St Paul is the place to go if you are looking for little green people. Its **flying-saucer landing pad** – which is still awaiting its first customer – is open for business. Residents built the 12m-high circular landing pad in 1967 as part of a Canadian Centennial project, declaring the land underneath the pad international (and, one can assume, intergalactic). It's billed as the world's largest, and only, UFO landing pad and UFO enthusiasts have been visiting ever since. Check out the **UFO Data Center** (☑780-645-6800, UFO hotline 888-733-8367; www.town.stpaul.ab.ca/Tourist-Information; 50 Avenue, St Paul; ⊙10am-6pm May-Sep) with its space-themed gift shop and book of 137 recorded local sightings, along with images and accounts of local cattle mutilations, abductions and crop circles. There's also a UFO hotline for people to report new sightings.

Hwy 63 is the main route into the province's northeastern wilderness interior. The highway, with a few small settlements and campgrounds on the way, leads to **Fort McMurray**, 439km northeast of Edmonton. Originally a fur-trading outpost, it's now home to the Athabasca Oil Sands, the world's largest single oil deposit and Alberta's economic bread and butter. The history of oil sands and the story of how crude oil is extracted from them is told through interactive displays at the **Oil Sands Discovery Centre** (☑780-743-7167; http://history.alberta.ca/oil sands; 515 MacKenzie Blvd, Fort McMurray; adult/child/family \$11/7/29; ⊙9am-5pm mid-May–mid-Sep, 10am-4pm Tue-Sun mid-Sep–mid-May). The town itself isn't particularly interesting; non–oil workers who do visit come to see the aurora borealis (northern lights). The town hit the world press in 2016 when a massive wildfire swept through; all residents were evacuated for months and many, sadly, didn't have a home to return to.

British Columbia

Best Places to Eat

➡ Bistro 694 (p176)

➡ Pilgrimme (p194)

➡ Vij's (p130)

➡ Ask for Luigi (p128)

➡ Nova Kitchen (p152)

Best Places to Sleep

➡ Free Spirit Spheres (p176)

➡ Wickaninnish Inn (p180)

➡ Shades of Jade Inn & Spa (p153)

➡ Skwachays Lodge (p124)

➡ Old Courthouse Inn (p154)

Why Go?

Visitors to Canada's westernmost province should pack a long list of superlatives to deploy here; the words 'wow,' 'amazing' and 'spectacular' will only go so far. Luckily, it's not too hard to wax lyrical about the mighty mountains, deep forests and dramatic coastlines here that instantly lower heart rates to tranquil levels.

There's much more to British Columbia (BC) than nature-hugging dioramas, though. Vancouver fuses cuisines and cultures from Asia and beyond, while mid-sized cities such as Victoria and Kelowna are creating their own vibrant scenes. It's also hard to beat the welcoming, sometimes quirky character of smaller communities – from Cumberland to Powell River and to Salt Spring – that are the beating heart of BC.

Wherever you head, the great outdoors will always call. Don't just point your camera at it: BC is unbeatable for skiing, kayaking and hiking experiences that can make this the trip of a lifetime.

When to Go
Vancouver, BC

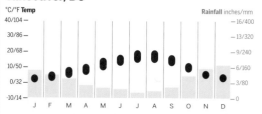

Dec–Mar Best powder action on the slopes of Whistler and Blackcomb mountains.

Jul & Aug Beaches, patios and a plethora of outdoor festivals in sun-dappled Vancouver.

Sep & Oct Dramatic surfing and the start of storm-watching season in beachy Tofino.

Parks & Wildlife

BC's national parks include snowcapped **Glacier** and the Unesco World Heritage sites of **Kootenay** and **Yoho**. The newer **Gulf Islands National Park Reserve** protects a fragile coastal region. Visit the website of **Parks Canada** (www.pc.gc.ca) for information.

The region's almost 1000 provincial parks offer 3000km of hiking trails. Notables include **Strathcona** and remote **Cape Scott**, as well as the Cariboo's canoe-friendly **Bowron Lake** and the Kootenays' Matterhorn-like **Mt Assiniboine**. Check the website of **BC Parks** (www.bcparks.ca) for information.

Expect to spot some amazing wildlife. Land mammals – including elk, moose, wolves, grizzlies and black bears – will have most visitors scrambling for their cameras, and there are around 500 bird varieties, including blue herons and bald eagles galore. Ocean visitors should keep an eye out for orcas.

ℹ Getting Around

The sheer size of BC can overwhelm some visitors: it's a scary-sounding 1508km drive from Vancouver to Prince Rupert, for example. While it's tempting to simply stick around Vancouver – the main point of entry for most BC-bound visitors – you won't really have experienced the province unless you head out of town.

Despite the distances, driving remains the most popular method of movement in BC. Plan your routes via the handy **DriveBC website** (www.drivebc.ca) and check out the dozens of services offered by the extensive **BC Ferries** (☎888-223-3779; www.bcferries.com) system.

VIA Rail (www.viarail.com) operates two BC train services. One trundles across the north from the coastline to Jasper. Pick up the second in Jasper for a ride back to Vancouver. A third line on Vancouver Island may also reopen in the coming years.

VANCOUVER

POP 604, 778

Walkable neighborhoods, drink-and-dine delights and memorable cultural and outdoor activities framed by dramatic vistas – there's a glassful of great reasons to love this lotusland metropolis.

Downtown is just the start of Vancouver. Walk or hop public transit and within minutes you'll be hanging with the locals in one of the city's many diverse and distinctive 'hoods. Whether discovering the coffee shops of Commercial Dr or the hipster

haunts of Main St, the indie bars and restaurants of Gastown or the heritage-house beachfronts and browsable stores of Kitsilano, you'll find this city perfect for easy-access urban exploration. Just be sure to chat to the locals wherever you go: they might seem shy or aloof at first, but Vancouverites love talking up their town.

History

The First Nations lived in this area for up to 16,000 years before Spanish explorers arrived in the late 1500s. When Captain George Vancouver of the British Royal Navy sailed up to these shores in 1792, he met a couple of Spanish captains who informed him of their country's land claim (the beach they met on is now called Spanish Banks). But by the early 1800s, as European settlers began arriving, the British crown had gained an increasing stranglehold.

Fur trading and a feverish gold rush soon redefined the region as a resource-filled Aladdin's cave. By the 1850s, thousands of fortune seekers had arrived, prompting the Brits to officially claim the area as a colony. Local entrepreneur 'Gassy' Jack Deighton seized the initiative in 1867 by opening a bar on the forested shoreline of Burrard Inlet. This triggered a rash of development – nicknamed Gastown – that became the forerunner of modern-day Vancouver.

But not everything went to plan. While Vancouver rapidly reached a population of 1000, its buildings were almost completely destroyed in an 1886 blaze (quickly dubbed the Great Fire, even though it only lasted 20 minutes). A prompt rebuild followed and the new downtown core soon took shape. Buildings from this era still survive, as does Stanley Park. Originally the town's military reserve, it was opened as a public recreation area in 1888.

Relying on its port, the growing city became a hub of industry, importing thousands of immigrant workers to fuel economic development. The Chinatown built at

BRITISH COLUMBIA VANCOUVER

British Columbia Highlights

1 Stanley Park (p110) Stretching your legs on the breathtaking 8.8km seawall stroll.

2 Tofino (p178) Surfing up a storm (or just watching a storm) on Vancouver Island's wild west coast.

3 Okanagan Valley (p198) Slurping some celebrated tipples on an ever-winding winery tour.

4 Whistler (p144) Skiing the Olympian slopes, then enjoying a warming après-ski beverage in the village.

5 Gwaii Haanas National Park Reserve (p236) Exploring the ancient and ethereal rainforest and kayaking the coastline for a bird's-eye view of the region.

6 Salt Spring Island (p190) Puttering around the lively Saturday Market and scoffing more than a few treats.

7 Alert Bay (p187) Walking the waterfront boardwalk and exploring evocative First Nations arts and culture.

8 Sea to Sky Gondola (p142) Hopping on the new gondola near Squamish for panoramic up-top views of the shimmering region.

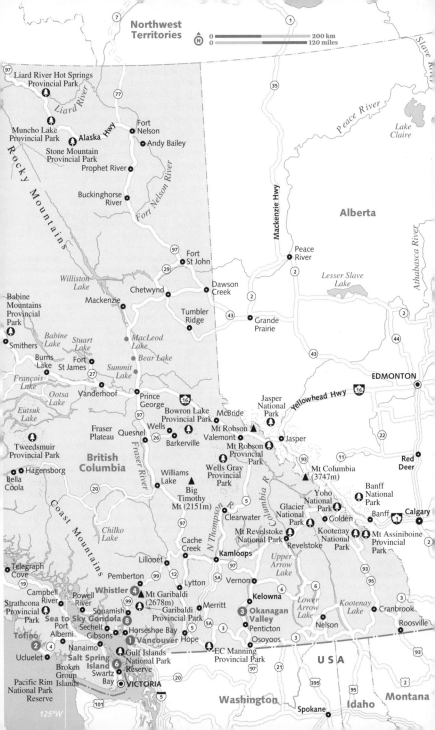

this time is still one of the largest in North America. But WWI and the 1929 Wall Street crash brought deep depression and unemployment. The economy recovered during WWII, when shipbuilding and armaments manufacturing added to the traditional economic base of resource exploitation.

Growing steadily throughout the 1950s and 1960s, Vancouver added an NHL (National Hockey League) team and other accoutrements of a midsize North American city. Finally reflecting on its heritage, Gastown – by now a slum – was saved for gentrification in the 1970s, becoming a National Historic Site in 2010.

In 1986 the city hosted a highly successful Expo World's Fair, sparking a wave of new development and adding the first of the mirrored skyscrapers that now define Vancouver's downtown core. A further economic lift arrived when the city staged the Olympic and Paralympic Winter Games in 2010. Even bigger than the Expo, it was Vancouver's chance to showcase itself to the world. But for many locals, 2013's 125th birthday party for Stanley Park was just as important: big events come and go, but Vancouverites aim to ensure the city's greatest green space is here forever.

◎ Sights

Few of Vancouver's main visitor attractions are located in the downtown core: the main museums are in Vanier Park and at the University of British Columbia, other top sights are in Stanley Park or Chinatown, and two of the region's main outdoor lures are on the North Shore. Luckily, the majority of these must-sees are easy to reach by car or a transit hop from the city center.

◉ Downtown & West End

You can easily spend a whole day exploring the attractions of Stanley Park. But the downtown core and the West End have their own appeals, including art galleries, historic buildings and bustling main streets that are the city's de facto promenades.

★ Stanley Park   PARK
(Map p114; P🅟🚾; 🚆19) This magnificent 404-hectare park combines excellent attractions with a mystical natural aura. Don't miss a stroll or cycle (rentals near the W Georgia St entrance) around the 8.8km seawall: a kind of visual spa treatment fringed by a 150,000-tree temperate rainforest, it'll take you past the park's popular totem poles.

Lost Lagoon   LAKE
(Map p114; 🚆19) This rustic area near Stanley Park's entrance was originally part of Coal Harbour. But after a causeway was built in 1916, the new body of water was renamed, transforming itself into a freshwater lake a few years later. Today it's a **nature sanctuary** – keep your eyes peeled for beady-eyed blue herons – and its perimeter pathway is a favored stroll for nature-huggers.

The **Stanley Park Nature House** (Map p114; 🖉604-257-8544; www.stanleyparkecology.ca; north end of Alberni St; free; ☉10am-5pm Tue-Sun Jul & Aug, 10am-4pm Sat & Sun Sep-Jun; 🚾; 🚆19) FREE provides exhibits and illumination on the park's wildlife, history and ecology. Ask about its fascinating park walks, covering everything from bird-watching strolls to artsy ambles around the park.

Vancouver Aquarium   AQUARIUM
(🖉604-659-3400; www.vanaqua.org; 845 Avison Way; adult/child $31/22; ☉9:30am-6pm Jul & Aug, 10am-5pm Sep-Jun; 🚾; 🚆19) Stanley Park's biggest draw, the aquarium is home to 9000 water-loving critters – including sharks, wolf eels and a somewhat shy octopus. There's also a small, walk-through rainforest area of birds, turtles and a statue-still sloth. The aquarium also keeps captive whales and dolphins and organizes animal encounters with these creatures, which may concern some visitors. Animal-welfare groups claim keeping cetaceans in enclosed tanks is harmful for these complex animals.

Stanley Park Train   MINIATURE RAILWAY
(🖉604-257-8531; adult/child $6/4.75; ☉10am-5pm mid-Jun–Aug, to 4pm Sat & Sun Apr & May, plus Easter, Halloween & Christmas; 🚾; 🚆19) This miniature train replica of the first passenger-rail service that rolled into Vancouver in 1887 is a firm family favorite. Its assumes several popular incarnations throughout the year, trundling through the sun-dappled trees in summer, then decorating itself for seasonal special trains at Easter, Halloween and Christmas.

English Bay Beach   BEACH
(Map p114; cnr Denman St & Beach Ave; 🚆5) Wandering south on Denman St, you'll spot a clutch of palm trees ahead announcing one of Canada's best urban beaches. Then you'll see Vancouver's most popular public artwork: a series of oversized laughing figures that makes everyone smile. There's a party atmosphere here in summer as locals catch rays and panoramic ocean views...or just ogle the volleyballers prancing around on the sand.

Vancouver

0 — 5 km
0 — 2.5 miles

Coquitlam River

Noons Creek

Indian Arm Provincial Park

Barnston Island

Mossom River

PORT COQUITLAM

Douglas Island

Fort Langley (8km)

Tynehead Regional Park

176th St

168th St

152nd St

SURREY

88th Ave

King George Hwy

96th Ave

128th St

120th St

72nd Ave

Nordel Way

ANMORE

Belcarra Regional Park

Mt Seymour Provincial Park

Indian Arm

BELCARRA

Como Lake Ave

Mundy Park

Austin Ave

COQUITLAM

Simon Fraser University

Burnaby Mountain Conservation Area

BURNABY

Discovery Centre

Fraser River

River Market

NEW WESTMINSTER

Annacis Island

Annacis Hwy

DELTA

River Rd

Green Timbers Urban Forest

Delta Nature Reserve

Grouse Mountain (1km)

Capilano Suspension Bridge

Maplewood Farm

Mt Seymour Pkwy

Dollarton Hwy

Second Narrows

Burrard Inlet

Confederation Park

E Hastings St

Lynn Canyon Park

Lynn Creek

Burnaby Lake Regional Park

Burnaby Village Museum

Deer Lake Park

Central Park

Rupert St

Boundary Rd

Kerr St

Marine Way

Kingsway

North Arm Fraser River

George Massey Tunnel

Lougheed Hwy

10th Ave

Canada Way

NORTH VANCOUVER

Lonsdale

Lonsdale Quay

Vancouver Harbour

First Narrows

Stanley Park

See Downtown Vancouver Map (p114)

Nanaimo St

Commercial Dr

Kingsway

Knight St

Main St

Oak St

Cambie St

Granville St

Queen Elizabeth Park

SOUTH MAIN

Mitchell Island

Bridgeport Rd

Richmond Summer Night Market

International Summer Night Market

RICHMOND

Richmond Hwy

Westminster Hwy

Blundell Rd

Steveston Hwy

No 1 Rd

Marine Dr

Lions Gate Bridge

English Bay

KITSILANO

W Broadway

16th Ave

W 41st Ave

WEST SIDE

Vancouver International Airport

Richmond Night Market

Richmond Nature Park

Kuan Yin Temple

STEVESTON

Britannia Shipyard

Gulf of Georgia Cannery

Burrard Inlet

West Bay

Sandy Cove

Lighthouse Park

Point Grey

Spanish Banks Beach Park

Jericho Beach

Wreck Beach

Museum of Anthropology

UBC Botanical Garden

UNIVERSITY OF BRITISH COLUMBIA

Pacific Spirit Regional Park

Marine Drive Foreshore Park

Musqueam Indian Reserve 2

Iona Island

Sea Island

Strait of Georgia

Bowen Island

Horseshoe Bay (2km); Bowen Island (7km); Whistler (105km)

Upper Levels Hwy

Tsawwassen (15km); Seattle (USA; 190km)

Roedde House Museum
MUSEUM

(Map p114; ☑ 604-684-7040; www.roeddehouse. org; 1415 Barclay St; $5; ☺11am-4pm Tue-Sat, 1-4pm Sun, reduced hours in winter; ☐5) For a glimpse of what the West End looked like before the apartment blocks arrived, drop by this handsome 1893 Queen Anne–style mansion, now a lovingly preserved museum. Designed by infamous British Columbia architect Francis Rattenbury, the house is packed with antiques and the garden is planted in period style. Admission comes with a guided tour while Sunday entry includes tour, tea and cookies for just $8.

★ Vancouver Art Gallery
GALLERY

(VAG; Map p114; ☑ 604-662-4700; www.vanart gallery.bc.ca; 750 Hornby St; adult/child $20/6; ☺10am-5pm Wed-Mon, to 9pm Tue; ☐5) The VAG has dramatically transformed since 2000, becoming a vital part of the city's cultural scene. Contemporary exhibitions – often showcasing Vancouver's renowned photoconceptualists – are now combined with blockbuster international traveling shows. Check out **FUSE** (Map p114; www.vanartgallery.bc.ca/fuse; admission $24; ☺8pm-midnight), a quarterly late-night party where you can hang out with the city's young arties over wine and live music.

Canada Place
LANDMARK

(Map p114; ☑ 604-775-7063; www.canadaplace. ca; 999 Canada Place Way; ☐; ☐Waterfront) Vancouver's version of the Sydney Opera House, – judging by the number of postcards it appears on –, this iconic landmark is shaped like sails jutting into the sky over the harbor.

Both a cruise-ship terminal and convention center (next door's grass-roofed expansion opened in 2010), it's also a stroll-worthy pier, providing camera-hugging views of the North Shore mountains and some busy floatplane action.

FlyOver Canada
THEATER

(Map p114; ☑ 604-620-8455; www.flyovercanada. com; 999 Canada Pl; adult/child $22/14; ☺10am-9pm, reduced hours in winter; ☐; ☐Waterfront) Canada Place's newest attraction, this breathtaking movie-screen simulator ride makes you feel like you're swooping across the entire country, waggling your legs over grand landscapes and city landmarks from coast to coast. En route, your seat will lurch, your face will be sprayed and you'll likely have a big smile on your face. And once the short ride is over, you'll want to do it all again.

Bill Reid Gallery of Northwest Coast Art
GALLERY

(Map p114; ☑ 604-682-3455; www.billreidgallery. ca; 639 Hornby St; adult/child $10/5; ☺11am-5pm mid-May–Sep, 11am-5pm Wed-Sun Oct–mid-May; ☐Burrard) Showcasing carvings, paintings and jewelry from Canada's most revered Haida artists and many others, this tranquil gallery is lined with fascinating and exquisite works – plus handy touch-screens to tell you all about them. The space centers on the Great Hall, where there's often a carver at work. Be sure to also hit the mezzanine level: you'll come face to face with an 8.5m-long bronze of intertwined magical creatures, complete with impressively long tongues.

VANCOUVER IN...

One Day

Begin with a heaping breakfast at **Templeton** (p124) before strolling south to the **Vancouver Art Gallery** (p112). Next, take a window-shopping wander along **Robson St**, then cut down to the waterfront for panoramic sea and mountain vistas. Walk west along the **Coal Harbour** seawall and make for the dense trees of **Stanley Park** (p110). Spend the afternoon exploring the beaches, totem poles and **Vancouver Aquarium** (p110) here before ambling to the **West End** for dinner.

Two Days

Follow the one-day itinerary, then the next morning head to clamorous Chinatown. Stop at the towering **Millennium Gate** and duck into the nearby **Dr Sun Yat-Sen Classical Chinese Garden & Park** (p113) for a taste of tranquility. Check out the colorful stores (and tempting pork buns) around the neighborhood before strolling south along Main St towards **Science World** (p116) for some hands-on fun. Afterwards hop on the SkyTrain at the nearby station, trundle to Waterfront Station, and then take the scenic SeaBus to North Vancouver's **Capilano Suspension Bridge Park** (p119). On your return, hit Gastown's **Alibi Room** (p131) for some craft beers.

Gastown & Chinatown

Just wandering the historic, sometimes cobbled streets of Gastown and Chinatown on foot is the best way to spend a few hours in this part of the city. But there are also a couple of unique, must-see attractions worth stopping off at.

Vancouver Police Museum   MUSEUM

(Map p114; ☑604-665-3346; www.vancouverpolice museum.ca; 240 E Cordova St; adult/child $12/8; ⊙9am-5pm Tue-Sat; ☐4) Illuminating the crime-and-vice-addled history of the region, this quirky museum is lined with confiscated weapons and counterfeit currency. It also has a former mortuary room where the walls are studded with preserved slivers of human tissue – spot the bullet-damaged brain slices. Consider adding a **walking tour** ($20) to learn all about the area's salacious olden days. And buy a toe tag T-shirt in the gift shop.

Dr Sun Yat-Sen Classical
Chinese Garden & Park   GARDENS

(Map p114; ☑604-662-3207; www.vancouver chinesegarden.com; 578 Carrall St; adult/child $14/10; ⊙9:30am-7pm mid-Jun–Aug, 10am-6pm Sep & May–mid-Jun, 10am-4:30pm Oct-Apr; ⑤Stadium-Chinatown) A tranquil break from clamorous Chinatown, this intimate 'garden of ease' reflects Taoist principles of balance and harmony. Entry includes a 45-minute guided tour, where you'll learn about the symbolism behind the placement of the gnarled pine trees, winding covered pathways and ancient limestone formations. Look out for the lazy turtles bobbing in the jade-colored water.

Steam Clock   LANDMARK

(Map p114; cnr Water & Cambie Sts; ⑤Waterfront) Halfway along Water St, this oddly popular tourist magnet lures the cameras with its tooting steam whistle. Built in 1977, the clock's mechanism is actually driven by electricity; only the pipes on top are fueled by steam (reveal it to the patiently waiting tourists and you might cause a riot). It sounds every 15 minutes, and marks each hour with little whistling symphonies.

Chinatown Millennium Gate   LANDMARK

(Map p114; cnr W Pender & Taylor Sts; ⑤Stadium-Chinatown) Inaugurated by Canadian prime minister Jean Chretien in 2002, Chinatown's towering entrance is the landmark most visitors look for. Stand well back, since the decoration is mostly on its lofty upper reaches, an elaborately painted section topped with a

---

BEST MUSEUMS

➡ Museum of Anthropology (p118)

➡ Museum of Vancouver (p118)

➡ Vancouver Police Museum (p113)

➡ Roedde House Museum (p112)

➡ Beaty Biodiversity Museum (p118)

➡ Vancouver Maritime Museum (p119)

---

terracotta-tiled roof. The characters inscribed on its eastern front implore you to 'Remember the past and look forward to the future.'

Yaletown & Granville Island

Granville Island is a self-guided sight unto itself – and it's not just about the market. Add a miniferry hop across False Creek and you can include some history- and sport-themed attractions from Yaletown on your grand day out.

★ Granville Island Public Market   MARKET

(Map p114; ☑604-666-6655; www.granvilleisland. com/public-market; Johnston St; ⊙9am-7pm; ☐50, ⚲miniferries) Granville Island's highlight is the covered Public Market, a multisensory smorgasbord of fish, cheese, fruit and bakery treats. Pick up some fixings for a picnic at nearby Vanier Park or hit the international food court (dine off-peak and you're more likely to snag a table). From June to September, there's also an alfresco **farmers market** outside where, depending on the harvest, you'll find BC cherries, peaches and blueberries.

Engine 374 Pavilion   MUSEUM

(Map p114; www.roundhouse.ca; Roundhouse Community Arts & Recreation Centre, 181 Roundhouse Mews; ⊙10am-4pm, reduced hours off-season; ☵; ⑤Yaletown-Roundhouse) **FREE** May 23, 1887 was an auspicious date for Vancouver. That's when Engine 374 pulled the very first transcontinental passenger train into the fledgling city, symbolically linking the country and kick-starting the eventual metropolis. Retired in 1945, the engine was, after many years of neglect, restored and placed in this splendid pavilion. The friendly volunteers here will show you the best angle for snapping the perfect photo of the engine.

BC Sports Hall of Fame & Museum   MUSEUM

(Map p114; ☑604-687-5520; www.bcsportshallof fame.com; Gate A, BC Place Stadium, 777 Pacific Blvd;

Downtown Vancouver

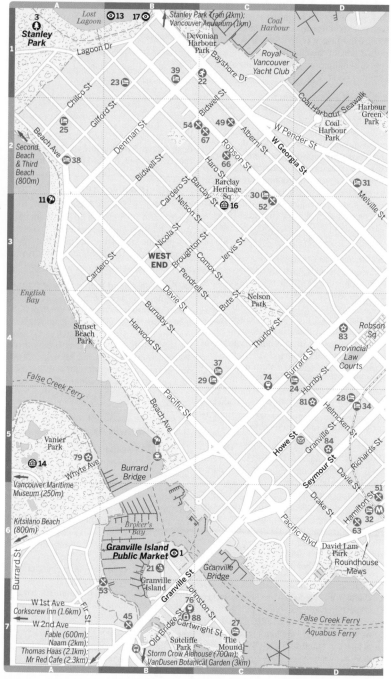

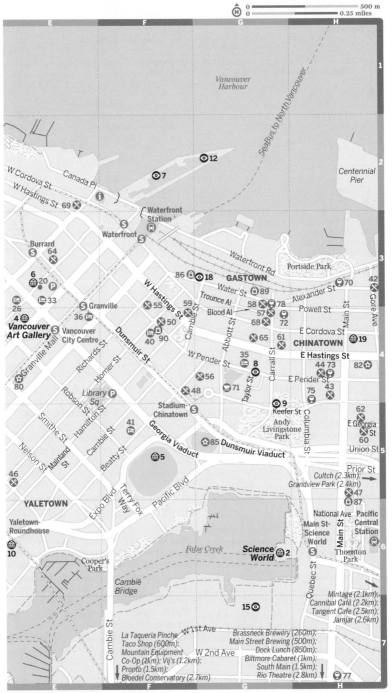

BRITISH COLUMBIA

0   500 m
0   0.25 miles

Vancouver
Harbour

Centennial
Pier

Canada Pl

W Cordova St

W Hastings St   69

Waterfront
Station

Waterfront

Waterfront Rd

Portside Park

Burrard
64

6   20

26   33

4   Vancouver
Art Gallery

Granville

Vancouver
City Centre

80

W Hastings St

Dunsmuir St

GASTOWN

86   18

Water St   89   Alexander St   70   42

Trounce Al

Blood Al

55   59   58   78

57   72

68   65   61

36   50

40   90

W Pender St

35   8

56

48   71

Powell St

E Cordova St

CHINATOWN   19

E Hastings St

44   73

E Pender St

75   43

82

Richards St

Homer St

Hamilton St

Cambie St

Beatty St

Library
Sq

41

Stadium-
Chinatown

Georgia Viaduct

9

Keefer St

Andy
Livingstone
Park

Columbia St

62

E Georgia
St

60

Union St

85   Dunsmuir Viaduct

Nelson St

Smithe St

Robson St

Mainland St

YALETOWN

46

Yaletown-
Roundhouse

10

Expo Blvd

Terry Fox
Way

Pacific Blvd

Cooper's
Park

Cambie
Bridge

5

Prior St

Cultch (2.3km);
Grandview Park (2.4km)

47

87

National Ave   Pacific
Central
Station

Main St-
Science
World

Thornton
Park

Science
World   2

15

False Creek

Quebec St

Mintage (2.1km);
Cannibal Café (2.2km);
Tangent Cafe (2.5km);
Jamjar (2.6km)

Cambie St

La Taqueria Pinche
Taco Shop (600m);
Mountain Equipment
Co-Op (1km); Vij's (1.2km);
Pronto (1.5km);
Bloedel Conservatory (2.7km)

W 1st Ave

W 2nd Ave

Brassneck Brewery (260m);
Main Street Brewing (500m);
Dock Lunch (850m);
Biltmore Cabaret (1km);
South Main (1.5km);
Rio Theatre (2.8km)

77

Downtown Vancouver

adult/child $15/12; ◎10am-5pm; ⊞; ⑤Stadium-Chinatown) Inside BC Place Stadium, this small but perfectly formed attraction showcases top BC athletes, both amateur and professional, with galleries devoted to each decade in sports. There are medals, trophies and sporting memorabilia on display (judging by the size of their shirts, hockey players were much smaller in the old days), and tons of hands-on activities to tire the kids out.

◉ Main Street & Commercial Drive

Anchored by a geodesic-domed attraction loved by local families, this area's other main lures are its rich array of independent private galleries. Many are clustered just off Main around 2nd Ave, while others popup around the area like splotches of fresh paint on an artist's palette.

The Drive itself is the main attraction here, acting as a bohemian promenade of cool stores and coffee shops. The center of the strip is Grandview Park, a handy green pit-stop in your stroll.

★ Science World
MUSEUM

(Map p114; ☑604-443-7440; www.scienceworld.ca; 1455 Quebec St; adult/child $25.75/17.75; ◎10am-6pm, to 8pm Thu Jul & Aug, reduced hours off-season; ℗⊞; ⑤Main St-Science World) Under Vancouver's favorite geodesic dome (okay, its only one), this ever-popular science and nature showcase has tons of exhibition space and a cool outdoor park crammed with hands-on fun (yes, you *can* lift 2028kg). Inside, there are two floors of educational play, from a walk-in hamster wheel to an air-driven ball maze.

Olympic Village
AREA

(Map p114; Athletes Way; ⑤Main St-Science World) Built as the home for 2800 athletes during the 2010 Olympic and Paralympic Winter Games, this glassy waterfront development became the city's newest neighborhood once the sporting types went home. It's taken a while to make the area feel like a community, but shops and restaurants – plus some cool public art – have helped. It is well worth a look on your seawall stroll.

BRITISH COLUMBIA VANCOUVER

Grandview Park PARK

(Commercial Dr, btwn Charles & William Sts; 📷20) The Drive's alfresco neighborhood hangout is named after the smashing views peeking between its trees: to the north are the North Shore mountains, while to the west is a cityscape vista of twinkling towers. Teeming with buskers, dreadlocked drummers and impromptu sidewalk sales, the park is a big summertime lure for nearby locals.

◎ Fairview & South Granville

Parks and botanical attractions are the main visitor sights in this area and they're easily accessible via transit along Cambie St and Oak St.

VanDusen Botanical Garden GARDENS

(☑604-257-8335; www.vandusengarden.org; 5251 Oak St; adult/child Apr-Sep $12.25/5.75, reduced off-season; ☉9am-8:30pm Jun-Aug, reduced hours off-season; 🅿🚹; 📷17) The city's favorite green-thumbed tranquility break, this 22-hectare, 255,000-plant idyll is a web of paths weaving through many small, specialized gardens: the **Rhododendron Walk**

blazes with color in spring, while the **Korean Pavilion** is a focal point for a fascinating Asian collection. Save time to get lost in the maze and look out for the herons and turtles that call the ponds here home. Check the online calendar for tours and events.

★**Bloedel Conservatory** GARDENS

(☑604-257-8584; www.vandusengarden.org; Queen Elizabeth Park, 4600 Cambie St; adult/child $6.75/3.25; ☉9am-8pm Mon-Fri, 10am-8pm Sat & Sun May-Aug, 10am-5pm daily Sep-Apr; 🅿🚹; 📷15) Cresting the hill in Queen Elizabeth Park, this balmy, triodetic-domed conservatory is an ideal rainy-day warm-up spot, as well as Vancouver's best-value attraction. For little more than the price of a latte, you'll find tropical trees and plants bristling with hundreds of free-flying, bright-plumaged birds. Look for the resident parrots but also keep your eyes peeled for rainbow-hued Gouldian finches, shimmering African superb starlings and maybe even a sparkling Lady Amherst pheasant, snaking through the undergrowth. The attendants might even let you feed the smaller birds from a bowl.

BRITISH COLUMBIA VANCOUVER

⊙ Kitsilano & University of British Columbia

Kitsilano's Vanier Park is home to a triumvirate of museums, with some of the city's best beaches stretching from here along the shoreline to the University of BC. The campus itself has more than enough attractions of its own to justify an alternative day out from the city center.

★ **Museum of Anthropology**   MUSEUM
(🖉604-822-5087; www.moa.ubc.ca; 6393 NW Marine Dr; adult/child $18/16; ⊙10am-5pm Wed-Sun, to 9pm Tue; 🅿; 🚍99B-Line) Vancouver's best museum is studded with spectacular First Nations totem poles and breathtaking carvings – but it's also teeming with artifacts from cultures around the world, from Polynesian instruments to Cantonese opera costumes. Take one of the free daily **tours** (check ahead for times) for some context, but give yourself at least a couple of hours to explore on your own. It's easy to immerse yourself here.

Museum of Vancouver   MUSEUM
(Map p114; 🖉604-736-4431; www.museumofvancouver.ca; 1100 Chestnut St; adult/child $15/5; ⊙10am-5pm, to 8pm Thu; 🅿🚼; 🚍22) The MOV has hugely improved in recent years with cool temporary exhibitions and evening events aimed at culturally minded adults. It hasn't changed everything, though. There are still evocative displays on local 1950s pop culture and 1960s hippie counterculture – a reminder that 'Kits' was once the grass-smoking

---

ℹ️ SAVE YOUR DOUGH

The **Vanier Park Explore Pass** costs adult/child $36/30 and covers entry to the Museum of Vancouver, Vancouver Maritime Museum and HR MacMillan Space Centre. It's available at each of the three attractions and can save you around $10 on individual adult entry. You can also save with the **UBC Museums and Gardens Pass**. It costs adult/child $33/28 and includes entry to the Museum of Anthropology, Botanical Garden, Nitobe Memorial Garden and Beatty Biodiversity Museum. Available at any of these attractions, it also includes discounts for the Greenheart TreeWalk, plus deals on campus parking, dining and shopping.

---

center of Vancouver's flower-power movement – plus a shimmering gallery of vintage neon signs from around the city.

Kitsilano Beach   BEACH
(cnr Cornwall Ave & Arbutus St; 🚍22) Facing English Bay, Kits Beach is one of Vancouver's favorite summertime hangouts. The wide, sandy expanse attracts buff Frisbee tossers and giggling volleyball players, and those who just like to preen while catching the rays. The ocean is fine for a dip, though serious swimmers should consider the heated **Kitsilano Pool** (🖉604-731-0011; www.vancouverparks.ca; 2305 Cornwall Ave; adult/child $5.86/2.95; ⊙7am-evening mid-Jun–mid-Sep), one of the world's largest outdoor saltwater pools.

UBC Botanical Garden   GARDENS
(www.botanicalgarden.ubc.ca; 6804 SW Marine Dr; adult/child $9/5; ⊙9:30am-4:30pm, to 8pm Thu mid-Mar–Oct, 9:30am-4pm Nov–mid-Mar; 🅿; 🚍99 B-Line, then C20) You'll find a giant collection of rhododendrons, a fascinating apothecary plot and a winter green space of off-season bloomers in this 28-hectare complex of themed gardens. Save time for the attraction's **Greenheart TreeWalk** (🖉604-822-4208; adult/child $20/10; ⊙10am-4:30pm daily , to 7:30pm Thu Apr-Oct; 🚼), which lifts visitors 17m above the forest floor on a 308m guided eco tour. A combined botanical garden and walkway ticket costs $20.

Beaty Biodiversity Museum   MUSEUM
(🖉604-827-4955; www.beatymuseum.ubc.ca; 2212 Main Mall; adult/child $12/10; ⊙10am-5pm Tue-Sun; 🚼; 🚍99B-Line) UBC's newest museum is also its most family-friendly. Showcasing two million natural history specimens that have never before been available for public viewing, the museum features fossil, fish and herbarium displays. The highlight is the 25m blue whale skeleton, artfully displayed in the museum's two-story main entrance, plus the first display case, which is crammed with tooth-and-claw taxidermy. Check the schedule for free tours and kids' activities.

HR MacMillan Space Centre   MUSEUM
(Map p114; 🖉604-738-7827; www.spacecentre.ca; 1100 Chestnut St; adult/child $18/13; ⊙10am-5pm Jul-Aug, 10am-3pm Mon-Fri, 10am-5pm Sat & noon-5pm Sun Sep-Jun; 🅿🚼; 🚍22) Popular with schoolkids – expect to have to elbow them out of the way to push the flashing buttons – this slightly dated science center illuminates the world of space. There's plenty of fun to be had battling aliens, designing spacecraft

or strapping yourself in for a simulator ride to Mars – as well as with movie presentations on all manner of spacey themes.

Vancouver Maritime Museum　MUSEUM
(www.vancouvermaritimemuseum.com; 1905 Ogden Ave; adult/child $11/8.50; ☺10am-5pm, to 8pm Thu, reduced hours off-season; **P**; 🚌22) Combining dozens of intricate models, detailed re-created ship sections and some historic boats, the prize exhibit in this waterfront A-frame museum is the *St Roch*, a 1928 Royal Canadian Mounted Police Arctic patrol vessel that was the first to navigate the legendary Northwest Passage in both directions. On a budget? Thursday entry (after 5pm) is by donation.

👁 North Shore

The North Shore is home to some of Metro Vancouver's favorite outdoor attractions. But North Van, in particular, is also starting to buzz as an urban visitor lure, especially at the shoreline end of Lonsdale Ave. Save some time to wander along the waterfront here, where gritty shipyard spaces are being reclaimed for market halls and public art. This is also the home of the striking new **Polygon Gallery**, which was under construction during our visit; see www.presentationhousegallery.org for updates.

Grouse Mountain　OUTDOORS
(☑604-980-9311; www.grousemountain.com; 6400 Nancy Greene Way, North Vancouver; Skyride adult/child $44/15; ☺9am-10pm; **P** 👪; 🚌236) The self-proclaimed 'Peak of Vancouver,' this mountaintop playground offers smashing views of downtown glittering in the water below. In summer, Skyride gondola tickets include access to lumberjack shows, alpine hiking, bird of prey displays and a grizzly bear refuge. Pay extra for **ziplining** and Eye of the Wind, a 20-story, elevator-accessed turbine tower with a panoramic viewing pod that will have your camera itching for action.

Capilano Suspension Bridge Park　PARK
(☑604-985-7474; www.capbridge.com; 3735 Capilano Rd, North Vancouver; adult/child $40/12, reduced off-season; ☺8:30am-8pm Jun-Aug, reduced off-season; **P** 👪; 🚌236) As you walk gingerly onto one of the world's longest (140m) and highest (70m) suspension bridges, swaying gently over the roiling Capilano Canyon, remember that its thick steel cables are embedded in concrete. That should steady your

feet – unless there are teenagers stamping across. Added park attractions include a glass-bottomed **cliffside walkway** and an elevated **canopy trail** through the trees.

Maplewood Farm　FARM
(☑604-929-5610; www.maplewoodfarm.bc.ca; 405 Seymour River Pl, North Vancouver; adult/child $7.80/4.70; ☺10am-4pm Apr-Oct, closed Mon Nov-Mar; 👪; 🚌239 from Lonsdale Quay, then C15) This popular farmyard attraction includes plenty of hands-on displays, plus more than 200 birds and domestic animals. Your wide-eyed kids can pet some critters, watch the milking demonstration and feed some squawking, ever-hungry ducks and chickens. The highlight is the daily round-up (3:30pm), when hungry critters streak back into their barn for dinner.

Mt Seymour Provincial Park　OUTDOORS
(www.bcparks.ca; 1700 Mt Seymour Rd, North Vancouver; ☺dawn-dusk) A popular rustic retreat from the downtown clamor, this giant, tree-lined park is suffused with summertime **hiking trails** that suit walkers of most abilities (the easiest path is the 2km Goldie Lake Trail). Many trails wind past lakes and centuries-old Douglas firs. This is also one of the city's main winter playgrounds.

LOCAL KNOWLEDGE

IT'S OFFICIAL

BC's provincial bird is the Steller's jay; its official mammal is the Kermode bear, a black bear with white fur.

The park is a great spot for **mountain biking** and has many dedicated trails. It's around 30 minutes from downtown Vancouver by car; drivers can take Hwy 1 to the Mt Seymour Parkway (near the Second Narrows Bridge) and follow it east to Mt Seymour Rd.

Lynn Canyon Park   PARK
(www.lynncanyon.ca; Park Rd, North Vancouver; ⊙7am-9pm; 🚻; 🚍229) Amid a dense bristling of ancient trees, the main feature of this popular park is its **suspension bridge**, a free alternative to Capilano. Not quite as big as its tourist-magnet rival, it nevertheless provokes the same jelly-legged reaction as you sway over the river that runs 50m below – and it's always far less crowded. **Hiking trails**, swimming areas and picnic spots will keep you busy here as well.

The park's **Ecology Centre** (www.lynncanyon ecologycentre.ca; 3663 Park Rd, North Vancouver; entry by suggested $2 donation; ⊙10am-5pm Jun-Sep, 10am-5pm Mon-Fri & noon-4pm Sat & Sun Oct-May; 🚻; 🚍227) 🖉 houses interesting displays, including dioramas and video presentations, on the area's rich biodiversity. It stages talks and events for kids, especially in summer.

🏃 Activities

Vancouver's variety of outdoorsy activities is a huge hook: you can ski in the morning and hit the beach in the afternoon; hike or bike scenic forests; windsurf along the coastline; or kayak to your heart's content – and it will be content, with grand mountain views as your backdrop. There's also a full menu of spectator sports to catch here.

Ecomarine Paddlesport Centres   KAYAKING
(Map p114; ☑604-689-7575; www.ecomarine. com; 1668 Duranleau St; kayak/paddleboard rental per 2hrs $39/29; ⊙9am-9pm Jun & Jul, to 8pm Aug, 10am-6pm Sep-May; 🚍50) Headquartered on Granville Island, the friendly folks at Ecomarine offer kayak and stand-up paddle board (SUP) rentals, as well as popular guided tours around the area. At the center's **Jericho Beach branch** (1300 Discovery St, Jericho Sailing Centre; ⊙10am-dusk Mon-Fri, 9am-

dusk Jun-Aug; 🚍4), events and seminars are organized where you can rub shoulders with local paddle nuts. Fancy exploring further? They also arrange multiday tours around some of BC's most magical marine regions.

Spokes Bicycle Rentals   CYCLING
(Map p114; ☑604-688-5141; www.spokesbicycle rentals.com; 1798 W Georgia St; adult bicycle rental per hour/day from $6.67/26.67; ⊙8am-9pm, reduced hours off-season; 🚍5) On the corner of W Georgia and Denman Sts, this is the biggest of the bike shops servicing the Stanley Park cycling trade. It can kit you and your family out with all manner of bikes, from cruisers to kiddie one-speeds. Ask for tips on riding the Seawall; it extends far beyond Stanley Park.

Grouse Mountain   SNOW SPORTS
(☑604-980-9311; www.grousemountain.com; 6400 Nancy Greene Way, North Vancouver; winter adult/child $58/25; ⊙9am-10pm mid-Nov–mid-Apr; 🚻; 🚍236) Vancouver's favorite winter hangout, family-friendly Grouse offers 26 ski and snowboard runs (including 14 night runs). There are classes and lessons available for beginners and beyond, and the area's forested snowshoe trails are magical. There are also a couple of dining options if you just want to relax and watch the snow with hot chocolate in hand.

Cypress Mountain   SNOW SPORTS
(☑604-926-5612; www.cypressmountain.com; Cypress Bowl Rd, West Vancouver; lift ticket adult/youth/child $71/57/38; ⊙9am-10pm mid-Dec–Mar, 9am-4pm mid-Nov–mid-Dec & Apr) Around 8km north of West Van via Hwy 99, Cypress Provincial Park transforms into Cypress Mountain resort in winter, attracting well-insulated locals with its 53 runs, 11km of snowshoe trails, cross-country ski access and a family-friendly six-chute snowtubing course. Upgraded for the 2010 Winter Olympics, the resort's newer facilities include an expanded lodge and upgrades to several runs.

👣 Tours

⭐**Forbidden Vancouver**   WALKING
(☑604-227-7570; www.forbiddenvancouver.ca; adult/senior/student $22/19/19) This quirky company offers highly entertaining tours: a delve into Prohibition-era Vancouver and a poke around the seedy underbelly of historic Gastown. Not recommended for kids. Every few months, it also offers an excellent behind-the-scenes history tour of the infamous

Penthouse nightclub, a strip joint that has a rich, somewhat glamorous and sometimes seedy past. Check the website for details.

Talaysay Tours WALKING
(604-628-8555; www.talaysay.com) Providing a range of authentic First Nations–led tours, including a signature Stanley Park walking option, this operator can also arrange guided kayak jaunts around the region.

Sewell's Marina BOATING
(604-921-3474; www.sewellsmarina.com; 6409 Bay St, Horseshoe Bay; adult/child $87/57; Apr-Oct; 250) West Vancouver's Horseshoe Bay is the departure point for Sewell's two-hour marine-wildlife-watching boat tours. Orcas are always a highlight but even if they're not around, you'll almost certainly spot harbor seals lolling on the rocks and pretending to ignore you. Seabirds and bald eagles are also big stars of the show.

Cycle City Tours TOURS
(Map p114; 604-618-8626; www.cyclevancouver. com; 648 Hornby St; tours from $59, bicycle rental per hour/day $8.50/34; 9am-6pm, reduced hours in winter; Burrard) Striped with an ever-increasing number of dedicated bike lanes, Vancouver is a good city for two-wheeled exploring. But if you're not great at navigating, consider a guided tour with this friendly operator. If you're a beer fan, aim for the Craft Beer Tour ($90), with nine tasty samples included. Alternatively, go it alone with a rental; there's a bike lane right outside.

⚔ Festivals & Events

Chinese New Year CULTURAL
(www.vancouver-chinatown.com; Jan or Feb) Festive kaleidoscope of dancing, parades and great food held in January or February.

Winterruption CULTURAL
(www.granvilleisland.com; mid-Feb) Granville Island brushes off the winter blues with tours, music and performances.

Vancouver International Wine Festival WINE
(www.vanwinefest.ca; late Feb) The city's oldest and best annual wine celebration, with a different regional focus every year.

Vancouver Craft Beer Week BEER
(www.vancouvercraftbeerweek.com; late May) A taste-tripping showcase for BC's amazing craft beer scene, with dozens of events around the city.

Vancouver International Children's Festival PERFORMING ARTS
(www.childrensfestival.ca; late May;) Storytelling, performance and activities around Granville island.

Vancouver International Jazz Festival MUSIC
(www.coastaljazz.ca; Jun & Jul) City-wide cornucopia of superstar shows and free outdoor events from mid-June.

Celebration of Light FIREWORKS
(www.hondacelebrationoflight.com; late Jul) FREE Three-night international fireworks extravaganza in English Bay.

Pride Week CARNIVAL, PARADE
(www.vancouverpride.ca; late Jul) Parties, concerts and fashion shows, as well as the city's biggest street parade.

Pacific National Exhibition CULTURAL
(www.pne.ca; Hastings Park; mid-Aug–Sep;) Family-friendly shows, music concerts and fairground fun (plus lots of naughty things to eat).

Vancouver International Film Festival FILM
(www.viff.org; late Sep) Popular two-week showcase of Canadian and international movies. Book ahead; tickets are hot items here.

Eastside Culture Crawl ART
(www.culturecrawl.ca; mid-Nov) Vancouver's best visual-arts festival: a four-day gallery and studio open house with hundreds of participants.

MAIN'S BEST FEST

If you make it to June's annual **Car Free Day** (www.carfreevancouver.org; mid-Jun) – staged along Main St, south of the Broadway intersection, for at least 30 blocks – you'll realize there's much more diversity to this area than you thought. Taking over the streets for this family-friendly community fest are live music, craft stalls, steaming food stands and a highly convivial atmosphere that makes for a party-like afternoon with the locals. And if you miss it? Consider checking out September's **Autumn Shift Festival** as well. It's just as much fun and has a sustainability theme.

ℹ FAMILY ATTRACTIONS

Vancouver has a wide of range of inviting sights to keep your kids happy, from a popular **aquarium** (p110) to an excellent **science center** (p116) – both of which are easily worth half-day visits. And if they want to get close to some local critters, there's a great city **farm** (p119) on the North Shore. Wherever you take them, be sure to go by train: the SkyTrain system here is popular with younger children, especially if they head to the front and pretend to drive. They can compare the experience to a more traditional journey via a ride on Stanley Park's **miniature train** (p110).

Santa Claus Parade CHRISTMAS
(www.rogerssantaclausparade.com; ⊙ early Dec; ▣) The city's main Christmas procession, centered on West Georgia St, complete with the great man himself.

🛏 Sleeping

Metro Vancouver is home to more than 25,000 hotel, B&B and hostel rooms – many in or around the downtown core. The city is packed with visitors in summer, so book ahead...unless you fancy sleeping against a damp log in Stanley Park. Rates peak in July and August, but there are good spring and fall deals, when you can also expect some accompanying 'Wet Coast' rainfall.

🛏 Downtown & West End

Samesun Backpackers Lodge HOSTEL $
(Map p114; ☑ 604-682-8226; www.samesun. com; 1018 Granville St; dm/r incl breakfast $35/100; ⊜ @ �s; ▣ 10) Vancouver's party hostel, the popular Samesun is right on the city's nightlife strip. Ask for a back room if you fancy a few hours of sleep or just head down to the large on-site bar (provocatively called the Beaver) to join the beery throng. Dorms are comfortably small, and there's a large kitchen. Continental breakfast is included.

HI Vancouver Central HOSTEL $
(Map p114; ☑ 604-685-5335; www.hihostels.ca/ vancouver; 1025 Granville St; dm/r incl breakfast $40/100; ⊜ ✳ �s; ▣ 10) On the Granville Strip, this warren-like hostel is more of a party joint than its **HI Downtown** (Map p114; ☑ 604-684-4565; 1114 Burnaby St; dm/r incl breakfast $40/100; ⊜ @ �s; ▣ 6) sibling. Some of the benefits of its past hotel incarnation remain, including air-conditioning and small rooms, some of which are now private, with the rest converted to dorm rooms with up to four beds. There are dozens of two-bed dorms (some en suite) for privacy fans.

★ St Regis Hotel BOUTIQUE HOTEL $$
(Map p114; ☑ 604-681-1135; www.stregishotel. com; 602 Dunsmuir St; d incl breakfast $299; ⊜ ✳ @ �s; ⑤ Granville) Transformed in recent years, this is now an art-lined boutique sleepover in a 1913 heritage shell. Befitting its age, almost all the rooms seem to be a different size, and they exhibit a loungey élan with leather-look wallpaper, earth-toned bedspreads, flatscreen TVs and multimedia hubs. Rates include value-added flourishes like cooked breakfasts, access to the nearby gym and free international phone calling.

Times Square Suites Hotel APARTMENT $$
(Map p114; ☑ 604-684-2223; www.timessquare suites.com; 1821 Robson St; d $225; ℗ ✳ �s ⓣ; ▣ 5) Superbly located a short walk from Stanley Park, this West End hidden gem (even the entrance can be hard to spot) is the perfect apartment-style Vancouver sleepover. Rooms are mostly one-bedroom suites and are spacious, with tubs, laundry facilities, full kitchens and well-maintained (if slightly 1980s) decor. Rates include nearby gym access.

Burrard Hotel HOTEL $$
(Map p114; ☑ 604-681-2331; www.theburrard. com; 1100 Burrard St; d from $229; ℗ ⊜ �s ⓣ; ▣ 22) A groovy makeover has transformed this 1950s downtown motel into a knowingly cool sleepover with a tongue-in-cheek retro-cool feel. The mostly quite compact rooms have been spruced up with mod flourishes and contemporary amenities such as fridges, flatscreens and Nespresso coffee machines. But not everything has changed: the hidden interior courtyard of Florida-style palm trees is _très_ cool.

Victorian Hotel HOTEL $$
(Map p114; ☑ 604-681-6369; www.victorianhotel. ca; 514 Homer St; d incl breakfast from $145; ⊜ @ �s; ⑤ Granville) The high-ceilinged rooms at this popular Euro-style, heritage-building hotel combine glossy hardwood floors, a sprinkling of antiques, an occasional bay window and plenty of historical charm. The best rooms are in the renovated extension, where raindrop showers, marble bathroom floors and flatscreen TVs add a slice of luxe. Rates

include continental breakfast, and rooms are provided with fans in summer.

Buchan Hotel HOTEL $$

(Map p114; ☑604-685-5354; www.buchanhotel. com; 1906 Haro St; d with/without bathroom $149/109; P⟲@🛜; 🚌5) The great-value 1926-built Buchan has bags of charm and is just steps from Stanley Park. Along corridors lined with prints of yesteryear Vancouver, its pension-style budget rooms – most with shared bathrooms – are clean, cozy and well maintained, although some furnishings have seen better days. The pricier rooms are correspondingly prettier, while the eastside rooms are brighter. The front desk is friendly.

Sylvia Hotel HOTEL $$

(Map p114; ☑604-681-9321; www.sylviahotel. com; 1154 Gilford St; d $199; P⟲🛜🐾; 🚌5) This ivy-covered 1912 charmer enjoys a prime location overlooking English Bay. Generations of guests keep coming back – many requesting the same room every year – for a dollop of old-world ambience, plus a side order of first-name service. The rooms, some with older furnishings, have a wide array of comfortable configurations, but the best are the large suites, which have kitchens and waterfront views.

Sunset Inn & Suites HOTEL $$

(Map p114; ☑604-688-2474; www.sunsetinn. com; 1111 Burnaby St; d incl breakfast $220; P❄@🛜; 🚌6) A good-value cut above most of Vancouver's self-catering suite hotels, the popular Sunset Inn offers larger-than-average rooms with full kitchens. Each has a balcony, and some – particularly those on south-facing higher floors – have partial views of English Bay. Rates include continental breakfast and, rare for Vancouver, gratis parking. The attentive staff is among the best in the city.

Listel Hotel BOUTIQUE HOTEL $$

(Map p114; ☑604-684-8461; www.thelistelhotel. com; 1300 Robson St; d $265; ⟲❄@🛜; 🚌5) A sophisticated, self-described 'art hotel,' the Listel attracts grown-ups through its on-site installations and package deals with local galleries. Many rooms display original artworks and all have a relaxing, mood-lit West Coast feel. Artsy types should check out the lobby sculptures for selfie opportunities, while the property's on-site bar and restaurant are arguably the best hotel drink and dine options in the city.

Loden Hotel BOUTIQUE HOTEL $$$

(Map p114; ☑604-669-5060; www.theloden.com; 1177 Melville St; d $449; P❄@🛜🐾; Ⓜ Burrard) The stylish Loden is the real designer deal, and one of the first boutique properties in years to give Yaletown's Opus (p124) a run for its money. The chic, mocha-hued rooms have a contemporary feel, with luxe accoutrements such as marble-lined bathrooms and those oh-so-civilized heated floors. Service is top-notch; try the lobby restobar as well as the complimentary London taxicab limo service.

Rosewood Hotel Georgia HOTEL $$$

(Map p114; ☑604-682-5566; www.rosewood hotels.com; 801 W Georgia St; d $520; ⟲❄@ 🛜🐾🐾; Ⓢ Vancouver City Centre) Vancouver's current 'It' hotel underwent a spectacular renovation a few years back that brought the 1927-built landmark back to its golden-age glory. Despite the abstract modern art lining its public areas, the hotel's rooms take a classic, elegant approach with warming earth and coffee tones, pampering treats such as deep soaker tubs and (in some rooms) sparkling downtown cityscape views.

Fairmont Hotel Vancouver HOTEL $$$

(Map p114; ☑604-684-3131; www.fairmont. com/hotelvancouver; 900 W Georgia St; d $399; P❄@🛜🐾🐾; Ⓢ Vancouver City Centre) Opened in 1939 by visiting UK royals, this sparkling grand dame is a Vancouver landmark. Despite the provenance, the hotel carefully balances comfort with elegance: the lobby is bedecked with crystal chandeliers but the rooms have an understated business-hotel feel. If you have the budget, check in to the Gold Floor for a raft of pampering extras.

English Bay Inn B&B $$$

(Map p114; ☑604-683-8002; www.englishbay inn.com; 1968 Comox St; d incl breakfast from $260; P⟲🛜; 🚌6) Each of the six antique-lined rooms in this Tudoresque B&B near Stanley Park has a private bathroom, and some have sumptuous four-poster beds. You'll think you've arrived in Victoria, BC's determinedly Olde English capital, by mistake. Rates include a lovely three-course breakfast – arrive in the dining room early for the alcove table. There's also a canopy-shaded garden for hanging out in summer.

Gastown & Chinatown

★**Skwachays Lodge**   BOUTIQUE HOTEL $$
(Map p114; ☎604-687-3589; www.skwachays.com; 29 W Pender St; d from $220; ❉🐾; Ⓢ Stadium-Chinatown) The 18 rooms at this First Nations art hotel include the captivating Forest Spirits Suite, with floor-to-ceiling birch branches, and the sleek Longhouse Suite, with its illuminated metalwork frieze. Deluxe trappings, from plasma TVs to eco-friendly toiletries, are standard and there's an on-site gallery for purchasing one-of-a-kind artworks to take home.

Yaletown & Granville Island

★**YWCA Hotel**   BUDGET HOTEL $
(Map p114; ☎604-895-5830; www.ywcahotel.com; 733 Beatty St; s/d/tr without bath $93/138/160; P🐾❉@🐾; Ⓢ Stadium-Chinatown) A good-value, well-located option offering nicely maintained (if spartan) rooms of the student accommodation variety. There's a wide range of configurations, from singles to five-bed rooms, plus shared, semi-private or private bathrooms. Each room has a minifridge and guests can use the three large communal kitchens. Rates include access to the YWCA Health & Fitness Centre, a 10-minute walk away.

Opus Hotel   BOUTIQUE HOTEL $$$
(Map p114; ☎604-642-6787; www.opushotel.com; 322 Davie St; d $390; P❉🐾🐾; Ⓢ Yaletown-Roundhouse) The Opus kick-started Vancouver's boutique hotel scene and, with regular revamps, it's remained one of the city's top sleepover options. The designer rooms have contemporary-chic interiors with bold colors, mod furnishings and feng-shui bed placements, while many of the luxe bathrooms have clear windows overlooking the streets (visiting exhibitionists take note).

Granville Island Hotel   BOUTIQUE HOTEL $$$
(Map p114; ☎604-683-7373; www.granvilleislandhotel.com; 1253 Johnston St; d $375; P🐾@🐾; 🖵50) This gracious boutique property hugs Granville Island's quiet southeastern tip, enjoying tranquil views across False Creek to Yaletown's mirrored towers. You'll be a stroll from the Public Market, with shopping and theater options on your doorstep. Rooms have a West Coast feel with some exposed wood flourishes. There's also a rooftop Jacuzzi, while the on-site brewpub-restaurant has one of the city's best patios.

Kitsilano & University of British Columbia

HI Vancouver Jericho Beach   HOSTEL $
(☎604-224-3208; www.hihostels.ca/vancouver; 1515 Discovery St; dm/d $34/80; ⊙May-Oct; P@🐾; 🖵4) One of Canada's largest hostels looks like a Victorian hospital but has a scenic, near-the-beach location. Basic rooms make this the least palatial Vancouver HI hostel, but it has a large kitchen, bike rentals and a recently revamped, licensed cafe. Dorms are also larger here. Book ahead for the popular, budget-hotel-style private rooms, which come in both shared and private bathroom options.

Corkscrew Inn   B&B $$
(☎604-733-7276; www.corkscrewinn.com; 2735 W 2nd Ave; d incl breakfast from $215; P🐾; 🖵4) This immaculate, gable-roofed property appears to have a drinking problem: it houses a little museum, available only to guests, that's lined with quirky corkscrews and antique vineyard tools. Aside from the boozy paraphernalia, this lovely century-old Craftsman home has five artsy, wood-floored rooms (we like the Art Deco room) and is just a short walk from the beach. Sumptuous breakfast included.

🍴 Eating

Vancouver has an amazing array of generally great-value dine-out options: top-drawer sushi joints, clamorous Chinese restaurants, inviting indie eateries, tempting food trucks and a fresh-picked farm-to-table scene are all on the menu. You don't have to be a local to indulge: just follow your tastebuds and dinner will become the most talked-about highlight of your Vancouver visit.

🍴 Downtown & West End

Templeton   DINER $$
(☎604-685-4612; www.thetempleton.ca; 1087 Granville St; mains $10-16; ⊙9am-11pm Mon-Wed, to 1am Thu-Sun; 🖉♿; 🖵10) A chrome-and-vinyl '50s-look diner with a twist, Templeton serves up plus-sized organic burgers, addictive fries, vegetarian quesadillas and perhaps the best hangover cure in town – the 'Big Ass Breakfast.' Sadly, the mini jukeboxes on the tables don't work, but you can console yourself with a waistline-busting chocolate ice-cream float. Avoid weekend peak times or you'll be queuing for ages.

Finch's
CAFE $

(Map p114; ☎604-899-4040; www.finchtea house.com; 353 W Pender St; mains $5-10; ⊗9am-5pm Mon-Fri, 11am-4pm Sat; 🖉; ᾡ4) For a coveted seat at one of the dinged old tables, arrive off-peak at this sunny corner cafe that has a 'granny-chic' look combining creaky wooden floors and junk-shop bric-a-brac. You'll be joining in-the-know hipsters and creative types who've been calling this their local for years. They come mainly for the freshly prepared baguette sandwiches (pear, Brie, prosciutto and roasted walnuts recommended).

Tractor
CANADIAN $

(Map p114; ☎604-979-0550; www.tractorfoods. com; Marine Building, 335 Burrard St; ⊗7am-9:30pm Mon-Fri, 11am-9:30pm Sat & Sun; 🖉; ⑤Waterfront) A healthy fast-food cafeteria tucked into the base of the Marine Building. Step up to the counter and choose from 10 or so hearty mixed salads, then add a half or whole grilled sandwich. Wholesome and satisfying, housemade soups and stews are also available but make sure you add a lemonade as well – there's usually a tempting flavor or two.

Sushi Itoga
JAPANESE $

(Map p114; ☎604-687-2422; www.itoga.com; 1686 Robson St; sushi combos $8-18; ⊗11:30am-2pm & 5-8pm Mon-Sat, 5-8pm Sun; ᾡ5) You'll be rubbing shoulders with other diners at the large communal dining table here, one of the best spots in town for a superfresh sushi feast in a casual setting. Check the ever-changing blackboard showing what's available and then tuck into expertly prepared and well-priced shareable platters of all your fave *nigiri*, *maki* and sashimi treats. Udon dishes are also available.

★Forage
CANADIAN $$

(Map p114; ☎604-661-1400; www.foragevan couver.com; 1300 Robson St; mains $16-29; ⊗6:30-10am & 5pm-midnight Mon-Fri, 7am-2pm & 5pm-midnight Sat & Sun; ᾡ5) 🖉 A champion of the local farm-to-table scene, this sustainability-hugging restaurant is the perfect way to sample the flavors of the region. Brunch has become a firm local favorite (turkey-sausage hash recommended), and for dinner the idea is to sample an array of tasting plates. The menu is innovative and highly seasonal, but look out for the seafood chowder with quail's egg.

★Guu with Garlic
JAPANESE $$

(Map p114; ☎604-685-8678; www.guu-izakaya. com; 1698 Robson St; small plates $4-9, mains $8-16; ⊗11:30am-2:30pm & 5:30pm-12:30am Mon-Sat, 11:30am-2:30pm & 5:30pm-midnight Sun; ᾡ5) One of the Vancouver's best *izakayas*, this welcoming, wood-lined joint is a cultural immersion. Hotpots and noodle bowls are available but it's best to experiment with some Japanese bar tapas, including black cod with miso mayo, deep-fried egg and pumpkin balls or finger-lickin' *tori-karaage* fried chicken. Garlic is liberally used in most dishes. It's best to arrive before opening time for a seat.

Royal Dinette
INTERNATIONAL $$

(Map p114; ☎604-974-8077; www.royaldinette. ca; 905 Dunsmuir St; mains $15-34; ⊗11:30am-2pm & 5-10pm; ⑤Burrard) Seasonal and regional are the foundations of this smashing downtown restaurant, but add friendly, unpretentious service and it becomes a winner. The lunchtime two- or three-course prix fixe ($30 or $35) is a good way to try the place out, but dinner is all about a lingering opportunity to savor international influences combined with local ingredients: the squid-ink spaghetti is our favorite.

Jam Cafe
BREAKFAST $$

(Map p114; ☎778-379-1992; www.jamcafes.com; 556 Beatty St; mains $11-16; ⊗8am-3pm; 🛜🖉; ⑤Stadium-Chinatown) The Vancouver outpost of Victoria's wildly popular breakfast and brunch superstar hit the ground running soon after opening here. It's typically packed, so you'll have to wait for a table (reservations not accepted) unless you're smart enough to dine very off-peak. You'll find a white-walled room studded with Canadian knick-knacks and a huge array of satisfying options, from chicken and waffles to red-velvet pancakes.

Timber
PUB FOOD **$$**

(Map p114; ☑604-661-2166; www.timbervancouver.com; 1300 Robson St; mains $10-19; ☺11am-1pm Mon-Thu, 10am-1pm Fri & Sat, 10am-midnight Sun; ☑5) One of two good dining options attached to the Listel Hotel, this resto-pub combines a great BC-focused craft beer menu along with a tongue-in-cheek array of Canadian comfort food. Snap some photos with the taxidermied beaver and Canada goose, then dive into bison burgers, ketchup-flavored potato chips (Canada's fave flavor) and deep-fried cheese curds. It's like a crash course in calorific Canadian grub.

Sura Korean Cuisine
KOREAN **$$**

(Map p114; ☑604-687-7872; www.surakoreancuisine.com; 1518 Robson St; mains $10-20; ☺11am-4pm & 5-10:30pm; ℗; ☑5) From the 1400-block of Robson St on and around onto Denman and Davie Sts, you'll find a smorgasbord of authentic Korean and Japanese eateries. A cut above its ESL-student-luring siblings, slick Sura offers awesome Korean comfort dishes in a cosy, bistro-like setting. Try the spicy beef soup, kimchi pancakes and excellent *bibimbap*: beef, veggies and a still-cooking egg in a hot stone bowl.

Indigo Age Cafe
VEGAN **$$**

(Map p114; ☑604-622-1797; www.indigoagecafe.com; 436 Richards St; mains $10-13; ☺10am-8pm Mon-Thu, to 9pm Fri & Sat; 🛜🖊; ☑14) 🖊 A cozy subterranean spot beloved of in-the-know Vancouver vegans and raw-food fans. Snag a log-slice table here and dive into a hearty array of house-made dishes. Pierogies, cabbage rolls and pizza have their fans here but we recommend the delicious zucchini pasta with Portobello mushroom 'steak.'

Fat Badger
BRITISH **$$$**

(Map p114; ☑604-336-5577; www.fatbadger.ca; 1616 Alberni St; mains $20-38; ☺5-11pm Tue-Sun; ☑5) A gourmet reinvention of a British pub in a gabled heritage-listed building, the atmospheric dark-wood interior here is the ideal setting for hunkering in a corner on a rainy night and stuffing yourself with Scotch eggs, lamb-and-Guinness pie and the kind of sticky toffee pudding that might make you propose marriage to your dessert (again).

Chambar
EUROPEAN **$$$**

(Map p114; ☑604-879-7119; www.chambar.com; 562 Beatty St; mains $27-34; ☺8am-3pm & 5-10pm; ℗; ⑤ Stadium-Chinatown) This giant, brick-lined cave is a great place for a romantic night out. The sophisticated Belgian-esque menu includes perfectly delectable *moules et frites* (mussels and fries) and a braised lamb shank with figs that's a local dining legend. An impressive wine and cocktail list (try a blue-fig martini) is also coupled with a great Belgian beer menu dripping with *tripels* and *lambics*.

🍴 Gastown & Chinatown

★Tacofino
MEXICAN **$**

(Map p114; ☑604-899-7907; www.tacofino.com; 15 W Cordova St; tacos $6-12; ☑14) Food-truck favorite Tacofino made an instant splash with this huge, handsome dining room (think stylish geometric-patterned floors and hive-like lampshades). The simple menu focuses on a handful of taco options (six at lunch, more at dinner), plus nachos, soups and a boozy selection of beer, agave and naughty tequila flights. Fish tacos are the top seller, but we love the super-tender lamb *birria* (stew).

★Purebread
BAKERY

(Map p114; ☑604-563-8060; www.purebread.ca; 159 W Hastings St; baked goods $3-6; ☺8:30am-5:30pm; 🛜; ☑14) When Whistler's favorite bakery opened here, salivating Vancouverites began flocking in en masse. Expect to stand slack-jawed in front of the glass panels as you try to choose from a cornucopia of cakes, pastries and bars. Cake-wise, we love the coconut buttermilk loaf, but make sure you also pick up a crack bar or salted caramel bar to 'go (or preferably both).

Bestie
GERMAN

(Map p114; ☑604-620-1175; www.bestie.ca; 105 E Pender St; mains $4-11; ☺11:30am-10pm Sun-Thu, to midnight Fri & Sat; 🛜; ☑3) Like a food truck with a permanent home, this white-walled hole-in-the-wall specializes in Berlin-style currywursts – hearty sausages slathered in curry sauce, served with crunchy fries. It's popular with passing hipsters, so arrive off-peak for a chance of snagging the little cubby-hole window table, the best in the house. There's always a small but well-curated array of local craft beers to add to the fun.

Ramen Butcher
RAMEN **$**

(Map p114; ☑604-806-4646; www.theramenbutcher.com; 223 E Georgia St; mains $10-12;

FOOD-TRUCK FRENZY

Keen to emulate the legendary street-food scenes of Portland and Austin, Vancouver jumped on the kitchen-equipped bandwagon in 2011, launching a pilot scheme with 17 food carts. Things took off quickly and there are now dozens dotted around the city, serving everything from halibut tacos to Korean sliders, pulled-pork sandwiches to French crepes. Prices are typically $8-12 per entree.

While there are a number of experimental fusion trucks, several have quickly risen to the top; look out for local favorites Le Tigre, Kaboom Box, TacoFino, Soho Road, Mom's Grilled Cheese and Vij's Railway Express – plus Johnny's Pops artisan ice lollies. Locating the trucks can sometimes be challenging; there are usually a couple outside the Vancouver City Centre Canada Line station and on busy stretches of downtown arteries like Georgia, Robson and around the Vancouver Art Gallery perimeter. Also look out for the trucks at city farmers markets and outside some microbreweries (you're allowed to eat your truck takeout in the brewery tasting rooms).

For listings, opening hours and locations, the handy www.streetfoodapp.com/vancouver website tells you excatly where to go. Alternatively, **Vancouver Foodie Tours** (604-295-8844; www.foodietours.ca; tours from $50) offers a tasty guided walk that includes samples at four trucks. But if you're keen to loosen your belt and sample as many as you can in one belly-busting afternoon, check out August's three-day-long **YVR Food Fest** (www.yvrfoodfest.com; Olympic Village; Main St-Science World), where dozens of food carts congregate to lure the deeply ravenous. And if you fancy an easy trip from town, August's one-day **Columbia StrEat Food Truck Fest** in New Westminster (easily reached via SkyTrain) is also well-worth checking out, with its 70+ trucks. See www.downtownnewwest.ca for details.

11am-3pm & 5-10pm Tue-Thu, 11am-10pm Fri-Sun; 3) One of several new Asian-themed restaurants arriving in Chinatown in recent years, this is the first North American foray of a well-known Japanese ramen franchise. The signature thin noodles come in several broth-bowl varieties with slabs of slow-cooked pork; we recommend the garlicky Red Ramen. Still have some soup in your bowl? They'll toss in a second serving of noodles for free.

Save On Meats
DINER $

(Map p114; 604-569-3568; www.saveonmeats.ca; 43 W Hastings St; mains $5-15; 7am-10pm Mon-Thu, 8am-10pm Fri & Sat, 8am-7pm Sun; ; 14) A former old-school butcher shop, Save On Meats has been transformed into a popular hipster diner. But it's not just about looking cool. Slide into a booth or take a perch at the long counter and tuck into comfort dishes, including a good-value $5 all-day breakfast, plus a menu of basic faves such as shepherd's pie, and mac and cheese.

MeeT in Gastown
VEGAN $$

(Map p114; 604-688-3399; www.eatmeet.ca; 12 Water St; mains $7-15; 11am-11pm Sun-Thu, to 1am Fri & Sat; ; Waterfront) Bringing great vegan comfort dishes to locals without the rabbit-food approach, this wildly popular spot can be clamorously busy at times. But it's worth the wait for a wide-ranging array of herbivore- and carnivore-pleasing dishes, from rice bowls and mac 'n' cheese (made from vegan nut 'cheese') to Portobello mushroom burgers and poutine-like fries slathered in cashew gravy (our recommendation).

Bodega
SPANISH $$

(Map p114; 604-565-8815; www.bodegaonmain.com; 1014 Main St; small plates $7-20; 11am-midnight Mon-Fri, 4:30pm-midnight Sat & Sun; 3) The newest of several recently arrived restaurants in this once-sketchy Main St stretch is actually the relocated reincarnation of one of Vancouver's oldest Spanish eateries. A downtown mainstay for decades, the new Bodega is a sumptuous room of bordello-red seats and paintings evoking the old country, plus a menu of lovely tapas favorites like meatballs, grilled octopus and slow-roasted rabbit.

Phnom Penh
VIETNAMESE, CAMBODIAN $$

(Map p114; 603-682-5777; 244 E Georgia St; mains $8-18; 10am-9pm Mon-Thu, to 11pm Fri-Sun; 3) The dishes at this bustling joint are split between Cambodian and Vietnamese soul-food classics. It's the highly addictive chicken wings and their lovely pepper sauce that keep regulars loyal. Once you've piled up the bones, dive back in for round two: papaya salad, butter beef and spring rolls show just how good a street-food-inspired Asian menu can be.

Nuba   MIDDLE EASTERN $$

(Map p114; ☑604-688-1655; www.nuba.ca; 207 W Hastings St; mains $9-30; ☺11:30am-10pm Mon-Fri, noon-10pm Sat, 5-10pm Sun; ☑; ☑14) Tucked under the landmark Dominion Building, this Lebanese restaurant attracts budget noshers and cool hipsters in equal measure. If you're not sure what to go for, split some tasty, surprisingly filling mezze dishes, including excellent hummus and falafel, or just dive straight into a shareable La Feast for two ($38) that covers all the bases (including the inevitable doggie-bag takeout).

Bao Bei   CHINESE $$

(Map p114; ☑604-688-0876; www.bao-bei.ca; 163 Keefer St; small plates $5-19; ☺5:30pm-midnight Mon-Sat, 5:30-11pm Sun; ☑; ☑3) Reinterpreting a Chinatown heritage-building interior with hipster-esque flourishes, this Chinese brasserie is the area's most seductive dinner destination. Bringing a contemporary edge to Asian cuisine are, tapas-sized, MSG-free dishes such as *shao bing* (stuffed Chinese flatbread), duck salad and steamed pork belly buns: there's also an inventive cocktail array to keep you occupied if you have to wait at the bar for your table.

★ Ask for Luigi   ITALIAN $$$

(Map p114; ☑604-428-2544; www.askforluigi.com; 305 Alexander St; mains $22-24; ☺11:30am-2:30pm & 5:30-10:30pm Tue-Fri, 9:30am-2:30pm & 5:30-11pm Sat, 9:30am-2:30pm & 5:30-9:30pm Sun; ☑4) Consider an off-peak lunch if you don't want to wait too long for a table at this white-clapboard, shack-look little charmer (reservations are not accepted). Inside, you'll find a checkerboard floor and teak-lined interior crammed with tables and delighted diners tucking into (and sharing) plates of scratch-made pasta that mama never used to make; think bison tagliatelle and borage-and-ricotta ravioli.

ℹ GUILT-FREE FISH & CHIPS

Seafood is BC's main dining choice. Support the sustainability of the region's aquatic larder by frequenting restaurants operating under the Ocean Wise banner; see www.oceanwise.ca.

L'Abattoir   FRENCH $$$

(Map p114; ☑604-568-1701; www.labattoir.ca; 217 Carrall St; mains $35-44; ☺5:30-10pm Sun-Thu, to 10:30pm Fri & Sat, brunch 10am-2pm Sat & Sun; ☑4) Gastown's most romantic top-end restaurant, this candlelit, brick-lined spot makes an art of attending to every detail. Be careful not to fill up on the warm bread before you tuck into a menu of French-influenced West Coast dishes. We recommend the lamb leg with spicy *merguez* sausage. Reservations are suggested: ask for a table in the delightful, window-walled back room.

✕ Yaletown & Granville Island

Go Fish   SEAFOOD $

(Map p114; ☑604-730-5040; 1505 W 1st Ave; mains $8-14; ☺11:30am-6:30pm Mon-Fri, noon-6:30pm Sat & Sun; ☑50) A short stroll westwards along the seawall from the Granville Island entrance, this almost-too-popular seafood stand is one the city's fave fish-and-chip joints, offering halibut, salmon and cod encased in crispy golden batter. The smashing (and lighter) fish tacos are also recommended, while ever-changing daily specials – brought in by the nearby fishing boats – often include scallop burgers or ahi tuna sandwiches.

★ Bistro 101   CANADIAN $$

(Map p114; ☑604-724-4488; www.picachef.com; 1505 W 2nd Ave; ☺11:30am-2pm & 6-9pm Mon-Fri; ☑50) Vancouver's best-value gourmet dining option, the training restaurant of the **Pacific Institute of Culinary Arts** is popular with in-the-know locals, especially at lunchtime, when $22 gets you a delicious three-course meal (typically three options for each course) plus service that's earnestly solicitous. The dinner option costs $8 more and there's a buffet offering on the first Friday of the month. Reservations recommended.

Rodney's Oyster House   SEAFOOD $$

(Map p114; ☑604-609-0080; www.rohvan.com; 1228 Hamilton St; mains $16-32; ☺11:30am-11pm; ⑤Yaletown-Roundhouse) Vancouver's favorite oyster eatery, Rodney's always has a buzz. And it's not just because of the convivial room with its nautical flourishes: these folks really know how to do seafood. While the fresh-shucked oysters with a huge array of sauces (try the spicy vodka) never fail to impress, there's also everything from sweet mussels to superb Atlantic lobster available here.

Flying Pig CANADIAN $$
(Map p114; ☑604-568-1344; www.theflyingpig
van.com; 1168 Hamilton St; mains $19-27;
⊙11am-midnight Mon-Fri, 10am-midnight Sat,
10am-11pm Sun; Ⓢ Yaletown-Roundhouse) Yale-
town's best midrange restaurant is a warm,
woodsy bistro that has mastered the art of
friendly service and saliva-triggering, gour-
met comfort food. Dishes focus on seasonal
local ingredients and are virtually guaranteed
to make your belly smile. Wine-braised short
ribs and roast chicken served with buttermilk
mash top our to-eat list but it's best to arrive
off-peak to avoid the crowds.

Blue Water Cafe SEAFOOD $$$
(Map p114; ☑604-688-8078; www.bluewater
cafe.net; 1095 Hamilton St; mains $29-48; ⊙5-
11pm; Ⓢ Yaletown-Roundhouse) Under celebrated executive chef Frank Pabst, this is one of
Vancouver's best high-concept seafood restaurants. Gentle music fills the brick-lined,
blue-hued interior, while top-notch char,
sablefish and butter-soft scallops grace the
tables inside and on the patio. Not a seafood
fan? There's also a small array of meaty 'principal plates' to sate your carnivorous appetite,
including Wagyu beef.

✖ Commercial Drive

★**Jamjar** LEBANESE $
(☑604-252-3957; www.jamjaronthedrive.com;
2280 Commercial Dr; small plates $6-12; mains
$17-22; ⊙11:30am-10pm; ☑; ☐20) This super-
friendly, cafe-style joint has a rustic-chic interior and a folky Lebanese menu of ethically
sourced ingredients and lots of vegetarian
options. You don't have to be a veggie to love
the crispy falafel balls or the utterly irresisti-
ble deep-fried cauliflower stalks – which will
have you fighting for the last morsel if you
made the mistake of ordering to share.

★**Cannibal Café** BURGERS $
(☑604-558-4199; www.cannibalcafe.ca; 1818
Commercial Dr; mains $11-16; ⊙11:30am-10pm
Mon-Thu, 11:30am-midnight Fri, 10am-midnight Sat,
10am-10pm Sun; ☐20) This is a punk-tastic
diner for fans of seriously real burgers made
with love. You'll find an inventive array from
classics to the recommended Korean BBQ
burger. Top-notch ingredients will ensure
you never slink into a fast-food chain again.
Check the board outside for daily specials
and keep in mind there are happy hour deals
from 3pm to 6pm weekdays.

Tangent Cafe DINER $
(☑604-558-4641; www.tangentcafe.ca; 2095
Commercial Dr; mains $11-14; ⊙8am-3pm Mon &
Tue, to midnight Wed & Thu, to 1am Fri & Sat, to 10pm
Sun; ☎; ☐20) Lined with 1970s-style wood-
paneling, this popular hangout combines
comfort-classic BLTs and burgers with several Malaysian curry options. But breakfast (served until mid-afternoon) is when
most locals roll in, often to cure hangovers
founded right here the night before. A great
craft beer menu (check the corner chalkboard) and live music (mostly jazz) three
nights a week makes this a popular nighttime haunt.

✖ Main Street

Hawkers Delight ASIAN $
(☑604-709-8188; 4127 Main St; mains $4-10;
⊙noon-9pm Mon-Sat; ☑; ☐3) It's easy to miss
this cash-only hole-in-the-wall, but it's worth
retracing your steps for authentic Malaysian
and Singaporean street food, made from
scratch at this family-run favorite. Prices
are temptingly low, so order to share – from
spicy *mee pok* to noodle-heavy *mee goreng*
and prawn-packed *laksa*. Check the counter
when ordering for the addictive veggie fritters – they're just $1 for two.

Slickity Jim's Chat 'N' Chew DINER $
(☑604-873-6760; www.skinnyfatjack.com; 3475
Main St; mains $8-14; ⊙8:30am-4pm Mon & Tue,
to 8pm Wed, Thur & Sun, to midnight Fri & Sat; ☑;
☐3) This local favorite gets jam-packed
with bleary-eyed locals soothing their
hangovers, but it's worth the wait for a
quirky, darkened room lined with the kind
of oddball art David Lynch probably favors
in his house. Menu-wise, they've nailed
breakfast here, with traditional as well as
inventive (and heaping) plates enlivened
with quirky names like the Breakfast of
Broken Dreams.

★**Dock Lunch** INTERNATIONAL $$
(☑604-879-3625; 152 E 11th Ave; mains $10-14;
⊙11:30am-5pm Mon-Fri, 11am-3pm Sat & Sun) Like
dining in a cool hippie's home, this utterly
charming room in a side-street house serves a
daily-changing menu of one or two soul-food
mains (think spicy tacos or heaping weekend
brunches). Arrive early and aim for one of the
two window seats and you'll soon be chatting
with the locals or browsing the cookbooks
and Huxley novels on the shelves.

DON'T MISS

UBC'S APPLETASTIC FOOD FESTIVAL

From Salish to Aurora Golden Gala and from Gravensteins to Cox's Orange Pippins, fans of the real king of fruit have plenty to bite into at the autumnal, weekend-long **UBC Apple Festival** (www.ubcbotanicalgarden.org/events; adult/child $4/free; ☺mid-Oct). Staged every October at the **UBC Botanical Garden** (p118), it's one of Vancouver's most popular community events. Along with live music and demonstrations on grafting and cider-making, there are lots of smile-triggering children's activities. But the event's main lure is the chance to nibble on a vast array of around 40,000 pounds of BC-grown treats that make most supermarket apples taste like hockey pucks.

The best way to sample as many as possible is to pay an extra $5 and dive into the **Tasting Tent**. Here, 60 locally grown heritage and more recent varieties are available for considered scoffing, including rarities such as Crestons and Oaken Pins. Before you leave, follow your nose to the sweet aroma of perhaps the best apple pie you'll ever taste. A highlight of the festival, the deep-dish, golden-crusted slices for sale here are an indulgence you could happily eat until you explode – with an apple-flavored smile on your face.

✖ Fairview & South Granville

★**La Taqueria Pinche Taco Shop** MEXICAN $
(☎604-558-2549; www.lataqueria.ca; 2549 Cambie St, Fairview; 4 tacos $8.50-10.50; ☺11am-8:30pm Mon-Sat, noon-6pm Sun; ☑; Ⓢ Broadway-City Hall) This popular taco spot expanded from its tiny Hastings St location (which is still there) with this larger storefront. It's just as crowded but luckily many of the visitors are going the take-out route. Snag a brightly painted table, then order at the counter from a dozen or so meat or veggie soft tacos (take your pick or ask for a selection).

★**Pronto** ITALIAN $$
(☎604-722-9331; www.prontocaffe.ca; 3473 Cambie St, Cambie Village; mains $14-22; ☺11:30am-9pm Sun, Tue & Wed, to 10pm Thu-Sat; ☐15) A delightful neighborhood eatery, this charming Cambie Village trattoria combines woodsy candlelit booths, perfectly prepared house-made pasta and the kind of welcoming service few restaurants manage to provide. Drop by for a lunchtime *porchetta* sandwich, or head here for dinner, when the intimate, wood-floored space feels deliciously relaxed. Check the blackboard specials or head straight for the gnocchi with pesto and pancetta.

★**Vij's** INDIAN $$$
(☎604-736-6664; www.vijsrestaurant.ca; 3106 Cambie St, Cambie Village; mains $19-27; ☺5:30-10pm; ☑; ☐15) A sparkling (and far larger) new location for Canada's favorite East Indian chef delivers a warmly sumptuous lounge coupled with a cavernous dining area and cool rooftop patio. The menu, a high-water mark of contemporary Indian cuisine, fuses BC ingredients, global flourishes and classic ethnic flavors to produce many inventive dishes. Results range from signature 'lamb popsicles' to flavorful meals like sablefish in yogurt-tomato broth.

✖ Kitsilano & University of British Columbia

Kitsilano's two main arteries – West 4th Ave and Broadway – offer a healthy mix of eateries: it's well worth the trek here to lounge on a beach or stroll the shopping areas, then end your day with a rewarding meal. The neighborhood's hippie past has left a legacy of vegetarian-friendly restaurants, but Kits' more recent wealth means there are also some top-notch high-end options well worth a splurge. If you're at UBC, there are some dining options available; alternatively, hop on a bus to nearby Kitsilano for a far superior selection.

★**Mr Red Cafe** VIETNAMESE $
(☎604-559-6878; 2680 W Broadway; mains $6-14; ☺11am-9pm; ☑; ☐9) Serving authentic northern Vietnamese homestyle dishes that look and taste like there's a lovely old lady making them out back. Reservations are not accepted; dine off-peak to avoid waiting for the handful of tables, then dive into shareable gems like pork baguette sandwiches, *cha ca han oi* (spicy grilled fish) and the ravishing pyramidical rice dumpling, stuffed with pork and a boiled quail's egg.

131

★ **Fable** CANADIAN $$
(📞604-732-1322; www.fablekitchen.ca; 1944 W 4th
Ave; mains $19-31; ⊙11:30am-2pm Mon-Fri, 5:30-
10pm Mon-Sat, brunch 10:30am-2pm Sat & Sun;
🖥4) One of Vancouver's favorite farm-to-
table restaurants is a lovely rustic-chic room
of exposed brick, wood beams and promi-
nently displayed red rooster logos. But looks
are just part of the appeal. Expect perfectly
prepared bistro dishes showcasing local sea-
sonal ingredients, such as duck, lamb and
halibut. It's great gourmet comfort food with
little pretension – hence the packed room
most nights. Reservations recommended.

Naam VEGETARIAN $$
(📞604-738-7151; www.thenaam.com; 2724 W 4th
Ave; mains $9-16; ⊙24hr; 🍴; 🖥4) An evocative
relic of Kitsilano's hippie past, this vegetarian
restaurant has the feel of a comfy farmhouse.
It's not unusual to have to wait for a table
at peak times, but it's worth it for the huge
menu of hearty stir-fries, nightly curry specials, bulging quesadillas and ever-popular
fries with miso gravy. It's the kind of veggie
spot where carnivores delightedly dine.

🍷 **Drinking & Nightlife**

Vancouverites spend a lot of time drinking.
And while British Columbia (BC) has a tasty
wine sector and is undergoing an artisanal
distilling surge, it's the regional craft beer
scene that keeps many quaffers merry. For a
night out with locally made libations as your
side dish, join savvy drinkers supping in the
bars of Gastown, Main St and around Commercial Dr.

★ **Alibi Room** PUB
(Map p114; 📞604-623-3383; www.alibi.ca; 157
Alexander St; ⊙5-11:30pm Mon-Thu, 5pm-12:30am
Fri, 10am-12:30am Sat, 10am-11:30pm Sun; 📶; 🖥4)
Vancouver's best craft beer tavern has an exposed brick bar that stocks a roster of around
50 drafts, mostly from celebrated BC breweries such as Driftwood, Four Winds and Yellow
Dog. Adventurous taste-trippers – hipsters
and veteran beer fans alike – enjoy the $11.50
'frat bat' of four samples: choose your own or
ask to be surprised. Check the board for ever-
changing guest casks.

★ **Storm Crow Alehouse** PUB
(📞604-428-9670; www.stormcrowalehouse.com;
1619 W Broadway, South Granville; ⊙11am-1am
Mon-Thu, 11am-2am Fri, 9am-2am Sat, 9am-1am
Sun; 🖥9) This large, nerdy pub welcomes
everyone from the Borg to beardy *Lord of*
the Rings dwarfs. They come to peruse the
memorabilia-studded walls (think Millennium Falcon models and a Tardis washroom
door), play the board games and dive into
apposite refreshments including Romulan
Ale and Pangalactic Gargleblasters. Hungry?
Miss the chunky chickpea fries at your peril.

★ **Brassneck Brewery** MICROBREWERY
(📞604-259-7686; 2184 Main St; ⊙2-11pm Mon-Fri,
noon-11pm Sat & Sun; 🖥3) Vancouver's favour-
ite microbrewery concocted more than 50
different beers in its first six months of operating and continues to win new fans with an
ever-changing chalkboard of intriguing libations with names like Bivouac Bitter, Stock-
holm Syndrome and Magician's Assistant.
Our recommendation? The delicious Passive
Aggressive dry-hopped pale ale. Arrive early
for a seat in the small tasting bar, especially
on weekends.

★ **Catfe** CAFE
(Map p114; 📞778-379-0060; www.catfe.ca; International Village Mall, 88 Pender St; with/without
cafe purchase $5/8; ⊙11am-9pm Fri- Wed; 🚼;
🚇Stadium-Chinatown) Vancouver's only cat
cafe; book online for your time slot (walk-
ins may also be available), buy a coffee and
then meet the moggies in the large feline
play room, where at least a dozen whiskered
wonders await. All the cats come from the
SPCA (Society for the Prevention of Cruelty
to Animals) and are available for adoption
via their usual procedures.

★ **Shameful Tiki Room** BAR
(www.shamefultikiroom.com; 4362 Main St;
⊙5pm-midnight Sun-Thu, to 1am Fri & Sat; 🖥3)
This windowless snug instantly transports
you to a Polynesian beach. The lighting –
including glowing puffer-fish lampshades
– is permanently set to dusk and the walls
are lined with tiki masks and rattan cover-
ings under a straw-shrouded ceiling. But it's
the drinks that rock: seriously well-crafted
classics from Zombies to Mai Tais to a four-
person Volcano Bowl.

Narrow Lounge BAR
(Map p114; www.narrowlounge.com; 1898 Main
St; ⊙5pm-1am Mon-Fri, to 2am Sat & Sun; 🖥3)
Enter through the doorway on 3rd Ave – the
red light tells you if it's open or not – then
descend the graffiti-lined stairway into Vancouver's coolest small bar. Little bigger than
a train carriage and lined with moth-eaten
taxidermy and junk-shop pictures, it's an

BRITISH COLUMBIA VANCOUVER

atmospheric nook that always feels like midnight. In summer, try the hidden alfresco bar out back.

Fountainhead Pub
GAY

(Map p114; ☑ 604-687-2222; www.thefountainheadpub.com; 1025 Davie St; ⊙ 11am-1am Sun-Thu, to 2am Fri & Sat; 🚍 6) The area's loudest and proudest gay neighborhood pub, this friendly joint is all about the patio, which spills onto Davie St like an overturned wine glass. Take part in the ongoing summer-evening pastime of ogling passing locals or retreat to a quieter spot inside for a few lagers or a naughty cocktail: anyone for a Porn Star or a Red Stag Sour?

Main Street Brewing
MICROBREWERY

(☑ 604-336-7711; www.mainstreetbeer.ca; 261 E 7th Ave; ⊙ 2-11pm Mon-Thu, noon-11pm Fri-Sun; 🚍 3) Tucked into an historic old brewery building, Main Street Brewing has a great, industrial-chic little tasting room and a booze roster divided into regular beers and casks. Start with a four-flight tasting sampler then dive in with a larger order. The Westminster Brown Ale is our favorite but there's usually an IPA or two worth quaffing here as well.

Diamond
COCKTAIL BAR

(Map p114; www.di6mond.com; 6 Powell St; ⊙ 5:30pm-1am Mon-Thu, to 2am Fri & Sat, to midnight Sun; 🚍 4) Head upstairs via the unassuming entrance and you'll find yourself in one of Vancouver's warmest little cocktail bars. A renovated heritage room studded with sash windows – try for a view seat – it's popular with local coolsters but is rarely pretentious. A list of perfectly nailed premium cocktails helps, coupled with a tapas menu that includes lots of Japanese-influenced options.

Fortune Sound Club
CLUB

(Map p114; ☑ 604-569-1758; www.fortunesoundclub.com; 147 E Pender St; ⊙ 9:30pm-3am Fri & Sat, plus special events; 🚍 3) Vancouver's best club has transformed a tired Chinatown spot into a slick space with the kind of genuine staff and younger, hipster-cool crowd rarely seen in Vancouver venues. Slide inside and you'll find a giant dance floor popping with party-loving locals just out for a good time. Expect weekend queues, and check out Happy Ending Fridays, when you'll possibly dance your ass off.

Keefer Bar
COCKTAIL BAR

(Map p114; ☑ 604-688-1961; www.thekeeferbar.com; 135 Keefer St; ⊙ 5pm-midnight Mon, to 1am Tue-Thu & Sun, to 2am Fri & Sat; Ⓜ Stadium-Chinatown) A dark, narrow and atmospheric Chinatown bar that's been claimed by local cocktail-loving coolsters from day one. Drop in for a full evening of liquid taste-tripping and you'll have a blast. From perfectly prepared rosemary gimlets and Siamese slippers to an excellent whiskey menu and some tasty tapas, it offers up a great night out.

★ Liberty Distillery
DISTILLERY

(Map p114; ☑ 604-558-1998; www.theliberty distillery.com; 1494 Old Bridge St; ⊙ 11am-8pm; 🚍 50) Vancouver's most attractive craft distillery has a saloon-like tasting room where you can gaze through windows at the shiny, steampunk-like booze-making equipment beyond. It's not all about looks, though. During happy hour (Monday to Thursday, 3pm to 6pm), sample house-made gin, vodka and white whiskey plus great cocktails for just $6 a pop. Tours are available ($10; Saturdays and Sundays; 11:30am and 1:30pm).

Six Acres
BAR

(Map p114; ☑ 604-488-0110; www.sixacres.ca; 203 Carrall St; ⊙ 11:30am-11:30pm Sun-Thu, to 12:30am Fri & Sat; ☎; 🚍 4) Gastown's coziest tavern; you can cover all the necessary food groups via the carefully chosen draft- and bottled-beer list here. There's a small, animated summer patio out front but inside (especially upstairs) is great for hiding in a chatty, candlelit corner and working your way through the brews – plus a shared small plate or three.

RAISE A GLASS: BC'S TOP BEERS

Fat Tug IPA Driftwood Brewery (www.driftwoodbeer.com)

Dive Bomb Porter Powell Street Craft Brewery (www.powellbeer.com)

Four Winds IPA Four Winds Brewing (www.fourwindsbrewing.ca)

Persephone Pale Ale Persephone Brewing Company (www.persephone-brewing.com)

Zunga Blonde Ale Townsite Brewing (www.townsitebrewing.com)

Red Racer India Red Ale Central City Brewers & Distillers (www.centralcitybrewing.com)

Father John's Winter Ale Howe Sound Brewing (www.howesound.com)

☆ Entertainment

You'll never run out of options if you're looking for a good time here. Vancouver is packed with activities from high- to low-brow, perfect for those craving a play one night, a soccer match the next, and a rocking live music show to follow. Ask the locals for tips and they'll likely point out grassroots happenings you never knew existed.

Live Music

★**Commodore Ballroom**   LIVE MUSIC
(Map p114; ☑604-739-4550; www.commodore ballroom.com; 868 Granville St; 🖳10) Local bands know they've made it when they play Vancouver's best mid-sized venue, a restored art deco ballroom that still has the city's bounciest dance floor – courtesy of tires placed under its floorboards. If you need a break from your moshing, collapse at one of the tables lining the perimeter, catch your breath with a bottled Stella and then plunge back in.

Rickshaw Theatre   LIVE MUSIC
(Map p114; ☑604-681-8915; www.liveatrickshaw. com; 254 E Hastings St; 🖳14) Revamped from its grungy 1970s incarnation, the funky Rickshaw shows that Eastside gentrification can be positive. The stage of choice for many punk and indie acts, it's an excellent place to see a band. There's a huge mosh area near the stage and rows of theater-style seats at the back.

Biltmore Cabaret   LIVE MUSIC
(☑604-676-0541; www.biltmorecabaret.com; 2755 Prince Edward St; 🖳9) One of Vancouver's best alt venues, the Biltmore is a firm favorite on the local indie scene. A low-ceilinged, good-vibe spot to mosh to local and touring musicians, there are also regular event nights: check the online calendar for upcoming happenings, including the hugely popular **Kitty Nights Burlesque shows** (www.kit-tynights.com), which end with a full-on DJ dance party.

Cinemas

★**Pacific Cinémathèque**   CINEMA
(Map p114; ☑604-688-3456; www.thecinema theque.ca; 1131 Howe St; tickets $11, double bills $16; 🖳10) This beloved cinema operates like an ongoing film festival with a daily-changing program of movies. A $3 annual membership is required – organize it at the door – before you can skulk in the dark with other chin-stroking movie buffs who probably named their children (or pets) after Fellini and Bergman.

Rio Theatre   CINEMA, THEATER
(☑604-879-3456; www.riotheatre.ca; 1660 E Broadway; ⑤Commercial-Broadway) Vancouver's most eclectic cinema, this restored 1980s movie house is like a community rep theater, staging everything from blockbuster and art-house movies to live music (there's an excellent sound system), improv comedy and saucy burlesque nights. Check the calendar to see what's on: the Gentlemen Heckler narrated movie screenings are recommended.

Vancity Theatre   CINEMA
(Map p114; ☑604-683-3456; www.viff.org/ theatre; 1181 Seymour St; tickets $12, double bills $18; 🖳10) The state-of-the-art headquarters of the Vancouver International Film Festival (p121) screens a wide array of movies throughout the year in the kind of auditorium that cinephiles dream of: generous legroom, wide armrests and great sight lines from each of its 175 seats. It's a place where you can watch a four-hour subtitled epic about a dripping tap and still feel comfortable.

Scotiabank Theatre   CINEMA
(Map p114; www.cineplex.com; 900 Burrard St; 🖳2) Downtown's shiny multiplex is big enough to have its own corporate sponsor and it's the most likely theater to be screening the latest must-see blockbuster. In contrast, it also shows occasional live broadcast performances from major cultural institutions such as London's National Theatre and New York's Metropolitan Opera. Drop by on Tuesdays for discounted admission.

Theater & Classical Music

★**Bard on the Beach**   PERFORMING ARTS
(Map p114; ☑604-739-0559; www.bardonthe beach.org; Vanier Park, 1695 Whyte Ave; tickets from $20-57; ☉Jun-Sep; 🖳22) Watching Shakespeare performed while the sun sets against the mountains beyond the tented stage is a Vancouver summertime highlight. There are usually three of Shakespeare's plays, plus one Bard-related work (*Rosencrantz and Guildenstern are Dead,* for example), to choose from during the run. Q&A talks are staged after Tuesday-night performances, along with regular opera, fireworks and wine-tasting nights throughout the season.

★**Cultch**   THEATER
(Vancouver East Cultural Centre; ☑604-251-1363; www.thecultch.com; 1895 Venables St; 🖳20) This once-abandoned church has been a

gathering place for performers and audiences since being officially designated as a cultural space in 1973. Following comprehensive renovations a few years back, the beloved Cultch (as everyone calls it) is now one of Vancouver's entertainment jewels, with a busy roster of local, fringe and visiting theatrical shows staging everything from spoken word to touring Ibsen productions.

Arts Club Theatre Company   THEATER
(☑604-687-1644; www.artsclub.com) Vancouver's largest, most popular and most prolific theater company, the Arts Club stages shows at three theaters around the city.

**Vancouver Symphony
Orchestra**   PERFORMING ARTS
(☑604-876-3434; www.vancouversymphony.ca) The city's orchestra plays classical and popular music concerts (think movie music) around the city and beyond. Venues range from the palatial Orpheum Theatre to large outdoor spaces in Stanley Park.

Sports

Vancouver Canucks   HOCKEY
(Map p114; ☑604-899-7400; canucks.nhl. com; Rogers Arena, 800 Griffiths Way; ⑤Stadium-Chinatown) Vancouver's National Hockey League (NHL) team toyed with fans in 2011's Stanley Cup finals before losing Game 7 to the Boston Bruins, triggering riots across the city. But love runs deep and 'go Canucks, go!' is still boomed out from a packed Rogers Arena at most games. Book your seat early or just head to a local bar for some raucous game-night atmosphere.

Vancouver Whitecaps   SOCCER
(Map p114; ☑604-669-9283; www.whitecapsfc. com; BC Place Stadium, 777 Pacific Blvd; tickets $30-150; ⊙Mar-Oct; ⓓ; ⑤Stadium-Chinatown) Using BC Place Stadium as its home, Vancouver's professional soccer team plays in North America's top-tier Major League Soccer (MLS). They've struggled a little since being promoted to the league in 2011, but have been finding their feet (useful for soccer players) in recent seasons. Save time to buy a souvenir soccer shirt to impress everyone back home.

BC Lions   FOOTBALL
(Map p114; ☑604-589-7627; www.bclions.com; BC Place Stadium, 777 Pacific Blvd; tickets from $35; ⊙Jun-Nov; ⓓ; ⑤Stadium-Chinatown) The Lions are Vancouver's team in the Canadian Football League (CFL), which is arguably more exciting than its US counterpart, the NFL.

They've had some decent showings in recent years but they haven't won the all-important Grey Cup championship since 2011. Tickets are easy to come by – unless the boys are laying into their arch enemies, the Calgary Stampeders.

🛍 Shopping

Vancouver's retail scene has developed dramatically in recent years. Hit Robson St's mainstream chains, then discover the hip, independent shops of Gastown, Main St and Commercial Dr. Granville Island is stuffed with artsy stores and studios, while South Granville and Kitsilano's 4th Ave serve up a wide range of ever-tempting boutiques.

★**Regional Assembly of Text**   ARTS & CRAFTS
(☑604-877-2247; www.assemblyoftext.com; 3934 Main St; ⊙11am-6pm Mon-Sat, noon-5pm Sun; ☑3) This ironic antidote to the digital age lures ink-stained locals with its journals, handmade pencil boxes and T-shirts printed with typewriter motifs. Check out the tiny under-the-stairs gallery showcasing zines from around the world, and don't miss the monthly **Letter Writing Club** (7pm, first Thursday of every month), where you can hammer on vintage typewriters, crafting erudite missives to your far-away loved one.

★**Paper Hound**   BOOKS
(Map p114; ☑604-428-1344; www.paperhound. ca; 344 W Pender St; ⊙10am-7pm Sun-Thu, to 8pm Fri & Sat; ☑14) Proving the printed word is alive and kicking, this small but perfectly curated bookstore opened a couple of years ago and has already become a dog-eared favorite among locals. A perfect spot for browsing your day away, you'll find tempting tomes (mostly used but some new) on everything from nature to poetry to chaos theory. Ask for recommendations: they really know their stuff here.

★**Mintage**   VINTAGE
(☑604-646-8243; www.mintagevintage.com; 1714 Commercial Dr; ⊙10am-7pm Mon-Sat, 11am-6pm Sun; ☑20) Where Drive hipsters add a little vintage glam to their look. There's a Western-saloon feel to the interior here, but don't be fooled – this is one of the city's most kaleidoscopically eclectic stores. Ladieswear dominates – you'll find everything from saris to tutus – while the menswear at the back is ideal for finding a velour leisure suit with 'matching' Kenny Rogers T-shirt.

★**Mountain Equipment
Co-Op** SPORTS & OUTDOORS
(☑604-872-7858; www.mec.ca; 130 W Broadway; ☺10am-9pm Mon-Fri, 9am-6pm Sat, 10am-6pm Sun, reduced hours off-season; ☐9) Grown hikers weep at the amazing selection of clothing, kayaks, sleeping bags and clever camping gadgets at this cavernous outdoors store: MEC has been encouraging fully fledged outdoor enthusiasts for years. You'll have to be a member to buy, but that's easy to arrange for just $5. Equipment – canoes, kayaks, camping gear etc – can be rented here.

Eastside Flea MARKET
(Map p114; www.eastsideflea.com; Ellis Building, 1014 Main St; $3; ☺6-10pm Fri, 11am-5pm Sat & Sun, third weekend of the month; ☐3) Running for years at halls around the city, the monthly Flea's new Ellis Building location means 50 new and vintage vendors, plus food trucks, live music and a highly inviting atmosphere. Arrive early so you can buy a top hat and swan around like the ironic out-of-time Victorian gentleman you've always wanted to be (bring your own waxed mustache).

John Fluevog Shoes SHOES
(Map p114; ☑604-688-6228; www.fluevog.com; 65 Water St; ☺10am-7pm Mon-Wed & Sat, to 8pm Thu & Fri, noon-6pm Sun; ⑤Waterfront) Like an art gallery for shoes, this alluringly cavernous store showcases the famed footwear of local designer Fluevog, whose men's and women's boots and brogues are what Doc Martens would have become if they'd stayed interesting and cutting-edge. Pick up that pair of thigh-hugging dominatrix boots you've always wanted or settle on some designer loafers that would make anyone walk tall.

Smoking Lily CLOTHING
(☑604-873-5459; www.smokinglily.com; 3634 Main St; ☺11am-6pm Mon-Sat, noon-5pm Sun; ☐3) Art-school-cool rules at this mostly womenswear boutique, with skirts, belts and halter-tops whimsically accented with prints of insects, narwhals and the periodic table. Anatomically correct heart motifs are also popular, appearing on shirts, jewelry and cushion covers. And there's a great array of accessories, including quirky purses and shoulder bags beloved of the local pale-and-interesting set.

★**Gallery of BC Ceramics** ARTS & CRAFTS
(Map p114; ☑604-669-3606; www.bcpotters. com; 1359 Cartwright St; ☺10:30am-5:30pm; ☐50) The star of Granville Island's arts-and-crafts shops and the public face of the Potters Guild of BC, this excellent spot exhibits and sells the striking works of its member artists. You can pick up one-of-a-kind ceramic tankards or swirly-painted soup bowls; the hot items are the cool ramen-noodle cups, complete with holes for chopsticks. It's well-priced art for everyone.

**Coastal Peoples
Fine Arts Gallery** ARTS & CRAFTS
(Map p114; ☑604-684-9222; www.coastalpeoples. com; 312 Water St; ☺10am-7pm mid-Apr–mid-Oct, to 6pm mid-Oct–mid-Apr; ⑤Waterfront) This museum-like store showcases an excellent array of Inuit and Northwest Coast aboriginal jewelry, carvings and prints. On the high-art side of things, the exquisite items here are ideal if you're looking for a very special souvenir for someone back home. Don't worry: they can ship the totem poles if you can't fit them in your suitcase.

Thomas Haas FOOD
(☑604-736-1848; www.thomashaas.com; 2539 W Broadway; ☺8am-5:30pm Tue-Sat; ☐9) This independent chocolatier is often bursting with locals purchasing its regular supplies of gourmet treats, such as caramel-pecan squares and chili-suffused bon-bons. But the stars of the glass cabinet are the choc-encased fruit jellies (raspberry ganache recommended). A good spot for Vancouver-made souvenirs like chunky chai and espresso chocolate bars.

Red Cat Records MUSIC
(☑604-708-9422; www.redcat.ca; 4332 Main St; ☺11am-7pm Mon-Thu, to 8pm Fri & Sat, to 6pm Sun; ☐3) The ideal destination to hang out on a Main St rainy day, Red Cat's wooden racks are home to a well-curated collection of new and used CDs and vinyl records in what is one of the coolest record stores in the city. It helps that it's co-owned by musicians; ask them for tips on whom to see live on the local scene.

Front & Company CLOTHING, ACCESSORIES
(☑604-879-8431; www.frontandcompany.ca; 3772 Main St; ☺11am-6:30pm; ☐3) A triple-fronted store where you could easily spend a couple of hours; the largest section here contains trendy consignment clothing (where else can you find that vintage velvet smoking jacket?). Next door houses new, knowingly cool housewares, while the third area includes must-have gifts and accessories such as manga figures, peace-sign ice trays and nihilist chewing gum (flavorless, of course).

ℹ️ Information

MEDICAL SERVICES

St Paul's Hospital (☑ 604-682-2344; 1081 Burrard St; 🚇 22) Downtown hospital for accidents and emergencies.

Shoppers Drug Mart (☑ 604-669-2424; 1125 Davie St; ⊘ 24hr; 🚇 6) Pharmacy chain.

Ultima Medicentre (☑ 604-683-8138; www.ultimamedicentre.ca; Plaza Level, Bentall Centre, 1055 Dunsmuir St; ⊘ 8am-5pm Mon-Fri; Ⓢ Burrard) Appointments not necessary.

MONEY

Vancouver Bullion & Currency Exchange (☑ 604-685-1008; www.vbce.ca; 800 W Pender St; ⊘ 9am-5pm Mon-Fri; Ⓢ Granville) Aside from the banks, try Vancouver Bullion & Currency Exchange for currency exchange. It often has a wider range of currencies and competitive rates.

POST

Howe St Postal Outlet (Map p114; ☑ 604-688-2068; 732 Davie St; ⊘ 9am-7pm Mon-Fri, 10am-5pm Sat; 🚇 6)

TOURIST INFORMATION

The **Tourism Vancouver Visitor Centre** (Map p114; ☑ 604-683-2000; www.tourismvancouver.com; 200 Burrard St; ⊘ 8:30am-5pm; Ⓢ Waterfront) is a large repository of resources for visitors, with a staff of helpful advisers ready to assist in planning your trip. Services and info available here include free maps, visitor guides, half-priced theater tickets, accommodation and tour bookings, plus a host of glossy brochures on the city and the wider BC region.

ℹ️ Getting There & Away

AIR

Canada's second-busiest airport, **Vancouver International Airport** (YVR; ☑ 604-207-7077; www.yvr.ca; 🛜) lies 13km south of downtown in the city of Richmond. There are two main terminals – international (including flights to the US) and domestic – just a short indoor stroll apart. A third (and much smaller) South Terminal is located a quick drive away; free shuttle-bus links are provided. This terminal services floatplanes, helicopters and smaller aircraft traveling on lower-capacity routes to small communities in BC and beyond. In addition, short-hop floatplane (p679) and helicopter services (p693) to and from Vancouver Island and beyond also depart from the city's downtown waterfront, near Canada Place.

The main airport has shops, food courts, currency-exchange booths and a tourist information desk. It's also dotted with handsome aboriginal artworks. Baggage carts are free (no deposit required) and there is also free wi-fi.

BOAT

BC Ferries (☑ 250-386-3431; www.bcferries.com) services arrive at Tsawwassen, an hour south of Vancouver, and at Horseshoe Bay, 30 minutes from downtown in West Vancouver. The company operates one of the world's largest ferry networks, including some spectacular routes throughout the province.

Main services to Tsawwassen arrive from Vancouver Island's Swartz Bay, near Victoria, and Duke Point, near Nanaimo. Services also arrive from the Southern Gulf Islands.

Services to Horseshoe Bay arrive from Nanaimo's Departure Bay. Services also arrive here from Bowen Island and from Langdale on the Sunshine Coast.

To depart Tsawwassen via transit, take bus 620 (adult/child $5.50/3.50) to Bridgeport Station and transfer to the Canada Line. It takes about 40 minutes to reach downtown.

From Horseshoe Bay to downtown, take bus 257 (adult/child $4/2.75, 45 minutes), which is faster than bus 250. It takes about 35 minutes.

Cruise ships, big business here from May to September, dock at downtown's Canada Place or at Ballantyne Pier, just to the east.

BUS

➤ Most intercity nontransit buses trundle to a halt at Vancouver's neon-signed **Pacific Central Station** (1150 Station St; Ⓢ Main St-Science World). It's the main arrival point for cross-Canada and transborder **Greyhound** buses (www.greyhound.com; www.greyhound.ca); cross-border budget bus services on **Bolt Bus** (www.boltbus.com); and services from Seattle and Seattle's Sea-Tac International Airport on **Quick Shuttle** (www.quickcoach.com).

➤ The station has a ticket office and left-luggage lockers, and is also the city's trans-Canada and cross-border train terminal.

➤ The Main St-Science World SkyTrain station is just across the street for connections to downtown and the suburbs.

➤ There are car-rental desks in the station and cabs are available just outside.

CAR & MOTORCYCLE

If you've rented a car in the US and are driving it into Canada, bring a copy of the rental agreement to save any possible hassles with border officials.

Gas is generally cheaper in the US, so be sure to fill up before you cross into Canada.

TRAIN

➤ **Pacific Central Station** (p136) is the city's main terminus for long-distance trains from across Canada on **VIA Rail** (www.viarail.com), and from Seattle (just south of the border) and beyond on **Amtrak** (www.amtrak.com). It's also the main arrival point for major intercity, including cross-border, bus services.

➡ The Main St-Science World SkyTrain station is just across the street for connections to downtown and beyond.

➡ There are car-rental desks in the station and cabs are also available just outside the building.

ℹ Getting Around

TO/FROM THE AIRPORT
Taxi
➡ Follow the signs from inside the airport terminal to the cab stand just outside. The fare to downtown, around 30 minutes away, will usually cost between $35 and $45, plus tip (15% is the norm).

➡ Alternatively, limo-car services are also available close to the main taxi stand. Expect to pay around $20 more for your ride to the city if you want to arrive in style.

Train
SkyTrain's 16-station **Canada Line** (see the route maps at www.translink.ca) operates a rapid-transit train service from the airport to downtown. Trains run every few minutes from early morning until after midnight and take around 25 minutes to reach downtown's Waterfront Station. The airport station is located just outside, between the domestic and international terminals. Follow the signs from inside either terminal and buy your ticket from the platform vending machines. These accept cash, and credit and debit cards – look for green-jacketed Canada Line staff if you're bleary-eyed and need assistance after your long-haul flight. Fares from the airport cost between $7.75 and $10.50, depending on your destination and the time of day.

BICYCLE
➡ Vancouver is a relatively good cycling city, with more than 300km of designated routes crisscrossing the region.

➡ Cyclists can take their bikes for free on SkyTrains, SeaBuses and transit buses, which are all now fitted with bike racks. Cyclists are required by law to wear helmets.

➡ In recent years, dedicated bike lanes have been created downtown and, in 2016, a new public bike-share scheme called **Mobi** (www. mobibikes.ca) was introduced.

➡ Pick up a free *Metro Vancouver Cycling Map* for details on area routes and bike-friendly contacts and resources – or download it via the TransLink website.

➡ If you're traveling sans bike, you can also rent wheels (often including inline skates) from businesses around the city, especially on Denman St near Stanley Park – home of Vancouver's most popular scenic cycling route.

BOAT
Operators offer day passes ($10 to $15) as well as discounted books of tickets for those making multiple water hops. Single trips cost from $3.50.

Aquabus Ferries (☑ 604-689-5858; www. theaquabus.com; adult/child from $3.50/1.75) Runs frequent minivessels (some big enough to carry bikes) between the foot of Hornby St and Granville Island. It also services several additional spots along the False Creek waterfront, as far as Science World.

False Creek Ferries (Map p114; ☑ 604-684-7781; www.granvilleislandferries.bc.ca; adult/child from $3.25/2) Operates a similar Granville Island service from Sunset Beach, and has additional ports of call around False Creek.

CAR & MOTORCYCLE
For sightseeing in the city, you'll be fine without a car (the city center is especially easy to explore on foot and transit routes are extensive). For visits that incorporate the wider region's mountains and communities, however, a vehicle makes life much simpler: the further you travel from downtown, the more limited your transit options become.

PUBLIC TRANSPORTATION
Bus
➡ Vancouver's **TransLink** (www.translink.ca) bus network is extensive. All vehicles are equipped with bike racks and all are wheelchair accessible. Exact change (or more) is required; buses use fare machines and change is not given. Fares cost adult/child $2.75/1.75 and are valid for up to 90 minutes of transfer travel. While Vancouver's transit system covers three geographic fare zones, all bus trips are regarded as one-zone fares.

➡ Bus services operate from early morning to after midnight in central areas. There is also a handy night-bus system that runs every 30 minutes between 1:30am and 4am. The last night-bus leaves downtown Vancouver at 3:09am. Look for night-bus signs at designated stops.

SeaBus
➡ The iconic SeaBus shuttle is part of the TransLink transit system (regular transit fares apply) and it operates throughout the day, taking 12 minutes to cross Burrard Inlet between Waterfront Station and Lonsdale Quay in North Vancouver. At Lonsdale you can then connect to buses servicing North Vancouver and West Vancouver; this is where you pick up bus 236 to both Capilano Suspension Bridge and Grouse Mountain.

➡ SeaBus services leave from Waterfront Station between 6:16am and 1:22am, Monday to Saturday (8:16am to 11:16pm on Sunday). Vessels are wheelchair accessible and bike-friendly.

➡ Tickets must be purchased from vending machines on either side of the route before boarding. The machines take credit and debit cards and also give change up to $20 for cash transactions.

SkyTrain

➡ TransLink's SkyTrain rapid-transit network currently consists of three routes and is a great way to move around the region, especially beyond the city center. A fourth route, the Evergreen Line, is scheduled to begin operations in 2017 and will link the suburban communities of Burnaby, Coquitlam and Port Moody.

➡ Compass tickets for SkyTrain trips can be purchased from station vending machines (change is given; machines also accept debit and credit cards) prior to boarding.

➡ SkyTrain journeys cost $2.75 to $5.50 (plus $5 more if you are traveling from the airport), depending on how far you are journeying.

TAXI

Vancouver currently does not allow Uber-type services. Try the following long-established taxi companies:

Black Top & Checker Cabs (☑ 604-731-1111; www.btccabs.ca; ☎)

Vancouver Taxi (☑ 604-871-1111; www.vancouver taxi.cab)

Yellow Cab (☑ 604-681-1111; www.yellowcab online.com; ☎)

LOWER MAINLAND

Stretching from coastal Horseshoe Bay as far inland as the verdant Fraser Valley, this region encompasses the towns and suburbs within an hour or two by car or transit from downtown Vancouver, including those communities immediately adjoining the city that together are known as Metro Vancouver. Ideal for day-tripping, the area is striped with looming mountains, forested coastal parks, wildlife sanctuaries and historic attractions.

Burnaby

Immediately east of Vancouver and accessible via SkyTrain from the city center, Burnaby is a quiet residential suburb with a half-day's worth of attractions. For information on the area, visit the **Tourism Burnaby** (☑ 604-419-0377; www.tourismburnaby.com) website.

The pathways of tranquil **Deer Lake Park** (6450 Deer Lake Park Ave) crisscross meadows and woodlands, circling a lake where birds and other wildlife hang out. In summer, it's home to the annual **Burnaby Blues + Roots Festival** (www.burnabybluesfestival.com; ⊙ Aug). The adjoining **Burnaby Village Museum** (www.burnabyvillagemuseum.ca; 6501 Deer Lake Ave; ⊙ 11am-4:30pm Tue-Sun May-Aug; ♿) **FREE** colorfully re-creates a pioneer town, complete with replica homes, businesses and a handsome 1912 carousel. To get directly there by car, take the Sperling Ave exit off Hwy 1 and follow the museum signs.

Topping Burnaby Mountain, 50-year-old **Simon Fraser University** (www.sfu.ca; 8888 University Dr; ☐ 135) is the Lower Mainland's second-biggest campus community. Small visitor attractions here include the **SFU Gallery** (☑ 778-782-4266; www.sfu.ca/galleries; ⊙ noon-5pm Tue-Fri) **FREE** and the **Museum of Archaeology & Ethnology** (☑ 778-782-3135; www.sfu.ca/archaeology/museum.html; ⊙ 10am-noon & 1-4pm Mon-Fri) **FREE**.

ⓘ Getting There & Away

TransLink's (☑ 604-953-3333; www.translink. ca) SkyTrain Expo and Millennium lines trundle from Vancouver into Burnaby every few minutes throughout the day. It's a two-zone transit hop between the two cities (two-zone fare $4).

Fort Langley

Little Fort Langley's tree-lined streets and 19th-century storefronts make it one of the Lower Mainland's most picturesque historic villages, ideal for an afternoon jaunt from Vancouver. Aside from the fort itself, cafes, boutiques and ice-cream-scoffing opportunities abound.

The highlight of a visit here is **Fort Langley National Historic Site** (☑ 604-513-4777; www.parkscanada.gc.ca/fortlangley; adult/child $7.80/3.90; ⊙ 10am-5pm; ♿), the region's most important and evocative old-school landmark.

A fortified trading post built in 1827, it's where James Douglas announced the creation of British Columbia in 1858, giving the site a legitimate claim to being the province's birthplace. With costumed reenactors, re-created artisan workshops and a gold-panning area that's a kid-friendly must-do (they also enjoy charging around the wooden battlements), it's an ideal destination for families aiming to add a little education to their trips.

If you need an introduction before you start wading into the buildings, there's a surprisingly entertaining time-travel-themed movie presentation on offer. Also check the website before arriving: there's a wide array of interpretive events and activities that bring the past to life here, including blacksmithing workshops (book ahead).

You won't go hungry in Fort Langley, where there are several enticing eateries a short stroll from the fort. But if you want to hang with the locals, drop into **Wendel's Bookstore & Cafe** (☑ 604-513-2238; www.wendelsonline.com; 9233 Glove Rd; dishes $8-14; ☺ 7:30am-10pm; 🛜 📶).

New Westminster

A short SkyTrain ride from downtown Vancouver, 'New West' is one of BC's most historic communities – it was briefly the capital of the new Colony of British Columbia in 1859. Its star faded during much of the last century but recent years have seen attempts at revival. It's easily worth a couple of hours of your time if you're looking for an accessible excursion from Vancouver.

Hop off at the New Westminster SkyTrain station and stroll downhill towards the Fraser River, where the **Waterfront Esplanade Boardwalk** includes a shoreline stroll studded with artsy flourishes and shimmering river views (looks for seals, herons and log-towing boats here).

The adjoining indoor **River Market** (☑ 604-520-3881; www.rivermarket.ca; 810 Quayside Dr; ☺ 10am-6pm) is a good lunch stop, and you'll also spot what claims to be **the world's largest tin soldier** looming over the shoreline. If you have time, nip into the **Fraser River Discovery Centre** (☑ 604-521-8401; www.fraserriverdiscovery.org; 788 Quayside Dr; suggested donation $6; ☺ 10am-4pm Jun-Aug, 10am-4pm Wed-Sat Sep-May; 📶) for the story of the mighty river flowing alongside. Then turn your back on the water and hit nearby Columbia St for the shops and historic buildings.

❶ Information

For more information on the area, connect with **Tourism New Westminster** (☑ 604-526-1905; www.tourismnewwestminster.com; 777 Columbia St; ☺ 10am-5pm Mon-Sat Jun-Sep, 10am-4pm Oct-May).

❶ Getting There & Away

Frequent **TransLink** (☑ 604-953-3333; www.translink.ca) SkyTrain services from downtown Vancouver take about 25 minutes to whisk you to New West. It's a two-zone fare ($4).

Richmond & Steveston

The region's modern-day Chinatown is easy to reach via Canada Line SkyTrain from Vancouver, making for an accessible half-day of Asian shopping malls followed by a taste-trip through Chinese, Japanese and Vietnamese restaurants. And don't miss the city's historic waterfront Steveston village – a popular destination for sunset-viewing locals with a penchant for great fish and chips, it also has a couple of great museums.

❂ Sights

Gulf of Georgia Cannery   MUSEUM
(☑ 604-664-9009; www.gulfofgeorgiacannery.org; 12138 4th Ave, Steveston; adult/child $10.20/6.30; ☺ 10am-5pm; 📶 ; Ⓜ Richmond-Brighouse, then bus 401) British Columbia's best 'industrial museum' illuminates the sights and sounds of the region's bygone era of labor-intensive fish processing. Most of the machinery remains and there's an evocative focus on the people who used to work here; you'll hear recorded testimonies from old employees percolating through the air like ghosts, bringing to life the days they spent immersed in entrails as thousands of cans rolled down the production line. Take one of the guided tours for the full story.

Britannia Shipyard   MUSEUM
(☑ 640-718-8038; www.britanniashipyard.ca; 5180 Westwater Dr, Steveston; ☺ 10am-5pm Fri-Wed, to 8pm Thu May-Sep, noon-5pm Sat & Sun Oct-Apr; Ⓜ Richmond-Brighouse, then bus 410) **FREE** A riverfront complex of historic sheds housing dusty tools, boats and reminders of the region's maritime past, this is one of the most evocative, fancy-free historic sites in the region. Check out the preserved **Murakami House**, where a large Japanese family lived before being unceremoniously interned during the war. Ask the volunteers plenty of questions: they have some great stories to tell.

Richmond Night Market   MARKET
(☑ 604-244-8448; www.richmondnightmarket.com; 8351 River Rd, Richmond; adult/child $3.25/free; ☺ 7pm-midnight Fri & Sat, to 11pm Sun mid-May–mid-Oct; Ⓢ Bridgeport) The larger of Richmond's

two Asian-flavored night markets and the easiest to reach via transit; expect to line-up for entry at this wildly popular summer tradition. Inside, you'll find the usual rows of blingy trinkets plus live entertainment and dozens of steaming, hunger-abating food stalls. Fans of fish balls, deep-fried squid and bubble tea? This is the place for you.

Panda Market   MARKET

(☑ 604-278-8000; www.pandamarket.ca; 12631 Vulcan Way, Richmond; ☺ 7pm-midnight Fri & Sat, to 11pm Sun May–mid-Sep; 🚍 407) **FREE** Originally known as the International Summer Night Market, thousands of hungry locals are lured here every weekend to check out the tacky vendor stands and – more importantly – the dozens of hawker food stalls. Don't eat before arriving and you can taste-trip through steaming Korean, Japanese and Chinese treats. Do not miss the spiral fried potatoes on sticks.

Richmond Olympic Oval   STADIUM

(☑ 778-296-1409; www.richmondoval.ca; 611 River Rd, Richmond; ☺ 6am-11pm; skytrain, 🚍 Brighouse, then 🚍 C94) The biggest new venue built for the 2010 Winter Olympics (it hosted long-track speed skating), this riverfront behemoth has since become a community sports facility shared by locals around the region. The five rings haven't been forgotten, though: the on-site **Richmond Olympic Experience** (www.therox.ca) offers a host of simulator experiences enabling you to pretend you won your own medal.

International
Buddhist Temple   BUDDHIST TEMPLE

(☑ 604-274-2822; www.buddhisttemple.ca; 9160 Steveston Hwy, Richmond; ☺ 9:30am-5:30pm; 🚍 403, 🚇 Richmond-Brighouse) **FREE** The highlight of this classical Chinese temple complex is the sumptuous Gracious Hall, complete with deep-red exterior walls and a gently flaring porcelain roof. Check out the colorful 100m Buddha mural and the golden, multi-armed Bodhisattva figure. The landscaped garden, with sculptures and bonsai trees, is another highlight. You don't have to be a Buddhist to visit and the monks are highly welcoming if you're keen to have a look around.

✖️ Eating

⭐ Pajo's   SEAFOOD $

(☑ 604-272-1588; www.pajos.com; The Wharf, Steveston; mains $9-16; ☺ 11am-7pm; skytrain, 🚇 Richmond-Brighouse, then 🚍 401) There's

no better spot to enjoy fish and chips than Steveston's boat-bobbing wharf. Follow your nose and descend the ramp to the little ordering hatch here and you'll be greeted by a friendly face and a menu more extensive than your average chippy. Go the traditional fresh fried cod, salmon or halibut route (with secret-recipe tartar sauce), adding mushy peas for the full effect.

Parker Place   FOOD COURT $

(☑ 604-273-0276; www.parkerplace.com; 4380 No 3 Rd, Richmond; mains $5-10; ☺ 11am-7pm Sun-Thu, to 9pm Fri & Sat; 🚇; 🚇 Aberdeen) There are several popular Asian shopping malls in Richmond, but while Aberdeen Centre and Lansdowne Centre are bigger, Parker Place has an authentic-feeling food court that evokes a Singaporean hawker market. It's beloved of Asian-Canadian locals. Dive in for good-value noodle, fish-ball and dragon's-beard candy dishes; buy a few plates and share 'em at your table.

Shibuyatei   RAMEN $

(☑ 778-297-1777; 2971 Sexsmith Rd, Richmond; mains $7-14; ☺ 11:30am-2pm & 5pm-9pm Mon-Sat) Inauspiciously located next to a car wash, this tiny, local-favorite hole-in-the-wall serves sushi but it's really all about great ramen bowls (with no MSG) and tasty Japanese curries, served with chicken or pork *katsu* (deep-fried). It's a one-man operation so avoid peak times if you don't want to wait too long.

Shanghai River Restaurant   CHINESE $$

(☑ 604-233-8885; 7381 Westminster Hwy, Richmond; mains $10-22; ☺ 11am-3pm & 5:30-10pm; 🚇 Richmond-Brighouse) Grab a seat at the kitchen window at this cavernous northern Chinese eatery and you'll be mesmerized by the handiwork that goes into folding some of the area's best dim-sum dumplings. Order plates to share – one dish per person is the usual ratio – and be careful not to squirt everyone with the juicy pork or shrimp dumplings.

Sushi Hachi   SUSHI $$

(☑ 604-207-2882; 8888 Odlin Cres, Richmond; rmains $8-22; ☺ 6pm-9pm Mon-Sat; 🚇 Aberdeen) An authentic, fancy-free mom-and-pop operation serving top-notch *nigiri* (raw fish or seafood on a rice ball) and sashimi to in-the-know locals, this place isn't like the hundreds of other similar-sized sushi joints in the region. Call ahead for a reservation and you'll soon be tucking into delectable flounder, octopus and jack mackerel. Add some sake for the full effect.

🛍 Shopping

Daiso DEPARTMENT STORE
(☑604-295-6601; www.daisocanada.com; 4151 Hazelbridge Way, Aberdeen Centre; ⊙9:30am-9pm; ⑤Aberdeen) Canada's first (and so far only) branch of Japan's favorite discount store has a cult-like following in Metro Vancouver. A visit to the large, two-floor store is as much a cultural exploration as a chance to buy temptingly low-priced stationery, rice bowls and Ultraman-type action figures, plus odd-ball plastic items that seem unfathomable, some of them adorned with hilarious 'Japanese English' slogans.

YVR Thrift Store THRIFT STORE
(www.yvrchaplain.com/thrift-store; 4871 Miller Rd, Vancouver International Airport; ⊙noon-5pm Fri; ⓂYVR-Airport) If you're at Vancouver International Airport with a spare hour, it's a 10-minute stroll from the terminal to this unusual thrift store. Wondering what happens to those scissors and nail clippers confiscated at airport security – not to mention the books and sweaters (and a stroller, on our visit) passengers leave behind before jetting in or out? This is their final resting place.

ℹ Information

For information on both areas, drop into the **Tourism Richmond Visitor Centre** (☑604-271-8280; www.tourismrichmond.com; 3811 Moncton St, Steveston; ⊙9:30am-6pm Jul-Aug, 9:30-5pm Mon-Sat & noon-4pm Sun Sep-Jun; ᗺ402).

ℹ Getting There & Away

TransLink's (☑604-953-3333; www.translink. ca) Canada Line SkyTrains trundle in from Vancouver every few minutes throughout the day. The service splits at Bridgeport Station, with some trains heading to the airport and others winding further into Richmond; make sure you're on the right one. Transit buses (including those to Steveston) connect to the Canada Line at Bridgeport and other stations.

BOWEN ISLAND

One of the best days out you can have from Vancouver – it's just a 20-minute boat hop from Horseshoe Bay but it feels a million miles from downtown – Bowen is like British Columbia in miniature. That means a sigh-triggering ferry ride to **Snug Cove**, a cute, village-like settlement with lots of quirky locals and lashings of outdoorsy appeal.

Stroll the Snug Cove boardwalks and drink-in the old-school ambience of dozens of wooden cottages and Tudor-look buildings. On weekends throughout July and August, there's an arts, crafts and food **market** to keep things lively. If you miss it, climb the fairly steep hill to **Artisan Square** for a loop of clapboard galleries and boutique shops – including **Cocoa West Chocolatier** (☑604-947-2996; www.cocoawest.com; 581C Artisan Ln; ⊙10am-5pm May-Sep, reduced hours off-season).

Visitors used to roll in here by steamship in the 1920s and 1930s; you can hear all about these halcyon days on a fascinating excursion with **Bowen Island Tours** (☑604-812-5041; www.bowenislandtours.com; tours from adult/child $25/12). Alternatively, explore the breathtaking woodland trails of **Crippen Regional Park** and **Killarney Lake** – see www.bowentrails.ca for tips. Look out for Opa, the island's grandest old-growth tree, said to be centuries old, or hit the water with **Bowen Island Sea Kayaking** (☑604-947-9266; www.bowenislandkayaking.com; Bowen Island Marina, Snug Cove; rentals/tours from $45/$75; ⊙Apr-Sep).

Plans for a hotel have been under discussion for years but there are several cool accommodation options on Bowen. Chocolate fans should consider the swish suite at Cocoa West Chocolatier, complete with a tasty welcome pack on your pillow. Alternatively, some of the old **Union Steamship Marina** (☑604-947-0707; www.ussc.ca; Snug Cove; d from $180; 🐾) cottages and buildings have been renovated as unique sleepovers; see their website for options.

A short stroll from the ferry, you'll find **Doc Morgan's Restaurant & Pub** (☑604-947-0808; 437 Bowen Island Trunk Rd; mains $16-22; ⊙noon-11pm Sun-Fri, 10-1am Sat).

ℹ Information

Drop into the **visitors center** (☑604-200-2399; www.tourismbowenisland.com; 432 Cardena Rd; ⊙9am-4pm mid-May–Sep), just steps from the ferry dock, for insider tips.

ℹ Getting There & Away

Take a **TransLink** (☑604-953-3333; www. translink.ca) transit bus from downtown Vancouver – the 257 express bus is best – and you'll be at the Horseshoe Bay **BC Ferries** (☑250-386-3431; www.bcferries.com) terminal in around 40 minutes. Ferry services depart from here to Bowen Island's Snug Cove throughout the day (adult/child/car $12.35/6.20/34.85, 20 minutes, 12 daily).

SEA TO SKY HIGHWAY

Otherwise known as Hwy 99, this breath-takingly picturesque cliffside roadway links a string of communities between West Van-couver and Lillooet and is the main route to Squamish and Whistler from Metro Vancouver. Upgraded in recent years, the winding road has several worthwhile stops – especially if you're an outdoor activity fan, history buff or lover of British Columbia's eye-poppingly scenic vistas.

❶ Getting There & Away

Most travelers visiting this area from Vancouver are driving via Hwy 99, which handily links the city to Squamish, Whistler and beyond. Intercity bus services ply the same route, including **Greyhound Canada** (www.greyhoundcanada.ca) and **Pacific Coach Lines** (☑604-662-7575; www.pacificcoach.com). If you're driving, tune into Mountain Radio (107.1FM) for handy traffic and road-condition updates.

Squamish & Around

An hour north of Vancouver and another hour to Whistler, Squamish sits at the meeting point of ocean, river and alpine forest. Originally just a grungy logging town, it's now a popular base for outdoor activities and is also a hub for top attractions nearby.

◉ Sights

Sea to Sky Gondola   GONDOLA
(☑604-892-2551; www.seatoskygondola.com; 36800 Hwy 99, Squamish; adult/child $40/14; ⊙10am-6pm daily May-Oct, to 8pm Fri & Sat May-Sep, reduced hours in winter) The biggest new Squamish-area attraction to open in years, this popular eco lure whisks visitors up the tree-studded mountainside then serves up a rich slab of breathtaking BC scenery from its summit viewing platforms. Once you've depleted your camera batteries snapping the Howe Sound vistas, shimmy over the lofty suspension bridge and check out the bird-lined forest trails and view-hugging restaurant. There are free **nature tours** in summer while winter visitors can access activities from **snow tubing** to backcountry snowshoeing.

Britannia Mine Museum   MUSEUM
(☑604-896-2260; www.britanniaminemuseum.ca; Hwy 99, Britannia Beach; adult/child $29/18.50; ⊙9am-5pm; ⚑) Once the British Empire's largest copper mine, this giant and superbly restored industrial museum is just 10 min-utes before Squamish on Hwy 99. The rattling underground train tour is highly recommended (included with entry) and there are plenty of kid-friendly exhibits, including hands-on gold panning. You'll never moan about your boss again as you discover just how grim it was to work a *real* job back in the day. Save time for the gift shop and a sparkly pyrite souvenir.

West Coast Railway Heritage Park   MUSEUM
(☑604-898-9336; www.wcra.org; 39645 Government Rd, Squamish; adult/child $18/13; ⊙10am-5pm; ⚑) Train nuts should continue just past central Squamish to this large, mostly alfresco museum that's lined with clapboard buildings and dozens of historic locomo-tives and carriages – including BC's legend-ary Royal Hudson steam engine, housed in the purpose-built Roundhouse. Spend time chatting to the volunteers – many are re-tired railway operators with lots of stories to share – and don't miss the old walk-through mail train. Check ahead for kid-friendly spe-cial events, particularly during Christmas and school holidays.

Garibaldi Provincial Park   PARK
(www.bcparks.ca; Hwy 99) Outdoorsy types should make a beeline for this 1950 sq km park, justly renowned for hiking trails colored by diverse flora, abundant wildlife and panoramic wilderness vistas. Summer hikers seem magnetically drawn here but the trails also double as cross-country ski routes in winter. There are five main trail areas – directions to each are marked by the blue-and-white signs you'll see off Hwy 99. Among the park's most popular trails, the **Cheakamus Lake hike** (3km) is relatively easy, with minimal elevation.

Stawamus Chief Provincial Park   PARK
(www.bcparks.ca; Hwy 99, Squamish) On the way into Squamish from Vancouver, you'll see a sheer, 652m-high granite rock face looming ahead. Attracting hardy climbers, it's called the 'Chief' and it's the highlight of Stawamus Chief Provincial Park. You don't have to gear up to experience the summit's breathtaking vistas: there are hiking routes up the back for anyone who wants to have a go. Consider Squamish Rock Guides (p143) for climbing assistance or lessons.

Shannon Falls Provincial Park   WATERFALL
(www.bcparks.ca; Hwy 99, Squamish) About 4km before you reach Squamish, you'll hear the

rushing waters of Shannon Falls Provincial Park. Pull into the parking lot and stroll the short trail to BC's third-highest waterfall, where water cascades down a 335m drop. A few picnic tables make this a lovely spot for an alfresco lunch.

Gillespie's Fine Spirits   DISTILLERY
(☑604-390-1122; www.gillespiesfinespirits.com; 38918 Progress Way, Squamish; ⊙noon-6pm Fri-Sun, Mon-Thu by appointment) Fiendishly well-hidden in an industrial area, this friendly little micro-distillery is worth the search. Drop by for Saturday or Sunday tours (2pm) or roll up to the tasting bar and grab one of their housemade gin, vodka and liqueurs – served in mismatched thrift-store glasses (3 samples for $5). Check their Facebook feed for evening lounge openings and bookable cocktail classes.

Brandywine Falls Provincial Park   PARK
(www.bcparks.ca; Hwy 99) A few kilometers north of Squamish and adjacent to Hwy 99, the focus of this tree-lined 143-hectare park is its spectacular 70m waterfall. A short stroll through the forest leads to a leg-jelly-lying platform overlooking the top of the falls, where water drops suddenly out of the trees like a giant faucet. A 7km looped trail leads further through the dense forest and ancient lava beds to **Cal-Cheak Suspension Bridge.**

🏃 Activities

Sea to Sky Air   SCENIC FLIGHTS
(☑604-898-1975; www.seatoskyair.ca; Squamish Airport, Squamish; from $109; ⊙9am-6pm Apr-Oct, to 5pm Thu-Sun & Tue Nov-Mar) Running a series of small airplane tours from the town's forest-fringed little airport, the friendly folk here will soon have you snapping photos over snow-peaked valleys and glittering glacier-fed lakes. But the best option is the Introductory Flight Experience ($199), where you'll start with a runway plane inspection, shimmy up into the sky alongside the pilot and then take the controls.

Squamish Spit   OUTDOORS
(Squamish) If you prefer to travel under your own steam, the Squamish Spit is a popular kiteboarding (and windsurfing) hot spot; the season runs from May to October. The **Squamish Windsports Society** (www.squamishwindsports.com) is your first point of contact for weather and water conditions and information on access to the spit.

WORTH A TRIP

KAOHAM SHUTTLE

One of British Columbia's smallest trains trundles locals and visitors through arguably the province's most scenic short rail journey. Call ahead to book your spot on the two-car **Kaoham Shuttle** (☑250-259-8300; www.tsalalh.net/shuttle.html; round-trip $10), especially in summer when the 30 seats fill up quickly. Aim for the Friday service, which is more feasible for day tripping. Then drive on Hwy 99 past Pemberton to Lillooet Station to hop abroad. It's less than two hours to **Seton Portage** and back but on the way you'll be immersed in spectacular lake and mountain views and frequent opportunities for wildlife-watching, often including bears, bighorn sheep and grouse skittering across the tracks ahead. The best part? It costs just $10 round-trip.

Squamish Rock Guides   CLIMBING
(☑604-892-7816; www.squamishrockguides.com; guided rock climbs half-day/day from $85/135) This outfit provides guided climbs and lessons for the Stawamus Chief Provincial Park (p142).

🛏 Sleeping & Eating

Alice Lake Provincial Park   CAMPGROUND $
(www.discovercamping.ca; Hwy 99, Brackendale; campsites $35) This large, family-friendly campground, 13km north of Squamish, has more than 100 sites. There are two shower buildings with flush toilets, and campers often indulge in activities like swimming, hiking and biking (rentals available). Consider an interpretive ranger tour through the woods (July and August only). Reserve far ahead; this is one of BC's most popular campgrounds.

Sunwolf   CABIN $$
(☑604-898-1537; www.sunwolf.net; 70002 Squamish Valley Rd, Brackendale; d $150; 🖗🖩) This idyllic place – with a clutch of 10 comfortable, well-maintained riverside cabins along a forested riverbank – is the perfect tranquility break from the city. Bald eagles flying overhead are common, while additional attractions include popular rafting excursions and a gabled on-site cafe that lures in-the-know locals – sit outside under a tree and feast on the area's best breakfast or brunch.

Howe Sound Inn   INN $$
(☑604-892-2603; www.howesoundinn.com; 37801 Cleveland Ave, Squamish; d $129; 🖗) Quality rustic

is the approach at this comfortable inn-style accommodation, where the rooms are warm and inviting with plenty of woodsy touches. Recover from your climbing escapades at the Stawamus Chief via the property's popular sauna – or just head to the downstairs **brewpub**. It serves some of BC's best housemade beers; inn guests can request free brewery tours.

Even if you're not staying, it's worth stopping in at the restaurant here for great pub grub with a gourmet twist.

Galileo Coffee Company CAFE **$**
(☑604-896-0272; www.galileocoffee.com; 173 Hwy 99; baked goods from $4; ☺6am-3pm Mon-Fri, 7am-3pm Sat & Sun) Across from the entrance to Britannia Mine Museum (p142), Galileo Coffee is everyone's favorite java pit stop en route to Whistler.

❶ Information

Head to the slick visitors center, named the **Squamish Adventure Centre** (☑604-815-5084; www.exploresquamish.com; 38551 Loggers Lane, Squamish; ☺8am-8pm; 🛜), to see what's on offer. It's crammed with good info on hiking and biking trails in the area.

❶ Getting There & Away

Greyhound Canada (www.greyhound.ca) buses arrive in Squamish from Vancouver ($16, 65 minutes, two daily) and Whistler ($12, 70 minutes, two daily). The more salubrious **Pacific Coach Lines** (☑604-661-1725; www.pacificcoach.com) buses also arrive here from downtown Vancouver ($60, 70 minutes, up to six daily). But ask the locals and they'll tell you they take the comfortable **Squamish Connector** (☑604-802-2119; www.squamishconnector.com) minibus shuttle between here and Vancouver ($25, one hour, two daily).

WHISTLER

POP 10,300

Named for the furry marmots that populate the area and whistle like deflating balloons, this gabled alpine village and 2010 Olympics venue is one of the world's most popular ski resorts. Nestled in the formidable shadow of the Whistler and Blackcomb Mountains, the village has a frosted, Christmas-card look in winter. But summer visitors now outnumber their ski-season equivalents, with many lured by the area's scenic hiking, biking and thrill-popping outdoor adventures. It's surprisingly easy to get lost walking around the labyrinthine little village but you're unlikely to find yourself too far from your destination once you turn around the next corner.

◉ Sights

★ **Audain Art Museum** GALLERY
(Map p146; ☑604-962-0413; www.audainartmuseum.com; 4350 Blackcomb Way; adult/child $18/free; ☺10am-5pm Sat-Mon & Wed, to 9pm Thu & Fri) BC's finest new art museum is housed in a dramatic angular building that's a landmark in itself. But inside is even better. The rooms display a jaw-dropping array of historic First Nations carvings followed by iconic paintings of the region by leading artists from Emily Carr to EJ Hughes. There's also a strong commitment to contemporary work, with sparkling photoconceptualist images by Jeff Wall, Rodney Graham et al. The final rooms showcase eye-popping modern First Nations works to great effect.

Peak 2 Peak Gondola GONDOLA
(☑604-967-8950; www.whistlerblackcomb.com/discover/360-experience; 4545 Blackcomb Way; adult/teen/child $57/50/29; ☺10am-4:45pm) Built to link the area's two main mountaintops, this record-breaking engineering marvel gently eases goggle-eyed passengers along a lofty 4.4km gondola ride that takes around 11 minutes to complete. En route, you'll be mesmerized by the unfolding panorama of forest-snow-and-peak vistas – especially if you snag one of the two glass-bottomed cars. Equally popular in summer and winter.

Whistler Museum & Archives MUSEUM
(Map p146; ☑604-932-2019; www.whistlermuseum.org; 4333 Main St; suggested donation $5; ☺11am-5pm, to 9pm Thu) Tucked into an anonymous green shed behind the library building and tracing Whistler development from wilderness outpost to Olympic resort, this great little museum has quirky exhibits that include an original 1965 ski lift gondola and a 2010 Olympic torch. New exhibitions were being planned in mid-2016, as well as a hoped-for larger venue. Check ahead for events and add one of their area walking tours in summer (by donation; 1pm daily, from June to August).

Squamish Lil'wat Cultural Centre MUSEUM
(☑604-964-0990; www.slcc.ca; 4584 Blackcomb Way; adult/child $18/8; ☺9:30am-5pm Apr-Sep, 10am-5pm Tue-Sun Oct-Mar) This handsome, wood-beamed facility showcases two quite different First Nations groups – one coastal

and one interior-based. Take a tour for the vital context behind the museum-like exhibits and keep your eyes open for on-site artist demonstrations during the summer, when there are also Tuesday-night barbecue dinners. If you miss it, the on-site cafe serves tasty bannock tacos while the recently-expanded gift shop offers an excellent array of BC-made arts and crafts.

🏃 Activities

Skiing & Snowboarding

Comprising 37 lifts and crisscrossed with over 200 runs, the **Whistler-Blackcomb** (☑ 604-967-8950; www.whistlerblackcomb.com; 2-day winter lift ticket adult/child $258/129) sister mountains are also physically linked by the resort's mammoth 4.4km Peak 2 Peak Gondola (p144). It takes just 11 minutes to shuttle wide-eyed powder hogs between the two high-alpine areas, so you can hit the slopes on both mountains on the same day.

More than half the resort's runs are aimed at intermediate-level skiers, and the season typically runs from late November to April on Whistler and November to June on Blackcomb – December to February is the peak for both.

You can beat the crowds with an early-morning (upload is between 7:15am and 8am) Fresh Tracks ticket ($20), available in advance at Whistler Village Gondola Guest Relations. Coupled with your regular lift ticket, it gets you an extra hour on the slopes and the ticket includes buffet breakfast at the Roundhouse Lodge up top.

Snowboard fans should also check out the freestyle terrain parks, mostly located on Blackcomb, including the **Snow Cross** and the **Big Easy Terrain Garden**. There's also the popular **Habitat Terrain Park** on Whistler.

If you didn't bring you own gear, **Mountain Adventure Centres** (☑ 604-967-8950; www.whistlerblackcomb.com/rentals; ◷ 8am-5pm) has several equipment rental outlets around town. It offers online reservations – choose your favorite gear before you arrive – as well as lessons for ski and snowboard first-timers.

Cross-country Skiing & Snowshoeing

A pleasant stroll or free shuttle bus away from the village, **Lost Lake** (☑ 604-905-0071; www.crosscountryconnection.ca; day pass adult/child $20/10; ◷ 8am-8pm mid-Dec–Mar) is the hub for 25km of wooded cross-country ski trails, suitable for novices and experts alike. Around 4km of the trail is lit for additional

nighttime skiing and there's a handy 'warming hut' providing lessons and equipment rentals. Snowshoers are also well served in this area: you can stomp off on your own on 15km of trails or rent equipment and guides.

Southwest of the village via Hwy 99, **Whistler Olympic Park** (☑ 604-964-0060; www.whistlersportlegacies.com; 5 Callaghan Valley Rd, Callaghan Valley; park access per vehicle weekdays/weekends $10/15) is a pristine, snow-swathed venue that hosted several 2010 Olympic Nordic events. Now perfect for visiting (and local) snowshoers and cross-country skiers, it has more than 130km of marked trails. In summer, it's also popular with hikers and bikers.

Mountain Biking

Colonizing the melted ski slopes in summer and accessed via lifts at the village's south end, **Whistler Mountain Bike Park** (☑ 604-967-8950; http://bike.whistlerblackcomb.com; 1-day lift ticket adult/child $59/35; ◷ May-Oct) offers barreling downhill runs and an orgy of jumps and bridges twisting through well-maintained forested trails. Luckily, you don't have to be a bike courier to stand the knee-buckling pace: easier routes are marked in green, while blue intermediate trails and black-diamond advanced paths are offered if you want to **Crank It Up** – the name of one of the most popular routes.

Outside the park area, regional trails include **Comfortably Numb** (a tough 26km with steep climbs and bridges); **A River Runs Through It** (suitable for all skill levels, it has teeter-totters and log obstacles); and the gentle **Valley Trail**, an easy 14km loop that encircles the village and its lake, meadow and mountain chateau surroundings – this is recommended for first-timers.

Hiking

With more than 40km of flower-and-forest alpine trails, most accessed via the Whistler Village Gondola, the region is ideal for those who like nature of the strollable variety. Favorite routes include the **High Note Trail** (8km), which traverses pristine meadows and has stunning views of the blue-green waters of Cheakamus Lake. Free route maps are available at the Whistler Visitors Centre (p151). Guided hikes are also offered by the friendly folk at **Mountain Skills Academy & Adventures** (Map p146; ☑ 604-938-9242; www.mountainskillsacademy.com; 4368 Main St; ◷ 8am-7pm reduced hrs off-season), who can also help with rock-climbing excursions.

Whistler

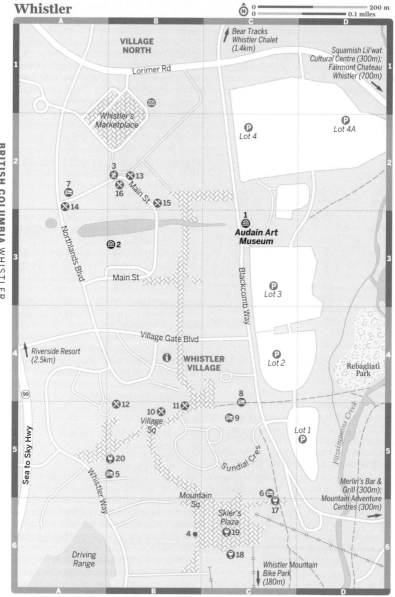

N 0 — 200 m
0 — 0.1 miles

VILLAGE NORTH

↑ Bear Tracks Whistler Chalet (1.4km)

Lorimer Rd

Squamish Lil'wat Cultural Centre (300m); Fairmont Chateau Whistler (700m) →

Whistler's Marketplace

P Lot 4

P Lot 4A

3
7
13
16
Main St
14

1
Audain Art Museum

2

Main St

Blackcomb Way

P Lot 3

Village Gate Blvd

↑ Riverside Resort (2.5km)

WHISTLER VILLAGE

P Lot 2

Rebagliati Park

Sea to Sky Hwy

99

12
10
Village Sq
11

8
9

Northlands Blvd

Sundial Cres

P Lot 1

Fitzsimmons Creek

20
5

Whistler Way

Mountain Sq

6
17

Merlin's Bar & Grill (300m); Mountain Adventure Centres (300m) →

Driving Range

4
Skier's Plaza
19

18

↓ Whistler Mountain Bike Park (180m)

Rafting

Tumbling waterfalls, dense forests and a menagerie of wildlife are some of what you might see as you lurch along the roiling stretches of local rivers on an adrenaline-charged rafting trip. **Wedge Rafting** (Map p146; ☎ 604-932-7171; www.wedgerafting. com; 4293 Mountain Sq; tours adult/child from $99/69; 🚣) offers paddle-like-crazy excursions, plus more gentler jaunts that are popular with kids.

Whistler

⚒ Festivals & Events

Winterpride   LGBT
(www.gaywhistler.com; ☉Jan) A week of gay-friendly snow action and late-night partying.

World Ski & Snowboard Festival   SPORTS
(www.wssf.com; ☉Apr) A multi-day showcase of pro ski and snowboard competitions, plus partying.

Crankworx   SPORTS
(www.crankworx.com; ☉Aug) An adrenaline-filled celebration of bike stunts, speed contests and mud-splattered shenanigans.

Cornucopia   FOOD & DRINK
(www.whistlercornucopia.com; ☉Nov) Bacchanalian food and wine fest crammed with parties.

⊨ Sleeping

Winter, especially December and January, is the peak for prices, but last-minute deals are still possible if you're planning an impromptu overnight from Vancouver – check the website of **Tourism Whistler** (www.whistler.com) for room sales and packages. Most hotels extort parking fees of up to $40 daily and some also slap on resort fees, so confirm these before you book.

HI Whistler Hostel   HOSTEL $
(☑604-962-0025;   www.hihostels.ca/whistler; 1035 Legacy Way; dm/r $37/97; @☎) Built as athlete accommodation for the 2010 Winter Olympics, this sparkling hostel is 7km south of the village, near Function Junction. Transit buses to/from town stop right outside. Book ahead for private rooms (with ensuite

bathrooms and TVs) or save by staying in a small dorm. Eschewing the sometimes institutionalized HI hostel feel, this one has IKEA-style furnishings, art-lined walls and a licensed cafe.

Riverside Resort   CAMPGROUND, CABIN $$
(☑604-905-5533; www.whistlercamping.com; 8018 Mons Rd; campsites/yurts/cabins $35/119/219; ☎☯) Just a few minutes past Whistler on Hwy 99, this facility-packed, family-friendly campground and RV park has elevated itself in recent years by adding cozy cabin and yurt options. The yurts come with basic furnishings, electricity and bedding provided, and are especially recommended. The resort's on-site Riverside Junction Cafe serves great breakfasts. Yurts and cabins have a two-night minimum stay.

Whistler Peak Lodge   HOTEL $$
(Map p146; ☑604-938-0878; www.whistlerpeaklodge.com; 4295 Blackcomb Way; d from $240; ☎) Brilliantly located in the heart of the village, this former Holiday Inn has been upgraded but still has some of the best rates in town (if you book far enough ahead). There's a wide array of rooms available but full kitchen or kitchenette facilities are standard – you're steps from many restaurants if you're feeling too lazy to cook.

Bear Tracks Whistler Chalet   B&B $$
(☑604-932-4187; www.beartrackswhistler.ca; 7461 Ambassador Crs; d from $130; ℗☎) A short walk from the village, this Bavarian-look B&B has several bright and sunny rooms – think pine furnishings and crisp white duvets – plus a garden that's ideal for a spot of

BRITISH COLUMBIA WHISTLER

FUNCTION JUNCTION

Take bus number 1 southbound from the village and within 20 minutes you'll be in the heart of a favorite locals' neighborhood. **Function Junction** started life as a hidden-among-the-trees area where industrial businesses carried on without affecting the village's Christmas-card visuals. But things have changed in recent years and many of its industrial units have given way to galleries and cafes.

The are a couple of streets to explore, but the best is **Millar Creek Rd**. Start with some bakery treats at **Purebread** (604-983-3013; www.purebread.ca; 1040 Millar Creek Rd; baked goods $3-6; ⊙ 8:30am-5pm), then nip across to **Whistler Brewing Company** (604-962-8889; www.whistlerbeer.com; 1045 Millar Creek Rd; tours $16; ⊙ 1-8pm Mon-Thu, to 10pm Fri, noon-7pm Sat & Sun). The area's very own beer maker is responsible for challenging the choke hold of factory-made suds at bars in the village. You can take a tour of the facilities and try a few brews in the taproom; with any luck, the sought-after Chestnut Ale will be available. For more options and information, visit the handy www.shopfunction.ca website.

evening wine quaffing. Or you can just hop in the hot tub and dream about the large breakfast coming your way in the morning.

Pinnacle Hotel Whistler HOTEL $$
(Map p146; 604-938-3218; www.whistlerpinnacle.com; 4319 Main St; d from $240; ⊙ ⊛ ⊠ ⊛) Just across the street from the museum, this friendly, well-established, adult-oriented lodge has the perfect extra in almost every room: a large, jetted soaker tub that dominates proceedings. Balconies and full kitchens are also de rigueur and there's an on-site restaurant if it's too cold to stray far from your room.

Adara Hotel BOUTIQUE HOTEL $$
(Map p146; 604-905-4009; www.adarahotel.com; 4122 Village Green; r from $209; ⊙ ⊛ ⊠ ⊛) Unlike all those lodges now claiming to be boutique hotels, the sophisticated and very centrally located Adara is the real deal. Studded with designer details, including a mod circular sofa in the lobby, it offers accommodations with spa-like bathrooms and fireplaces that look like TVs. Despite the ultra-cool aesthetics, service is warm and relaxed. Check ahead for packages and off-season deals.

Whistler Village Inn & Suites HOTEL $$
(Map p146; 604-932-4004; www.whistlervillageinnandsuites.com; 4429 Sundial Pl; d $189; ⊙ ⊠ ⊛) Superbly located in the heart of the village action, just a few steps from the Whistler Village Gondola, this comfy 1980s-stye hotel has been renovated in recent years and now offers a wide range of accommodation options. The studios and standard rooms are fine, but the loft suites

are the way to go with their contemporary furnishings and handy kitchenettes.

Nita Lake Lodge BOUTIQUE HOTEL $$$
(604-966-5700; www.nitalakelodge.com; 2135 Lake Placid Rd; d from $240; ⊙ ⊛) Adjoining the handsome Creekside railway station, this swanky timber-framed lodge is perfect for a pampering retreat. Hugging the lakeside, the chic but cozy rooms feature individual patios, rock fireplaces and bathrooms with heated floors and large tubs; some also have handy kitchens. Creekside lifts are a walkable few minutes away and there's an on-site spa to soothe your aching muscles.

The hotel also has an excellent West Coast restaurant but a free shuttle can whisk you to the village if you want to dine further afield.

Pan Pacific Whistler Mountainside HOTEL $$$
(Map p146; 604-905-2999; www.panpacific.com; 4320 Sundial Cres; d from $240; ⊛ ⊙ ⊠) One of Whistler's two Pan Pacifics, the Mountainside wins for its slope-hugging views of the skiers swishing down to the base of Whistler Mountain. Rooms are apartment-style and comfortable with full kitchens and cozy fireplaces, but for many the (heated) outdoor swimming pool, with its surrounding vista of snow-capped peaks, is a key lure.

Eating

★ **Purebread** BAKERY $
(Map p146; 604-962-1182; www.purebread.ca; 4338 Main St; baked goods $3-6; ⊙ 8:30am-5:30pm) When this Function Junction legend finally opened a village branch, the locals came running and they've been

queuing ever since. They're here for the cornucopia of drool-worthy bakery treats, including salted caramel bars, sour-cherry choc-chip cookies and the amazing Crack, a naughtily gooey shortbread cookie bar. There's savory here, too; go for the hearty homity or pudgie pie.

Peaked Pies
AUSTRALIAN $
(Map p146; ☑604-962-4115; www.peakedpies. com; 4369 Main St; mains $7-13; ⊙8am-9pm) A chatty little nook that's very busy at mealtimes (takeout recommended), this is the place to dive into Australia's age-old pie infatuation. Check the glass cabinet for the day's available offerings – kangaroo is included but the butter chicken is our favorite – and 'peak it' with added toppings of mashed potato, mushy peas and gravy. Add a lamington cake dessert for the full Aussie effect.

La Cantina Urban Taco Bar
MEXICAN $
(Map p146; ☑604-962-9950; www.tacoslacantina. ca; 4340 Lorimer Rd; mains $8-14; ⊙11am-9pm) A busy corner eatery where you order at the counter and then grab a perch (the high stools down the side usually have some empty spots), aim for a selection of $3 tacos or dive into a bulging burrito if you're really hungry. This place gets jam-packed at peak times so consider a takeout rather than resorting to fisticuffs to find a seat.

Gone Village Eatery
CAFE $
(Map p146; ☑604-938-1990; www.gonevillage eatery.com; 4205 Village Sq; mains $10-12; ⊙6:30am-9pm; 🖝🍴) This well-hidden locals' fave (just behind the store Armchair Books) serves a wide range of hearty, good-value comfort grub of the chili, pad Thai and salmon burger variety. This is where many fuel up for a day on the slopes and have a Mars-bar coffee when they return. There's a patio out back for summer evening basking.

Add a Howe Sound Brewing beer to the mix – just $5.50 for a real pint. There are also lots of options here for vegetarians.

Mount Currie Coffee Co
CAFE $
(Map p146; ☑604-962-2288; www.mountcur riecoffee.com; 4369 Main St; mains $5-9; ⊙7am-6pm; 🖝) One of Whistler's favorite independent coffee pit stops, this outpost of the popular Pemberton company also offers plenty of baked treats to tempt you from your java-only diet (carrot cake recommended). Croissants and panini are also popular at lunchtimes.

Sachi Sushi
JAPANESE $$
(Map p146; ☑604-935-5649; www.sachisushi. com; 106-4359 Main St; mains $7-32; ⊙noon-2pm Tue-Fri, & 5pm-late daily) This popular Japanese spot is a sushi specialist but they also serve everything from pork gyoza to spicy hotpots and stomach-warming udon noodle bowls – the tempura noodle bowl is best. A relaxing après-ski hangout, it's great for a glass of hot sake on a cold winter's day.

Red Door Bistro
FRENCH $$$
(☑604-962-6262; www.reddoorbistro.ca; 2129 Lake Placid Rd; $22-38; ⊙5pm-late) As soon as you know you're coming to Whistler, call for a reservation at this hot little Creekside eatery that delighted locals love as much as in-the-know visitors. Taking a French bistro approach to fine, mostly West Coast ingredients means mouthwatering lamb and seafood dishes plus a highly-recommended cassoulet that's brimming with everything from duck to smoked pork.

Bar Oso
SPANISH $$$
(Map p146; ☑604-962-4540; www.baroso.ca; 4222 Village Square; small plates $7-27; ⊙3pm-late) Taking a Spanish approach ('oso' translates as 'bear') to BC's cornucopia of great ingredients, the top-notch small plates (don't miss the lamb meatballs) and housemade charcuterie plates are a taste-tripping delight here – especially if you're able to snag a seat at the dramatic swirly-stone bar and add a cocktail or two to the proceedings.

Christine's on Blackcomb
INTERNATIONAL $$$
(☑604-938-7437; Rendezvous Lodge, Blackcomb Mountain; mains $28-32) A viewtastic gondola-accessed mountaintop restaurant where the swish menu combines with diners dressed in ski gear, Christine's is the best place to eat during your skiing or hiking day out. Book ahead (or try to avoid the lunch rush) then dive into the smashing Keralan fish curry. Can't get a table? The adjoining cafeteria serves everything from burgers to burritos and ramen bowls.

Araxi Restaurant & Bar
CANADIAN $$$
(Map p146; ☑604-932-4540; www.araxi.com; 4222 Village Sq; mains $28-48; ⊙dinner from 5pm daily) Whistler's best splurge restaurant, Araxi cooks up an inventive and exquisite Pacific Northwest menu and has charming and courteous service. Try the seared wild scallops and drain the 15,000-bottle wine selection but save room for dessert: a regional cheese plate or the amazing chocolate ganache tart...or both.

WORTH A TRIP

DETOUR TO COWBOY COUNTRY

If you're craving an alternative to bustling Whistler Village (but you don't want to head into the wilderness like Grizzly Adams on a day out), the next community north along Hwy 99 is **Pemberton**. Founded as a farming and cowboy town, it still has a distant-outpost feel, with enough to keep you occupied for a half-day. You can get the 99 Pemberton Commuter transit bus here from Whistler ($4.50, 40 minutes, four times daily) but a car will enable you to explore much more effectively. Plan ahead via www.tourismpemberton.com.

Start with coffee and a giant cinnamon bun at the woodsy little **Blackbird Bakery** (☑ 604-894-6226; www.blackbirdbread.com; 7424 Frontier St; baked goods & sandwiches $3-8; ⊙ 6am-8pm Mon-Sat, 7am-8pm Sun) in the former train station, then head over to **Pemberton Museum** (☑ 604-894-5504; www.pembertonmuseum.org; 7455 Prospect St; ⊙ 10am-5pm May-Oct) for the lowdown on how this quirky little town started. Ask them about the Pemberton mascot, a neckerchief-wearing potato dressed like a cowboy.

Next, drive over to **Pemberton Distillery** (☑ 604-894-0222; www.pembertondistillery.ca; 1954 Venture Pl; ⊙ noon-5pm Wed & Thu, to 6pm Fri & Sat Jun–early Sep, reduced hours in winter). A pioneer of BC's latter-day artisan booze movement, they have tours and a tasting room. And while they started with silky potato vodka, they've expanded production to include top-selling gin and a seductive whiskey and wild-honey liqueur. Next – with designated driver at the wheel – trundle 20 minutes out of town and uphill to **Joffre Lakes**. There's a lovely two-hour hike from the trailhead here or you can just snap some breathtaking glacier photos from the parking lot.

Finally, when dinner beckons, weave back into town and find a table at the rustic, red-walled **Pony** (☑ 604-894-5700; www.thepony.ca; 1392 Portage Rd; mains $9-18; ⊙ 6:30am-late; ☑). The town's main dining hangout, it serves an elevated comfort-food menu (pizzas recommended) and some choice BC craft beers.

Here in July? Book ahead for the mountain-framed **Pemberton Music Festival** (www.pembertonmusicfestival.com), one of the best and biggest in BC.

Drinking & Nightlife

Merlin's Bar & Grill   PUB

(☑ 604-938-7700; 4553 Blackcomb Way; ⊙ 11am-1am) If you must drink fizzy Kokanee beer this is the place to do it. A cavernous party pub with a huge patio at the base of Blackcomb, the log-lined walls, ceiling-mounted lift cars and bra-draped moose head add to the casual ambience. Food covers the pub-grub classics (there's also better beer than Kokanee available) and there's often live music during peak season.

Garibaldi Lift Company   PUB

(Map p146; ☑ 604-905-2220; 4165 Springs Lane, Whistler Village Gondola; ⊙ 11am-1am) The closest bar to the slopes, you can smell the sweat of the skiers or mountain bikers hurtling past the patio at this cavernous bar that's known by every local as the GLC. The furnishings have the scuffs and dings of a well-worn pub, and the best time to come is when DJs or bands turn the place into a clubbish mosh pit.

Dubh Linn Gate   PUB

(Map p146; ☑ 604-905-4047; www.dubhlinngate.com; 4320 Sundial Cres; ⊙ 8am-1am Mon-Fri, 7am-1am Sat & Sun) Whistler's favorite Irish pub, this dark, wood-lined joint would feel just like an authentic Galway watering hole if not for the obligatory heated patio facing the slopes. Tuck yourself into a shady corner table inside and revive your inner leprechaun with a stout – there's Guinness as well as Murphy's. Even better is the slightly pricey BC-craft-brew menu and regular live music, often of the trad Irish variety.

Moejoe's   CLUB

(Map p146; ☑ 604-935-1152; www.moejoes.com; 4155 Golfer's Approach; ⊙ 9pm-2am) Popular with the kind of party-hard international under-30s that work in Whistler shops and coffeehouses so they can ski the slopes as much as possible, this is the best place in town if you like dancing yourself into a drooling heap. Locals will tell you that Fridays are the best nights.

Longhorn Saloon & Grill   PUB

(Map p146; ☑ 604-932-5999; www.longhorn saloon.ca; 4284 Mountain Sq; ⊙ 9am-1am) Across from lifts at the base of Whistler Mountain, the sprawling patio here sometimes threatens to take over the village (especially with its pumping party soundtrack). Popular with twentysomethings, it's all about downing jugs of fizzy lager and eyeing up potential partners from your chair. The food is nothing special, but it's hard to beat the atmosphere on hopping winter evenings.

ℹ Information

Post Office (Map p146; www.canadapost. ca; 4360 Lorimer Rd; ☺8am-5pm Mon-Fri, to noon Sat)

Whistler Visitors Centre (Map p146; ☑604-935-3357; www.whistler.com; 4230 Gateway Dr; ☺8am-8pm Sun-Wed, 8am-10pm Thu-Sat Jun-Aug, reduced hours off-peak) Flyer-lined visitors center with friendly staff.

Public Library (☑604-935-8433; www.whistler-library.ca; 4329 Main St; ☺11am-7pm Mon-Thu, 10am-6pm Fri, 11am-5pm Sat & Sun; ☎) Free wi-fi plus internet-accessible computers on-site (free for up to one hour per person per day).

Northlands Medical Clinic (☑604-932-8362; www.northlandsclinic.com; 4359 Main St; ☺9am-5:30pm) Walk-in medical center.

ℹ Getting There & Away

While most visitors arrive by car from Vancouver via Hwy 99, **Greyhound Canada** (www.greyhound. ca) buses also service the route, arriving at Creekside and Whistler Village from the city ($26, 2½ hours, four daily). Buses are equipped with free wi-fi.

Pacific Coach Lines (☑604-662-7575; www. pacificcoach.com) services also arrive from Vancouver ($55, two hours, six daily) and Vancouver International Airport and drop off at Whistler hotels. **Snowbus** (☑604-451-1130; www.snowbus.com) operates a wintertime service from Vancouver (adult $38, up to three hours, up to three daily).

Whistler Transit System (www.bctransit.com/whistler) buses (single fare/one-day pass $2.50/$7) are equipped with ski and bike racks. In summer, there's a free service from the village to Lost Lake.

SUNSHINE COAST

Fringing the forested coastline for 139km from Langdale in the south to Lund in the north, the Sunshine Coast – separated from the Lower Mainland by the Coast Mountains and the Strait of Georgia – has an independent, island-like mentality that belies the fact it's just a short hop by ferry or plane from Metro Vancouver. Hwy 101 handily strings together the key communities of Gibsons, Roberts Creek, Sechelt and Powell River, making this an easy and leisurely region to explore. Popular with hikers, kayakers and mountain bikers, there's also a lively and welcoming arts scene. Peruse the website of **Sunshine Coast Tourism** (www. sunshinecoastcanada.com) for information and pick up the *Recreation Map & Activity Guide* – available in upper and lower region versions – for outdoorsy suggestions throughout the area.

Gibsons

POP 4500

If you're arriving on the Sunshine Coast via BC Ferries from Horseshoe Bay, your first port of call after docking in Langdale and driving or busing into town will be the pretty waterfront strip called Gibsons Landing. A rainbow of painted wooden buildings overlooking the marina, its streets are lined with browsable boutiques and tempting eateries while its wharf is a summer-hugging promenade for languid boat watching.

Transformation was coming to the Gibsons Landing waterfront on our visit, with a new hotel breaking ground and a handsome public market building being renovated nearby. Drop into the **visitor centre** (☑604-886-2374; www.gibsonsvisitorinfo.com; 417 Marine Dr; ☺10am-4pm Wed-Sat & Mon, 10am-3pm Sun) for the latest news.

Eavesdrop on locals gossiping about the changes to the town at **Gibsons Public Art Gallery** (☑604-886-0531; www.gpag.ca; 431 Marine Dr; ☺11am-4pm Thu-Mon) **FREE**, where new shows pop-up monthly.

Need to hit the water? Book a rental or guided tour via the friendly folk at **Sunshine Kayaking** (☑604-886-9760; www. sunshinekayaking.com; Molly's Lane; kayak rentals 2hr/24hr $35/85; ☺9am-7pm, call ahead for reservations).

Accommodation-wise, the lovely **Bonniebrook Lodge** (☑604-886-2887; www. bonniebrook.com; 1532 Ocean Beach Esplanade; d from $199; ☎) is an historic wood-built inn overlooking a quiet waterfront stretch. The area also abounds with B&Bs, including the homely, family-friendly **Arcturus Retreat Bed & Breakfast** (☑604-886-1940; www. arcturusretreat.ca; 160 Pike Rd; d from $160; ☎), handily located just up the hill from the ferry dock. They can also point you to the nearby **Sprockids Mountain Bike Park**.

SUNSHINE COAST GALLERY CRAWL

Pick up the free *Purple Banner* flyer at area visitor centers for the location of dozens of studios and galleries throughout the region. Many are open for drop-in visitors (especially in summer) – look out for the purple flags along the road on your travels – and they're a great way to meet the locals and find unique souvenirs. For further information, see www.suncoastarts.com. Also, if you're here in October, don't miss the three-day **Sunshine Coast Art Crawl** (www.sunshine coastartcrawl.com), a party-like showcase of local studios, galleries and events.

If you're thirsty for Sunshine Coast beer, head to **Persephone Brewing Company** (☑778-462-3007; www.persephonebrewing.com; 1053 Stewart Rd; ⊙11am-7pm Tue-Thu & Sun, 10am-9pm Fri & Sat, reduced hours in winter) – especially on summer weekends, when its rustic tasting lounge spills outside for growler supping at log tables; there's also live music and a pizza food truck. Don't miss their delicious Pale Ale but look out for intriguing seasonals as well.

✕ Eating

Smoke on the Water
BBQ Shack   BARBECUE $

(☑604-840-0004; www.smokeonthewaterbbq.ca; 611 School Rd; $10-16; ⊙11am-6:30pm, Apr-Oct) Follow your nose along the wharf for this shingle-sided gourmet barbecue shack, like a food truck with a permanent (albeit seasonal) location. Brisket or pulled-pork sandwiches are staples but look out for the occasional barbecued salmon special – it disappears quickly. If you miss it, console yourself with their amazing meat-lovers poutine (your calorie intake for the week).

Smitty's Oyster House   SEAFOOD $$

(☑604-886-4665; www.smittysoysterhouse.com; 643 School Rd Wharf; mains $12-24; ⊙noon-late Tue-Sat, to 8pm Sun, reduced hours in winter) The best spot for seafood in Gibsons (especially if you snag a seat at the communal long table alongside the marina boardwalk), Smitty's sparked a renaissance in local dining when it opened a few years back. It's still as popular as ever, especially on summer evenings when this is the perfect place to scoff a pile of fresh-shucked bivalves.

The Nova Kitchen   BISTRO $$$

(☑604-886-5858; www.thenovakitchen.com; 546 Gibsons Way; $19-30; ⊙4:30pm-9pm Tue-Thu, to 9:30pm Fri & Sat) While the steep climb to get here seems off-putting, it's worth it for this smashing little farm-to-table bistro – especially if you snag a patio table with its dramatic views over Gibsons Landing and the shoreline panorama. The seasonal menu can include BC-sourced treats like Chilliwack pork or Yarrow Meadow duck, lovingly prepared and served with delicious sides and super-warm service.

❶ Getting There & Away

BC Ferries (☑250-386-3431; www.bcferries.com) services arrive at Langdale, 6km northeast of Gibsons, from West Vancouver's Horseshoe Bay (passenger/vehicle $16.15/54, 40 minutes, nine daily).

Pacific Ferries (☑778-866-5107; www.pacific ferries.ca) runs passenger-only services between Gibsons Landing and Horseshoe Bay ($15, 30 minutes, two daily).

Regular **Sunshine Coast Regional Transit System** (www.busonline.ca) buses arrive in Gibsons from the Langdale ferry terminal and other Sunshine Coast communities (adult/child $2.25/1.75).

Roberts Creek

Just off Hwy 101 via Roberts Creek Rd, the funky 'downtown' here looks like a little hobbit community, if hobbits had gone through a hippie phase. Poke around the wood-built, shack-like stores and eateries and then wander downhill to the beach, checking out the huge, ever-changing **Community Mandala** painted on the ground.

Join the locals for coffee and baked goodies (including excellent pizza) at the wood-floored **Gumboot Cafe** (1057 Roberts Creek Rd; mains $8-11; ⊙7am-6pm Mon-Fri, 8am-6pm Sat & Sun; ☏). But save yourself for dinner at the nearby **Gumboot Restaurant** (☑604-885-4216; www.gumbootrestaurant.com; 1041 Roberts Creek Rd; mains $14-27; ⊙10am-8:30pm Mon-Thu, 9am-9pm Fri & Sat, 9am-8:30pm Sun), which serves lovingly-prepared, often organic West Coast dishes from lamb to seafood.

⌂ Sleeping

Up the Creek Backpackers B&B   HOSTEL $

(☑604-837-5943; www.upthecreek.ca; 1261 Roberts Creek Rd; dm/r $28/80; ☏) The Sunshine

Coast's best hostel includes small dorms plus private rooms aimed at couples and families – the back garden cabin is a cozy delight. Tent pitches are available ($14) and they'll even rent you a two-person tent if you've left yours at home ($28). The small shared kitchen is well-equipped and there's an active eco approach including rigorous recycling.

Shades of Jade Inn & Spa

B&B $$

(☑ 604-885-3211; www.shadesofjade.ca; 1489 Henderson Rd; d from $189; ☎) Aimed at tranquility-craving adults, this luxe two-unit B&B – with its Asian–West Coast fusion decor approach – couldn't be more relaxing. Each spacious room (we love the upstairs one with its hidden little deck) is equipped with a kitchen and steam shower while there's an outdoor hot tub plus on-site spa treatments to provide you with multiple reasons to never leave.

ℹ Getting There & Away

Regular **Sunshine Coast Regional Transit System** (www.busonline.ca) buses run from the ferry terminal at Langdale into Roberts Creek and beyond (adult/child $2.25/1.75).

Sechelt

POP 9775

Not quite as alluring as Gibsons, Roberts Creek or Powell River, Sechelt is nevertheless a good stop-off on your Sunshine Coast jaunt: there are tasty places to fuel up plus access to some cool outdoor activities – including a camera-triggering stroll along the town's waterfront.

With a good kayak launch site and a sandy beach, fir-and-cedar-forested **Porpoise Bay Provincial Park** (www.bcparks.ca; Hwy 101) is 4km north of Sechelt along East Porpoise Bay Rd. There are trails throughout the park and a large **campground** (www.discovercamping.ca; campsites $29) with handy hot showers.

For visiting paddlers, **Pedals & Paddles** (☑ 604-885-6440; www.pedalspaddles.com; 7425 Sechelt Inlet Rd; kayak rentals 2/24hr $37/95) organizes kayak rentals and can also take you on kayak, Zodiac or SUP tours of the inlet's wonderfully tranquil waters. Alternatively, dive in (not literally) with a First Nations interpretive kayak or hiking tour organized by **Talaysay Tours** (☑ 604-628-8555; www.talaysay.com; Porpoise Bay Provincial Park; tours from $59; ⊙ Apr-Sep).

If you like secluded waterfront retreats, check out the cottage and two spacious suites at **Beachside by the Bay** (☑ 604-741-0771; www.beachsidebythebay.com; 5005 Sunshine Coast Hwy; d from $199; ☎). You'll be waking up to spectacular Davis Bay panoramas. Alternatively, continue on Hwy 101 for 30 minutes past Sechelt to lovely **Halfmoon Bay** for a night overlooking the water from your spacious villa at **Painted Boat Resort Spa & Marina** (☑ 604-883-2122; www.paintedboat.com; 12849 Lagoon Rd; d from $385; ☎ ☒) – units have full kitchens and there's a handy supermarket nearby (plus a celebrated on-site restaurant).

Back in Sechelt, drop into downtown's hip **Basted Baker** (☑ 604-885-1368; bastedbaker.com; 5685 Cowrie St; $9-12; ⊙ 8:30am-5pm Mon-Fri, 9:30am-4pm Sat & Sun; ☎) for a bulging biscuit sandwich (check the specials before ordering) along with a housemade sweet treat to go. Alternatively, aim for a heartier meal at local favorite **Ty's Fine Foods & Bistro** (☑ 604-740-9818; www.tysfinefoods.com; 5500 Trail Ave; $12-18; ⊙ 11am-5pm Mon-Fri, 11am-3pm Sat), where tapas, soups and sandwiches are prepared with care.

ℹ Information

For more information, drop by the **Sechelt Visitor Centre** (☑ 604-885-1036; www.sechelt visitorcentre.com; 5790 Teredo St; ⊙ 9am-5pm Jul & Aug, 9am-5pm Mon-Sat Jun & Sep, reduced hours in winter).

ℹ Getting There & Away

Regular **Sunshine Coast Regional Transit System** (www.busonline.ca) buses arrive in Sechelt from the Langdale ferry terminal and other Sunshine Coast communities (adult/child $2.25/1.75).

Harbour Air Seaplanes (☑ 604-885-2111; www.harbourair.com) flies floatplanes from downtown Vancouver to Sechelt three times a day ($118, 20 minutes).

Powell River

POP 12,900

An historic paper mill town founded more than a century ago, this upper Sunshine Coast community has been busy reinventing itself in recent years. The result is an increasingly hip town – especially in the historic Townsite area – that's also a gateway to splendid outdoor activities.

BRITISH COLUMBIA SECHELT

DON'T MISS

THE OTHER WEST COAST TRAIL

••••••••••••••••••••••••••••••••••••

Vancouver Island's West Coast Trail is so popular it's hard not to run into other hikers en route. But the Sunshine Coast offers its own under-the-radar version that many BC locals have only just started discovering. Running from Sarah Point to Saltery Bay, the 180km-long **Sunshine Coast Trail** is a wilderness paradise of ancient forests, eagle-dotted waterfronts and breath-taking snowcapped vistas. Unlike the West Coast Trail, this one is free and reservations are not required – there are also 12 free-use sleeping huts dotted along the route. For more information, visit www.sunshinecoasttrail.com.

◉ Sights & Activities

Pick up a free walking tour flyer from the visitors centre (p154) and wander the Townsite's heritage buildings, including many carefully restored arts-and-crafts constructions. Highlights include **Dr Henderson's House** (6211 Walnut Ave) and the lovely **Patricia Theatre** (📞604-483-9345; www.patriciatheatre. com; 5848 Ash Ave), Canada's oldest continually operating cinema. Step inside to peruse its mural-painted interior. Also touch base with the **Townsite Heritage Society** (📞604-483-3901; www.powellrivertownsite.com; 6211 Walnut Ave, Dr Henderson's House; $5), which often runs guided tours of the historic neighborhood in summer.

Conclude your wander with a free tour at **Townsite Brewing** (📞604-483-2111; www. townsitebrewing.com; 5824 Ash Ave; ⊙11am-7pm Apr-Oct, 11am-7pm Tue-Sat Nov-Mar) (Saturdays year-round plus Thursdays in summer) in the old post office building. For $8, you'll get a tasty, four-beer sample flight – don't miss the lip-smacking Suncoast Pale Ale, which is only available here. Need some booze for your Sunshine Coast Trail hike? Buy one of their sought-after steel growlers to go (don't forget to fill it).

If you need to blow away a few cobwebs, hit the water for a refreshing paddle with **Powell River Sea Kayak** (📞604-483-2160; www.bcseakayak.com; 10676 Crowther Rd; 3/12hr rental $35/44).

🛏 Sleeping & Eating

When it's time to rest your weary noggin, it's hard to beat the highly welcoming **Old Courthouse Inn** (📞604-483-4000; www. oldcourthouseinn.ca; 6243 Walnut St; d from $129; 🖥), an immaculately restored Tudoresque antique-lined hotel. Each room, individualized with its own knickknacks, feels like a cozy home-away-from-home decorated by a nostalgic aunt with artistic appreciation. Rates include cooked breakfast in the lovely **Edie Rae's Diner** (homemade biscuits recommended), where there's also a great Monday-night dinner deal offered every week.

Need a mid-morning coffee? **Base Camp** (📞604-485-5826; www.basecamp-coffee.com; 4548 Marine Dr; mains $8-16; ⊙7am-7pm Sun-Thu, 7am-9pm Fri & Sat; 🖥) serves every local in town at some point during the day. And when lunch beckons, drop in for tacos at the tiny, brightly painted **Costa del Sol** (📞604-485-2227; www.costadelsollatincuisine.com; 4578 Marine Ave; mains $10-16; ⊙11:30am-late, Wed-Mon; 🍴) nearby. Alternatively, hit the view-tastic deck for craft beers and comfort food – chicken-and-waffle sandwich recommended – at **Coastal Cookery** (📞604-485-5568; www. coastalcookery.com; 4553 Marine Ave; mains $12-28; ⊙11:30am-late Mon-Sat, 4pm-late Sun) across the street. The menu changes seasonally and there's a tasty commitment to BC-sourced ingredients (and top-flight beer).

ℹ Information

Visitors Centre (📞604-485-4701; www. powellriver.info; 4670 Joyce Ave; ⊙9am-6pm Jul & Aug, to 5pm Mon-Sat Sep-Jun)

ℹ Getting There & Away

If you're driving here from the lower Sunshine Coast, you'll hop the **BC Ferries** (📞250-386-3431; www.bcferries.com) service between Earls Cove and Saltery Bay en route (passenger/vehicle $15.85/52.60, 50 minutes, up to 7 daily). From there, it's a 40-minute drive to Powell River. The company also operates Powell River services to and from Texada Island (passenger/vehicle $11.45/26.95, 35 minutes, up to 9 daily) and Vancouver Island's Comox (passenger/vehicle $15.90/45.70, 90 minutes, up to 5 daily).

Pacific Coastal Airlines (📞604-273-8666; www.pacificcoastal.com) flies into Powell River from the South Terminal of Vancouver International Airport four times daily (from $106, 35 minutes).

VANCOUVER ISLAND

The largest populated landmass between western North America and New Zealand – around 500km long and 100km wide – Vancouver Island is studded with colorful, quirky communities, many founded on logging or fishing and featuring the word 'Port' in their name.

The locals are a friendly bunch, proud of their region and its distinct differences. You'll find a wide range of attractions, experiences and activities that feel many miles from the bustle of mainland Vancouver. Which reminds us: to make a good impression, don't mistakenly refer to the place as 'Victoria Island.'

While the history-wrapped BC capital Victoria is the arrival point for many, it shouldn't be the only place you visit here. Food and wine fans will love the Cowichan Valley farm region; outdoor-activity enthusiasts shouldn't miss the surf-loving wild west coast radiating from Tofino; and visitors venturing north will find an uncrowded region of independent communities fringed by rugged wilderness.

ⓘ Information

For an introduction to the island, contact **Tourism Vancouver Island** (☑ 250-754-3500; www.vancouver island.travel) for listings and resources.

Victoria

POP 85,000

With a wider metro population approaching 380,000, this picture-postcard provincial capital was long-touted as North America's most English city. Thankfully, the tired theme-park version of old-fashioned England is no more. Fueled by an increasingly younger demographic, a quiet revolution has seen lame tourist pubs, eateries and stores transformed into the kind of brightly painted bohemian shops, coffee bars and innovative restaurants that would make any city proud. It's worth seeking out these enclaves on foot, but activity fans should also hop on their bikes: Victoria has more cycle routes than any other Canadian city. Once you've finished pedaling, there's BC's best museum, a park fringed by a windswept seafront and outdoor activities from kayaking to whale-watching.

◉ Sights

★ Miniature World   MUSEUM

(Map p160; ☑ 250-385-9731; www.miniature world.com; 649 Humboldt St; adult/child $15/10; ⊙ 9am-9pm mid-May–mid-Sep, to 5pm mid-Sep–mid-May; ⛟; ☒ 70) Tucked along the side of the Empress Hotel, this old-school hidden gem is a must-see, especially if you appreciate the craft of extremely intricate modelmaking. Lined with dozens of diminutive diorama scenes, divided into themes from Camelot to space and from fairyland to Olde England, there's plenty of push-button action, several trundling trains and the chance to see yourself on a miniature movie theater screen. An immaculately maintained reminder of innocent yesteryear attractions.

★ Craigdarroch Castle   MUSEUM

(☑ 250-592-5323; www.thecastle.ca; 1050 Joan Cres; adult/child $14/5; ⊙ 9am-7pm mid-Jun–Aug, 10am-4:30pm Sep–mid-Jun; ℗; ☒ 14) One of Canada's finest stately home attractions, this elegant turreted mansion illuminates the lives of the city's Victorian-era super-rich. Lined with sumptuous wood paneling and stained-glass windows, the rooms are teeming with period antiques, giving the impression the residents have just stepped away from their chairs. Climb the tower's 87 steps for distant views of the Olympic Mountains. Save time to read up on the often tragic story behind the family that lived here.

Royal BC Museum   MUSEUM

(Map p160; ☑ 250-356-7226; www.royalbcmuseum. bc.ca; 675 Belleville St; adult/child from $16/11; ⊙ 10am-5pm daily, to 10pm Fri & Sat mid-May–Sep; ⛟; ☒ 70) Start in the natural history gallery of BC's best museum and say hello to the hulking woolly mammoth exhibit. From there, wander alongside evocative dioramas, then head up to the First Peoples exhibit with its fascinating mask gallery – complete with a ferret-faced white man. The museum's highlight, though, is the walk-through colonial street with its chatty Chinatown and detailed storefronts.

Beacon Hill Park   PARK

(www.beaconhillpark.ca; Douglas St; ℗⛟; ☒ 3) Fringed by crashing ocean, this waterfront park is ideal for feeling the breeze in your hair – check out the windswept trees along the clifftop. You'll also find a gigantic totem pole, Victorian cricket pitch and

BRITISH COLUMBIA VICTORIA

Vancouver Island

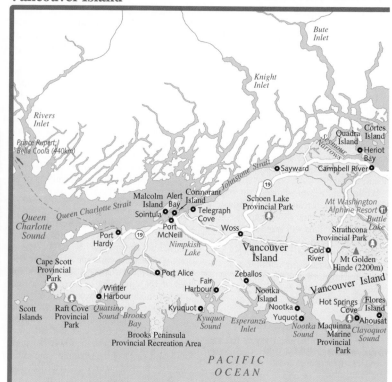

a marker for Mile 0 of Hwy 1, alongside a statue of Canadian legend Terry Fox. If you're here with kids, you should consider the popular **children's farm** (www.beacon hillchildrensfarm.ca) as well.

Victoria Bug Zoo
ZOO

(Map p160; ☑250-384-2847; www.victoria bugzoo.com; 631 Courtney St; adult/child $12/8; ⊙10am-5pm Mon-Fri, to 6pm Sat & Sun, reduced hours off-season; ☻; ☑70) The most fun any kid can have in Victoria without realizing it's educational. Step inside the brightly painted main room for a cornucopia of show-and-tell insect encounters. New owners have spruced the place up with more tanks but it's still all about the enthusiasm of the young guides who are great at firing up your enthusiasm for atlas beetles, dragon-headed crickets and thorny devils. There are plenty of chances to snap shots of your kids handling the goods (under supervision).

Parliament Buildings
HISTORIC BUILDING

(Map p160; ☑250-387-3046; www.leg.bc.ca; 501 Belleville St; ⊙tours 9am-5pm mid-May–Aug, 9am-5pm Mon-Fri Sep–mid-May; ☑70) **FREE** This dramatically handsome confection of turrets, domes and stained glass is the province's working legislature and is also open to history-loving visitors. Peek behind the facade on a colorful (and free) 45-minute guided tour then stop for lunch at the 'secret' politicians' restaurant inside. Return in the evening when the elegant exterior is illuminated like a Christmas tree.

Robert Bateman Centre
GALLERY

(Map p160; ☑250-940-3630; www.bateman centre.org; 470 Belleville St; adult/child $12.50/6; ⊙10am-5pm daily, to 9pm Fri & Sat Jun-Aug; ☑70) Colonizing part of the Inner Harbour's landmark old Steamship Terminal building, this gallery showcases the photo realistic work of Canada's most popular nature painter, along with a revolving roster of works by other art-

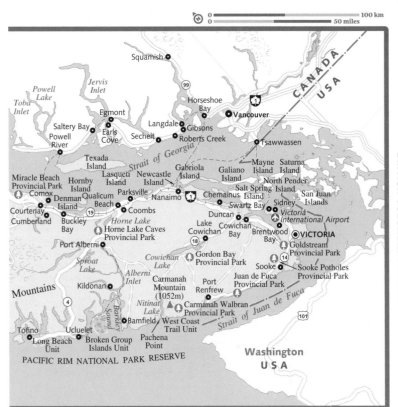

0   100 km
0   50 miles

ists. Start with the five-minute intro movie, then check out the dozens of achingly beautiful paintings showing animals in their natural surroundings in BC and beyond.

Art Gallery of Greater Victoria GALLERY
(☎250-384-4171; www.aggv.ca; 1040 Moss St; adult/child $13/2.50; ☻10am-5pm Mon-Sat, noon-5pm Sun, closed Mon mid-Sep–mid-May; 🚍14) Head east of downtown on Fort St and follow the gallery street signs to one of Canada's best Emily Carr collections. Aside from Carr's swirling nature canvases, you'll find an immersive array of Asian art and an ever-changing menu of temporary exhibitions. Check online for events, including lectures and frequent guided tours. Admission is by donation on the first Tuesday of every month.

Emily Carr House MUSEUM
(☎250-383-5843; www.emilycarr.com; 207 Government St; adult/child $6.75/4.50; ☻11am-4pm Tue-Sat May-Sep; 🅿; 🚍3) The birthplace of

BC's best-known painter, this bright-yellow gingerbread-style house has plenty of period rooms, plus displays on the artist's life and work. There's an ever-changing array of local contemporary works on display, but head to the Art Gallery of Greater Victoria if you want to see more of Carr's paintings. On your visit here, look out for the friendly house cats.

🏃 Activities

Whale-watching

Raincoat-clad tourists head out by the boatload throughout the May to October viewing season. The whales don't always show, so most excursions also visit the local haunts of lolling sea lions and portly elephant seals.

Eagle Wing Tours WHALE WATCHING
(☎250-999-0502; www.eaglewingtours.ca; 12 Erie St, Fisherman's Wharf; adult/child $125/95; ☻Mar-Oct) Long-established whale-watching boat tour operator, based at Fisherman's Wharf.

Victoria

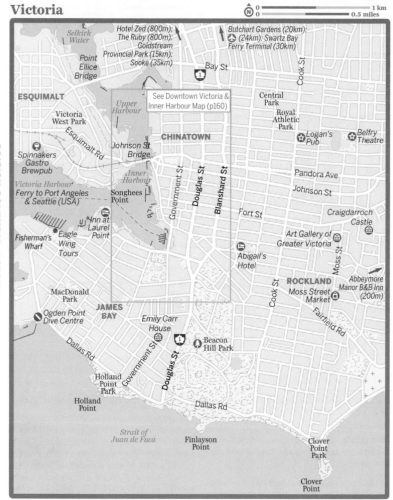

0 — 1 km
0 — 0.5 miles

Hotel Zed (800m);
The Ruby (800m);
Goldstream
Provincial Park (15km);
Sooke (35km)

Butchart Gardens (20km);
(24km); Swartz Bay
Ferry Terminal (30km)

Bay St

Cook St

Point Ellice Bridge

Selkirk Water

See Downtown Victoria & Inner Harbour Map (p160)

Central Park

ESQUIMALT

Upper Harbour

Royal Athletic Park

Victoria West Park

Esquimalt Rd

Johnson St Bridge

CHINATOWN

Logan's Pub

Belfry Theatre

Spinnakers Gastro Brewpub

Inner Harbour

Government St

Douglas St

Blanshard St

Pandora Ave

Johnson St

Victoria Harbour

Ferry to Port Angeles & Seattle (USA)

Songhees Point

Fort St

Craigdarroch Castle

Inn at Laurel Point

Art Gallery of Greater Victoria

Fisherman's Wharf

Eagle Wing Tours

Abigail's Hotel

Moss St

Abbeymore Manor B&B Inn (200m)

MacDonald Park

ROCKLAND

Cook St

Moss Street Market

JAMES BAY

Ogden Point Dive Centre

Dallas Rd

Emily Carr House

Government St

Beacon Hill Park

Fairfield Rd

Holland Point Park

Douglas St

Dallas Rd

Holland Point

Strait of Juan de Fuca

Finlayson Point

Clover Point Park

Clover Point

Prince of Whales
WHALE WATCHING

(Map p160; 📞250-383-4884; www.princeof whales.com; 812 Wharf St; adult/child from $120/95; 🚻) Long-established local operator offering several ways to check out the local whales and marine life from the water.

Springtide Charters
WHALE WATCHING

(Map p160; 📞250-384-4444; www.springtide charters.com; 1119 Wharf St; adult/child $105/85; ⏰8am-10pm, reduced hours off-season) This experienced operator has been offering local whale-watching tours for more than two decades and is one of the city's most popular marine excursion companies.

Water Sports

Paddling around the coastline is the perfect way to see this region, especially if you spot soaring eagles and starfish-studded beaches. If you like what you see on the surface, consider a dive below.

Ocean River Sports
KAYAKING

(Map p160; 📞250-381-4233; www.oceanriver. com; 1824 Store St; rental per 2hr $40, tours from $75; ⏰9:30am-6pm Mon-Fri, to 6pm Sat, 10am-5pm Sun) Rentals and popular kayak day tours in the area (including evening options). Stand-up paddling and multi-day tours also available.

Ogden Point Dive Centre
DIVING
(☑ 250-380-9119; www.divevictoria.com; 199 Dallas Rd; ⊙ 9am-6pm) Dive courses and rentals a few minutes from the Inner Harbour.

☞ Tours

Harbour Air
SCENIC FLIGHTS
(Map p160; ☑ 250-384-2215; www.harbourair.com; Inner Harbour; tours from $109) For a bird's-eye Victoria view, these breathtaking floatplane tours from the Inner Harbour are fab, especially when they dive-bomb the water on landing.

Pedaler
CYCLING
(Map p160; ☑ 778-265-7433; www.thepedaler.ca; 719 Douglas St; tours from $49, rentals from $10; ⊙ 9am-6pm, reduced hours off-season) Offering bike rentals and several guided two-wheeled tours around the city, including the Hoppy Hour Ride with its craft-beer-sampling focus.

Hike Victoria
HIKING
(☑ 250-889-3008; www.hikevictoria.com; tours from $65) Guided nature hikes (they pick you up from your hotel) on the outskirts of Victoria, with a focus on taking great scenic photos.

Big Bus Victoria
BUS
(☑ 250-389-2229; www.bigbusvictoria.com; 1 day adult/child $36/21; ⊙ May-Oct) Handy hop-on hop-off bus service that covers most of Victoria major attractions: one-day and two-day options are available.

★☆ Festivals & Events

Victoria Day Parade
PARADE
(www.gvfs.ca; ⊙ mid-May) Street fiesta, with dancers, marching bands and 50,000-plus spectators.

Victoria Ska & Reggae Fest
MUSIC
(www.victoriaskafest.ca; ⊙ mid-Jun) The largest music festival of its kind in Canada.

Victoria International JazzFest
MUSIC
(www.jazzvictoria.ca; ⊙ late Jun) Toe-tapping jazz shows over 10 days.

Victoria International Buskers Festival
PERFORMING ARTS
(www.victoriabuskers.com; ⊙ mid-Jul) Ten days of street performing action from local and international artists.

Victoria Fringe Theater Festival
THEATER
(www.victoriafringe.com; ⊙ late Aug) Two weeks of quirky short plays and stand-up performances throughout the city.

Rifflandia
MUSIC
(www.rifflandia.com; ⊙ Sep) Victoria's coolest music festival sees indie bands playing around the city.

🛏 Sleeping

From heritage B&Bs to cool boutiques and high-end options, Victoria is stuffed with accommodation for all budgets. Off-season sees great deals. Tourism Victoria's **room reservation service** (☑ 250-953-2033, 800-663-3883; www.tourismvictoria.com/hotels) can show you what's available. Keep in mind that most downtown accommodation also charge for parking.

Ocean Island Inn
HOSTEL $
(Map p160; ☑ 250-385-1789; www.oceanisland.com; 791 Pandora Ave; dm/d $28/96; @ 🛜; 🚌 70) This brightly painted hostel combines a labyrinth of small dorms with three en suite pension-style private rooms adorned with Indonesian craft flourishes and with their own TVs and fridges. Dorms also have fridges and sleep a maximum of six, while there are plenty of private bathrooms on each floor. A simple breakfast is included and there's a busy events roster (including weekly pub crawls).

HI Victoria Hostel
HOSTEL $
(Map p160; ☑ 250-385-4511; www.hihostels.ca/victoria; 516 Yates St; dm/d $33/80; @ 🛜; 🚌 70) This quiet downtown hostel situated in a high-ceilinged heritage building has two large single-sex dorms, three small coeds and a couple of private rooms. A games room and a book-lined reading area keep guests busy but you're also in the heart of the action if you want to do your own thing. Free city tours are also regularly scheduled. Free breakfast, tea and coffee included.

Hotel Zed
MOTEL $$
(☑ 250-388-4345; www.hotelzed.com; 3110 Douglas St; d from $175; P 🛜 ⛺ 🐾; 🚌 70) Accommodation Austin Powers would love, this motel has been given a tongue-in-cheek retro makeover, complete with rainbow paintwork and free VW van rides to downtown (a 10-minute walk away). The rooms are also fun: 1970s phones, bathroom comic books and brightly painted walls. Loaner bikes and free coffee are provided via the front desk and there's also a great diner if you're hungry.

BRITISH COLUMBIA VICTORIA

Downtown Victoria & Inner Harbour

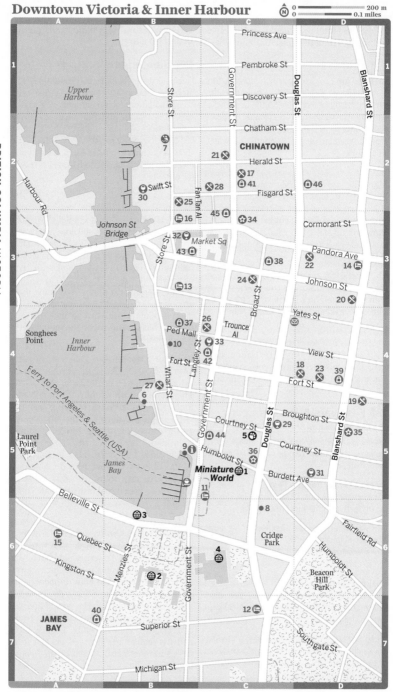

Downtown Victoria & Inner Harbour

⊙ Top Sights
1 Miniature World	C5

⊙ Sights
2 Parliament Buildings	B6
3 Robert Bateman Centre	B6
4 Royal BC Museum	C6
5 Victoria Bug Zoo	C5

⊙ Activities, Courses & Tours
6 Harbour Air	B4
7 Ocean River Sports	B2
8 Pedaler	C6
9 Prince of Whales	B5
10 Springtide Charters	B4

⊜ Sleeping
11 Fairmont Empress Hotel	C5
12 Helm's Inn	C7
13 HI Victoria Hostel	B3
14 Ocean Island Inn	D3
15 Royal Scot Hotel & Suites	A6
16 Swans Suite Hotel	B3

⊗ Eating
17 Brasserie L'École	C2
18 Crust Bakery	D4
19 Fishhook	D4
20 Foo Asian Street Food	D3
21 Jam Cafe	C2
22 John's Place	D3
23 La Taqueria	D4
Legislative Dining Room	(see 2)
24 Lotus Pond Vegetarian Restaurant	C3
25 Olo	B2
26 ReBar	C4
27 Red Fish Blue Fish	B4
28 Venus Sophia	C2

⊙ Drinking & Nightlife
29 Big Bad John's	C5
30 Canoe Brewpub	B2
31 Clive's Classic Lounge	D5
32 Drake	B3
33 Garrick's Head Pub	C4

⊙ Entertainment
34 McPherson Playhouse	C3
35 Royal Theatre	D5
36 Vic Theatre	C5

⊙ Shopping
37 Bastion Square Public Market	B4
38 Cherry Bomb Toys	C3
39 Ditch Records	D4
40 James Bay Market	A7
41 Milkman's Daughter	C2
42 Munro's Books	C4
43 Regional Assembly of Text	B3
44 Rogers' Chocolates	C5
45 Silk Road	C3
46 Victoria Public Market	D2

Helm's Inn
HOTEL **$$**

(Map p160; ☑250-385-5767; www.helmsinn.com; 600 Douglas St; d from $140; 🅿 @ 🛜; 🖵70) One of downtown's best value hotels (you're also just a couple of blocks away from the Inner Harbour), the 42 well-maintained rooms at this three-building, motel-style property all have handy kitchen facilities (either full kitchens or fridges and microwaves). Family-run for three decades, coin laundry is also available and the front-desk staff has plenty of suggestions for how to enjoy your stay in the city.

Swans Suite Hotel
BOUTIQUE HOTEL **$$**

(Map p160; ☑250-361-3310; www.swanshotel. com; 506 Pandora Ave; d from $145; 🛜🏠; 🖵70) This former brick-built warehouse has been transformed into an art-lined boutique hotel. Most rooms are spacious loft suites where you climb upstairs to bed in a gabled nook, and each is decorated with a comfy combination of wood beams, rustic chic furniture and deep leather sofas. The full kitchens are handy but there's also a brewpub downstairs for liquid sustenance.

Royal Scot Hotel & Suites
HOTEL **$$**

(Map p160; ☑250-388-5463; www.royalscot. com; 425 Quebec St; d from $230; 🅿 🛜 🏊 🏠; 🖵70) The best of several midrange options crowding the banks of the Inner Harbour near the Parliament Buildings, rooms at the Royal Scot are spotlessly maintained. Expect a friendly welcome and lots of cruise-ship seniors in the lobby. Rooms come in a variety of configurations, some with full kitchens. A free local shuttle service is available.

Inn at Laurel Point
HOTEL **$$$**

(☑250-386-8721; www.laurelpoint.com; 680 Montreal St; d from $260; 🌸 @ 🛜 🏊 🏠; 🖵70) Tucked along the Inner Harbour a short seaside stroll from the downtown action, this friendly, art-lined and ever-comfortable hotel is all about the views across the waterfront. Spacious rooms come with private balconies for drinking in the mesmerizing sunsets. Still owned by a local family, with a resort-like level of calm relaxation. In-room spa treatments and bike rentals are also available.

Fairmont Empress Hotel HOTEL $$$
(Map p160; ☎250-384-8111; www.fairmont.com/
empress-victoria; 721 Government St; d from $340;
P✸@⩗⬚; ☐70) Undergoing an upgrade
on our visit (including the removal of the
Bengal Lounge bar), this century-old Inner
Harbour landmark is Victoria's favorite ho-
tel. Aim for a room overlooking the water
and expect classic decor and effortlessly so-
licitous service. Add a sumptuous high tea
on the lobby level and, even if you're not
staying here, stroll through and soak up the
Old World charm.

Abbeymoore Manor B&B Inn B&B $$$
(☎250-370-1470; www.abbeymoore.com; 1470
Rockland Ave; d from $199; P@⬚; ☐14) A
romantic 1912 arts-and-crafts mansion,
Abbeymoore's handsome colonial exterior
hides seven antique-lined rooms furnished
with Victorian knickknacks. Some units
have kitchens and jetted tubs and the hearty
breakfast will fuel you up for a day of exploring: Craigdarroch Castle (p155) and the
Art Gallery of Greater Victoria (p157) are
nearby.

Abigail's Hotel B&B $$$
(☎250-388-5363; www.abigailshotel.com; 906 Mc-
Clure St; d from $249; P@⬚; ☐7) One of Vic-
toria's most romantic sleeping options, this
sumptuous guest house is a short walk from
the Inner Harbour. Behind its Tudoresque
facade, accommodations range from flow-
ery standard rooms to antique-lined, gable-
ceilinged suites with canopy beds, marble
fireplaces and Jacuzzi tubs. Whatever their

STROLLABLE 'HOODS

Start your exploration of Canada's old-
est, and possibly smallest, **Chinatown**
at the handsome gate near the corner
of Government and Fisgard Sts. From
here, Fisgard is studded with neon signs
and traditional grocery stores, while
Fan Tan Alley, a narrow passageway
between Fisgard St and Pandora Ave, is
a small warren of traditional and trendy
stores hawking cheap and cheerful
trinkets, cool used records and funky
artworks. If you crave company, con-
sider a guided Chinatown amble with
Discover the Past (☎250-384-6698;
www.discoverthepast.com; adult/child
$15/13; ⊙10:30am Sat year-round, plus Tue
& Thu Jun-Aug).

---

price bracket, all guests enjoy a great break-
fast: a three-course belt-buster of regionally
sourced ingredients. Adults only.

Eating

Victoria's dining scene has been radically
upgraded in recent years. Pick up the free
Eat Magazine to check out the latest foodie
happenings. Looking for browsable options?
Check out downtown's Fort St, the city'sde
factodining row.

Crust Bakery BAKERY $
(Map p160; ☎250-978-2253; www.crustbakery.
ca; 730 Fort St; baked goods $3-6; ⊙8am-5:30pm;
☐14) Arrive early for the best selection at
Victoria's favorite new bakery. A fresh-baked
egg, bacon and rosemary Danish should
start you off nicely but be sure to fill your
backpack with tartlets and top-selling cro-
nuts, as well as chocolate and coconut bread
and butter pudding; you may be able to
trade them on the streets for ten times their
face value.

La Taqueria MEXICAN $
(Map p160; ☎778-265-6255; www.lataqueria.
com; 766 Fort St; tacos up to $3 each; ⊙11am-8:30
pm Sun-Thu, to 11pm Fri & Sat; ☑; ☐14) The
huge, aquamarine-painted satellite of Van-
couver's popular and authentic Mexican
joint, this ultra-friendly spot specializes in
offering a wide array of soft taco options
(choose four for $10.50, less for vegetarian
options), including different specials every
day. Quesadillas are also available and you
can wash everything down with margaritas,
Mexican beer or mezcal – or all three.

Red Fish Blue Fish SEAFOOD $
(Map p160; ☎250-298-6877; www.redfish-blue
fish.com; 1006 Wharf St; mains $6-16; ⊙11am-
7pm; ☐70) ⚑ On the waterfront boardwalk
at the foot of Broughton St, this freight-
container takeout shack serves fresh-made,
finger-licking sustainable seafood. High-
lights like jerk fish poutine, amazing chow-
der and tempura-battered oysters (you can
also get traditional fish and chips, of course).
Expanded new seating has added to the ap-
peal but watch out for hovering gull mob-
sters as you try eat.

Foo Asian Street Food ASIAN $
(Map p160; ☎250-383-3111; www.foofood.ca;
769 Yates St; mains $9-14; ⊙11:30am-10pm Mon-
Sat, to 9pm Sun; P; ☐70) Like a permanent
food truck tucked inauspiciously in a park-
ing lot, this locals' fave food shack focuses

on hearty dishes inspired by Asian hawker stalls. Grab a perch inside or out, check the specials board and dive into fresh-cooked, good-value options, from saag paneer to octopus salad. Beer-wise, there's a love for local-made brews from the likes of Hoyne and Driftwood.

Jam Cafe
BREAKFAST $

(Map p160; ☑778-440-4489; www.jamcafevictoria. com; 542 Herald St; mains $9-16; ☻8am-3pm; 🛜🍴) The locals won't tell you anything about this slightly off-the-beaten-path place. But that's not because they don't know about it – it's because they don't want you to increase the lineups for Victoria's best breakfast. The wide array of Benedict varieties is ever popular, but we also recommend the amazing, and very naughty, chicken French toast. Arrive early or off-peak; there are no reservations.

Fishhook
SEAFOOD $$

(Map p160; ☑250-477-0470; www.fishhookvic. com; 805 Fort St; mains $13-24; ☻11am-9pm) 🍴 Don't miss the smokey, coconutty chowder at this Indian-and-French influenced seafood gem but make sure you add a tartine open-faced sandwich: it's the house specialty. If you still have room (and you're reluctant to give up your perch at the communal table) split a seafood *biryani* platter with your dining partner. Focused on local and sustainable fish supplies.

Venus Sophia
VEGETARIAN $$

(Map p160; ☑250-590-3953; www.venussophia. com; 540 Fisgard St; mains $10-19; ☻10am-6pm Jul & Aug, 11am-6pm Wed-Sun Sep-Jun; 🍴; 🚇70) A delightful cream-walled tearoom combining traditional tea service (including a lovely afternoon tea) with beautifully presented vegetarian lunches, this is a uniquely tranquil respite from Chinatown's sometimes busy streets. Try the blue-cheese-and-pear panino and add an organic tea (served in mismatched vintage cups) from the wide selection. Our favorite? The delicious cream Earl Grey.

John's Place
DINER $$

(Map p160; ☑250-389-0711; www.johnsplace.ca; 723 Pandora Ave; mains $9-17; ☻7am-9pm Mon-Fri, 8am-4pm & 5-9pm Sat & Sun; 🛜🍴; 🚇70) This ever-friendly, wood-floored hangout is lined with quirky memorabilia, while its enormous menu is a cut above standard diner fare. They'll start you off with a basket of addictive housemade bread, but save room for heaping pasta dishes, piled-high salad mains

or a pancake or Tex-Mex brunch. A near-perfect breakfast spot; save time to peruse the signed celebrity photos on the walls.

The Ruby
DINER $$

(☑250-507-1325; www.therubyvictoria.com; 3110 Douglas St; mains $13-18; ☻8am-9pm; 🅿🛜) The Hotel Zed's upmarket diner lures locals (arrive off-peak to avoid the crush) with its breakfast tacos and eggs Benedict platters (Mexi Benny recommended) but the rest of the day is all finger-licking comfort dishes, typically including succulent rotisserie chicken. Local ingredients are key and extras like meat rubs and hot sauce are made from scratch. Check out the serious vinyl record collection.

Lotus Pond Vegetarian Restaurant
CHINESE, VEGETARIAN $$

(Map p160; ☑250-380-9293; www.lotuspond 1998.ca; 617 Johnson St; mains $9-17; ☻11:30am-3pm & 5-9pm Tue-Sat, noon-3pm & 5-8pm Sun; 🍴; 🚇70) This no-frills downtown spot was satisfying local vegetarians long before meat-free diets became fashionable. Superior to most Chinese eateries and with a menu that easily pleases carnivores as well as veggie types, the best time to come is lunch, when the busy buffet lures everyone in the vicinity. Don't miss the turnip cakes, a house specialty.

Legislative Dining Room
CANADIAN $$

(Map p160; ☑250-387-3959; www.leg.bc.ca; 501 Belleville St, Parliament Buildings; mains $9-18; ☻hours vary Mon-Fri; 🚇70) One of Victoria's best-kept dining secrets, the Parliament Buildings has its own subsidized, old-school restaurant where both MLAs and the public can drop by for a silver-service menu of regional dishes, ranging from salmon salads to velvety steaks and a BC-only wine list. Entry is via the security desk just inside the building's main entrance; photo ID is required.

ReBar
VEGETARIAN, FUSION $$

(Map p160; ☑250-361-9223; www.rebarmodern food.com; 50 Bastion Sq; mains $9-17; ☻11:30am-9pm Mon-Fri, 9:30am-9pm Sat & Sun; 🍴; 🚇70) A beloved local fave with new monochrome-painted exterior (although the same riotously colorful tablecloths inside), this is the best place in town for vegetarians and carnivores to dine together without one side feeling cheated. The signature almond burger is one of many excellent veggie options, while meaty-types will find lots of fish and chicken options. Also a popular weekend brunch spot.

BRITISH COLUMBIA VICTORIA

WORTH A TRIP

HIT THE TRAILS

Easily accessed along the Island Hwy just 16km from Victoria, **Goldstream Provincial Park** (☑250-478-9414; www.goldstreampark.com; 2930 Trans-Canada Hwy; P), at the base of Malahat Mountain, makes for a restorative nature-themed day trip from the city. Dripping with ancient, moss-covered cedar trees and a moist carpet of plant life, it's known for its chum-salmon spawning season from late October to December. Hungry bald eagles are attracted to the fish and bird-watchers come ready with their cameras. Head to the park's **Freeman King Visitors Centre** (☑250-478-9414; 2390 Trans-Canada Hwy; ⊙9am-4:30pm) for area info and natural history exhibits.

Aside from nature watching, you'll also find great hiking: marked trails range from tough to easy and some are wheelchair accessible. Recommended treks include the hike to 47.5m-high **Niagara Falls** (not *that* one) and the steep, strenuous route to the top of **Mt Finlayson**, one of the region's highest promontories. The visitors center can advise on trails and will also tell you how to find the park's forested **campground** (www.discover camping.ca; campsites $35; P) if you feel like staying over.

Olo
CANADIAN $$$

(Map p160; ☑250-590-8795; www.olorestaurant. com; 509 Fisgard St; mains $24-30; ⊙5pm-midnight Sun-Thu, to 1am Fri & Sat; ☑) Slightly confusingly re-invented from the Ulla restaurant that used to be here, version 2.0 ploughs the farm-to-table furrow even deeper. The sophisticated seasonal menu can include anything from Quadra Island scallops to local smoked duck breast, but the multicourse, family-style tasting menu is the way to go if you're feeling flush (from $45 per person).

Brasserie L'École
FRENCH $$$

(Map p160; ☑250-475-6260; www.lecole.ca; 1715 Government St; mains $18-50; ⊙5:30-11pm Tue-Sat; ☑70) Preparing West Coast ingredients with French-bistro flare, this warm and ever-popular spot is perfect for an intimate night out. The dishes constantly change to reflect seasonal highlights, like figs, salmonberries and heirloom tomatoes, but we recommend any seafood you find on the menu, or the ever-available *steak frites* (steak and fries) with a red-wine and shallot sauce.

🍷 Drinking & Nightlife

Victoria is one of BC's best beer towns; look out for local-made craft brews at pubs around the city. Rest assured: repeated first-hand research was undertaken for this section.

★Drake
BAR

(Map p160; ☑250-590-9075; www.drakeeatery. com; 517 Pandora Ave; ⊙11:30am-midnight; ☎; ☑70) Victoria's best taphouse, this hangout has more than 30 amazing craft drafts, including revered BC producers like Townsite, Driftwood and Four Winds. Arrive on a rainy afternoon and you'll find yourself still here several hours later. Food-wise, the smoked tuna club is a top-seller but the cheese and charcuterie plates are ideal for grazing.

Spinnakers Gastro Brewpub
PUB

(☑250-386-2739; www.spinnakers.com; 308 Catherine St; ⊙11am-11pm; ☎; ☑15) One of Canada's first craft brewers, this wood-floored smasher is a short hop from downtown via Harbour Ferry. Sail in for copper-colored Nut Brown Ale and the lip-smacking Lion's Head Cascadia Dark Ale and check out the daily casks to see what's on special. Save room to eat: the menu here is true gourmet gastropub grub.

Garrick's Head Pub
PUB

(Map p160; ☑250-384-6835; www.garrickshead. com; 66 Bastion Sq; ⊙11am-late; ☑70) Great spot to dive into BC's brilliant craft beer scene. Pull up a perch at the long bar and you'll be faced with 55-plus taps serving a comprehensive menu of beers from Driftwood, Phillips, Hoyne and beyond. There are always 10 rotating lines with intriguing tipples (ask for samples) plus a comfort-grub menu of burgers et al to line your boozy stomach.

Clive's Classic Lounge
LOUNGE

(Map p160; ☑250-361-5684; www.clivesclassic lounge.com; 740 Burdett Ave; ⊙4pm-midnight Mon-Thu, 4pm-1am Fri, 5pm-1am Sat, 5pm-midnight Sun; ☑70) Tucked into the lobby level of the Chateau Victoria Hotel, this is the best spot in town for perfectly prepared cocktails. Completely lacking the snobbishness of big-city cocktail haunts, this ever-cozy spot is totally dedicated to its mixed-drinks menu, which means timeless classic cocktails, as well as cool-ass fusion tipples that are a revelation.

Canoe Brewpub PUB

(Map p160; ☑250-361-1940; www.canoebrew
pub.com; 450 Swift St; ⊙11:30am-11pm Sun-Wed,
to midnight Thu, to 1am Fri & Sat; ☑70) The cavernous brick-lined interior is great on rainy
days, but the patio is also the best in the city
with its usually sunny views over the harbor.
Indulge in on-site-brewed treats, like the
hoppy lager and the summer-friendly honey
wheat ale. Grub is also high on the menu,
with the mussels recommended.

Big Bad John's PUB

(Map p160; ☑250-383-7137; www.strathcona
hotel.com; 919 Douglas St; ⊙noon-2am; ☑70)
Easily missed from the outside, this dark
little hillbilly-themed bar feels like you've
stepped into the backwoods. But rather than
some dodgy banjo players with mismatched
ears, you'll find good-time locals enjoying the
cave-like ambience of peanut-shell-covered
floors and a ceiling dotted with old bras. A
good spot to say you've been to, at least once.

☆ Entertainment

Check the weekly freebie *Monday Maga-
zine* for the lowdown on local happenings.
Entertainment resources online include
Live Victoria (www.livevictoria.com) and
Play in Victoria (www.playinvictoria.net).

Logan's Pub LIVE MUSIC

(☑250-360-2711; www.loganspub.com; 1821 Cook
St; ⊙3pm-1am Mon-Fri, 10am-1am Sat, 10am-
midnight Sun; ☑6) A 10-minute walk from
downtown, this no-nonsense pub looks like
nothing special from the outside, but its roster of shows is a fixture on the local indie
scene. Fridays and Saturdays are your best
bet for performances; check the online calendar to see what's coming up.

Vic Theatre CINEMA

(Map p160; ☑250-389-0440; www.thevic.ca;
808 Douglas St; ☑70) Screening arthouse and
festival movies in the heart of downtown. A
$2 membership is required alongside your
ticket admission here.

Belfry Theatre THEATER

(☑250-385-6815; www.belfry.bc.ca; 1291 Gladstone Ave; ☑22) A 20-minute stroll from
downtown, the celebrated Belfry Theatre
showcases contemporary plays in its lovely
former-church-building venue.

Royal Theatre THEATER

(Map p160; ☑888-717-6121, 250-386-6121; www.
rmts.bc.ca; 805 Broughton St; ☑70) With a ro-

coco interior, the Royal Theatre hosts mainstream theater productions, and is home to
the Victoria Symphony and Pacific Opera
Victoria.

McPherson Playhouse THEATER

(Map p160; ☑888-717-6121, 250-386-6121; www.
rmts.bc.ca; 3 Centennial Sq; ☑70) One of Victoria's main stages, McPherson Playhouse
offers mainstream visiting shows and performances.

Shopping

While Government St is a souvenir shopping
magnet, those looking for more original pur-
chases should head to the Johnson St stretch
between Store and Government, which is
lined with cool independent stores.

Regional Assembly of Text STATIONERY

(Map p160; ☑778-265-6067; www.assemblyof
text.com; 560 Johnson St; ⊙11am-6pm Mon-Sat,
noon-5pm Sun; ☑70) The satellite of Vancouver's charming hipster stationery store
is socked into a quirky space resembling a
hotel lobby from 1968. You'll find the same
clever greeting cards and cool journals, plus
the best Victoria postcards you'll ever find;
postage is available. Add the button-making

DON'T MISS

TO MARKET, TO MARKET

On rainy days, **Victoria Public Market**
(Map p160; ☑778-433-2787; www.
victoriapublicmarket.com; 1701 Douglas
St; ⊙10am-6pm Mon-Sat, 11am-5pm
Sun; ☑4) serves up a couple of dozen
food-focused vendors – from artisan tea
to chocolate and cheese – in its downtown heritage building location. But if
the weather's fine, slap on the suntan
lotion and head outside.

Bastion Square Public Market
(Map p160; www.bastionsquare.ca; Bastion
Sq; ⊙11am-4:30pm Thu-Sat, 11am-4pm Sun
May-Sep; ☑70) offers art-and-craft stalls
all summer, while **James Bay Market**
(Map p160; www.jamesbaymarket.com;
494 Superior St; ⊙9am-3pm Sat mid-
May–mid-Sep; ☑27) and the large **Moss
Street Market** (www.mossstreetmarket.
com; 1330 Fairfield Rd; ⊙10am-2pm Sat
May-Oct; ☑7) offer a community-focused
combo of both arts and food. Come hun-
gry: there is plenty to eat at these two.

table, typewriter stations and a *Mister Mitten* chapbook purchase and you'll be happier than a shiny new paper clip.

Munro's Books
BOOKS

(Map p160; ☑250-382-2464; www.munrobooks. com; 1108 Government St; ◷9am-6pm Mon-Wed, 9am-9pm Thu-Sat, 9:30am-6pm Sun; ☑70) Like a cathedral to reading, this high-ceilinged bookstore lures legions of locals and visitors who love communing with the written word. There's a good array of local-interest tomes, as well as a fairly extensive travel section at the back on the left. Check out the piles of bargain books, too – they're not all copies of *How to Eat String, Volume II* from 1974.

Silk Road
TEA

(Map p160; ☑250-704-2688; www.silkroadtea. com; 1624 Government St; ◷10am-6pm Mon-Sat, 11am-5pm Sun; ☑70) A pilgrimage spot for regular and exotic tea fans where you can pick up all manner of leafy paraphernalia. Alternatively, sidle up to the tasting bar to quaff some adventurous brews. There's also a small on-site spa, where you can indulge in oil treatments and aromatherapy.

Milkman's Daughter
CLOTHING, GIFTS

(Map p160; www.themilkmansdaughter.ca; 1713 Government St; ◷10am-6:30pm Mon-Thu & Sat, 10am-8pm Fri, noon-5pm Sun; ☑70) This shop is a hipster's dream, with an array of clothing as well as must-have artisan creations from both locals and those from further afield, mostly from the West Coast. It's an eclectic mix, from jewelry to pottery and from buttons to notebooks, but it's easy to find something to fall in love with.

ON YER BIKE

Take your bike across on the ferry from the mainland to Swartz Bay, Vancouver Island, from where you can hop onto the easily accessible and well-marked **Lochside Regional Trail**. The 29km, mostly flat route to downtown Victoria is not challenging – there are only a couple of overpasses – and it's an idyllic, predominantly paved ride through small urban areas, waterfront stretches, rolling farmland and forested countryside. You'll find several spots to pick up lunch en route and, if you adopt a leisurely pace, you'll be in town within four hours or so.

Rogers' Chocolates
FOOD

(Map p160; ☑250-881-8771; www.rogerschoco lates.com; 913 Government St; ◷9:30am-7pm; ☑70) This charming, museum-like confectioner serves the best ice-cream bars, but repeat offenders usually spend their time hitting the menu of rich Victoria Creams, one of which is usually enough to substitute for lunch. Varieties range from peppermint to seasonal specialties and they're good souvenirs, so long as you don't scoff them all before you get home (which you will).

Ditch Records
MUSIC

(Map p160; ☑250-386-5874; 784 Fort St; ◷10am-6pm Mon-Sat, 11am-5pm Sun; ☑14) A fave record store among the locals, Ditch is lined with tempting vinyl, plenty of CDs and many furtive musos perusing releases by acts like Frazey Ford and Nightmares on Wax. An ideal rainy-day hangout; if it suddenly feels like time to socialize, you can book gig tickets here, too.

Cherry Bomb Toys
TOYS

(Map p160; ☑250-385-8697; www.cherrybomb toys.com; 1410 Broad St; ◷10am-6pm Mon-Sat, noon-5pm Sun; ☷; ☑70) The nostalgically inclined will love this large toy emporium of collectibles, especially if they head upstairs to the mezzanine-level **toy museum**. It's crammed with everything from vintage GI Joes to antique Lego plus old computer game consoles that will likely trigger Proustian flashbacks. They encourage donations if you want to visit the museum but it's free if you buy anything downstairs.

ℹ Information

Downtown Medical Centre (☑250-380-2210; 622 Courtney St; ◷8:30am-5pm Mon-Fri; ☑70) Handy walk-in clinic.

Main Post Office (Map p160; 709 Yates St; ◷9am-5pm Mon-Fri; ☑70) Near the corner of Yates and Douglas Sts.

Tourism Victoria Visitor Centre (Map p160; ☑250-953-2033; www.tourismvictoria.com; 812 Wharf St; ◷8:30am-8:30pm mid-May– Aug, 9am-5pm Sep-May; ☑70) Busy, flyer-lined visitors center overlooking the Inner Harbour.

ℹ Getting There & Away

AIR

Victoria International Airport (☑250-953-7500; www.victoriaairport.com) is 26km north of the city via Hwy 17. Frequent **Air Canada** (www.aircanada.com) services arrive from Vancouver ($169, 25 minutes), while **Westjet**

(www.westjet.com) flights arrive from Calgary ($265, 1½ hours). Both offer cross-Canada connections.

YYJ Airport Shuttle (☑778-351-4995; www.yyjairportshuttle.com) buses run between the airport and downtown Victoria ($25, 30 minutes). In contrast, a taxi to downtown costs around $50.

Harbour Air (☑250-384-2215; www.harbourair.com) flies into the Inner Harbour from downtown Vancouver ($205, 30 minutes) throughout the day. Similar **Helijet** (www.helijet.com) helicopter services arrive from Vancouver ($245, 35 minutes).

BUS

Buses rolling into the city include **Greyhound Canada** (www.greyhound.ca) services from Nanaimo ($26, two hours, up to six daily) and **Tofino Bus** (☑250-725-2871; www.tofinobus.com) services from points across the rest of the island. Frequent **BC Ferries Connector** (☑778-265-9474; www.bcfconnector.com) services, via the ferry, arrive from Vancouver (from $45, 3½ hours) and Vancouver International Airport ($50, four hours).

BOAT

BC Ferries (☑250-386-3431; www.bcferries.com) arrive from mainland Tsawwassen (adult/vehicle $17/56, 1½ hours) at Swartz Bay, 27km north of Victoria via Hwy 17. Services arrive frequently throughout the day in summer, less often off-season.

Victoria Clipper (☑250-382-8100; www.clippervacations.com) services arrive in the Inner Harbour from Seattle (adult/child US $109/54, three hours, up to twice daily). **Black Ball Transport** (☑250-386-2202; www.ferrytovictoria.com) boats also arrive here from Port Angeles (adult/child/vehicle US$18.50/9.25/64, 1½ hours, up to four daily).

❶ Getting Around

BICYCLE

Victoria is a great cycling capital, with routes crisscrossing the city and beyond. Check the website of the **Greater Victoria Cycling Coalition** (www.gvcc.bc.ca) for local resources. Bike rentals are offered by **Cycle BC Rentals** (☑250-380-2453; www.cyclebc.ca; 685 Humboldt St; ▯1).

BOAT

Victoria Harbour Ferry (Map p160; ☑250-708-0201; www.victoriaharbourferry.com; fares from $6) covers the Inner Harbour and beyond with its colorful armada of little boats.

BUS

Victoria Regional Transit (www.bctransit.com/victoria) buses (fare/day pass $2.50/5) cover a wide area from Sidney to Sooke, with some routes served by modern-day double-deckers. Children under five travel free.

TAXI

Yellow Cab (☑250-381-2222; www.yellowcabvictoria.com)

BlueBird Cabs (☑250-382-2222; www.taxicab.com)

Southern Vancouver Island

Not far from Victoria's madding crowds, southern Vancouver Island is a laid-back region of quirky little towns that are never far from tree-lined cycle routes, waterfront hiking trails and rocky outcrops bristling with gnarly Garry oaks. The wildlife here is abundant and you'll likely spot bald eagles swooping overhead, sea otters cavorting on the beaches and perhaps the occasional orca sliding silently by just off the coast.

Saanich Peninsula & Around

Home to Vancouver Island's main airport and busiest ferry terminal, this peninsula north of Victoria has plenty to offer day-trippers looking to escape from the city.

SIDNEY

At the peninsula's northern end, seafront Sidney is a pleasant afternoon diversion, with a walkable waterfront, strollable shops (especially bookstores) and laid-back places to eat.

The popular **Shaw Ocean Discovery Centre** (☑250-665-7511; www.oceandiscovery.ca; 9811 Seaport Pl; adult/child $15/8; ⊙10am-4:30pm) is Sidney's kid-luring highlight. Enter through a dramatic Disney-style entrance – it makes you think you're descending below the waves – then step into a gallery of aquatic exhibits, including alien-like jellyfish, a large touch tank with purple starfish and an octopus that likes to unscrew a glass jar to snag its fresh crab dinner. Continue your marine education aboard a whale-watching boat trek with **Sidney Whale Watching** (☑250-656-7599; www.sidneywhalewatching.com; 2537 Beacon Ave; adult/child $115/89; ⊙Mar-Oct), located a few steps away.

If you decide to stick around, the swish **Sidney Pier Hotel & Spa** (☑250-655-9445; www.sidneypier.com; 9805 Seaport Pl; d from $209; @🛜🐾) situated on the waterfront fuses West Coast lounge – cool with beach pastel colors.

BOOKSTORE CENTRAL

Beacon Avenue is lined with shops and there are more than half a dozen bookstores here if that's what you're into. **Tanner's Books** (☑ 250-656-2345; www.tannersbooks.com; 2436 Beacon Ave; ☺8am-9pm) is a cavernous corner shop with a large array of magazines and a comprehensive travel-book section. They also organize evening book readings, typically at the Red Brick Cafe across the street – check their website for listings. Also, save time for **Beacon Books** (☑ 250-655-4447; 2372 Beacon Ave; ☺10am-5:30pm Mon-Sat, noon-4pm Sun). It's a multi-room shop piled high with used tomes guarded by a house-cat who may or may not let you stroke her (probably not). Look out for the collection of vintage postcards, then send one home, pretending you're vacationing in 1942.

If it's time to eat, check out **Sabhai Thai** (☑ 250-655-4085; www.sabhai.ca; 2493 Beacon Ave; mains $12-18; ☺11:30am-2pm & 5-9pm), a cozy locals' favorite with a bonus patio and a good line in authentic curry and *phad* dishes. The lunch combos (around the $10 mark) are good value and include rice and spring rolls.

Serving the best coffee in Sidney, **Toast Cafe** (☑ 250-665-6234; 2400 Bevan Ave; mains $6-12; ☺6:30am-4pm Mon-Sat; ☎) is a wood-floored, just-off-the-main-drag corner joint that makes great breakfast wraps and thick-cut, superbly satisfying, salad-accompanied sandwiches. On sunny days, aim for a perch at the communal table outside and fill your belly – check the daily special on the chalk-board inside before you order, though.

BRENTWOOD BAY

A 30-minute drive from Victoria, this countryside swath has some attractions of its own, including one of BC's most popular visitor destinations.

The rolling farmlands of Brentwood Bay are home to the immaculate, green-thumbed **Butchart Gardens** (☑ 250-652-5256; www.butchartgardens.com; 800 Benvenuto Ave; adult/teen/child $32.10/16.05/3; ☺9am-10pm, reduced hours off-season; 🖬75), Vancouver Island's most visited attraction. It's divided into separate gardens where there's always something in bloom; the tour buses roll in relentlessly

throughout the summer here but Saturday-night fireworks in July and August make it all worthwhile. Tea fans take note: the **Dining Room Restaurant** serves a smashing afternoon tea; leave your diet at the door. Also ask about November's fascinating behind-the-scenes **greenhouse tours**.

If you have time, also consider nearby **Victoria Butterfly Gardens** (☑ 250-652-3822; www.butterflygardens.com; 1461 Benvenuto Ave; adult/child $16/5; ☺10am-4pm mid-Mar–Oct, 10am-3pm Oct–mid-Mar), which offers a kaleidoscope of thousands of fluttering critters, from around 75 species, in a free-flying environment. As well as watching them flit about and land on your head, you can learn about ecosystem life cycles, and eyeball exotic fish, plants and birds. Look out for Spike, the long-beaked puna ibis, who struts around the trails as if he owns the place.

Sooke & Around

Rounding Vancouver Island's rustic southern tip towards Sooke, a 45-minute drive from Victoria, Hwy 14 is lined with twisted Garry oaks and unkempt hedgerows, while the houses – often artisan workshops or homely B&Bs – seem spookily hidden in the forest shadows.

◎ Sights & Activities

Sharing the same building and hours as the visitors center, the fascinating **Sooke Region Museum** (☑ 250-642-6351; www.sookeregionmuseum.com; 2070 Phillips Rd; ☺9am-5pm mid-May–mid-Oct, closed Mondays mid-Oct–mid-May) **FREE** illuminates the area's rugged pioneer days. Check out Moss Cottage in the museum grounds: built in 1869, it's the oldest residence west of Victoria.

If you're craving some thrills, find your inner screamer on the forested zip-line tours operated by **Adrena LINE** (☑ 250-642-1933; www.adrenalinezip.com; 5128 Sooke Rd; adult/child from $80/70; ☺9am-5pm Mar-Oct). Its full-moon zips are the most fun (book ahead) and, if you don't have your own transport, they can also shuttle you to and from Victoria for an extra $15.

A more relaxed way to encounter the natural world is the **Sooke Potholes Provincial Park** (☑ 250-474-1336; www.bcparks.ca; Sooke River Rd), a 5km drive from Hwy 14 (the turnoff is east of Sooke). With rock pools and potholes carved into the river base during the last ice age, it's ideal for summertime swimming and tube floating.

Juan de Fuca Marine Trail HIKING
(www.juandefucamarinetrail.com) The 47km Juan de Fuca Marine Trail in **Juan de Fuca Provincial Park** (✎250-474-1336; www. bcparks.ca; Hwy 14) rivals the West Coast Trail as a must-do trek. From east to west, its trail-head access points are China Beach, Sombrio Beach, Parkinson Creek and Botanical Beach. It takes around four days to complete the route, but you don't have to go the whole hog if you want to take things easier.

Be aware that some sections are often muddy and difficult to hike, while bear sightings and swift weather changes are not uncommon. The most difficult stretch is between Bear Beach and China Beach. The route has several basic backcountry camp-sites and you can pay your camping fee ($10 per adult) at any of the trailheads. The most popular spot to pitch your tent is the more salubrious, family-friendly **China Beach Campground** (✎800-689-9025, 519-826-6850; www.discovercamping.ca; campsites $20; ⊙mid-May–mid-Sep), which has pit toilets and cold-water taps but no showers. There's a waterfall at the western end of the beach and booking ahead in summer is essential.

Booking ahead is also required on the **West Coast Trail Express** (✎888-999-2288, 250-477-8700; www.trailbus.com; fares from $30; ⊙May-Sep) minibus that runs between Victoria, the trailheads and Port Renfrew.

🛏 Sleeping & Eating

You'll find B&Bs dotted along the route here but, for one of the province's most delightful and splurge-worthy options, head to Whiffen Spit's **Sooke Harbour House** (✎250-642-3421; www.sookeharbourhouse.com; 1528 Whiffen Spit Rd; d from $329; ☎❄). The restaurant is also a great place for fine West Coast dining, whether or not you're staying here.

Located between Sooke and Jordan River, the rustic, locally beloved **Shirley Delicious Cafe** (✎250-528-2888; 2794 Sheringham Point Rd; mains $4-10; ⊙8am-5pm) is bristling with home-baked treats, bulging sandwiches and hearty soups.

Port Renfrew

Conveniently nestled between the Juan de Fuca and West Coast Trails, delightfully re-mote Port Renfrew is a great access point for either route. There are several places to rest your weary head and also fuel up with great grub here.

If you've had enough of your sleeping bag, **Wild Renfrew** (✎250-647-5541; www.wildren frew.com; 17310 Parkinson Rd; lodge d from $139, cabin from $249; ☎❄) has woodland cabins and lodge rooms that have all been upgrad-ed in recent years. There are many ways to unplug from the city and sink into the retreat-like feel of the rainforest here. The woodsy seaside cottages are best and each includes a kitchen for preparing your alfres-co balcony breakfast in the morning – there's also a pub nearby if you're feeling lazy.

For a respite from campground pasta, **Coastal Kitchen Cafe** (✎250-647-5545; 17245 Parkinson Rd; mains $8-16; ⊙7am-9pm) is a laid-back, locally loved hangout that serves hearty comfort grub from breakfast to din-ner (add a glass of BC craft beer to the lat-ter). The dish to have here? Miss the halibut and chips at your peril.

Tacked onto the historic Port Renfrew Hotel, summer drinking at **Renfrew Pub** (✎250-647-5541; 17310 Parkinson Rd; $12-24; ⊙noon-8pm Mon-Fri, 8am-8pm Sat, 8am-7pm Sun) is all about snagging a spot on the patio alongside the wharf. On lazy days, it's hard to peel yourself away from the shimmering shoreline views, especially if you've had a huge bowl of seafood chowder and a round or two of BC craft ale.

Cowichan Valley

A swift Hwy 1 drive northwest of Victoria, the farm-filled Cowichan Valley region is ripe for discovery, especially if you're a trave-ling foodie or an outdoor activity nut.

Contact **Cowichan Regional Visitor Centre** (✎250-746-4636; www.tourismcowichan. com; 2896 Drinkwater Rd; ⊙9am-5pm Sun-Tue, to 6pm Wed-Sat Jun-Aug, reduced hours in winter) for more information.

Duncan

Developed as a logging industry railroad stop, Duncan is the valley's main communi-ty. A useful base for regional exploration, it's known for its dozens of totem poles, which dot downtown like sentinels.

If your First Nations curiosity is piqued, head to the **Quw'utsun' Cultural & Confer-ence Centre** (✎250-746-8119; www.quwutsun.ca; 200 Cowichan Way; adult/child $15/8; ⊙10am-4pm Mon-Sat Jun-Sep) to learn about carving and traditional salmon runs. Its on-site **Riverwalk Cafe** serves First Nations–inspired cuisine.

Save time during your Duncan visit for a selfie with the **World's Largest Hockey Stick**, a 62-meter-long behemoth attached to the **Island Savings Centre** on James St.

Also, drive 3km north of town to the **BC Forest Discovery Centre** (☑250-715-1113; www.bcforestdiscoverycentre.com; 2892 Drinkwater Rd; adult/child $16/11; ☺10am-4:30pm Jun-Aug, reduced hours off-season; ▣), complete with pioneer-era buildings, logging machinery and a working **steam train** you can hop aboard for a trundle (check website for the schedule).

✖ Eating & Drinking

Duncan Garage Cafe & Bakery CAFE $
(☑250-748-6223; 3330 Duncan St; mains $7-12; ☺7am-6pm Mon-Sat, 8:30am-5pm Sun; ☑) This always-busy and ever-chatty hangout is the main attraction in the red-painted Duncan Garage heritage building across from the old train station (there's also a bookstore and food shop here). The entirely vegetarian chalkboard menu is crammed with tempting breakfast, lunch and bakery treats but aim for the rice bowls or poutine if you're feeling especially hungry.

Old Firehouse Wine Bar WEST COAST $$
(☑250-597-3473; www.theoldfirehouse.ca; 40 Ingram St; mains $13-22; ☺11:30am-11pm Tue-Sat,

reduced hours off-season) Divided into several rooms, this surprisingly large, dark-painted resto-bar is a popular spot for evening cocktails in the center of town. But it's also a great dining option with a well-executed menu of seasonally changing dishes – the flatbreads are menu mainstays (try the fig and prosciutto).

Hudson's on First WEST COAST $$
(☑250-597-0066; www.hudsonsonfirst.ca; 163 First St; mains $12-32; ☺11am-2pm Tue, 11am-late Wed-Fri, 10am-late Sat, 10am-2pm Sun) In an immaculately restored heritage building, the ever-changing seasonal menu here fuses local ingredients with subtle European influences. For lunch, go for the gourmet fish and chips (add the housemade soup) or drop by for an excellent eggs Benedict brunch on the weekend. But if you come for dinner, start with a cocktail in the tin-ceilinged bar.

Craig Street Brew Pub PUB FOOD $$
(☑250-737-2337; www.craigstreet.ca; 25 Craig St; mains $8-18; ☺11am-11pm Mon-Thu, to midnight Fri & Sat, to 10pm Sun; ☎☑) An inviting, multi-floor locals' hangout (aim for the top-floor patio in summer), this dark-wood boozer offers a huge menu of elevated pub grub, from taco salads to finger-licking pizzas (a favorite among diners). They also make their own beer. Go for a five-glass sampler ($12) and make sure it includes a seasonal plus the top-selling pilsner-style Cow Bay Lager.

❶ Getting There & Away

Greyhound Services (www.greyhound.ca) trundle in from Nanaimo (up to six times daily, one hour, $20) and Victoria (up to three times daily, one hour, $19.40).

Cowichan Bay

'Cow Bay' to the locals, the region's most attractive pit stop is a colorful string of wooden buildings perched over a mountain-framed ocean inlet. It's well worth an afternoon of your time, although it might take that long to find parking on a busy summer day.

Start your visit with a fresh-baked snack at **True Grain Bread** (☑250-746-7664; www.truegrain.ca; 1725 Cowichan Bay Rd; ☺8am-6pm, closed Mon Nov-Feb) then duck into the **Maritime Centre** (☑250-746-4955; www.classicboats.org; 1761 Cowichan Bay Rd; suggested donation $5; ☺dawn-dusk May-Sep, reduced hours in winter) to peruse the salty boat-building exhibits and intricate models. Next, stroll

VANCOUVER ISLAND BOOZE TRAIL

Vancouver Island's blossoming local food movement has spread to booze in recent years, with wineries, breweries, cideries and distilleries popping up across the region, giving visitors plenty of reason to appoint a designated driver. But unless you know where to go, many of these artisan operators can be hard to find. Here are some thirst-slaking recommendations for visitors.

In the Comox Valley, **Cumberland Brewing** (p184) is one of the island's tastiest new beer makers – don't miss their Red Tape Pale Ale. A weave around the Cowichan region delivers **Cherry Point Vineyards** (☑ 250-743-1272; www.cherrypointvineyards. com; 840 Cherry Point Rd, Cobble Hill; ◷ 10am-5pm), with its lip-smacking blackberry port; **Averill Creek** (☑ 250-709-9986; www.averillcreek.ca; 6552 North Rd, Duncan; ◷ 11am-5pm), with its patio views and lovely pinot noirs; and the rustic-chic **Merridale Estate Cidery** (☑ 250-743-4293; www.merridalecider.com; 1230 Merridale Rd, Cobble Hill; ◷ 11am-5pm, reduced hours off-season), an inviting apple-cider producer that also makes brandy and has a great patio bistro.

Further south in Saanich – just a short drive from Victoria – organic apples are also on the taste-tripping menu at **Sea Cider** (☑ 250-544-4824; www.seacider.ca; 2487 Mt St Michael Rd, Saanichton; ◷ 11am-4pm Jun-Sep, 11am-4pm Wed-Sun Oct-May). Booze of a stronger hue is the approach at Sidney's **Victoria Distillers** (☑ 250-544-8218; www.victoriadistillers.com; 9891 Seaport Pl; tours $7; ◷ 10am-5pm Sat & Sun Apr-Sep), where the lovely Oaken Gin is recommended. Both offer tours and tastings.

---

the shoreline to **Cowichan Estuary Nature Centre** (☑ 250-597-2288; www.cowichanestuary. ca; 1845 Cowichan Bay Rd; suggested donation $2; ☝) for illuminating displays on the region's flora and fauna, including an aquarium touch tank.

This region is filled with welcoming B&B options, including the delightful **Ambraden Pond B&B** (☑ 250-743-2562; www.ambraden. com; 971 Aros Rd, Cobble Hill; d from $175; ☎), with its secluded natural setting, two spacious rooms (plus self-catering carriage house suite) and Lulu, the welcoming house dog. It's a 10-minute drive from Cow Bay.

When you're ready for a lunchtime fuel-up, hook a waterfront table at **Rock Cod Cafe** (☑ 250-746-1550; www.rockcodcafe.com; 1759 Cowichan Bay Rd; mains $10-18; ◷ 11am-9pm Jul & Aug, 11am-7pm Sun-Thu, to 8pm Fri & Sat Sep-Jun; ☝) for fish and chips or a bowl of chowder, but save some belly space for an elongated dinner on the waterfront deck at the charming **Masthead Restaurant** (☑ 250-748-3714; www.themastheadrestaurant.com; 1705 Cowichan Bay Rd; mains $26-35; ◷ 5-10pm). The three-course tasting menu is surprisingly good value and you can add a bottle of local wine to keep things lively.

Chemainus

After the last sawmill shut down in 1983, tiny Chemainus became the model for BC communities dealing with declining resource jobs. Instead of submitting to a slow death, town officials commissioned a giant wall mural depicting local history. More than 45 artworks were later added and a tourism industry was born.

Stroll the Chemainus streets (expect a permanent aroma of fresh-cut logs from the nearby sawmill) on a mural hunt and you'll pass artsy boutiques and tempting ice-cream shops, some housed in heritage buildings, others in attractive faux-historic piles. In the evening, the surprisingly large **Chemainus Theatre** (www.chemainustheatrefestival.ca; 9737 Chemainus Rd; tickets from $25) stages professional productions, mostly popular plays and musicals, to keep you occupied.

Nearby, the town's **Chemainus Inn** (☑ 250-246-4181; www.chemainushotel.com; 9573 Chemainus Rd; d from $169; ☀☀☀) is like a midrange business hotel transplanted from a much larger town; the rooms here are slick and comfortable and many include kitchen facilities. Rates include breakfast.

Drop by the handsome yellow heritage building housing **Willow Street Café** (☑ 250-246-2434; www.willowstreetcafe.com; 9749 Willow St; mains $13-15; ◷ 8am-5pm; ☎). With a menu founded on wraps, sandwiches and quesadillas, this cafe in the heart of town has a popular summertime patio out front. Save room for a slab of cheesecake then jog around the building a dozen times to work it off.

Check in at the **visitors center** (🖉250-246-3944; www.visitchemainus.ca; 9799 Waterwheel Cres; ⊘9:30am-5pm mid-Jun–Aug, reduced hours in winter) for mural maps and further information, plus the little community museum in the same building.

Nanaimo

POP 85,000

Vancouver Island's 'second metropolis,' Nanaimo will never have the allure of tourist-magnet Victoria but the Harbour City has undergone some quiet upgrades since the 1990s with the emergence, especially on Commercial St, of some good shops and eateries, plus a good museum. With dedicated ferry services from the mainland, the city is also a handy hub for exploring the rest of the island.

◎ Sights

Nanaimo Museum   MUSEUM
(Map p173; 🖉250-753-1821; www.nanaimomuseum.ca; 100 Museum Way; adult/child $2/75¢; ⊘10am-5pm daily, closed Sun Sep–mid-May) Just off the Commercial St main drag, this popular museum showcases the region's heritage, from First Nations to colonial, maritime, sporting and beyond. Highlights of the eclectic collection include exhibits on Nanaimo bars and bathtub racing plus a carved golden beaver from an 1890s tugboat. Ask at the front desk about the museum's guided walking tour program as well as summertime entry to the nearby **Bastion**, an 1853 wooden tower fortification.

**Newcastle Island Marine
Provincial Park**   PARK
(www.newcastleisland.ca) 🏄 Nanaimo's rustic outdoor gem offers 22km of **hiking** and **biking** trails, plus beaches and wildlife spotting. Traditional Coast Salish land, it was the site of shipyards and coal mines before becoming a popular summer excursion for locals in the 1930s when a tea pavilion was added. Accessed by a 10-minute ferry hop from the harbor (adult/child return $9/5), there's a seasonal eatery and regular First Nations dancing displays.

Wild Play Element Parks   AMUSEMENT PARK
(🖉250-716-7874; www.wildplay.com; 35 Nanaimo River Rd; adult/child $35/20; ⊘10am-6pm mid-May–Sep, reduced hours off-season; 🚼) The perfect spot to tire your kids out, this tree-lined adventure playground is packed with adrenaline-pumping fun, from bungee jumping to scream-triggering zip-lining. Along with its fun obstacle courses, there's plenty of action to keep the family occupied, from walking trails to busy volleyball courts.

Old City Quarter   AREA
(Map p173; www.oldcityquarter.com; cnr Fitzwilliam & Wesley Sts) A steep hike uphill from the waterfront on Bastion and Fitzwilliam Sts delivers you to a strollable heritage hood of independent stores, galleries and eateries in brightly painted old buildings. Highlights include McLeans Specialty Foods; A Wee Cupcakery; and Taphouse Restaurant, a large pub that has taken over the town's old train station. Look out for the heritage plaques on buildings in this area.

🛏 Sleeping

Painted Turtle Guesthouse   HOSTEL $
(Map p173; 🖉250-753-4432; www.paintedturtle.ca; 121 Bastion St; dm/r $38/99; @☎) New owners have not diminished the quality at this top-notch, well-maintained HI-affiliated hostel where small dorms combine with 10 hotel-style private rooms (there are also two family rooms). The hardwood floors and IKEA-style furnishings line a large and welcoming kitchen-lounge combo and you can book tours from the front desk if you've had enough of strumming the hostel's guitar.

Buccaneer Inn   MOTEL $$
(🖉250-753-1246; www.buccaneerinn.com; 1577 Stewart Ave; d/ste from $100/160; ☎) Handy for the Departure Bay ferry terminal, this friendly, family-run motel has a gleaming white exterior that makes it hard to pass by. It's worth staying in as the neat-and-tidy approach is carried over into the maritime-themed rooms, most of which have kitchen facilities. Splurge on a spacious suite and you'll have a fireplace, full kitchen and flatscreen TV.

Coast Bastion Hotel   HOTEL $$
(Map p173; 🖉250-753-6601; www.coasthotels.com; 11 Bastion St; d from $175; ❄@☎🐾) Downtown's best hotel has an unbeatable location overlooking the harbor, with most guests enjoying waterfront views. Rooms have been well refurbished with a lounge-modern élan in recent years, adding flatscreen TVs and, in most rooms, small fridges. The lobby restaurant-bar is a popular hangout and there's a spa if you want to chillax.

Nanaimo

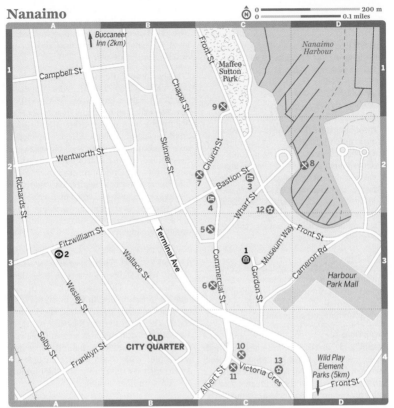

Nanaimo

Inn on Long Lake   HOTEL **$$**
(☑ 250-758-1144; www.innonlonglake.com; 4700 Island Hwy; d from $160; ❄ 🐾 🛜 🚲) This family-owned motel property is handily located just off the highway. But don't worry about noise: all the rooms face the tranquil lake. A large-scale renovation has transformed rooms with kitchen facilities and new bathrooms, and rates include a good continental-breakfast buffet.

✖ Eating

★**Gabriel's Gourmet Café**   INTERNATIONAL **$**
(Map p173; ☑ 250-714-0271; www.gabrielscafe. ca; 39 Commercial St; mains $9-13; ☺ 8am-7pm; 🛜 🚲) An expanded new location for Nanaimo's best farm-to-table eatery (check out the tables made from old bowling-alley wood) means a larger menu of international-influenced comfort dishes. But some things never change, including favorites like

DON'T MISS

EAT & DRINK LIKE A LOCAL

With Nanaimo's bar scene decidedly underwhelming, it's worth packing your beer belly and heading out of town (with a designated driver, of course). A 20-minute weave from the city via Hwy 1, Cedar Rd and Yellow Point Rd delivers you to the **Crow and Gate** (☑ 250-722-3731; www. crowandgate.ca; 2313 Yellow Point Rd, Cedra; ☺ 11am-11pm), the best Brit-style pub in British Columbia. With a dark, wood-beam interior and a grassy beer garden – plus a lip-smacking menu of housemade pies, Scotch eggs as well as bangers and mash that far exceed most pubs back in the home country – this idyllic country-side watering hole is a great spot to spend a languid summer evening.

the spoon-licking Malaysian-peanut-sauce chicken rice bowl. Vegetarians are well looked after (quinoa and chickpea fritter recommended) and there's some sidewalk seating if you need some sun.

Vault Cafe CAFE $
(Map p173; ☑ 778-441-2950; 499 Wallace St; mains $13-16; ☺ 8am-10pm Mon & Tue, 8am-midnight Wed-Sat, 10am-4pm Sun; 🛜) A cavernous former bank building colonized with mismatched old sofas, junk-shop knickknacks and some striking local artwork, the Vault is a laid-back coffeehouse and lunch spot (with bulging toasted sandwiches) by day and a bohemian hangout by night, when there are often bands, open-mic events or film screenings.

2 Chefs Affair DINER $
(Map p173; ☑ 250-591-4656; www.twochefsaffair. com; 123b Commercial St; mains $13-15; ☺ 8am-3pm; 🛜) Focused on great comfort food at great prices, with a fresh, made-from-scatch approach, this highly welcoming locals' haunt in the heart of downtown is a great spot for breakfast – go the eggs Benedict route. Lunch is arguably even more enticing: ask for the 'Cheating Heart' sandwich and you won't be disappointed.

Pirate Chips FAST FOOD $
(Map p173; ☑ 250-753-2447; www.pirate-chips. com; 75 Front St; mains $10-18; ☺ 11am-9pm Tue-Thu, to 10pm Fri & Sat, to 8pm Sun) A sparkling new location for this former Nanaimo hole-in-the-wall means the old faves – fish and chips, and deep-fried Nanaimo bars – have been joined by a wide array of new, most-ly seafood dishes. Try the bannock tacos, in meat or seafood varieties, and aim for an outside seat in summer.

Thirsty Camel Café MIDDLE EASTERN $
(Map p173; ☑ 250-753-9313; www.thirstycamel cafe.ca; 14 Victoria Cres; mains $8-16; ☺ 11am-4pm Mon-Wed, 11am-7pm Thu & Fri, noon-4pm Sat; 🍴) Partake of a lip-smacking Middle East-ern feast at this cheery little family-owned joint, tucked into an elbow of Victoria Cres. Everything's prepared from scratch, which makes for addictive hummus, spicy soups and the region's best felafel. The shareable platters, especially the spice-encrusted Per-sian chicken, are recommended and there are several excellent vegetarian options that even meat eaters will love.

Penny's Palapa MEXICAN $$
(Map p173; ☑ 250-753-2150; www.pennyspalapa. com; 10 Wharf St, Dock H; mains $8-18; ☺ 11am-8pm May-Sep; 🍴) This flower-and-flag-decked floating hut and patio in the harbor is love-ly for an alfresco meal among the jostling boats. The inventive, well-priced menu of Mexican delights includes seasonal seafood specials (the signature halibut tacos are great) plus some good vegetarian options. Arrive early, as the dining area fills rapidly on balmy summer evenings.

Modern Cafe INTERNATIONAL $$
(Map p173; ☑ 250-754-5022; www.themodern cafe.ca; 221 Commercial St; mains $12-22; ☺ 11am-11pm Mon-Wed, 11am-midnight Thu-Sat, 10am-11pm Sun) This reinvented old coffee shop has cool, loungy interiors combining exposed brick and comfy booths and, for when it's sunny, a ray-warmed street-side patio. The menu includes some great gourmet comfort food – go for the lobster ravioli – and the weekend brunch draws the locals.

☆ Entertainment

Port Theatre THEATER
(Map p173; ☑ 250-754-8550; www.porttheatre. com; 125 Front St) Presenting local and touring live theater shows.

Queen's Hotel LIVE MUSIC
(Map p173; ☑ 250-754-6751; www.thequeens. ca; 34 Victoria Cres) The city's best live music and dance spot, hosting an eclectic roster of performances and club nights, ranging from indie to jazz and country.

❶ Information

For tourist information, drop into the main **Nanaimo Visitor Centre** (☑ 250-751-1556; www.tourismnanaimo.com; 2450 Northfield Rd; ☺ 9am-6pm, reduced hours off-season) or, in summer, hit the satellite branch located at the Bastion historic site on the waterfront.

❶ Getting There & Away

AIR

Nanaimo Airport (☑ 250-924-2157; www.nanaimoairport.com) is 18km south of town via Hwy 1. Frequent **Air Canada** (www.aircanada.com) flights arrive here from Vancouver (from $150, 25 minutes) throughout the day.

Frequent and convenient **Harbour Air** (☑ 250-714-0900; www.harbourair.com) floatplane services also arrive in the inner harbor from downtown Vancouver ($100, 20 minutes).

BOAT

BC Ferries (☑ 250-386-3431; www.bcferries.com) from Tsawwassen (passenger/vehicle $17/56, two hours) arrive at Duke Point, 14km south of Nanaimo. Services from West Vancouver's Horseshoe Bay (passenger/vehicle $17/56, 95 minutes) arrive at Departure Bay, 3km north of the city center via Hwy 1.

BUS

Greyhound Canada (www.greyhound.ca) buses arrive from Victoria ($28, two hours, up to 6 daily).

❶ Getting Around

Downtown Nanaimo, around the harbor, is highly walkable, but after that the city spreads out and a car or strong bike legs are required. Be aware that taxis are expensive here.

Nanaimo Regional Transit (www.bctransit.com; single trip/day pass $2.50/6.25) Buses stop along Gordon St, west of Harbour Park Mall. Bus 2 goes to the Departure Bay ferry terminal. No city buses run to Duke Point.

Nanaimo Airporter (www.nanaimoairporter.com; from $26) Provides door-to-door service to downtown from both ferry terminals, as well as handy airport drop-off and pick-up.

Parksville & Qualicum

This popular mid-island seaside region, which also includes rustic Coombs, has been a traditional destination for vacationing families for decades – hence the water parks and miniature golf attractions. It's a great spot to take a breather on your trip up or down island.

◉ Sights & Activities

Morningstar Farm   FARM
(☑ 250-954-3931; www.morningstarfarm.ca; 403 Lowry's Rd, Parksville; ☺ 9am-5pm; 🖶) **FREE** Check out the region's 'locavore' credentials at this delightful and highly welcoming working farmstead. Let your kids run wild – most will quickly fall in love with the rabbits – then hunt down some samples from the on-site Little Qualicum Cheeseworks and Mooberry Winery: Bleu Claire cheese is recommended, along with a bottle of velvety blueberry wine to go.

Coombs Old Country Market   MARKET
(☑ 250-248-6272; www.oldcountrymarket.com; 2326 Alberni Hwy, Coombs; ☺ 9am-7pm) The mother of all pit stops, this sprawling, ever-expanding indoor food and crafts menagerie is stuffed with bakery and produce delectables. It attracts huge numbers of visitors on summer days, when cameras are pointed at the grassy roof, where a herd of goats spend the season. Nip inside for giant ice-cream cones, heaping pizzas and the deli makings of a great picnic. Souvenir required? Grab a Billy Gruff chocolate bar.

Save some time to explore the attendant store and attractions around the site, from clothing emporiums to an Italian trattoria.

Horne Lake Caves & Outdoor Centre   PARK
(☑ 250-248-7829; www.hornelake.com; tours from $24; ☺ 10am-5pm) A 45-minute drive from Parksville delivers you to BC's best spelunking. Some caves are open to the public for self-exploration, though the excellent guided tours are recommended, from family-friendly to extreme; book ahead for these. To get there, take Hwy 19 towards Courtenay, then exit 75 and proceed for 12km on the gravel road; if you get lost en route give them a call.

Milner Gardens & Woodland   GARDENS
(☑ 250-752-6153; www.milnergardens.org; 2179 W Island Hwy, Qualicum Beach; adult/youth/child $11/$6.50/free; ☺ 10am-5pm mid-Apr–Aug, 10am-5pm Thu-Sun Sep–mid-Oct) This idyllic outdoor attraction combines rambling forest trails shaded by centuries-old trees with flower-packed gardens planted with magnificent trilliums and rhododendrons. Meander down to the 1930s **tearoom** on a stunning bluff overlooking the water. Then tuck into a full afternoon tea ($21) on the porch and drink in views of the bird-lined shore and snowcapped peaks shimmering on the horizon.

BRITISH COLUMBIA PARKSVILLE & QUALICUM

🛏 Sleeping & Eating

★ Free Spirit Spheres   CABIN **$$**
(📞 250-757-9445; www.freespiritspheres.com; 420 Horne Lake Rd, Qualicum Beach; cabins from $175) These unique, spherical tree houses enable guests to cocoon themselves in the forest canopy. Compact inside, 'Eve' is small and basic, while 'Eryn' and 'Melody' are lined with built-in cabinets. It's all about communing with nature (TVs are replaced by books) and guests receive snacks for their stay on arrival. There's also a ground-level facilities block with sauna, BBQ and hotel-quality showers.

Blue Willow Guest House   B&B **$$**
(📞 250-752-9052; www.bluewillowguesthouse.com; 524 Quatna Rd, Qualicum Beach; d from $140) A surprisingly spacious, delightfully tranquil Victorian-style cottage, this lovely B&B has a book-lined lounge, exposed beams and a fragrant country garden. The two rooms and one self-contained suite are lined with antiques and each is extremely homey. The attention to detail carries over to the gourmet breakfast: served in the conservatory, it's accompanied by finger-licking home-baked treats.

Crown Mansion   BOUTIQUE HOTEL **$$**
(📞 250-752-5776; www.crownmansion.com; 292 E Crescent Rd, Qualicum Beach; d from $209; 🛜) A sumptuous family home built in 1912, this handsome, white-painted mansion has been restored to its former glory and opened as a unique hotel. Recall past guests Bing Crosby and John Wayne as you check out the family crest in the library fireplace, then retire to your elegant room. Rates include continental breakfast; arrive early to snag the window table.

Bistro 694   CANADIAN **$$**
(📞 250-752-0301; www.bistro694.com; 694 Memorial Ave, Qualicum Beach; mains $21-30; ⏱4pm-9pm Wed-Sun) Ask the locals and they'll tell you to cancel your dinner plans and head straight here. You'll find an intimate, candlelit dining room little bigger than a train carriage and a big-city menu fusing top-notch regional ingredients with knowing international nods. We favor the seafood route, especially if the Balinese prawn curry or highly addictive seafood crepes are available. Reserve ahead.

Fish Tales Café   SEAFOOD **$$**
(📞 250-752-6053; www.fishtalescafe.com; 3336 Island Hwy W, Qualicum Beach; mains $12-25; ⏱11:30am-9pm Tue-Fri, 8am-9pm Sat & Sun) This Tudoresque landmark has the look of an old English tea shop, but it's been reeling in visitors with its perfect fish and chips for years. It's worth exploring the non-deep-fried dishes; the grilled salmon dinner is recommended. If you arrive early enough, grab a table in the flower-studded, fairy-lighted garden.

ℹ Information

For more information on the area, visit www.parksvillequalicumbeach.com.

ℹ Getting There & Away

Tofino Bus services arrive in Parksville from Victoria ($35, two to three hours, three daily) and Nanaimo ($17, 30 minutes, three daily) among others.

Port Alberni

With resource jobs declining, Alberni – located on Hwy 4 between the island's east and west coasts – has been dipping its toe into tourism in recent years. And while the downtown core is a little run-down, there are some good historical attractions and outdoorsy activities to consider before you drive through.

◉ Sights & Activities

Cathedral Grove   PARK
(www.bcparks.ca; MacMillan Provincial Park) Between Parksville and Port Alberni, this spiritual home of tree huggers is the mystical highlight of **MacMillan Provincial Park**. It's often overrun with summer visitors – try not to knock them down as they scamper across the highway in front of you. The accessible forest trails wind through a dense, breathtaking canopy of vegetation, offering glimpses of some of BC's oldest trees, including centuries-old Douglas firs more than 3m in diameter. Try hugging that.

Alberni Valley Museum   MUSEUM
(📞 250-723-2181; www.alberniheritage.com; 4255 Wallace St; by donation; ⏱10am-5pm Tue-Sat, to 8pm Thu) Don't be put off by the unassuming concrete exterior: this is one of Vancouver Island's best community museums. Studded with fascinating First Nations displays – plus an eclectic array of vintage exhibits ranging from bottle caps to dresses and old-school toys – it's worth an hour of anyone's time. History buffs should also hop aboard the summertime **Alberni Pacific Railway steam train** (www.albernisteamtrain.ca) for a trundle to McLean Mill; it's a National Hiistoric Site.

MV Frances Barkley
CRUISE

(☑ 250-723-8313; www.ladyrosemarine.com; 5425 Argyle St; round-trip $60-82) This historic boat service is a vital link for the region's remote communities, ferrying freight, supplies and passengers between Alberni and Bamfield thrice weekly. In summer, with its route extended to Ucluelet and the beautiful Broken Group Islands, it lures kayakers and mountain bikers, but it's also open for those who just fancy an day cruise up Barkley Sound.

The company recently purchased a decommissioned BC Ferries vessel which they'll also be deploying on the route.

🛏 Sleeping & Eating

Hummingbird Guesthouse
B&B $$

(☑ 250-720-2111; www.hummingbirdguesthouse. com; 5769 River Rd; ste from $140; 🛜) With four large suites and a huge deck with its own hot tub, this modern B&B has a home-away-from-home feel. There's a shared kitchen on each of the two floors and each suite has satellite TV; one has its own sauna. For families, there's a teen-friendly games room out back.

All Mex'd Up
MEXICAN $

(☑ 250-723-8226; 5440 Argyle St; mains $4-10; ⊙ 11am-4pm Sun-Fri, 9am-4pm Sat) A funky and highly colorful Mexican eatery near the waterfront, this fairy-lighted little spot makes everything from scratch and focuses on local ingredients as much as possible. Tuck into a classic array of made-with-love tacos, quesadillas and big-ass burritos and you'll be full for your day of exploring, especially if you add a side of nachos with spicy *pico de gallo* (salsa).

Bare Bones Fish & Chips
FISH & CHIPS $$

(☑ 250-720-0900; 4824 Johnston Rd; mains $9-21; ⊙ 11:30am-7:30pm Sun-Thu, to 8pm Fri & Sat) Colonizing a decommissioned wooden church, this smashing fry-joint serves cod, salmon and halibut in three different styles (beer-battered recommended), adding a tangle of delicious chips and their own lemon-dill dip. Arrive off-peak to avoid the rush (this place is a true local favorite) and add a prawn side dish if you're still hungry (you won't be).

ℹ Information

For more on what to do in the region, visit www. albernivalleytourism.com

ℹ Getting There & Away

Tofino Bus services arrive here from Victoria ($46, four hours, three daily) and Tofino ($29, two hours, three daily) among others.

Pacific Rim National Park Reserve

Dramatic, wave-whipped beaches and mist-licked forests make the **Pacific Rim National Park Reserve** (☑ 250-726-3500; www. pc.gc.ca/pacificrim; 2040 Pacific Rim Hwy; park day-pass adult/child $7.80/3.90) a must-see for anyone interested in encountering BC's raw West Coast wilderness. The 500-sq-km park comprises the northern Long Beach Unit, between Tofino and Ucluelet; the Broken Group Islands Unit in Barkley Sound; and, to the south, the ever-popular West Coast Trail Unit. If you're stopping in the park, you'll need to pay and display a pass, available from the visitors center or from the yellow dispensers dotted along the highway.

Long Beach Unit

Attracting the lion's share of park visitors, Long Beach Unit is easily accessible by car along the Pacific Rim Hwy. Wide sandy beaches, untamed surf, lots of beachcombing nooks, plus a living museum of dense, old-growth rainforest, are the main reasons for the summer tourist clamor. **Cox Bay Beach** alone is an ideal hangout for surfers and families. Seabirds, sand dollars, and purple and orange starfish abound.

For an introduction to the area's natural history and First Nations heritage, visit the **Kwisitis Visitor Centre** (Wick Rd; ⊙ 10am-5pm Jun-Oct, 11am-3pm Fri-Sun Nov-May) FREE overlooking Wickaninnish Beach. If you're suddenly inspired to plunge in for a stroll, try one of the following **walking trails**, keeping your eyes peeled for swooping bald eagles and giant banana slugs. Safety precautions apply: tread carefully over slippery surfaces and never turn your back on the mischievous surf.

➡ **Long Beach** Great scenery along the sandy shore (1.2km; easy).

➡ **Rainforest Trail** Two interpretive loops through old-growth forest (1km; moderate).

➡ **Schooner Trail** Through old- and second-growth forests with beach access (1km; moderate).

➡ **Shorepine Bog** Loops around a moss-layered bog (800m; easy and wheelchair accessible).

West Coast Trail Unit

The 75km West Coast Trail is BC's best-known hiking route. It's also one of the toughest, not for the uninitiated. There are two things you'll need to know before tackling it: it will hurt and you'll want to do it again next year.

The trail winds along the wave-licked rainforest shoreline between trailhead information centers at Pachena Bay, 5km south of Bamfield on the north end, and Gordon River, 5km north of Port Renfrew on the southern tip. The entire stretch takes between six and seven days to complete. Alternatively, a mid-point entrance at Nitinat Lake, operated by the **Ditidaht First Nation** (☎ 250-745-3999; www.westcoasttrail.com), can cut your visit to a two-or three-day adventure. Check their website for packages.

Open from May to the end of September, access to the route is limited to 60 overnight backpackers each day and **reservations** (☎ 519-826-5391, 877-737-3783; www.reservation.pc.gc.ca; nonrefundable reservation fee $11) are required. Book as far ahead as you can – reservations open in January every year. All overnighters must pay a trail-user fee ($127.50), plus a per-person reservation fee ($24.50) and the price of the short ferry crossings along the length of the route. All overnighters must attend a detailed orientation session before departing. If you don't have a reservation on the day you arrive, your name can be added to a standby list for any remaining spots (don't count on this, though, especially during the summer peak).

If you don't want to go the whole hog (you wimp), you can do a day hike or hike half the trail from Pachena Bay, considered the easier end of the route. Overnight hikers who only hike this end of the trail can exit from Nitinat Lake. Day hikers are exempt from the pricey trail-user fee, but they need to get a day-use permit at one of the trailheads.

West Coast Trail walkers must be able to manage rough, slippery terrain, stream crossings and severe, suddenly changing weather. There are more than 100 little, and some not-so-little, bridges and 70 ladders. Be prepared to treat or boil all water and cook on a lightweight camping stove; you'll be bringing in all your own food. Hikers can rest their weary muscles at any of the basic campsites along the route, most of which have solar-composting outhouses. It's recommended that you set out from a trailhead at least five hours before sundown to ensure you reach a campsite before nightfall – stumbling around in the dark is the prime cause of accidents on this route.

West Coast Trail Express (☎ 250-477-8700; www.trailbus.com; from $60; ⊙ daily mid-Jun–mid-Sep, odd-numbered days May–mid-Jun & last two weeks of Sep) runs a handy shuttle service to and from the trailheads. Book ahead.

Broken Group Island Unit

Comprising some 300 islands and rocks scattered across 80 sq km around the entrance to Barkley Sound, this serene natural wilderness is beloved of visiting kayakers – especially those who enjoy close-up views of whales, porpoises and multitudinous birdlife. Compasses are required for navigating here, unless you fancy paddling to Hawaii.

If you're up for a trek, **Lady Rose Marine Services** (☎ 250-723-8313; www.ladyrosemarine.com) will ship you and your kayak from Port Alberni to its Sechart Lodge three hours away in Barkley Sound. The lodge rents kayaks if you'd rather travel light and it also offers accommodations (single/double $164/263, including meals).

From there, popular paddle destinations include **Gibraltar Island**, one hour away, with its sheltered campground and explorable beaches and tidal pools. **Willis Island** (1½ hours from Sechart) is also popular. It has a campground and, at low tide, you can walk to the surrounding islands. Remote **Benson Island** (four hours from Sechart) has a campground, grazing deer and a blowhole.

Camping fees are $9.80 per night, payable at Sechart or to the boat-based staff who patrol the region – they can collect additional fees from you if you decide to stay longer. The campgrounds are predictably basic and have solar composting toilets, but you must carry out all your garbage. Bring your own drinking water since island creeks are often dry in summer.

Tofino
POP 2050

Transforming from resource outpost to hippie enclave and now a resort town, Tofino is Vancouver Island's favorite outdoorsy retreat. It's not surprising that surf fans, families and city-escaping Vancouverites keep coming: packed with activities and blessed with spectacular local beaches, it sits on Clayoquot Sound, where forested mounds rise from roiling, ever-dramatic waves.

⊙ Sights

Tofino Botanical Gardens GARDENS
(☑ 250-725-1220; www.tbgf.org; 1084 Pacific Rim Hwy; 3-day admission adult/child $12/free; ⊙ 8am-dusk Jun-Aug, reduced hours off-season) Explore what coastal temperate rainforests are all about by checking out the frog pond, forest boardwalk, native plants and educational workshops at this smashing, bird-packed attraction. New sculptures have been added to the garden in recent years, many by local artists. Pick up a self-guided field guide from the front desk to illuminate your exploration.There's a $1 discount on admission if you arrive car-free.

Tofino Brewing Company BREWERY
(☑ 250-725-2899; www.tofinobrewingco.com; 681 Industrial Way; ⊙ 11am-10pm Jun-Aug, reduced hours off-season) Hidden around the back of an unassuming industrial building, this smashing little brewery makes islanders very merry, which is why its brews are in restaurants around town and beyond. Roll up to the tasting bar and check out a few samples (four-glass flights are $6). Always ask for the seasonal offerings and check out the excellent Kelp Stout and Tuff Session Ale.

Maquinna Marine Provincial Park PARK
(www.bcparks.ca) One of the most popular day trips from Tofino, the highlight here is **Hot Spring Cove**. Tranquility-minded trekkers travel to the park by Zodiac boat or seaplane, watching for whales and other sea critters en route. From the boat landing, 2km of boardwalks lead to the natural **hot pools**.

Eagle Aerie Gallery GALLERY
(☑ 250-725-3235; royhenryvickers.com; 350 Campbell St; ⊙ 10am-5pm) Showcasing the work of First Nations artist Roy Henry Vickers, this dramatic, longhouse-style building is a downtown landmark. Inside you'll find beautifully presented paintings and carvings as well as occasional opportunities to meet the man himself.

Ahousat PARK
(www.wildsidetrail.com) Situated on remote Flores Island and accessed by tour boat or kayak, Ahousat is the mystical location of the spectacular **Wild Side Heritage Trail**, a moderately difficult path that traverses 11km of forests, beaches and headlands between Ahousat and Cow Bay. There's a natural warm spring on the island and it's also home to a First Nations band. A popular destination for kayakers, camping (no facilities) is allowed.

Meares Island PARK
Visible through the mist and accessible via kayak or tour boat from the Tofino waterfront, Meares Island is home to the **Big Tree Trail**, a 400m boardwalk through old-growth forest that includes a stunning 1500-year-old red cedar. The island was the site of the key 1984 Clayoquot Sound anti-logging protest that kicked off the region's latter-day environmental movement.

🏃 Activities

Surf Sister SURFING
(☑ 250-725-4456; www.surfsister.com; 625 Campbell St; lessons $79) Introductory lessons for kids, families and beginner adults.

T'ashii Paddle School CANOEING
(☑ 250-266-3787; www.tofinopaddle.com; 1258 Pacific Rim Hwy; tour from $65) Tour the regional waters in a canoe (you'll also be doing the paddling) with a First Nations guide who provides an evocative interpretive narration. Walking tours also available.

Ocean Outfitters BOATING
(☑ 250-725-2866; www.oceanoutfitters.bc.ca; 368 Main St; adult/child $99/79) Whale-watching tours, with bear and hot-springs treks as well as fishing charters also offered.

STORMING TOFINO

Started as a clever marketing ploy to lure off-season visitors, **storm watching** has become a popular reason to visit the island's wild west coast between November and March. View spectacularly crashing winter waves, then scamper back inside for hot chocolate with a face freckled by sea salt. There are usually good off-peak deals to be had in area accommodations during storm-watching season and many hotels can supply you with loaner 'Tofino tuxedos,' otherwise known as waterproof gear. The best spots to catch a few crashing spectacles are Cox Bay, Chesterman Beach, Long Beach, Second Bay and Wickaninnish Beach. Just remember not to get too close or turn your back on the waves: these gigantic swells will have you in the water within seconds given half the chance.

DON'T MISS

PACIFIC RIM PIT STOP

Don't drive too fast in your rush to get to end-of-the-highway Tofino or you'll miss the locals' favorite stomping ground. Ostensibly known as the **Beaches Shopping Centre** area, 1180 Pacific Rim Hwy is home to dozens of cool little wood-built businesses where you could easily spend a happy half-day. Start with a java at **Tofitian** (1180 Pacific Rim Hwy; ⊘ 7:30am-5pm Jun-Aug, reduced hours off-season; 🛜) then add some chocolate and maybe an ice-cream at **Chocolate Tofino** just around the corner (salted caramels recommended). When lunch beckons, join the line-up at **Tacofino** (📞 250-726-8288; www.tacofino.com; 1184 Pacific Rim Hwy; mains $5-13; ⊘ 11am-7pm, reduced hours off-season) (or call your order in like the locals do) or avoid queuing completely by heading to **Wildside Grill** (📞 250-725-9453; www.wildsidegrill. com; 1180 Pacific Rim Hwy; mains $6-18; ⊘ 9am-9pm, reduced hours off-season) for panko-fried prawns.

Jamie's Whaling Station BOATING
(📞 250-725-3919; www.jamies.com; 606 Campbell St; adult/child $109/79) Spot whales, bears and sea lions on Jamie's boat jaunts. Short or multiday kayak tours are also available.

🛏 Sleeping

Whalers on the Point Guesthouse HOSTEL $
(📞 250-725-3443; www.hihostels.ca; 81 West St; dm/r $45/129; 🛜) Close to the action, but with a secluded waterfront location, this excellent HI hostel is a comfy, wood-lined retreat. Dorms are mercifully small (the female-only one has the best waterfront views) and there are some highly sought-after private rooms. Facilities include a BBQ patio, games room and a wet sauna. Reservations are essential in summer. Bike rentals are available ($35 for 24 hours).

Tofino Inlet Cottages CABIN $$
(📞 250-725-3441; www.tofinoinletcottages.com; 350 Olsen Rd; ste from $130; 🛜) Located in a pocket of tranquility just off the highway, this hidden gem is perfect for waking up to glassy-calm waterfront views. It consists of two 1960s-built A-frame cottages, divided into suites, and a spacious woodsy house, which has a lovely circular hearth and is ideal for families.

Ecolodge HOSTEL $$
(📞 250-725-1220; www.tbgf.org; 1084 Pacific Rim Hwy; r from $159; @ 🛜) In the grounds of the botanical gardens, this quiet, wood-built education center has a selection of rooms, a large kitchen and an on-site laundry. Popular with families and groups, there's a bunk room that's around $40 each per night in summer for groups of four. Rates include garden entry and there's a copy of Darwin's *The Origin of Species* in every room.

Ocean Village Beach Resort CABIN $$$
(📞 250-725-3755; www.oceanvillageresort.com; 555 Hellesen Dr; ste from $229; 🛜🏊🐾) This immaculate beachside resort of beehive-shaped cedar cabins – hence the woodsy aroma when you step in the door – is a family favorite, with a Scandinavian look. Each unit faces the nearby shoreline and all have handy kitchens. If your kids tire of the beach, there's a saltwater pool and lots of loaner board games to keep them occupied. No in-room TVs.

Pacific Sands Beach Resort RESORT $$$
(📞 250-725-3322; www.pacificsands.com; 1421 Pacific Rim Hwy; d from $350; 🛜🐾) Combining comfortable lodge rooms, all with full kitchens, plus spectacular three-level beach houses, this family-friendly resort hugs dramatic Cox Bay Beach. Wherever you stay, you'll be lulled to sleep by the sound of the nearby rolling surf. The spacious, contemporary-furnished beach houses are ideal for groups and have stone fireplaces and top-floor bathtubs with views. Free summertime kids' camps.

Wickaninnish Inn HOTEL $$$
(📞 250-725-3100; www.wickinn.com; Chesterman Beach; d from $420; 🛜🐾) Cornering the market in luxury winter-storm-watching packages, 'the Wick' is worth a stay any time of year. Embodying nature with its recycled-wood furnishings, natural stone tiles and the ambience of a place grown rather than constructed, the sumptuous guest rooms have push-button gas fireplaces, two-person hot tubs and floor-to-ceiling windows. It's one of BC's most romantic hotels.

🍴 Eating

Common Loaf Bake Shop BAKERY $
(📞 250-725-3915; 1801 First St; menu items $8-12; ⊘ 8am-6pm) The locals' favorite bakery hangout, this red-painted back street hangout is lined with local art and has a little community library box outside if you

need something to read over your java and croissant. Lunch-hungry visitors should head down the grilled cheese sandwich route, while apposite egg-based sandwiches are also available for breakfasters. Cash only.

Schooner SEAFOOD $$
(☑250-725-3444; www.schoonerrestaurant.ca; 331 Campbell St; mains $18-32; ⊙9am-10pm) A Tofino fixture for almost 70 years, this local legend has never rested on its laurels. Start your evening with a cocktail, then launch your voyage into the region's seafood bounty; the giant, two-person Admiral's Plate blowout of local salmon, scallops et al is the way to go. Come back the next morning for a crab Benedict brunch.

Sobo CANADIAN $$
(☑250-725-2341; www.sobo.ca; 311 Neill St; mains $14-33; ⊙11:30am-9:30pm) This local favorite launched as a food truck but has been a popular sit-down eatery for years. The focus at Sobo – meaning Sophisticated Bohemian – is seasonal West Coast ingredients prepared with international influences. A brilliant place to dive into fresh-catch seafood, there's a hearty, well-priced lunch menu if you need an early fill-up; chowder, fish tacos and gourmet pizzas are recommended.

Wolf in the Fog CANADIAN $$$
(☑250-725-9653; www.wolfinthefog.com; 150 Fourth St; mains $15-45; ⊙9am-late, dinner from 5pm) Reserve ahead for your table at this sparkling regional- and seasonal-focused restaurant that's won awards as Canada's best new restaurant in recent years. The larger plates to share are the best way to go (expect anything from Fraser Valley duck to delectable shellfish) but make sure you also add a taste-bud-popping cedar-sour cocktail.

❶ Information

Tourism Tofino Visitor Centre (☑250-725-3414; www.tourismtofino.com; 1426 Pacific Rim Hwy; ⊙9am-8pm Jun-Aug, reduced hours off-season) A short drive south of town, the visitors center has detailed information on area accommodations, hiking trails and hot surf spots. There's also a kiosk in the town center in summer that dispenses advice to out-of-towners.

❶ Getting There & Away

Orca Airways (☑604-270-6722; www.flyorcaair.com) Flights arrive at Tofino Airport from Vancouver International Airport's South Terminal ($217, one hour, up to five daily).

Tofino Bus (www.tofinobus.com) Services arrive from Port Alberni ($29, two hours), Nanaimo ($46, three to four hours), Victoria ($69, six to seven hours) and beyond. Their 'Beach Bus' service rolls in along Hwy 4 from Ucluelet ($17, 40 minutes).

Ucluelet
POP 1,500

Threading along Hwy 4 through the mountains to the west coast, you'll arrive at a junction sign proclaiming that Tofino is 33km to your right, while just 8km to your left is Ucluelet. Sadly, most still take the right-hand turn, which is a shame, since sleepier 'Ukee' has more than a few charms of its own (especially in the culinary department) and is a good reminder of what Tofino was like before tourism arrived.

◉ Sights & Activities

Ucluelet Aquarium AQUARIUM
(☑250-726-2782; www.ucluelletaquarium.org; Main Street Waterfront Promenade; adult/child $14/7; ⊙10am-5pm mid-Mar–Nov) ✔ This excellent catch-and-release facility on the waterfront focuses on illuminating the marine critters found in the region's local waters, which can mean anything from alien-looking sea cucumbers to a squirming, and frankly mesmerizing, Pacific octopus or two. But it's the enthusiasm of the young staff that sets this place apart, along with the ability to educate on issues of conservation without browbeating. A great kid-friendly facility – you can expect to walk away with renewed excitement about the wonders of ocean wildlife.

Wild Pacific Trail HIKING
(www.wildpacifictrail.com) This 10km nature trail provides smashing, easy-access views of the wave-whipped shoreline. From the intersection of Peninsula and Coast Guard Rds, it winds around the cliffs past the lighthouse (get your camera out) and along the craggy shore fringing the town. Seabirds are abundant and it's a good storm-watching spot; stick to the trail or the waves might pluck you from the cliffs.

Subtidal Adeventures WILDLIFE
(☑250-726-7336; www.subtidaladventures.com; 1950 Peninsula Rd; adult/child $99/79) A long-established local company offering popular Zodiac boat tours that illuminate the regional wildlife scene, with options including a summer favorite that often includes sightings

of bears, several types of whales, lots of sea-birds and maybe a sea otter (if you're lucky).

Relic Surf Shop
SURFING

(☑ 250-726-4421; www.relicsurfshop.com; 1998 Peninsula Rd; rentals from $35) The perfect place if you want to practice the ways of the surf – rentals, lessons and stand-up paddle boarding included.

🛏 Sleeping

Surfs Inn Guesthouse
CABIN, HOSTEL $

(☑ 250-726-4426; www.surfsinn.ca; 1874 Peninsula Rd; dm/cottages from $28/139; 🛜) It's hard to miss this blue-painted house near the center of town, with its small, recently upgraded dorm rooms. But the real find is hidden out back: two cute cabins ideal for groups and families. One is larger and self-contained while the other is divided into two suites with kitchenettes. Each has a BBQ. Ask about surf packages if you fancy hitting the waves.

C&N Backpackers
HOSTEL $

(☑ 250-726-7416; www.cnnbackpackers.com; 2081 Peninsula Rd; dm/r $28/70; ⊙ Apr-Oct; 🛜) Take your shoes off at the door and slide into this large, woodsy hostel, where the gigantic out-back garden is the best place to hang (in a hammock) on lazy evenings. A spacious downstairs kitchen and recently renovated bathrooms add to the appeal, while the dorms are joined by three sought-after private rooms.

Whiskey Landing Lodge
HOTEL $$

(☑ 855-726-2270; www.whiskeylanding.com; 1645 Cedar Rd; d from $219; 🛜🐕) Right on the harbor (expect to wake to honking seals), this wood-beamed, apartment-style hotel is steps from Ukee's main restaurants. But since each of its 15 studios and suites also has its own kitchen, you can chef up your own meals as well (there's a supermarket up the hill). Don't forget to say hello to Pebbles, the lodge dog.

🍴 Eating

Zoe's Bakery & Cafe
BAKERY $

(☑ 250-726-2253; 250 Main St; sandwiches $8-10; ⊙ 7am-4pm Tue-Sun, reduced hours off-season) Most locals visit this sunny, centrally located bakery at least once a day, dropping by for coffee, Black Magic Bars or the lunch-time soup and sandwich special. Local, organic ingredients are deployed wherever possible and if you're here early enough you

can scoop up a slice of our favorite break-fast: a finger-licking savory bread-pudding egg bake.

Ravenlady
SEAFOOD $$

(www.ravenlady.ca; 1801 Bay St; mains $15-18; ⊙ noon-2pm & 5-8pm Fri-Tue) The sole exponent of Ucluelet's food-truck scene is far superior to many bricks-and-mortar seafood restaurants. Specializing in fresh-shucked regional oysters, there are also gourmet delights from octopus linguini to baguette po'boys stuffed to the gills with albacore tuna or *panko*-fried oysters. You can also order these *panko* delights separately ($5), while snagging a picnic table seat in the sun.

Howler's
PUB FOOD $$

(☑ 250-726-2211; 1992 Peninsula Rd; mains $14-18; ⊙ noon-midnight; 🛜🍺) The place to meet the locals, this family-friendly, pub-style restaurant covers a lot of bases: heaping plates of pasta, wraps and burgers (go for the elk), craft beers from Tofino Brewing, a four-lane bowling alley and a backroom of billiard tables and arcade games. Complete with friendly service, it's the kind of place you can easily hang out all evening.

Norwoods
CANADIAN $$$

(☑ 250-726-7001; www.norwoods.ca; 1714 Peninsula Rd; mains $24-38; ⊙ 5-10pm) Showing how far Ucluelet's dining scene has elevated itself in recent years, this lovely candlelit room would easily be at home in Tofino. The ever-changing menu focuses on seasonal regional ingredients; think halibut and duck breast. All are prepared with a sophisticated international approach, plus there's a full menu of BC (and beyond) wines, many offered by the glass.

ℹ Information

Ucluelet Visitors Centre (www.ucluelet. ca; 1604 Peninsula Rd; ⊙ 9am-5pm Jun-Aug, 9:30am-4:30pm Mon-Fri Sep-May) For a few good reasons to stick around in Ukee, including a dining scene that finally has some great options, make for the handy downtown visitors center for tips.

ℹ Getting There & Away

Tofino Bus (www.tofinobus.com) services arrive from Port Alberni (from $26, 1½ hours, three daily), Nanaimo (from $46, three to four hours, three daily) and Victoria (from $34, six hours, four daily), among others. Their 'Beach Bus' comes into town along Hwy 4 from Tofino ($17, 40 minutes, up to three daily).

Denman & Hornby Islands

The main Northern Gulf Islands, Denman and Hornby share laid-back attitudes, artistic flair and some tranquil outdoor activities. You'll arrive by ferry at Denman first from Buckley Bay on Vancouver Island, then hop from Denman across to Hornby. Stop at **Denman Village**, near the first ferry dock, and pick up a free map and attractions guide for both islands.

Denman has three provincial parks: **Filongley**, with easy hiking and beachcombing; **Boyle Point**, with a beautiful walk to the lighthouse; and **Sandy Island**, only accessible by water from north Denman.

Among Hornby's provincial parks, **Tribune Bay** features a long sandy beach with safe swimming, while **Helliwell** offers notable hiking. **Ford's Cove**, on Hornby's south coast, offers the chance for divers to swim with six-gilled sharks. The island's large **Mt Geoffrey Regional Park** is crisscrossed with hiking and mountain-biking trails.

If you fancy hitting the water, **Denman Hornby Canoes & Kayaks** (☑250-335-0079; www.denmanpaddling.ca; 4005 East Rd, Denman Island; ☺rental/tour from $50/120) offers rentals and guided tours.

🛏 Sleeping & Eating

Blue Owl
B&B $$

(☑250-335-3440; www.blueowlondenman.ca; 8850 Owl Cres, Denman Island; d $140; 🐾) An idyllically rustic retreat for those craving an escape from city life, this woodsy little cottage is a short walk from the ocean. Loaner bikes are freely available if you fancy exploring (there's a swimmable lake nearby), but you might want to just cozy up for a night in. There's a two-night minimum stay policy.

Sea Breeze Lodge
HOTEL $$

(☑250-335-2321; www.seabreezelodge.com; 5205 Fowler Rd, Hornby Island; adult/child $200/70) This 12-acre retreat, with 16 cottages overlooking the ocean, is a popular island fixture. Rooms are comfortable rather than palatial and some have fireplaces and full kitchens. You can swim, kayak and fish or just flop lazily around in the cliffside hot tub. Rates are per person.

Cardboard House Bakery
BAKERY $

(☑250-335-0733; www.thecardboardhousebakery. com; 2205 Central Rd, Hornby Island; mains $5-10; ☺8:30am-9pm Tue-Sun, to 4pm Mon, reduced hours off-season) It's easy to lose track of time at this old shingle-sided farmhouse that combines a hearty bakery and cozy cafe. It's impossible not to stock up on a bag full of oven-fresh muffins, cookies and croissants for the road. Stick around for an alfresco crepe lunch in the adjoining orchard, which also stages live music Wednesday and Sunday evenings in summer.

Island Time Café
CAFE $

(3464 Denman Rd, Denman Island; mains $7-12) This village hangout specializes in fresh-from-the-oven bakery treats, like muffins and scones, plus organic coffee, as well as bulging breakfast wraps and hearty house-made soups. The pizza is particularly recommended, and is served with a side order of gossip from the locals. If the sun is cooperating, you can sit outside and catch some rays.

ℹ Information

For more information on the islands, see www. visitdenmanisland.ca and www.hornbyisland. com.

ℹ Getting There & Away

BC Ferries (☑250-386-3431; www.bcferries. com) Services arrive throughout the day at Denman from Buckley Bay (passenger/vehicle $10.50/24.35, 10 minutes). Hornby Island is accessed by ferry from Denman (passenger/vehicle $10.50/24.35, 10 minutes).

Comox Valley

Comprising the towns of Comox and Courtenay as well as the hipster-favorite village of Cumberland, this is a region of rolling mountains, alpine meadows and colorful communities. A good outdoor adventure base and a hotbed for mountain biking, its activity highlight is Mt Washington.

⊙ Sights & Actvities

Courtenay and District Museum & Palaeontology Centre
MUSEUM

(☑250-334-0686; www.courtenaymuseum.ca; 207 4th St, Courtenay; by donation; ☺10am-5pm Mon-Sat, noon-4pm Sun, closed Mon & Sun in winter; 🐾) With its life-sized replica of an elasmosaur (a prehistoric marine reptile first discovered in the area) this excellent small museum also houses pioneer and First Nations exhibits. Pick up a dino-themed chocolate bar from the gift shop: the perfect edible souvenir.

Cumberland Museum
MUSEUM

(☑ 250-336-2445; www.cumberlandmuseum.ca; 2680 Dunsmuir Ave, Cumberland; adult/child $5/4; ⊙ 10am-5pm Jun-Aug, 10am-5pm Wed-Sun Sep-May) A wonderfully quirky museum located on a row of clapboard buildings that looks like a Dodge City movie set, there are evocative exhibits on the area's pioneer past and Japanese and Chinese communities here. There's also a walk-through mine tunnel that offers a glimpse of just how tough the job would have been (the frightening iron lung exhibited upstairs does the same).

Mt Washington Alpine Resort
OUTDOORS

(☑ 250-338-1386; www.mountwashington.ca; winter lift ticket adult/child $85/43) The main reason for winter visits, this has long been the island's skiing and snowboarding spot, with dozens of runs, plus snowshoeing and tubing options. But there are also great summer activities, including some of the region's best hiking and biking trails.

🛏 Sleeping

★ Riding Fool Hostel
HOSTEL $

(☑ 250-336-8250; www.ridingfool.com; 2705 Dunsmuir Ave, Cumberland; dm/r $28/60; @ 🛜) One of BC's finest hostels colonizes a restored Cumberland heritage building with its rustic wooden interiors, large kitchen and lounge areas and, along with small dorms, the kind of immaculate family and private rooms often found in midrange hotels. Bicycle rentals are available (this is a great hostel to meet mountain bikers) but you'll need to book ahead for the summer peak.

Cona Hostel
HOSTEL $

(☑ 250-331-0991; www.theconahostel.com; 440 Anderton Ave, Courtenay; dm/r $26/65; @ 🛜) It's hard to miss this orange riverside hostel, popular along mountain-bikers gearing up for the area's multitudinous trails. The friendly folks at the front desk have plenty of other suggestions for what to explore, but you might want to just stay indoors as there's a large kitchen, foosball table and beer growlers you can fill up for cheap at a nearby microbrewery.

Old House Village Hotel & Spa
HOTEL $$

(☑ 250-703-0202; www.oldhousevillage.com; 1730 Riverside Ln, Courtenay; d from $149; 🛜 🛗) Neither an old house nor in a village, this superior lodge-look apartment-style hotel has full kitchens, heated bathroom floors and excellent front-desk staff are ready with helpful suggestions for area sightseeing and dining. There's also an on-site restaurant as well as a spa if you don't fancy straying too far from the building.

🍴 Eating & Drinking

Waverley Hotel Pub
BURGERS $$

(☑ 250-336-8322; www.waverleyhotel.ca; 2692 Dunsmuir Ave, Cumberland; mains $13-18; ⊙ 11am-10:30pm Sun-Thu, 11am-late Fri & Sat; 🛜 ☑) Hit this historic, antler-studded saloon for a pub-grub dinner while you flick through a copy of glossy local magazine *CV Collective*. There are a dozen or so craft drafts to keep you company, while the menu ranges from the recommended Thai green curry to some excellent burgers (the Big Wave is the locals' fave). Check ahead for live music.

Mad Chef Café
CANADIAN, FUSION $$

(☑ 250-871-7622; www.madchefcafe.ca; 444 Fifth St, Courtenay; mains $13-16; ⊙ 11am-8pm Mon-Thu, to 9pm Fri & Sat; ☑) A large new location for this super-friendly neighborhood favorite hasn't changed the approach. There's still a great selection of made-from-scratch pizzas, wraps and gigantic salads (seafood bowl recommended). Whatever you choose, be sure to add a bowl of the signature Miso Yummy soup, unless you're having the mammoth Death by Bacon Burger, in which case you won't be able to eat anything else.

Atlas Café
FUSION $$

(☑ 250-338-9838; www.atlascafe.ca; 250 6th St, Courtenay; mains $12-18; ⊙ 8:30am-9:30pm Tue-Thu, to 10pm Fri & Sat, to 3:30pm Sun; ☑) One of Courtenay's favorite dining options has a pleasing modern bistro feel with a global menu that fuses Asian, Mexican and Mediterranean flourishes. Check out the gourmet fish tacos, plus ever-changing seasonal treats. Good vegetarian options, too. Looking for weekend breakfast? Aim for the blue-crab Benedict.

Cumberland Brewing
BREWERY

(☑ 250-400-2739; www.cumberlandbrewing.com; 2732 Dunsmuir Ave, Cumberland; ⊙ noon-9pm Sun, Tue, & Wed, noon-9pm Thu-Sat) A microbrewery that's mastered the neighborhood-pub vibe, this tasty spot combines a woodsy little tasting room with a larger outdoor seating area striped with communal tables. Dive into a tasting flight of four beers; make sure it includes the Red Tape Pale Ale.

Gladstone Brewing Company BREWERY

(www.gladstonebrewing.ca; 244 4th St, Courtanay; ⊙10am-late) Order a pizza at the adjoining servery and grab a parasol table outside this excellent addition to the region's drinking scene. Check the chalkboard for the current roster of brews then order a four-glass tasting flight ($8). The porter is a favorite but there are usually some intriguing Belgian-influenced beers to whet your whistle as well.

❶ Information

Vancouver Island Visitors Centre (✏885-400-2882; www.discovercomoxvalley.com; 3607 Small Rd, Cumberland; ⊙9am-5pm) Drop by the slick visitors center for tips on exploring the area.

❶ Getting There & Away

The area's three main communities are linked by easy-to-explore highway routes, while **Tofino Bus** (✏250-725-2871; www.tofinobus.com) services trundle into Courtenay at least twice a day from communities across the island.

If you're flying in from the mainland, **Pacific Coastal Airlines** (✏604-273-8666; www.pacificcoastal.com) services arrive at **Comox Valley Airport** (✏250-890-0829; www.comoxairport.com) from Vancouver's South Terminal ($132, 55 minutes, up to nine daily).

Campbell River

POP 33,400

Southerners will tell you this marks the end of civilization on Vancouver Island, but Campbell River is a handy drop-off point for wilderness tourism in **Strathcona Provincial Park** and is large enough to have plenty of attractions and services of its own. Head to the waterfront for seal and boat-bobbing marina views or wander the shops and restaurants on Pier St.

◉ Sights

Discovery Passage Aquarium AQUARIUM

(✏250-914-5500; www.discoverypassageaquarium.ca; 705 Island Hwy; adult/child $8/5; ⊙10am-5pm May-Sep; ␧) Repurposing the old blue shed aquarium that was moved here from Ucluelet, this smashing little marine-critter attraction can be found at the entrance to the Discovery Pier. A showcase of local aquatic life: look out for starfish, eel grass beds and (if you're lucky) an octopus or two. Great spot for kids on a rainy day.

Museum at Campbell River MUSEUM

(✏250-287-3103; www.crmuseum.ca; 470 Island Hwy; adult/child $8/5; ⊙10am-5pm mid-May–Sep, noon-5pm Tue-Sun Oct–mid-May) This fascinating museum is worth an hour of anyone's time. Its diverse collection showcases aboriginal masks, an 1890s pioneer cabin and video footage of the world's largest artificial, non-nuclear blast (an underwater mountain in Seymour Narrows that caused dozens of shipwrecks before it was blown apart in a controlled explosion in 1958).

Discovery Pier LANDMARK

Since locals claim the town as the 'Salmon Capital of the World,' you should wet your line off the downtown Discovery Pier (rental rods available) or just stroll along with the crowds and see what everyone else has caught. Much easier than catching your own lunch: you can also buy fish and chips here.

🍴 Sleeping & Eating

Heron's Landing Hotel HOTEL $$

(✏250-923-2848; www.heronslandinghotel.com; 492 S Island Hwy; d from $130; @ 🛜 🐾) Superior motel-style accommodation with renovated rooms, including large loft suites ideal for families. Rates include breakfast but rooms also have their own kitchens if you need to chef up your own eggs-and-bacon special. There are also handy coin-operated laundry facilities on-site.

Dick's Fish & Chips FISH & CHIPS $

(✏250-287-3336; www.dicksfishandchips.com; 660 Island Hwy; mains $7-16; ⊙10:30am-dusk) The locals' favorite fish and chip shop, this gable-roofed restaurant a short walk from the Discover Pier is often busy, so consider an off-peak visit. Alongside the usual golden-battered meals, you'll find popular salmon, oyster and halibut burgers, as well as house-made mushy peas that some Vancouver Islanders just can't live without.

❶ Getting There & Away

Pacific Coastal Airlines (✏604-273-8666; www.pacificcoastal.com) Flights from Vancouver ($132, 45 minutes, up to six daily) arrive throughout the day.

Campbell River Transit (✏250-287-7433; www.bctransit.com; adult/child $2/1.75) Operates buses throughout the area and beyond.

Tofino Bus (✏250-725-2871; www.tofinobus.com) Services roll in from points around Vancouver Island, including Nanaimo, Victoria and Port Hardy.

WORTH A TRIP

QUADRA ISLAND HOP

For a day out with a difference, take your bike on the 10-minute **BC Ferries** (p175) trip from Campbell River to rustic **Quadra Island**. There's an extensive network of trails across the island; maps are sold in local stores. Many of the forested trails are former logging routes, and the local community has spent a lot of time building and maintaining the trails for mountain bikers of all skill levels. If you don't have your wheels, you can rent a bike on the island or in Campbell River. For more information on visiting the island, see www.quadraisland.ca.

Quadra's fascinating **Nuyumbalees Cultural Centre** (www.nuyumbalees.com; 34 Weway Rd; adult/child $10/5; ☺10am-5pm May-Sep) illuminates the heritage and traditions of the local Kwakwaka'wakw First Nations people, showcasing carvings and artifacts and staging traditional dance performances. But if you just want to chill out with the locals, head to **Spirit Sq**, where performers entertain in summer.

If you decide to stick around for dinner, head for the waterfront pub or restaurant at the handsome **Heriot Bay Inn & Marina** (☑250-285-3322; www.heriotbayinn.com; Heriot Bay; d/cabins from $109/229) where, if you have a few too many drinks, you might also choose to stay the night. The hotel has motel-style rooms and charming rustic cabins.

Strathcona Provincial Park

Centered on Mt Golden Hinde (2200m), the island's highest point, **Strathcona Provincial Park** (☑250-474-1336; www.bcparks.ca) is a magnificent pristine wilderness crisscrossed with enticing trail systems. Give yourself plenty of time and you'll soon be communing with waterfalls, alpine meadows, glacial lakes and mountain crags.

On arrival at the park's main entrance, get your bearings at **Strathcona Park Lodge & Outdoor Education Centre**. A one-stop shop for park activities, including kayaking, zip-lining, guided treks and rock climbing, this is a great place to rub shoulders with outdoorsy types. All-in adventure packages are available, some aimed specifically at families. Head to the **Whale Room** or **Myrna's** eateries for a fuel-up before you get too active.

Notable park hiking trails include **Paradise Meadows Loop** (2.2km), an easy amble in a delicate wildflower and evergreen ecosystem; and **Mt Becher** (5km), with its great views over the Comox Valley and mountain-lined Strait of Georgia. Around Buttle Lake, easier walks include **Lady Falls** (900m) and the trail along **Karst Creek** (2km), which winds past sinkholes, percolating streams and tumbling waterfalls.

The park's **lodge** (☑250-286-3122; www.strathconaparklodge.com/escape/accommodation; 41040 Gold River Hwy; r/cabin from $139/250; ▣) offers good accommodations, ranging from rooms in the main building to secluded timber-framed cottages. If you are a true back-to-nature fan, there are also several campsites available in the park. Consider pitching your tent at **Buttle Lake Campground** (☑519-826-6850, 800-689-9025; www.discovercamping.ca; campsites $20; ☺Apr-Oct); the swimming area and playground alone make it a great choice for families.

North Vancouver Island

Down-islanders, meaning anyone south of Campbell River, will tell you, 'There's nothing up there worth seeing,' while locals here will respond, 'They would say that, wouldn't they?' Parochial rivalries aside, what this giant region, covering nearly half the island, lacks in towns, infrastructure and population, it more than makes up for in character and natural beauty. Despite the remoteness, some areas are remarkably accessible to hardy hikers, especially along the North Coast Trail.

Port McNeill

Barreling down the hill almost into the harbor, Port McNeill is a useful pit stop for those heading to Port Hardy or craving a coffee before boarding the ferry to delightful (and highly recommended) Alert Bay.

Check out the **museum** (351 Shelley Cres; ☺10am-5pm Jul-Sep, 1pm-4pm Sat & Sun Oct-Jun) for the region's backstory and don't miss the **World's Biggest Burl** as you stroll towards the entrance. A giant warty outgrowth from a huge tree, it's the best selfie opportunity in the area. If you fancy communing further with the local wilderness, book a backcountry guided hike with **North Island Daytrippers** (☑ 800-956-2411; www.islanddaytrippers.com).

More a superior motel than a resort, the hilltop **Black Bear Resort** (☑ 250-956-4900; www.port-mcneill-accommodation.com; 1812 Campbell Way; d/cabin incl breakfast from $162/212; @🛜🐾) overlooks the town and is located across from the shops and restaurants. Standard rooms are small but clean and include microwaves and fridges; full-kitchen units are also available and a string of roadside cabins was added a few years back.

For a perfect coffee stop before boarding the Alert Bay ferry, check out **Mugz** (☑ 250-956-3466; 1597 Beach Dr; pastries & sandwiches $3-11; ☺ 7am-8pm Mon-Sat, 7am-7pm Sun; 🛜). There's also ice cream and a lunch panini to tempt you at this popular locals hangout. In summer, snag a perch on the patio.

Drop into the gabled **visitors center** (☑ 250-956-3881; www.town.portmcneill.bc.ca; 1594 Beach Dr; ☺ 8:30am-5:30pm May-Sep, reduced hours in winter) for regional insights.

Tofino Bus (☑ 250-287-7151; www.tofinobus. com) services roll in from places including Port Hardy ($17, 50 minutes, daily) and Campbell River ($44, two to three hours, daily).

Alert Bay

Hop the 45-minute BC Ferries service from Port McNeil for one of the region's best days out. Located on Cormorant Island and radiating from the ferry dock along easily strolled waterfront boardwalks, Alert Bay's brightly painted shacks and houses-on-piles are highly photogenic – even the ones that are crumbling into the briny. Home to the Namgis First Nation, there are lots of ways to experience indigenous culture here, plus some cozy spots to eat or sleep. Expect eagles and ravens to be whirling overhead.

● Sights & Activities

This area is highly explorable on foot, so poke along the waterfront boardwalk from the ferry; head right for the breathtaking **Original Namgis Burial Grounds**, with its incredible totem poles, or left for the **Culture Shock Interactive Gallery** (☑ 250-974-2484; www.cultureshockgallery.ca; 10 Front St; ☺ 9:30am-6pm Jul-Sep, closed Sun May, Jun & Oct, reduced hours in winter), a store crammed with contemporary First Nations crafts, T-shirts and jewelry. There's a coffee shack alongside the gallery plus a summer program of cultural experiences for visitors ranging from

storytelling to salmon barbecues; check the website to see what's coming up.

Also, don't miss the **U'mista Cultural Centre** (☑ 250-974-5403; www.umista.ca; 1 Front St; adult/child $12/5; ☺ 9am-5pm Jul & Aug, 9am-5pm Tue-Sat Sep-May), a longhouse-like facility proudly displaying dozens of culturally priceless indigenous artifacts confiscated when potlatch ceremonies were outlawed in Canada. These were distributed to museums and collections around the world, but the Centre has been slowly negotiating their return and the main gallery here is a spine-tingling celebration of these efforts. Summer programs include book readings and cedar-bark weaving demonstrations (check the Facebook page for events) while the gift shop is a treasure trove of ethically sourced First Nations art.

And if the ocean is calling, **Seasmoke Whale Watching** (☑ 250-974-5225; www. seasmokewhalewatching.com; adult/child $120/95; ☺ tours mid-May–Sep) offers five-hour marine wildlife-spotting voyages on its yacht, including afternoon tea.

🍽 Sleeping & Eating

There are some B&Bs and woodsy cabins available here if you're looking to stay. Contact the **visitors center** (☑ 250-974-5024; www.alertbay.ca; 118 Fir St; ☺ 9am-5pm Jul & Aug, 9am-5pm Mon-Fri Jun, Sep & Oct) for suggestions, especially in summer, when availability is limited. Aim for a secluded sleepover with **Alert Bay Cabins** (☑ 604-974-5457; www. alertbaycabins.net; 390 Poplar Rd; d from $135).

There are several homestyle eateries along the boardwalk but the best of the bunch is **Pass 'n Thyme** (☑ 250-974-2670; www.passnthyme.com; 4 Maple Rd; mains $13-21; ☺ 11am-8pm Tue-Thu & Sat, 11am-9pm Fri).

❶ Getting There & Away

BC Ferries (☑ 250-386-3431; www.bcferries. com) arrive in Alert Bay from Port McNeil (adult/vehicle $12.35/28.40, 45 minutes, up to six daily).

Telegraph Cove

Built as a one-shack telegraph station, this charming destination has since expanded into one of the north's main visitor lures. Its pioneer-outpost feel is enhanced by the dozens of brightly painted wooden buildings perched around the marina on stilts. Be aware that it can get very crowded with summer day trippers.

◉ Sights & Activities

Head first along the boardwalk to the smashing **Whale Interpretive Centre** (☑ 250-928-3129; www.killerwhalecentre.org; by donation adult/child $5/3; ☺ 9am-5pm mid-May–Oct), bristling with hands-on artifacts and artfully displayed skeletons of cougars and sea otters. But the main lure at this unique, rustic-barn-like museum are the whale skeletons, mostly hanging from the ceiling. Minke, grey, fin and pygmy are part of the menagerie; give yourself plenty of time to peruse everything carefully.

You can also see whales of the live variety just offshore: this is one of the island's top marine-life viewing regions and **Stubbs Island Whale Watching** (☑ 250-928-3185; www.stubbs-island.com; adult/child $99/84; ☺ May–Oct) will get you up close with the orcas on a boat trek; you might also see humpbacks, dolphins and sea lions. Mid-July to mid-September is prime time for orca-viewing.

For a bear-tastic alternative, **Tide Rip Grizzly Tours** (☑ 250-339-5320; www.tiderip.com; tours $299-340; ☺ May-Sep) leads full-day trips to local beaches and inlets in search of the area's furry locals.

🍴 Sleeping & Eating

The well-established **Telegraph Cove Resorts** (☑ 250-928-3131; www.telegraphcoveresort.com; campsites/cabins from $32/150) provides accommodations in forested tent spaces and a string of rustic cabins, while the nearby **Dockside 29** (☑ 250-928-3163; www.telegraphcove.ca; d from $185; 🛜) is a good, motel-style alternative.

Seahorse Cafe   CAFE $
(☑ 250-527-1001; www.seahorsecafe.org; mains $9; ☺ 8:30am-7pm May-Sep) This popular dockside cafe has plenty of outdoor picnic tables for you to relax at while digging into barbecued Bavarian smokies, bison burgers, salmon burgers and home-cut fries.

Killer Whale Café   BISTRO $$
(☑ 250-928-3155; mains $14-18; ☺ mid-May–mid-October) Killer Whale Café is the cove's best eatery – the salmon, mussel and prawn linguine is recommended. Aim for a window seat in this creaky-floored heritage building so you can gaze over the marina.

ⓘ Getting There & Away

Telegraph Cove is a winding but well-signposted turnoff drive from Hwy 19.

Port Hardy

A handy hub for exploring the north's many rugged outdoor experiences, this is also the spot for catching your breath before hopping aboard the breathtaking BC Ferries Inside Passage route.

◉ Sights & Activities

North Island Lanes   BOWLING ALLEY
(☑ 250-949-6307; 7210 Market St; per game incl shoes $6; ☺ 1pm-3pm Tue, 5pm-9:30pm Wed-Sun, to 10pm Fri & Sat) With old-school bowling alleys tumbling like knocked-over pins across BC, this immaculately preserved six-lane hangout is a must-see even if you don't want to play. Like stepping into the 1970s, the yellow-painted walls with retro-cool back lights is like a living museum. But rather than being a mothballed old exhibit, it's also one of the friendliest and liveliest evening hangouts in town, especially on Fridays and Saturdays when 'cosmic bowling' takes over.

Quatse Salmon Stewardship Centre   FARM
(☑ 250-949-9022; www.thesalmoncentre.org; 8400 Byng Rd; ☺ 10am-5pm Wed-Sun mid-May–Sep; 👪) Bring your kids and they'll learn all about the salmon life-cycle at this off-the-beaten-path hatchery attraction. Besides lots of hands-on action (as well as a cylindrical fish tank you can pop your head into) there are also hatchery tours for a more in-depth education.

Nakwakto Rapids Tours   BOATING
(☑ 250-230-3574; www.nakwaktorapidstours.com; 154 Tsulquate Reserve; tour $100; ☺ by appointment) There's more to this four-hour boat tour than experiencing the roiling waters of 'the world's fastest tidal surge.' Your First Nations guides also provide a rich interpretive narration as well as taking you to some of the region's most scenically remote areas.

🍴 Sleeping & Eating

North Coast Trail Backpackers Hostel   HOSTEL $
(☑ 250-949-9441; www.northcoasthostel.com; 8635 Granville St; dm/r $29/64; @ 🛜) This spacious, homey hostel is a warren of small and larger dorms, overseen by friendly owners with plenty of tips on how to encounter the region. The hostel's hub is a large rec room and, while the kitchen is small, the adjoining mural-painted cafe can keep you well fueled. Pension-style private rooms are available and traveling families are also welcomed.

Pier Side Landing
HOTEL **$$**

(☑ 250-949-7437; www.piersidelanding.com; 8600 Granville St; d from $120; ☞) It's hard to beat the location of this elevated motel-style property that has recently been fully renovated: in the center of town, on the waterfront and (if you get an 'ocean view' rather than a 'mountain view' room) offering smashing vistas along a shoreline bristling with bald eagles. Rooms are spacious (not all have balconies, though) and the in-room fridges are handy.

Café Guido
CAFE **$**

(☑ 250-949-9808; www.cafeguido.com; 7135 Market St; mains $6-8; ⊘ 7am-6pm Mon-Fri, 8am-6pm Sat, 8am-5pm Sun; ☞) You'll easily end up sticking around for an hour at this friendly locals' hangout, especially if you also purchase a tome to read from the bookstore downstairs. The grilled 'Gladiator' pesto flatbread sandwich is ever-popular at lunchtime but save room for the raspberry-lemon scones. Say hi to resident pooch Lucy, who's usually hanging out in the upstairs craft store.

Sporty Bar & Grill
PUB FOOD **$$**

(☑ 250-949-7811; www.sportybar.ca; 8700 Hastings St; mains $11-24; ⊘ 11:30am-11pm; ☞) Great service and pub grub push this neighborhood bar to the top of the Port Hardy dine-out tree. Sporty's offers hearty burgers, pizzas and fish and chips but there's also a great-value Cobb salad ($13) that's well worth faceplanting into. Beer-wise, eschew the Lucky Lager (the north's traditional favorite) and go for Victoria-brewed Hermann's Dark Lager.

❶ Information

Port Hardy Visitor Information Centre
(☑ 250-949-7622; www.visitporthardy.com; 7250 Market St; ⊘ 9am-6pm Jun-Sep, 8am-4pm Mon-Fri Oct-May) Lined with flyers and staffed by locals who can help you plan your visit in town and beyond, this your first port of call. They're especially adept with area hiking tips.

❶ Getting There & Away

Pacific Coastal Airlines (www.pacific-coastal.com) Services arrive from Vancouver ($209, 65 minutes, up to four daily).

BC Ferries (☑ 250-386-3431; www.bcferries.com) Services arrive from Prince Rupert (passenger/vehicle $206/469, 16 hours, schedules vary) via the scenically splendid Inside Passage.

Tofino Bus (☑ 250-725-2871; www.tofinobus.com) Services roll in from southern destinations, including Port McNeil ($17, 50 minutes, daily).

North Island Transportation (☑ 250-949-6300; shuttle $8) Operates a handy shuttle to/from the ferry and area hotels.

Cape Scott Provincial Park

It's more than 550km from Victoria to the nature-hugging trailhead of this remote park on the island's crenulated northern tip. This should be your number-one destination if you really want to experience the raw, ravishing beauty of BC, especially its unkempt shorelines, breeze-licked rainforests and stunning sandy bays animated with tumbling waves and beady-eyed seabirds.

Hike the park's well-maintained 2.5km **San Josef Bay Trail** and you'll stroll from the shady confines of the trees right onto one of the best beaches in BC, a breathtaking, windswept expanse of roiling water, forested crags and the kind of age-old caves that could easily harbor lost smugglers. You can camp right here on the beach or just admire the passing ospreys before plunging back into the trees.

One of the area's shortest trails (2km), in adjoining **Raft Cove Provincial Park** (www.bcparks.ca), brings you to the wide, crescent beach and beautiful lagoons of Raft Cove. You're likely to have the entire 1.3km expanse to yourself, although the locals also like to surf here – it's their secret, so don't tell anyone.

If you really like a challenge, consider the 55km **North Coast Trail**, which typically takes up to seven days. You'll be passing sandy coves, deserted beaches and dense, wind-whipped rainforest woodland, as well as a couple of river crossings on little cable cars. The trail is muddy and swampy in places, so there are boardwalks to make things easier. The area is home to elk, deer, cougars, wolves and black bears; make sure you know how to handle an encounter before you set off. The trail is for experienced and well-equipped hikers only. There are backcountry campsites at Nissen Bight, Laura Creek and Shuttleworth Bight.

❶ Getting There & Away

If you're aiming to tackle the North Coast Trail, take an early morning **Cape Scott Water Taxi** (☑ 250-949-6541; www.capescottwater-taxi.ca; 6555 Port Hardy Bay Rd) service to Shushartie Bay and, after your hike, hop the **North Coast Trail Shuttle** (☑ 250-949-6541; www.northcoasttrailshuttle.com) minibus back to Port Hardy. Book ahead for both services.

SOUTHERN GULF ISLANDS

Stressed Vancouverites love escaping into the restorative arms of these laid-back islands, strung like a shimmering necklace between the mainland and Vancouver Island. Formerly colonized by hippies and US draft dodgers, Salt Spring, Galiano, Mayne, Saturna, and North and South Pender deliver on their promise of rustic, sigh-triggering getaways. For additional visitor information, see www.sgislands.com.

Salt Spring Island

POP 10,500

The busiest and most developed of the islands, Salt Spring has a reputation for palatial vacation homes, but it's also lined with artist studios and artisan food and drink producers who welcome visitors. Well worth a long weekend visit, the heart of the community is Ganges, home of Salt Spring's awesome summer market.

◉ Sights & Activities

★ **Saturday Market**   MARKET

(www.saltspringmarket.com; Centennial Park, Ganges; ◷ 9am-4pm Sat Apr-Oct) The best market in British Columbia, this gigantic cornucopia of produce, edible goodies and locally made artworks lures everyone like a magnet on summer Saturdays. Arrive in the morning; it can be oppressively jam-packed at times. Alternatively, join the locals at the smaller, produce-only Tuesday market.

Salt Spring Island Cheese   FARM

(☑ 250-653-2300; www.saltspringcheese.com; 285 Reynolds Rd; ◷ 11am-5pm May-Sep, to 4pm Oct-Apr; ⊕) A family-friendly farmstead with a strollable garden, wandering chickens and a winery-like tasting room and shop, this must-see spot produces goat and sheep milk chèvres, feta and Camembert styles; the soft-goat cheese rounds in several flavors (the garlic one is recommended) are the farm's specialty. You can watch the handmade production through special windows but look out for glimpses of the farm's gamboling goats.

Saltspring Island Ales   BREWERY

(☑ 250-653-2383; www.saltspringislandales.com; 270 Furness Rd; ◷ noon-5pm) Colonizing a rustic, cedar-built shack between the trees, this microbrewery's woodsy little tasting room offers a roster of all-organic brews, from malty Extra Special Bitter to smooth Heatherdale Ale. There are always intriguing seasonal beers to try as well; growlers are available if you need a takeout.

Mistaken Identity Vineyards   WINERY

(☑ 250-538-9463; www.mistakenidentityvineyards. com; 164 Norton Rd; ◷ 11am-6pm) If you're on a picnic-gathering push and need an accompanying libation, consider an exploratory tasting visit (with designated driver) to this locals'-favorite vineyard. The lovely Bliss rosé is recommended.

Ruckle Provincial Park   PARK

(www.bcparks.ca) A southeast gem with ragged shorelines and gnarly arbutus forests: there are trails for all skill levels here, with **Yeo Point** making an ideal pit stop.

Salt Spring Adventure Co   KAYAKING

(☑ 250-537-2764; www.saltspringadventures.com; 126 Upper Ganges Rd, Ganges; rentals/tours from $30/55; ◷ 8:30am-6pm Jun-Sep) When it's time to hit the water, touch base with this well-established local operator. They can kit you out for a bobbling kayak tour around Ganges Harbour, but they also serve the stand-up paddleboard crowd. Bike rentals and extended kayak tours around the region are also on the menu.

Salt Spring Studio Tour   TOURS

(www.saltspringstudiotour.com) Art fans should hit the trail on Salt Spring by checking out gallery and studio locations via the free downloadable *Studio Tour Map*. Highlights include **Blue Horse Folk Art Gallery** (☑ 250-537-0754; www.bluehorse.ca; 175 North View Dr; ◷ 10am-5pm Sun-Fri Mar-Dec) and **Duthie Gallery** (☑ 250-537-9606; www.duthiegallery.com; 125 Churchill Rd, Ganges; ◷ 11am-5pm Thu-Mon, reduced hours off-season).

🛏 Sleeping & Eating

Oceanside Cottages   COTTAGE $$

(☑ 250-653-0007; www.oceansidecottages.com; 521 Isabella Point Rd; d from 135) These four unique cottages are nooks of bliss. Each is exceedingly private and filled with eclectic artwork and creative flourishes. We especially love the groovy little Love Shack, with its retro, Austin Powers vibe.

Salt Spring Inn   HOTEL $$

(☑ 250-537-9339; www.saltspringinn.com; 132 Lower Ganges Rd, Ganges; d from $90; ☎) In the heart of Ganges and located above a popular bar, the small but well-maintained rooms at

Southern Gulf Islands

10 km
5 miles

Point Roberts

Ferry to Tsawwassen

USA
CANADA

Washington
British Columbia

Patos Island

Waldron Island

East Point

Tumbo Island

Cabbage Island Day Use Area

Narvaez Bay Day Use Area

Taylor Point Day Use Area

East Point Rd

Saturna

Narvaez Bay Rd

Saturna Island

South Pender Island

Strait of Georgia

Fernhill Rd

Bennett Bay

Winter Cove

Samuel Island

Payne Rd

Gowland Point Rd

Mayne

Mayne Island

Village Bay

Dinner Bay Park

Naty Channel

Otter Bay

North Pender Island

Mt Norman (244m)

Canal Rd

Medicine Beach

Moresby Island

Sturdies Bay Rd

Gossip Island

Sturdies Bay

Bluffs Park

Active Pass

Swanson Channel

Montague Harbour Marine Provincial Park

Georgeson Island

Prevost Island

Ruckle Provincial Park

Portland Island

Swartz Bay (2km)

Galiano Island

Bodega Ridge Provincial Park

Portlier Pass Rd

Montague Harbour

Parker Island

Long Harbour

Captain Passage

Beddis Beach

Fulford Harbour

Piers Island

Dionisio Point Provincial Park

Secretary Islands

Wallace Island

Trincomali Channel

Upper Ganges Rd

Ganges

Beddis Rd

Salt Harbour

Fulford Ganges Rd

Fulford Harbour

Satellite Channel

Reid Island

Hall Island

Norway Island

Southey Point

North End Rd

Vesuvius Bay

Ganges

Mt Maxwell Provincial Park

Baynes Peak (588m)

Thetis Island

Kuper Island

Tent Island

Sunset Dr

Booth Bay

Mt Maxwell Rd

Salt Spring Island

Cowichan Bay

Victoria (60km)

Willy Island

Stuart Channel

Sansum Narrows

Crofton

Maple Mountain Centennial Park

Vancouver Island

Maple Bay

Quamichan Lake

Cowichan Bay

Island Hwy

this friendly inn are popular with midrange travelers. The pricier deluxe rooms have sea views, en suite bathrooms and fireplaces, while the standard rooms share bathrooms. All are well maintained and well located if you're stumbling up from the bar below after a few too many.

Wisteria Guest House
B&B $$

(☑250-537-5899; www.wisteriaguesthouse.com; 268 Park Dr; d/cottage from $120/180; 🐾) This home-away-from-home B&B has brightly painted guest rooms in the main building, some with shared bathrooms. There are also a pair of private-entrance studios and a small cottage with a compact kitchen – the immaculate studio 1 is our favorite. Breakfast is served in the large communal lounge, surrounded by a rambling, flower-strewn garden. A two-night minimum stay sometimes applies; check ahead.

Hastings House Hotel
HOTEL $$$

(☑800-661-9255; www.hastingshouse.com; 160 Upper Ganges Rd, Ganges; d from $350; 🐾) This smashing rustic-chic hotel with 17 rooms is just up the hill from the main Ganges action, but it feels like staying in a country cottage estate in England. The immaculate grounds are strewn with locally made artworks and the waterfront views will have your camera itching to be used. The **restaurant** is high-end gourmet; breakfast is recommended.

Salt Spring Coffee
CAFE $

(☑250-537-0825; www.saltspringcoffee.com; 109 McPhillips Ave, Ganges; baked goods $3-8; ⊙6:30am-4pm Mon-Fri, 7am-4pm Sat, 8am-4pm Sun, reduced hours off-season) The perfect place to catch up on local gossip over some coffee – if you want to partake of the conservation, ask your neighbor whether or not they support expanding the Saturday Market. Soups and pies are also part of the mix at this ever-animated local legend.

★Tree House Café
CANADIAN $$

(☑250-537-5379; www.treehousecafe.ca; 106 Purvis Lane, Ganges; mains $8-17; ⊙8am-10pm Wed-Sun, to 4pm Mon & Tue July & Aug, reduced hours off-season) At this magical outdoor dining experience, you'll be sitting in the shade of a large plum tree as you choose from a menu of comfort pastas, Mexican specialties and gourmet burgers and sandwiches. The tuna melt is a local fave, perhaps washed down with a Saltspring Island Ales porter. There's live music Wednesday to Sunday nights here in summer.

Restaurant House Piccolo
CANADIAN $$$

(☑250-537-1844; www.housepiccolo.com; 108 Hereford Ave, Ganges; mains $27-34; ⊙5-10pm Wed-Sun) White-tablecloth dining in a beautifully intimate heritage-house setting, this is the locals' top spot for a romantic night out. It's focused on local seasonal ingredients prepared with knowing international flourishes; you'll find memorable seafood and duck dishes, as well as soft venison. Wine fans will find the best drinks menu on the island.

❶ Information

Salt Spring Island Visitor Information Centre
(☑250-537-5252; www.saltspringtourism.com; 121 Lower Ganges Rd, Ganges; ⊙9am-4pm May-Oct, 11am-3pm Nov-Apr) A one-stop shop for activity suggestions and accommodation ideas.

❶ Getting There & Away

BC Ferries (☑250-386-3431; www.bcferries.com) Frequent services arrive at Long Harbour, Fulford Harbour and Vesuvius Bay from the mainland, Vancouver Island and the other islands.

Salt Spring Air (☑250-537-9880; www.saltspringair.com) Floatplane services from Vancouver's downtown harbour arrive in Ganges Harbour ($135, up to four times daily)

North & South Pender Islands

POP 2250

Once joined by a sandy isthmus, North and South Pender Islands attract those looking for a quiet retreat. With pioneer farms, old-time orchards and dozens of coves and beaches, the islands – now linked by a single-lane bridge – are a good spot for bikers and hikers. For visitor information, check www.penderislandchamber.com.

◉ Sights & Activities

Sea Star Vineyards
WINERY

(☑250-629-6960; www.seastarvineyards.ca; 6621 Harbour Hill Dr; ⊙11am-5pm May-Sep) A verdant, 26-acre vineyard that's become a BC favorite, despite only being in operation for a few years; drop into the tasting room here and sample as much as you can. Crisp whites are a specialty. Expect to be greeted by Hudson, the friendly retriever.

Pender Islands Museum
MUSEUM

(www.penderislandmuseum.org; 2408 South Otter Bay Rd, North Pender; ⊙10am-4pm Sat & Sun Jul & Aug, reduced hours off-season) **FREE** Colonizing

THE NORTH'S BEST BREAKFAST

Whether you're driving up or down island, look for road signs to Sayward and you'll soon find yourself double-taking at the quirkiest streetside diner you've ever seen. The **Cable Cook House Cafe** (☑250-282-3433; Sayward Rd; mains $8-14; 🚗) is completely enveloped in 2500 meters of thick steel cable (it took three months to coil it around the building) and it's a beloved local landmark to those in the know. Once you've perused the menagerie of rusting logging machinery dotted around the grounds (and the painted outhouses out back), head inside for a traditional breakfast and a few giant cinnamon buns to go. But don't miss the murals at the back of the room. Painted by Len Whelan in the 1970s, these humorous folk-art masterpieces depict scenes from the area's logging camps. Look out for an endless logging truck winding around a mountain and a man having coffee poured over his head.

an historic white-clapboard farmhouse, this community museum includes an eclectic array of exhibits tracing the human heritage of the area, including thousands of years of First Nations history. Look out for some evocative photos of the early pioneer days.

Pender Island Arts TOURS
(www.penderarts.com) Many artists call Pender home and you can find them via the handy listings on Pender Island Arts website. Most are on North Pender, where you can visit several within easy walking distance of each other. If you're here in mid-July, don't miss the annual **Art Off The Fence** event, where you'll likely meet every creative in the area.

Pender Island Kayak Adventures KAYAKING
(☑250-629-6939; www.kayakpenderisland.com; 4605 Oak Rd, North Pender Island; rentals/tours from $59/35) Hit the water with a paddle (and hopefully a boat) via the friendly folks here. They also rent stand-up paddleboards as well as bicycles, and run popular guided kayak tours; the sunset tour is especially recommended. They also run multi-day tours around the region – great if you want to go in-depth (while still remaining in your kayak).

🛏 Sleeping & Eating

Woods on Pender CABIN $$
(☑250-629-3353; www.woodsonpender.com; 4709 Canal Rd, North Pender; d/cabin/Airstream from $100/200/200; 🚗) With lodge rooms and rustic cabins also available, the stars here are the six self-catering Airstream caravans, each with their own barbecue-equipped decks. The tree-lined site also includes hot tubs, outdoor games (bocce included) and a restaurant serving comfort grub and dozens of board games. There's a three-night minimum stay for cabins and Airstreams in summer.

Poet's Cove Resort & Spa HOTEL $$$
(☑250-629-2100; www.poetscove.com; 9801 Spalding Rd, Bedwell Harbour, South Pender; d from $350; 🚗) This luxurious harbor-front lodge has arts-and-crafts-accented rooms, most with great views across the glassy water. Extras include an activity center that books eco-tours and fishing excursions, and an elegant West Coast restaurant, Aurora, where you can dine in style. The resort also offers kayak treks plus a full-treatment spa, complete with that all-important steam cave.

Pender Island Bakery Cafe CAFE $
(4605 Bedwell Harbour Rd, Driftwood Centre, North Pender; mains $6-20; ⊙7am-5pm; 🚗) At the locals' fave coffeehouse, the coffee is organic, as are many of the bakery treats, including cinnamon buns, which will have you wrestling an islander for the last one. This is a good spot to stock up on croissants for breakfast; see if you can hang on until morning or end up scoffing one in the middle of the night.

Cafe at Hope Bay CANADIAN $$
(☑250-629-2090; www.thecafeathopebay.com; 4301 Bedwell Harbour Rd, North Pender; mains $10-23; ⊙11am-8:30pm Mon-Sun) West Coast ingredients with international influences rule at this bistro-style spot just a few minutes from the Otter Bay ferry dock, closely followed by the sterling views across Plumper Sound. The fish and chips is predictably good, but dig deeper into the menu for less-expected treats, like the lip-smacking coconut-curried mussels and prawns.

ℹ Getting There & Away

BC Ferries (p192) Frequent services arrive from Tsawwassen (adult/child/car $19.80/9.90/72.80), Swartz Bay (adult/child/car $13.45/6.75/41.90) and other islands.

Seair Seaplanes (604-273-8900; www.seairseaplanes.com) Services arrive on North Pender from Vancouver International Airport ($119, three times a day)

Pender has a cool **'community transit' system**, where car-driving locals pick people up at designated stops across the islands.

Galiano Island

POP 1150

With the most ecological diversity of the Southern Gulf Islands, this skinny landmass – named after a 1790s Spanish explorer – offers activities for marine enthusiasts and landlubbers alike.

The Sturdies Bay ferry end is busier than the rest of the island (with restaurants and shops to match) while the island becomes ever more forested and tranquil as you drive away from the dock.

◉ Sights & Activities

Once you've got your bearings – that is, driven off the ferry – head for **Montague Harbour Marine Provincial Park** for trails to beaches, meadows and a cliff carved by glaciers. In contrast, **Bodega Ridge Provincial Park** is renowned for eagle and cormorant birdlife plus spectacular vistas.

The protected waters of **Trincomali Channel** and the more chaotic waters of Active Pass satisfy paddlers of all skill levels. **Galiano Kayaks** (250-539-2442; www.seakayak.ca; 3451 Montague Rd; 2hr/day rental from $35/60, tours from $60) can help with rentals and guided tours. If you fancy exploring on land, rent a moped from **Galiano Adventure Company** (250-593-3443; www.galianoadventures.com; Montague Harbour Marina; rental per hour from $20; ⊗May-Sep).

🛏 Sleeping & Eating

Among the island's sleeping options, sophisticates will enjoy **Galiano Inn** (250-539-3388; www.galianoinn.com; 134 Madrona Dr; d from $249; 🗟🕸), close to the Sturdies Bay ferry dock. Those craving a nature retreat should head to **Bodega Ridge** (250-539-2677; www.bodegaridge.com; 120 Manastee Rd; cabins $275; 🗟), a tranquil woodland clutch of cedar cabins at the other end of the island.

Fuel up on breakfast, treats and local gossip at **Sturdies Bay Bakery** (250-539-2004; 2450 Sturdies Bay Rd; mains $6-12; ⊗7am-3pm Mon-Thu, to 5pm Fri-Sun; 🗟). Once you're done exploring the island, drop in for beer and fish and chips at the venerable, forest-fringed **Hummingbird Pub** (250-539-5472; www.hummingbirdpub.com; 47 Sturdies Bay Rd; mains $12-17). But make time for dinner at **Pilgrimme** (250-539-5392; www.pilgrimme.ca; 2806 Montague Rd; mains $16-30; ⊗5pm-10pm Wed-Mon), an innovative, top-notch eatery that would still be massively popular in a far bigger community. Seasonal, regional and often locally foraged, the regular menu features highlights including duck and Pacific octopus.

❶ Information

Drop into the **visitors info booth** (www.galianoisland.com; 2590 Sturdies Bay Rd; ⊗10am-5pm Mon-Sat, Jun-Aug, reduced hours off-season) before you leave the ferry area. If it's closed, nearby **Galiano Island Books** (250-539-3340; www.galianoislandbooks.com; 76 Mardona Dr; ⊗10am-5:30pm Sun-Fri, 9:30am-5:30pm Sat) has a great selection and friendly staffers who can point you in the right direction.

❶ Getting There & Away

BC Ferries (p192) Frequent services arrive at the Sturdies Bay dock from Tsawwassen (adult/child/car $19.80/9.90/72.80), Swartz Bay (adult/child/car $13.45/6.75/41.90) and other islands.

Seair Seaplanes (p194) Flights from Vancouver International Airport arrive at Montague Harbour ($119, twice daily).

Saturna Island

POP 350

Suffused with tranquility, tiny Saturna is a natural retreat remote enough to deter casual visitors. Almost half the island, laced with curving bays, stunning rock bluffs and towering arbutus trees, is part of the **Gulf Islands National Park Reserve** and the only crowds you'll see are feral goats that have called this munchable area home. If you've had enough of civilization, this is the place to be.

On the north side of the island, **Winter Cove** has a white-sand beach that's popular for swimming, boating and fishing. Great for a hike is **Mt Warburton Pike** (497m), where you'll spot wild goats, soaring eagles and panoramic views of the surrounding islands: focus your binoculars and you might spy a whale or two sailing quietly along the coast.

If you're here on Canada Day (July 1), join the locals at the annual **Lamb Barbecue** (www.saturnalambbbarbeque.com; adult/child $23/12). It's the biggest party on the island.

Alongside campsites and B&Bs, you'll find a small selection of other sleeping options. Aim for **Saturna Lodge** (📞250-539-2254; www.saturna.ca; 130 Payne Rd; d from $145; 🛜), a peaceful respite surrounded by a garden.

Dining is generally of the rustic variety here. Not far from the ferry dock, **Wild Thyme Coffee House** (📞250-539-5589; www.wildthymecoffeehouse.com; 109 East Point Rd; mains $6-10; ⏱5:45am-4:30pm Mon-Fri, 8am-4:30pm Sat & Sun; 🛜🍴) is a delightful converted double-decker bus (seats and tables inside and out) serving wholesome breakfasts, soup and sandwich lunches, and baked treats, all made with foodie love. There's a focus on local ingredients and fair-trade coffee.

ℹ️ Information

Saturna Island Tourism Association (www.saturnatourism.com) Visit the Saturna Island Tourism Association website for more information.

ℹ️ Getting There & Away

BC Ferries (p192) Services dock at Lyall Harbour on the west of the island from Tsawwassen (adult/child/car $19.80/9.90/72.80), Swartz Bay (adult/child/car $13.45/6.75/41.90) and other islands.

Seair Seaplane (p194) Services arrive Lyall Harbour from Vancouver International Airport ($119, three times daily)

Mayne Island

POP 1,100

Once a stopover for gold-rush miners, who nicknamed it 'Little Hell,' Mayne is the region's most historic island. Long past its importance as a commercial hub, it now houses a colorful clutch of resident artists. For further visitor information, see www.mayneislandchamber.ca.

The heritage **Agricultural Hall** in Miners Bay hosts the lively **Farmers Market** (📞250-222-0034; 430 Fernhill Rd, Agricultural Hall; ⏱10am-1pm Sat May-Oct) of local crafts and produce. But if it's time to explore, the south shore's **Dinner Bay Park** (Dinner Point Rd) has a lovely sandy beach, as well as an immaculate **Japanese Garden**, built by locals to commemorate early-20th-century Japanese residents. If you're feeling active, **Bennett Bay Kayaking** (📞250-539-0864; www.bennettbaykayaking.com; 494 Arbutus Dr; kayak rentals/tours from $37/66; ⏱Apr-Oct) can help kayakers and stand-up paddleboarders get out on the water via rentals and tours.

If you're just too tired to head back to the mainland, **Mayne Island Resort** (📞250-539-3122; www.mayneislandresort.com; 494 Arbutus Dr; d from $159; 🛜🍴🐾) combines ocean-view rooms in a century-old inn with swanky luxe beach cottages. There's also a spa and large restaurant-bar. Alternatively, go the heritage B&B route at the charming **Fairview Farm** (📞604-539-5582; www.fairviewonmayne.com; 601 Bell Bay Rd; d from $125).

If it's time for treats, head to **Sunny Mayne Bakery Cafe** (📞250-539-2323; www.sunnymaynebakery.com; 472 Village Bay Rd; mains $4-10; ⏱6am-6pm) – don't miss the sausage rolls. But when dinner is required, aim for a water-view seat at **Bennett Bay Bistro** (📞250-539-3122; www.bennettbaybistro.com; 494 Arbutus Dr; mains $12-22; ⏱11:30am-8:30pm).

ℹ️ Getting There & Away

BC Ferries (p192) Frequent services arrive at Village Bay from Tsawwassen (adult/child/car $19.80/9.90/72.80), Swartz Bay (adult/child/car $13.45/6.75/41.90) and other islands.

Seair Seaplanes (p194) Flights arrive from Vancouver International Airport at Miners Bay ($119, twice daily).

FRASER & THOMPSON VALLEYS

Those looking for an inland escape from Vancouver can shoot east on Hwy 1 through the fertile plains of places such as Abbotsford. Mostly people just whiz past this farmland, and you should too, unless you have a hankering to see a turnip in the rough. That said, the Fraser Canyon thrills with stunning river-gorge beauty and the Thompson River looks little changed in decades.

ℹ️ Information

About 150km east of Vancouver, Hope has a good **visitors center** (📞604-869-2021; www.hopebc.ca; 919 Water Ave; ⏱9am-5pm) with plenty of information about the local provincial parks and the region.

EC Manning Provincial Park

This 708-sq-km **provincial park** (📞604-795-6169; www.bcparks.ca; 🅿), 30km southeast of Hope, is a hint of bigger – much bigger – things to come as you head east,

Fraser & Thompson Valleys

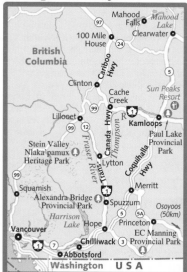

away from the farmlands of the Lower Mainland, towards the Rocky Mountains. It packs in a lot: dry valleys dark; mountainous forests; roiling rivers and alpine meadows. The park makes a good pause along Hwy 3, but don't expect solitude, as there are scores of folk from the burgs west seeking the same thing.

Sights & Activities

Manning is a four-seasons playground. Manning Park Resort (p196) has winter sports. In summer boat rentals are available on Lightning Lake, and you can enjoy the alpine splendor on day hikes.

The following walks are easily reached from Hwy 3:

➡ **Dry Ridge Trail** Crosses from the dry interior into an alpine climate; excellent views and wildflowers (3km round-trip, one hour).

➡ **Canyon Nature Trail** Nice loop trail with a river crossing on a bridge (2km, 45 minutes).

➡ **Lightning Lake Loop** The perfect intro: a level loop around this central lake (9km, two hours). Look for critters in the evening.

Sleeping

Lightning Lake Campground CAMPGROUND $
(reservations 800-689-9025; www.discover-camping.ca; EC Manning Provincial Park; campsites $35) A popular campground that accepts advance reservations.

Manning Park Resort RESORT $$
(800-330-3321, 250-840-8822; www.manning-park.com; 7500 Hwy 3; dm from $35, r from $120; P ⌂ ⌘) Manning Park Resort has the only indoor accommodations in the park. The 73 rooms are housed in the lodge and cabins. All provide use of a hot tub, requisite after a day of downhill **skiing** and **snowboarding** (adult/child day pass $53/33). It also has 100km of groomed trails for cross-country skiing and snowshoeing.

Information

The park's **visitor center** (604-668-5953; Hwy 3; ⌚ 9am-6pm mid-Jun–mid-Sep) is 30km inside the western boundary. It has detailed hiking descriptions, and a relief model of the park and nearby beaver ponds.

Getting There & Away

The park is east of Hope on Hwy 3. **Greyhound Canada** (800-661-8747; www.greyhound.ca) has buses from Hope ($20, one hour, one daily).

Fraser River Canyon

The name alone makes **Spuzzum** a fun stop along Hwy 1 on its way to Cache Creek, 85km west of Kamloops. The road shadows the swiftly flowing Fraser River through the eponymous canyon and, as you'd expect, white-water rafting is huge here. Grand scenery and several good provincial parks make this a winning trip.

North from Spuzzum, **Stein Valley Nla-ka'pamux Heritage Park** (250-371-6200; www.bcparks.ca; Stein Valley Rd, Lytton; P) is an ecologically diverse park that is managed together with the Lytton First Nation. It offers some excellent long-distance **hiking** through dry valleys and snow-clad peaks amid one of the best-preserved watersheds in lower BC.

Two kilometers north of Spuzzum, **Alexandra Bridge Provincial Park** (604-795-6169; www.bcparks.ca; off Hwy 1; P) makes for a scenic stop, where you can picnic while gazing up at the bridge's historic 1926 span.

White-water rafting down the Fraser and its tributaries' fast-flowing rapids is popular and **Fraser River Raft Expeditions** (☑ 604-863-2336; www.fraserraft.com; 30950 Hwy 1, Yale; trips from $160) covers all the main waterways in the area. **Kumsheen Rafting Resort** (☑ 800-663-6667; www.kumsheen.com; Hwy 1, 5km east of Lytton; campsites/tipis from $35/130; ℗) also offers a variety of trips and funky accommodations.

Kamloops

POP 89,500

If you've opted to follow Hwy 1 from Vancouver east to the Rockies and Banff, Kamloops makes a useful break in the journey. Motels abound, and there's a walkable heritage center. Historically, the Shuswap First Nation found the area's many rivers and lakes useful for transportation and salmon fishing. Traders set up camp for fur hunting in 1811.

The focus of the downtown area is tree-lined Victoria St, which is a lively place on sunny days; very busy train tracks separate the wide Thompson River from downtown. Franchises and malls line the highlands along Hwy 1.

The 2017 *Power Rangers* movie was filmed here.

◎ Sights

Using Victoria St as your anchor, stroll downtown, stopping at the art gallery and museum. Pick up the *Downtown Cultural Heritage Walking Tour* brochure from the visitor center (p198).

Look for **back-alley art**, a series of murals in the alley between Victoria and Seymour Sts east of 2nd Ave.

Kamloops Heritage Railway   HISTORIC RAILWAY
(☑ 250-374-2141; www.kamrail.com; 510 Lorne St; adult/child from $25/12; ⊙ Aug; ℗) Across the train tracks from downtown, the Kamloops Heritage Railway runs steam-engine-powered excursions. Confirm the schedule in advance.

Kamloops Art Gallery   GALLERY
(☑ 250-377-2400; www.kag.bc.ca; 465 Victoria St; adult/child $5/3; ⊙ 10am-5pm Mon-Sat, to 9pm Thu) Suitably loft-like in feel, this gallery has an emphasis on contemporary Western and aboriginal works by regional artists.

WORTH A TRIP

BC'S PARK GEM

From Kamloops, Hwy 5 runs north toward the Alberta border and Jasper National Park, 440km from Kamloops. Along the way, it passes near **Wells Gray Provincial Park** (p231), 125km from Kamloops, one of BC's finest and a haven for those who really want to get away from civilization.

Kamloops Museum & Archives   MUSEUM
(☑ 250-828-3576; www.kamloops.ca/museum; cnr Seymour St & 2nd Ave; adult/child $3/1; ⊙ 9:30am-4:30pm Tue-Sat; ☀) Kamloops Museum is in a vintage building and has a suitably fitting collection of historic photographs. Come here for the scoop on river-namesake David Thompson, and an entire floor dedicated to exhibits for kids.

Paul Lake Provincial Park   PARK
(☑ 250-819-7376; www.bcparks.ca; Pinantan Rd; ℗) On the often-hot summer days, the beach at Paul Lake Provincial Park beckons and you may spot falcons and coyotes. There is a 20km **mountain-biking loop**, and campsites ($18). It's 24km northeast of Kamloops, via Hwy 5.

🛏 Sleeping

Older and shabbier motels can be found along a stretch of Hwy 1 east of downtown. Columbia St, from the center up to Hwy 1 above town, has another gaggle of chain and older indie motels, some with sweeping views. The nearby parks have good camping.

★ Plaza Hotel   HOTEL $$
(☑ 877-977-5292, 250-377-8075; www.plazaheritage hotel.com; 405 Victoria St; r $75-200; ℗ ⊕ ❄ 🖤) In a town of bland modernity as far as lodgings go, the Plaza reeks of character. This 67-room, six-story classic has changed little on the outside since its opening in 1928. Rooms are nicely redone in a chic heritage style, though, and the included breakfast is excellent.

Scott's Inn   MOTEL $$
(☑ 250-372-8221; www.scottsinn.com; 551 11th Ave; r from $100; ℗ ❄ @ 🖤 🖤) Unlike many of its competitors, Scott's is close to the center and very well run. The 51 rooms are nicely furnished for a motel, and extras include an indoor pool, hot tub, cafe and rooftop sun deck.

South Thompson Inn
Guest Ranch
LODGE $$

(☐ 250-573-3777; www.stigr.com; 3438 Shuswap Rd E; r $160-260; P✳☎☀) Some 20km west of town via Hwy 1, this luxe waterfront lodge is perched on the banks of the South Thompson River and set amid rolling grasslands. Its 57 rooms are spread between the wood-framed main building, a small manor house and some converted stables.

✕ Eating & Drinking

Art We Are
CAFE $

(www.theartweare.com; 246 Victoria St; mains from $8; ☺9am-9pm Mon-Sat; ☎☑) Tea joint, local artist venue, hangout, bakery and more – this funky cafe is a great place to let some Kamloops hours slip by. The organic menu changes daily. Saturday night has live rock or blues.

Hello Toast
CAFE $

(☐ 250-372-9322; www.facebook.com/hellodouble; 428 Victoria St; mains $5-12; ☺7:30am-3pm; ☑) As opposed to Good Morning Croissant, this veggie-friendly, organic cafe offers whole grains for some, and fried combos of bacon and eggs or burgers for others. Nice open front and sidewalk tables.

★ Noble Pig
PUB FOOD $$

(☐ 778-471-5999; www.thenoblepig.ca; 650 Victoria St; mains $12-20; ☺11:30am-11pm Mon-Wed, to midnight Thu-Sat, 3-10pm Sun) This large and slick microbrewery has a rotating lineup of seven of its own beers (its excellent IPA is always on tap) plus other top BC brews. The food is equally good and includes salads, burgers, pizza and various specials. Try the fries. The inside is warm and welcoming; in summer you can't beat the huge patio.

Commodore
PUB

(☐ 250-851-3100; www.commodorekamloops.com; 369 Victoria St; ☺11am-late Mon-Sat) An old-style pub with a long menu that highlights burgers and fondue (mains from $12), the Com is the place on Friday nights for live jazz and funk. Other nights, DJs spin pretty much anything. Enjoy the sidewalk seating.

❶ Information

The **visitor center** (☐ 250-374-3377, 800-662-1994; www.tourismkamloops.com; 1290 W Hwy 1, exit 368; ☺8am-6pm; ☎) is just off Hwy 1, overlooking town.

❶ Getting There & Away

Greyhound Canada (p196) is about 1km southwest of the center off Columbia St W. Destinations include the following:

Jasper $70, 5½ hours, one daily
Kelowna $37, 2½ hours, two daily
Prince George $89, seven hours, one daily
Vancouver $59, five hours, six daily

VIA Rail (p107) serves Kamloops North Station, 11km from town off Hwy 5, with the tri-weekly *Canadian* on its run from Vancouver (9½ hours) to Jasper (another 9½ hours) and beyond. Fares vary greatly by season and class of service.

❶ Getting Around

Kamloops Transit System (☐ 250-376-1216; www.bctransit.com/kamloops; fares $2) runs local buses.

Sun Peaks

The hills looming northeast of Kamloops are home to the **Sun Peaks Resort** (☐ 800-807-3257; www.sunpeaksresort.com; 1280 Alpine Rd; lift tickets adult/child $92/46, mountain biking $45/27). This ever-growing resort boasts 135 ski runs (including some 8km-long powder trails), 12 lifts and a pleasant base-area village. In summer, lifts provide access to more than two dozen mountain-bike trails.

Sun Peaks has many lodges, B&Bs and luxury condos. **Sun Peaks Hostel** (☐ 250-578-0057; www.sunpeakshostel.com; 1140 Sun Peaks Rd; dm/d from $27/75; ☎) has a mix of dorms and private rooms in a woodsy lodge setting.

Sun Peaks is 50km northeast of Kamloops via Hwy 5. In winter there are shuttles from Kamloops ($15).

OKANAGAN VALLEY

It's hard to know which harvest is growing faster in this fertile and beautiful valley midway between Vancouver and Alberta: tourists or fruit. The 180km-long Okanagan Valley is home to orchards of peaches and apricots, and scores of excellent wineries whose vines spread across the terraced hills, soaking up some of Canada's sunniest weather. The valley has provided a summertime escape for generations of Canadians, who frolic in the string of lakes linking the Okanagan's towns.

Okanagan Valley

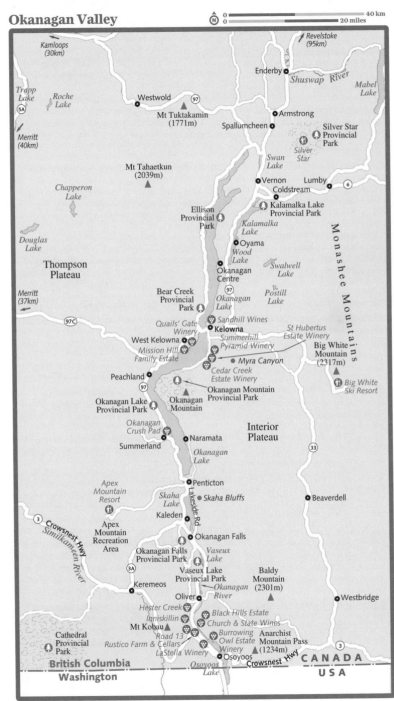

N 0 ———————— 40 km
   0 ———————— 20 miles

Kamloops
(30km)

Revelstoke
(95km)

Enderby

Shuswap River

Mabel
Lake

Trapp
Lake

Roche
Lake

Westwold

97

Mt Tuktakamin
(1771m)

Armstrong

Silver Star
Provincial
Park

5A

Spallumcheen

Silver
Star

Merritt
(40km)

Swan
Lake

Vernon

Lumby

6

Mt Tahaetkun
(2039m)

Coldstream

Chapperon
Lake

Kalamalka Lake
Provincial Park

Ellison
Provincial
Park

Kalamalka
Lake

Douglas
Lake

Oyama

Wood
Lake

Swalwell
Lake

Thompson
Plateau

Okanagan
Centre

Postill
Lake

Merritt
(37km)

Bear Creek
Provincial
Park

97

Okanagan
Lake

Sandhill Wines

97C

Quails' Gate
Winery

Kelowna

St Hubertus
Estate Winery

Monashee Mountains

West Kelowna

Summerhill
Pyramid Winery

Mission Hill
Family Estate

Myra Canyon

Big White
Mountain
(2317m)

Peachland

Cedar Creek
Estate Winery

Big White
Ski Resort

97

Okanagan Lake
Provincial Park

Okanagan
Mountain

Okanagan Mountain
Provincial Park

Okanagan
Crush Pad

Interior
Plateau

Summerland

Naramata

Okanagan
Lake

33

Apex
Mountain
Resort

Penticton

Lakeside Rd

Skaha
Lake

Skaha Bluffs

Beaverdell

Apex
Mountain
Recreation
Area

Kaleden

3

Crowsnest Hwy

Similkameen River

Okanagan Falls

3A

Okanagan Falls
Provincial Park

Vaseux
Lake

Keremeos

Vaseux Lake
Provincial Park

Baldy
Mountain
(2301m)

Westbridge

Okanagan
River

Cathedral
Provincial
Park

Oliver

Hester Creek

Black Hills Estate

Inniskillin

Church & State Wines

Mt Kobau

Road 13

Burrowing
Owl Estate
Winery

Anarchist
Mountain Pass
(1234m)

Rustico Farm & Cellars

LaStella Winery

Osoyoos

3

British Columbia

Osoyoos
Lake

Crowsnest Hwy

CANADA

Washington

USA

OKANAGAN VALLEY WINERIES

The abundance of sunshine, fertile soil and cool winters have allowed the local wine industry to thrive. Kelowna and the region in the valley's north are known for whites, such as Pinot Grigio. South, near Penticton and Oliver, reds are the stars, especially ever-popular Merlot.

A majority of the more than 120 wineries are close to Hwy 97, which makes tasting a breeze. Most offer tours and all will gladly sell you a bottle or 20; in fact, many of the best wines are only sold at the cellar door. Some wineries feature excellent cafes and bistros that offer fine views and complex regional fare to complement what's in the glass.

Festivals

Okanagan seasonal **wine festivals** (www.thewinefestivals.com) are major events, especially the one in fall.

The usual dates are fall (early October), winter (mid-January), spring (early May) and summer (early August). Events take place at wineries across the valley.

Information

Good sources of information on Okanagan Valley wines include the **BC Wine Information Centre** situated in Penticton's **visitor center** (p207) and the **BC Wine Museum** (p208) located in Kelowna. *John Schreiner's Okanagan Wine Tour Guide* is an authoritative guidebook.

Tours

Numerous companies allow you to do the sipping while they do the driving.

Club Wine Tours (☎250-762-9951; www.clubwinetours.com; tours from $75) The 'signature' tour includes four wineries and lunch in a vineyard.

Distinctly Kelowna Tours (☎250-979-1211; www.distinctlykelownatours.ca; tours from $100) Offers winery tours by valley region; many include stops for lunch.

Visiting the Wineries

Wine tastings at those wineries open to visitors vary greatly. Some places have just a couple of wines on offer; others offer dozens of vintages. Some tasting rooms are glorified sales areas; others have magnificent views of the vineyards, valley and lakes. Some charge; others are free.

Among the dozens of options, the following (listed north to south) are recommended. Summerhill Pyramid and Cedar Creek Estate are south of Kelowna along the lake's east shore. The rest of the wineries can be reached via Hwy 97.

Sandhill Wines (☎250-762-2999; www.sandhillwines.ca; 1125 Richter St, Kelowna; ⊙10am-6pm; P) Formerly known as Calona Vineyards, Sandhill Wines was the Okanagan's first winery when it kicked off production in 1932. Its architecturally striking tasting room is an atmospheric spot to try its ever-popular, melon-note Pinot Blanc.

Summerhill Pyramid Winery (☎250-764-8000; www.summerhill.bc.ca; 4870 Chute Lake Rd, Kelowna; ⊙9am-6pm; P) In the hills along the lake's eastern shore is one of the Okanagan's most colorful wineries. Summerhill Pyramid Winery combines a traditional tasting room with a huge pyramid where every Summerhill wine is aged in barrels. The winery's **Sunset Organic Bistro** (p211) offers locally sourced dishes; the wines are organic.

Cedar Creek Estate Winery (☎250-764-8866; www.cedarcreek.bc.ca; 5445 Lakeshore Rd, Kelowna; ⊙10am-7pm Jul & Aug, 11am-5pm Sep-Jun; P) Known for excellent tours, its Riesling and its Ehrenfelser, a refreshing fruity white wine. Its **Vineyard Terrace** (☎778-738-1027; mains $20-35; ⊙11am-9pm Jun–mid-Sep) has the kind of view that makes you want to eat here twice.

Quails' Gate Winery (☎250-769-2501; www.quailsgate.com; 3303 Boucherie Rd, West Kelowna; ⊙10am-8pm; P) A small winery with a huge reputation; it's known for its Pinot Noir, Chardonnay and Chenin Blanc. The **Old Vines Restaurant** (☎250-769-4451; mains $20-35; ⊙11:30am-2pm & 5-9pm) is among the best.

Mission Hill Family Estate (☎250-768-7611; www.missionhillwinery.com; 1730 Mission Hill Rd, West Kelowna; ⊙10am-6pm; P) As if it were a Tuscan hill town, this winery's architecture wows. Go for a taste of one of the blended reds (try the Bordeaux) or the excellent Syrah. **Terrace** (p208) is one of the valley's best restaurants and sources fine foods locally; book ahead.

Okanagan Crush Pad (☎250-494-4445; www.okanagancrushpad.com; 16576 Fosbery Rd, Summerland; ⊙10:30am-5:30pm; P) Ages many of its wines in concrete tanks, reviving a centuries-old practice that largely died out when the industry shifted to stainless steel. Tastings range across more than 20 varieties from the multiple labels that are produced here.

Hester Creek (☎250-498-4435; www.hestercreek.com; 877 Road 8, Oliver; ⊙10am-7pm; P) Has a sweeping location, a great new tasting room and is known for its reds, especially its richly flavored Cabernet Franc. **Terrafina** (p204) has a Med accent.

Inniskillin (☎250-498-4500; www.inniskillin.com; 7857 Tucelnuit Dr, Oliver; ⊙10am-5pm; P) BC's first producer of Zinfandel is also home to the elixirs known as ice wines, which are harvested when the grapes are frozen on the vine; go for the golden-hued Riesling.

Road 13 (☎250-498-8330; www.road13vineyards.com; 799 Ponderosa Rd, Road 13, Oliver; ⊙10am-5:30pm May-Oct, 11am-4pm Mon-Sat Nov-Apr; P) Its very drinkable reds (Pinot Noir) and whites (Chenin Blanc) win plaudits. The no-frills vibe extends to its picnic tables with gorgeous views and the motto 'It's all about dirt.' The attractive lounge has views of the grapes.

Rustico Farm & Cellars (☎250-498-3276; www.rusticowinery.com; 4444 Golden Mile Dr, Oliver; ⊙10am-6pm Apr-Oct; P) Who says winemaking is serious? For Bruce Fuller, it's a hoot. Set in a 19th-century bunk house now covered in vines, this winery produces fine reds and whites such as the Bonanza Old Vine Zinfandel. There is an Old West feel here, helped along by the cowboy-hat-wearing Fuller.

Black Hills Estate (☎250-498-0666; www.blackhillswinery.com; 4190 Black Sage Rd, Oliver; guided tastings $10-30; ⊙10am-5pm Apr-Nov; P) The tasting room here is an arresting vision of glass and metal, with deeply shaded patios for sunset tippling. Besides vintages such as Viognier, there are many blends, including Alibi, a blend of Sauvignon Blanc and Semillon. It offers a sunset happy hour with local transport in summer from 4pm to 7pm.

Church & State Wines (☎250-498-2700; www.churchandstatewines.com; 4516 Ryegrass Rd, Oliver; ⊙11am-6pm; P) Making a big splash at its Coyote Bowl vineyards, especially with its full-bodied, luscious Syrahs. Also home to the Lost Inhibitions label, which produces popularly priced wines with names such as Chill the F*uck Out and I Freakin' Love You.

Burrowing Owl Estate Winery (☎250-498-0620; www.burrowingowlwine.ca; 500 Burrowing Owl Pl, Oliver; ⊙10am-6pm mid-Fed–mid-Dec; P) 🌿 Wine with an eco-accent that includes organic farm techniques; try the Syrah. Other award-winners include the Cabernet Franc and Meritage. This Golden Mile landmark includes a hotel and the excellent **Sonora Room** (p204) restaurant.

LaStella Winery (p202) A beautiful vision of Italy rises up near Osoyoos Lake. Terracotta roof tiles and floors and granite touches combine for one of the valley's most beautiful wineries. The Cabernet Sauvignon–based Maestoso is highly regarded.

Osoyoos, near the US border, is almost arid, but things become greener heading north. Central Kelowna is a fast-growing city that's a heady mix of lakeside beauty and fun.

In July and August the entire valley is as overburdened as a grapevine before harvest; the best times to visit are in the late spring and early fall, when the crowds lessen. Snowy winters also make nearby Big White resort an attraction for skiers and snowboarders.

Osoyoos

POP 5100

Once-modest Osoyoos has embraced an upscale future. The town takes its name from the First Nations word *soyoos*, which means 'sand bar across'; even if the translation is a bit rough, the definition is not: much of the town is indeed on a narrow spit of land that divides Osoyoos Lake. It is ringed with beaches, and the waters irrigate the lush farms, orchards and vineyards that line Hwy 97 going north out of town.

Nature's bounty aside, this is the arid end of the Okanagan Valley and locals like to say that the town marks the northern end of Mexico's Sonoran Desert; much of the town is done up in a style that loses something across borders. From the cactus-speckled sands to the town's cheesy faux-tile-and-stucco architecture, it's a big change from the BC image of pine trees and mountains found in both directions on Hwy 3.

◉ Sights & Activities

Osoyoos Lake is one of the warmest in the country. That, together with Osoyoos' sandy beaches, means great swimming, a huge relief when the summer temp hits 42°C (108°F). Many lakeside motels and campgrounds hire out kayaks, canoes and small boats.

Osoyoos Desert Centre PARK
(☑250-495-2470; www.desert.org; off Hwy 97; adult/child $7/6; ⊗9:30am-4:30pm mid-May–mid-Sep, shorter hours mid-Sep–mid-May; ℗) Hear the rattle of a snake and the songs of birds at the Osoyoos Desert Centre, 3km north of town, where interpretive kiosks along raised boardwalks meander through the dry land. The nonprofit center offers 90-minute **guided tours**. Special gardens focus on delights such as delicate wildflowers.

Nk'Mip Desert & Heritage Centre MUSEUM
(☑250-495-7901; www.nkmipdesert.com; 1000 Rancher Creek Rd; adult/child $14/10; ⊗9:30am-5:30pm May-Sep, shorter hours Oct-Apr; ℗) Part of a First Nations empire, the Nk'Mip Desert & Heritage Centre features cultural demonstrations and tours of the arid ecology. Located off 45th St north of Hwy 3, it also has a desert **golf course**, the noted winery **Nk'Mip Cellars**, a resort and more.

LaStella Winery WINERY
(☑250-495-8180; www.lastella.ca; 8123 148 Ave, Osoyoos; ⊗10:30am-6:30pm Apr-Oct; ℗) A beautiful vision of Italy rises up near Osoyoos Lake. Terra-cotta roof tiles and floors and granite touches combine for one of the valley's most beautiful wineries. The Cabernet Sauvignon–based Maestoso is highly regarded.

Cathedral Provincial Park PARK
(☑604-795-6169; www.bcparks.ca; Ashnola Rd; ℗) About 30km west of Keremeos, Cathedral Provincial Park is a 330-sq-km mountain wilderness that's a playground for the truly adventurous. The park offers excellent backcountry camping ($13) and **hiking** around wildflower-dappled alpine expanses and turquoise waters.

ATB Watersports WATER SPORTS
(☑250-498-9044; www.atbwatersports.com; 5815 Oleander Dr, Safari Beach Resort; SUP rental per hour from $25; ⊗Jun-Sep) Osoyoos Lake is mirror-flat, perfect for paddleboarding hijinks. Rent or take lessons. Also available: kayaks and canoes.

🛏 Sleeping & Eating

The eastern edge of the lake is lined with campgrounds. More than a dozen modest motels line the narrow strip of land that splits Osoyoos Lake, but beware of shabby older properties. Many cluster around Hwy 3 and there's another clump on the southwest shore near the border. Chains can be found at the junction.

Nk'Mip Campground & RV Resort CAMPGROUND $
(☑250-495-7279; www.campingosoyoos.com; 8000 45th St; campsites/RV sites from $35/48, cabins from $170; ℗🛜) Choose from more than 300 sites at this year-round lakeside resort off Hwy 3. Now offers large cabins as well.

Avalon Inn
MOTEL $$

(☎ 250-495-6334; www.avaloninn.ca; 9106 Main St; r $90-180; P ❋ 🛜) Away from the lake but close to good restaurants, this 20-unit indie motel has large rooms and gardens that get more ornate by the year. Some rooms have kitchens.

Walnut Beach Resort
RESORT $$$

(☎ 250-495-5400; www.walnutbeachresort.com; 4200 Lakeshore Dr; r $150-350; P ❋ 🛜 🏊) This large resort is an upscale addition to the east shore of the southern half of the lake. There are 112 large suites (some with two bedrooms) and a vast terrace surrounding a pool.

Roberto's Gelato
GELATERIA $

(☎ 250-495-5425; www.robertosgelato.com; 15 Park Dr, Watermark Beach Resort; gelato from $3; ⊙ noon-10pm Jun-Sep, shorter hours Oct-May) Located downtown near the lake, Roberto's always offers at least 24 house-made flavors.

★ Dolci Socialhaus
CAFE $$

(☎ 250-495-6807; www.dolcideli.com; 8710 Main St; mains $14-25; ⊙ 11:30am-9pm Tue-Sat) Tucked into a small storefront mid-block, this cafe is easy to miss – but to do so would be a mistake. The simple fare is transcendent thanks to a passionate flair for food provenance – even the bacon is smoked in-house. Go for a table on the terrace and graze the farm board.

❶ Information

The large **visitor center** (☎ 250-495-5070; www.destinationosoyoos.com; cnr Hwys 3 & 97; ⊙ 9am-6pm; 🛜) has info, maps and books, and it can book bus tickets and accommodations for you.

❶ Getting There & Away

Greyhound Canada (p196) runs to Vancouver ($77, seven hours, one daily), departing from outside the visitor center. One bus runs north up the valley daily, including to Penticton ($20, 70 minutes).

Oliver

POP 5200

Oliver has emerged as a hub of excellent wineries and other natural bounty. Over the 20km drive between Oliver and Osoyoos, Hwy 97 plunges through orchard after orchard laden with lush fruits, earning it the moniker 'The Golden Mile.' Roadside stands display the ripe bounty and many places will let you pick your own.

---

❶ IT'S TIME FOR FRUIT

Roadside stands and farms where you can buy and even pick your own fruit line Hwy 97 between Osoyoos and Penticton. Major Okanagan Valley crops and their harvest times:

Cherries Mid-June to late July

Apricots Mid-July to mid-August

Peaches Mid-July to mid-September

Pears Mid-August to late September

Apples Early September to late October

Table Grapes Early September to late October

◉ Sights & Actvities

The small roads through the vineyards around Oliver are made for exploring by bike. Local walking and biking routes include the excellent 18.4km **International Bike Trail**.

Pick up the heritage walking-tour brochure from the tourist office to fully appreciate this traditional orchard town.

Double O Bikes
CYCLING

(☎ 250-535-0577; www.doubleobikes.com; 6246 Main St; bicycle rental per day from adult/child $24/20; ⊙ 9:30am-5pm) Bike rental and good route advice. Has another store that is located in Osoyoos.

🛏 Sleeping & Eating

Mount View Motel
MOTEL $$

(☎ 250-498-3446; www.mountviewmotel.com; 5856 Main St; r $80-120; P ❋ 🛜) Close to the center of town, seven units sunbathe around a flower-bedecked vintage motor court. All have kitchens – and corkscrews. The decor features new wood floors and a contemporary style.

★ Burrowing Owl Guest House
BOUTIQUE HOTEL $$$

(☎ 250-498-0620; www.burrowingowlwine.ca; 500 Burrowing Owl Pl, off Black Sage Rd; r $170-350; ⊙ May-Oct, reduced hours Nov-Apr; P ❋ 🛜 🏊) What is one of the Okanagan's best wineries has 10 rooms with patios facing southwest over the vineyards. There's a big pool, a hot tub, king-size beds and corporate mission-style decor. The Sonora Room (p204) is noted for its fusion cuisine. It's 13km south of Oliver, off Hwy 97.

Hester Creek
INN $$$

(☑250-498-4435; www.hestercreek.com; 877 Road 8; r $200-300; P❉☎) One of the valley's top wineries, Hester Creek has six suites in a Mediterranean-style villa with a sweeping view over the vineyards. The trappings are plush, with fireplaces, soaking tubs and more. On-site Terrafina (p204) serves excellent Tuscan-accented fare using foods from the region.

Medici's Gelateria
GELATERIA $

(☑250-498-2228; www.medicisgelateria.ca; 9932 350th Ave/Fairview Rd; treats from $3; ☺10am-5pm) Frozen delights so good you'll worship them – appropriate, given the setting in an old church. Also serves good coffee, plus soups, panini and more, all made with local produce. It's just west of Hwy 97.

Farmers Market
MARKET $

(Lion's Park, Hwy 97; ☺8am-1pm Sat & 5-8pm Wed summer) A vibrant market that celebrates the region's bounty.

★Terrafina
ITALIAN $$$

(☑250-495-3278; www.terrafinarestaurant.com; 887 Road 8, Oliver; mains $20-35; ☺11:30am-9pm daily Jun-Sep, Wed-Sun Oct-May) This intimate restaurant at Hester Creek Estate Winery serves up exquisite Tuscan-flavored dishes. Its outdoor terrace is one of the valley's finest.

Sonora Room
FUSION $$$

(☑250-498-0620; www.burrowingowlwine.ca; 500 Burrowing Owl Pl, Burrowing Owl Estate; mains $20-35; ☺11:30am-9pm May–mid-Oct, shorter hours mid-Apr–Apr) Fresh fare with light Italian and French touches is the hallmark at this very attractive Tuscan-style restaurant in one of the valley's warmest corners. It offers transport to/from the resorts in Osoyoos for $25.

❶ Information

The **visitor center** (☑778-439-2363; www.winecapitalofcanada.com; 6431 Station St; ☺9am-5pm) has affable staff and is located in the old train station near the center of town. It has regional info, and walking and biking maps.

Vaseaux Lake

About 10km north of Oliver on Hwy 97, nature reasserts itself at this lake – an azure gem, framed by sheer granite cliffs.

If you're not in a hurry, the small roads on the east side of Skaha Lake between Okanagan Falls and Penticton are more interesting for their wineries and views than Hwy 97.

Vaseux Lake Provincial Park (www.bcparks.ca; Hwy 97) has a 300m boardwalk for viewing oodles of birds, bighorn sheep, mountain goats and some of the 14 species of bat. You can also hike to the **Bighorn National Wildlife Area** and the **Vaseux Lake National Migratory Bird Sanctuary**, which has more than 160 bird species.

Penticton

Penticton combines the idle pleasures of a beach resort with its own edgy vibe. It's long been a final stop in life for Canadian retirees, which adds a certain spin to its Salish-derived name Pen-Tak-Tin, meaning 'place to stay forever.' The town today is growing fast, along with the rest of the Okanagan Valley.

Penticton makes a good base for your valley pleasures. There are plenty of activities and diversions to fill your days, even if you don't travel further afield. Ditch Hwy 97, which runs west of the center, for Main St and the attractively walkable downtown area, which extends about 10 blocks southward from the picture-perfect lakefront; avert your eyes from the long stretch of strip malls and high-rise condos further south.

❂ Sights

Okanagan Beach boasts about 1300m of sand, with average summer water temperatures of about 22°C (72°F). If things are jammed, quieter shores are often found at 1.5km-long **Skaha Beach**, south of the center.

★SS Sicamous Inland Marine Museum
HISTORIC SITE

(☑250-492-0405; www.sssicamous.ca; 1099 Lakeshore Dr W; adult/child $6/3; ☺10am-5:30pm) Back when the best way to get around inland BC was by boat, the SS *Sicamous* hauled passengers and freight on Okanagan Lake from 1914 to 1936. Now the boat has been restored and permanently moored; a tour is an evocative self-guided ramble.

Skaha Bluffs Provincial Park
PARK

(www.bcparks.ca; Smythe Dr; ☺Mar-Nov) Propelled by the dry weather and compact gneiss rock, climbers from all over the world come to this park to enjoy **climbing** on more than 400 bolted routes. The local climbing group has comprehensive info on the bluffs (see www.skaha.org), which are off Lakeside Rd on the east side of Skaha Lake.

Penticton Museum   MUSEUM
(☑ 250-490-2451; www.pentictonmuseum.com; 785 Main St; by donation; ☺ 10am-5pm Tue-Sat) Inside the library, the Penticton Museum has delightfully eclectic displays, including the de rigueur natural-history exhibit with stuffed animals and birds, and everything you'd want to know about the juicy fruits of the Peach Festival (p206).

Art Gallery of Southern Okanagan   GALLERY
(☑ 250-493-2928; www.pentictonartgallery.com; 199 Marina Way; adult/child $2/free; ☺ 10am-5pm Tue-Fri, 11am-4pm Sat & Sun) The beachfront Art Gallery of Southern Okanagan displays a diverse collection of regional, provincial and national artists.

🏃 Activities

Aquatic fun abounds, and classic, cheesy resort diversions such as miniature golf await at the west end of Okanagan Beach.

Water Sports

Okanagan and Skaha Lakes both enjoy some of the best sailboarding, boating and paddling conditions in the Okanagan Valley.

There are several water-sports rental places on Okanagan Lake.

The paved **Okanagan River Channel Biking & Jogging Path** follows the rather arid channel linking Okanagan Lake to Skaha Lake. But why pound the pavement when you can float on the water?

★ Coyote Cruises   WATER SPORTS
(☑ 250-492-2115; www.coyotecruises.ca; 215 Riverside Dr; rentals & shuttle $12; ☺ 10am-5pm mid-Jun–Sep) Coyote Cruises rents out inner tubes that you can float on to a midway point on the Okanagan River Channel. It then buses you back to the start near Okanagan Lake. If you have your own floatable, it's $5 for the bus ride.

Pier Water Sports   WATER SPORTS
(☑ 250-493-8864; www.pierwatersports.com; Rotary Park, Lakeshore Dr W; party barges per 2hr from $275, SUP rentals 1hr/$20, kayak rentals 1hr/$15; ☺ 9am-7pm May-Sep) Rents several types of boats as well as kayaks, SUPs and pretty much anything else that floats.

Penticton Cruises   BOATING
(☑ 250-215-2779; www.pentictoncruises.com; Penticton Marina, 293 Marina Way; adult/child $25/12.50; ☺ May-Sep) Stimulate your inner seafarer with a one-hour, open-air lake tour on a faux stern wheeler. There are multiple daily sailings at summer's peak.

Mountain Biking & Cycling

Long dry days and rolling hills add up to perfect conditions for mountain biking. Get to popular rides by heading east out of town, toward Naramata. Follow signs to the city dump and **Campbell's Mountain**, where you'll find a single-track and dual-slalom course, both of which aren't too technical. Once you get there, the riding is mostly on the right-hand side, but once you pass the cattle guard, it opens up and you can ride anywhere.

Cyclists can try the route through Naramata and onto the Kettle Valley Rail Trail (p212). Other good options include the small, winery-lined roads south of town and east of Skaha Lake.

Freedom – The Bike Shop   CYCLING
(☑ 250-493-0686; www.freedombikeshop.com; 533 Main St; bicycle rental per day from $40; ☺ 9am-5:30pm Mon-Sat) Rents bikes and offers a wealth of information. Can arrange transport to/from the Kettle Valley Rail Trail.

Rock Climbing

Propelled by the dry weather and compact gneiss rock, climbers from all over the world come to Skaha Bluffs Provincial Park (p204) to enjoy climbing on more than 400 bolted routes. The local climbing group's website www.skaha.org has comprehensive info on the bluffs, which are off Lakeside Rd on the east side of Skaha Lake.

★ Skaha Rock Adventures   CLIMBING
(☑ 250-493-1765; www.skaharockclimbing.com; 437 Martin St; 1-day intros from $160; ☺ by appointment) Skaha Rock Adventures offers advanced technical instruction, as well as introductory courses for anyone venturing into a harness for the first time.

Snow Sports

Apex Mountain Resort   SKIING
(☑ 877-777-2739, condition report 250-487-4848; www.apexresort.com; off Green Mountain Rd; lift tickets adult/child $78/48) One of Canada's best small ski resorts is 37km west of Penticton. It has more than 68 downhill runs for all ability levels, but the mountain is known for its plethora of double-black-diamond and technical runs; the drop is more than 600m. It is usually quieter than nearby Big White.

★✫ Festivals & Events

Elvis Festival
MUSIC

(www.pentictonelvisfestival.ca; ⊙ late Jun) Dozens of Elvis impersonators could be your idea of heaven or hound-dog hell, especially on the afternoon of open-microphone singalongs.

Peach Festival
CULTURAL

(☑ 250-487-9709; www.peachfest.com; ⊙ early Aug) The city's premier event is basically a party that has taken place since 1948, loosely centered on the ripe succulent orbs and the crowning of a Peach Queen.

Pentastic Jazz Festival
MUSIC

(☑ 250-770-3494; www.pentasticjazz.com; ⊙ early Sep) More than a dozen bands perform at five venues over three days.

🛏 Sleeping

HI Penticton Hostel
HOSTEL $

(☑ 250-492-3992, reservations 866-782-9736; www.hihostels.ca; 464 Ellis St; dm/r from $35/76; ✳@🛜) This 47-bed hostel is near the center in a heavily worn 1908 house. Arranges activities, including wine tours.

Bowmont Motel
MOTEL $$

(☑ 800-811-1377; www.bowmontmotel.com; 80 Riverside Dr; r $80-180; P✳🛜🏊) Look past the dubious faux-Southwestern facade and you'll find an excellent indie motel near the lake. The 45 rooms are immaculate and all share terraces or balconies. Each has a full kitchen and there is a gas barbecue near the pool.

Tiki Shores Beach Resort
MOTEL $$

(☑ 250-492-8769; www.tikishores.com; 914 Lakeshore Dr W; condos $150-300; P✳🛜🏊) This lively resort across from the beach has 40 condo-style units with kitchens, most with separate bedrooms. Rooms have a light color scheme that seems ideal for a freshwater lakeside holiday.

Quidni Estate Winery Guest Rooms
APARTMENT $$$

(☑ 250-490-5251; www.quidniwine.com; 1465 Naramata Rd; r from $350; P✳🛜) Three plush suites await at this winery on the lovely Naramata Rd, 5km from Penticton. Views open up across the vineyards and down to the lake. Bathrooms feature marble and the soft furnishings are luxe. Cyclists enjoying the many local routes are well catered for here (spare tire tubes available etc). Enjoy tastings of the winery's products.

Crooked Tree Bed & Breakfast
B&B $$$

(☑ 250-490-8022; www.crooked-tree.com; 1278 Spiller Rd; suite $175-215; P🛜) All of Okanagan Lake glistens below you from this mountainside retreat that's 9km east of downtown Penticton. The three large apartments each have multiple decks amid this woodsy aerie and are well stocked with luxuries. Minimum stay two nights.

✕ Eating & Drinking

★Burger 55
BURGERS $

(☑ 778-476-5529; www.burger55.com; 52 Front St; mains $9-15; ⊙ 11am-9pm) Best burger in Canada? It's your own fault if it isn't, as you have myriad ways to customize at this downtown restaurant. Six kinds of buns, 10 kinds of cheese, and toppings that include roasted garlic and *pico de gallo* are just some of the options. Sides, such as fries, are equally excellent. There's a fine patio and a good beer list.

★Penticton Farmers Market
MARKET

(☑ 250-583-9933; www.pentictonfarmersmarket. org; 100 Main St; ⊙ 8:30am-1pm Sat May-Oct) Penticton definitely has its share of good eats. The farmers market, based at Gyro Park on Main St, has large numbers of local organic producers.

Bench Market
CAFE $

(☑ 250-492-2222; www.thebenchmarket.com; 368 Vancouver Ave; meals $9-12; ⊙ 7am-5pm) Always buzzing – and not just because of the excellent organic coffee – this neighborhood fave is consistently busy. The patio is where locals meet and exchange gossip. Egg dishes star at breakfast; lunch is about sandwiches and salads. Great baked goods and other deli items are sold through the day.

Il Vecchio Deli
DELI $

(☑ 250-492-7610; 317 Robinson St; sandwiches $6; ⊙ 9am-5pm Mon-Sat) The smell that greets you as you enter confirms your choice. The best lunch sandwiches in town can be consumed at a couple of tables in this atmospheric deli, but will taste better on a picnic. Choices are many; we like the sandwich with garlic salami and marinated eggplant.

Theo's
GREEK $$

(☑ 250-492-4019; www.eatsquid.com; 687 Main St; mains $10-25; ⊙ 11am-10pm) The place for dating locals. Serves up authentic Greek-island cuisine in the atmospheric, fire-lit interior or out on the patio. The *garithes uvetsi* is a starter symphony of shrimp.

Dream Cafe
FUSION $$

(☑ 250-490-9012; www.thedreamcafe.ca; 67 Front St; mains $11-25; ⊙ 11am-9pm Tue-Sun; ⚡) The heady aroma of spices hits as you enter this pillow-bedecked, upscale-yet-funky bistro. Asian and Indian flavors mix on the menu, which has numerous veggie options. There's live acoustic music by touring pros on many nights; tables outside hum all summer long.

Hooded Merganser
PUB FOOD $$

(☑ 250-493-8221; www.hoodedmerganser.ca; Penticton Lakeside Resort, 21 Lakeshore Dr; mains $12-30; ⊙ 7am-midnight) Named for a small breed of duck noted for its vibrant plumage, this huge lakeside pub attracts plenty of birds of a similar feather. On a summer afternoon its waterfront terrace literally heaves. Food is designed for sharing, with some steaks and burgers tossed into the mix.

Hillside Bistro
BISTRO $$$

(☑ 250-493-6274; www.hillsidewinery.ca; 1350 Naramata Rd; mains $16-35; ⊙ 11:30am-2pm & 5-9pm mid-Jun–Sep) Beautifully set among its namesake vineyards about 5km from Penticton, this casual eatery has great lakeside views from its various open-air decks. The menu includes upscale versions of burgers, pasta and other dishes made from ingredients sourced locally. Enjoy a glass of Mosaic, the house Bordeaux-style blended red.

★ Mile Zero Wine Bar
WINE BAR

(☑ 250-488-7944; www.milezerowinebar.ca; 200 Ellis St; ⊙ 3pm-midnight) Long overdue! This sleek, industrial-edged wine bar is right in the center and is a magnificent place to sample the region's wine bounty. There are always 10 varieties on tap and dozens more available by the glass. Enjoy live jazzy tunes on Friday nights; note that this is where the local vintners like to party.

ⓘ Information

The **visitor center** (☑ 250-276-2170; www.visitpenticton.com; 553 Vees St, off Hwy 97; ⊙ 9am-6pm; 📶) has a full range of info on area activities and wine.

ⓘ Getting There & Away

Greyhound Canada (p196) Has services to Vancouver ($69, six hours, one daily) and Kelowna ($20, one hour, four daily).
Penticton Transit (☑ 250-492-5602; www.bctransit.com; single trips/day pass $2/4) Runs between both waterfronts.

DON'T MISS

SCENIC DRIVE TO NARAMATA

On all but the busiest summer weekends, you can escape many of Penticton's mobs by taking the road less traveled, 18km north from town along the east shore of Okanagan Lake. The route through the **Naramata Bench** (www.naramatabench.com) is lined with more than 30 wineries, as well as farms producing organic lavender and the like. This is a good route for cycling and at several points you can access the Kettle Valley Rail Trail (p212). There are numerous places to hike, picnic, bird-watch or do whatever else occurs to you in beautiful and often secluded surroundings. Naramata itself is a cute little village.

Penticton to Kelowna

Lakeside resort town **Summerland**, 18km north of Penticton on Hwy 97, features some fine 19th-century heritage buildings on the hillside above the ever-widening and busy highway. There are some good wineries here, too.

Hugging the lake below Hwy 97, some 25km south of Kelowna, the little town of **Peachland** is good for a quick, breezy stroll along the water amid parks and interesting shops.

Between Peachland and Kelowna, urban sprawl becomes unavoidable, especially through the billboard-lined nightmare of **West Kelowna** (aka Westbank).

◎ Sights & Activities

Zipzone Peachland
ADVENTURE SPORTS

(☑ 855-947-9663; www.zipzone.ca; Princeton Ave, Peachland; adult/child from $110/80; ⊙ 9am-5pm May-Oct) Zoom along Canada's highest zip lines at Zipzone Peachland, where you can sail high over Deep Creek Canyon.

Kettle Valley Steam Railway
RAIL

(☑ 877-494-8424; www.kettlevalleyrail.org; 18404 Bathville Rd, Summerland; adult/child $25/16; ⊙ May-Oct) The Kettle Valley Steam Railway is an operating, 16km remnant of the famous tracks. Ride behind an old steam locomotive in open-air cars and enjoy orchard views.

🛏 Sleeping & Eating

A View of the Lake
B&B $$

(📞 250-769-7854; www.aviewofthelake.com; 1877 Horizon Dr, West Kelowna; r $120-185; 🅿 ❄ 🛜) Set on the west side of Okanagan Lake, this B&B offers privacy and magnificent views. Book the Grandview Suite for a lake vista that extends even to the air-jet bathtub. Rooms are peaceful; beds are comfy; and the three-course breakfast on the deck is gourmet.

★ Peach Pit
MARKET $

(📞 778-516-7003; cnr Hwy 97 & Jones Flat Rd, Summerland; treats from $3; ⊙ 9am-6pm May-Oct) Amid oodles of competition, this roadside stand on Hwy 97 on the north side of Summerland stands out. The owners have an orchard right behind the market. They also have deals with some of the valley's very best producers (the $3 tub of raspberries will have you checking local real-estate prices) and they create wonderful baked goods.

★ Terrace
MODERN AMERICAN $$$

(📞 250-768-6467; www.missionhillwinery.com; 1730 Mission Hill Rd, Mission Hill Family Estate, West Kelowna; mains $25-35; ⊙ 11am-9pm Jun-Oct) A suitably impressive restaurant to go with a very impressive winery. Terrace (yes, there are views) exemplifies farm-to-table with its fresh and inventive menu.

Kelowna

POP 123,500

A kayaker paddles past scores of new tract houses on a hillside: it's an iconic image for ever-growing Kelowna, the unofficial 'capital' of the Okanagan and the sprawling center of all that's good and not-so-good with the region.

Entering from the north, the ever-lengthening urban sprawl of tree-lined Hwy 97/ Harvey Ave seems to go on forever. Once past the ceaseless waves of chains and strip malls, the downtown is a welcome respite. Museums, culture, nightlife and the park-lined lakefront feature. You can spend a day strolling here. About 2km south of the center is **Pandosy Village**, a charming and upscale lakeside enclave.

◉ Sights

The focal point of the city's shoreline, the immaculate downtown **Kelowna City Park** (Map p210) is home to manicured gardens, water features and **Hot Sands Beach** (Map p210), where the water is a respite from the hot summer air.

Restaurants and pubs take advantage of the uninterrupted views of the lake and forested shore opposite. North of the marina, **Waterfront Park** (Map p210; Lakefront) has a variegated shoreline and a popular open-air stage.

Among the many outdoor statues near the lake, look for the one of the **Ogopogo** (Map p210; Kelowna City Park), the lake's mythical – and hokey – monster. More prosaic is **Bear** (Map p210; Water St), a huge, lacy confection in metal. The visitor center has a lavish public art guide.

Be sure to pick up the **Cultural District** walking-tour brochures at the visitor center (p212) and visit www.kelownamuseums.ca for exhibitions info.

BC Orchard Industry Museum
MUSEUM

(Map p210; 📞 250-763-0433; www.kelowna museums.ca; 1304 Ellis St; by donation; ⊙ 10am-5pm Mon-Sat, 11am-4pm Sun) Located in the historic Laurel Packing House, the BC Orchard Industry Museum recounts the Okanagan Valley from its ranchland past, grazed by cows, to its present, grazed by tourists. The old fruit-packing-crate labels are works of art.

Carmelis Goat Cheese Artisan
FARM

(📞 250-764-9033; www.carmelisgoatcheese.com; 170 Timberline Rd; tours $5; ⊙ 10am-6pm May-Sep, 11am-5pm Mar, Apr & Oct, closed Nov-Feb; 🅿 👶) Call ahead to book a tour of the dairy, milking station and cellar. Even without the tour, you can sample soft-ripened cheeses with names such as Moonlight and Heavenly, or the hard-ripened Smoked Carmel or Goatgonzola. For those with a milder palate, there are super-soft unripened versions, such as feta and yogurt cheese. And then there's the goat's-milk gelato!

BC Wine Museum
MUSEUM

(Map p210; 📞 250-763-2417; www.kelowna museums.ca; 1304 Ellis St; by donation; ⊙ 10am-5pm Mon-Sat, 11am-4pm Sun) Housed in the historic Laurel Packinghouse and newly expanded in 2016, the museum offers a look at celebrated bottles, labels and equipment, along with an overview of winemaking in the region.

Okanagan Lavender Farm
FARM

(📞 250-764-7795; www.okanaganlavender.com; 4380 Takla Rd; tours $5-15; ⊙ 10am-6pm, tours 10:30am Jun-Aug; 🅿 👶) Visiting Okanagan Lavender Farm is a heady experience. Rows and rows of more than 60 types of lavender waft in the breeze against a backdrop of the Okanagan Lake. Enjoy a guided or self-guided tour of the aromatic acres, and pop into the shop for everything from bath products to lavender lemonade. Your wine-soaked palate will be well and truly cleansed. The farm is 9km south of the center.

Okanagan Heritage Museum MUSEUM
(Map p210; ☑250-763-2417; www.kelowna museums.ca; 470 Queensway Ave; by donation; ⊙10am-5pm Mon-Sat) The Okanagan Heritage Museum looks at centuries of local culture in an engaging manner that includes a First Nations pit house, a Chinese grocery and a Pandosy-era trading post.

Kelowna Art Gallery GALLERY
(Map p210; ☑250-979-0888; www.kelownaart gallery.com; 1315 Water St; $5; ⊙10am-5pm Tue, Wed, Fri & Sat, to 9pm Thu, 1-4pm Sun) The airy Kelowna Art Gallery features works by Canadian artists.

🏃 Activities

The balmy weather makes Kelowna ideal for fresh-air fun, whether on the lake or in the surrounding hills.

You'll find great **hiking** and **mountain biking** opportunities all around town. The 17km **Mission Creek Greenway** is a meandering, wooded path following the creek along the south edge of town. The western half is a wide and easy expanse, but to the east the route becomes sinuous as it climbs into the hills.

Knox Mountain, which sits at the northern end of the city, is another good place to hike or ride. Populated with bobcats and snakes, the 235-hectare park has well-maintained trails and rewards visitors with excellent views from the top.

Cycling on the Kettle Valley Rail Trail (p212) and amid the vineyards is popular.

★**Monashee Adventure Tours** CYCLING
(☑250-762-9253; www.monasheeadventuretours. com; bicycle rental per day from $30) Offers scores of biking and hiking tours of the Okanagan Valley, its parks, Kettle Valley Rail Trail (from $120) and wineries. Many tours are accompanied by entertaining local guides. Prices usually include bike hire, lunch and a shuttle to the route. Shuttles can also be used by independent riders looking for one-way transport. Offers snowshoe tours in winter.

Myra Canyon Bike Rentals CYCLING
(☑250-878-8763; www.myracanyonrental.com; Myra Canyon; bicycle rental per half-day from adult/child $40/30, bike tours from $70; ⊙9am-5:30pm mid-May–mid-Oct) Offers bike rentals and tours at the Kettle Valley Rail Trail (p212) head.

Okanagan Rent A Boat BOATING
(Map p210; ☑250-862-2469; www.lakefrontsports. com; 1310 Water St, Delta Grand Okanagan Resort; kayak rental per 2hr $40; ⊙May-Sep) Rent speedboats (starting at $145 per hour), canoes, kayaks, wakeboards, pedal boats and much more from this seasonal booth on the lakefront.

🛌 Sleeping

Kelowna Samesun International Hostel HOSTEL $
(Map p210; ☑250-763-9814; www.samesun.com; 245 Harvey Ave; dm/r from $33/100; P☀@🛜) Near the center and the lake, this purpose-built hostel has 88 dorm beds in four- and eight-bed dorms, plus private rooms. There is a hot tub; activities include various group outings.

Kelowna International Hostel HOSTEL $
(☑250-763-6024; www.kelowna-hostel.bc.ca; 2343 Pandosy St; dm/r from $25/60; @🛜) About 1km south of City Park, this small hostel is in a '50s home on a tree-lined residential street. Neighbors no doubt enjoy the regular keg parties, free bongo drums and other social events that keep the cheery place hopping. Ask for Greyhound pickup.

Willow Creek Family Campground CAMPGROUND $
(☑250-762-6302; www.willowcreekcampground.ca; 3316 Lakeshore Rd; campsites/RV sites from $30/42; P🛜) South of the center, close to Pandosy Village and a beach, this 82-site facility has a laundry. Tent sites are on a grassy verge.

Hotel Zed MOTEL $$
(Map p210; ☑250-763-7771; www.hotelzed.com; 1627 Abbott St; r $90-180; P☀🛜💦) An old Travelodge has been reborn as this throwback to a 1960s that never existed. The 52 rooms come in many shapes and sizes; all are in cheery colors. Extras such as free bike rentals, ping-pong, hot tub, comic books in the bathrooms and much more are way cool. It's located downtown and across from City Park.

Accent Inns Kelowna MOTEL $$
(☑250-862-8888; www.accentinns.com; 1140 Harvey Ave; r $90-180; P☀🛜) Best of the chain motels near the center, this three-storey property

Kelowna

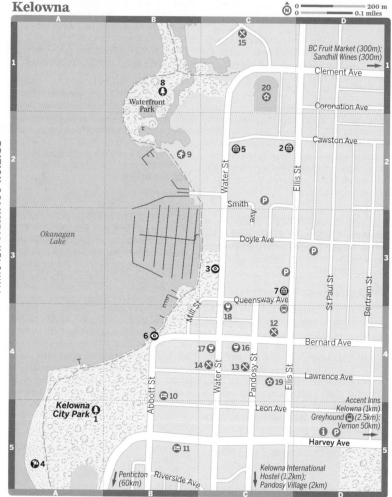

is a 10-minute walk from the lake. The 102 rooms are roomy and have many thoughtful extras, such as office supplies in the desks, plus fridges and microwaves. Flowers adorn the walkways, and the staff are charmers.

Lakeshore Bed & Breakfast B&B **$$**
(☏250-764-4375; www.lakeshorebb.ca; 4186 Lakeshore Rd; r $115-175; P❋⊛) This bright, two-room B&B has a prime lakefront location, 6km south of the center, complete with its own tiny strip of sand. The larger of the two rooms is a real deal, with broad water views

and a private outdoor sitting area. Furnishings are modern and upscale.

★**Hotel Eldorado** HOTEL **$$$**
(☏250-763-7500; www.hoteleldoradokelowna. com; 500 Cook Rd; r $180-400; P❋⊛⊠) This historic lakeshore retreat, south of Pandosy Village, has 19 heritage rooms where you can bask in antique-filled luxury. A modern, low-key wing has 30 more rooms and six opulent waterfront suites. It's classy, artful and funky all at once. Definitely the choice spot for a luxurious getaway.

Kelowna

Eating

Little Hobo
CAFE $

(Map p210; ☑778-478-0411; www.thelittlehobo. com; 438 Lawrence Ave; mains $7-12; ☺10am-2pm Mon-Fri) This unadorned sandwich shop is hugely popular and for good reason: the food is excellent. Custom sandwiches are good, but the daily specials really shine (meatloaf, pasta, pierogi etc) and the variety of soups is simply superb.

Kelowna Farmers Market
MARKET $

(☑250-878-5029; cnr Springfield Rd & Dilworth Dr; ☺8am-1pm Wed & Sat Apr-Oct) The farmers market has more than 150 vendors, including many with prepared foods. Local artisans also display their wares. It's located off Hwy 97.

BC Tree Fruits Market
MARKET $

(☑250-763-8872; www.bctree.com; 826 Vaughan Ave; fruit from $1; ☺9am-5pm Mon-Sat) Run by the local fruit-packing cooperative, BC Tree Fruits Market has dozens upon dozens of the Okanagan's best fruits on display and available for tasting. Prices are half of that in supermarkets. An adjoining tasting room sells locally produced ciders.

Pulp Fiction Coffee House
CAFE $

(Map p210; ☑778-484-7444; www.pulpfiction coffeehouse.com; 1598 Pandosy St; coffee $2; ☺7am-10pm) Baked goods, paninis and soups go with your excellent coffee or tea at this sharp, category-busting cafe right downtown. It includes an antiques and rare-book store.

★ RauDZ Regional Table
FUSION $$

(Map p210; ☑250-868-8805; www.raudz.com; 1560 Water St; mains $12-30; ☺5-10pm) Noted chef Rod Butters has defined the farm-to-table movement with his casual bistro that's a temple to Okanagan produce and wine. The dining room is as airy and open as the kitchen. The seasonal menu takes global inspiration for its Mediterranean-infused dishes, which are good for sharing, and serves steaks and seafood. Suppliers include locally renowned Carmelis goat's cheese.

Sunset Organic Bistro
BISTRO $$

(☑250-764-8000; www.summerhill.bc.ca; 4870 Chute Lake Rd, Summerhill Pyramid Winery, Kelowna; mains $15-30; ☺11am-9pm) ✔ Acclaimed chef Alex Lavroff has created excellent locally sourced and organic menus for lunch and dinner. In between, there is an exquisite selection of small dishes, which go well with an afternoon of organic wine tasting.

Waterfront Restaurant & Wine Bar
BISTRO $$$

(Map p210; ☑250-979-1222; http://waterfront restaurant.ca; 1180 Sunset Dr; mains $25-38; ☺5-10pm) Chef and sommelier Mark Filatow has created his vision for a farm-to-table restaurant in Kelowna that celebrates the bounty of the region, both on the plate and in a glass. The tapas menu is long and encourages sharing. Many local wines are available by the glass. The atmosphere is sleek and contemporary.

🍸 Drinking & Nightlife

The local microbrewer, Tree Brewing, has an excellent range of beers that are sold around town. Downtown Kelowna's clubs are mostly at the west end of Leon and Lawrence Aves.

Micro PUB

(Map p210; 📞 778-484-3500; www.microkelowna.com; 1500 Water St; ⊙11:30am-3pm Thu-Sun, 3pm-late daily) This great small bar from the team behind local bistro RauDZ is hard to leave. Craft beers, local wines and fine cocktails are served. Small bites are fresh and inventive, good for sharing – or for lunch. Gather at the wood-block bar or at a sidewalk table.

Sturgeon Hall PUB

(Map p210; 📞 250-860-3055; 1481 Water St; ⊙11am-late Mon-Sat) Fanatical fans of the Kelowna Rockets hockey team feast on excellent burgers and thin-crust pizza (mains from $10 to $20) while quaffing brews at the bar or outside at sidewalk tables. In season, this Kelowna institution shows hockey on every TV.

Doc Willoughby's PUB

(Map p210; 📞 250-868-8288; 353 Bernard Ave; ⊙11:30am-2am) Right downtown, this pub boasts a vaulted interior lined with wood, as well as tables on the street. Perfect for a drink or a meal; the fish and chips are good (mains cost $10 to $20). The beer selection is excellent, including brews from Tree Brewing and Penticton's Cannery Brewing.

☆ Entertainment

Blue Gator LIVE MUSIC

(Map p210; 📞 250-860-1529; www.bluegator.net; 441 Lawrence Ave; ⊙3pm-late Tue-Sun) Head for blues, rock, acoustic jam and more at the valley's sweaty dive for live music and cold beer.

Kelowna Rockets HOCKEY

(Map p210; 📞 250-860-7825; www.kelownarockets.com; tickets from $25; ⊙Sep-Mar) The much-beloved local WHL hockey team is a perennial contender, playing in the 6000-seat stadium **Prospera Place** (Map p210; 📞 250-979-0888; www.prosperaplace.com; cnr Water St & Cawston Ave). Home games see the local pubs fill before and after the match.

ⓘ Information

Kelowna Visitor Center (Map p210; 📞 250-861-1515; www.tourismkelowna.com; 544 Harvey Ave; ⊙9am-6pm) Near the corner of Ellis St and Hwy 97; a good source for free maps and tour info.

DON'T MISS

KETTLE VALLEY RAIL TRAIL

The famous **Kettle Valley Rail Trail** vies with wine-drinking and peach-picking as the attraction of choice for the region's visitors – smart ones do all three.

Once stretching 525km in curving, meandering length, the railway was built so that silver ore could be transported from the southern Kootenays to Vancouver. Finished in 1916, it remains one of the most expensive railways ever built, on a per-kilometer basis. It was entirely shut by 1989, but it wasn't long before its easy grades (never more than 2.2%) and dozens of bridges were incorporated into the **Trans Canada Trail (TCT)**.

Of the entire Kettle Valley Rail Trail, the most spectacular stretch is close to Kelowna. The 24km section through the **Myra Canyon** has fantastic views of the sinuous canyon from **18 trestles** that span the gorge for the cliff-hugging path. That you can enjoy the route at all is something of a miracle, as 12 of the wooden trestles were destroyed by fire in 2003. All have been rebuilt; much credit goes to the **Myra Canyon Trestle Restoration Society** (www.myra-trestles.com), the website of which has downloadable maps and info. The broad views sweep down to Kelowna and the lake, more than 900m below. You can see alpine meadows reclaiming the fire-cleared landscape.

To reach the area closest to the most spectacular trestles from Kelowna, follow Harvey Ave (Hwy 97) east to Gordon Dr. Turn south and then go east 2.6km on KLO Rd and then join McCulloch Rd for 7.4km after the junction. Look for the Myra Forest Service Rd; turn south and make a winding 8.7km climb on a car-friendly gravel road to the parking lot. It's about a 40-minute drive from Kelowna's center.

Myra Canyon is just part of an overall 174km network of trails in the Okanagan that follow the old railway through tunnels, past Naramata and as far south as Penticton and beyond. You can easily access the trail at many points, or book hiking and cycling tours. **Myra Canyon Bike Rentals** (p209) offers bike rentals and tours at the main trail head.

❶ Getting There & Away

From **Kelowna International Airport** (www.kelownaairport.com; 5533 Airport Way, off Hwy 97), Westjet serves major cities in Canada. Air Canada Jazz serves Vancouver and Calgary. Alaska Air serves Seattle. The airport is 20km north of the center on Hwy 97.

Greyhound Canada (☑ 250-860-2364; www.greyhound.ca; 2366 Leckie Rd) is inconveniently located east of the downtown area, off Hwy 97. City buses 9 and 10 make the run from downtown (every 30 minutes between 6:30am and 9:45pm). Routes include: Golden ($67, 5½ hours, one daily), Kamloops ($37, three hours, two daily), Penticton ($20, one hour, four daily) and Vancouver ($69, six hours, four daily).

❶ Getting Around

Kelowna Regional Transit System (☑ 250-860-8121; www.transitbc.com; single fare/day pass $2.50/6.50) runs local bus services. All downtown buses pass through **Queensway Station** (Map p210; Queensway Ave, btwn Pandosy & Ellis Sts). Bus 97 serves West Kelowna.

All major car-rental companies are found at **Kelowna International Airport**. Taxi companies include **Kelowna Cabs** (☑ 250-762-4444, 250-762-2222; www.kelownacabs.ca).

Vernon

POP 38,900

The Okanagan glitz starts to fade before you reach Vernon. Maybe it's the weather. Winters have more of the traditional inland BC bite here and wineries are few, but that doesn't mean the area is without its charms. The orchard-scented valley is surrounded by three lakes – Kalamalka, Okanagan and Swan – that attract fun-seekers all summer long.

Downtown life is found along 30th Ave, known as Main St. Confusingly, 30th Ave is intersected by 30th St in the middle of downtown, so mind your streets and avenues. The north side of town is a mess of strip malls.

◉ Sights & Activities

Davison Orchards   FARM
(☑ 250-549-3266; www.davisonorchards.ca; 3111 Davison Rd; ⊙ 8am-8pm Apr-Oct; P ⊕) FREE Has tractor rides, homemade ice cream, fresh apple juice, winsome barnyard animals and more. Follow 25th Ave west, turn north briefly on 41st St, then go west on Bella Vista Rd and watch for signs.

BIG WHITE SKI RESORT

Perfect powder is the big deal at **Big White Ski Resort** (☑ 250-765-8888, snow report 250-765-7669; www.bigwhite.com; off Hwy 33; 1-day lift pass adult/child $91/51), located 56km east of Kelowna off Hwy 33. With a vertical drop of 777m, it features 15 lifts and 118 runs that offer excellent downhill and backcountry skiing, while deep gullies make for killer snowboarding. Because of Big White's isolation, most people stay up here on-site. The resort includes numerous restaurants, bars, hotels, condos, rental homes and a hostel. The website has lodging info and details of the ski-season shuttle to Kelowna.

Planet Bee   FARM
(☑ 250-542-8088; www.planetbee.com; 5011 Bella Vista Rd; ⊙ 8am-6pm; P) FREE Planet Bee is a working honey farm where you can learn all the sweet secrets of the golden nectar and see a working hive up close. Follow 25th Ave west, turn north briefly on 41st St, then go west on Bella Vista Rd and watch for signs. It's near Davison Orchards.

Kalamalka Lake Provincial Park   PARK
(☑ 250-545-1560; www.bcparks.ca; off Hwy 6; P) The beautiful 9-sq-km Kalamalka Lake Provincial Park lies south of town on the eastern side of the warm, shallow lake. The park offers great swimming at Jade and Kalamalka Beaches, good fishing and a network of mountain-biking and hiking trails. Innerspace Watersports operates a seasonal booth in the park.

Innerspace Watersports   WATER SPORTS
(☑ 250-549-2040; www.innerspacewatersports.com; 3006 32nd St; canoe rental per hour $25; ⊙ 10am-5:30pm Mon-Sat) Offers canoe and stand-up paddleboard rentals at Kalamalka Lake Provincial Park; has a full-service store located in town, which has scuba gear. Park location open mid-June to August.

⊨ Sleeping & Eating

Ellison Provincial Park   CAMPGROUND $
(☑ info 250-494-6500, reservations 800-689-9025; www.discovercamping.ca; Okanagan Landing Rd; campsites $32; ⊙ Apr-Oct; P) Some 16km southwest of Vernon, this is a great tree-shaded, 219-acre place near the lake. The 71 campsites fill up early, so reserve in advance.

BRITISH COLUMBIA VERNON

Tiki Village Motel   MOTEL $$

(☑250-503-5566; www.tikivillagevernon.com; 2408 34th St; r $70-150; P❄☎🛜🏊) An ode to the glory days of decorative concrete blocks, the Tiki has suitably expansive plantings and 30 rooms with a vaguely Asian minimalist theme. All rooms have fridges; some have kitchenettes.

Beaver Lake Mountain Resort   LODGE $$

(☑250-762-2225; www.beaverlakeresort.com; 6350 Beaver Lake Rd; campsites from $29, cabins $85-180; P@) Set high in the hills east of Hwy 97, about midway between Vernon and Kelowna, this postcard-perfect lakeside resort has a range of rustic log cabins and some more-luxurious cabins that sleep up to six people.

Little Italy   ITALIAN $

(☑778-475-5898; http://littleitalymarketdeli.food pages.ca; 3105 35th Ave; mains $10-20; ⊙9am-5pm Mon-Sat; 🛜) Order a cup of authentic Italian coffee and enjoy it on the porch at this cute little market and deli just east of Hwy 97.

Vernon Farmers Market   MARKET

(☑250-351-5188; www.vernonfarmersmarket.ca; 3445 43rd Ave, Kal Tire Place; ⊙8am-1pm Mon & Thu) The market draws more than 150 vendors. It's just west of Hwy 97.

★Bamboo Beach Fusion Grille   FUSION $$

(☑250-542-7701; www.facebook.com/Bamboo BeachFusionGrille; 3313 30th Ave; mains $12-25; ⊙noon-9pm; 🍴) Flavors from across Asia season popular local foods at this sprightly restaurant. Look for Japanese, Korean and Thai influences in the halibut curry, the fish and chips, and much more. The curry soba noodles show the talent of the Japanese-trained chef.

❶ Information

The **visitor center** (☑250-542-1415; www.tourismvernon.com; 3004 39th Ave; ⊙9am-6pm; 🛜) is near the town center.

BC MASCOTS

Some BC towns have their own quirky mascots, which sometimes appear at community events. On your travels, look out for **Knuckles** the grey whale in Ucluelet; **Peter Pine** the tree in Princeton; **Mr PG** in Prince George; and, our favorite, **Potato Jack** in Pemberton – a jaunty tuber dressed as a cowboy, complete with spurs and a neckerchief.

❶ Getting There & Away

Greyhound Canada (☑800-661-8747; www.greyhound.ca; 3102 30th St, cnr 31st Ave) Services from Vernon include Kelowna ($17, 45 minutes, four daily) and Revelstoke ($31, 2½ hours, one daily).

Vernon Regional Transit System (☑250-545-7221; www.transitbc.com; fares from $2) Buses leave downtown from the bus stop at the corner of 31st St and 30th Ave. For Kalamalka Lake, catch bus 1; for Okanagan Lake, bus 7.

North of Vernon

Just north of Vernon, beautiful Hwy 97 heads northwest to Kamloops via tree-clad valleys punctuated by lakes. **Armstrong**, 23km north of Vernon, is a cute little village. Attractions are few in this area, which is more notable for its major highway connections.

Home to the O'Keefe family between 1867 and 1977, the **O'Keefe Ranch** (www.okeeferanch.ca; 9380 Hwy 97N; adult/child $14/9; ⊙10am-5pm May, Jun & Sep, to 6pm Jul & Aug) retains its original log cabin, and has lots of live displays of old ranching techniques. Before orchards – and later grapes – covered the valley, ranching as portrayed here was the typical way of life. The ranch is 12km north of Vernon, 4km after Hwy 97 splits from Hwy 97A, which continues northeast to Sicamous and Hwy 1.

Silver Star

Classic inland BC dry powder makes **Silver Star** (☑250-542-0224, snow report 250-542-1745; www.skisilverstar.com; 123 Shortt St, Silver Star Mountain; 1-day lift ticket adult/child $92/48) a very popular ski resort.

The ski resort has all types of accommodations, from hostels to condos. **Samesun Lodge** (☑250-545-8933; www.samesun.com; 9898 Pinnacles Rd, Silver Star; dm/r from $32/80; P@🛜) runs a very popular and almost posh backpacker hostel.

To reach Silver Star, take 48th Ave off Hwy 97. The resort is 22km northeast of Vernon. Check with your accommodations for various seasonal van and bus services to the resort.

Shuswap Region

Rorschach-test-like **Shuswap Lake** anchors a somewhat bland but pleasing region of green, wooded hills, some farms and two small towns, **Sicamous** and **Salmon Arm**. The former has a lakefront park that's good for picnics, just northwest of Hwy 1.

The entire area is home to several lake-based provincial parks and is a popular destination for families looking for outdoor fun. Many explore the lakes via houseboats.

The main attraction here is the annual spawning of sockeye salmon at **Roderick Haig-Brown Provincial Park** (☑250-851-3000; www.bcparks.ca; off Hwy 1, Saquilax). The 10.59-sq-km park protects both sides of the Adams River between Shuswap Lake and **Adams Lake**, a natural bottleneck for the bright-red sockeye when they run upriver every October. The fish population peaks every four years, when as many as four million salmon crowd the Adams' shallow riverbed. The next big spawn is due in 2018.

Meet the cows, then lick the ice cream at **D Dutchmen Dairy** (☑250-836-4304; www.dutchmendairy.ca; 1321 Maeir Rd; treats from $3; ☺8am-9pm Jun-Sep), an off-beat dairy close to Hwy 1. There are dozens of flavors of traditional frozen treats.

THE KOOTENAYS & THE ROCKIES

You can't help sighing as you ponder the plethora of snow-covered peaks in the Kootenay Region of BC. Deep river valleys cleaved by white-water rivers, impossibly sheer rock faces, alpine meadows and a sawtooth of white-dappled mountains stretching across the horizon inspire awe, action and even mere contemplation.

Coming from the west, the mountain majesty builds as if choreographed. The roughly parallel ranges of the Monashees and the Selkirks striate the West Kootenays, with the Arrow Lakes adding texture. Appealing towns such as Revelstoke and Nelson nestle against the mountains and are centers of year-round outdoor fun. The East Kootenays cover the Purcell Mountains region below Golden, taking in Radium Hot Springs and Fernie.

BC's Rocky Mountains national parks (Mt Revelstoke, Glacier, Yoho and Kootenay) don't have the profile of Banff and Jasper National Parks over the border, but for many that's an advantage: each has its own spectacular qualities, often relatively unexploited by the Banff-bound hordes.

Revelstoke

POP 7700

Gateway to serious mountains, Revelstoke doesn't need to toot its own horn – the ceaseless procession of trains through the center does that. Built as an important point on the Canadian Pacific transcontinental railroad that first linked Eastern and Western Canada, Revelstoke echoes not just with whistles but with history. The compact center is lined with heritage buildings, yet it's more than a museum piece. There's a vibrant local arts community, and most locals take full advantage of the boundless opportunities for hiking, kayaking and, most of all, skiing.

It's more than worth a long pause as you pass on Hwy 1, which bypasses the town center to the northeast. The main streets include 1st St and Mackenzie Ave.

⦿ Sights

Grizzly Plaza, between Mackenzie and Orton Aves, is a pedestrian precinct and the heart of downtown, where free live-music performances take place every evening in July and August.

While outdoor activities are Revelstoke's real drawcard, a stroll of the center and a moment spent at the museums is a must. Pick up the *Public Art* and *Heritage* walking-tour brochures at the tourist office.

★**Mt Revelstoke National Park**   PARK
(www.pc.gc.ca/revelstoke; off Hwy 1; adult/child incl Glacier National Park $8/4) Grand in beauty if not in size, this 260-sq-km national park, just northeast of its namesake town, is a vision of peaks and valleys – many of which are all but untrodden.

There are several good **hiking trails** from the summit. To overnight in the wild, you must have a Wilderness Pass camping permit ($10, in addition to your park pass), which is available from the **Parks Canada Revelstoke Office** (☑250-837-7500; revglacier.reception@pc.gc.ca; 301 3rd St, Revelstoke; ☺8am-4:30pm Mon-Fri) or from the Rogers Pass Centre (p219) inside Glacier National Park (p219). Both centers also have excellent hiking info on trails long and short; don't miss the 30-minute **Skunk Cabbage Trail**.

Revelstoke Railway Museum   MUSEUM
(☑250-837-6060; www.railwaymuseum.com; 719 Track St W; adult/child $10/2; ☺9am-5pm May-Sep,

The Kootenays & The Rockies

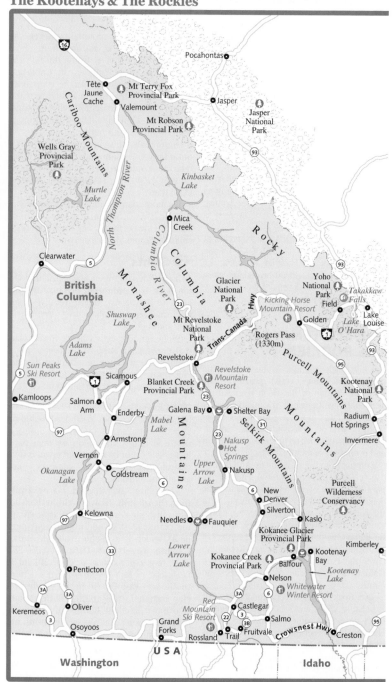

0 ——————————— 100 km
0 ——————————— 50 miles

Alberta

Red ○
Deer

Banff
○ National
Park

○ Banff
Canmore ○
○ Mt Assiniboine
○ Provincial Park

Calgary ○

Mountains

○ Fairmont
Hot Springs

○ Elkford

○ Skookumchuck

○ Wasa
Fort   ○ Sparwood
Steele   Mt Fernie
○ Provincial
○ Cranbrook Park
○ Fernie

Lethbridge,
Alberta (100km)

○ Elko

○ Roosville

Montana

shorter hours Oct-Apr; [P]) In an attractive building across the tracks from the town center, Revelstoke Railway Museum contains restored steam locomotives, including one of the largest steam engines ever used on Canadian Pacific Railway (CPR) lines. Photographs and artifacts document the construction of the CPR, which was instrumental – actually, essential – in linking Eastern and Western Canada.

Revelstoke Museum   MUSEUM
([☎] 250-837-3067; www.revelstokemuseum.ca; 315 1st St W; adult/child $5/free; ⊙ 10am-6pm Mon-Sat year-round, 11am-5pm Sun Jul & Aug) Furniture and historical odds and ends – including mining, logging and railway artifacts that date back to the town's establishment in the 1880s – line the rooms. The local skiing history displays are worthwhile.

🏃 Activities

Sandwiched between the vast but relatively unknown Selkirk and Monashee mountain ranges, Revelstoke draws serious snow buffs looking for vast landscapes of crowd-free powder. It's where North America's first ski jump was built, in 1915.

For **cross-country skiing**, head to the 22km of groomed trails at Mt MacPherson Ski Area, 7km south of town on Hwy 23; see www.revelstokenordic.org for information.

All that white snow turns into white water come spring and **rafting** is big here. **Mountain biking** is also huge; pick up trail maps from the visitor center.

Revelstoke Mountain Resort   SKIING
([☎] 888-837-2188; www.revelstokemountainresort. com; Camozzi Rd; 1-day lift ticket adult/child $86/26) Just 6km southeast of town, the Revelstoke Mountain Resort has ambitions to become the biggest ski resort this side of the Alps. It has seemingly endless virgin slopes and 65 runs. In one run you can ski both 700m of bowl and 700m of trees. At 1713m, the vertical drop is the greatest in North America.

Apex Rafting Co   RAFTING
([☎] 250-837-6376; www.apexrafting.com; 112 1st St E; adult/child $95/80; ⊙ Jun-Aug; 👶) Runs kid-friendly two-hour guided trips on the Illecillewaet River in spring and summer.

Wandering Wheels   CYCLING
([☎] 250-814-7609; www.wanderingwheels.ca; lessons per hour from $35, tours from $60; ⊙ Jun-Oct) Offers bike shuttle services, lessons and tours.

BRITISH COLUMBIA REVELSTOKE

ⓘ AVALANCHE WARNING

The Kootenays are the heart of avalanche country. Such events kill more people in BC each year than any other natural phenomenon. The toll is stubbornly high every year.

Avalanches can occur at any time, even on terrain that seems relatively flat. Roughly half the people caught in one don't survive. It's vital that people venturing out onto the snow make inquiries about conditions first; if an area is closed, don't go there. Whether you're backcountry ski touring or simply hiking in the alpine region, you'll want to rent a homing beacon; most outdoor shops can supply one.

In Revelstoke, **Avalanche Canada** (☑ 250-837-2141; www.avalanche.ca) tracks avalanche reports and offers forecasts for BC and the Canadian Rockies. It has a vital website and a phone app.

Revelstoke Dogsled Adventures   ADVENTURE SPORTS
(☑ 250-814-3720; www.revelstokedogsledadventures.ca; from $200; ☉ winter) Thrill at winter wonders while a team of huskies pulls you through the Kootenay wilderness.

Skookum Cycle & Ski   CYCLING
(☑ 250-814-0090; www.skookumrevelstoke.com; 118 Mackenzie Ave; mountain bike rental per day from $40; ☉ 10am-5pm) Pick up trail maps and rent bikes in summer, skis in winter.

Natural Escapes Kayaking   KAYAKING
(☑ 250-837-7883; www.naturalescapes.ca; rental per 4hr from $60, tours from $70; ☉ Jun-Sep) Has tours, lessons and rents kayaks and canoes.

Free Spirit Sports   SNOW SPORTS, WATER SPORTS
(FSS; ☑ 250-837-9453; www.freespiritsports.com; 203 1st St W; SUP rental per day $50; ☉ 10am-5pm Mon-Sat) Rents a wide variety of summer and winter gear, including essential avalanche equipment for skiers.

Mica Heliskiing   SKIING
(☑ 877-837-6191; www.micaheli.com; 207 Mackenzie Ave; per day from $1500; ☉ Dec-Apr) Mica Heliskiing offers trips to remote bowls accessible by helicopter.

🛏 Sleeping

Samesun Backpacker Lodge   HOSTEL $
(☑ 250-837-4050; www.samesun.ca; 400 2nd St W; dm/r from $30/80; 🅿 @ 🛜) Ramble though the numerous rooms in this perennial backpacker favorite. The 80 beds (in four-bed dorms) are often full, so book ahead. It has bike and ski storage, plus summer barbecues and free passes to the town's aquatic center.

Blanket Creek Provincial Park   CAMPGROUND $
(☑ 800-689-9025; www.discovercamping.ca; Hwy 23; campsites $28; 🅿) This park, 25km south of Revelstoke, includes more than 60 campsites, with flush toilets and running water. It has a playground, and there's a waterfall nearby.

Courthouse Inn   B&B $$
(☑ 250-837-3369; www.courthouseinnrevelstoke.com; 312 Kootenay St; r $130-200; 🅿 ❄ 🛜) A posh 10-room B&B close to the center. Extras include a lavish breakfast, boot and glove driers for winter and lots of personal service. You can't beat the quiet location; rooms have no TVs or phones.

Regent Inn   HOTEL $$
(☑ 250-837-2107; www.regenthotel.ca; 112 1st St E; r $100-200; 🅿 ❄ 🛜 🍽) The poshest place in the center is not lavish, but it is comfy. The 42 modern rooms bear no traces of the hotel's 1914 roots and exterior. The restaurant and lounge are justifiably popular. Many guests bob the night away in the outdoor hot tub.

Revelstoke Lodge   MOTEL $$
(☑ 250-837-2181; www.revelstokelodge.com; 601 1st St W; r $90-180; 🅿 ❄ 🛜 🍽) Thanks to its downtown location this 42-room, maroon-hued motel overcomes inherent flaws, such as its all-encompassing parking area and stark cinder-block construction. Redecorated rooms have fridges and microwaves. Take heed of the motel slogan: 'Your mom called and said to stay here.'

🍴 Eating & Drinking

★ **Modern Bakeshop & Café**   CAFE $
(☑ 250-837-6886; 212 Mackenzie Ave; mains from $6; ☉ 7am-5pm Mon-Sat; 🛜) Try a *croque monsieur* (grilled ham-and-cheese sandwich) or an elaborate pastry for a taste of Europe at this cute art-deco cafe. Many items, such as the muffins, are made with organic ingredients.

Taco Club   MEXICAN $
(☑ 250-837-0988; www.thetacoclub.ca; 206 Mackenzie Ave; mains $6-14; ☉ 11am-10pm) Once Revelstoke's favorite food truck, Taco Club has now laid down some roots in a building downtown. Tacos and burritos are excellent, and all the usual suspects for sides are available.

Farmers Market MARKET **$**
(Grizzly Plaza; ⊙8:30am-1pm Sat May-Oct) The farmers market sprawls across Grizzly Plaza.

⭐**Woolsey Creek** FUSION **$$**
(🗷250-837-5500; www.woolseycreekbistro.ca; 604 2nd St W; mains $20-30; ⊙5-10pm; 🗷) The food at this lively and fun place is both artistic and locally sourced. There are global influences across the menu, which features meat, fish and a fine wine list.

Cabin BAR
(🗷250-837-2144; www.cometothecabin.com; 200 1st St E; ⊙5pm-midnight Tue-Sat) Bowling alley, bar, outdoor-gear store and gallery: it's a cool spot serving a few snacks to go with the beers.

❶ Information

The **visitor center** (🗷250-837-5345; www.see revelstoke.com; 301 Victoria Rd; ⊙9am-6pm) is an excellent source for hiking and mountain-biking info and maps.

❶ Getting There & Away

Greyhound Canada (🗷250-837-5874; www. greyhound.ca; 122 Hwy 23 N; ⊙9am-6pm) is located west of town, just off Hwy 1; it has storage lockers. Buses go east to Calgary ($63, six hours, four daily) via Golden and Banff, and west to Kelowna ($49, 3½ hours, one daily). In winter there are various shuttles to Kelowna's international **airport** (p213) and up to the ski resort. Check with the visitor center for details.

Revelstoke to Golden

Keep your eyes on the road or, better yet, let someone else drive as you traverse the Trans-Canada Hwy (Hwy 1) for 148km between Revelstoke and Golden. Stunning mountain peaks follow one after another as you go.

Glacier National Park (www.pc.gc.ca/glacier; adult/child incl Mt Revelstoke National Park $8/4) should be called '430 Glaciers National Park'. The annual snowfall can be as much as 23m, and due to the sheer mountain slopes, this is one of the world's most active avalanche areas. For this reason, skiing, caving and mountaineering are regulated; you must register with park wardens before venturing into the backcountry. Check the weather and get an avalanche report (p218) in season. **Rogers Pass** ranks as one of the most beautiful mountain passes you'll ever traverse. Be sure to pause at the **Hemlock Grove Trail**, 54km east of Revelstoke, where a 400m boardwalk winds through an ancient hemlock rainforest.

Not far from Rogers Pass are Glacier National Park's three **campgrounds** (Rogers Pass, off Hwy 1; campsites $16-22; ⊙late Jun–early Sep): Illecillewaet, Mount Sir Donald and Loop Brook. Sites are available on a first-come, first-served basis.

Rogers Pass Centre (🗷250-814-5233; off Hwy 1; ⊙8am-7pm mid-Jun–early Sep, shorter hours mid-Sep–mid-Jun) displays Canadian Pacific Railway (CPR) dioramas, 72km east of Revelstoke and 76km west of Golden. Shows films about Glacier National Park and organizes guided walks in summer. Has an excellent bookstore run by the Friends of Mt Revelstoke & Glacier.

Golden

POP 3850

Golden is well situated for national-park explorations – there are six nearby. White-water rafting excitement lies even closer, where the Kicking Horse River converges with the Columbia.

Don't just breeze past the strip of franchised yuck on Hwy 1 or you'll miss the tidy town center down by the tumbling river.

❍ Sights & Activities

Golden is the center for **white-water rafting** trips on the turbulent and chilly Kicking Horse River. Along with the powerful grade III and IV rapids, the breathtaking scenery along the sheer walls of the Kicking Horse Valley makes this rafting experience one of North America's best.

Note that access to the lower canyon, where the best rapids are located, is threatened by the Canadian National Railway, which at random times has cut off vital access across its tracks.

⭐**Alpine Rafting** RAFTING
(🗷250-344-6778; www.alpinerafting.com; 101 Golden Donald Upper Rd; raft trips $25-180; ⊙Jun-Sep; 🗷) Offers several good family rafting options, including a white-water run for kids aged four years and over, right up to the more extreme class IV+ 'Kicking Horse Challenge'.

---

❶ **WATCH YOUR GAS**

The closure of services at **Rogers Pass** means that there is no gas (petrol) available along the 148km stretch between Revelstoke and Golden on Hwy 1.

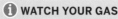

DON'T MISS

TWO PERFECT WALKS

Easily accessible, **Skunk Cabbage Trail**, 28km east of Revelstoke on Hwy 1, is a 1.2km boardwalk along the Illecillewaet River that's lined with its huge namesakes. Another 4km east, the **Giant Cedars Boardwalk** winds a 500m course up and down and all around a grove of huge old-growth cedars.

Northern Lights Wolf Centre   PARK
(☑ 250-344-6798; www.northernlightswildlife.com; 1745 Short Rd; adult/child $12/6; ⊙ 9am-7pm Jul & Aug, 10am-6pm May, Jun & Sep, noon-5pm Oct-Apr; P) This small wildlife center houses a small pack of gray wolves and wolf-husky crosses, all born and bred in captivity. Visits include an introduction to the resident wolves – although most of the viewing is done through wire-frame pens.

Kicking Horse Mountain Resort   SKIING, MOUNTAIN BIKING
(☑ 866-754-5425, 403-254-7669; www.kickinghorseresort.com; Kicking Horse Trail; 1-day lift ticket adult/child winter $90/36, summer $41/21) Some 60% of the 120 ski runs at Kicking Horse Mountain Resort are rated advanced or expert. With a 1260m (4133ft) vertical drop and a snowy position between the Rockies and the Purcells, the resort's popularity grows each year. It's renowned for its summer mountain biking, which includes the longest cycling descent in Canada.

🛏 Sleeping & Eating

There are scores of chain motels along busy, charmless Hwy 1.

★ Dreamcatcher Hostel   HOSTEL $
(☑ 250-439-1090; www.dreamcatcherhostel.com; 528 9th Ave N; dm/r from $35/90; P🛜) Run by two veteran travelers, this centrally located hostel has everything a budget traveler could hope for. There are 33 beds across eight rooms, as well as a vast kitchen and a comfy common room with a stone fireplace. Outside there's a garden and a barbecue.

Golden Eco-Adventure Ranch   CAMPGROUND $
(☑ 250-344-6825; www.goldenadventurepark.com; 872 MacBeath Rd; tent & RV sites $35, yurts $52; ⊙ early Apr–late Sep) Spread over 160 hectares (395 acres) of mountain meadow 5km south of Golden on Hwy 95, this great camp-

ground-cum–outdoors center feels a world away from the cramped confines of municipal camping. Sites are spacious; there are full RV hookups; and you can even sleep in a Mongolian yurt if you're tired of your tent.

Mary's Motel   MOTEL $$
(☑ 250-344-7111; www.marysmotel.com; 603 8th Ave N; r $80-150; P✳🛜🏊) In town, right on the roaring river, Mary's has 81 rooms spread across several buildings; get one with a patio. There's a large outdoor pool, plus an indoor one and two hot tubs. It's an easy walk to nightlife.

Kicking Horse Canyon B&B   GUESTHOUSE $$
(☑ 250-344-6848; www.kickinghorsecanyonbb.com; 644 Lapp Rd; d $125-145; P🛜) Hidden away among the hills to the east of Golden (phone for directions), this endearingly offbeat B&B takes you into the bosom of the family the minute you cross the threshold. Run by genial host Jeannie Cook and her husband, Jerry, it's a real alpine home-away-from-home, surrounded by private grassy grounds with views across the mountains.

Canyon Ridge Lodge   GUESTHOUSE $$
(☑ 250-344-9876; www.canyonridgelodge.com; 1392 Pine Dr; d $109-125; P🛜) Three white rooms and a smart, high-ceilinged studio suite are on offer at this lovely timber-framed home, 1km from Golden's visitor center just off Golden Donald Upper Rd. It's nicely finished (underfloor heating, slate-tiled private bathrooms) and there's a communal hot tub.

Bacchus Cafe   CAFE $
(☑ 250-344-5600; www.bacchusbooks.ca; 409 9th Ave N; mains $6-12; ⊙ 9am-5:30pm Mon-Sat, 10am-4pm Sun) This bohemian hideaway at the end of 8th St is a favorite haunt for Golden's artsy crowd. Browse for books (new and secondhand) in the downstairs bookstore, then head upstairs to find a table for tea among the higgledy-piggledy shelves. Sandwiches, salads and cakes are all made on the premises, and the coffee is as good as you'll find in Golden.

★ Wolf's Den   PUB FOOD $$
(☑ 250-344-9863; www.thewolfsdengolden.ca; 1105 9th St; mains $10-20; ⊙ 4-10pm) An excellent pub with live music on Sundays. It's popular with locals, who love the burgers and hearty fare, which is way above average. The beer menu includes some of BC's best on tap. It's south of the river from downtown.

Eleven22
FUSION **$$**

(☑ 250-344-2443; www.eleven22.ca; 1122 10th Ave S; mains $12-26; ◷5-10pm) A cross between a restaurant and a home dinner party, this appealing option has art on the walls of the dining rooms and all the stars you can count out on the patio. Watch the kitchen action from the lounge area while sharing small plates.

❶ Information

The **visitor center** (☑ 250-344-7125; www. tourismgolden.com; 500 N 10th Ave; ◷9am-5pm daily May-Sep, to 4pm Tue-Fri Oct-Apr) is 1km east on Hwy 1 from the Hwy 95 turnoff into Golden.

❶ Getting There & Away

Delays may offset improvements on Hwy 1 east of Golden as the road is reconstructed from scratch; see www.kickinghorsecanyon.ca.

Greyhound Canada (p196) Serves Vancouver ($128, nine to 13 hours, five daily) and Calgary ($48, 3½ hours, five daily) via Banff.

Sun City Coachlines (☑ 250-417-3117; www.suncity.bc.ca) Runs one daily bus each way on Hwy 95 between Golden and Cranbrook ($70, four hours).

Yoho National Park

The surging waters of glacier-fed, ice-blue Kicking Horse River that plow through a valley of the same name are an apt image for dramatic Yoho National Park. This spectacular park is home to looming peaks, pounding waterfalls, glacial lakes and patches of pretty meadows.

◉ Sights & Activities

★**Burgess Shale Fossil Beds** NATIONAL PARK
This World Heritage site protects the amazing Cambrian-age fossil beds on Mt Stephen and Mt Field. These 515-million-year-old fossils preserve the remains of marine creatures that were some of the earliest forms of life on earth. You can only get to the fossil beds by guided hikes, which are led by naturalists from the **Burgess Shale Geoscience Foundation** (☑ 800-343-3006; www.burgess-shale.bc.ca; 200 Kicking Horse Ave, Field; tours adult/child from $95/65; ◷mid-Jun–mid-Sep). Reservations are essential.

Kicking Horse Pass & Spiral Tunnels
VIEWPOINT
The historic Kicking Horse Pass between Banff and Yoho National Parks is one of the most important passes in the Canadian Rockies. It was discovered in 1858 by the Palliser Expedition, which was tasked with discovering a possible route across the Rockies for the Canadian Pacific Railway. Accessible 8km east of Field from the west-bound lanes of Hwy 1, the viewing area is often closed and the view obscured by vegetation.

Takakkaw Falls
WATERFALL
A thundering torrent of water tumbles from its source in the nearby Daly Glacier over a sheer cliff face for 255m, making it the second-highest waterfall in Canada. At the end of the road, a trail leads for around 800m from the Takakkaw parking lot to the base of the falls. The road is open from late June to early October.

Emerald Lake
LAKE
For most visitors, this vividly colored lake is Yoho's most unmissable sight. Ringed by forest and silhouetted by impressive mountains, including the iconic profile of **Mt Burgess** to the southeast, it's a truly beautiful – if incredibly busy – spot. Escape the mobs in a rental canoe. The lake road is signed off Hwy 1 just to the southwest of Field and continues for 10km (6.2 miles) to the lake shore.

Twin Falls & the Whaleback
HIKING
This moderate 8.2km route from Takakkaw Falls parking lot through pine forest takes in four waterfalls: the **Angel's Staircase**, **Point Lace Falls**, **Laughing Falls** and the double-tiered Twin Falls.

Yoho Lake & Wapta Highline
HIKING
This strenuous route ranks among the finest (and hardest) day hikes in the Rockies. The route starts at the Whiskey Jack trailhead near Takakkaw Falls, and climbs to Yoho Lake before ascending onto the sky-top flanks of Wapta Mountain.

▙ Sleeping

The four campgrounds within Yoho all close from mid-October to mid-May. In addition to a couple of lodges in the park, you can find a range of lodgings in Field.

HI-Yoho National Park
HOSTEL **$**
(Whiskey Jack Hostel; ☑ 403-670-7580; www.hihostels.ca; Yoho Valley Rd, Yoho National Park; dm from $28; ◷Jul-Sep) Yoho National Park's Takakkaw Falls are so close you can see them from the hostel's timber deck. Three nine-bed dorms and a basic kitchen comprise the rudimentary facilities; it's usually booked out in summer.

BRITISH COLUMBIA YOHO NATIONAL PARK

Kicking Horse Campground CAMPGROUND $
(Map p69; Yoho Valley Rd; tent & RV sites $28; ⊙May-Oct; 🐕) This is probably the most popular campground in Yoho. It's in a nice forested location, with plenty of space between the 88 sites, and there are showers. Riverside sites (especially 68 to 74) are the pick of the bunch.

Takakkaw Falls Campground CAMPGROUND $
(Yoho Valley Rd; campsites $18; ⊙Jul-Oct) This appealing campground, 13km along a gravel road, has 35 walk-in (200m) campsites for tents only.

Emerald Lake Lodge LODGE $$$
(✉403-410-7417; www.crmr.com/emerald; Emerald Lake Rd, Yoho National Park; r $250-450; 🅿🐕) Commanding a picture-perfect five-hectare site accessed by a bridge and situated right beside the tranquil shores of Emerald Lake, this lodge couldn't have a better position. The interiors are disappointingly old-fashioned, however, so sit back on the porch and enjoy the lake view.

❶ Information

Yoho National Park Information Centre
(✉250-343-6783; off Hwy 1, Field; ⊙9am-7pm May-Oct) provides maps and trail descriptions; however, this vital resource is often closed due to budget cuts. Rangers can advise on itineraries and conditions. Alberta Tourism staffs a desk here in summer.

Lake O'Hara

Perched high in the mountains, Lake O'Hara is an encapsulation of the Rockies region, and worth the significant hassle to reach it. Compact wooded hillsides, alpine meadows, snow-covered passes, mountain vistas and glaciers wrap around the stunning lake. A day trip is rewarding, but if you stay overnight in the backcountry you'll be able to access many **hiking trails** – some quite difficult, and all quite spectacular. The **Alpine Circuit** (12km) has a bit of everything.

🛏 Sleeping

You can camp or stay in Lake O'Hara Lodge, but reserve well in advance and prepare to jump through hoops to secure a spot.

Lake O'Hara Campground CAMPGROUND $
(✉reservations 250-343-6433; Yoho National Park; tent sites $10, reservation fee $12; ⊙Apr-Oct) Reserve three months in advance to snare one of 30 campsites. Available spots are of-

ten taken in the first hour that reservation phone lines are open (from 8am Mountain time). If you don't have advance reservations, three to five campsites are set aside for 'standby' users; call at 8am the day before you wish to stay.

★Lake O'Hara Lodge LODGE $$$
(✉250-343-6418; www.lakeohara.com; Yoho National Park; s/d from $500/665, cabins $940; ⊙Jan-Apr & Jun-Oct) 🌿 Leaving guests slack-jawed for more than 80 years, the lodge is the only place to stay at the lake if you're not traveling with a tent. It's luxurious in a rustic way, and its environmental practices are lauded. Food comes from BC producers and is excellent. There's a two-night minimum stay.

❶ Getting There & Away

To reach the lake, take the **shuttle bus** (✉reservations 877-737-3783; adult/child return $15/8, reservation fee $12; ⊙mid-Jun–Sep) from the Lake O'Hara parking lot, 15km east of Field on Hwy 1. A quota system governs bus access to the lake. Given the lake's popularity, reservations are basically mandatory, unless you want to walk. That said, if you don't have advance reservations, six day-use seats on the bus are set aside for 'standby' users. Call at 8am the day before and think 'lucky'.

You can freely walk the 11km from the parking area, but no bikes are allowed. The area around Lake O'Hara usually remains covered with snow or else stays very muddy until mid-July.

Field

Right off xHwy 1, this historic railroad town is worth a stop for its dramatic overlook of the river and quaint yet unfussy atmosphere. Many buildings date from the early days of the railways, when the town was the Canadian Pacific Railway's headquarters for exploration and, later, for strategic planning, when engineers were working on the problem of moving trains over Kicking Horse Pass.

🛏 Sleeping & Eating

Fireweed Hostel HOSTEL $
(✉250-343-6999; www.fireweedhostel.com; 313 Stephen Ave; dm/r from $40/125; 🐕) This four-room hostel in Field is a real find, beautifully finished in rustic pine. Dorms are small but smart; each room has two pine bunk beds and a shared bathroom off the hallway, and all have full use of a kitchen and sitting room.

Canadian Rockies Inn   GUESTHOUSE **$$**
(☑ 250-343-6046; www.canadianrockiesinn.com;
Stephen Ave; r $125-190; P ⏵) Spotless rooms
and enormous beds are the main attrac-
tions. All rooms have microwaves, kettles
and fridges.

Truffle Pigs   FUSION **$$$**
(☑ 250-343-6303; www.trufflepigs.com; 100 Cen-
tre St; mains $12-30; ⊘11am-3pm & 5-9pm Mon-
Fri, 8am-3pm & 5-9pm Sat & Sun; ⏵) ⯃ A legendary cafe serving inventive, high-concept
bistro fare that's locally sourced and usually
organic. The menu changes seasonally.

Kootenay National Park

Kootenay is the the only national park in
Canada to contain both glaciers and cacti.
From BC you can create a fine driving loop
via Kootenay and Yoho National Parks;
many of the top sights are easily reached
by car.

The very remote **Mt Assiniboine Provincial Park** (www.bcparks.ca) offers true adventurers a remarkable wilderness experience.

◉ Sights

Kootenay National Park   NATIONAL PARK
(Map p69; ☑ 250-347-9505; www.pc.gc.ca/
kootenay; Hwy 93; adult/child $10/5, campsites
$22-39; ⊘camping May-Oct) Shaped like a
lightning bolt, Kootenay National Park is
centered on a long, wide, tree-covered valley
shadowed by cold, gray peaks. Encompassing 1406 sq km, Kootenay has a more moderate climate than other Rocky Mountains
parks and, in the southern regions especially, summers can be hot and dry, which is a
factor in the frequent fires.

The interpretive **Fireweed Trail** (500m or
2km) loops through the surrounding forest
at the north end of Hwy 93. Panels explain
how nature is recovering from a 1968 fire.
Some 7km further on, **Marble Canyon** has
a pounding creek flowing through a nascent
forest. Another 3km south on the main road
you'll find the easy 2km trail through forest
to ochre pools known as the **Paint Pots**.
Panels describe both the mining history of
this rusty earth and its importance to Aboriginal people.

Learn how the park's appearance has
changed over time at the **Kootenay Valley
Viewpoint**, where informative panels vie
with the view. Just 3km south, **Olive Lake**
makes a perfect picnic or rest stop. A 500m

ⓘ CHECK YOUR WATCH

It is a constant source of confusion
that the East Kootenays lie in the
Mountain time zone, along with Alberta, unlike the rest of BC, which falls
within the Pacific time zone. West on
Hwy 1 from Golden, the time changes
at the east gate of Glacier National
Park. Going west on Hwy 3, the time
changes between Cranbrook and Creston. Mountain time is one hour later
than Pacific time.

---

lakeside interpretive trail describes some of
the visitors who've come before you.

🛏 Sleeping

Kootenay National Park has a few lodges
and campgrounds inside its border, and
nearby Radium Hot Springs has a huge
number of lodgings. Mt Assiniboine Provincial Park is limited to wilderness camping, a
few huts and a remote lodge.

Marble Canyon Campground   CAMPGROUND **$**
(off Hwy 93, Kootenay National Park; campsites
$22; ⊘Jul-Sep) This high-country 61-pitch
campground is situated near the Marble
Canyon trail, and has flush toilets but no
showers. Most sites have tree cover to shel-
ter from the wind. The eastern side has the
best views.

**McLeod Meadows
Campground**   CAMPGROUND **$**
(off Hwy 93, Kootenay National Park; campsites
$22; ⊘Jun-Sep) An 80-pitch campground
located on the banks of the Kootenay River
just a 2.6km walk to the shores of pretty Dog
Lake. There are plentiful trees and spacious,
grassy sites.

Kootenay Park Lodge   CABIN **$$**
(☑ 403-762-9196; www.kootenayparklodge.com;
Hwy 93, Vermilion Crossing, Kootenay National
Park; d cabins $135-200; ⊘mid-May–late Sep; P)
The pick of the few places to stay inside the
park, this lodge has a range of cute log cab-
ins complete with verandas, fridges and hot
plates. Think rustic charm.

ⓘ Information

The main **Kootenay National Park visitor
center** (p224) is in Radium Hot Springs. It has
excellent resources for hikers.

Radium Hot Springs

Lying just outside the southwest corner of Kootenay National Park, Radium Hot Springs is a major gateway to the entire Rocky Mountains national park area.

Radium boasts a large resident population of bighorn sheep, which often wander through town, but the big attraction is the namesake hot springs, 3km north of town.

The **hot springs'** (☑250-347-9485; www.pc.gc.ca/hotsprings; off Hwy 93; adult/child $7/6; ☉9am-11pm) pools are quite modern and can get very busy in summer. The water comes from the ground at 44°C, enters the first pool at 39°C and hits the final one at 29°C.

Radium glows with lodging. **Cedar Motel** (☑250-347-9463; www.cedarmotel.ca; 7593 Main St W; r $85-100; ℗🐾) is clean, cheap and (as its name suggests) cedar-clad. This Swiss-run place is one of the more attractive motels in Radium. The rooms are boxy but bright, with large beds and Technicolor bedspreads. Some have teeny kitchenettes.

Village Country Inn (☑250-347-9392; www.villagecountryinn.bc.ca; 7557 Canyon Ave; r $120-175; ℗🐾) is a cute gabled house just off the main drag, with rooms decked out in country fashion. The same folksy feel runs into the downstairs tea room, where afternoon tea is served on bone china and frilly doilies.

An ideal road-trip breaker is **Meet on Higher Ground Coffee House** (☑250-347-6567; www.meetonhigherground.com; 7527 Main St; snacks $3-10; ☉6am-5pm; 🐾), where you can refuel with coffee and a cinnamon bun or something more savory.

Parks Canada rangers and the Radium tourism people share space at the **Kootenay National Park & Radium Hot Springs Visitors Centre** (☑250-347-9331; www.radiumhotsprings.com; 7556 Main St E, Hwy 93/95; ☉visitor center 9am-5pm year-round, Parks Canada May-Oct; 🐾), and they provide excellent local hiking info. There are some good displays on the park.

Sun City Coachlines (p221) runs one daily bus each way on Hwy 95 to Golden ($27, one hour) and Cranbrook ($43, three hours).

Radium Hot Springs to Fernie

South from Radium Hot Springs, Hwy 93/95 follows the wide Columbia River valley between the Purcell and Rocky Mountains. It's not especially interesting, unless you're into the area's industry (ski resort construction), agriculture (golf courses) or wild game (condo buyers).

South of Skookumchuck on Hwy 93/95, the road forks. Go left on Hwy 95 and you'll come to **Fort Steele Heritage Town** (☑250-426-7342; www.fortsteele.ca; 9851 Hwy 93/95; adult/child $12/5; ☉9:30am-6pm mid-Jun–Aug, shorter hours winter), a re-created 1880s town that's less irritating than many of similar ilk. In summer there are all manner of activities and re-creations, which taper off to nothing in winter, although the site stays open.

From Fort Steele it's 95km to Fernie along Hwys 93 and 3.

Fernie

POP 4800

Surrounded by mountains on four sides – that's the sheer granite Lizard Range you see looking west – Fernie defines cool. Once devoted solely to lumber and coal, the town has used its sensational setting to branch out. Skiers love the 8m-plus of dry powder that annually blankets the runs seen from town. In summer, this same dramatic setting lures scores of hikers and mountain bikers.

Despite the town's discovery by pleasure seekers, it still retains a down-to-earth, vintage-brick vibe, best felt in the cafes, bars, shops and galleries along Victoria (2nd) Ave in the historic center, three blocks south of Hwy 3 (7th Ave).

◉ Sights & Activities

One of many disasters suffered, Fernie experienced a devastating fire in 1908, which resulted in a brick-and-stone building code. Today you'll see numerous fine **early 20th-century buildings**, many of which were built out of local yellow brick, giving the town an appearance unique in the East Kootenays. Get a copy of *Heritage Walking Tour* ($5), a superb booklet produced by the **Fernie Museum** (☑250-423-7016; www.ferniemuseum.com; 491 2nd Ave; adult/child $5/free; ☉10am-5:30pm).

★**Fernie Alpine Resort**   SKIING
(☑250-423-4655; www.skifernie.com; 5339 Ski Area Rd; 1-day pass adult/child $90/36) In fall, all eyes turn to the mountains for more than just their beauty: they're looking for snow. A five-minute drive from downtown, fast-growing Fernie Alpine Resort boasts 142 runs, five bowls and almost endless dumps of powder. Most hotels run shuttles here daily.

Mt Fernie Provincial Park PARK
(☑250-422-3003; www.bcparks.ca; Mt Fernie Park Rd, off Hwy 3) Mountain biking is popular at Mt Fernie Provincial Park, which is just 3km south of town. It also offers hikes for all skills and interests, plus camping.

Fernie Bike Guides CYCLING
(☑250-423-3650; www.ferniebikeguides.ca; guiding per hr $30) Raise your mountain-biking game with expert coaching, and let them show you the far reaches of the Elk Valley.

Mountain High River Adventures RAFTING
(☑250-423-5008; www.raftfernie.com; 100 Riverside Way, Standford Resort; trips adult/child from $140/100; ☉May-Sep) The Elk River is a classic white-water river, with three grade IV rapids and 11 grade III rapids. In addition to rafting, Mountain High offers kayaking, floats, rentals and more on the surging waters.

Ski & Bike Base SKIING, CYCLING
(☑250-423-6464; www.skibase.com; 432 2nd Ave; bicycle rental per day from $45; ☉10am-6pm Mon-Sat year-round, 11am-5pm Sun Jun-Aug) One of several excellent all-season gear-sales and -rental shops on 2nd Ave.

🛏 Sleeping

Being a big ski town, Fernie's high season is winter. You'll have the most fun staying in the center.

Fernie Central Reservations (☑250-423-2077; www.ferniecentralreservations.com) can book you a room at the ski resort.

HI Raging Elk Hostel HOSTEL $
(☑250-423-6811; www.ragingelk.com; 892 6th Ave; dm/r from $30/76; @☎) Wide decks allow plenty of inspirational mountain-gazing at this well-run central hostel. Raging Elk has good advice for those hoping to mix time on the slopes or trails with seasonal work. The pub (open from 4pm to 11pm) is a hoot (and offers cheap beer).

Mt Fernie Provincial Park CAMPGROUND $
(☑800-689-9025; www.discovercamping.ca; Mt Fernie Park Rd, off Hwy 3; campsites $30; ☉May-Sep) Only 3km south of town, this campground has 41 sites, flush toilets, waterfalls and access to mountain-bike trails.

Park Place Lodge HOTEL $$
(☑250-423-6871; www.parkplacelodge.com; 742 Hwy 3; r $130-240; ❄@☎❋) The nicest lodging close to the center, Park Place offers 64 comfortable rooms with fridges and micro-

waves, and access to an indoor pool and hot tub. Some have balconies and views.

Snow Valley Motel & RV Park MOTEL $$
(☑250-423-4421; www.snowvalleymotel.com; 1041 7th Ave, Hwy 3; RV campsites $35; r $65-140; ❄@☎) Great value in the middle of town. The 20 motel units are large and come equipped with microwaves and fridges; some have full kitchens. Nothing is fancy here, but there is a barbecue deck with a hot tub and views.

🍴 Eating & Drinking

Blue Toque Diner CAFE $
(☑250-423-4637; 601 1st Ave; mains from $12; ☉9am-2:30pm Thu-Mon; ☑) Part of the Arts Station community gallery, this is *the* place for breakfast. The menu features lots of seasonal and organic vegetarian specials.

Big Bang Bagel BAKERY $
(☑250-423-7778; www.bigbangbagels.com; 502 2 Ave; mains $4-10; ☉7am-5pm) The wooden floors creak in accompaniment to the anticipatory growls of your stomach at this popular corner bakery. Everything from bagels to sandwiches to lunch mains are good. Excellent coffee.

★Yamagoya JAPANESE $$
(☑250-430-0090; www.yamagoya.ca; 741 7th Ave, Hwy 3; small dishes $4-8, mains $11-30; ☉5-10pm) As compact as a California roll, this gem of a sushi place serves up a wide range of classics, from sashimi to tempura. The miso soup is good, especially after a day of skiing. In addition to sake, there's a great beer selection. Also has outdoor seating.

Bridge Bistro CANADIAN $$
(☑250-423-3002; 301 Hwy 3; mains $11-25; ☉11am-10pm) Enjoy the views of the Elk River and surrounding peaks from the deck, but save some attention for the long menu of tasty burgers, steaks, salads and pizza.

Royal Hotel PUB
(☑250-946-5395;www.facebook.com/RoyalFernie; 501 1st Ave; ☉9pm-2am Mon-Sat) A local institution. This old brick bar has live music many nights, from blues to punk. On any night, it's good for a drink and a chat.

❶ Information

The **visitor center** (☑250-423-6868; www.ferniechamber.com; 102 Commerce Rd; ☉9am-5pm Mon-Fri Sep-Jun, daily Jul & Aug) is east of town off Hwy 3, just past the Elk River crossing.

It includes the **Fernie Nature Centre**, which has displays on local critters. The **Fernie Museum** (p224) also has tourist info.

🛈 Getting There & Away

Shuttles operate between town and the ski resort. **Greyhound Canada** (✆ 250-423-5577; www.greyhound.ca; 1561 9th Ave) runs buses west to Kelowna ($108, 11 hours, one daily) and Nelson ($62, five hours, one daily), and east to Calgary ($63, 6½ hours, one daily). The stop is near Hwy 3, just north of the center.

Kimberley

When big mining left Kimberley in 1973, a plan was hatched to transform the little mountain village at 1113m altitude into a tourist destination with a Bavarian theme. The center became a pedestrian zone named the Platzl; locals were encouraged to prance about in lederhosen and dirndl; and sausage was added to many a menu. Now, more than three decades later, that shtick is long-gone. There's still a bit of fake half-timbering here and there, but for the most part Kimberley is a diverse place that makes a worthwhile detour off Hwy 95 between Cranbrook and Radium Hot Springs.

Take a 15km ride on **Kimberley's Underground Mining Railway** (✆ 250-427-7365; www.kimberleysundergroundminingrailway.ca; Gerry Sorensen Way; adult/child $25/10; ☉ tours 11am-3pm May-Sep, trains to resort 10am Sat & Sun), where the tiny train putters through the steep-walled Mark Creek Valley toward some sweeping mountain vistas.

At the end of the Underground Mining Railway, a chair lift takes you up to the **Kimberley Alpine Resort** (✆ 250-427-4881; www.skikimberley.com; 301 N Star Blvd; 1-day lift pass adult/child $73/29). (You can also drive up if you wish.) In winter, the resort has more than 700 hectares of skiable terrain, including 80 runs, and mild weather.

🛈 Information

The **visitor center** (✆ 778-481-1891; www.tourismkimberley.com; 270 Kimberley Ave; ☉ 10am-5pm daily Jul & Aug, closed Sun Sep-Jun) sits in the large parking area behind the Platzl.

Cranbrook

The region's main center, 31km southeast of Kimberley, Cranbrook is a modest crossroads. Hwy 3/95 bisects the town, which is a charmless array of strip malls.

The one great reason for stopping in Cranbrook? The **Cranbrook History Centre** (✆ 250-489-3918; www.cranbrookhistorycentre.com; 57 Van Horne St S, Hwy 3/95; from $15; ☉ 10am-5pm daily Jun-Aug, Tue-Sat Sep-May), which includes the **Canadian Museum of Rail Travel**. It has some fine examples of classic Canadian trains, including the luxurious 1929 edition of the **Trans-Canada Limited**, a legendary train that ran from Montréal to Vancouver.

Cranbrook to Rossland

Hwy 3 twists and turns its way 300km from Cranbrook to Osoyoos at the south end of the Okanagan Valley. Along the way it hugs the hills close to the US border and passes eight border crossings.

Creston, 123km west of Cranbrook, is known for its orchards and as the home of Columbia Brewing Co's Kokanee True Ale. Hwy 3A heads north from here for a scenic 80km to the free **Kootenay Lake Ferry**, which connects to Nelson.

Some 85km west of Creston, **Salmo** is notable mostly as the junction with Hwy 6, which runs north for a bland 40km to Nelson. The Crowsnest Hwy splits 10km to the west. Hwy 3 bumps north through **Castlegar**, notable for the closest large airport to Nelson and a very large pulp mill. Hwy 3B dips down through the cute cafe-filled town of **Fruitvale** and industrial **Trail**.

🔾 Sights

Columbia Brewery · · · · · · · · · · · · · · · · BREWERY
(✆ 250-428-9344; www.columbiabrewery.ca; 1220 Erikson St; tours $5; ☉ 9:30am-3pm Jul & Aug, 9:30am-2:30pm Mon-Fri mid-May–Jun & Sep–mid-Oct) This is the home of the Columbia Brewery, creators of the Kokanee and Kootenay brands. The brewery offers tours (four to six daily) and visits to the sample room.

Creston Valley Wildlife Management Area · · · · · · · · · WILDLIFE RESERVE
(✆ 250-402-6900; www.crestonwildlife.ca; 1760 West Creston Rd; ☉ dawn-dusk) This wildlife spot 11km west of Creston is a good place to spot oodles of birds, including blue herons, from the 1km boardwalk.

🛏 Sleeping & Eating

Valley View Motel · · · · · · · · · · · · · · · · · MOTEL **$**
(✆ 250-428-2336; www.valleyviewmotel.info; 216 Valley View Dr, Creston; r from $90; ❋ 🕱) In the

motel-ville of Creston, this could be your best bet. On a view-splayed hillside, it's clean, comfortable and quiet.

Retro Cafe
FRENCH $

(☑ 250-428-2726; www.retrocafe.ca; 1431 NW Blvd, Creston; mains from $6; ⊙ 7am-5pm Mon-Fri, to 3pm Sat) A French mirage in Creston, 'retro' will probably be the last thing on your mind as you scour the hand-scrawled blackboard and tuck into *très délicieux* crepes.

Rossland

Rossland is a world apart. High in the Southern Monashee Mountains (1023m), this old mining village is one of Canada's best places for **mountain biking**. A long history of mining has left the hills crisscrossed with old trails and abandoned rail lines, all of which are perfect for riding.

Free-riding is all the rage as the ridgelines are easily accessed and there are lots of rocky paths for plunging downhill. The **Seven Summits & Dewdney Trail** is a 35.8km single track along the crest of the Rossland Range. The **Kootenay Columbia Trails Society** (www.kcts.ca) has good maps online.

Red Mountain Ski Resort (☑ 250-362-7384, snow report 250-362-5500; www.redresort.com; Hwy 3B; 1-day lift pass adult/child $84/42) draws mountain bikers in summer and plenty of ski enthusiasts in winter. Red, as it's called, includes the 1590m-high Red Mountain, the 2075m-high Granite Mountain and the 2048m-high Grey Mountain, for a total of 1670 hectares of challenging, powdery terrain and 110 runs.

ⓘ Information

The **visitor center** (☑ 250-362-7722; www.rossland.com; 1100 Hwy 3B, Rossland Museum; ⊙ 9am-5pm May-Sep) is located in the Rossland Museum building, at the junction of Hwy 22 (coming from the US border) and Hwy 3B.

Nelson

POP 11,100

Nelson is an excellent reason to visit the Kootenays and should feature on any itinerary in the region. Tidy brick buildings climb the side of a hill overlooking the west arm of deep-blue Kootenay Lake, and the waterfront is lined with parks and beaches. The thriving cafe, culture and nightlife scene is a bonus. However, what really propels Nelson is its personality: a funky mix of hippies, creative types and rugged individualists. You can find all these along Baker St, the pedestrian-friendly main drag where wafts of patchouli mingle with hints of fresh-roasted coffee.

Born as a mining town in the late 1800s, Nelson embarked on a decades-long heritage-preservation project in 1977. Today there are more than 350 carefully preserved and restored period buildings. The town is also an excellent base for hiking, skiing and kayaking the nearby lakes and hills.

⊙ Sights

Almost a third of Nelson's **historic buildings** have been restored to their high- and late-Victorian architectural splendor. Pick up the superb *Heritage Walking Tour* from the visitor center. It gives details of more than 30 buildings in the center and offers a good lesson in Victorian architecture.

Lakeside Park
PARK

(Lakeside Dr; Ⓟ) By the iconic Nelson Bridge, Lakeside Park is a flower-filled, shady park and a beach, and has a great summer cafe.

Touchstones Nelson
MUSEUM

(☑ 250-352-9813; www.touchstonesnelson.ca; 502 Vernon St; adult/child $8/4; ⊙ 10am-5pm Mon-Wed, Fri & Sat, to 8pm Thu, 10am-4pm Sun Jun-Aug, closed Mon Sep-May) An enormous renovation transformed what was once a baronial old city hall (1902) into Touchstones Nelson, a museum of local history and art. Every month brings new exhibitions, many of which celebrate local artists. The history displays are engaging and interactive, banishing images of musty piles of poorly labeled artifacts.

⚡ Activities

From the center, follow the **Waterfront Pathway**, which runs along the length of the shore – its western extremity passes the airport and has a remote river vantage. You might choose to walk to Lakeside Park and then ride **Streetcar 23** (☑ 250-352-7672; www.nelsonstreetcar.org; Waterfront Pathway; adult/child $3/2; ⊙ 11am-4:30pm mid-May–mid-Nov) back along the 2km track from the park to the wharf at Hall St.

★ Kokanee Glacier Provincial Park
HIKING

(☑ trail conditions 250-825-3500; www.bcparks.ca; Kokanee Glacier Rd) This park boasts 85km of some of the area's most superb hiking trails. The fantastic summer-only 2.5km (two hour) round-trip hike to **Kokanee Lake** on a well-marked trail can be continued to the treeless, boulder-strewn expanse around the glacier. Turn off Hwy 3A 20.5km northeast of Nelson, then head another 16km on Kokanee Glacier Rd.

Kootenay Kayak Company KAYAKING
(☑ 250-505-4549; www.kootenaykayak.com; kayak rentals per day $40-50, tours from $55) Rents kayaks and has a variety of guided kayak tours.

Sacred Ride MOUNTAIN BIKING
(☑ 250-354-3831; www.sacredride.ca; 213b Baker St; bicycle rental per day $45-100; ☺ 9am-5:30pm Mon-Sat) Sacred Ride has a wide variety of rentals. Also sells *Your Ticket to Ride,* an extensive trail map.

Pulpit Rock HIKING
(www.pulpitrocknelson.com) The two-hour climb to Pulpit Rock, just across the lake, affords fine views of Nelson and Kootenay Lake. The trailhead starts at the parking lot on Johnstone Rd.

Great Northern Rail Trail HIKING
Extending 42km from Nelson to Salmo along an old rail line, this trail has stunning views amid thick forest. Turn back whenever you want, but the first 6km have many highlights. The trailhead is at the corner of Cherry and Gore Streets.

Whitewater Winter Resort SKIING
(☑ 250-354-4944, snow report 250-352-7669; www.skiwhitewater.com; off Hwy 6; 1-day lift ticket adult/child $76/38) Known for its heavy powdery snowfall, this laid-back resort 12km south of Nelson off Hwy 6 has a small-town charm. Lifts are few, but so are the crowds, who enjoy a drop of 623m on 81 runs. There are 11 groomed Nordic trails.

🛌 Sleeping

★ HI Dancing Bear Inn HOSTEL $
(☑ 250-352-7573; www.dancingbearinn.com; 171 Baker St; dm/r from $28/59; P @ ☎) ⌀ The brilliant management here offers advice and smooths the stay of guests in the 14 shared and private rooms, all of which share bathrooms. There's a gourmet kitchen, a library, patio and a laundry.

City Tourist Park CAMPGROUND $
(☑ 250-352-7618; campnels@telus.net; 90 High St; campsites from $25; ☺ May-Sep; P ☎) Just a five-minute walk from central Baker St, this small municipal campground has 43 shady sites, showers, a kitchen and a laundry.

★ Hume Hotel HOTEL $$
(☑ 250-352-5331; www.humehotel.com; 422 Vernon St; r incl breakfast $100-200; P ❄ ☎) This 1898 classic hotel maintains its period grandeur. The 43 rooms vary greatly in shape and size; ask for the huge corner rooms with views of the hills and lake. Rates include a delicious breakfast. It has several appealing nightlife venues.

Adventure Hotel HOTEL $$
(☑ 250-352-7211; www.adventurehotel.ca; 616 Vernon St; r $80-160; P ❄ ☎) Rooms come in three flavors at this renovated hotel: budget (tiny, two bunk beds, shower down the hall), economy (full private bath) and deluxe (a choice of beds). Common areas include a lounge, patio, a gym and a rooftop sauna. The decor is IKEA-basic, in warm hues.

Victoria Falls Guest House INN $$
(☑ 250-505-3563; www.victoriafallsguesthouse. com; cnr Victoria & Falls Sts; r $85-165; P ☎) The wide porch wraps right around this festive, yellow, renovated Victorian. The five suites have sitting areas and cooking facilities. Decor ranges from cozy antiques to family-friendly bunk beds. There is a barbecue.

Cloudside Inn B&B $$
(☑ 250-352-3226; www.cloudside.ca; 408 Victoria St; r $125-215; P ❄ ☎) Live like a silver baron at this vintage mansion, where the seven rooms are named after trees. Luxuries abound, and a fine patio looks over the terraced gardens and the town. Most rooms have private bathrooms.

Mountain Hound Inn GUESTHOUSE $$
(☑ 250-352-6490; www.mountainhound.com; 621 Baker St; r $80-140; ❄ ☎) The 19 rooms are small, but have an industrial edge – to go with the cement-block walls. It's ideally located in the center and is a good-value, no-frills choice. There's a public laundry right next door.

🍴 Eating & Drinking

★ Cottonwood Community Market MARKET $
(www.ecosociety.ca; 199 Carbonate St, Cottonwood Falls Park; ☺ 9:30am-3pm Sat mid-May–Oct) ⌀ Close to downtown and next to the surging Cottonwood waterfall, this market encapsulates Nelson. There's great organic produce; fine baked goods, many with heretofore-unheard-of grains; and various craft items with artistic roots in tie-dyeing. A second event, the Downtown Market, is less colorful.

Full Circle Cafe
DINER $
(✆250-354-4458; 402 Baker S; mains $8-15; ⊙6:30am-2:30pm) A downtown diner beloved for its omelettes, the Full Circle will have you doing just that as you return for skillfully made breakfast classics, such as eggs Benedict. It gets popular on weekends, so prepare for a wait.

Downtown Market
MARKET $
(400 block Baker St; ⊙9:30am-3pm Wed mid-Jun–Sep) Nelson's mid-week market.

Cantina del Centro
MEXICAN $$
(✆250-352-3737; 561 Baker St; small plates $6-10; ⊙11am-late) Bright and vibrant, Cantina del Centro gets jammed with diners. The tacos and other small plates reflect the vivid colors of the Mexican tile floor. You can watch your meal being grilled behind the counter while you chill with a margarita. Opt for the buzz of an outdoor table.

Bibo
FUSION $$
(✆250-352-2744; www.bibonelson.ca; 518 Hall St; mains $18-30; ⊙5pm-late) Bibo is all about exposed brick inside, while outside tables on the hillside terrace overlook the lake and mountains beyond. Small plates celebrate local produce: enjoy tapas or a cheese and charcuterie plate accompanied by flights of wine. The short list of upscale mains includes burgers and seafood.

★All Seasons Cafe
FUSION $$$
(✆250-352-0101; www.allseasonscafe.com; 620 Herridge Lane; mains $23-36; ⊙5-10pm) Sitting on the patio here beneath little lights twinkling in the huge maple above you is a Nelson highlight; in winter, candles inside provide the same romantic flair. The eclectic menu changes with the seasons but always celebrates BC foods. Presentations are artful; service is gracious.

Royal
BAR
(✆250-354-7014; www.royalgrillnelson.com; 330 Baker St; ⊙5pm-2am Tue-Sat) This gritty old pub on Baker gets some of the region's best music acts. It has a whole section of tables outside on the street and serves decent pub food.

Oso Negro
CAFE
(✆250-532-7761; www.osonegrocoffee.com; 604 Ward St; coffee from $2; ⊙7am-5pm; ☎) This local favorite corner cafe roasts its own coffee in 20 blends. Outside there are tables in a garden that burbles with water features amid statues. Enjoy baked goods and other snacks.

🛍 Shopping

★Still Eagle
HOMEWARES
(✆250-352-3844; www.stilleagle.com; 476 Baker St; ⊙10am-8pm Mon-Sat, 11am-7pm Sun) 🍃 Fair-trade and Kootenay-produced clothing, kitchen goods and products for the home are sold in this large store, which has a deep environmental commitment. Many products are made from recycled materials.

Otter Books
BOOKS
(✆250-352-7525; 398 Baker St; ⊙9:30am-5:30pm Mon-Sat, 11am-4pm Sun) A good local indie with books and maps.

ℹ Information

The **visitor center** (✆250-352-3433; www.discovernelson.com; 91 Baker St; ⊙8:30am-6pm daily May-Oct, to 5pm Mon-Fri Nov-Apr) is housed in the beautifully restored train station. It offers excellent brochures detailing driving and walking tours.

Listen to the Nelson beat on **Kootenay Co-Op Radio** (93.5FM).

ℹ Getting There & Away

Castlegar Airport (www.wkrairport.ca; Hwy 3A) The closest airport to Nelson is 42km southwest.

Greyhound Canada (✆250-352-3939; 1128 Lakeside Dr, Chahko-Mika Mall) Buses serve Fernie ($69, 4¾ hours, one daily) and Kelowna ($62, 5¼ hours, one daily).

Queen City Shuttle (✆250-352-9829; www.kootenayshuttle.com; one-way adult/child $25/10) Links with Castlegar Airport (one hour); reserve in advance.

West Kootenay Transit System (✆855-993-3100; www.bctransit.com; fares $2) Buses 2 and 10 serve Chahko-Mika Mall and Lakeside Park. The main stop is at the corner of Ward and Baker Sts.

Nelson to Revelstoke

Heading north from Nelson to Revelstoke, there are two options, both scenic. Hwy 6 heads west for 16km before turning north at South Slocan. The road eventually runs alongside pretty Slocan Lake for about 30km before reaching New Denver, 97km from Nelson.

Going north and east from Nelson on Hwy 3A is the most interesting route. Head 34km northeast to Balfour, where the free Kootenay Lake Ferry (✆250-229-4215; www2.gov.bc.ca/gov/content/transportation/passenger-travel) connects to Kootenay Bay (35 minutes). The ferry's a worthwhile side trip for its long lake vistas of blue mountains rising sharply from the water. From Kootenay Bay, Hwy 3A heads 80km south to Creston. Continuing north from the ferry at Balfour, the road becomes Hwy 31 and follows the lake 34km to Kaslo, passing cute towns along the way. From Kaslo to New Denver is spectacular. North of there you pass the village of Nakusp and another ferry before reaching Revelstoke. This is a great all-day trip.

Kaslo

A cute little town, Kaslo is an underrated gem with a beautiful lakeside setting.

Don't miss the restored 1898 lake steamer **SS Moyie** (☑250-353-2525; http://klhs.bc.ca; 324 Front St; adult/child $10/4; ☺10am-5pm mid-May–mid-Oct). It also has tourist info on the myriad ways to kayak and canoe the sparkling-blue waters.

There's a range of acommodations in and around town, including the appealing downtown **Kaslo Hotel** (☑250-353-7714; www.kaslohotel.com; 430 Front St; r $150-220; ✷☏), a veteran hotel (1896) which has lake views and a good pub. Rooms have balconies and porches.

New Denver

Wild mountain streams are just some of the spectacular highlights on Hwy 31A, which goes up and over some rugged hills west of Kaslo. At the end of this twisting 47km road, you reach New Denver, which seems about five years away from ghost-town status. But that's not necessarily bad, as this historic little gem slumbers away peacefully right on the clear waters of Slocan Lake. The equally sleepy old mining town of **Silverton** is just south.

Housed in the 1897 Bank of Montreal building, the **Silvery Slocan Museum** (☑250-358-2201; www.newdenver.ca; 202 6th Ave; adult/child $5/free; ☺9am-4pm Jun-Aug) features well-done displays from the booming mining days, a tiny vault and an untouched tin ceiling. It also has visitor info.

Nakusp

Situated right on Upper Arrow Lake, Nakusp was forever changed by BC's orgy of dam building in the 1950s and 1960s. The water level here was raised and the town was relocated to its current spot, which is

why it has a 1960s-era look. It has some attractive cafes and a tiny museum.

The **Nakusp Hot Springs** (☑250-265-4528; www.nakusphotsprings.com; 8500 Hot Springs Rd; adult/child $10/9; ☺9:30am-9:30pm), 12km northeast of Nakusp off Hwy 23, feel a bit artificial after receiving a revamp. However, you'll forget this as you soak away your cares amid an amphitheater of trees.

CARIBOO, CHILCOTIN & THE COAST

This vast and beautiful region covers a huge swath of BC north of Whistler. It comprises three very distinct areas. The Cariboo region includes numerous ranches, and terrain that's little changed from the 1850s, when the 'Gold Rush Trail' passed through from Lillooet to Barkerville.

Populated with more moose than people, the Chilcotin lies to the west of Hwy 97, the region's north–south spine. Its mostly wild, rolling landscape has a few ranches and some Aboriginal villages. Traveling west along Hwy 20 from Williams Lake leads you to the Bella Coola Valley, a spectacular bear-and-wildlife-filled inlet along the coast.

Much of the region can be reached via Hwy 97, enabling you to build a circle itinerary to other parts of BC via Prince George in the north. The Bella Coola Valley is served by ferry from Port Hardy on Vancouver Island, which makes for even cooler circle-routes.

❶ Getting There & Away

Hwy 97 forms the spine of the region; it's a good-quality road that continues to be improved. A twice-daily **Greyhound Canada** (p196) service runs along Hwy 97; Cache Creek to Prince George takes six hours.

Williams Lake to Prince George

Cattle and lumber have shaped **Williams Lake**, the hub for the region. Some 206km north of the junction of Hwys 1 and 97, this small town has a pair of **museums**.

In the tiny town center, sprightly **New World Café** (☑778-412-5282; www.newworld-coffee.ca; 72 Oliver St, Wiliams Lake; mains $7-15; ☺8am-5pm Mon-Wed, to 8pm Thu-Sat) has a bakery and excellent coffee. Get a sandwich to go, or eat in to enjoy the menu of soups, salads, hot specials and more.

Quesnel, 124km north of Williams Lake on Hwy 97, is all about logging. From Quesnel, Hwy 26 leads east to the area's main attractions, **Barkerville Historic Park** and **Bowron Lake Provincial Park**. North of Quesnel it's 116km on Hwy 97 to Prince George.

❶ Information

Williams Lake has a superb **visitor center** (☑ 250-392-5025; www.williamslake.ca; 1660 Broadway S, off Hwy 97; ◷ 9am-5pm) in a huge log building. It has full regional info and gives the lowdown for trips west to the coast on Hwy 20.

Barkerville & Around

In 1862 Billy Barker, previously of Cornwall, struck gold deep in the Cariboo. **Barkerville** soon sprung up, populated by the usual fly-by-night crowds of prostitutes, tricksters and just plain prospectors. Today it's a compelling attraction, a time capsule of the Old West.

You can visit more than 125 restored heritage buildings in **Barkerville Historic Town** (☑ 888-994-3332; www.barkerville.ca; Hwy 26; adult/child $14.50/4.75; ◷ reception 8am-8pm mid-Jun–Aug, 8:30am-4pm mid-May–mid-Jun & Sep), which also has shops, cafes and a couple of B&Bs. In summer, people dressed in period garb roam through town and, if you can tune out the crowds, it feels more authentic than forced. At other times of the year, you can wander the town for free, but don't expect to find much open.

Barkerville lies 82km east of Quesnel along Hwy 26. Historic **Cottonwood House**, a park-like area, makes an atmospheric stop on the way. Nearby **Wells** is an offbeat town.

❶ Information

The **visitor center** (☑ 250-994-2323, 877-451-9355; www.wellsbc.com; 4120 Pooley St; ◷ 9am-5pm May-Sep) has regional info and a small museum.

Bowron Lake

The place heaven-bound canoeists go when they die, **Bowron Lake Provincial Park** (☑ 778-373-6107; www.bowronlakecanoe.com; off Hwy 26; ◷ May-Sep; ℗) is a fantasyland of 10 lakes surrounded by snowcapped peaks.

Forming a natural circle with sections of the Isaac, Cariboo and Bowron Rivers, Bowron Lake Provincial Park's 116km **canoe circuit** (permits $30 to $60) is one of the

world's finest. There are eight portages, with the longest (2km) over well-defined trails. The park website has maps, and details everything you'll need to know for planning your trip, including mandatory reservations, which sometimes book up in advance. Campsites cost $18. You can rent, canoes, kayaks and carriers at the park.

The whole canoe circuit takes between six and 10 days, and you'll need to be completely self-sufficient. September is a good time to visit, both for the bold colors of changing leaves and the lack of summertime crowds.

Whitegold Adventures (☑ 866-994-2345; www.whitegold.ca; Hwy 26, Wells; 8-day canoe circuit from $1620) offers four- to eight-day guided paddles of Bowron Lake. There is also a one-day paddle trip ($120).

For accommodations, **Bowron Lake Lodge** (☑ 800-519-3399, 250-992-2733; www.bowronlakelodge.com; Bowron Lake; campsites $35, r from $100; ◷ May-Sep) is picture-perfect and right on the lake. It has simple cabins and motel rooms, and rents canoes, kayaks and gear.

Wells Gray Provincial Park

Plunging 141m onto rocks below, **Helmcken Falls** may only be Canada's fourth-highest waterfall but it is one of the undiscovered facets of Wells Gray Provincial Park, itself an under-appreciated gem.

Clearwater, the town near the park entrance, has everything you'll need for a visit.

◉ Sights & Activities

Wells Gray Provincial Park   PARK
(☑ 250-587-2090; www.bcparks.ca; Wells Gray Rd) BC's fourth-largest park is bounded by the Clearwater River and its tributaries, which define the park's boundaries. Highlights for visitors include five major lakes, two large river systems, scores of waterfalls such as **Helmcken Falls** and most every kind of BC land-based wildlife. Many hiking trails and sights, such as Helmcken Falls, are accessible off the main park road, which ends at **Clearwater Lake**.

You'll find opportunities for **hiking**, **cross-country skiing** and **horseback riding** along more than 20 trails of varying lengths. Rustic backcountry campgrounds dot the area around four of the lakes.

Clearwater Lake Tours
WATERSPORTS

(☑ 250-674-2121; www.clearwaterlaketours.com; canoe/kayak rental per day from $55) Rents canoes and kayaks, and also leads tours of the park.

🛏 Sleeping

In addition to camping in the park, you'll find all manner of holiday accommodations outside the park around Clearwater.

Wells Grey Provincial Park
Campgrounds
CAMPGROUND $

(☑ reservations 800-689-9025; www.discovercamping.ca; Wells Grey Provincial Park; campsites $20-23) There are three vehicle-accessible yet simple campgrounds in the park. Woodsy **Pyramid Campground** is just 5km north of the park's south entrance and is close to Helmcken Falls. There's also plenty of **backcountry camping** ($5).

Dutch Lake Resort
LODGE $$

(☑ 888-884-4424, 250-674-3351; www.dutchlake.com; 361 Ridge Dr, Clearwater; campsites $31-44, cabins $140-210) This family-friendly waterfront resort has cabins and 65 campsites. Rent a canoe and practice for more fun in the park.

Wells Gray Guest Ranch
LODGE $$

(☑ 250-674-2792, 866-467-4346; www.wellsgrayranch.com; Clearwater Valley Rd; campsites from $25, r $175-290) Wells Gray Guest Ranch has cabins and cozy rooms in the main lodge building. It's inside the park, 27km north of Clearwater. There are horse rides and many more activities.

ℹ Information

Clearwater's **visitor center** (☑ 250-674-3334; www.wellsgraypark.info; 416 Eden Rd, off Hwy 5, Clearwater; ⊙ 9am-6:30pm May-Oct; 🛜) is a vital info stop for the park. It books rooms and fun-filled white-water-rafting trips.

Chilcotin & Highway 20

Meandering over the lonely hills west of the Chilcotin, Hwy 20 runs 450km from Williams Lake to the Bella Coola Valley. You'll come across a few aboriginal villages, as well as gravel roads that lead off to the odd provincial park and deserted lake.

Long spoken about by drivers in hushed and concerned tones, Hwy 20 has received steady improvement and is now more than 90% paved. However, the unpaved section remains a doozy: **The Hill** is a 30km stretch of gravel that's 386km west of Williams Lake. It descends 1524m from Heckman's Pass to the valley, which is nearly at sea level, through a series of sharp switchbacks and 11% grades. But by taking your time and using low gear, you'll actually enjoy the stunning views. It's safe for all vehicles – visitors in rented SUVs will be humbled when a local in a Ford beater zips past.

Bella Coola Valley

The verdant Bella Coola Valley is at the heart of Great Bear Rainforest, a lush land of huge stands of trees, surging white water and lots of bears. It's a spiritual place: Nuxalk First Nation artists are active here and, for many creative types from elsewhere, this is literally the end of the road. The valley lies west of the dry expanses of the Chilcotin.

The valley stretches 53km to the shores of the **North Bentinck Arm**, a deep, glacier-fed fjord that runs 40km inland from the Pacific Ocean. The two main towns, **Bella Coola** on the water and **Hagensborg** 15km east, almost seem as one, with most places of interest in or between the two.

◉ Sights & Activities

There's really no limit to activities here. You can hike into the hills and valleys, accessible from roads (consider **Odegaard Falls**) or at points only reachable by boat along the craggy coast.

Walk amid 500-year-old cedars just west of Hagensborg at **Walker Island Park**, on the edge of the wide and rocky Bella Coola River floodplain.

Tweedsmuir Provincial Park
PARK

(☑ 250-398-4414; www.bcparks.ca; off Hwy 20) Spanning the Chilcotin and the east end of the valley, the southern portion of Tweedsmuir Provincial Park is the second-largest provincial park in BC. It's a seemingly barely charted place, perfect for challenging backcountry adventures. Day hikes off Hwy 20 in the valley follow trails into lush and untouched coastal rainforest. Campsites $20.

★ Kynoch Adventures
ADVENTURE, WILDLIFE

(☑ 250-982-2298; www.bcmountainlodge.com; 1900 Hwy 20, Hagensborg; tours from adult/child $90/45) Specializes in critter-spotting trips down local rivers and wilderness hikes. Highly recommended float trips to spot the valley's renowned **grizzly bear** population run from late August into October ($150 per person).

🛏 Sleeping

There are B&Bs and small inns along Hwy 20.

Rip Rap Camp CAMPGROUND $
(📞 250-982-2752; www.riprapcamp.com; 1854 Hwy 20, Hagensborg; campsites $20-28, cabins $60-125; ☻May-Oct; 🅿🐾) A much-lauded campground, Rip Rap has plenty of services and a great viewing deck overlooking the river.

Tallheo Cannery GUESTHOUSE $$
(📞 604-992-1424; www.bellacoolacannery.com; campsites $15, r incl transport $125) One of BC's most unusual places to stay is 3km across the inlet from Bella Coola in an old cannery. The adventurous will find that the views (stunning), explorations (it's an entire village with its own beach) and mystery (abandoned detritus of an old cannery) make this a fascinating stay. Transport for campers is $10; tours for day-trippers cost $50.

Bella Coola Mountain Lodge INN $$
(📞 250-982-2298; www.bcmountainlodge.com; 1900 Hwy 20, Hagensborg; r $100-160; 🅿@🐾) 📶 The 14 rooms, many with kitchen facilities, are huge and there's an excellent espresso bar. The owners also run Kynoch Adventures (p232), which offers river tours and wilderness hikes.

ℹ Information

The volunteer-run **Bella Coola Valley Tourism visitor center** (📞 250-799-5202; www.bellacoola.ca; 442 MacKenzie St, Copper Sun Art Gallery, Bella Coola; ☻10am-6pm Jun-Sep) has oodles of info and advice, including trail guides. The visitor center in Williams Lake is also a good resource.

The Bella Coola visitor center and your accommodations will point you to guides and gear for skiing, mountain biking, fishing, rafting and much more. Car repair, ATMs, laundry and groceries are available. Most tourist services are closed October to April.

ℹ Getting There & Away

BC Ferries (📞 888-223-3779; www.bcferries.com) links to Bella Coola. The route to reach Port Hardy or Prince Rupert (adult/child $200/100, car from $400) requires a transfer in Bella Bella, a small Inside Passage town – a major inconvenience. Schedules allow a trip every few days in summer (much less often in winter) and it can take 18 or more hours to reach the final port.

There are no buses along Hwy 20 from Williams Lake, but you can go by charter plane. **Pacific Coastal Airlines** (📞 800-663-2872; www.pacificcoastal.com) has daily one-hour flights from Vancouver.

NORTHERN BRITISH COLUMBIA

Northern British Columbia is where you'll truly feel that you've crossed that ethereal border into some place different. Nowhere else are the rich cultures of Canada's Aboriginal people so keenly felt, from the Haida on Haida Gwaii to the Tsimshian on the mainland. Nowhere else does land so exude mystery, whether it's the storm-shrouded coast and islands or the silent majesty of glaciers carving passages through entire mountain ranges. And nowhere else is so alive with fabled fauna, from orcas to moose to grizzlies.

It's also a region of promise. Highways such as the fabled Alaska or the awe-inspiring Stewart-Cassiar encourage adventure, discovery or even a new life. Here, your place next to nature will never be in doubt; you'll revel in your own insignificance.

Prince Rupert

POP 12,700

People are always 'discovering' Prince Rupert, and realising what a find it is. This intriguing city with a gorgeous harbor is not just a transportation hub for ferries heading south to Vancouver Island, west to Haida Gwaii and north to Alaska: it's a destination in its own right. It has two excellent museums, fine restaurants and a culture that draws much from its aboriginal heritage. Yet the city struggles to attract the huge cruise ships plying the Inside Passage.

It may rain 220 days a year, but that doesn't stop the drip-dry locals enjoying activities in the misty mountains and waterways. Originally the dream of Charles Hays, who built the railroad here before going to a watery grave on the *Titanic*, Rupert always seems one step behind a bright future. But its ship may finally have come in, or at least anchored offshore: the city's expanding container port speeds cheap tat from China to the US.

◎ Sights

A short walk from the center, **Cow Bay** is a delightful place for a stroll. The eponymous spotted decor is everywhere, but somehow avoids seeming clichéd. There are shops, cafes and a good view of the waterfront, especially from the cruise ship docks at the Atlin Terminal.

You'll see **totem poles** all around town; two flank the statue of Charlie Hays beside City Hall on 3rd Ave. Also watch around town for more than 30 huge **murals** adorning buildings. Noted artist Jeff King paints history and nature.

★ North Pacific Cannery National Historic Site   HISTORIC SITE

(☑ 250-628-3538; www.northpacificcannery.ca; 1889 Skeena Dr; adult/child $12/8; ☉ 10am-5pm daily Jul & Aug, Tue-Sun May, Jun & Sep) Explore the history of fishing and canning along the Skeena River. This fascinating all-wood complex was used from 1889 to 1968; exhibits document the miserable conditions of the workers, and tours cover the industrial process or cannery life. Prince Rupert Transit has bus service to the site. Situated about 20km south of Prince Rupert, near the town of Port Edward,

★ Museum of Northern BC   MUSEUM

(☑ 250-624-3207; www.museumofnorthernbc. com; 100 1st Ave W; adult/child $6/2; ☉ 9am-5pm daily Jun-Aug, Tue-Sat Sep-May) Residing in a building styled after an aboriginal longhouse, this museum is a don't-miss. It shows how local civilizations enjoyed sustainable cultures that lasted for thousands of years – you might say they were ahead of their time. The displays include a wealth of excellent Haida, Gitksan and Tsimshian art and plenty of info on totem poles. The bookshop is excellent.

★ Activities

Among the many local walks, a good place to start is the **Butze Rapids Trail**, a 4.5km loop beginning 3km south of town. It has interpretive signs.

Further afield, **Khutzeymateen Grizzly Bear Sanctuary** is a natural area home to more than 50 of the giants; it can be visited through **Prince Rupert Adventure Tours** (☑ 250-627-9166; www.adventuretours.net; 210 Cow Bay Rd, Atlin Terminal; bear tours $225, whale tours $115).

Skeena Kayaking   KAYAKING

(☑ 250-624-1921; www.skeenakayaking.ca; kayak rentals from $50) Offers both kayak rentals and custom tours of the area, which has a seemingly infinite variety of places to put in the water.

★ Sleeping

Rupert has a range of accommodations, including more than a dozen B&Bs. When all of the three ferries are docked, competition gets fierce, so book ahead.

Black Rooster Guesthouse   GUESTHOUSE $

(☑ 250-627-5337; www.blackrooster.ca; 501 6th Ave W; dm $35, r $65-150; P @ 🛜) This renovated house just 400m up the hill from the center has a patio and a bright common room. Rooms range from spartan singles to large apartments.

Pioneer Hostel   HOSTEL $

(☑ 250-624-2334; www.pioneerhostel.com; 167 3rd Ave E; dm $30-40, r $60-95; P @ 🛜) Located between Cow Bay and downtown, Pioneer Hostel has spotless, compact rooms accented with vibrant colors. There's a small kitchen and barbecue facilities out back.

Prince Rupert RV Campground   CAMPGROUND $

(☑ 250-624-5861; www.princeruperttrv.com; 1750 Park Ave; campsites from $21, RV sites $33-48; P 🛜) Located near the ferry terminal, this somewhat barren campground has 77 sites, hot showers, laundry facilities and a small playground.

★ Crest Hotel   HOTEL $$

(☑ 250-624-6771; www.cresthotel.bc.ca; 222 1st Ave W; r $130-300; P 🛜) Prince Rupert's premier hotel has harbor-view rooms that are worth every penny, right down to the built-in bay-window seats with loaner binoculars. Avoid the smallish rooms overlooking the parking lot. Suites are opulent.

Inn on the Harbour   MOTEL $$

(☑ 250-624-9107; www.innontheharbour.com; 720 1st Ave W; r incl breakfast $110-260; P 🛜) Sunsets may dazzle you to the point that you don't notice the humdrum exterior at this modern harbor-view motel. The 49 rooms have a plush, contemporary look.

Eagle Bluff B&B   B&B $$

(☑ 250-627-4955; www.eaglebluff.ca; 201 Cow Bay Rd; r $85-155; @ 🛜) In an ideal location on Cow Bay, this pier-side B&B is in a heritage building that has a striking red-and-white paint job. Inside, the seven rooms have harbor views – some quite spectacular; two share bathrooms.

★ Eating

Cowpuccino's   CAFE $

(☑ 250-627-1395; 25 Cow Bay Rd; coffee $2; ☉ 7am-9pm; 🛜) This woodsy local cafe will make you forget the rain with its coffee and fine selection of baked goods (great cookies) and sandwiches. Good for picnics or eating in.

★ Charley's Lounge · PUB FOOD $$

(☑250-624-6771; www.cresthotel.bc.ca; 222 1st Ave W, Crest Hotel; mains $12-25; ☺noon-10pm) Locals flock to trade gossip while gazing out over the harbor from the heated patio. The food matches the view: the pub menu features some of Rupert's best seafood.

Fukasaku · JAPANESE $$

(☑250-627-7874; www.fukasaku.ca; 215 Cow Rd; mains $15-30; ☺5-8:30pm) 🍴 This excellent sushi place has a menu crafted with certified sustainability in mind. Enjoy uberfresh seafood in rolls, sashimi, *donburi* etc. The dining area is properly minimalist.

Smiles Seafood · SEAFOOD $$

(☑250-624-3072; www.smilesseafoodcafe.ca; 113 Cow Bay Rd; mains $8-30; ☺9am-9pm) Since 1934 Smiles has served classic, casual seafood meals. Slide into a vinyl booth and enjoy a shrimp club sandwich or a fresh halibut steak. Also has fine diner-style breakfasts.

Cow Bay Café · ITALIAN $$

(☑250-627-1212; www.cowbaycafe.com; 205 Cow Bay Rd; mains $16-25; ☺11:30am-2pm & 5-9pm Tue-Sat, 1-8pm Sun) This bistro is right in Cow Bay and has wraparound water views. Serves a menu that's heavy on red sauce.

Waterfront Restaurant · FUSION $$$

(☑250-624-6771; www.cresthotel.bc.ca; 222 1st Ave W, Crest Hotel; mains $15-40; ☺6:30am-9pm Mon-Fri, 7am-9pm Sat & Sun) Nab a table with a fantastic waterfront view and dig into delicious, fresh ingredients used with color and flair.

❶ Information

Prince Rupert Visitor Center (☑250-624-5637; www.visitprincerupert.com; 215 Cow Bay Rd, Atlin Terminal; ☺9am-5pm) Has regional info. Located next to a display promoting the ever-growing port.

❶ Getting There & Away

The ferry and train terminals are 3km southwest of the center.

AIR

Prince Rupert Airport (☑250-622-2222; www.ypr.ca) Located on Digby Island, across the harbor from town. The trip involves a bus and ferry; pickup is at the Highliner Hotel (815 1st Ave) about two hours before flight time. Confirm all the details with your airline or the airport.

Air Canada Jazz (☑888-247-2262; www.aircanada.com) Flies to Vancouver.

BOAT

Alaska Marine Highway System (☑250-627-1744, 800-642-0066; www.ferryalaska.com) One or two ferries each week ply the spectacular Inside Passage to the Yukon gateways of Haines and Skagway in Alaska.

BC Ferries (☑250-386-3431; www.bcferries.com) Sails the Inside Passage run to Port Hardy, hailed for its amazing scenery. There are three services per week in summer and one per week in winter on the *Northern Expedition*.

BUS

Greyhound Canada (p196) Buses depart for Prince George ($142, 10½ hours) once a day in summer, less often other times. Check to see if a mooted **BC Transit bus** (www.bctransit.com) is also running on this route.

TRAIN

VIA Rail (p107) Operates tri-weekly services to Prince George (12½ hours) and, after an overnight stop, Jasper in the Rockies. Much of the run is spectacular, especially between Rupert and Smithers.

Haida Gwaii

Haida Gwaii forms a dagger-shaped archipelago of some 450 islands lying 80km west of the BC coast, and offers a magical trip for those who make the effort. The number-one attraction here is remote Gwaii Haanas National Park, which makes up the bottom third of the archipelago. Attention has long focused on the many unique species of flora and fauna to the extent that 'Canada's Galápagos' is a popular moniker. But each year it becomes more apparent that the real soul of the islands is the Haida culture itself.

Haida reverence for the environment is protecting the last stands of superb old-growth rainforests, where the spruce and cedars are some of the world's largest. Amid this sparsely populated, wild and rainy place are bald eagles, bears and much more wildlife. Offshore in marine-protected waters, sea lions, whales and orcas abound, and once-rare right whales and sea otters have been spotted.

◉ Sights

The Haida Gwaii portion of the **Yellowhead Hwy** (Hwy 16) heads 110km north from Queen Charlotte (known as QCC) past Skidegate, Tlell and Port Clements. The last was where a golden spruce tree, famous for its colour, that stood on the banks of the Yakoun River was cut down by a demented forester in 1997. The incident is detailed in the best-selling *The Golden Spruce* by John Vaillant, an excellent book on the islands and Haida culture.

All along the road to **Masset**, look for seaside pullouts, oddball boutiques and cafes that are typical of the islands' character.

★ **Gwaii Haanas National Park Reserve, National Marine Conservation Area Reserve & Haida Heritage Site**   NATIONAL PARK
(☑ 250-559-8818; www.parkscanada.ca/gwaii haanas; Haida Gwaii) This huge Unesco World Heritage site with a name that's a mouthful encompasses Moresby and 137 smaller islands at its southern end. It combines a time-capsule look at abandoned Haida villages with hot springs, amazing natural beauty and some of the continent's best kayaking.

Access to the park is by boat or plane only. A visit demands a decent amount of advance planning and usually requires several days. From May to September, you must obtain a reservation, unless you're with a tour operator.

Archaeological finds have documented more than 500 ancient Haida sites, including villages and burial caves throughout the islands. The most famous village is **SGang Gwaay** (Ninstints) on Anthony Island, where rows of weathered totem poles stare eerily out to sea. Other major sights include the ancient village of **Skedans**, on Louise Island, and **Hotspring Island**, whose natural hot springs are back on after being disrupted by earthquakes in 2012. The sites are protected by Haida Gwaii caretakers, who live on the islands in summer.

In 2013 the **Gwaii Haanas Legacy Pole** was raised at Windy Bay, the first new pole in the protected area in 130 years.

Contact Parks Canada (p238) with questions. The website has links to the essential annual trip planner. Any visitor not on a guided tour must attend a free orientation at the park office. All visitors must register.

The number of daily reservations is limited: plan well in advance. User fees apply (adult/child $20/10 per day). Fees are waived if you have a Parks Canada Season Excursion Pass. A few much-coveted standby spaces are made available daily: call Parks Canada.

The easiest way to get into the park is with a tour company. Parks Canada can provide you with lists of operators; tours last from one day to two weeks. Many can also set you up with rental kayaks (average per day/week $60/300) and gear for independent travel.

★ **Haida Heritage Centre at Kay Llnagaay**   MUSEUM
(☑ 250-559-7885; www.haidaheritagecentre.com; Hwy 16, Skidegate; adult/child $16/5; ☺ 10am-6pm Mon-Wed, to 8pm Thu-Sun Jun-Aug, 10am-5pm Tue-Sat Sep-May) One of the top attractions in the north is this marvelous cultural center. With exhibits on history, wildlife and culture, it would be enough reason to visit the islands just by itself. The rich traditions of the Haida are fully explored in galleries, programs and work areas, where contemporary artists create works such as the totem poles lining the shore. Look for the remarkable model of Skidegate before colonial times.

In summer there are worthwhile free tours of the collection. There are also frequent talks and walks by Parks Canada rangers.

Naikoon Provincial Park   PARK
(☑ 250-626-5115; www.bcparks.ca; off Hwy 16) Much of the island's northeastern side is devoted to the beautiful 726-sq-km Naikoon Provincial Park, which combines sand dunes and low sphagnum bogs, surrounded by stunted and gnarled lodgepole pine, and red and yellow cedar. The starkly beautiful **beaches** on the north coast feature strong winds, pounding surf and flotsam from across the Pacific. They can be reached via the stunning 26km-long Tow Hill Rd, east of Masset.

Dixon Entrance Maritime Museum   MUSEUM
(☑ 250-626-6066; 2182 Collinson Ave; adult/child $3/free; ☺ 1-6pm daily Jun-Aug, 2-4pm Sat & Sun Sep-May) Housed in what was once the local hospital, the museum features exhibits on the history of this seafaring community, with displays on shipbuilding, medical pioneers, military history, and nearby clam and crab canneries.

Port Clements Museum   MUSEUM
(☑ 250-557-4576; www.portclementsmuseum.ca; 45 Bayview Dr; adult/child $3/free; ☺ 10am-4pm Jun–mid-Sep, 2-4pm Sat & Sun mid-Sep–May) Learn about early logging practices and check out toys and tools from pioneering days. Nearby is the fenced-in cutting of the famous but felled **Golden Spruce**. It's alive but rather shrub-like.

🏃 Activities

Away from the park, Haida Gwaii has myriad other natural places to explore on land and sea.

Yakoun Lake   HIKING

(☑ 250-557-6810) Hike 20 minutes through ancient stands of spruce and cedar to pristine **Yakoun Lake**, a large wilderness lake towards the west side of Graham Island. A small beach near the trail is shaded by gnarly Sitka alders. Dare to take a dip in the bracing waters, or just enjoy the sweeping views.

The trailhead is at the end of a rough track off a branch from the main dirt-and-gravel logging road between Queen Charlotte (QCC) and Port Clements – watch for signs for the lake, about 20km north of QCC. It runs for 70km. On weekdays, phone for info on active logging trucks. This is 4WD country.

★**Moresby Explorers**   ADVENTURE

(☑ 800-806-7633, 250-637-2215; www.moresby-explorers.com; Sandspit; 1-day tours from $215) Offers one-day Zodiac tours, including the Louise Island trip that takes in the town of Skedans and its important totem poles, as well as much longer trips (the four-day trip is highly recommended). Also rents kayaks and gear, and provides logistics.

Archipelago Ventures   KAYAKING

(☑ 250-652-4913, 888-559-8317; www.tourhaidagwaii.com; 6-day tours from $2350) Runs multi-day kayak trips that fully explore the Gwaii Haanas National Park Reserve. Guests are housed on the mothership MV *Island Bay*, and emphasis is placed on building a cohesive group, eg chores are shared, etc. Itineraries are flexible and the guides take care to see that guests' desires are met.

Haida Style Expeditions   CULTURAL

(☑ 250-637-1151; www.haidastyle.com; tours $275-375; ☺ May–mid-Sep) Buzz through the Gwaii Haanas National Park Reserve in a large inflatable boat. This Haida-run outfit runs four different one-day tours (eight to 12 hours) that together take in the most important sights in the park.

🛏 Sleeping

Small inns and B&Bs are mostly found on Graham Island. There are numerous choices in Queen Charlotte (QCC) and Masset, with many in between and along the spectacular north coast. Naikoon Provincial Park has two campgrounds, including a dramatic, windswept one on deserted Agate Beach, 23km east of Masset.

Agate Beach Campground   CAMPGROUND $

(☑ 250-557-4390; www.env.gov.bc.ca/bcparks; Tow Hill Rd, North Shore, Naikoon Provincial Park; campsites $18; P) This stunning, wind-whipped campground is right on the beach on the north shore. Frolic on the sand, hunt for its namesake rocks and see if you can snare some flotsam.

★**Premier Creek Lodging**   INN $$

(☑ 250-559-8415, 888-322-3388; www.qcislands.net/premier; 3101 3rd Ave, QCC; dm from $30, r $50-160; P 🐾) Dating from 1910, this friendly Queen Charlotte lodge run by Lenore has eight beds in a hostel building out back, and 12 rooms in the main building that range from tiny but great-value singles to spacious rooms with views, kitchens and porches.

THE GREAT BEAR RAINFOREST

It's the last major tract of coastal temperate rainforest left on the planet. The Great Bear Rainforest is a wild region of islands, fjords and towering peaks. Covering 64,000 sq km (7% of British Columbia), it stretches south from Alaska along the BC coast and Haida Gwaii to roughly Campbell River on Vancouver Island (which isn't itself part of the forest). The forests and waters are remarkably rich in life: whales, salmon, eagles, elk, otters and more thrive. Remote river valleys are lined with forests of old Sitka spruce, Pacific silver fir and various cedars that are often 100m tall and 1500 years old.

In 2016, BC's provincial government announced that 85% of the Great Bear Rainforest region would be permanently protected from industrial logging. However, the area is still under threat from a proposed Northern Gateway Pipelines project. For an introduction to the campaign to save the area, head to www.savethegreatbear.org.

From Bella Coola you can arrange boat trips and treks to magical places in the Great Bear, including hidden rivers where you might see a rare **Kermode bear**, a white-furred offshoot of the black bear known in tribal legend as the 'spirit bear' and the namesake of the rainforest.

HAIDA HISTORY

Haida Gwaii, which means 'Islands of the People,' is home to the Haida, one of the most advanced and powerful First Nations. The people suffered terribly after Westerners arrived; however, their culture is resurgent and can be found across the islands in myriad ways beyond their iconic totem poles, and contributes greatly to the protection of the islands' spectacular natural environment.

Haida Gwaii was formerly known as Queen Charlotte Islands, which name was officially dropped as a name in 2010.

North Beach Cabins   CABIN $$

(☑250-557-2415; www.northbeachcabins.com; Km 16, Tow Hill Rd, North Shore; cabins $100-175; P) ✈ Tucked into the dunes of beautiful North Beach are six cozy escapes. You're totally off the grid, but thanks to propane you can cook, which will be about the only diversion from the fabulous views and endless sandy strolls.

All The Beach You Can Eat   CABIN $$

(☑250-626-9091; www.allthebeachyoucaneat.com; Km 15, Tow Hill Rd, North Shore; cabins $100-190; P) ✈ On beautiful North Beach, five cabins are perched in the dunes, back from the wide swath of sand that runs for miles east and west. One, the lovely little Sweety Pie, has views that seem to reach to Japan. Similar to other properties with rental cabins out here, there is no electricity; cooking and lighting are fueled by propane. It's off the grid and out of this world.

Copper Beech House   B&B $$

(☑250-626-5441; www.copperbeechhouse.com; 1590 Delkatla Rd, Masset; r $100-160; P🔊) This legendary B&B in a rambling old house on Masset Harbor is owned by poet Susan Musgrave. It has five unique rooms, and there's always something amazing cooking in the kitchen.

✗ Eating

The best selection of restaurants is in Queen Charlotte (QCC), and there are also a few in Skidegate and Masset. Ask at the visitor centers about local Haida feasts, where you'll enjoy the best salmon and blueberries you've ever had. Good supermarkets are found in QCC and Masset.

Moon Over Naikoon   BAKERY $

(☑250-626-5064; 16443 Tow Hill Rd, Masset; snacks from $3; ⊘8am-5pm Jun-Aug) Embodying the spirit of its location, on a road to the end of everything, this tiny community center–cum–bakery is housed in an old school bus in a clearing about 6km from Masset. The baked goods and coffee are brilliant.

Queen B's   CAFE $

(☑250-559-4463; 3201 Wharf St, QCC; mains $3-10; ⊘9am-5pm) This funky place in Queen Charlotte excels at baked goods, which emerge from the oven all day long. There are tables with water views outside, and lots of local art inside.

★ Charters Restaurant   SEAFOOD $$

(☑250-626-3377; 1650 Delkatla Rd, Masset; mains $15-30; ⊘5-9pm Wed-Sun) The numbers are small: six tables, three entrees. But the pleasure is great: simply delicious food, such as seafood fettuccine and fresh local halibut. The changing menu also features burgers, ribs, salads and more. The attention to detail is extraordinary: the greens used to ornament plates are grown under lights in the kitchen. Reserve ahead.

Haida House   SEAFOOD $$

(☑855-557-4600; www.haidahouse.com; 2087 Beitush Rd, Tlell; mains $20-30; ⊘5-7:30pm Tue-Sun mid-May–mid-Sep) This Haida-run restaurant has excellent, creative seafood and other dishes with island accents, such as Haida favorites with berries. Also rents plush rooms.

ℹ Information

Download, browse online or pick up a free copy of the encyclopedic annual *Haida Gwaii Visitors Guide* (www.gohaidagwaii.ca).

Parks Canada (☑250-559-8818, reservations 877-559-8818; www.parkscanada.ca/gwaii-haanas; Haida Heritage Centre at Kay Llnagaay, Skidegate; ⊘office 8:30am-noon & 1-4:30pm Mon-Fri) Has a lot of information online.

QCC Visitor Centre (☑250-559-8316; www.queencharlottevisitorcentre.com; 3220 Wharf St, QCC; ⊘9am-8pm Mon-Sat, noon-8pm Sun May-Sep, shorter hours other times) Handy visitor center that can make advance excursion bookings by phone.

Sandspit Airport Visitor Center (☑250-637-5362; Sandspit Airport; ⊘9:30-11:30am & 1-4pm) Useful visitor center.

❶ Getting There & Away

The main airport for Haida Gwaii is at Sandspit on Moresby Island, 12km east of the ferry landing at Aliford Bay. Note that reaching the airport from Graham Island is time-consuming: eg if your flight is at 3:30pm, you'll need to line up at the car ferry at Skidegate Landing at 12:30pm (earlier in summer). There's also a small airport at Masset.

Air Canada (www.aircanada.com) flies daily between Sandspit and Vancouver.

The **BC Ferries** (☑ 250-386-3431; www. bcferries.com) service is the most popular way to reach the islands. Mainland ferries dock at Skidegate Landing on Graham Island, which houses 80% of residents. Services run between Prince Rupert and Skidegate Landing five times a week in summer and three times a week in winter on the *Northern Adventure*. Travel time is six to seven hours; fares cost adults $39 to $48, children half-price, and for cars $139 to $169. Cabins are useful for overnight schedules (from $90).

❶ Getting Around

The main road on Graham Island is Hwy 16, which is fully paved. It links Skidegate with Masset, 101km north, passing the small towns of Tlell and Port Clements. The principal town is Queen Charlotte (previously Queen Charlotte City and still known by its old QCC acronym), 7km west of Skidegate. Off paved Hwy 16, most roads are gravel or worse. There is no public transit.

BC Ferries link Graham and Moresby Islands at Skidegate Landing and Alliford Bay (adult/child $11/5.50, cars from $25, 20 minutes, every two hours from 7am to 10pm). Schedules seem designed to inconvenience air passengers.

Eagle Transit (☑ 250-559-4461, 877-747-4461; www.eagletransit.net; airport shuttle adult/child $30/22) buses meet Sandspit flights and serve Skidegate and QCC.

Renting a car can cost roughly the same ($60 to $100 per day) as bringing one over on the ferry. Local companies include **Budget** (☑ 250-637-5688; www.budget.com; Sandspit Airport). There are several small, locally owned firms.

You can rent bikes at the small **Sandspit Airport Visitor Center** (p238) for $30 per day and take them across to Graham Island on the ferry.

Prince Rupert to Prince George

You can cover the 725km on Hwy 16 between BC's Princes in a day or a week. There's nothing that's an absolute must-see, but there's much to divert and cause you to pause if so inclined. With the notable exception of

Skeena River, the scenery along much of the road won't fill your memory card, but it is a pleasing mix of mountains and rivers.

Prince Rupert to Smithers

For the first 150km out of Prince Rupert, Hwy 16 hugs the wide and wild **Skeena River**. This is four-star scenic driving and you'll see glaciers and jagged peaks across the waters.

Tatty **Terrace** is nobody's idea of a reward at the end of the stretch. From Terrace, Hwy 16 continues 93km east to Kitwanga, where the **Stewart-Cassiar Hwy** (Hwy 37) strikes north towards the Yukon and Alaska.

Just east of Kitwanga is the **Hazelton** area, comprising New Hazelton, Hazelton and South Hazelton. It's the center of some interesting aboriginal sites, including **'Ksan Historical Village & Museum** (☑ 250-842-5544; www.ksan.org; off Hwy 16, Hazelton; from $2; ⊙ 10am-9pm Jun-Aug, shorter hours Sep-Jul). The re-created site of the Gitksan people features longhouses, a museum, various outbuildings and totem poles. The narrated tour ($10) is a must.

Smithers

Smithers is a largish town with a cute old downtown, roughly halfway between Prince Rupert and Prince George. It's the hub of the vibrant Bulkley Valley cultural scene.

Great hiking is found at **Babine Mountains Provincial Park** (☑ 250-847-7329; www.bcparks.ca; Old Babine Lake Rd) nearby. It's a 324-sq-km park with trails to glacier-fed lakes and subalpine meadows. Backcountry cabins cost $5 to $10 per person.

You can't beat the location of **Stork Nest Inn** (☑ 250-847-3831; www.storknestinn.com; 1485 Main St; r $90-110; [P][✳][🖥]), right across Hwy 16 from the center. The 23 rooms are large, and a good full breakfast is included. The owners offer great area advice.

All sorts of joy emerges from **Caravan** (☑ 778-210-1074; www.facebook.com/caravanhwy16; cnr Main St & Broadway Ave; mains $8-14; ⊙ 11am-3pm Tue-Sat), an excellent food truck that draws up in a small park in the heart of town. The menu changes daily and uses what's fresh from the many local suppliers. If the steak sandwich with onion rings is on, order it!

Named after the Mountain Pine Beetle, the **Bugwood Bean** (☑ 250-877-3505; www.bugwoodbean.com; 2nd & Main Sts; coffee $2; ⊙ 7:30am-4:30pm; 🖥) has homemade baked goods and great organic, fresh-roasted coffee.

Smithers to Prince George

Heading south and then east from Smithers along Hwy 16 for 146km will have you passing through **Burns Lake**, the center of a popular fishing district. Continue another 128km towards **Vanderhoof**, where you can either detour north or carry on along Hwy 16 for 100km toward Prince George. The highway passes through a region filled with dead trees typical of those seen across the north. These dark-grey specimens are victims of mountain pine beetles, whose explosive population growth is linked to comparatively milder winters due to climate change. Note the many sawmills processing the dead trees.

From Vanderhoof, Hwy 27 heads 66km north to **Fort St James National Historic Site** (☑ 250-996-7191; www.pc.gc.ca; Kwah Rd; adult/child $8/4; ☉ 9am-5pm Jun-Sep). The former Hudson's Bay Company trading post that's on the tranquil southeastern shore of Stuart Lake has been restored to its 1896 glory.

Prince George

POP 72,700

In First Nations times, before outsiders arrived, Prince George was called Lheidli T'Enneh, which means 'people of the confluence,' an appropriate name given that the Nechako and Fraser Rivers converge here. Today the name would be just as fitting, although it's the confluence of highways that matters most. A mill town since 1807, it is a vital BC crossroads, and you're unlikely to visit the north without passing through at least once.

Hwy 97 from the south cuts through the center of town on its way north to Dawson Creek (360km) and the Alaska Hwy. Hwy 16 becomes Victoria St as it runs through town westward to Prince Rupert (724km), and east to Jasper (380km) and Edmonton. The downtown, no beauty-contest winner, is compact and has some good restaurants.

◉ Sights

Prince George Railway & Forestry Museum MUSEUM
(☑ 250-563-7351; www.pgrfm.bc.ca; 850 River Rd, Cottonwood Island Nature Park; adult/child $8/5; ☉ 10am-5pm daily Jun-Aug, 11am-4pm Tue-Sat Sep-May) This museum honors trains, the beaver and local lore. It's located in **Cottonwood**

Island Nature Park, which has sylvan walks alongside the river.

Exploration Place MUSEUM
(☑ 250-562-1612; www.theexplorationplace.com; 333 Becott Pl, Fort George Park; adult/child $11/8; ☉ 9am-5pm; ⊞) Southeast of downtown (follow 20th Ave east of Gorse St), Exploration Place has various kid-friendly galleries devoted to science, and natural and cultural history.

🛏 Sleeping

Hwy 97 (Central St) makes an arc around the center, where you'll find legions of modest motels.

97 Motor Inn MOTEL $
(☑ 250-562-6010; www.97motorinn.ca; 2713 Spruce St; r $70-100; ⓟ ❋ 🛜) This modern motel is located on – yes, you guessed it – Hwy 97, near the junction with Hwy 16. Some of the 19 basic rooms have balconies and kitchens.

Economy Inn MOTEL $
(☑ 250-563-7106; www.economyinn.ca; 1915 3rd Ave; r $65-95; ⓟ ❋ 🛜) Close to the center, this simple blue-and-white motel has 30 rooms with fridges, microwaves and a spa bath. Celebrate your savings on accommodation with a Dairy Queen dip cone from across the street.

Bee Lazee Campground CAMPGROUND $
(☑ 250-963-7263; www.beelazee.ca; 15910 Hwy 97 S; campsites $25-32; ☉ May-Sep; ⓟ 🛜 ♨) About 15km south of town, this RV-centric place features full facilities, including (free) hot showers, fire pits and laundry.

Coast Inn of the North HOTEL $$
(☑ 250-563-0121; www.coasthotels.com; 770 Brunswick St; r $100-160; ⓟ ❋ 🛜 ♨) One of the nicest stays in a town with few options, the Coast is a high-rise with 153 very comfy rooms, some with balconies. There's an indoor pool, which is handy during the long months of cold temperatures. It's close to the center and its nightlife.

🍴 Eating

★ Nancy O's PUB FOOD $$
(☑ 250-562-8066; www.nancyos.ca; 1261 3rd Ave; mains $10-25; ☉ 11am-late Mon-Fri, from 10am Sat & Sun) Nancy O's may make you want to spend two nights in Prince George. Locally sourced ingredients are combined to create fabulous food: burgers, veggie specials, a

NORTH TO THE YUKON

There are three main ways to go north from BC by vehicle. All are good routes, so you have several ways of creating a circle itinerary to the Yukon, and even Alaska.

Alaska Highway

Proposed for many years but not constructed until WWII, this historic and epic route starts in Dawson Creek (364km northeast of Prince George) and weaves through northeast BC to Watson Lake (944km). It's most convenient for those coming from Edmonton and the east.

Stewart-Cassiar Highway

The Stewart-Cassiar (Hwy 37) runs 700km through wild scenery from the junction with Hwy 16, 240km east of Prince Rupert and 468km west of Prince George. A side trip to the incomparable glaciers around Stewart is essential and easy. This route is convenient for people coming from most areas of BC, Alberta and the western US. It ends at the Alaska Hwy, near Watson Lake, in the Yukon.

Alaska Marine Highway System

We love Alaska's car ferries (www.ferryalaska.com) that sail the Inside Passage. Free of frills, they let you simply relax and view one of the world's great shows of marine life while enjoying the same scenery that cruise-ship passengers spend thousands to see. You can take a three-day cruise on boats heading from Bellingham (north of Seattle), in Washington, US, to Haines and Skagway in southeast Alaska, on the Yukon border. Or catch ferries in Prince Rupert for service to those same two Alaskan towns. The ferries, especially cabins, fill up fast in summer, so reserve.

great avocado salad and a truly amazing *steak frites*. The bottled beer selection is fab (Belgian and BC), and there's live music and DJs many nights. The vibe is hipster-comfy.

Cimo MEDITERRANEAN **$$**
(☑ 250-564-7975; www.cimo.ca; 601 Victoria St; mains $12-30; ⊙ 11:30am-2pm & 5-9:30pm Mon-Sat) The authentic Mediterranean dishes never disappoint here. Dine or simply enjoy a glass of BC wine in the stylish interior or outside on the patio. Much of the produce comes from Cimo's kitchen garden. Great BC wine list and specials.

❶ Information

Prince George Visitor Center (☑ 250-562-3700; www.tourismpg.com; 1300 1st Ave, VIA Rail Station; ⊙ 8am-6pm Jun-Aug, shorter hours other times; ☎) This excellent visitor center can make bookings, such as ferry tickets. Loans out free (!) bikes and fishing rods.

❶ Getting There & Away

Prince George Airport (☑ 250-963-2400; www.pgairport.ca; 4141 Airport Rd) is off Hwy 97. **Air Canada Jazz** (☑ 888-247-2262; www.aircanada.com) and **Westjet** (☑ 888-937-8538; www.westjet.com) serve Vancouver.

Greyhound Canada (☑ 800-661-8747; www.greyhound.ca; 1566 12th Ave) Bus services may run less than daily in winter. Services include Dawson Creek ($85, six hours), Jasper ($70, 5½ hours), Prince Rupert ($142, 10½ hours) and Vancouver ($93, 11 hours).

VIA Rail (www.viarail.ca; 1300 1st Ave) Trains head west three times a week to Prince Rupert (12½ hours) and east three times a week to Jasper (7½ hours). Through passengers from either direction must overnight in Prince George.

Prince George to Alberta

Look for lots of wildlife as well as some good parks along the 380km stretch of Hwy 16 that links Prince George with Jasper, just over the Alberta border. **McBride** is good for a pause.

About 113km east of Prince George is the site of BC's newest park, **Ancient Forest/Chun T'oh Whudujut Park** (www.ancientcedar.ca; off Hwy 16). The Ancient Forest Trail leads 1km to some real behemoths of the temperate inland rainforest: old-growth red cedars and hemlocks that reach heights of 60m, are more than 1000 years old and are 16m in circumference. Short trails, including a 500m boardwalk, access the trees.

WORTH A TRIP

STEWART & HYDER

Awesome. Yes, the word is almost an automatic cliché, but when you gaze upon the **Salmon Glacier**, you'll understand why it was coined in the first place. This horizon-spanning expanse of ice is more than enough reason to make the 67km detour off Hwy 37; the turnoff is 158km north of Meziadin Junction. In fact, your first confirmation comes when you encounter the iridescent blue expanse of the **Bear Glacier** looming over Hwy 37A.

The sibling border towns of **Stewart** and **Hyder**, Alaska, perch on the coast at the head of the Portland Canal. Stewart, the much more businesslike of the pair, has excellent places to stay and eat.

Among several campgrounds and motels, Stewart's real star is **Ripley Creek Inn**.

Hyder ekes out an existence as a 'ghost town.' Some 40,000 tourists come through every summer, avoiding any border hassle from US customs officers (because there aren't any), although going back to Stewart you'll pass through beady-eyed Canadian customs. It has muddy streets and two businesses of note: the **Glacier Inn**, a bar you'll enjoy if you ignore the touristy 'get Hyderized' shot-swilling shtick; and the **Seafood Express**.

The enormous, horizon-filling Salmon Glacier is 33km beyond Hyder, up a winding dirt road that's OK for cars when it's dry. Some 3km into the drive, you'll pass the **Fish Creek viewpoint**, an area alive with bears and doomed salmon in late summer.

Northern BC's major mountain attraction abuts Jasper National Park, but on the BC side of the border. Uncrowded **Mt Robson Provincial Park** (Map p90; ☑ 250-964-2243; www.bcparks.ca; off Hwy 16) has steep glaciers, prolific wildlife and backcountry hiking that is overshadowed by its famous neighbor. Campsites are available ($22 to $28).

Stewart-Cassiar Highway

The 700km Stewart-Cassiar Hwy (Hwy 37) is a viable and ever-more-popular route between BC and the Yukon and Alaska. But it's more than just a means to get from Hwy 16 (via Meziadin Junction) in BC to the Alaska Hwy in the Yukon (7km west of Watson Lake) – it's a window onto one of the largest remaining wild and woolly parts of the province. It's also the road to Stewart (p242), a near-mandatory detour to glaciers, and more.

Gitanyow, a mere 15km north of Hwy 16, has an unparalleled collection of totem poles and you can often see carvers creating another.

Boya Lake Provincial Park (☑ 250-771-4591; www.bcparks.ca; off Hwy 37), a serene little park less than 90km south of the Yukon border, surrounds Boya Lake, which seems to glow turquoise. You can camp on the shore (campsites $20).

🍴 Sleeping & Eating

There's camping along the highway and a motel in Dease Lake. Otherwise stay in Smithers, Stewart or Watson Lake.

Ripley Creek Inn   GUESTHOUSE $$
(☑ 250-636-2344; www.ripleycreekinn.com; 306 5th Ave, Stewart; r $60-150; P 🛜) The 40 rooms in various heritage buildings are decorated with new and old items; decor varies greatly. There's a huge collection of vintage toasters.

Seafood Express   SEAFOOD $$
(☑ 250-636-9011; Hyder, Alaska; mains $12-25; ☺noon-8pm Jun-Sep) Serves the tastiest seafood ever cooked in a school bus.

Glacier Inn   BAR
(☑ 250-636-9248; International St, Hyder, Alaska; ☺noon-late) You'll enjoy this grizzled, old bar if you ignore the touristy 'get Hyderized' shot-swilling shtick and settle in with the crusty but affable locals.

ℹ Getting There & Away

All major roads linking to the Stewart-Cassiar Hwy are in excellent condition. Except for areas of construction, the highway is sealed and suitable for all vehicles. At any point, you should not be surprised to see bears, moose and other large mammals. Note that the region's untouched status is waning as projects such as the invasive Northwest Transmission Line are carved across the wilderness.

There's never a distance greater than 150km between gas stations. BC provides **road condition reports** (☑ 800-550-4997; www.drivebc.ca). When it's dry in summer, people drive from Stewart to Whitehorse (1043km) or from Smithers to Watson Lake (854km) in a single day, taking advantage of the long hours of daylight. But this a real haul, so prepare.

Alaska Highway

Even in Prince George you can start to smell the Alaska Hwy. As you travel north along Hwy 97, the mountains and forests give way to gentle rolling hills and farmland. Nearing Dawson Creek (360km), the landscape resembles the prairies of Alberta. There's no need to dawdle.

From **Chetwynd** you can take Hwy 29 along the wide vistas of the Peace River valley north via Hudson's Hope to join the Alaska Hwy north of Fort St John.

Dawson Creek is *the* starting point (Mile 0) for the Alaska Hwy and it capitalizes on this at the **Alaska Highway House** (☑ 250-782-4714; 10201 10th St, Dawson Creek; by donation; ⊙ 9am-5pm), an engaging museum in a vintage building overlooking the milepost. The nearby downtown blocks make a good stroll and have free wi-fi, and there's a **walking tour** of the old buildings. The **visitor center** (☑ 866-645-3022, 250-782-9595; www.tourismdawsoncreek.com; 900 Alaska Ave, Dawson Creek; ⊙ 8am-5:30pm mid-May–Sep, shorter hours other times; ☎) is housed in the old train station and has lots of Alaska Hwy info. Note that this corner of BC stays on Mountain Standard Time year-round. So in winter, the time is the same as Alberta, one hour later

than BC. In summer, the time is the same as Vancouver.

Now begins the big drive. Heading northwest from Dawson Creek, Fort St John is a stop best not made. In fact, the entire 430km to **Fort Nelson** gives little hint of the wonders to come.

Fort Nelson has seen boom and bust in recent years with the fluctuation of oil prices. This is the last place of any size on the Alaska Hwy until Whitehorse in the Yukon – most 'towns' along the route are little more than a gas station and motel or two.

Around 140km west of Fort Nelson, **Stone Mountain Provincial Park** (☑ 250-427-5452; www.bcparks.ca; off Hwy 97) has hiking trails, with backcountry camping and a campground. The stretches of road often have dense concentrations of wildlife, including moose, bears, bison, wolves, elk and much more. From here, the Alaska Hwy rewards whatever effort it took getting this far.

A further 75km brings you to **Muncho Lake Provincial Park** (www.bcparks.ca; off Hwy 97), centered on the emerald-green lake of the same name and boasting spruce forests, vast rolling mountains and some truly breathtaking scenery. There are two campgrounds by the lake, plus a few lodges scattered along the highway.

Finally, **Liard River Hot Springs Provincial Park** (☑ 250-427-5452; www.bcparks.ca; off Hwy 97; adult/child $5/3) has a steamy ecosystem that allows a whopping 250 species of plants to thrive. After a long day in the car, you'll thrive, too, in the soothing waters. From here it's 220km to Watson Lake and the Yukon.

BRITISH COLUMBIA ALASKA HIGHWAY

Yukon Territory

Best Places to Eat

➡ Drunken Goat Taverna (p264)

➡ Klondike Kate's (p264)

➡ Klondike Rib & Salmon (p251)

➡ Antoinette's (p251)

Best Places to Sleep

➡ Coast High Country Inn (p250)

➡ Robert Service Campground (p250)

➡ Bombay Peggy's (p263)

➡ Klondike Kate's (p263)

➡ Kathleen Lake Campground (p256)

Why Go?

This vast and thinly populated wilderness, where most four-legged species far outnumber humans, has a grandeur and beauty only appreciated by experience. Few places in the world today have been so unchanged over the course of time. Aboriginal people, having eked out survival for thousands of years, hunt and trap as they always have. The Klondike Gold Rush of 1898 was the Yukon's high point of population, yet even its heritage is ephemeral, easily erased by time.

Any visit will mean much time outdoors: Canada's five tallest mountains and the world's largest ice fields below the Arctic are all within Kluane National Park, while canoe expeditions down the Yukon River are epic. And don't forget the people: get set to appreciate the offbeat vibe of Dawson City and the bustle of Whitehorse, and join the growing numbers of people who've discovered the Yukon thanks to TV shows such as *Yukon Gold* and *Dr Oakley: Yukon Vet*.

When to Go
Dawson City

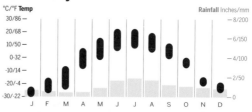

Nov–Apr Days of snowy winter solitude end when the river ice breaks up.

Jun–Aug Summers are short but warm, with long hours of daylight.

Sep You can feel the north winds coming. Trees erupt in color, crowds thin and places close.

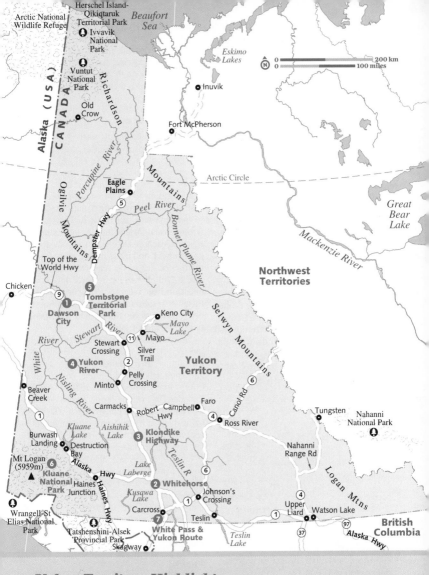

Yukon Territory Highlights

1 Dawson City (p259) Getting caught up in the modern vibe of Canada's funkiest historic town.

2 Whitehorse (p247) Spending an extra day in this surprising city filled with culture.

3 Klondike Hwy (p257) Counting moose and bears along this stunning road – they may outnumber cars.

4 Yukon River (p249) Living the dream of kayakers and canoeists on this legendary river.

5 Tombstone Territorial Park (p259) Losing yourself in this vast park, where the grandeur of the north envelops you.

6 Kluane National Park (p255) Finding and naming one of the 100 unnamed glaciers in this untamed Unesco-listed park.

7 White Pass & Yukon Route (p252) Sitting back and enjoying the ride on the fabled Gold Rush railroad.

History

There's evidence that humans were eating animals in the Yukon some 15,000 to 30,000 years ago, depending on your carbon-dating method of choice. However, it's widely agreed that these people were descended from those who crossed over from today's Siberia while the land bridge was in place. There's little recorded history otherwise, although it's known that a volcanic eruption in AD 800 covered much of the southern Yukon in ash. Similarities to the Athapaskan people of the southwest United States have suggested that these groups may have left the Yukon after the volcano ruined hunting and fishing.

In the 1840s Robert Campbell, a Hudson's Bay Company explorer, was the first European to travel the district. Fur traders, prospectors, whalers and missionaries all followed. In 1870 the region became part of the Northwest Territories (NWT). But it was in 1896 when the Yukon literally hit the map, after gold was found in a tributary of the Klondike River, near what was to become Dawson City. The ensuing gold rush attracted upward of 40,000 hopefuls from around the world. Towns sprouted overnight to support the numerous wealth-seekers, who were quite unprepared for the ensuing depravities.

In 1898 the Yukon became a separate territory, with Dawson City as its capital. Building the Alaska Hwy (Hwy 1) in 1942 opened up the territory to development. In 1953 Whitehorse became the capital, because it had the railway and the highway. Mining continues to be the main industry, followed by tourism, which accounts for over 330,000 visitors a year.

Local Culture

The 33,000-plus hardy souls who live in the Yukon Territory take the phrase 'rugged individualist' to heart. It's safe to say that the average Yukoner enjoys the outdoors (in all weather conditions!), relishes eating meats seldom found on menus to the south and has a crack in their truck's windshield (caused by one of the many dodgy roads).

More than 70% of the territory's annual revenue each year comes from the federal government, and it has been used to fund all manner of services at relatively comfortable levels. Whitehorse, for instance, has a range of cultural and recreational facilities that are the envy of southern Canadian communities many times its size. More than 5000 people have government jobs.

Thanks to the Yukon's long isolation before WWII, the 14 First Nations groups have maintained their relationship with the land and their traditional culture, compared to groups forced to assimilate in other parts of Canada. They can be found across the territory and in isolated places such as Old Crow, living lives not fundamentally changed in centuries. It's not uncommon to hear various aboriginal dialects spoken by elders.

Light – or the lack thereof – does play an important role in local life. Many people adjust to the radical variations in daylight through the year, but others do not. Every year you hear of longtime residents and newcomers alike who one day (often in February) announce enough is enough and move south for good.

Parks

The Yukon has a major Unesco World Heritage site in raw and forbidding Kluane National Park, which sits solidly within the Yukon abutting Tatshenshini-Alsek Provincial Park in British Columbia. Glacier Bay and Wrangell-St Elias National Parks are found in adjoining Alaska.

The Yukon has a dozen parks and protected areas (www.yukonparks.ca), but much of the territory itself is parklike and government campgrounds can be found throughout.

EXTREME YUKON

Tough conditions spawn tough contests:

Yukon Quest (www.yukonquest.com; ☺Feb) This legendary 1600km dogsled race goes from Whitehorse to Fairbanks, AK, braving winter darkness and -50°C temperatures. Record time: eight days, 14 hours, 21 minutes, set in 2014.

Yukon River Quest (www.yukonriverquest.com; ☺late Jun) The world's premier canoe and kayak race, which covers the classic 742km run of the Yukon River from Whitehorse to Dawson City. Record times include team canoe (39 hours, 32 minutes) and solo kayak (42 hours, 49 minutes).

Klondike Trail of '98 Road Relay (www.klondikeroadrelay.com; ☺early Sep) Some 100 running teams of 10 athletes each complete the overnight course from Skagway to Whitehorse.

Tombstone Territorial Park is remote, yet accessible via the Dempster Hwy, so you can absorb the horizon-sweeping beauty of the tundra and majesty of vast mountain ranges.

ℹ️ Information

There are excellent visitor information centers (VICs) covering every entry point in the Yukon: Beaver Creek, Carcross, Dawson City, Haines Junction, Watson Lake and Whitehorse.

The Yukon government produces enough literature and information to supply a holiday's worth of reading. Among the highlights are *Camping on Yukon Time, Art Adventures on Yukon Time,* the very useful *Yukon Wildlife Viewing Guide* and lavish walking guides to pretty much every town with a population greater than 50. Start your collection at the various visitors centers online (www.travelyukon.com). Another good internet resource is www.yukoninfo.com.

ℹ️ Getting There & Around

Whitehorse is linked by air to Vancouver, Kelowna, Calgary and Edmonton. There are even flights nonstop to Germany during summer. Dawson City has flights to Whitehorse, and to Inuvik in the Northwest Territories.

There are three major ways to reach the Yukon by road: first by ferry to the entry points of Skagway and Haines, AK; by the Alaska Hwy from Dawson Creek, British Columbia (BC); and by the Stewart-Cassiar Hwy from northwest BC that joins the Alaska Hwy near Watson Lake.

You can reach Whitehorse from British Columbia by bus. From there a patchwork of companies provides links to Alaska and Dawson. Rental cars (and Recreational Vehicles) are expensive and only available in Whitehorse. The Alaska Hwy and Klondike Hwy are paved and have services every 100km to 200km.

To check the territory's road conditions, contact **511Yukon** (📞511; www.511yukon.ca).

WHITEHORSE

POP 26,500

The capital city of the Yukon Territory (since 1953, to the continuing regret of much smaller and isolated Dawson City), Whitehorse will likely have a prominent role in your journey. The territory's two great highways, the Alaska and the Klondike, cross here; it's a hub for transportation (it was a terminus for the White Pass & Yukon Route railway from Skagway in the early 1900s, and during WWII was a major center for work on the Alaska Hwy). You'll find all manner of outfitters and services for explorations across the territory.

Not immediately appealing, Whitehorse rewards the curious. It has a well-funded arts community (with an especially vibrant visual arts community), good restaurants and a range of motels. Exploring the sights within earshot of the rushing Yukon River can easily take a day or more. Look past the bland commercial buildings and you'll see many heritage ones awaiting discovery.

⊙ Sights

You can explore Whitehorse's main sights in a day, mostly on foot.

★ MacBride Museum   MUSEUM
(Map p248; 📞867-667-2709; www.macbride museum.com; cnr 1st Ave & Wood St; adult/child $10/5; ⊙9:30am-5pm) The Yukon's attic covers the gold rush, First Nations, intrepid Mounties and much more. Old photos vie with old stuffed critters, and daily demonstrations, such as gold-panning, are good fun. Various buildings colorfully re-create the Yukon's past; don't miss the stuffed albino moose.

★ SS Klondike   HISTORIC SITE
(Map p248; 📞867-667-4511; www.parkscanada. ca; cnr South Access Rd & 2nd Ave; ⊙9:30am-5pm May-Aug) **FREE** Carefully restored, this was one of the largest stern-wheelers used on the Yukon River. Built in 1937, it made its final run upriver to Dawson in 1955 and is now a national historic site.

Whitehorse Waterfront   AREA
One look at the surging Yukon River and you'll want to spend time strolling its bank. The beautiful **White Pass & Yukon Route Station** (Map p248; 1109 1st Ave) has been restored and anchors an area that's in the midst of a revitalization. **Rotary Peace Park** (Map p248; off 2nd Ave) at the southern end is a great picnic spot, the Kwanlin Dün

Whitehorse

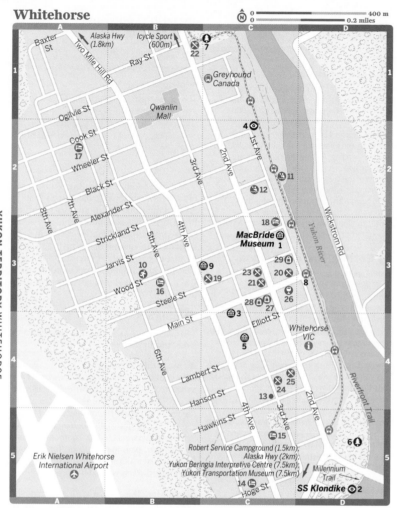

Cultural Centre is a dramatic addition in the middle, and **Shipyards Park** (Map p248; off 2nd Ave) at the northern end has a growing collection of historic structures moved here from other parts of the Yukon.

Linking it all is a cute little **waterfront trolley** (☑867-667-6355; www.yukonrails.com; one-way $3; ☉10am-6pm Jun-Aug).

Arts Underground   GALLERY
(Map p248; ☑867-667-4080; 305 Main St, Hougen Centre lower level; ☉10am-5pm Tue-Sat) Operated by the Yukon Arts Society. There are carefully selected and well-curated rotating exhibits.

Whitehorse Fishway   LANDMARK
(☑867-633-5965; Nisutlin Dr; by donation; ☉9am-5pm Jun-Aug) Stare down a salmon at the Whitehorse Fishway, a 366m wooden fish ladder (the world's longest) past the hydroelectric plant south of town. Large viewing windows let you see chinook salmon swim past starting in late July (before that it's grayling).

The fishway is easily reached on foot via the Millennium Trail.

Whitehorse

Yukon Transportation Museum   MUSEUM

(☑ 867-668-4792; www.goytm.ca; 30 Electra Cres; adult/child $10/5; ⊗ 10am-8pm Tue, to 6pm Wed-Mon mid-May–Aug, noon-5pm Sun & Mon Sep–mid-May) Find out what the Alaska Hwy was really like back in the day; let's just say mud was a dirty word. Exhibits cover planes, trains and dogsleds. The museum is near the Beringia Centre. Look for the iconic **DC-3 weather vane** (yes, it spins!) out front.

Yukon Beringia Interpretive Centre   MUSEUM

(☑ 867-667-8855; www.beringia.com; Km 1473 Alaska Hwy; adult/child $6/4; ⊗ 9am-6pm) This place focuses on Beringia, a mostly ice-free area that encompassed the Yukon, Alaska and eastern Siberia during the last ice age. Engaging exhibits re-create the era, right down to the actual skeleton of a 3m-long giant ground sloth – although some prefer the giant beaver.

Kwanlin Dün Cultural Centre   CULTURAL CENTER

(Map p248; ☑ 867-456-5322; www.kwanlin dunculturalcentre.com; 1171 1st Ave; by donation; ⊗ 9am-5pm Mon-Fri, 10am-4pm Sat & Sun) Opened in 2012, the striking Kwanlin Dün Cultural Centre has changing exhibits and a permanent collection of First Nations art.

Yukon Artists@Work   GALLERY

(Map p248; ☑ 867-393-4848; www.yaaw.com; 4129 4th Ave; ⊗ 11am-6pm Tue-Sat, to 4pm Sun) Operated by local artists, some of whom may be busily creating when you visit.

Old Log Church   HISTORIC BUILDING

(Map p248; ☑ 867-668-2555; www.oldlogchurch museum.ca; 303 Elliott St; adult/child $6/5; ⊗ 10am-6pm May-Aug) The only log-cabin-style cathedral in the world is a 1900 downtown gem. Displays include the compelling story of Rev Isaac Stringer, who boiled and ate his boots while lost in the wilderness for 51 days. Fittingly, all that's left is his sole. There are summer guided tours.

⭐ Activities

The VIC (p252) can guide you to numerous local hikes and activities year-round. Otherwise, Whitehorse is a major outfitting center for adventures on Yukon waterways.

Canoeing & Kayaking

Whitehorse is the starting place for popular canoeing and kayaking trips to Carmacks or on to Dawson City. It takes an average of eight days to the former and 16 days to the latter. Outfitters offer gear of all kinds (canoes and kayaks are about $40 to $50 per day), guides, tours, lessons and planning services, and can arrange transportation back to Whitehorse. Most paddlers use the map *The Yukon River: Marsh Lake to Dawson City*; available at www.yukonbooks.com.

Kanoe People   CANOEING

(Map p248; ☑ 867-668-4899; www.kanoepeople. com; cnr 1st Ave & Strickland St; 1-day Yukon River paddle tour $95) At the river's edge. Can arrange any type of trip including paddles down Teslin and Big Salmon Rivers. Gear, maps and guides for sale, bikes for rent.

Up North Adventures
CANOEING

(Map p248; ☑ 867-667-7035; www.upnorth adventures.com; 103 Strickland St; 19-day Yukon River canoe trip for beginners $3000; ⊙ 9am-7pm) Offers guided tours, rentals and transportation on the major rivers. Also paddling lessons, guided mountain-bike trips and winter sports.

Cycling

Whitehorse has scores of bike trails along the Yukon River and into the surrounding hills. The VIC has maps.

Cadence Cycle
CYCLING

(Map p248; ☑ 867-633-5600; www.cadencecycle. squarespace.com; 508 Wood St; bike/electric bike rental per day from $35/45; ⊙ 10am-6pm Mon-Sat) Sells and rents good used mountain bikes and does repairs.

Icycle Sport
CYCLING

(☑ 867-668-7559; www.icyclesport.com; 9002 Quartz Rd; bike rental per day from $45; ⊙ 10am-6pm Mon-Sat, noon-6pm Sun) Rents top-end mountain bikes, plus skis in winter.

Walking & Hiking

You can walk a scenic 5km loop around Whitehorse's waters that includes a stop at the fishway. From the SS *Klondike* go south on the **Millennium Trail** until you reach the Robert Service Campground and the **Rotary Centennial Footbridge** over the river. The fishway is just south. Head north along the water and cross the Robert Campbell Bridge and you are back in the town center.

Yukon Conservation Society
HIKING

(Map p248; ☑ 867-668-5678; www.yukon conservation.org; 302 Hawkins St; ⊙ Tue-Sat Jun-Aug) **FREE** Discover the natural beauty all around Whitehorse with a free Yukon Conservation Society nature hike. There are various itineraries ranging from easy to hard. Many focus on the drama of Miles Canyon.

🛏 Sleeping

Whitehorse can get almost full during the peak of summer, so book ahead. Whitehorse has a lot of midrange motels that earn the sobriquet 'veteran.' Check a room first before you commit.

★ Robert Service Campground
CAMPGROUND $

(☑ 867-668-3721; www.robertservicecampground. com; 120 Robert Service Way; tent sites $20; ⊙ mid-May–Sep; @ 🕏) It's a pretty 15-minute walk from town on the Millennium Trail to the 70 sites at this tents-only campground on the river 1km south of town. Sites have picnic tables and fire pits. The on-site cafe has excellent coffee, baked goods and ice cream.

Hi Country RV Park
CAMPGROUND $

(☑ 867-667-7445; www.hicountryrv.com; 91374 Alaska Hwy; campsites $22-42; ⊙ May-Sep; P 🕏) At the top of Robert Service Way, this woodsy 130-site campground offers hookups, showers, laundry and a playground.

Beez Kneez Bakpakers
HOSTEL $

(Map p248; ☑ 867-456-2333; www.bzkneez.com; 408 Hoge St; dm/r $35/70; 🕏) Like the home you've left behind, this cheery hostel has a garden, deck, grill and bikes. Two simple cabins are much in demand.

Boréale Ranch
GUESTHOUSE $$

(☑ 888-488-8489; www.be-yukon.com; Klondike Hwy; r $100-200; P 🕏) A lodge with an emphasis on cycling, 30 minutes' drive south of Whitehorse. There are four rooms in the appealingly minimalist main building. Outside there's a hot tub. Guests can use fat-tire bikes for free and there are numerous cycling programs. There are also summer-only yurts and tents with hardwood floors. The food wins plaudits.

Midnight Sun Inn
B&B $$

(Map p248; ☑ 867-667-2255; www.midnightsunbb. com; 6188 6th Ave; r $115-155; P ❄ @ 🕏) A modern B&B in a sort of overgrown suburban-style house with six rooms – some with themes, some sharing bathrooms. The Sun has a loyal following, is downtown, and serves big breakfasts.

★ Coast High Country Inn
HOTEL $$

(Map p248; ☑ 800-554-4471; www.highcountryinn. yk.ca; 4051 4th Ave; r $110-220; P ❄ 🕏) Towering over Whitehorse (four stories!), the High Country is popular with business travelers and groups. The 84 rooms are large – some have huge whirlpools right in the room. The pub is popular.

Historical House B&B
B&B $$

(Map p248; ☑ 867-668-2526; www.yukongold. com; cnr 5th Ave & Wood St; r $105-130; 🕏) A classic wooden home from 1907 with three guest rooms. Top-floor rooms have individual bathrooms one floor down and angled ceilings. A larger unit has a huge kitchen. Rooms have high-speed internet, and there's a nice garden.

River View Hotel MOTEL **$$**
(Canada's Best Value Inn; Map p248; ☑ 888-315-2378; www.riverviewhotel.ca; 102 Wood St; r $100-170; **P @ ☎**) The floors sound hollow here, but many of the 53 rooms have the views implied by the name (ask for one) and all are very large. It's close to everything, yet on a quiet street. Plus your car can bunk up almost as well as you: there's heated indoor parking in winter.

✗ Eating & Drinking

Ignore the influx of chain eateries and enjoy one of Whitehorse's excellent downtown restaurants. There's a great range; look for fresh Yukon salmon in season.

Baked Café & Bakery CAFE **$**
(Map p248; ☑ 867-633-6291; www.facebook.com/bakedcafewhitehorse; 100 Main St; mains from $6; ☉ 7am-7pm; ☎) ✐ In summer, the outdoor tables at this buzzing cafe are packed. Smoothies, soups, daily lunch specials, baked goods and more. Don't miss the raspberry pecan scones and take-out sandwiches.

Yukon Meat & Sausage DELI **$**
(Map p248; ☑ 867-667-6077; 203 Hanson St; sandwiches from $7; ☉ 8:30am-5:30pm Mon-Sat) The smell of smoked meat wafts out to the street and you walk right in; there's a huge selection of prepared items and custom-made sandwiches. Great for picnics, or dine in the simple table area.

★ Klondike Rib & Salmon CANADIAN **$$**
(Map p248; ☑ 867-667-7554; www.klondikerib.com; 2116 2nd Ave; mains $12-25; ☉ 11am-9pm May-Sep) It looks touristy and it seems touristy and it *is* touristy, but the food is excellent at this sprawling casual place with two decks. Besides the namesakes (the salmon kabobs are tops), there are other local faves.

Burnt Toast BISTRO **$$**
(Map p248; ☑ 867-393-2605; www.burnttoastcafe.ca; 2112 2nd Ave; mains $8-25; ☉ 8am-9pm Mon-Sat, 9:30am-2pm Sun) The food is far better than the coy name suggests! Brunch is excellent at this inviting bistro (try the French toast) and lunch and dinner specials abound. Food is local and seasonal; consult the blackboard. Good salads, sandwiches and Yukon meats.

Sanchez Cantina MEXICAN **$$**
(Map p248; ☑ 867-668-5858; 211 Hanson St; mains $14-25; ☉ 11:30am-3pm & 5-9:30pm Mon-Sat) You have to head south across two borders to find Mexican this authentic. Burritos are the thing – get them with the spicy mix of red and green sauces. Settle in for what may be a wait on the broad patio.

★ Antoinette's FUSION **$$$**
(Map p248; ☑ 867-668-3505; www.antoinettesfoodcache.ca; 4121 4th Ave; dinner mains $20-35; ☉ 11am-2pm & 4:30-9pm Mon-Fri, 4:30-9pm Sat) Antoinette Oliphant runs one of the most creative kitchens in the Yukon. Her eponymous restaurant has an ever-changing, locally sourced menu. Many dishes have a Caribbean flair. There is often live bluesy, loungey music on weekends.

Fireweed Community Market MARKET
(Map p248; www.fireweedmarket.ca; Shipyards Park; ☉ 3-8pm Thu mid-May–early Sep) The Fireweed Community Market draws vendors from the region; the berries are fabulous. There is a second, smaller market midday summer Saturdays near the White Pass & Yukon Route Station on the river.

★ Dirty Northern Public House PUB
(Map p248; ☑ 867-633-3305; www.facebook.com/dirtynorthernpublichouse; 103 Main St; ☉ 3pm-late) There are hints of style at this upscale pub, which has a great draft-beer selection and makes excellent mixed drinks. Grab a booth and chase the booze with a wood-fired pizza. Top local acts perform many nights.

🛍 Shopping

★ Mac's Fireweed Books BOOKS
(Map p248; ☑ 867-668-2434; www.macsbooks.ca; 203 Main St; ☉ 8am-8pm Mon-Sat, to 6pm Sun) Mac's has an unrivaled selection of Yukon titles. It also stocks topographical maps, road maps and periodicals.

North End Gallery ARTS & CRAFTS
(Map p248; ☑ 867-393-3590; www.yukonart.ca; 1116 1st Ave; ☉ 9am-7pm Mon-Sat, to 5pm Sun) High-end Canadian art featuring top Yukon artists.

Midnight Sun Emporium ARTS & CRAFTS
(Map p248; ☑867-668-4350; www.midnight
sunemporium.com; 205c Main St; ◷9am-7pm
Mon-Sat) Has a good selection of Yukon arts,
crafts and products.

❶ Information

Among local newspapers, the *Yukon News* (www.
yukon-news.com) is feisty.

VIC (Map p248; ☑867-667-3084; www.travel
yukon.com; 100 Hanson St; ◷8am-8pm) An
essential stop with vast amounts of territory-
wide information.

Whitehorse General Hospital (☑867-393-
8700; www.yukonhospitals.ca; 5 Hospital Rd;
◷24hr) The top hospital in the territory.

❶ Getting There & Away

AIR

**Erik Nielsen Whitehorse International
Airport** (YXY; Map p248; ☑867-667-8440;
www.gov.yk.ca/yxy; off Alaska Hwy; 🛜) is five
minutes west of downtown. Air Canada and
Westjet serve Vancouver. Locally owned Air
North (www.flyairnorth.com) serves Dawson
City (with flights on to Inuvik, NWT, and Old
Crow), plus Vancouver, Kelowna, Edmonton
and Calgary. Condor (www.condor.com) has
weekly summer flights to/from Frankfurt.

BUS

Check the latest bus service information with
the VIC.

Alaska/Yukon Trails (☑907-479-2277; www.
alaskashuttle.com) Serves Fairbanks, AK
(US$385, thrice weekly June to mid-September),
via Dawson City.

Greyhound Canada (Map p248; ☑867-667-
2223; www.greyhound.ca; 2191 2nd Ave) Runs
south along the Alaska Hwy to Dawson Creek
($285, 20 hours, thrice weekly); connects with
buses for the rest of BC and Canada.

Husky Bus (☑867-993-3821; www.huskybus.
ca) Serves Dawson City ($110, thrice weekly)
and makes all stops along the Klondike Hwy.
Departures are from the VIC. It will do pickups
of paddlers and canoes along the Klondike Hwy
with advance arrangement.

White Pass & Yukon Route (☑867-633-5710;
www.wpyr.com; 1109 1st Ave; adult/child one-
way $130/65; ◷ticket office 9am-5pm Mon-
Sat mid-May–mid-Sep) Offers a jaw-droppingly
scenic daily 10-hour rail and bus connection to/
from Skagway, AK, via Fraser, BC in season. On
some days the bus meets the train in Carcross,
which maximizes the beautiful train ride (this is
the preferred option).

❶ Getting Around

TO/FROM THE AIRPORT

A **Yellow Cab** (☑867-668-4811) taxi to the
center (10 minutes) will cost around $22.

BUS

Whitehorse Transit System (☑867-668-7433;
$2.50; ◷Mon-Sat) runs through the center.
Route 3 serves the airport, Route 5 passes the
Robert Service Campground.

CAR & RECREATIONAL VEHICLE

Check your rental rate very carefully as it's
common for a mileage charge to be added
after the first 100km, which will not get you far
in the Yukon. Also understand your insurance
coverage and ask whether damage from Yukon's
rugged roads is included.

Budget (☑867-667-6200; www.budget.com;
Erik Nielsen Whitehorse International Airport)

Fraserway RV Rentals (☑867-668-3438;
www.fraserwayrvrentals.com; 9039 Quartz Rd)
Rents all shapes and sizes of RV from $200 per
day depending on size (it matters) and season.
Mileage extra; rates can quickly add up.

Whitehorse Subaru (☑867-393-6550; www.
whitehorsesubaru.com; 17 Chilkoot Way) Has good
rates; most cars have manual transmissions.

ALASKA HIGHWAY

It may be called the Alaska Hwy, but given
that its longest stretch (958km) is in the Yukon, perhaps another name is in order...

Roughly 2450km in length from Dawson
Creek, BC, to Delta Junction, far inside Alaska, the Alaska Hwy has a meaning well beyond just a road; it's also a badge, an honor,
an accomplishment. Even though today it's
a modern thoroughfare, the very name still
evokes images of big adventure and getting
away from it all.

As you drive the Alaska Hwy in the Yukon,
you're on the most scenic and varied part of
the road. From little villages to the city of
Whitehorse, from meandering rivers to the
upthrust drama of the St Elias Mountains,
the scenery will overwhelm you.

British Columbia to Whitehorse

You'll never be far from an excuse to stop
on this stretch of the highway. Towns, small
parks and various roadside attractions appear at regular intervals. None are a massive
draw, but overall it's a pretty drive made compelling by the locale.

Watson Lake

Originally named after Frank Watson, a British trapper, Watson Lake is the first town in the Yukon on the Alaska Hwy and is just over the border from British Columbia (BC). It's mostly just a good rest stop, except for the superb **VIC** (☑867-536-7469; www.travelyukon.com; off Alaska Hwy; ☺8am-8pm May-Sep), which has a good museum about the highway and a passel of territory-wide info.

The town is famous for its **Sign Post Forest** just outside the VIC. The first signpost, 'Danville, Illinois,' was nailed up in 1942. Others were added and now there are 72,000 signs, many purloined late at night from municipalities worldwide.

Some 136km west on the Alaska Hwy, past the 1112 Km marker, look for the **Rancheria Falls Recreation Site**. A boardwalk leads to powerful twin waterfalls. It's an excellent stop.

For accommodations, the **Air Force Lodge** (☑867-536-2890; www.airforcelodge.com; off Alaska Hwy; s/d $85/95; P☏) has spotless rooms with shared bathrooms in a historic 1942 barracks for pilots. Just west of the junction with the Stewart-Cassiar Hwy (Hwy 37), family-run **Nugget City** (☑867-536-2307; www.nuggetcity.com; Alaska Hwy; campsites from $25, r $65-130; P☏) has accommodations and food that are three cuts above the Alaska Hwy norm. Stop just for the baked goods, especially the berry pie. Choose from a variety of cabins and suites.

Teslin

Teslin, on the long, narrow lake of the same name, is 260km west of Watson Lake. It's long been a home to the Tlingits (lin-*kits*), and the Alaska Hwy brought both prosperity and rapid change to this aboriginal population.

This engrossing **George Johnston Museum** (☑867-390-2550; www.gjmuseum.yk.net; Alaska Hwy; adult/child $5/2.50; ☺9am-6pm May-Aug) details the life and culture of a 20th-century Tlingits leader through photographs, displays and artifacts.

Johnson's Crossing

Some 50km northwest of Teslin is Johnson's Crossing, at the junction of the Alaska Hwy and Canol Rd (Hwy 6). During WWII the US army built the Canol pipeline at tremendous

WORTH A TRIP

ROBERT CAMPBELL HIGHWAY

To get right off the beaten path, consider this lonely gravel road (Hwy 4), which runs 585km from Watson Lake north and west to Carmacks, where you can join the Klondike Hwy (Hwy 2) for Dawson City. Along its length, the highway parallels various rivers and lakes. Wilderness campers will be thrilled.

Around 360km from Watson Lake, at the junction with Canol Rd (Hwy 6) is **Ross River**, home to the Kaska First Nation and a supply center for the local mining industry. There are campgrounds and motels in town.

human and financial expense to pump oil from Norman Wells in the NWT to Whitehorse. It was abandoned after countless hundreds of millions of dollars (in 1943 money, no less) were spent.

The Teslin River Bridge offers sweeping views.

Whitehorse to Alaska

For long segments west of Whitehorse, the Alaska Hwy has been modernized to the point of blandness. Fortunately, this ends abruptly in Haines Junction. From here the road parallels legendary Kluane National Park and the St Elias Mountains. The 300km to Beaver Creek is the most scenic part of the entire highway.

Haines Junction

It's goodbye flatlands when you reach Haines Junction and see the sweep of imposing peaks looming over town. You've reached the stunning Kluane National Park and this is the gateway. The town makes an excellent base for exploring the park or for staging a serious four-star mountaineering, backcountry or river adventure.

The magnificent Haines Hwy heads south from here to Alaska. The four-hour drive to Haines, traversing raw alpine splendor, is one of the north's most beautiful.

Oh, and that thing that looks like an acid-trip cupcake at the main junction? It's a **sculpture** that's meant to be a winsome tableau of local characters and critters.

SPRUCE BEETLES

Even as beetles wreak havoc on forests across British Columbia and the Rockies, the forests of the Yukon are recovering. The millions upon millions of trees killed by the spruce beetle since 1994 have shed their brown needles and are now a ghostly gray. Meanwhile, fast-growing opportunists are adding a bright green hue to the tableaux.

Many reasons for the tree deaths center on climate change, including warmer winters, allowing far more beetles than usual to survive from one year to the next. In recent years, however, several factors have been working against the beetles: dead trees mean less food, a very cold winter killed many beetles and there is now a population explosion of beetle-eaters. Meanwhile, nature has opened the door to other trees, including birch and alder, which grow relatively quickly.

To get a sense of the devastation caused by beetles in the last two decades stop at the short **Spruce Beetle Loop**, 17km northwest of Haines Junction, just off the highway. It has interpretive signs.

◉ Sights & Activities

Although Kluane National Park will most likely be your focus, there are some good activities locally. For a hike after hours of driving, there's a pretty 5.5km **nature walk** along Dezadeash River where Hwy 3 crosses it at the southern end of town.

Da Ku Cultural Centre   CULTURAL CENTER
(☑ 867-634-4200; www.cafn.ca/da-ku-cultural-centre; 280 Alaska Hwy; ⊙ 8:30am-6pm mid-May–Aug) FREE This large and impressive facility has a variety of exhibit areas that showcase the culture and history of the Champagne and Aishihik people. It has a picnic area.

★**Kluane Glacier Air Tours**   SCENIC FLIGHTS
(☑ 867-634-2916; www.kluaneglacierairtours.com; off Alaska Hwy, Haines Junction Airport; tours from $250) Kluane Glacier Air Tours offers flight-seeing of Kluane and its glaciers that will leave you limp with amazement. Options begin with a one-hour tour. There are several other air-tour outfits at the airport.

Tatshenshini Expediting   RAFTING
(☑ 867-393-3661; www.tatshenshiniyukon.com; rafting trip from $135, kayak rental per day $35; ⊙ May-Sep) Tatshenshini Expediting leads white-water rafting trips on the nearby Tatshenshini River, which has rapids from grade II to grade IV. Trips leave from Haines Junction and Whitehorse. It also arranges custom river trips and rents gear.

🛏 Sleeping & Eating

There's a cluster of motels and RV parks in Haines Junction. There's a beach and shade at Pine Lake, a territorial campground 6km east of town on the Alaska Hwy.

Wanderer's Inn   HOSTEL $
(☑ 867-634-5321; www.wanderersinn.ca; 191 Backe St; campsite/dm/r $25/40/90; ⊙ May-Sep, by reservation Oct-Apr; P 🛜) This modern house is right in the center of town amid a grove of trees. It has a kitchen and a common deck.

Alcan Motor Inn   MOTEL $$
(☑ 867-634-2371; www.alcanmotorinn.com; cnr Alaska & Haines Hwys; r $110-180; P ❄ 🛜) The modern two-story Alcan has 23 large rooms with great views of the jagged Auriol Range; some rooms have full kitchens. The on-site Northern Lights cafe has hearty fare.

★**Village Bakery & Deli**   BAKERY $
(☑ 867-634-2867; cnr Kluane & Logan Sts; mains $6-12; ⊙ 7am-7pm May-Sep; 🛜) The bakery here turns out excellent goods all day, while the deli counter has tasty sandwiches you can enjoy on the large deck. On Friday night there's a popular barbecue with live folk music. It has milk and other very basic groceries.

Frosty's Freeze   BURGERS $
(☑ 867-634-7070; Alaska Hwy; mains $7-11; ⊙ 11am-9pm May-Sep) What looks like a humdrum fast-food joint is several orders of magnitude better. The shakes are made with real ice cream, the sundaes feature fresh berries, and the burgers (try the mushroom-Swiss number) are huge and juicy.

ℹ Information

The **VIC** (☑ 867-634-2345; www.travelyukon.com; 280 Alaska Hwy, Da Ku Cultural Centre; ⊙ 8am-8pm May-Sep) has Yukon-wide info.

Parks Canada (✆ 867-634-7250; www.parks canada.gc.ca/kluane; 280 Alaska Hwy, Da Kų Cultural Centre; ⊙ 9am-7pm) has full Kluane details, including hiking info. Both share space in the First Nations' Da Kų Cultural Centre (p254). There are excellent films about the park, as well as engrossing exhibits on the park and aboriginal life.

For local info beyond the VIC, see www.haines junctionyukon.com.

❶ Getting There & Away

Haines Junction is a hub of highways: the Haines Hwy (Hwy 3) and the Alaska Hwy (Hwy 1) meet here.

Who What Where Tours (✆ 867-333-0475; www.whitehorsetours.com) offers the only public service between Whitehorse and Haines Junction (one way $73, twice weekly June to September).

Kluane National Park & Reserve

Unesco-recognized as an 'empire of mountains and ice,' Kluane National Park and Reserve looms south of the Alaska Hwy much of the way to the Alaska border. This rugged and magnificent wilderness covers 22,015 sq km of the southwest corner of the territory. Kluane (kloo-wah-neee) gets its far-too-modest name from the Southern Tutchone word for 'Lake with Many Fish.'

With British Columbia's Tatshenshini-Alsek Provincial Park to the south and Alaska's Wrangell-St Elias National Park to the west, this is one of the largest protected wilderness areas in the world. Deep beyond the mountains you see from the Alaska Hwy are over 100 named glaciers and as many unnamed ones.

Winters are long and harsh. Summers are short, making mid-June to early September the best time to visit. Note that wintery conditions can occur at any time, especially in the backcountry.

◉ Sights

The park consists primarily of the **St Elias Mountains** and the world's largest non-polar **ice fields**. Two-thirds of the park is glacier interspersed with valleys, glacial lakes, alpine forest, meadows and tundra. The **Kluane Ranges** (averaging a height of 2500m) are seen along the western edge of the Alaska Hwy. A greenbelt wraps around the base of these mountains, where most of the animals and vegetation live. Turquoise **Kluane Lake** is the Yukon's largest. Hidden

are the immense ice fields and towering peaks, including **Mt Logan** (5959m), Canada's highest mountain, and **Mt St Elias** (5489m), the second highest. Partial glimpses of the interior peaks can be found at the Km 1622 **viewpoint** on the Alaska Hwy and also around the **Donjek River Bridge**, but the best views are from the air.

In Haines Junction, Kluane Glacier Air Tours (p254) offers highly recommended flight-seeing of Kluane and its glaciers.

🏃 Activities

There's excellent hiking in the forested lands at the base of the mountains, along either marked trails or less defined routes. There are about a dozen in each category, some following old mining roads, others traditional aboriginal paths. Detailed trail guides and topographical maps are available at the information centers. Talk to the rangers before setting out. They will help select a hike and can provide updates on areas that may be closed due to bear activity. Overnight hikes require backcountry permits ($10 per person per night).

A good pause during an Alaska Hwy drive is the **Soldier's Summit Trail**, an easy 1km hike up from the Tachal Dhal information center. It has views across the park and plaques commemorating the inauguration of the Alaska Hwy at this point on November 20, 1942. You can listen to the original CBC broadcast of the opening.

The Tachal Dhal information center is also the starting point for **Ä'äy Chù (Slim's West)**, a popular 45km round-trip trek to **Kaskawulsh Glacier** – one of the few that can be reached on foot. This is a difficult route that takes from two to four days to complete and includes sweeping views from Observation Mountain (2114m).

An easy overnight trip is the 15km **Auriol loop**, which goes from spruce forest to subalpine barrens and includes a wilderness campground. It's 7km south of Haines Junction.

READING THE YUKON

A great way to get a feel for the Yukon and its larger-than-life stories is to read some of the vast body of Yukon novels. Start with Jack London – *Call of the Wild* is free online at www.online-literature.com.

Fishing is good and wildlife-watching plentiful. Most noteworthy are the thousands of Dall sheep that can be seen on **Sheep Mountain** in June and September. There's a large and diverse population of grizzly bear, as well as black bears, moose, caribou, goats and 150 varieties of birds, among them eagles and the rare peregrine falcon.

Many park visitors enjoy skiing or snow-shoeing, beginning in February.

🛏 Sleeping

⭐ Kathleen Lake Campground
CAMPGROUND $

(www.parkscanada.gc.ca/kluane; off Haines Hwy; campsites $16) Cerulean waters highlight Kathleen Lake, which has a Parks Canada campground and is 24km south of Haines Junction off the highway. The lake is a good stop by day and there are frequent ranger tours and programs in summer.

ℹ Information

Parks Canada has two information centers. One is in Haines Junction (p255) and the other is at T**achal Dhal** (Sheep Mountain; Alaska Hwy; ⊘ 9am-4pm mid-May–Aug), 130km west of Haines Junction, which has excellent resources and views of Sheep Mountain. Rangers have wildlife and hiking info.

At both, get a copy of the park guide, which shows the scope of the park (and how little is actually easily accessible). The map shows hikes ranging from 10 minutes to 10 days.

Destruction Bay

This small village on the shore of huge Kluane Lake is 106km northwest of Haines Junction. It was given its evocative name after a storm tore through the area during construction of the highway during WWII. Most of the residents are First Nations, who live off the land through the year.

Stop in at the local motel, or head 17km east of town on the Alaska Hwy to **Congdon Creek**, which has an 81-site territorial campground and a fine lakeside setting.

Burwash Landing

Burwash Landing boasts a spectacular setting, with Kluane National Park on one side and Kluane Lake on the other. It's a good place to stretch those legs and visit the excellent museum. The town was established by fur traders in 1909.

Commune with an enormous, albeit stuffed, moose at the **Kluane Museum** (✆ 867-841-5561; www.kluanemuseum.ca; Alaska Hwy; adult/child $5/3; ⊘ 9am-6:30pm mid-May–mid-Sep). Enjoy intriguing wildlife exhibits and displays on natural and aboriginal history.

Beaver Creek

Wide-spot-in-the-road Beaver Creek is a beacon for sleepy travelers or those who want to get gas – certainly its lackluster eateries will ensure the latter. The Canadian border checkpoint is just north of town; the US border checkpoint is 27km further west. Both are open 24 hours.

A strange **sculpture garden** just north tempts the silly (or intoxicated) into unnatural acts.

Of the four motels in town, the **1202 Motor Inn** (✆ 867-862-7600; www.1202motorinn.ca; 1202 Alaska Hwy; r $90-100; ⊘ 8am-11pm; P❄🛜) is the most appealing. The 30 rooms are basic and functional. Get one away from the idling trucks.

The **VIC** (✆ 867-862-7321; www.travelyukon.com; Km 1202 Alaska Hwy; ⊘ 8am-8pm May-Sep) has information on all of the Yukon.

HAINES HIGHWAY

If you're doing only a short loop between Haines and Skagway in Alaska via Whitehorse, this 259km road might be the highlight of your trip. In fact, no matter what length your Yukon adventure, the Haines Hwy (Hwy 3) might be the high point. In a relatively short distance you'll see glaciers, looming snow-clad peaks, lush and wild river valleys, windswept alpine meadows and a river delta dotted with the shadows of bald eagles.

Heading south of Haines Junction, look west for a close-up of the St Elias Mountains, those glaciers glimpsed at the top stretch all the way to the Pacific Ocean. About 80km south, look for the **Tatshenshini River viewpoint**. This white-water river flows through protected bear country and a valley that seems timeless.

About 10km further, you'll come to **Million Dollar Falls**. For once the sight lives up to the billing, as water thunders through a narrow chasm. As you drive, watch for glacier views.

The highway crosses into British Columbia for a mere 70km, but you'll hope for more as you traverse high and barren alpine wilderness, where sudden snow squalls happen year-round. At the 1070m **Chilkat Pass**, an ancient aboriginal route into the Yukon, the road suddenly plunges down for a steep descent into Alaska. The US border is 72km north of Haines, along the wide Chilkat River Delta.

The delta is home to scores of bald eagles year-round; the handsome birds flock like pigeons each fall when they mass in the trees overlooking the rivers, drawn by the comparatively mild weather and steady supply of fish. Pullouts line the Haines Hwy (Hwy 7 in Alaska), especially between mileposts 19 and 26. Take your time driving and find a place to park. Just a few feet from the road it's quiet, and when you see a small tree covered with 20 pensive – and sizable – bald eagles, you can enjoy your own raptor version of *The Birds*.

Note that the weather can turn nasty any time of the year on the road's higher reaches. Otherwise it is smooth and very well-maintained.

KLONDIKE HIGHWAY

Beginning seaside in Skagway, AK, the 716km Klondike Hwy climbs high to the forbidding Chilkoot Pass before crossing into stunning alpine scenery on the way to Carcross. For much of its length, the road generally follows the **Gold Rush Trail**, the route of the Klondike prospectors. You'll have a much easier time of it than they did.

North of Whitehorse, the road passes through often-gentle terrain that has been scorched by wildfires through the years. Signs showing the dates let you chart nature's recovery.

Carcross

Long a forgotten gold-rush town, cute little Carcross, 73km south of Whitehorse, is an evocative stop. There are four trains weekly in summer from Skagway to Carcross (and vice versa) on the **White Pass & Yukon Route** (☑800-343-7373; www.wpyr.com; one-way from Skagway adult/child $165/82.50; ☺Jun-Aug). These five-hour rides over White Pass access a lot of remote scenery that the shorter regular trips to Bennett don't cover. There are packages that include bus transport in one direction to allow Skagway-based day trips. Some old buildings are being restored and the site on Lake Bennett is superb. (Although Klondike prospectors who had to build boats here to cross the lake didn't think so.)

The old **train station** has good displays on local history.

Carcross Desert, often considered the world's smallest desert, is the exposed sandy bed of a glacial lake. It's 2km north of town.

VIC (☑867-821-4431; www.travelyukon.com; ☺8am-8pm May-Sep) In a modern complex with seasonal shops and cafes. Get the excellent walking-tour brochure.

Carmacks

This small village sits right on the Yukon River and is named for one of the discoverers of gold in 1896, George Washington Carmack. A rogue seaman wandering the Yukon, it was almost by luck that Carmack (with Robert Henderson, Tagish Charlie and Keish – aka Skookum Jim Mason) made their claim on Bonanza Creek. Soon he was living the high life and it wasn't long before he abandoned his First Nations family and

WORTH A TRIP

CHILKOOT TRAIL

Arduous at best, and deadly at its worst in 1898, the Chilkoot Trail was the route most prospectors took to get over the 1110m Chilkoot Pass from Skagway and into the Yukon. Today, hikers reserve spots months in advance to travel the same route.

The well-marked 53km trail begins near **Dyea**, 14km northwest of Skagway, and heads northeast over the pass. It then follows the Taiya River to Lake Bennett in British Columbia (BC), and takes three to five days to hike. It's a hard route in good weather and often treacherous in bad. You must be in good physical condition and come fully equipped. Layers of warm clothes and rain gear are essential.

Hardware, tools and supplies dumped by the prospectors still litter the trail. At several places there are wooden shacks where you can put up for the night, but these are usually full, so a tent and sleeping bag are required. There are 10 designated campgrounds along the route, each with bear caches.

At the Canadian end you can either take the White Pass & Yukon Route train from Bennett back to Skagway or further up the line to Fraser in BC, where you can connect with a bus for Whitehorse.

The Chilkoot Trail is a primary feature of the **Klondike Gold Rush National Historical Park** (www.nps.gov/klgo), a series of sites managed by both Parks Canada and the US National Park Service that stretches from Seattle, WA, to Dawson City. Each Chilkoot hiker must obtain one of the 50 permits available for each day in summer; reserve well in advance. Parks Canada/US National Park Service charge $55 for a permit plus $12 for a reservation. Each day eight permits are issued on a first-come, first-served basis. For information, contact the **Chilkoot Trail Centre** (cnr Broadway & 2nd Ave; ⊙8am-5pm Jun-Aug) in Skagway or go online to the park's website. Necessary preplanning includes determining which campsites you'll use each night.

headed south to the US. Given his record as a husband and father, it's fitting that Carmack be honored by this uninspired collection of gas stations and places to stay. Like elsewhere in the territory, residents here are keenly attuned to the land, which supplies them with game and fish throughout the year. A pretty 15-minute **interpretive walk** by the river provides a glimmer of insight into this life.

The main reason to stop off for a visit to Carmacks is the excellent **Tagé Cho Hudän Interpretive Centre** (⊠867-863-5831; off Hwy 2; by donation; ⊙9am-6pm May-Sep), where volunteers explain aboriginal life past and present.

Besides the interpretive center, there are things to see on the Klondike Hwy north and south of Carmacks.

About 25km north of Carmacks, the **Five Finger Rapids Recreation Site** has excellent views of the treacherous stretch of the rapids that once tested the wits of riverboat captains traveling between Whitehorse and Dawson. There's a steep 1.5km walk down to the rapids.

Heading out on the road south, there are a series of water features starting with **Twin Lakes**, located 23km from Carmacks, followed by **Fox Lake**. Situated another 24km

south, you can't miss serene **Lake Laberge**. The final 40km to Whitehorse is marked by low trees and a few cattle ranches.

Minto

Easily missed (unless you're toting a canoe or kayak), Minto is where the Klondike Hwy leaves the route of the Gold Rush Trail. This is a popular place to put in for the four- to five-day trip down the Yukon River to Dawson City. It's about 75km north of Carmacks.

Stewart Crossing

Another popular place to get your canoe wet, Stewart Crossing is on the Stewart River, which affords a narrow and somewhat more rugged experience before it joins the Yukon to the west for the trip to Dawson.

Otherwise unexceptional, the village is situated at the junction of the Klondike Hwy (Hwy 2) and the **Silver Trail** (Hwy 11), which makes a 225km round-trip to the nearly abandoned town of **Keno City** and the tiny village of **Mayo**.

DAWSON CITY

POP 1400

If you didn't know its history, Dawson City would be an atmospheric place to pause for a while, with a seductive, funky vibe. That it's one of the most historic and evocative towns in Canada is like gold dust on a cake: unnecessary but damn nice.

Set on a narrow shelf at the confluence of the Yukon and Klondike Rivers, a mere 240km south of the Arctic Circle, Dawson was the center of the Klondike Gold Rush. Today, you can wander the dirt streets of town, passing old buildings with dubious permafrost foundations, and discover Dawson's rich cultural life (that person passing by may be a dancer, filmmaker, painter or miner).

Dawson can be busy in the summer, especially during its festivals. But by September the days are getting short, the seasonal workers have fled south and the 1400 year-round residents are settling in for another long, dark winter.

History

In 1898 more than 30,000 prospectors milled the streets of Dawson – a few newly rich, but most without prospects and at odds with themselves and the world. Shops, bars and prostitutes relieved these hordes of what money they had, but Dawson's fortunes were tied to the gold miners and, as the boom ended, the town began a decades-long slow fade.

The territorial capital was moved to Whitehorse in 1952 and the town lingered on, surviving on the low-key but ongoing gold-mining industry. By 1970 the population was under 900. But then a funny thing happened on the way to Dawson's demise: it was rediscovered. Improvements to the Klondike Hwy and links to Alaska allowed the first major influx of summertime tourists, who found a charmingly moldering time capsule from the gold rush. Parks Canada designated much of the town as historic and began restorations.

◎ Sights

Dawson is small enough to walk around in a few hours, but you can easily fill three or more days with the many local things to see and do. If the summertime hordes get you down, head uphill for a few blocks to find timeless old houses and streets.

After draconian government budget cuts during the Harper era, Parks Canada is now enjoying greatly increased budgets, which mean programs and restorations are showing new vigor in Dawson. Check out the pass options, good for the many Parks Canada sites.

★ **Klondike National Historic Sites** HISTORIC SITE
(☑ 867-993-7210; www.pc.gc.ca/dawson; Parks Canada passes adult $7-31) It's easy to relive the gold rush at myriad preserved and restored places. Parks Canada runs walking tours (p262) through the day that allow access into various examples of the 26 restored buildings. Take several tours so you can see a wide variety. Outside of tours, various buildings such as the **Palace Grand Theatre** (Map p260; King St) are open for free on a rotating basis, usually 4:30pm to 5:30pm.

★ **Bonanza Creek Discovery Site** HISTORIC SITE
(Bonanza Rd) FREE Some 1.5km up the valley from Dredge No 4, this national historic site is roughly where gold was first found in 1896. It's a quiet site today with a little water burbling through the rubble. A fascinating 500m-long walk passes interpretive displays. Pick up a guide ($2.50) at the VIC (p247).

★ **Dredge No 4** LANDMARK
(☑ 867-993-5023; Bonanza Creek Rd; adult/child $20/10, return transport from Dawson $10; ◎ 10am-4pm May-Sep, tour times vary) The

YUKON TERRITORY DAWSON CITY

> **WORTH A TRIP**
>
> ## TOMBSTONE DETOUR
>
> **Tombstone Territorial Park** (☑ 867-667-5648; www.yukonparks.ca; Dempster Hwy), which lies along Dempster Hwy for about 50km, is an easy day trip from Dawson City. Shades of green and charcoal color the wide valleys here and steep ridges are dotted with small glaciers and alpine lakes. Summer feels tentative but makes its statement with a burst of purple wildflowers in July. Clouds sweep across the tundra, bringing squalls punctuated by brilliant sun. Stand amid this and you'll know the meaning of the sound of silence.
>
> The park's excellent **Interpretive Centre** (Dempster Hwy; ◎ 9am-7pm Jun-early Sep), which offers walks and talks, is 71km from the start of Hwy 5.

Dawson City

scarred valleys around Dawson speak to the vast amounts of toil that went into the gold hunt. Most emblematic is Bonanza Creek, where gold was first found and which still yields some today. Dredge No 4, 13km off the Klondike Hwy, is a massive dredging machine that tore up the Klondike Valley and left the tailings, which remain as a blight on the landscape. Tours of this Parks Canada site are run by Goldbottom Tours (p262).

Learn about this huge machine, which worked something like a freakish giant worm in a science-fiction novel.

★ **Jack London**
Interpretive Centre   MUSEUM
(Map p260; ☑ 867-993-5575; Firth St; adult/child $5/free; ⊙ 11am-6pm May-Aug) In 1898 Jack London lived in the Yukon, the setting for his most popular stories, including *Call of the Wild* and *White Fang*. At the writer's cabin there are excellent daily interpretive talks. A labor of love by the late historian Dick North, Dawne Mitchell and others, this place is a treasure trove of stories – including the search for the original cabin.

Dawson City

Crocus Bluff VIEWPOINT
(off Mary McLeod Rd) Near Dawson's cemeteries, there's a short path out to pretty Crocus Bluff, which has excellent views of Dawson and the Klondike and Yukon Rivers. If driving, take New Dome Rd and turn at Mary McLeod Rd (ignoring the 'No Exit' signs). It is a short walk up King St from town. You can also take the 400m **Crocus Bluff Connector** path off the **Ninth Avenue Trail**, which intersects with numerous streets along its 2.5km.

Fortymile Gold Workshop/Studio GALLERY
(Map p260; ☑ 867-993-5690; 3rd Ave, btwn York & King Sts; ◷ 9am-6pm May-Sep) Watch as jewelry is made from local refined gold, which is silky and has a rich yellow color, as opposed to the bling you see peddled on late-night TV. Examples of gold from various local claims and locations shows how old miners could tell where gold originated.

Midnight Dome VIEWPOINT
(New Dome Rd) The slide-scarred face of this hill overlooks the town to the north, but to reach the top you must travel south of town about 1km, turn left off the Klondike Hwy onto New Dome Rd, and continue for about 7km. The Midnight Dome, at 880m above sea level, offers great views of the Klondike Valley, Yukon River and Dawson City. There's also a steep **trail** that takes 90 minutes from Judge St in town; maps are available at the VIC (p247).

Robert Service Cabin HISTORIC SITE
(Map p260; cnr 8th Ave & Hanson St; Parks Canada admission $7; ◷ several events daily May-Aug) The 'Bard of the Yukon,' poet and writer Robert W Service, lived in this typical gold rush cabin from 1909 to 1912. Each day in season there are dramatic readings, guided walks and tours.

Harrington's Store MUSEUM
(Map p260; cnr 3rd Ave & Princess St; ◷ 9:30am-8:30pm) **FREE** This restored old shop has historic photos from Dawson's heyday.

Commissioner's Residence HISTORIC BUILDING
(Map p260; Front St; Parks Canada admission $7; ◷ 1:30-4:30pm May-Sep) Built in 1901 to house the territorial commissioner, this proud building was designed to give potential civic investors confidence in the city. The building was the longtime home of Martha Black, who came to the Yukon in 1898, owned a lumberyard and was elected to the Canadian Parliament at age 70. (*Martha Black* by Flo Whyard is a great book about this remarkable woman.)

SS Keno HISTORIC SITE
(Map p260; cnr Front & Queen Sts; Parks Canada admission $7; ◷ noon-4pm May-Aug) The SS *Keno* was one of a fleet of paddle wheelers that worked the Yukon's rivers for more than half a century. Grounded along the waterfront, the boat re-creates a time before any highways.

Dawson City Museum
MUSEUM

(Map p260; ☑ 867-993-5291; 5th Ave; adult/child $9/7; ◷10am-6pm May-Aug) Make your own discoveries among the 25,000 gold-rush artifacts at this museum. Engaging exhibits walk you through the grim lives of the miners. The museum is housed in the landmark 1901 Old Territorial Administration building.

Cemeteries
CEMETERY

(Mary McLeod Rd) A 15-minute walk up King St and Mary McCloud Rd near town leads to 10 cemeteries that are literally filled with characters. Among them is Joe Vogler, who fought to have Alaska secede from the US. He was buried here in 1993, having vowed never to be buried in an Alaska that wasn't free. Todd Palin (husband of Sarah) is among his acolytes.

Dänojà Zho Cultural Centre
NOTABLE BUILDING

(Map p260; ☑ 867-993-6768; www.trondekheritage. com; Front St; adult/child $7/free; ◷10am-5pm Mon-Sat Jun-Sep) Inside this impressive riverfront wood building there are displays and interpretative talks on the Tr'ondëk Hwëch'in (River People) First Nations. The collection includes traditional artifacts and a re-creation of a 19th-century fishing camp.

Klondike Institute for Art & Culture
NOTABLE BUILDING

(KIAC; Map p260; ☑ 867-993-5005; www.kiac. org; cnr 3rd Ave & Queen St) The Klondike Institute for Art & Culture is part of Dawson's thriving arts community. It has an impressive studio building, galleries and educational programs.

ODD Gallery
GALLERY

(Map p260; ☑ 867-993-5005; www.kiac.ca/odd gallery; cnr 2nd Ave & Princess St; ◷hours vary) The exhibition space of the Klondike Institute for Art & Culture, this gallery has regular shows.

🏃 Activities

Besides arriving by canoe or kayak, many people also exit Dawson City via the Yukon River. A popular trip good for novices goes from Dawson for three days and 168km downstream to Eagle, AK.

A three-hour hike to **Moosehide**, an old First Nations village, is popular. The trail follows hillsides above the river north of town. Be sure to get a map at the VIC.

You can explore much of the Dawson area by bike, including the 33km **Ridge Road**

Heritage Trail, which winds through the gold fields south of town.

Dawson City River Hostel
CANOEING, CYCLING

(www.yukonhostels.com; bike rental per day from $25; ◷May-Sep) Arranges all manner of canoe rentals, trips and transportation from Whitehorse and points further downstream to Dawson and from Dawson to the Alaskan towns of Eagle and Circle.

Dawson Trading Post
CANOEING

(Map p260; ☑ 867-993-5316; Front St; canoe rental per day from $40; ◷9am-5pm Jun-Aug) Rents out canoes and can arrange trips.

☞ Tours

★ Parks Canada Walking Tours
WALKING

(single tour $7, unlimited tours $31; ◷May-Aug) Parks Canada docents, often in period garb, lead excellent walking tours. On each tour, learn about a few of the 26 restored buildings and the many characters that walked the streets (many of whom could be called 'streetwalkers'). There are also self-guided 90-minute audio tours (adult $7, 9am to 5pm).

★ Goldbottom Tours
HISTORY

(Map p260; ☑ 867-993-5750; www.goldbottom. com; tours with/without transport from Dawson $55/45; ◷May-Sep) Run by the legendary Millar mining family. Tour their placer mine 15km up Hunker Creek Rd, which meets Hwy 2 just north of the airport. The three-hour tours include a gold-panning lesson; you get to keep what you find. You can also just pan for gold on their site for $20. The ticket office is on Front St.

Klondike Experience
BUS

(Map p260; ☑ 867-993-3821; www.klondike-experience.com; 954 2nd Ave; tours $25-120; ◷May-Aug) Runs various tours that include Midnight Dome (75 minutes), the Goldfields (three hours) and Tombstone Park (7½ hours). The latter is highly recommended.

Klondike Spirit
BOATING

(Map p260; ☑ 867-993-5323; www.klondikespirit. com; tours $50-65; ◷May-Sep) This faux old stern-wheeler cruises the river on various tours. Purchase tickets from the Triple J Hotel on the corner of 5th Avenue and Queen St.

★ Festivals & Events

Dawson City Music Festival
MUSIC

(☑ 867-993-5384; www.dcmf.com; ◷mid-Jul) Popular – tickets sell out months in advance and the city fills up; reservations are essential.

THE KLONDIKE GOLD RUSH

The Klondike Gold Rush continues to be the defining moment for the Yukon. Certainly it was the population high point. Around 40,000 gold seekers washed ashore (some literally) in Skagway, hoping to strike it rich in the gold fields of Dawson City, some 700km north.

To say that most were ill-prepared for the enterprise is an understatement. Although some were veterans of other gold rushes, a high percentage were American men looking for adventure. Clerks, lawyers and waiters were among those who thought they'd just pop up North and get rich. The reality was different. Landing in Skagway, they were set upon by all manner of flimflam artists, most working for the incorrigible Soapy Smith. Next came dozens of trips hefting their 1000lb of required supplies over the frozen Chilkoot Pass. Then they had to build boats from scratch and make their way across lakes and the Yukon River to Dawson. Scores died trying.

Besides more scamsters, there was another harsh reality awaiting in Dawson: by the summer of 1897 when the first ships reached the West Coast of the US with news of the discoveries on Dawson's Bonanza Creek, the best sites had all been claimed. The Klondike gold-rush mobs were mostly too late to the action by at least a year. Sick and broke, the survivors glumly made their way back to the US. Few found any gold and most sold their gear for pennies to merchants who in turn resold it to incoming gold seekers for top dollar. Several family fortunes in the Yukon today can be traced to this trade.

Today, even the hardiest folk seem like couch potatoes when compared to the protagonists of these harrowing stories. The deprivation, disease and heartbreak of these 'dudes' of the day make for fascinating reading. Among the many books about the Klondike Gold Rush, the following are recommended (and easily found in the Yukon):

➡ *The Klondike Fever* by Pierre Berton is the classic on the gold rush.

➡ *Sailor on Snowshoes* by Dick North traces Jack London's time in the Yukon and the hunt for his cabin. London's stories of the gold rush made his name as a writer.

➡ *The Floor of Heaven* by Howard Blum is a fabulous read. It details the lives of George Carmack, who was a gold discoverer; Soapy Smith, a legendary Skagway-based con man; and Charlie Siringo, a private cop who saved Carmack from Soapy.

★ **Discovery Days** CULTURAL
(www.dawsoncity.ca; ⊙ 3rd Mon in Aug) Celebrates the you-know-what of 1896 with parades and picnics. Events begin days before, including an excellent art show. It's a hoot!

🛏 Sleeping

Reservations are a good idea in July and August, although the VIC can help. Many places will pick you up at the airport; ask in advance.

Dawson City River Hostel HOTEL $
(☏ 867-993-6823; www.yukonhostels.com; dm $22, r from $48; ⊙ May-Sep) 🚭 This delightfully eccentric hostel is across the river from town and five minutes up the hill from the ferry landing. It has good views, cabins, platforms for tents, and a communal bathhouse. Tent sites are $14. Owner Dieter Reinmuth is a noted Yukon author and all-around character.

Yukon River Campground CAMPGROUND $
(campsites $12; ⊙ May-Sep; P) On the western side of the river about 250m up the road to the right after you get off the ferry; has 98 shady sites.

★ **Bombay Peggy's** INN $$
(Map p260; ☏ 867-993-6969; www.bombaypeggys. com; cnr 2nd Ave & Princess St; r $95-220; ⊙ Mar-Nov; 🛜) 🚭 A renovated former brothel with alluring period furnishings and spunky attitude. Budget 'snug' rooms share bathrooms. Rooms are plush in a way that will make you want to wear a garter.

★ **Klondike Kate's** LODGE $$
(Map p260; ☏ 867-993-6527; www.klondikekates. ca; cnr King St & 3rd Ave; cabins $140-200; ⊙ Apr-Sep; P 🛜) 🚭 The 15 cabins behind the restaurant of the same name are rustic without the rusticisms. Some units have microwaves and fridges. All have porches, perfect for decompressing. Green practices are many.

Aurora Inn
INN **$$**

(Map p260; ☑ 867-993-6860; www.aurorainn.ca; 5th Ave; r $110-210; P ☎) All 20 rooms in this European-style inn are large and comfortable. And if there's such a thing as old-world cleanliness, it's here: the admonishments to remove your (invariably) muddy shoes start at the entrance.

Triple J Hotel
HOTEL **$$**

(Map p260; ☑ 867-993-5323; www.triplejhotel.com; cnr 5th Ave & Queen St; r $100-180; P ☎) The 47 rooms in this modern motel with a throwback look are in a modern (retro-looking) wing, in the renovated main building or in a cabin. It's a good mainstream choice.

✖ Eating

Alchemy Cafe
CAFE **$**

(Map p260; ☑ 867-993-3831; www.alchemycafe.ca; 878 3rd Ave; mains $8-15; ☺ 8:30am-5pm Tue-Fri, 9:30am-5pm Sat & Sun; ☎ ☑) ✔ Groovy in the best sense of the word, Alchemy combines fantastic vegetarian food with a life-affirming green ethos. The coffees are way cool (in a hot sort of way) and special events include music, talks and, yes, rap sessions. The newly built vintage-style building has an alluring porch.

Cheechako's Bake Shop
BAKERY **$**

(Map p260; ☑ 867-993-5303; cnr Front & Princess Sts; mains $4-9; ☺ 7am-4pm Mon-Sat) A real bakery and a good one, on the main strip. Muffins, cookies and treats vie for your attention with sandwiches made on homemade bread.

Farmers Market
MARKET **$**

(Map p260; Front St; ☺ 11am-5pm Sat May-Sep) A farmers market thrives by the iconic waterfront gazebo. The sweet-as-candy carrots are the product of very cold nights. Try some birch syrup.

★ Klondike Kate's
CANADIAN **$$**

(Map p260; ☑ 867-993-6527; www.klondikekates.ca; cnr King St & 3rd Ave; mains $8-25; ☺ 4-9pm Mon-Sat, 8am-3pm & 4-9pm Sun Apr-Oct)

> ### ⓘ STREET NUMBERS & OPENING HOURS
> Street numbers are a rarity in Dawson and, unless noted otherwise, sights, attractions and many businesses are closed outside of the summer high season.

Two ways to know spring has arrived: the river cracks up and Kate's reopens. Locals in the know prefer the latter. The long and inventive menu has fine sandwiches, pastas and fresh Yukon fish. Look for great specials. Excellent list of Canadian craft brews.

★ Drunken Goat Taverna
GREEK **$$**

(Map p260; ☑ 867-993-5800; www.drunkengoattaverna.com; 2nd Ave; mains $14-28; ☺ noon-9pm) Follow your eyes to the flowers, your ears to the Aegean music and your nose to the excellent Greek food, run year-round by the legendary Tony Dovas. A new terrace out back is a fine place to while away an evening.

🍷 Drinking & Nightlife

The spirit(s) of the prospectors lives on in several saloons. On summer nights the action goes on until dawn, which would mean something if it weren't light all night.

★ Bombay Peggy's
PUB

(Map p260; ☑ 867-993-6969; www.bombaypeggys.com; cnr 2nd Ave & Princess St; ☺ 11am-11pm Mar-Nov) There's always a hint of pleasures to come swirling around the tables of Dawson's most inviting bar. Enjoy good beers, wines and mixed drinks inside or out.

Billy Goat
PUB

(Map p260; ☑ 867-993-5800; 2nd Ave; ☺ 5pm-late) Not a branch of the famed Chicago original, but a friendly lounge from Tony of Drunken Goat fame. Serves food from the Drunken Goat menu until late. Note the murals on the walls.

Downtown Hotel
PUB

(Map p260; ☑ 867-993-5346; www.downtownhotel.ca; cnr Queen St & 2nd Ave; ☺ 11am-late) This unremarkable bar comes to life at 9pm in summer for what can best be called the 'Sourtoe Schtick.' Tourists line up to drink a shot of booze ($10) that has a pickled human toe floating in it.

It's a long-running gag that's delightfully chronicled in Dieter Reinmuth's *The Saga of the Sourtoe.* (That the toe – it is real – looks much like a bit of beef jerky should give pause to anyone used to late-night Slim Jim jonesing...) And if you swallow it, the fee is $2500.

Bars at Westminster Hotel
BAR

(Map p260; ☑ 867-993-5339; 3rd Ave; ☺ noon-late) These two legendary bars carry the mostly affectionate monikers 'Snakepit,' 'Armpit' or simply 'Pit.' Theses are places for serious drinkers, with live music many nights.

DAWSON CITY TO ALASKA

From Dawson City, the free ferry crosses the Yukon River to the scenic **Top of the World Hwy** (Hwy 9). Only open in summer, the mostly paved 106km-long ridgetop road to the US border has superb vistas across the region.

You'll continue to feel on top of the world as you cross the border. The land is barren alpine meadows with jutting rocks and often grazing caribou. The border crossing (open 9am to 9pm Yukon time/8am to 8pm Alaska time 15 May to 15 September) has strict hours – if you're late you'll have to wait until the next day.

On the US side, Alaska shows its xenophobic side, as the 19km connection to the Taylor Hwy (Hwy 5) is mostly dirt and often impassable after storms (expect to get dirt in parts of your vehicle and person you didn't think possible). The old gold-mining town of Eagle on the Yukon River is 105km north. Some 47km south over somewhat better roads, you encounter **Chicken**, a delightful place of free thinkers happy to sell you a stupid T-shirt at one of the gas-station cafes or offer their views regarding government bureaucrats. Another 124km south and you reach the Alaska Hwy, where a turn east takes you to the Yukon. Just a tick west, **Tok** has services and motels. Alaska time is one hour earlier than the Yukon.

☆ Entertainment

★ **Diamond Tooth Gertie's Gambling Hall** CASINO
(Map p260; ☑ 867-993-5575; cnr Queen St & 4th Ave; $10; ⊙ 7pm-2am Mon-Fri, 2pm-2am Sat & Sun May-Sep) This popular re-creation of an 1898 saloon is complete with small-time gambling, a honky-tonk piano and dancing girls. The casino helps promote the town and fund culture. Each night there are three different floor shows with singing and dancing, which are often surprisingly contemporary.

ℹ Information

Much of Dawson is closed October to May. The biweekly, volunteer-run *Klondike Sun* (www. klondikesun.com) covers special events and activities.

CIBC ATM (2nd Ave; ⊙ 24hr) Near Queen St.

Northwest Territories Information Centre (Map p260; ☑ 867-993-6167; www.spectacularnwt.com; Front St; ⊙ 9am-7pm May-Sep) Has maps and information on the NWT and the Dempster Hwy.

VIC (Map p260; ☑ 867-993-5566; www.travel yukon.com; cnr Front & King Sts; ⊙ 8am-8pm May-Sep) Combines tourist and Parks Canada information (buy activity tickets and passes here). It also has essential schedules of events and activities.

ℹ Getting There & Away

Dawson City is 527km from Whitehorse. Public transportation to/from Whitehorse is often in flux. Should you fly in, there are no rental cars.

Dawson City Airport is 19km east of Dawson.
Air North (☑ 800-661-0407; www.flyairnorth. com) serves Whitehorse and Old Crow, and Inuvik in the NWT.

Alaska/Yukon Trails (☑ 907-479-2277; www. alaskashuttle.com) Runs buses to Fairbanks, AK ($285, thrice weekly June to mid-September).

Husky Bus (Map p260; ☑ 867-993-3821; www.huskybus.ca) Serves Whitehorse ($110, thrice weekly) and makes all stops along the Klondike Hwy. Departures are from the VIC. Husky will do pickups of paddlers and canoes along the Klondike Hwy with advance arrangement . Uses the Klondike Experience (p262) office.

DEMPSTER HIGHWAY

Rather than name this road for an obscure Mountie (William Dempster), this road should be named the Michelin Hwy or the Goodyear Hwy for the number of tires it's sent to an explosive demise. This 736km thrill ride is one of North America's great adventure roads, winding through stark mountains and emerald valleys, across huge tracts of tundra, and passing through Tombstone Territorial Park (p259).

The Dempster (Hwy 5 in the Yukon, Hwy 8 in the NWT) starts 40km southeast of Dawson City off the Klondike Hwy and heads north over the Ogilvie and Richardson Mountains beyond the Arctic Circle and on to Inuvik in the NWT, near the shores of the Beaufort Sea.

Road Conditions

Built on a thick base of gravel to insulate the permafrost underneath (which would otherwise melt, causing the road to sink without a trace), the Dempster is open most of the year, but the best time to travel is between June and early September, when the ferries over the Peel and Mackenzie Rivers operate. In winter, ice forms a natural bridge over the rivers, which become ice roads. The Dempster is closed during the spring thaw and the winter freeze-up; the timing of these vary by the year and can occur from mid-April to June and mid-October to December, respectively.

Check road conditions in the Yukon (p247) and the **NWT** (☑ 800-661-0750; www. dot.gov.nt.ca); the Northwest Territories Information Centre (p265) in Dawson City is a good resource. It takes 10 to 12 hours to drive to Inuvik without stopping for a break. (Given that William Dempster regularly made 700km dogsled journeys in subzero weather, this rugged and challenging road is properly named after all.)

🛏 Sleeping & Eating

Accommodations and vehicle services along the route are few. The Yukon government has three campgrounds: at **Tombstone** (with the interpretive centre, 71km from the start of the highway), **Engineer Creek** (194km) and **Rock River** (447km). There's also a NWT government campground at **Nitainlaii Territorial Park**, 9km south of Fort McPherson. Sites at these campgrounds are $12.

The Eagle Plains Hotel (☑ 867-993-2453; eagleplains@northwestel.net; Dempster Hwy; r $100-160; P @) is open year-round and offers 32 rooms in a low-rise building in a stark setting. The next service station is 180km further north at Fort McPherson in the NWT.

ARCTIC PARKS

North of the Arctic Circle, the Yukon's population numbers a few hundred. It's a lonely land with little evidence of humans and only the hardiest venture here during the short summers.

The 280-person village of **Old Crow** is home to the Vuntut Gwitch'in First Nations and is unreachable by vehicle. Residents subsist on caribou from the legendary 130,000-strong Porcupine herd, which migrates each year between the Arctic National Wildlife Refuge (ANWR) in Alaska and the Yukon.

On the Yukon side of this vast flat arctic tundra, a large swath of land is now protected in the adjoining **Vuntut National Park** and **Ivvavik National Park**. Information on both can be obtained from the Parks Canada office (p781) in Inuvik, NWT, where you can get information on the very limited options for organizing visits to the parks. There are no facilities of any kind in the parks.

The aboriginal name **Herschel Island-Qikiqtaruk Territorial Park** (☑ 867-777-4058; www.yukonparks.ca) means 'It is Island' and indeed it is. Barely rising above the waters of Mackenzie Bay on the Beaufort Sea, the park has a long tradition of human habitation. In the late 1800s American whalers set up shop at Pauline Cove. Abandoned in 1907, Pauline Cove has several surviving wooden buildings left behind by the whalers. Summer visits to Herschel Island are possible via tours from Inuvik.

Today, Inuvialuit families use the island for traditional hunting, although climate change is causing the island to dissolve into the sea.

Understand BC & the Canadian Rockies

BC & the Canadian Rockies Today

Locals in Western Canada's big cities will tell you that rising living costs are increasingly bumping up against flat-lining wages. Vancouverites have seen house prices leap by double-digit percentage points in recent years while salaries remain unchanged. And while Alberta's economy has long been hitched to oil, British Columbia is also craving a bigger slice of the resource-sector pie, to the chagrin of those decrying the potential despoiling of wilderness regions. Optimism remains high, though, and rising house prices may yet turn out to be a historic blip.

Best on Film

The Grey Fox (1982) Evocative Canadian Western covering the story of the country's first great train robbery.
City of Gold (1957) Delightful short film comparing gold rush Dawson City to 60 years later. Narrated by noted Canadian author Pierre Berton.
Carts of Darkness (2008) Documentary about shopping-cart races among Vancouver's homeless.
Mount Pleasant (2007) Gritty drama about family life in Vancouver.

Best in Print

City of Glass (Douglas Coupland; 2000) Vancouver's most celebrated contemporary writer offers a quirky guide to his hometown.
Craft Beer Revolution (Joe Wiebe; 2015) Profiles the lip-smacking breweries and beer-makers of BC.
The Call of the Wild (Jack London; 1903) The story of a dog during the Klondike gold rush.
Whistle Post West: Railway Tales from British Columbia, Alberta and Yukon (Various authors; 2015) Riveting stories from the region's golden age of rail.
The Jade Peony (Wayson Choy; 1995) Poignant coming-of-age story set in Vancouver's 1930s and '40s Chinatown.

Global Exposure

Vancouver's Expo '86 world exposition and its 2010 Winter Olympics were almost 25 years apart but they had similar effects on the city: each showcased the region's billion-dollar good looks and enticed the world to visit. But while tourism boomed, the benefits for locals were harder to grasp. Both events triggered real-estate stampedes that saw house prices leap beyond the reach of Vancouverites with everyday jobs. One result of this is that younger people, especially young families, are now looking far beyond the city for housing. Price spikes are taking place around the province in communities from Victoria to Nanaimo and from Cumberland to Powell River.

Resource Rumble

Alberta had its own Winter Olympics back in 1988. But oil has been a far bigger influence on its economy, enabling it to sidestep global recessions better than most via its vast oil sands and its reputation as a low-taxation, big-business capital. But with oil prices declining, has Alberta erroneously placed all its economic eggs in one basket? The province is still seeking to build infrastructure to support its biggest industry, including a controversial mega-pipeline that aims to send bitumen oil through remote, sensitive areas of BC wilderness to a tanker terminal on the coast.

BC is dealing with its own resource controversies. Many locals are up in arms about the gigantic Site C hydroelectric dam being built in the province's remote northeastern region, while a proposed Liquid Natural Gas (LNG) terminal has also become a focus for environmental ire. It remains to be seen how BC will deal with the challenge of balancing potential economic boons against the danger of permanently degrading swaths of pristine environment.

Roller-Coaster Loonie

On par with its US counterpart just a couple of years back, the Canadian dollar – known as the 'Loonie' because of the loon bird depicted on its $1 coins – has a huge influence on the regional economy; the country's southern neighbor will always be its biggest trading partner. And while dollar parity meant fewer American tourists were traveling north five years ago, a recent slide by as much as 25% in the loonie's value has seen them returning in droves, along with surging numbers from China, Australia and the UK. Cities such as Vancouver and Victoria have been posting impressive increases in tourism numbers since early 2015, but it's clear these figures could easily fall if the Canadian dollar rises again.

POPULATION: **4.7 MILLION**

UNEMPLOYMENT RATE: **6.2%**

GDP: **$205 BILLION**

GDP GROWTH: **3%**

Meanwhile in the Yukon

Although BC and the Yukon share a border, they share little else. The history of the Yukon has always been more closely linked to that of neighboring Alaska. The Yukon remains in many ways as it was 200 years ago: a forbidding wilderness bursting into life during a brief summer. Its politics lean towards the conservative, an outgrowth of the area's popular image of self-reliance. But while the Yukon has remained quietly under the radar, things may soon change dramatically.

Few doubt that enormous energy and mineral riches lie under the Yukon. While the territory's remoteness currently limits efforts towards further exploration, that will eventually change. Time will tell if the region will adopt an Alberta-style oil-sands approach or struggle with environmental considerations similar to those faced by BC.

if British Columbia were 100 people

74 would be white   3 would be Aboriginal
20 would be Asian   1 would be black
2 would be Latino

population per sq km

☀ ≈ 4 people

Alberta's Mammoth Wildfire

Canadians were glued to their TV screens in May 2016 when one of the country's biggest-ever wildfires swept through northern Alberta and into Saskatchewan, consuming 5900 sq km before being officially declared under control in early July. Horrified Canadians donated millions of dollars in aid while watching the community of Fort McMurray, including thousands of homes, become engulfed in flames. Online videos showed an estimated 70,000 people fleeing the raging fire – the largest wildfire evacuation in Alberta history – while a provincial state of emergency was swiftly declared.

International assistance also flooded in from the US, Mexico, Australia and beyond, while – eventually – surreal images emerged of devastated, ash-covered streets looking like apocalypse movie sets. Billions of dollars in damage was caused by the fire, which investigations indicate was started by human activity, and the event was reportedly the most expensive disaster in Canadian history.

History

This region's human history began at least 15,000 years ago when thriving Aboriginal communities emerged along the salmon-rich coastline and in the foothills of the Rockies. Everything changed rapidly, though, when the Europeans arrived in the 1700s. Finding untold abundance and locals without guns, they quickly transformed the area with trade, industry and pioneer settlements. Much of this tumultuous heritage is accessible to visitors, with national historic sites – from forts to famous homes – studding British Columbia, Alberta and the Yukon.

First Peoples Kick Things Off

The ancestors of Western Canada's Aboriginal peoples were settlers who showed up in North America at least 15,000 years ago. The most prominent theory is that, after the last Ice Age, they crossed to Alaska on a land bridge over what is now the Bering Strait. Some settled along the Pacific Coast, while others found their way to the interior – Alberta, the Yukon and beyond – ultimately populating the rest of North America. This theory is not without its detractors: in recent years archaeologists have discovered the remnants of communities that appear to pre-date the arrival of the Bering Strait settlers.

Whatever the true story, there is little dispute over who was here first. The Aboriginal peoples of this region, thriving on abundant food and untold resources, developed sophisticated cultures and intricate trade networks over many thousands of years. Coastal peoples dwelled as extended families in large, single-roofed cedar lodges, while inland and mountain communities generally had a tougher time, facing extremes of weather and leading nomadic subsistence lives: in the north they hungrily pursued migratory herds of animals such as moose and caribou, while in the south they chased down bison.

Best Museums

Royal BC Museum, Victoria

Glenbow Museum, Calgary

Whyte Museum of the Canadian Rockies, Banff

Craigdarroch Castle, Victoria

West Coast Railway Heritage Park, Squamish

Europeans Poke Around

During the 18th century, European explorers hungry for new sources of wealth appeared off the west coast as well as in the Rockies region after traveling through the wilderness from eastern Canada. Russian Alexsey

TIMELINE	800	1754	1774
	An ash-spewing eruption of the Yukon volcano now known as Mt Churchill causes many people to flee to southwest USA, where they may have evolved into the Navajo and Apaches.	The first European, fur trader Anthony Henday, manages to reach Alberta from eastern Canada. He spends the winter living with Aboriginal locals, hunting buffalo alongside them.	Spanish ships gingerly sail northwards along the Pacific Ocean coastline, nosing not very far into what would later become BC. They are the first Europeans to arrive by boat.

Chirikov is thought to have been first on the coast in 1741, followed by the Spaniards: they sent three expeditions between 1774 and 1779 in search of the fabled Northwest Passage. They ended up by the entrance to Nootka Sound on Vancouver Island but didn't initially venture into the Strait of Georgia.

British explorer Captain James Cook also elbowed in from the South Pacific in 1778. He had a similar Northwest Passage motive, and a similar result: he hit the west coast of Vancouver Island and believed it to be the mainland. It wasn't until 1791 that the mainland-lined Strait of Georgia was properly explored. Spanish navigator José María Narváez did the honors, sailing all the way into Burrard Inlet. He named part of this area Islas de Langara.

Next up was Captain George Vancouver, a British navigator who had previously sailed with Cook. In 1792 he glided into the inner harbor and spent one day there, meeting briefly with Spanish captains Valdez and Galiano who had already claimed the area. Then he sailed away, not thinking twice about a place that would eventually carry his name.

Despite Captain Vancouver's seeming indifference, the British interest in the area grew as its abundant resources became obvious. Finally, a treaty signed with the Spanish in 1794 saw war averted and the British assuming control.

Fur: The New Gold

The fur trade was the main lure for pioneers who followed on the heels of the first European forays, and trade grew rapidly as Western Canada's easy prey became clear. Fur trader Anthony Henday was reputedly the first European to arrive in Alberta, exploring in 1754 the outback areas now known as Edmonton and Red Deer. The region's Aboriginal people – inland and on the coast – soon came into contact with the Europeans.

Legendary trappers such as Alexander Mackenzie, Simon Fraser and David Thompson also explored overland routes from the east during this period. At the same time, the Hudson's Bay Company (HBC) rapidly became the catalyst for settler development, building fort communities and fostering trade routes throughout the region.

Of these early explorers, Mackenzie is probably the most interesting. Often compared to the Lewis and Clark expedition in the US, he traversed Canada in 1793, more than 10 years before the Americans crossed their country to the south. Exploring the Rockies, the continental divide and the Fraser River, he later produced a book on his exploits titled *Voyages... to the Frozen and Pacific Oceans*.

By the 1840s the US was making its own claims on the area and the HBC dispatched James Douglas to Vancouver Island, where he

---

Best Historical Sites

Klondike National Historic Sites, Yukon

Barkerville, BC

Fort Langley, BC

Head-Smashed-In Buffalo Jump, Alberta

Gulf of Georgia Cannery, BC

HISTORY FUR: THE NEW GOLD

1792	1805	1827	1871
Captain George Vancouver, of the British Royal Navy, sails in to the same area for one day, little knowing that the region would eventually take his name. He never returned.	The Northwest Trading Company establishes a fur-trading post at Hudson's Hope in northeast BC. It is later taken over by the Hudson's Bay Company.	The Hudson's Bay Company builds the strategically vital Fort Langley on BC's Fraser River. It's now one of the province's most popular historic attractions.	BC joins the Canadian Confederation and is promised a rail link from eastern Canada to sweeten the deal – it eventually arrives, 16 years later.

established Fort Victoria. A few years later the British and Americans settled their claims and the border was solidified.

Despite its relative remoteness, the Yukon was also becoming part of the action. The HBC's Robert Campbell became the first European to travel extensively in the region, followed by a ragtag wave of fur traders, prospectors, whalers and – as always – missionaries. Campbell established Fort Selkirk on the Yukon River as a trading post.

Gold: The New Fur

The discovery of gold along BC's Fraser River in 1858 brought a tidal wave of avaricious visitors to the region. A second wave arrived when the yellow stuff was discovered further north in the Cariboo area. Although the gold rush only lasted a few years, many of those who came remained afterwards. You can experience a sanitized version of a gold rush town – ie without the effluent, drunkenness and prostitution – at the restored Barkerville Historic Town.

By this stage, desperate travelers were panning and scraping for gold across the region, with large imaginary nuggets forming like misshapen pupils in their eyes. But for every prospector who made their fortune, there were hundreds who failed to find more than a whiff of the elusive treasure.

Alberta and BC are home to several 'castles of the north,' grand hotels built during the golden age of railway travel to entice the wealthy to travel by train. These remain as some of the region's finest historic sleepovers, including Banff Springs, the Hotel Vancouver and Victoria's Empress Hotel.

Of course, that didn't stop people trying. For years the Yukon became a byword for broken dreams and shattered fortune hunters...right up until 1896, when a discovery on a tributary of the Klondike River near what became Dawson City changed everything. The region's ensuing gold rush attracted further hopefuls from around the world – more than 99% of whom found no fortune while losing what they had.

Rail Link Opens the West

After mainland BC and Vancouver Island were united, Victoria was named BC's new provincial capital in 1868. Meanwhile, in 1867, the UK government had passed the British North American Act, creating the Dominion of Canada. The eastern provinces of Canada united under this confederation, while BC joined in 1871 and Alberta joined in 1905.

But rather than duty to the Crown, it was the train that made them sign on the dotted line. Western Canada remained a distant and forbidding frontier but the fledgling Canadian government promised to build a railway link to the rest of the country within a decade. The Canadian Pacific Railway rolled into Alberta in 1883, nosing into BC four years later.

The construction of the transcontinental railway is one of the most impressive and important chapters in the region's history. The railroad was crucial in unifying the distant east and west wings of the vast country in order to encourage immigration and develop business opportu-

1886	1896	1905	1920
The City of Vancouver is incorporated. Within weeks, the fledgling metropolis burns to the ground in the Great Fire. A prompt rebuild ensues, with stone and brick much in evidence.	Sparkly stuff found in Bonanza Creek near today's Dawson City, Yukon, sets off the legendary Klondike gold rush. After three frantic years and many shattered dreams the madness subsides.	Alberta becomes a province, but it is another 25 years before the federal government allows it to control its own resources. This would prove useful quite a few years later.	Having dropped significantly since the turn of the century, the population of the Yukon falls below 5000. It doesn't increase greatly until after the Alaska Hwy is built in 1942–43.

nities. But it came with a large price: the much-quoted statistic that a Chinese laborer died for every mile of track built is almost certainly true.

With the train link came a modicum of law and order. Aiming to tame the 'wild west,' the government created the North-West Mounted Police (NWMP) in 1873, which later became the Royal Canadian Mounted Police (RCMP). Nicknamed 'Mounties,' they still serve as the country's national police force.

Also during this period, wealth from gold and revenue from the people looking for it helped the Yukon become a separate territory in 1898, with Dawson City the capital. But the northern party was short-lived: by 1920 economic decline had set in and the population dropped to just 5000, a fraction of its gold-rush heyday. And although the construction of the Alaska Hwy in 1942 opened up the territory to development and provided it with its first tangible link to BC, the glory days were over.

Big Cities Emerge...Then Burn Down

While all this nation-building was going on, the region's first cities were quietly laying their foundations. And while some – Prince Rupert and New Westminster, for example – were considered as potential regional capitals (New West actually held the position in BC until Victoria took over), it was eventually Vancouver that became Western Canada's biggest metropolis. But it's worth remembering that the City of Glass almost didn't make it.

In 1867, near the middle of what's now called Maple Tree Sq, John 'Gassy Jack' Deighton opened a waterfront saloon for thirsty sawmill workers. Attracting an attendant ring of squalid shacks, the ramshackle area around the bar soon became known as Gastown. As the ad hoc settlement grew, the colonial administration decided to formalize it, creating the new town of Granville in 1870. Most people still called it Gastown, especially when Deighton opened a larger saloon nearby a few years later.

In 1886 the town's name was officially changed to Vancouver and plans were laid for a much larger city, encompassing the old Gastown/Granville area. But within a few weeks, a giant fire swept rapidly through the fledgling city, destroying around 1000 mostly wooden buildings in less than an hour.

When reconstruction began, stone replaced wood – which explains why this area of Vancouver is now packed with old brick and rock buildings that look like they were constructed to last forever. It's now home to many of Vancouver's best bars – Gassy Jack, now standing atop a whiskey barrel in statue form near the site of his first bar, would be proud.

Many of those who toiled to build the railway link across Canada came from China. But the government also lured dozens of miners from Wales to work on the Crows Nest Pass section of the project in 1897. They were offered the princely sum of $1.50 per day.

Inspector Constantine of the North-West Mounted Police arrived in the Yukon with a team of 20 hardy men in 1895. Their mission was to maintain law and order and uphold Canadian sovereignty, which included acting as magistrates, customs collectors and Dominion of Canada land agents.

1947	1960	1964	1971
Alberta makes a major oil discovery at Leduc, not far from Edmonton. As more oil and gas is discovered, the province changes forever, bringing vast wealth into the region.	Aboriginals finally get the right to vote in BC, a key advance in a decades-long initiative to restore the rights of the province's original residents and agree to compensation.	Implementation of the Columbia River Treaty starts the construction of huge dams that forever change the Kootenays. One creates Arrow Lakes, causing Nakusp to be moved, while obliterating other towns.	Greenpeace is founded in Vancouver. A small group of activists sets sail in a fishing boat to 'bear witness' to US underground nuclear tests on an island off Alaska.

Aboriginal Turmoil

Despite the successes of colonization, the Aboriginal people, who had thrived here for centuries, were almost decimated by the arrival of the Europeans. Imported diseases – especially smallpox – wiped out huge numbers of people who had no natural immunity or medicines for dealing with them. At the same time, highly dubious land treaties were 'negotiated,' which gave the Europeans title to land that had been traditional Aboriginal territory. In exchange, the locals were often reduced to living on small reserves.

But the treatment of the Aboriginal people went further than a mere land grab. In what is now regarded as one of the darkest chapters in Canada's history, a process of cultural strangulation took place that ranged from attempting to indoctrinate Aboriginal people (especially children) with Christianity and preventing them from practicing certain age-old rites, including the potlatch (gift-giving ceremonial feast). Only in the past 50 years have governments attempted to make amends, launching new treaty negotiations and finally (in 1951) repealing the anti-potlatch laws.

Moving On & Making Amends

After WWII Western Canada embraced mining and logging and a lot of money flowed into the region. Road and rail links were pushed into all manner of formerly remote places, such as those along the Stewart-Cassiar Hwy. The 1961 Columbia River Treaty with the US resulted in massive dam-building projects that flooded pristine valleys and displaced people. The Americans paid BC to hold back huge amounts of water that could be released to hydroelectric plants south of the border whenever power use demanded.

Vancouver hung out the welcome sign to the world in a big way starting in the 1980s, when Expo '86 showcased the city globally. Calgary had its own moment in the spotlight two years later when it became the first city in Canada to host the Winter Olympic Games – Vancouver joined the party in 2010 by hosting them, too.

BC has also made progress in making amends for past Aboriginal injustices. The first modern-day treaty – signed with the Nisga'a peoples in 1998 – provided about $200 million and allowed some self-governance. But this new process is highly controversial and not everyone is on board: many non-Aboriginal locals do not want the claims to go too far. So far only 20% of Aboriginal groups have begun negotiations.

BC's official coat of arms was unveiled by Queen Elizabeth II in 1987. It is the only coat of arms in the world to incorporate the Queen's own Royal Crest. It also includes the Latin motto 'splendor sine occasu,' which is often translated as 'splendor without diminishment.'

Party Time & Hangovers

Alberta has always been better at making money than BC, and the region has enjoyed astonishing economic success by exploiting its oil sands. Located in northern Alberta, this is a controversial enterprise involving

1988	1998	2001	2003
Calgary hosts the Olympic Winter Games, introducing Eddie 'The Eagle' Edwards to an amused world. Twenty-two years later, he shows up as a commentator at the Vancouver Olympics.	BC, the federal government and the Nisga'a Aboriginal peoples agree on the first modern-day treaty, a huge settlement for the impoverished people living at Nass Camp near the Nisga'a Lava Bed.	The Vancouver Canucks make the Stanley Cup hockey finals for the first time since 1994, but lose to Boston. Street riots featured both years.	BC and Ontario lead the way in North America by making same-sex marriage legal. Many gay and lesbian couples travel from across the continent to Vancouver to be married.

the labor-intensive extraction of bitumen. It has attracted the ire of environmentalists who believe it's one of the dirtiest and most ecologically damaging methods for producing oil. The companies involved – some of the world's biggest petroleum corporations – state that they operate to the highest standards and follow all government guidelines. With oil prices declining in recent years, though, the enterprise is not the lucrative license-to-print-money it may once have seemed.

Healthy profits of a different kind were enjoyed by suppliers and developers involved with the biggest party to hit Canada in decades: the 2010 Winter Olympic and Paralympic Games, staged in Vancouver and Whistler. Maple-leaf flags and face tattoos became the norm as Vancouverites transformed the city into a wandering carnival of family-friendly bonhomie. When the flame was extinguished at the closing ceremony, the locals wiped off the red face paint and trudged back to their regular lives.

The breathtaking images of the region's pristine beauty that circulated around the world as a result of the games, at the same time as international surveys proclaimed Vancouver to be one of the globe's best cities to live in, enticed more people to move to the city. Vancouver house prices rose rapidly as a result and many locals have since struggled with an increasing lack of affordability.

BC, Alberta and the Yukon are still relatively young enterprises at the start of their development, however, and there remains a sense that perhaps the best is yet to come for this part of the world.

Vancouver leads BC's frothy surge of modern-day craft beer microbreweries. But the city used to have many small beer producers, all of which had disappeared by the 1950s. These included Vancouver Brewery, Lion Brewing, Landsdowne Brewery and Cedar Cottage Brewery.

HISTORY PARTY TIME & HANGOVERS

2010	2013	2016	2016
Vancouver hosts the Olympic and Paralympic Winter Games, in front of a global TV audience estimated to be more than two billion. There's plenty of flag-waving and anthem-singing.	Calgary and other areas of southern Alberta receive their worst flooding in living memory, displacing more than 100,000 locals. The region shows its mettle with a giant clean-up drive.	70,000 Albertans are evacuated from the city of Fort McMurray in one of the province's largest-ever wildfires. A regional state of emergency is declared as flames spread to 5900 sq km before being brought under control.	Justin Trudeau becomes the first sitting Canadian prime minister to march in Vancouver's Pride Parade. He's cheered on by hundreds of thousands of locals.

Wildlife

British Columbia, Alberta and the Yukon offer a jaw-dropping safari of wildlife-spotting opportunities. While locals may be blasé, visitors frequently rave about the impressive animals they've seen in Canada's best critter-watching region. Expect a spine-tingling frisson when you see your first bear nonchalantly scoffing berries or a bald eagle dive-bombing a salmon-stuffed river. Then there are the whales: boat tours to see orca pods are extremely popular on the West Coast and the word 'magical' doesn't even come close to the experience.

Bears

An unmissable sighting for many visitors, grizzly bears – *Ursus arctos horribilis* to all you Latin scholars – are most commonly viewed in the Rockies. Identifiable by their distinctive shoulder hump, they stand up to 3m tall and are solitary mammals with no natural enemies (except humans; try to resist the need for a selfie). While they enjoy fresh-catch meals of elk, moose and caribou, most of their noshing centers on salmon and wild berries. Black bears are also fairly common on the mainland of BC (especially in the north) as well as in the north and west regions of Vancouver Island.

Confusingly, grizzlies are almost black, while their smaller and much more numerous relation, the black bear, is sometimes brown. More commonly spotted in the wild than grizzlies, black bears reside in large numbers in northern BC and in the Banff and Jasper areas, where 'wildlife jams' are a frequent issue among rubbernecking motorists. You may also see these bears as far south as Whistler and in the foothills of North Vancouver.

In 1994 coastal BC's Khutzeymateen Grizzly Bear Sanctuary (near the northern town of Prince Rupert) was officially designated for protected status. More than 50 grizzlies currently live on this 450-sq-km refuge. A few ecotour operators have permits for viewing these animals if you want to check them out face-to-face. There are also tiny bear sanctuaries in Banff and on Grouse Mountain in North Vancouver.

Kermode bears, sometimes called spirit bears, are a subspecies of the black bear but are whitish in color. They're unique to BC, and are found in the north, from Bella Coola through the Great Bear Rainforest to Stewart, mostly along the lower Skeena River Valley.

E-Fauna BC (http://ibis.geog.ubc.ca/biodiversity/efauna) is a fascinating online digital atlas of the province's flora and fauna, from amphibians to mammals. It has lots of great photos of birds to look out for on your visit to the region.

Whales

Whale-watching is a must-do activity on the West Coast and tours (typically up to three hours for around $100 per person) are justifiably popular. The waters around Vancouver Island, particularly in Johnstone Strait, teem with orcas every summer, and tours frequently depart from Tofino, Telegraph Cove, Victoria, Richmond and beyond. The Inside Passage cruise ship and ferry route between Port Hardy and Prince Rupert is also a popular long-haul viewing spot.

While orcas – also known as killer whales – dominate the region's viewing, you might sight some of the 20,000 Pacific gray whales that migrate along the coastline here twice a year. If you're lucky, you'll also see majestic humpbacks, which average 15m in length.

Orcas get their 'killer' moniker from the fast-paced way they pursue and attack the area's marine life and not from attacks on humans, which are more rare than whale sightings in the Rockies. On your tour you'll likely spot the orcas' preferred nosh languishing on rocks or nosing around your boat – keep your camera primed for porpoises, dolphins, seals, Steller sea lions and sea otters.

Prime orca-viewing season is from May to mid-July; for gray whales, it's mid-August to October; and for humpbacks, it's August to October.

This region is home to the gray wolf, also known as the timber wolf. They hunt in packs of up to a dozen strong and mate for life. The females give birth to as many as 11 pups each spring.

Wolves

Wolves are perhaps the most intriguing and mysterious of all Canada's wild animals. They hunt cleverly and tenaciously in packs and have no qualms about taking on prey much larger than themselves. Human attacks are extremely rare but you'll nevertheless feel nervous excitement if you're lucky enough to spot one in the wild – typically in the distance, across the other side of a wide river.

The Rockies are your most likely spot for seeing a wolf. You may also hear them howling at the moon at night if you're camping in the bush. An intriguing and elusive subspecies of 'sea wolves' has been increasingly studied in recent years. Genetically related but distinct from their inland cousins, they live primarily along the coastline of BC's Great Bear Rainforest, living off deer as well as salmon and sea lions.

It's extremely unlikely that you'll be approached by a wolf, but they sometimes become habituated to human contact, typically through access to uncovered food on campsites. If a wolf approaches you and seems aggressive or unafraid, wave your arms in the air to make yourself appear larger; reverse slowly and do not turn your back; and make noise and throw sticks and/or stones.

BEAR AWARE

Bears are rarely in the business of attacking humans but, if provoked, they'll certainly have a go. And it won't be pretty. Most bear attacks on tourists result from ignorance on the part of the visitor, so keep the following points in mind when you're on the road in bear country:

➡ When on foot, travel in groups. Consider wearing bear bells as a way to make some noise – bears will generally steer clear of you if they know where you are.

➡ Follow any notices you see about bears in the area and ask park staff about recent sightings.

➡ Keep pets on a leash and do not linger near any dead animals.

➡ Never approach a bear, and keep all food and food smells away from bears; always use bear-resistant food containers.

If the above fails and a bear attacks, do the following:

➡ Don't drop your pack – it can provide protection.

➡ Try to walk backwards slowly without looking the bear in the eye – this is seen as a challenge.

➡ Don't run – a bear will always outrun you.

➡ Try to get somewhere safe, like a car.

➡ If attacked, use bear spray. If this fails, deploy one of the following approaches, depending on the type of bear: for black bears, try to appear larger, shout a lot and fight back; for grizzlies, playing dead, curling into a ball and protecting your head is recommended.

TOP WILDLIFE-WATCHING SPOTS

➡ Icefields Parkway – the 230km drive between Banff and Jasper is lined with monumental mountain peaks and a regular chorus of deer, bighorn sheep and black bears.

➡ Maligne Lake Rd – eagles, deer, elk, bighorn sheep and maybe a moose are likely spottings in this Jasper National Park area.

➡ Khutzeymateen Grizzly Bear Sanctuary – dozens of grizzlies live in this northern BC refuge, and ecotour operators have permits for viewing.

➡ Bella Coola Valley – boat tours along rivers are thick with sightings of grizzly bears wandering the banks.

Elk, Caribou & Deer

Male elk have been known on occasion to charge into vehicles in Jasper after spotting their reflection in the shiny paintwork, perhaps believing they've met a rival for their harem of eligible females. But mostly they're docile creatures. It's common to see this large deer species wandering around the edges of the town site for much of the year. November's rut is the best time to visit, though: you'll see the bugling males at their finest, strutting around and taking on their rivals with head-smashing displays of strength.

More common in other Canadian regions, woodland caribou show up in small groups in BC and the Rockies, although the Jasper population almost wiped itself out a couple of years ago by triggering an avalanche that buried nearly all of them.

Deer are common sights away from the cities in much of BC and beyond. Expect to spot leaping white-tailed deer and mule deer flitting among the trees and alongside the roads in the Rockies. You might also spot the Columbia black-tailed deer, a small subspecies native to Vancouver Island and BC's west coast.

Edited by Alison Parkinson, *Parks and Nature Places Around Vancouver* is a comprehensive guide to the top spots in and around the city where you're likely to see memorable flora and fauna. Many of the listings can be easily accessed on public transportation.

Moose

Western Canada's postcard-hogging shrub-nibbler is the largest member of the deer family, and owes its popularity to a distinctively odd appearance: skinny legs supporting a humongous body and a cartoonish head that looks inquisitive and clueless at the same time. And then there are the antlers: males grow a spectacular rack every summer, only to discard them in November.

You'll spot moose foraging for twigs and leaves – their main diet – near lakes, muskegs and streams, as well as in the mountain forests of the Rockies and the Yukon.

Moose are generally not aggressive, and will often stand stock-still for photographs. They can be unpredictable, though, so don't startle them. During mating season (September), the giant males can become belligerent, so keep your distance: great photos are not worth a sharply pronged antler charge from a massive, angry moose.

If you manage to photograph one particular fabled local, you'll likely have an Instagram viral hit on your hands: Bigfoot or Sasquatch is said to roam the region's forests, avoiding cameras. Keep your eyes peeled in the BC interior and near Tofino, where 'sightings' have been reported.

Bighorn Sheep

Often spotted clinging tenaciously to the almost-sheer cliff faces overlooking the roads around Banff and Jasper, bighorn sheep are a signature Rockies sight. They're here in large numbers, so are one of the easiest animals to spot. On the drive between Banff and Jasper via the Icefields Parkway, you'll likely spy them looking like sculptures standing sentinel on the rocks. The best viewing season is during September and October when the rut is on and the males are smashing their heads together to prove their mate-worthy credentials.

Birdlife

Of the region's 500-plus bird species, the black-and-blue Steller's jay is among the most famous; it was named BC's official bird after a government-sponsored contest. Other prominent feathered locals include ravens, herons, great horned owls and peregrine falcons. You don't have to trek into the wilderness for an up-close glimpse: head to Lost Lagoon on the edge of Vancouver's Stanley Park and you'll discover a feather-fringed oasis just a few steps from the city. In fact, you don't even have to stray that far; keep your eyes peeled on Vancouver's residential streets for local and visiting hummingbirds as well as resident northern flickers, a woodpecker with a distinctive spotted plumage.

The most visually arresting birds in Western Canada are eagles, especially of the bald variety. Their wingspans can reach up to 2m and, like wolves, they are a spine-tingling sight for anyone lucky enough to see one in the wild. Good viewing sites include Brackendale, near Squamish in BC, where thousands nest in winter and an annual bird count lures visitors. Also train your camera lens on Vancouver Island's southern and western shorelines: it won't be long before something awesome sweeps into view.

Sealife

Divers off the BC coastline can encounter a startling and often bizarre range of aquatic life. The swimming scallop looks rather like a set of false teeth; in fact, it's a fascinating symbiotic creature able to move under its own power, nabbing floating nutrients while a sponge attached to its shell provides protection. Giant Pacific octopuses with tentacles of up to 2m in length are found on shallow rocky ocean bottoms. The record weight of one of these creatures is 272kg. Wolf eels are known for darting out of crevices to inspect wetsuit-clad visitors and often snuggling into the crooks of their arms.

Salmon Runs

After years of depressingly declining returns, the 2010 wild Pacific sockeye salmon run on BC's Fraser River surprised and delighted scientists and local fishing operators by being the largest for almost 100 years. More than 34 million gasping salmon reportedly pushed themselves up the river to lay their eggs and die, a spectacle that turned regional rivers red with the sight of millions of crimson sockeye. However, while restaurants fell over themselves to offer wild salmon dishes for several months, scientists correctly predicted that the record run was a flash-in-the-pan and not an indication of long-term recovery in the salmon sector.

Urban Wildlife

You don't necessarily have to travel far into the wilderness to catch sight of Western Canada's multitudinous critters. As cities have expanded outwards, the areas that once teemed with unfettered wildlife have come into direct contact with human habitation. Some animals have

WILDLIFE BIRDLIFE

Resident Birds

Anna's hummingbird

Bald eagle

Northern flicker

Steller's jay

Cormorant

Other Local Critters

Coyote

Raccoon

Skunk

Marmot

Cougar

Lynx

Porcupine

Beaver

Wolverine

Douglas squirrel

BY THE NUMBERS

This region is home to more than 150 mammal species, 510 bird species, almost 500 fish species, 20 reptile species and 20 types of amphibian. About 140 species (including most of the whales, the burrowing owl, the sea otter and the Vancouver Island marmot) are considered endangered but many more are also at risk. Ecosystems are at their most diverse in southern BC, but that's also where threats from human pressures are at their greatest.

BC author JB MacKinnon's fascinating 2013 book *The Once and Future World* illuminates the ecosystems of the past and explores the urgent need for modern society to reconnect with this natural order before it's too late.

responded by retreating further into the wilderness, while others have adapted their way of life to co-exist with two-legged locals. It's not always an easy relationship.

In small towns such as Whistler, Dawson City and Tofino, grainy images of bears roaming around people's backyards usually light up social media platforms around the region several times a year. But some creatures have taken it a step further. In metro Vancouver, there are an estimated 3000 coyotes that live and forage in or near populated neighborhoods: it's common to see notices posted around the region during denning season (the time when pups are raised) warning local dog owners to be aware of aggressively protective coyote mothers.

In contrast, the animal-human problem is mostly deer-shaped in the town of Jasper, Alberta. Here, drivers are used to watching the road ahead of them for oblivious road-crossers – they can cause massive damage (to both animals and cars) in a collision. And if you're a gardener in this region, you have to either give up your green-thumbed ways or embark on a serious fortification of your plot: a favorite deer supper here often involves flowers, vegetables and fruit trees.

Artistic Side

It's easy to think Western Canada doesn't have much of an arts scene. How can moun-tain bikers or die-hard cowboys be interested in art, theater and literature? But in reali-ty, this region is a roiling hotbed of creativity, especially at the grassroots level. The trick is to hit the major cultural attractions first, then to latch on to some artsy locals and ask for tips on the coolest off-the-beaten-path events, exhibitions and happenings. You'll likely be well rewarded for your efforts.

Visual Arts

British Columbia's Emily Carr (1871–1945) made her name by painting Ab-original villages and swirling forest landscapes on Vancouver Island. She's often referred to as an honorary member of Canada's legendary Group of Seven. But she isn't the only great painter to have come from this region. Transforming canvases a few decades later, EJ Hughes (1913–2007) created rich, stylized work that vividly depicted coastal life along the West Coast.

In recent years Vancouver has been Western Canada's contemporary art capital, with photoconceptualism especially revered here. Stan Doug-las and Rodney Graham (who also works in multimedia) are celebrated but it's Jeff Wall, a photorealist whose large works have the quality of cinematic production, who has attained global recognition, which in-cludes having his work exhibited at New York's Museum of Modern Art (MoMA). Vancouver's art gallery showcases artists such as these, and the sparkling new Audain Art Museum in Whistler is dedicated to the best of BC's historic and modern-day creatives.

But the region's art scene isn't just about landmark galleries. Many Vancouver locals will tell you their favorite annual art event is Novem-ber's weekend-long Eastside Culture Crawl (www.culturecrawl.ca), dur-ing which about 450 East Vancouver artists open their home studios and galleries to a strolling mass of locals. Recently marking its 20th anniver-sary, Eastside Culture Crawl is the most enjoyable way to meet the city's grassroots artists as well as artistically inclined Vancouverites.

A strong commitment to public art across the region is apparent. Stat-ues and installations can be found in Alberta's Calgary and Edmonton, and in BC's Victoria and Richmond. But big-city Vancouver leads the way with hundreds of camera-loving installations studding the city, many of the most dramatic appearing under its popular Vancouver Biennale ini-tiative. And the city's most photographed public artwork? A clutch of 14 oversized bronze figures near English Bay Beach, which are laughing and smiling as if they're having a ball.

Top Art Galleries

Vancouver Art Gallery, Vancouver

Audain Art Museum, Whistler

Art Gallery of Alberta, Edmonton

Contemporary Calgary, Calgary

Art Gallery of Greater Victoria, Victoria

Brilliant Biennale

Operating for two-year stretches since 2005, the Vancouver Biennale installs large, sometimes challenging landmarks on the streets of the city, aiming to create an open-air art museum for locals and visitors to enjoy. While some of the works stay just for the duration of the event, others have become per-manent Vancouver fixtures by utilizing sponsorship and corporate support. These include the 10m-high *Trans Am Totem,* five scrapped cars stacked

BEST READS

The Cremation of Sam McGee (Robert W Service; 1907) Written by the renowned Bard of the Yukon, this is a classic of regional prose about two gold miners, the cold and what men will sometimes do. It's Service at his peak.

Runaway: Diary of a Street Kid (Evelyn Lau; 1989) Tells the true story of the author's dangerous life on the streets of downtown Vancouver.

Red Dog, Red Dog (Patrick Lane; 2008) Follows two brothers trying to navigate tough times in 1950s Okanagan Valley. It's a gripping look at heartbreak, corruption and the tough lives of those who settled Canada.

Stanley Park (Timothy Taylor; 2001) Stirs together a haute-cuisine chef with a park's dark secrets. The result is a story capturing Vancouver's quirky modern ambience.

Klondike Tales (Jack London; 2001) A collection of stories drawing on the author's first-hand experiences to show the hardships, triumphs and betrayals of the Yukon gold rush in 1897. *The Call of the Wild* wins new fans every year.

atop a cedar tree trunk; and *A-maze-ing Laughter,* bronze characters near the beach at English Bay, the city's most selfie-inviting street feature. For the location of these and other talked-about local Biennale works, check out the self-guided tours at www.vancouverbiennale.com.

Riotous Artwork

Look for the large London Drugs store in the Woodwards building on W Hastings St in Vancouver and enter the building's courtyard, which is carved from what was originally the interior of one of the city's largest department stores. The space is now dominated by the city's most evocative – and perhaps provocative – public artwork.

Measuring 15m by 9m and created by Stan Douglas, *Abbott & Cordova, 7 August 1971* is a mammoth double-sided black-and-white photo montage depicting a key moment in the history of local social protest: the night when police in full riot gear broke up a pro-marijuana smoke-in being staged in the Downtown Eastside.

The action (the image shows mounted police pushing against unarmed locals, and miscreants being stuffed into police wagons) soon spiraled out of control, with pitched battles and general chaos triggering a siege-like atmosphere on the area's streets. Later, the event became known as the 'Gastown Riot' and 'The Battle of Maple Tree Square.'

BC's Sunshine Coast boasts dozens of home-based artists. Find out their location via the Purple Banner link at www.suncoastarts.com.

Literature

Perhaps due to those long Albertan winters and the month-long rain fests on the BC coast, Western Canadians are big readers. And there's no shortage of local tomes to dip into: BC has an estimated 1500 professional authors and dozens of publishers to provide material for the region's insatiable bookworms.

The bulging bookshelf of historic authors includes WP Kinsella (author of *Shoeless Joe,* the story that became the 1989 *Field of Dreams* movie); William Gibson (sci-fi creator of cyberpunk); and Malcolm Lowry, who wrote his *Under the Volcano* (1947) masterpiece here. Don't miss the writings of celebrated BC painter Emily Carr (1871–1945), especially *Klee Wyck* (1941), which evocatively recounts her experiences with local First Nations communities.

A rich vein of contemporary work exists, too. One of Canada's most revered artists and authors, Douglas Coupland lives in West Vancouver and has produced genre-defining titles such as *Generation X, Girlfriend in a Coma* and the excellent 'alternative guidebook' *City of Glass,* which showcases his love for Vancouver with quirky mini-essays and evocative photography. Coupland's latest offering is *Bit Rot* (2016).

A celebrated nonfiction scene has also developed in the region in recent years, with books from local lads Charles Montgomery and JB Mackinnon winning prestigious national awards. Mackinnon's most recent title, *The Once and Future World* (2013), explores the natural abundance of the past to inspire a new way of looking at our environment today.

While Alberta falls short of the heady heights of BC when it comes to literary output, you should consider dipping into the following books before arrrival for a richer understanding of the area: *The Wild Rose Anthology of Alberta Prose* (2003), edited by George Melnyk and Tamara Seiler, and *Writing the Terrain: Travelling Through Alberta with the Poets* (2005), edited by Robert Stamp.

And if you make it to the Yukon, drop into Dawson City. Bookish-types will love nosing around the Jack London Interpretive Centre, a cabin evoking the time when the celebrated author lived in the region. In fact, bring a book along for the trip: preferably *Sailor on Snowshoes* (2006) by Dick North, which explores London's time in the area. Alternatively, dip into almost anything written by the legendary Robert W Service (1874–1958) during his pioneer-era time here; it'll exponentially increase your understanding of this rugged region.

Many BC writers live on the Southern Gulf Islands. For an introduction to their work (and the work of other BC authors), visit the annual literary festival on tranquil Galiano Island (www.galianoliterary festival.com).

Yukon Shooting Star

Only one Yukoner has a star on the Hollywood Walk of Fame: that's Victor Jory. Like any good northerner, his story is better than the plots of the 200 or so movies and TV shows that have his name in the credits. He was born in 1902 to a single mother who ran a rooming house near Dawson City. Hanging around Hollywood got him his first role in 1930, and over the next 50 years he had parts in big pictures (eg quarrelsome field boss in *Gone with the Wind*) and small ones (the lead in *Cat-Women of the Moon*). Reflecting the ethos of the Yukon, he never said no to anything that might put food on his plate.

Theater & Dance

Local theaters can be found throughout Western Canada, with even the smallest communities providing a venue for grassroots performing troupes and visiting shows. Bigger cities such as Vancouver, Victoria, Edmonton and Calgary often have several large auditoria with their own repertory theater companies – Vancouver's Arts Club Theatre Company (www.artsclub.com) is the region's largest, staging shows at three venues around the city. The performance season usually runs from October to June, but shows frequently tread the boards outside this period. It pays to dig a little for some hidden gems: there are dozens of smaller venues, with a fringe-theater approach, throughout the region.

Fans of the small stage may wish to time their visits with fringe-theater events. Edmonton hosts the oldest and biggest fringe festival in North America (www.fringetheatre.ca), while there are also popular festivals in Vancouver (www.vancouverfringe.com) and Victoria (www.victoriafringe.com).

ALL THE WORLD'S A STAGE

Vancouver's Bard on the Beach (www.bardonthebeach.org) is a quintessentially West Coast way to catch a show. The event includes a roster of three or four Shakespeare and Shakespeare-related plays performed in tents on the Kitsilano waterfront, from June to September, with the North Shore mountains in the background. It regularly sells to capacity, making it one of North America's most successful and enduring Shakespeare festivals.

ARTISTIC SIDE YUKON SHOOTING STAR

Vancouver is a major Canadian capital for dance, second only to Montréal. It hosts frequent annual events, from classical to challenging modern interpretations. If you're a true dance buff, consider picking up a copy of *Dancing Through History: In Search of the Stories that Define Canada* (2102) by Vancouver-based author and dancer Lori Henry. The fascinating book explores the nation's culture through its traditional dances.

Cinema & Television

Western Canada is a hot spot for TV producers and moviemakers looking for a handy stand-in for American locations, hence the name 'Hollywood North,' used to describe the film sector up here. Blockbusters such as *Rise of the Planet of the Apes* (2011), *50 Shades of Grey* (2015) and *Godzilla* (2014) were filmed in and around metro Vancouver, while big-budget films including *Inception* (2010) and *The Revenant* (2015) were at least partly filmed in Alberta.

But it's not all about making US-set flicks. Canada has a thriving independent filmmaking sector. Catching a couple of locally made movies before you arrive can provide some handy insights into the differences between the US and Canada. Look out for locally shot indie flicks including *Mount Pleasant* (2006) and *Carts of Darkness* (2008).

The region also has a great reputation for special effects and postproduction work, with *Avatar* (2009), *Life of Pi* (2012) and the recent *Star Wars* and *Star Trek* reboots using local studios for added visual spectacle.

It's not unusual to spot movie trucks and trailers on your travels here – especially in downtown Vancouver – and you might like to try your hand at becoming an extra on your visit. See www.creativebc.com for the lowdown on what's filming and which productions are looking for 'background performers.'

Popular movie, TV and media festivals throughout the year include the Calgary International Film Festival, Edmonton International Film Festival, Vancouver International Film Festival and Whistler Film Festival.

Music

Ask visitors to name Canadian musicians and they'll stutter to a halt after Justin Bieber and Celine Dion. But ask the locals in BC, Alberta and the Yukon, and they'll hit you with a roster of local performers you've never heard of, plus some that you probably thought were American.

Superstars Michael Bublé, Bryan Adams, Sarah McLachlan and Diana Krall are all from BC, and their slightly less stratospheric colleagues include Nelly Furtado and Spirit of the West. For those who like their music with an indie hue, Black Mountain, Dan Mangan and CR Avery are among the area's popular grassroots performers.

Alberta has also spawned several big names: Joni Mitchell was born there for starters. Fans of indie rock are likely familiar with Feist, as well as Tegan and Sarah. Pop and country music singer-songwriter k.d. lang hails from Edmonton.

Bars are a great place to start if you want to take the pulse of the local music scene, some with free or minimal covers. Larger cities such as Vancouver, Calgary and Edmonton offer a wide range of dedicated venues for shows, from stadiums to cool underground spaces.

Even better, the region is bristling with great music festivals. Look out for toe-tapping options including the Vancouver International Jazz Festival and the Calgary Folk Music Festival.

Whatever your musical tastes, the best way to access the live scene on a grassroots level is to pick up local weekly newspapers and duck into small independent record stores. Cities large and small often have vinyl-selling shops staffed by musicians who know all there is to know about who's hot on the local scene.

The website of the National Film Board of Canada (www.nfb.ca) is a treasure trove of north-of-the-border films available for free online viewing. Recommended is *Carts of Darkness* (2008), a riveting exploration of shopping-cart races among the homeless in North Vancouver.

Aboriginal Cultures

Western Canada's original inhabitants have called this region home for thousands of years. While first contact with Europeans ultimately had a hugely detrimental impact on these communities, many of whom continue to face severe struggles in a society dominated by non-Aboriginals, recent history has been characterized by attempted reconciliation and a growing respect for the area's earliest locals. On your travels you'll find fascinating aboriginal museums, cultural centers and public art installations that will be highlights of your visit.

Early History

The prevailing theory that the region's first human inhabitants arrived many thousands of years ago by crossing a land bridge over the Bering Strait, near what's now known as Alaska, has been challenged (and, in some quarters, discredited) in recent years. Opposing theories have suggested that the earliest residents may have arrived on the east coast via boats from Asia, Polynesia or Siberia. What is known for sure is that the current Aboriginal communities in this region are descendants of the people who called this area home more than 10,000 years ago.

Some of these communities settled the forested foothills of the mountains to the east, while many others stayed on the ocean coastline, reaping the seemingly endless supply of juicy salmon, deer and rich local vegetation. Inland BC didn't provide the same bounty, however, and the Aboriginal Salish people in places such as the Okanagan Valley had to devote much more of their time to subsistence living and surviving the long winters. In the far north, the Tagish, Gwich'in and others depended on migrating moose and caribou.

While a common perception of these peoples is that they lived in teepees and smoked peace pipes, there was, in fact, a huge variety of groups, each living in distinctly different ways. For example, the first Vancouverites lived in villages of wood-planked houses arranged in rows, often

There are 34 aboriginal languages and 61 dialects in BC alone, making the province the most linguistically diverse for First Nations languages in Canada. For more on this rich linguistic heritage, see www.fpcc.ca.

TOP 10 ABORIGINAL ATTRACTIONS

➡ Museum of Anthropology (p118), Vancouver

➡ Royal BC Museum (p155), Victoria

➡ Haida Heritage Centre at Kay Llnagaay (p236), Haida Gwaii

➡ U'mista Cultural Centre (p187), Alert Bay

➡ Museum of Northern BC (p234), Prince Rupert

➡ Head-Smashed-In Buffalo Jump (p98), Fort Macleod

➡ Blackfoot Crossing Historical Park (p102), Canadian Badlands

➡ Nk'mip Desert & Heritage Centre (p202), Osoyoos

➡ Squamish Lil'wat Cultural Centre (p144), Whistler

➡ Bill Reid Gallery of Northwest Coast Art (p112), Vancouver

ABORIGINAL TOUR OPERATORS

On your travels around BC, look out for Aboriginal-themed or -led tours and excursions with the following operators. They're often a great way to gain a different perspective on the region.

Haida Style Expeditions (www.haidastyle.com) Cultural and fishing tours.

Talaysay Tours (www.talaysay.com) Kayaking and walking tours.

T'ashii Paddle School (www.tofinopaddle.com) Interpretive canoe tours.

Spirit Eagles Experiences (www.spiriteagle.ca) Guided canoe and cultural tours.

Tuckkwiowhum Aboriginal Interpretive Village (www.tuckkwiowhum.com) Heritage sleepover, teepee camping and guided tours.

Aboriginal Journeys (www.aboriginaljourneys.com) Wildlife-watching tours to spot everything from orcas to grizzlies.

It wasn't until 1949 that BC's First Nations were given the right to vote in provincial elections. The legislation, which was highly controversial at the time, also gave the vote to Canadian residents of Chinese and Japanese origin.

surrounded by a stockade. Nearby, totem poles would be set up as an emblem of a particular family or clan.

The distinct communities that formed in this area at that time included the Musqueam – who mostly populated the area around English Bay, Burrard Inlet and the mouth of the Fraser River – as well as the Squamish, who had villages in what are now called North Vancouver, West Vancouver, Jericho Beach and Stanley Park. Other groups that resided in the area included the Kwantlen, Tsawwassen and Coast Salish peoples.

How We Used to Live

There is very little evidence today about exactly how these early locals went about their daily lives. Most settlements have crumbled into the ground and few have been rediscovered by archaeologists. In addition, communities mostly deployed oral records, which meant telling each other the stories and legends of their ancestors, often in song, rather than writing things down. It's important to recall that this method would have been highly successful until the Europeans arrived, at which time generations of locals were quickly wiped out by disease or military attack.

One universally accepted aspect of these early societies is that art and creativity were a key presence in many communities. Homes were often adorned with exterior carvings and totem poles, and these illustrated a reverential regard for nature. This suggests that the region's first people enjoyed a symbiotic relationship with their surroundings – in many ways, they were the founders of Western Canada's current green movement.

European Contact

Bannock, a traditional flatbread originally imported to Canada by Scottish pioneers, is a staple of First Nations dining. There are many recipes, often passed down through generations. Vancouver's Salmon n' Bannock (www.salmonandbannock. net) restaurant is a good spot to try it.

Disease imported by early European visitors, such as Captain Cook, started the long slide for these peoples. Outright racism was rampant as well as official discrimination – perhaps the worst instance of which was the residential school system, which removed Aboriginal children from their families in order to strip them of their language and culture. In 1859 the governor of BC, James Douglas, declared that all the land and any wealth underneath it belonged to the Crown.

Laws enacted during much of the 20th century brutalized Aboriginal culture. A notorious law banned the potlatch, a vital ceremony held over many days by communities to mark special occasions, and establish ranks and privileges. Dancing, feasting and elaborate gift-giving from the chief to his people are features.

In the Rockies region of Alberta, similar devastating challenges were faced by the Sioux, Cree and Blackfoot peoples. This region is also the traditional home of the Métis, which translates from the French word for mixed blood and historically refers to the children born from Cree and French fur traders. It now refers to anyone born of mixed Cree and Aboriginal ancestry. Métis account for one-third of Canada's Aboriginal population and Edmonton is home to one of the country's largest populations.

Head-Smashed-in Buffalo Jump

Winning kudos among most visitors for having the most eye-poppingly impressive name of any cultural attraction in Canada, Head-Smashed-In Buffalo Jump (p98) is a celebrated Unesco World Heritage site. Situated at the junction of the Rocky Mountains and the Great Plains in Alberta, the archaeological destination lures thousands of visitors every year with its evocative exhibits and displays highlighting 6000 years of Aboriginal settlement.

But, like the label says, one aspect of historic life intrigues visitors more than most others. This site was where local Aboriginal people, over many centuries, perfected the buffalo jump method of hunting. The practice involved forcing bison to stampede over a steep precipice, from where their carcasses were dragged (relatively easily) to nearby blood-splattered camps for butchering. The name, in fact, tells you all you need to know.

Aboriginal Communities Today

The last 50 years have seen both an effort by governments to reverse the grim course of previous decades and a resurgence of Aboriginal culture. A long and difficult process has begun to settle claims from the 1859 proclamation through negotiations with the various bands. Negotiations include several stages but, so far, only one treaty has been finalized, with the Nisga'a peoples. It provides about $200 million and allows some self-governance. Given the money involved, the treaty process is contentious in Western Canada; much of the land under downtown Vancouver is subject to Aboriginal claims. But with Justin Trudeau as Canada's prime minister, many are hopeful for swifter and more meaningful progress; Trudeau is a strong supporter of Aboriginal communities and seems well positioned to lead a more productive relationship.

BC Aboriginal communities have succeeded in having indigenous names officially applied to several areas. For example, the former Queen Charlotte Islands is now Haida Gwaii; an area of southern BC ocean has been designated as the Salish Sea; and some locals have called for Stanley Park to be renamed Xwayxway.

ABORIGINAL CULTURES HEAD-SMASHED-IN BUFFALO JUMP

HISTORY OF TOTEMS

The artistry of Northwest Coast native groups – Tsimshian, Haida, Tlingit, Kwakwaka'wakw and Nuxalk – is as intricate as it is simple. One of the most spectacular examples of this is the totem pole, which has become such a symbolic icon that it's part of popular culture.

The carving of totem poles was largely quashed after the Canadian government outlawed the potlatch (gift-giving ceremonial feast) in 1884. Most totems only last 60 to 80 years, though some on Haida Gwaii are more than 100 years old. When a totem falls, tradition says that it should be left there until another is erected in its place.

Today, totem carving is again widespread, though the poles are often constructed for nontraditional uses, such as public art. Modern totems commissioned for college campuses, museums and public buildings no longer recount the lineage of any one household but instead stand to honor the Aboriginals, their outstanding artistry and their beliefs.

ABORIGINAL CULTURES YUKON FIRST NATIONS

Yukon First Nations

Today the Yukon region is home to 14 First Nations, which share eight languages. These First Nations include the Kluane, Teslin Tlingit and Ross River Dena communities. An estimated one-quarter of all Yukoners can trace their Aboriginal ancestry.

These communities often work together to share issues and raise concerns. At their annual general assembly in 2013, the Council of Yukon First Nations passed a resolution calling for the Yukon government to ban fracking (a controversial method of oil and gas extraction) throughout the region.

Aboriginal Arts

In the past there has been little outside recognition of the art produced by Canada's Aboriginal communities. But over the last several decades, there's been a strong and growing appreciation of this unique creative force. For most visitors, totem poles are their entry point, but the region's cultural treasures go way beyond that. Artworks such as masks, drums and paintings feature the distinctive black and red sweeping brush strokes that depict wolves, ravens and other animals from the spirit world.

Although most Aboriginal groups lack formal written history as we know it, centuries of cultural traditions live on. Art has long been a method of expression, intimately linked with historical and cultural preservation, religion and social ceremony.

Today, artist Lawrence Paul Yuxweluptun explores politics, the environment and aboriginal issues with his paintings that take inspiration from Coast Salish mythology. Shuswap actor and writer Darrell Dennis tackles aboriginal stereotypes head-on in his thrilling one-man show *Tales of an Urban Indian*.

Tofino-based Roy Henry Vickers fuses mystical and traditional themes with contemporary approaches, while Lawrence Paul Yuxweluptun and Brian Jungen have gained national and international recognition for their challenging abstract approaches.

Cultural Experiences

It seems to have taken Canada many years to realize that international visitors are eager to experience Aboriginal culture, and to encounter and understand the country's first inhabitants – and not just by viewing a dusty diorama of an 'Indian village' in a forgotten corner of a local museum.

Large and impressive cultural centers have sprung up in BC and Alberta in recent years. These include the award-winning Blackfoot Crossing Historical Park (p102) in Alberta, where you can learn from the locals about the authentic exhibits, watch a spectacular cultural dance display (look out for the Chicken Dance, typically performed by the community's young males), and stay overnight in a woodland teepee, with the sound of area coyotes howling at the moon to lull you to sleep.

Southern Alberta's ancient Siksika Nation is still renowned for its dancing prowess, especially its celebrated Chicken Dance. Inspired by the courtship moves of a chicken, it's performed by young males in the community. Check out June's World Chicken Dance Championship at the Blackfoot Crossing National Historical Park (www.blackfoot-crossing.ca).

For aboriginal experiences, attractions and activities, peruse the handy websites of Aboriginal Tourism BC (www.aboriginalbc.com) and the Yukon First Nations Culture and Tourism Association (www.yfnct.ca).

Pauline Johnson (1861–1913) was Vancouver's most famous poet. The daughter of a Mohawk chief and a middle-class English woman, she recited her works dressed in traditional aboriginal buckskin. She was hugely popular in the city, and her funeral was the largest ever held in Vancouver at the time. Johnson is also the only person to be officially buried in Stanley Park.

ABORIGINAL WINERY

Nk'Mip Cellars (pronounced 'in-ka-meep') became North America's first Aboriginal-owned and -operated winery when it opened its doors in Osoyoos, in the heart of BC's winery-heavy Okanagan region. The swanky, state-of-the-art winery was an immediate hit with visitors, many of whom drop by for tours as well as tastings. The winery, which is run by the Osoyoos Band, also has its own vineyard. Varietals produced include merlot, chardonnay, pinot noir and riesling ice wine.

The breathtaking Haida Heritage Centre (p236) in Haida Gwaii, BC, offers deep immersion into the history and rich creative impulses of the fascinating Haida people. The archipelago's Gwaii Haanas National Park Reserve (p236) also offers the chance to peruse evocative former villages on its southern shoreline, where decaying totem poles face the mist-streaked ocean as if they're telling a story. Unsurprisingly, this region is viewed as one of BC's most magical and mystical, with visitors frequently citing the area as one of the unforgettable highlights of their vacation.

Vancouver itself is crammed with First Nations encounters, such as a First Nations restaurant and an aboriginal art-themed hotel, plus pertinent art in public buildings and galleries throughout the city. But if you only have time for one spot, make it the University of British Columbia. It's home to the dramatic Museum of Anthropology (p118), which is teeming with astonishing art and artifacts that illustrate the rich heritage of Aboriginal culture and society throughout this region. The regular (and free) guided tours are highly recommended.

Haida Make History

Hundreds of locals, visitors and dignitaries gathered in Haida Gwaii a few years back to mark a special and highly symbolic event. The first such ceremony in the area for more than a century, a three-story-high totem pole was manually raised (with ropes) in the Gwaii Haanas National Park Reserve. The colorful, highly intricate pole took more than a year to carve, and its symbols were chosen to show that the islands are protected from harm.

There's more to the pole than its creation: it was carved to mark the two-decade anniversary of a treaty between the Haida and the Canadian government that allows both groups to protect and co-manage this region. It was also sited on Lyell Island, where the Haida protested logging of the area in 1985. The tense standoff made national headlines and ultimately culminated in the creation of Gwaii Haanas National Park Reserve. That protest is remembered on the pole itself: a carved area showing five men locking arms together in solidarity.

It is estimated that aboriginal tourism contributes around $50 million to the local economy in BC. There are now more than 200 aboriginal tourism businesses across the province.

West Coast Cuisine

Fine dining in the region used to mean choosing between doughnut varieties at a Tim Hortons outlet (maple cream recommended). But Western Canada is now sitting at the grown-ups' table when it comes to eating out. Seafood fans can stuff themselves to the gills with marine treats in British Columbia, while carnivores love Canada's steak-capital Rockies region. Throughout the area, a romance with local ingredients has transformed restaurant menus, many of which offer Canada's best international dining.

Seafood

If you're buying fresh wild salmon, look out for the following signs of freshness: it should not smell 'fishy'; the gills should have a red hue; the eyes should be bright and clear. For more tips and information on the region's tasty salmon, see www.bcsalmon.ca.

Atlantic Canada might pretend otherwise, but the West Coast is the country's undeniable seafood capital. A trip to the region that doesn't include throwing yourself into BC's brimming marine larder is like visiting Italy without having pasta: you can do it, but what's the point?

If you're starting in Vancouver, you'll find an astonishing array of innovative seafood dishes. This is the world's best sushi city outside Japan, and there are hundreds of spots to dip into, from slick joints with sake bars to cheap-and-cheerful hole-in-the-walls where you'll be rubbing shoulders with homesick overseas language students.

You'll also find a full table of traditional and innovative dishes in the area's Chinese restaurants, from the chatty Chinatown dim-sum dining rooms to contemporary fusion joints in Richmond, a bustling Hong Kong–like foodie heaven. If you're feeling adventurous, look out for locally harvested *geoduck* (pronounced 'gooey duck'), a giant saltwater clam. It's a delicacy in Chinese dining and is shipped to chefs across the world.

But it's not only multicultural approaches that bring BC's seafood to local diners. Many Pacific Northwest restaurants (more typically called West Coast restaurants on this side of the border) feature seasonal fresh catches. And as you travel around the region, you'll find the same amazing seafood almost everywhere you go. Juicy wild salmon is a signature here and in the autumn it dominates menus; do not miss it. Almost as popular is the early spring spot prawn season when the sweet, crunchy crustaceans turn up on tables throughout BC.

If you fancy meeting the fishers and choosing your grub straight off the back of a boat, you can also do that. The boats bobbing around the government wharf near Vancouver's Granville Island are a good spot to try, as is the evocative boardwalk area in Steveston. The south Richmond heritage fishing village is an ideal destination for seafood fans: there are two excellent museums recalling the area's days as the center of the once-mighty regional fishing fleet, and there are several finger-licking restaurants offering BC's best fish and chips.

If you're lucky enough to make it to Haida Gwaii, you'll encounter some of the best seafood you've ever had in your life, typically caught that day and prepared in a simple manner that reveals the rich flavors of the sea. Keep your appetite primed for halibut, scallops and crab, often plucked from the shallow waters just off the beach by net-wielding locals walking along the sand.

Local Flavors

Vancouver arguably surpasses Montréal and Toronto as Canada's fine-dining capital, and also beats both those cities with its surfeit of excellent multicultural dining options. You'll be hard-pressed to find a bad Chinese or Japanese restaurant here, while its West Coast dining choices (usually fused with intriguing international influences) bring the best of the region to tables across the city.

In recent years, some of the country's most innovative chefs have set up shop, inspired by the twin influences of an abundant local larder of unique flavors and the most cosmopolitan – especially Asian – population in Canada. Fusion is the starting point here, but there's also a high level of authenticity in traditional multicultural dining: amazing sushi bars and Japanese izakayas jostle for attention with superb Vietnamese and Korean eateries that feel like they've been transported from halfway around the world.

Outside Vancouver, the urban areas of Vancouver Island – especially in downtown Victoria – as well as the Okanagan Valley offer additional top-notch eateries. And if you're heading up to Whistler, you can expect plenty of surprisingly gourmet restaurants to restore your energy after an exhilarating day on the slopes.

Eating well is not just about fine dining, of course, and you'll find many welcoming places to nosh in more rustic areas of BC, Alberta and the Yukon, many of them delivering some taste-bud-thrilling surprises. Follow the locals to waterfront seafood diners in coastal communities such as Gibsons, Salt Spring Island and Prince Rupert for the kind of freshly caught aquatic treats that would cost several times more in the big city.

Even the smallest towns can usually rustle up a decent meal – including those ubiquitous 'Chinese and Canadian' eateries where the menu usually combines deep-fried cheeseburgers with gelatinous sweet-and-sour pork dishes. There are also many family-oriented, mid-priced eateries and chatty diners for those traveling with kids. And unlike pubs in the UK and other countries, bars here are usually just as interested in serving food as they are beer.

Foodie nirvana stretches across the Rockies into Alberta, Canada's cowboy country. This is the nation's beef capital, and you'll find top-notch Alberta steak on menus at leading restaurants across the country. But it's not all about steak here: look out for caribou and venison, both rising in popularity in recent years. If you're offered 'prairie oysters,' though, you might want to know (or maybe you'd prefer not to) that

REGIONAL FOOD & WINE MAGAZINES

Avenue Magazine (www.avenuecalgary.com) Lifestyle publication illuminating the Calgary restaurant scene for hungry locals. Separate Edmonton edition (www.avenueedmonton.com) also available.

City Palate (www.citypalate.ca) Covering Calgary's food and dining scene.

Eat Magazine (www.eatmagazine.ca) Free mag covering BC food and wine happenings.

Edible Vancouver (www.ediblecommunities.com/vancouver) Free quarterly with an organic and Slow Food bent, available at choice local food shops.

Growler (www.thegrowler.ca) Vancouver-based beer publication, showcasing beer-producers throughout the province.

Vancouver Magazine (www.vanmag.com) City lifestyle glossy with good coverage of local restaurants and culinary happenings.

they're bull's testicles prepared in a variety of intriguing ways designed to take your mind off their origin.

Wherever your taste buds take you, try to score some unique local flavors with a sampling of aboriginal food. Canada's Aboriginal people have some fascinating and accessible culinary traditions. Reliant on meat and seafood (try a juicy halibut stew on BC's Haida Gwaii), aboriginal tradition also includes bannock bread, imported by the Scots and appropriated by Canada's original locals. And if you think you're an expert on desserts, try some 'Indian ice cream.' Made from whipped soapberries, it's sweetened with sugar to assuage its bitter edge.

Eat Streets

Farmers markets are exploding across the region, bringing home-grown produce to the tables of locals and epicurious visitors. Look out for seasonal fresh-picked peaches, cherries, blueberries and apples. For BC market locations, see www.bcfarmersmarket.org; for Alberta, check www.albertamarkets.com. In the Yukon, hit Whitehorse's Fireweed Community Market.

Some thoroughfares in the region are permanently suffused with the aroma of great cooking, as well as an attendant chorus of satisfied-looking diners rubbing their bellies and surreptitiously loosening their straining belts. If you're hungry, heading to these areas is the way to go – you'll have a great regional meal, and meet the locals into the bargain.

If you're in Vancouver, there are several tasty options to choose from. Near Stanley Park, the West End's Denman St is teeming with good-value midrange restaurants. There's a huge variety here, from Vietnamese to Ukrainian and from pizza to tapas. The menu is similarly diverse on Commercial Dr, Main St and Kitsilano's West 4th Ave. But if fine dining floats your boat, check out Hamilton St and Mainland St in Yaletown: both are lined with fancy joints for that romantic, special-occasion meal.

Across the region, Richmond's 'Golden Village' area (Alexandra Rd here is also known as 'Eat St') is packed with superb Asian dining. The streets radiating from Chinatown in Victoria house some treats, and the city's Fort St has a few tempting joints. Up north in Prince Rupert, you won't have to go hungry: head to Cow Bay Rd for fish and chips and some great bistro options.

Over in Alberta, the Whyte Ave stretch of Edmonton's Old Strathcona neighborhood offers some excellent independent dining options, including plenty of taste-tripping international eateries. In Calgary – where the dining scene has jumped in quality in recent years – the top dining thoroughfares are downtown's Stephen St and in the neighborhoods of Kensington, Mission and Inglewood.

STREET EATS

Vancouver's sidewalk-dining revolution kicked off in mid-2010 with the introduction of 17 diverse food carts across the city. Suddenly barbecued pulled pork, organic tacos and gourmet Korean-fusion takeout were available to hungry locals. The network has since expanded to more than 100 carts. Grab delicious tacos from Tacofino and sit on the sunny steps of the Vancouver Art Gallery to watch the world go by, or dive into a creamy curry at Vij's Railway Express nearby. Visit www.streetfoodapp.com/vancouver for the latest listings and locations. If you're in the city in August, don't miss the YVR Food Fest (www.yvrfoodfest.com), during which you can sample fare from dozens of food trucks.

Since Vancouver kick-started the region's street-eats trend, Calgary and Edmonton have jumped on board with their own growing scenes, while trucks often pop up at smaller towns, too.

And if you can't find a cart, just head to Richmond, BC. The city hosts two Asian-style night markets on weekends throughout the summer. These are stuffed with steaming food stands serving everything from spicy fish balls to 'tornado potatoes' – thin-cut spirals of fried potato served on skewers.

MEET YOUR MAKERS

Ask Vancouverites where the food on their tables comes from and most will point vacantly at a nearby supermarket, but others will confidently tell you about the Fraser Valley. This lush interior region starts about 50km from the city and has been studded with busy farms for decades. In recent years, farmers and the people they feed have started to get to know one another on a series of five **Circle Farm Tours**. These self-guided driving tours take you around the communities of Langley, Abbotsford, Chilliwack, Agassiz and Harrison Mills, and Maple Ridge and Pitt Meadows, pointing out recommended pit stops – farms, markets, wineries and eateries – along the way. To add a cool foodie adventure to your BC trip, download the free tour maps at www.circlefarmtour.ca.

Festivals & Events

Food and drink is the foundation of having a good time in BC, Alberta and the Yukon. Languid summer barbecues, fall's feast-like Thanksgiving Day and winter family get-togethers at Christmas traditionally center on tables groaning with meat and seafood dishes, diet-eschewing fruit desserts, and plentiful wine and beer.

In addition there's a full menu of annual festivals where you can dive into the flavors of the region and bond with locals over tasty treats. Recommended events include the following:

Cornucopia (www.whistlercornucopia.com) A bacchanalian November food and wine fest in Whistler.

Dine Out Vancouver (www.dineoutvancouver.com) A three-week-long January event where local restaurants offer great-value two- or three-course tasting menus.

Feast of Fields (www.feastoffields.com) Local produce and top chefs at alfresco dinner-party days in metro Vancouver, the Okanagan Valley and on Vancouver Island.

Feast Tofino (www.feasttofino.com) A multi-week menu of Tofino events in May focused on local seafood.

Saturna Island Lamb Barbecue (www.saturnalambbarbeque.com) Pagan-esque Canada Day party in the Southern Gulf Islands.

Savour Cowichan Festival (www.savourcowichan.com) A late-September celebration of regional food and wine on Vancouver Island.

Taste Festival (www.victoriataste.com) Four-day fiesta of Vancouver Island food and wine treats.

Taste of Edmonton (www.tasteofedm.ca) A nine-day outdoor event in July showcasing local eateries and producers. There's also a similar, smaller event in Calgary (www.tasteofcalgary.com) in August.

In *The Boreal Gourmet: Adventures in Northern Cooking,* Whitehorse-based Michele Genest explores the Yukon's regional food specialties at the same time as offering insights into life in the region. Anyone for moose cooked in locally brewed espresso stout?

Vegetarians & Vegans

Traveling herbivores will find a full roster of vegetarian and vegan options in urban BC, with Vancouver especially undergoing a recent and inventive surge in meat-free dining options.

Eat heartily before you leave the city, though, as your options diminish as the towns shrink in size. In the smaller settlements of BC and the Yukon, vegetarian options can be limited to salads, sandwiches or portobello mushroom burgers, with the occasional veggie-only joint standing out like a beacon in the carnivorous darkness.

Crossing into the meat-loving Rockies, your choices will diminish faster than an ice cube on a sunny sidewalk. But it's not all doom and gloom: Calgary and Edmonton have their own dedicated veggie eateries, and you can usually find some meat-free pasta options available in Banff and Jasper restaurants.

TASTY LOCAL COOKBOOKS

A Taste of Haida Gwaii: Food Gathering and Feasting at the Edge of the World (Susan Musgrave; 2015) Recipes and food-themed recollections from the islands' own poet.

Calgary Cooks: Recipes from the City's Top Chefs (Gail Norton and Karen Ralph; 2014) Leading chefs from around the city offer up some tempting recipes.

Dirty Apron Cookbook (David Robertson; 2014) A greatest hits of top recipes from Vancouver's favorite cooking school.

Fresh: Seasonal Recipes Made with Local Foods (John Bishop; 2007) A celebration of BC produce and its dedicated growers, this sumptuous 100-recipe book underlines Bishop's credentials as the city's leading sustainable restaurateur.

Ocean Wise Cookbook 2 (Jane Mundy; 2015) Showcases a great array of sustainable seafood recipes from chefs and eateries in Vancouver and beyond.

Culinary Tours

If following your nose is an unreliable method for tapping into the region's culinary scene, consider an escort: BC is especially well served by operators who can guide you through the area's flavors on a tasty tour. Slip into a pair of pants with an elasticized waist and hit the road for what may well be the highlight of your visit.

If you're attracted to Vancouver Island's cornucopia of great produce, consider an educational tour of the verdant Cowichan Valley farm region, offered by Travel with Taste (www.travelwithtaste.com). You'll meet and sample from artisan cheese-makers and boutique vintners before tucking into a gourmet lunch of wild BC salmon. The company also offers lip-smacking guided tours around Victoria and Salt Spring Island.

In Vancouver, consider a Granville Island Market tour with Vancouver Food Tours (www.foodietours.ca) or a Stanley Park food-foraging tour via the Forager Foundation (www.foragertours.com).

Over in Calgary, consider a guided tour of the Calgary Farmers Market with Calgary Food Tours (www.calgaryfoodtours.com). The company also offers a full range of taste-tripping tour options around the region.

When to Eat

You can get virtually anything your belly craves throughout the day in Vancouver, but outside the region's main metropolis restaurants may shut early, even in seemingly hip places such as Victoria, Edmonton and Whistler. If it's time for dinner, be at the restaurant by 8pm outside peak summer weekends or you may find yourself out of luck.

Breakfast is usually eaten between 7am and 10am. Many hotels offer at least a continental breakfast (a hot drink, juice, toast, muffins and maybe cereal) during these hours, with higher-end joints typically serving cooked options – various varieties of eggs Benedict are very popular here (go for the smoked salmon). Most local residents eat breakfast at home on weekdays or grab a quick bite on the run with their morning coffee. But on weekends, a leisurely breakfast or brunch at a cafe or restaurant is a favorite pastime. Weekend brunch service often stretches well into the afternoon at restaurants and is one of the most popular ways for locals to socialize, especially in brunch-loving Victoria and Vancouver.

The midday meal is typically taken between 11am and 1pm. It can be as simple as a snack bought from a farmers market or street-food cart, or a picnic taken on your hike. Dinner is served anytime from about 5pm to 8pm, often later on weekends and in large cities as well as resort areas, such as Whistler and Banff.

Dress is casual almost everywhere. For more formal restaurants, the cliched 'smart casual' is perfectly acceptable.

The Yukon Gold is one of Canada's favorite premium potato varieties. With a yellow color and nugget-sized appearance, it was named after the country's gold rush region. It is popular for boiling, baking and frying, mainly because it retains its distinctive yellow hue.

Drinking BC & Beyond

Gone are the days when drinkers were perfectly content to quaff generic fizzy beers or rocket-fuel wines made from foraged berries. Mirroring the recent rise in distinctive regional cuisine, Western Canada has developed one of the nation's most sophisticated tipple scenes. Vineyards in BC's Okanagan Valley and beyond quench the thirst of wine fans, while the province also leads in craft beer production, with dozens of flavorful producers, and fosters an emerging trend towards tasty craft cideries and distilleries.

Wine Regions

Visitors are often surprised to learn that wine is produced here, but their skepticism is usually tempered after a choice drink or two. BC's wines have gained ever-greater kudos in recent years, and while smaller-scale production and the industry dominance of wine regions such as Napa means they'll never be a global market leader, there are some surprisingly top-quality treats.

The best way to sample any wine is to head straight to the source. Consider doing some homework and locating the nearest vineyards on your visit: they'll likely be a lot closer than you think. The Okanagan Valley (p200) and Vancouver Island are the region's main wine areas, but you'll also find wineries – alone or in mini-clusters – in BC's Fraser Valley and on the Southern Gulf Islands. And while Alberta has far fewer wineries, keep your eyes peeled while you're on the road: there are a handful of friendly (mostly fruit-wine) joints worth stopping at.

Wherever your tipple-craving takes you, drink widely and deeply. And make sure you have plenty of room in your suitcase – packing materials are always available if you want to take a bottle or two home with you.

For background and further information before you arrive, peruse the Wines of British Columbia website (www.winebc.com) as well as the insightful John Schreiner on Wine blog (www.johnschreiner.blogspot.ca).

John Schreiner's Okanagan Wine Tour Guide (2014) is an in-depth tome covering the region for visiting oenophiles. It's packed with great suggestions on how to make the most of a wine-based trawl around the area.

Okanagan Valley

The rolling hills of this lakeside BC region are well worth the five-hour drive from Vancouver. Studded among the vine-striped slopes, approximately 175 wineries enjoy a diverse climate that fosters both crisp whites and bold reds. With varietals including pinot noir, pinot gris, pinot blanc, merlot and chardonnay, there's a wine here to suit almost every palate. Many visitors base themselves in Kelowna, the Okanagan's wine capital, before fanning out to well-known blockbuster wineries such as Mission Hill, Quails' Gate, Cedar Creek and Summerhill Pyramid Winery (yes, it has a pyramid). Many of them have excellent vista-hugging restaurants. For more information on Okanagan wines and wineries, visit www.okanaganwines.ca.

Oliver & Osoyoos

Some of BC's best Okanagan wineries are centered south of the valley between Oliver and Osoyoos, where the hot climate fosters a long, warm, growing season. Combined with gravel, clay and sandy soils, this area is

A SIX-PACK OF TOP BEERS

On your travels around the region, look out for these taste-tested top brews:

Driftwood Brewery's Fat Tug IPA (www.driftwoodbeer.com)

Powell Street Craft Brewery's Dive Bomb Porter (www.powellbeer.com)

Four Winds Brewing's IPA (www.fourwindsbrewing.ca)

Persephone Brewing's Persephone Pale Ale (www.persephonebrewing.com)

Central City Brewing's Red Racer India Red Ale (www.centralcitybrewing.com)

Howe Sound Brewing's Father John's Winter Ale (www.howesound.com)

ideally suited to varietals such as merlot, chardonnay, gewürztraminer and cabernet sauvignon. The 40 or so wineries here include celebrated producers Burrowing Owl, Tinhorn Creek and Road 13 Vineyards, making this an ideal touring area. Don't miss Nk'Mip Cellars, a First Nations winery in Osoyoos that's on the edge of a desert. For more information on this region's imbibing opportunities, see www.oliverosoyoos.com.

Vancouver Island & the Gulf Islands

Long-established as a farming area, Vancouver Island's verdant Cowichan Valley is home to some great little wineries. A short drive from Victoria, you'll find Averill Creek, Blue Grouse, Cherry Point Vineyards and Venturi-Schulze Vineyards. Also consider the delightful Merridale Estate Cidery, which produces several celebrated ciders on its gently sloped orchard grounds.

A lesser-known winery region, the bucolic Gulf Islands are home to several small, island-based wineries, including two on Salt Spring Island that welcome visitors. If you plan to visit Salt Spring on a summer weekend, gather picnic fixings at the treat-packed Saturday Market (local-made cheese recommended) before picking up an island-made libation to accompany your alfresco feast.

For more information on Vancouver Island and Gulf Islands wineries, visit www.wineislands.ca.

Here for the Beer?

While the usual round of bland factory suds and international suspects (you know the ones we mean) are readily available, a little digging – actually, hardly any digging at all – uncovers a thriving regional microbrewing scene overflowing with distinctive craft beers.

From Tofino to Prince Rupert, BC is packed like a Friday-night pub with almost 200 breweries, many of them only established in the past 10 years. On your thirst-slaking travels, look out for taps from celebrated producers such as Four Winds (Delta), Townsite (Powell River), Driftwood (Victoria), Persephone (Gibsons), Central City (Surrey), Howe Sound (Squamish) – and Powell Street (Vancouver), which crafts an utterly delicious Dive Bomb Porter.

Victoria kick-started the region's microbrewery golden age a few years back but Vancouver has seized the initiative in recent years. The reason? Breweries in Vancouver (of which there are at least three dozen) are much more likely to have tasting rooms, each operating like de facto neighborhood pubs. That means crawl-worthy brewery districts have popped up in the city, including those on Main St (don't miss Brassneck and Main Street Brewing) and another in East Vancouver (look out for Callister, Powell Street and Off the Rail).

The legal drinking age in BC and the Yukon is 19; in Alberta it's 18. If you look young you should expect to be asked for identification. Canada is very serious about curbing drink-driving, and you may encounter mandatory roadside checkpoints, especially on summer evenings or around winter holidays.

You don't have to go thirsty in the Rockies region, either: travelers in Alberta should hunt down local beverages from Calgary's Village Brewery and Tool Shed Brewing; Edmonton's Alley Kat Brewing; Red Deer's Blindman Brewing; and the popular Jasper Brewing Company brewpub, evocatively located in the heart of Jasper National Park. And if you're way up north, it has to be Yukon Brewing (start with a pint of Yukon Gold).

For the lowdown on BC's burgeoning craft beer scene, pick up a copy of *The Growler* (www.thegrowler.ca) at area breweries.

The smaller the brewery, the more likely it is to produce tipples that make generic fizzy beers taste like something you'd rather wash your car with. Ales, bitters, lagers, pilsners, porters, stouts, sours and even hemp beers are often available at pubs, bars and restaurants throughout the region. Some bars also host weekly cask nights, when they crack open a guest keg of something special: check ahead and find out what's available during your visit.

If you want to see how it's all done – and stoke your thirst in the process – Granville Island Brewing in Vancouver and Big Rock Brewery in Calgary are among those offering short tours coupled with satisfyingly leisurely sample tastings. Cheers!

Artisan Distilling

Craft distilling has become Western Canada's latest wave of artisan booze-making. You'll find intriguing operations, most of them with inviting tasting rooms, across the region. Many are selling housemade vodka and gin, always a delightful, aromatic surprise for those of us more used to bland factory varieties that dominate the market. These drops are typically smooth enough to drink neat, and you can expect to pay around $40 to $50 for a savor-worthy bottle; samples are always available.

As these distillery operations mature (most of them are less than five years old), they plan to also sell aged whiskies – ask about this wherever you visit. Distilleries to look out for include Liberty in Vancouver; Gillespie's in Squamish; Pemberton Distillery in Pemberton; Sheringham on Vancouver Island; and Eau Claire near Calgary.

Take the opportunity to try as many drops as you can handle under one roof at Vancouver's annual BC Distilled (www.bcdistilled.ca) festival, usually held in March.

Festivals & Events

Time your visit well and you'll be sipping glasses of wine or downing pints of beer at a series of regional events. Large or small, they're a great way to hang out with the locals.

DRINKING ICE WINE IN THE SNOW

There are many good reasons to visit the Winter Okanagan Wine Festival (www.thewinefestivals.com) – for instance, the accessible educational seminars, the dinner events, a cozy alpine-lodge ambience and some of BC's best outdoor winter activities – but the evening Progressive Tasting is the best reason of all. During the event, wineries set up stalls and offer more than 100 wines at locations throughout Sun Peaks ski-resort village, while increasingly tipsy visitors stumble between them in an attempt to keep their glasses as full as possible.

The annual mid-January festival is particularly renowned for celebrating a distinctive tipple that's become a signature of Canadian wineries. Made from grapes frozen on the vine at -8°C (note, there are plenty of fakes on the market that don't meet this simple criterion), Canadian ice wine is a premium, uber-sweet dessert wine sold in distinctive slender bottles at upwards of $50 a pop. While Austria, Germany and other countries produce their own ice wines, it's a product that reflects Canada's enduring international image as a snowy winter wonderland.

A recent change means farmers markets around BC can now offer sales and booze samples to shoppers. Look out for wine, beer and distillery stalls wherever you go.

Wine-lovers are well served in the Okanagan, where several events are held throughout the year. The biggest is the 10-day Fall Wine Festival, while January's Winter Okanagan Wine Festival is evocatively hosted in an icicle-draped ski resort: there's usually plenty of ice wine to go around here. For information on the region's events, see www.thewinefestivals.com.

If you're in Vancouver in February, connect with the Vancouver International Wine Festival (www.vanwinefest.ca). It's the city's largest and oldest wine-based celebration and it focuses on one wine region each year.

Combining drinks and grub, Alberta's Rocky Mountain Wine and Food Festival (www.rockymountainwine.com) takes place on different dates in Calgary and Edmonton.

And if beer floats your boat, you can sample all those BC microbrews you've been craving at the ever-popular Vancouver Craft Beer Week (www.vancouvercraftbeerweek.com) in late May. It's the province's biggest beer event, but it's not the only one: check out Victoria's Great Canadian Beer Festival (www.gcbf.com) as well as the five annual events staged under the Alberta Beer Festivals banner (www.albertabeerfestivals.com).

If you're looking for something stronger, don't miss November's annual Hopscotch Festival (www.hopscotchfestival.com) staged in Vancouver and Kelowna; it covers all the boozy bases by focusing on beer, whiskey and other spirits.

Where to Drink

You don't have to visit wineries, breweries or distilleries to find a good drink in the region: BC, Alberta and the Yukon are well stocked with watering holes, from traditional pubs to slick wine bars and sparkling cocktail joints, although finding a perfect Moscow Mule in smaller towns may be a tough ask. Keep in mind that most bars follow the North American table service approach: servers come to the table for your order rather than expecting you to order your own drink at the bar. The (potential) downside is that table service means tipping is standard.

While craft booze is taking off across the region, brewpubs are still underrepresented in some areas: you'll find a handful in Vancouver and Victoria, plus single beacons of beery delight in towns such as Banff, Jasper and Kelowna. In contrast, many craft breweries in BC (with the notable exception of most in Victoria) have small, highly welcoming tasting rooms that are among the best places in the province to drink a beer with the locals. Try Persephone in Gibsons, Townsite in Powell River, Brassneck in Vancouver and Wheelhouse in Prince Rupert.

Survival Guide

Directory A–Z

Accommodations

British Columbia and Alberta offer a good range of hotels, B&Bs and hostels, with reduced options in northern BC and the Yukon. Booking ahead is advisable in summer (and in winter at ski resorts), especially in Vancouver, Victoria and the main Rockies destinations.

Booking Services

Hello BC (www.hellobc.com) Official Destination British Columbia (BC) accommodations search engine.

Travel Alberta (www.travelalberta. com) Accommodations booking engine on the province's official visitor site.

Travel Yukon (www.travelyukon. com) Online accommodations listings.

Tourism Vancouver (www.tourism vancouver.com) Wide range of accommodations listings and package deals.

BC Bed & Breakfast Innkeepers Guild (www.bcsbestbnbs. com) Wide range of B&Bs around the province.

Camping & RV in BC (www. campingrvbc.com) Resources and site listings for the province.

Lonely Planet (www.lonely planet.com/canada/hotels) Recommendations and bookings.

B&Bs

North American B&Bs are typically more upscale than the casual, family-style pensions found in Europe. There are thousands to choose from across the region, many of which are unique or romantic.

➡ Book ahead: B&Bs often have only one to three rooms.

➡ Check the rules: many B&Bs are adults-only. Others only open seasonally and/or require a two-night minimum stay.

➡ Parking is usually free.

➡ Local visitor centers usually have good B&B listings for their particular areas. Also see Bed & Breakfast Online (www. bbcanada.com) for listings across the region.

Camping & Holiday Parks

This region is a campers' paradise with thousands of government-run and private campgrounds.

➡ Options range from basic pitches nestled in the remote wilderness to highly accessible, amenities-packed campgrounds popular with families.

➡ Campgrounds are typically open from May to September but dates vary by location.

➡ Many popular sites are sold out months in advance: booking ahead is recommended, especially for holiday weekends and the summer peak season.

➡ Facilities vary widely. Expect little more than pit toilets and a fire ring at backcountry sites, while larger campgrounds may have shower blocks and guided interpretive programs.

➡ Camping in national or provincial parks can cost up to $45 per night, although many are around the $25 mark. Private sites may offer more facilities and charge a little more.

➡ See Parks Canada (www. pccamping.ca), BC Parks (www.discovercamping.ca) and Alberta Parks (www. reserve.albertaparks.ca) for information, listings and bookings for government-run sites in national and local parks.

BOOK YOUR STAY ONLINE

For more accommodations reviews by Lonely Planet authors, check out http://lonelyplanet.com/hotels/. You'll find independent reviews, as well as recommendations on the best places to stay. Best of all, you can book online.

Guest Ranches

BC and Alberta have dozens of enticing guest ranches, which is the euphemism for horse-centered dude ranches where you can join a trail ride or sit by a mountain lake. The Cariboo-Chilcotin region is a guest ranch hotbed.

Hostels

Independent and Hostelling International (HI) hostels are easy to find in popular visitor destinations, with some areas enjoying healthy competition between several establishments.

→ Dorms (typically $25 to $45) may be small or sleep up to 20 people, and facilities usually include shared bathrooms, a kitchen and common areas. Laundry facilities, bike storage and wi-fi are common.

→ Private rooms in hostels are increasingly popular: they are also the most sought-after, so book far ahead.

→ Many outdoorsy hostels offer extras such as bike or kayak rentals, while city-based hostels often have free or low-cost social programs that include guided tours or pub nights.

→ City hostels are often open 24 hours; those in other areas may be closed during the day – check ahead.

→ Booking ahead for hostels in popular destinations such as Tofino, Whistler and Banff is essential in summer.

→ For locations, listings and bookings across the region, see Hostelling International (www.hihostels.ca), SameSun (www.samesun.com) and Backpackers Hostels Canada (www.backpackers.ca).

Hotels & Motels

→ Hotel rates vary tremendously around the region. Plan to spend at least $150 for a basic double room with a private bathroom during summer peaks in Vancouver and Victoria. In less-visited areas, $100 is closer to the norm.

→ Boutique properties and high-end hotels are readily available in Vancouver and Victoria, with chateaux-like resorts common in Whistler and the Rockies.

→ Wilderness retreats are dotted around the BC coastline and in some parts of the Rockies, offering spas and top-notch dining packages.

→ Midrange hotel and motel rooms typically include a private bathroom, one or two large beds, a tea and coffee maker, and free wi-fi.

→ Your hotel may not include air-conditioning. If this is a deal-breaker, check before you book.

→ In distant areas such as northern BC, the Alberta outback and remote Yukon spots, you'll find hotels folksy at best.

→ Many motels (and an increasing number of suite-style hotels) offer handy (and money-saving) kitchenettes.

→ Children can often stay free in the same room as their parents; check to see if there's a charge for rollaway beds.

Taxes & Fees

Be aware that there will be some significant additions to most quoted room rates, including provincial taxes (up to 13% in BC) and also, in some areas, Hotel Room Tax of up to 3%. On top of this, some hotels also charge a Destination Marketing Fee of around 1.5%. Parking fees don't help either: overnight parking, especially at higher-end hotels, can be expensive, sometimes as much as $50 per night. Keep in mind that B&Bs usually include parking free of charge. Check all these potential extra charges at time of booking to avoid any unpleasant surprises.

Children

Family-friendly Western Canada is stuffed with activities and attractions for kids, and there's a good attitude in most restaurants and many accommodations to traveling families. For general advice on family travel, see Lonely Planet's *Travel with Children*.

Equipment Strollers, booster seats, toys and other equipment can be rented from Wee Travel (www.weetravel.ca).

Resources Pick up the free *Kids' Guide Vancouver* around town and visit www.kidsvancouver.com for local tips, resources and family-focused events.

Blogs Check out www.rockiesfamilyadventures.com for inspirational stories on how to cover the region with your family.

Parks Canada Canada's national park system offers plenty of (mostly summer) programs for visiting kids; check individual park and historic site attractions online (www.pc.gc.ca) for detailed information.

Practicalities

Accommodations Children can often stay with parents at hotels for no extra charge. Cots may also be available in some accommodations. Some hostels have family rooms. Hotels can recommend trusted babysitting services for you to book.

Dining out Not all restaurants will have high chairs available; call ahead before you arrive to check and reserve one.

Child safety seats Hire-car companies can provide these if you book head.

Breastfeeding in public This is rarely a problem for the locals in Western Canada.

Customs Regulations

→ Check in with the **Canada Border Services Agency** (☎204-983-3500; www.cbsa.gc.ca) for the latest customs lowdown.

→ Duty-free allowance coming into Canada is 1.14L (40oz) of liquor, 1.5L (or two 750mL bottles) of wine, or 24 cans or bottles of beer, as well as up to 200 cigarettes, 50 cigars or 200g of tobacco.

→ You are allowed to bring in gifts up to a total value of $60. Gifts above $60 are subject to duty and taxes on the over-limit value.

→ Fresh and prepared foods are the subject of myriad rules and regulations here. Just buy what you need in Canada.

Discount Cards

Parks Canada Discovery Pass (www.pc.gc.ca/ar-sr/lpac-ppri/ced-ndp.aspx) Good-value pass if you're planning to visit national parks and historic sites across the region (adult/child/family $68/33/136).

Vancouver City Passport (www.citypassports.com) Discounts at attractions, restaurants and activities across the city for up to two adults and two children ($25).

Vanier Park ExplorePass (www.spacecentre.ca/explore-pass) Combined entry pass covering three Vancouver attractions: the Museum of Vancouver, Vancouver Maritime Museum and HR MacMillan Space Centre (adult/child $36/30).

Electricity

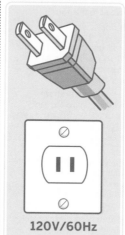

120V/60Hz

120V/60Hz

Food & Drink

The region has a fine range of eating options. See p290 for an introduction to the region's food scene. Tables at the most popular restaurants in cities such as Vancouver, Victoria and Calgary need to be booked in advance.

Restaurants A full menu of options, from mom-and-pop operations to high-end spots for special occasions.

Cafes From sandwich-serving coffee shops to chatty local haunts, cafes are common and usually good value.

Bars Most bars also serve food, typically of the pub-grub variety.

Food trucks Vancouver is the food-truck capital and you'll find pockets of wheeled wonders elsewhere throughout the region.

Farmers markets Ubiquitous in summer; a great way to sample regional produce and local-made treats.

Health

A high level of hygiene in the region means most common infectious diseases will not be a major concern for travelers. No special vaccinations are required, but all travelers should be up to date with standard immunizations, such as tetanus and measles.

Before You Go
HEALTH INSURANCE

The Canadian healthcare system is one of the best in the world and excellent care is widely available. Benefits are generous for Canadian citizens, but foreigners aren't covered, which can make treatment prohibitively expensive.

Make sure you have travel-health insurance if your regular policy doesn't apply when you're abroad. Find out

---

EATING PRICE RANGES

• • • • • • • • • • • • • • • • • • • •

The following price ranges refer to the cost of a standard main course, excluding taxes and services charges.

$ less than $15

$$ $15–25

$$$ more than $25

in advance if your insurance plan will make payments directly to providers or reimburse you later for overseas health expenditures.

MEDICATIONS

Bring medications in their original containers, clearly labeled. A signed, dated letter from your physician describing all medical conditions and medications, including generic names, is also a good idea. If carrying syringes or needles, be sure to have a physician's letter documenting their medical necessity.

In BC & the Canadian Rockies

AVAILABILITY & COST OF HEALTH CARE

If you have a choice, treatment at a university hospital may be preferable to a community hospital, although you can often find superb medical care in small local hospitals, and the waiting time is usually shorter. If the problem isn't urgent, you can call a nearby hospital and ask for a referral to a local physician – less expensive than a trip to the emergency room.

Pharmacies are abundantly supplied; however, you may find that some medications that are available over the counter in your home country require a prescription in Canada. In the largest cities you'll be able to find 24-hour pharmacies, although most drugstores typically keep regular store hours.

INFECTIOUS DISEASES

Be aware of the following, particularly if you're traveling in wilderness areas:

Giardiasis A parasitic infection of the small intestine. Symptoms may include nausea, bloating, cramps and diarrhea, and may last for weeks. Avoid drinking directly from lakes, ponds, streams and rivers, which may be contaminated by animal or human feces.

Lyme Disease Transmitted by tiny deer ticks. Mostly occurs in late spring and summer in southern areas. First symptom is usually an expanding red rash. Flu-like symptoms, including fever, headache, joint pains and body aches, are also common.

West Nile Virus Recently observed in provinces including Alberta. Transmitted by Culex mosquitoes, which are active in late summer and early fall and generally bite after dusk. Most infections are mild, but the virus may infect the central nervous system, leading to fever, headache, confusion, coma and sometimes death.

MEDICAL SERVICES

For immediate medical assistance:

BC, Alberta & Whitehorse (Yukon) ☎911

Yukon (except Whitehorse) ☎867-667-5555

Generally, if you have a medical emergency, it's best to find the nearest hospital emergency room.

Insurance

Make sure you have adequate travel insurance to cover your trip. Cover for luggage theft or loss is handy, but health coverage for medical emergencies and treatment is vital: medical treatment for non-Canadians is expensive.

Worldwide travel insurance is available at www.lonely planet.com/travel-insurance. You can buy, extend and claim online anytime – even if you're already on the road.

Internet Access

➡ Wi-fi connections are almost standard in accommodations across BC, Alberta and the Yukon.

➡ You'll find wi-fi and internet-access computers in libraries, and free wi-fi in coffee shops and other businesses.

➡ The ☎ symbol in our listings shows where wi-fi access is available, while the @ symbol indicates where computers are available for public or guest use.

Legal Matters

➡ The Canadian federal government permits the use of marijuana for medicinal purposes, but prescription cannabis is strictly regulated.

➡ It's illegal to consume alcohol anywhere other than at a residence or licensed premises; parks, beaches and other public spaces are (officially) off-limits.

➡ Stiff fines, jail time and penalties apply if caught driving under the influence of alcohol or any illegal substance. The blood-alcohol limit is 0.08%, which is reached after just two beers.

➡ Canada has strict regulations banning smoking in all indoor public places and workplaces. Best bet is lighting up in the middle of a big empty parking lot.

LGBTI Travelers

In BC and Alberta, attitudes toward gays and lesbians are relaxed, especially in urban areas such as Vancouver and Calgary where there are dedicated rainbow-hued nightlife scenes.

While you won't find such an open gay and lesbian culture in other parts of the region, attitudes are generally tolerant throughout the provinces and in the Yukon. That said, the lack of prominent gay and lesbian communities outside urban centers tends to mean that most people keep their orientation to themselves.

The following are useful resources for gay travelers:

Travel Gay Canada (www. visitgaycanada.com) National and regional resources for LGBT visitors.

PRACTICALITIES

DVDs Canada is in DVD region 1.

Newspapers Most towns have a daily or weekly newspaper. The *Vancouver Sun* and *Calgary Herald* provide reasonable regional coverage.

Radio Signs at the entrances to towns provide local frequencies for CBC Radio One.

Smoking Banned in indoor public places and workplaces throughout Canada. This includes restaurants and bars.

Weights & Measures The metric system is used throughout Canada, although popular references to the imperial system (as used in the US) still survive.

Qmunity (www.qmunity.ca) Online resources for the community throughout BC.

Daily Xtra (www.dailyxtra.com) Source for gay and lesbian news nationwide.

Gay Van (www.gayvan.com) Listings and events in Vancouver and beyond.

Maps

➡ Bookstores, gas stations and convenience stores sell a wide variety of maps ranging from regional overviews to detailed street atlases.

➡ Topographic maps are recommended for extended hikes or multiday backcountry treks. The best are the series of 1:50,000 scale maps published by the government's Centre for Topographic Information (www.nrcan.gc.ca). These are sold around the country; check the website for vendors. You can also download and print maps from www.geobase.ca.

➡ Gem Trek Publishing (www.gemtrek.com) offers some of the best Rocky Mountains maps in scales from 1:35,000 to 1:100,000.

Money

ATMs & Eftpos

ATMs are common throughout BC, Alberta and the larger towns of the Yukon. Cana-dian ATM fees are generally low but your bank at home may also charge a fee.

Credit & Debit Cards

Credit and debit cards are almost universally accepted; in fact, you'll find it hard or impossible to rent a car, book a room or buy tickets online or over the phone without one.

Currency

The Canadian dollar ($) is divided into 100 cents (¢). Coins come in 5¢ (nickel), 10¢ (dime), 25¢ (quarter), $1 (loonie) and $2 (toonie) pieces. Notes come in $5, $10, $20, $50 and $100 denominations; $100 bills can prove difficult to cash.

Money Changers

➡ Currency exchange counters are located at international airports such as Vancouver and Calgary. Exchange offices are common in bigger towns, cities and in tourist destinations such as Whistler and Banff.

➡ Larger banks may exchange currency, and rates are usually better.

➡ US dollars are often accepted by businesses at larger tourist towns such as Victoria and Whistler – especially in gift shops – but rates typically are not favorable.

Taxes & Refunds

BC, Alberta and the Yukon have different consumer tax rates. The federal Goods and Services Tax (GST) adds 5% to nearly every product, service or transaction in Alberta and the Yukon.

In BC a 5% GST levy applies as well as 7% Provincial Sales Tax (PST). Not all items will attract both rates, but many will. Some items attract higher PST rates: alcohol is taxed at 10%, for example.

Some areas also levy a hotel tax, including a 3% Municipal and Regional District Tax on overnight accommodations in Vancouver.

There are almost no tax-rebate schemes for visitors; you may be eligible for a rebate if you paid taxes on a tour package – ask your tour provider for further information.

Tipping

Tipping is expected in Canada. Typical rates:

Bar servers $1 per drink

Hotel bellhops $1 to $2 per bag

Hotel room cleaners $2 per day

Restaurant wait staff 15%

Taxi drivers 10% to 15%

Opening Hours

The following standard opening hours apply throughout the region. Note that many attractions have reduced hours in the low season.

Banks 9am or 10am to 5pm Monday to Friday; some open 9am to noon Saturday

Bars 11am to midnight or later; some only open from 5pm

Post offices 9am to 5pm Monday to Friday; some open on Saturday

Restaurants breakfast 7am to 11am, lunch 11:30am to 2pm, dinner 5pm to 9:30pm (8pm in rural areas)

Shops 10am to 5pm or 6pm Monday to Saturday; noon to 5pm Sunday; some (especially in malls) open to 8pm or 9pm Thurday and/or Friday

Supermarkets 9am to 8pm; some open 24 hours

Post

→ Canada Post (www.canadapost.ca) is reliable and easy to use. Red storefronts around towns and cities denote main branches.

→ Full-service Canada Post counters are ubiquitous in the back of convenience stores, drug stores and supermarkets. Look for the signs in windows. Often have longer opening hours than branches.

→ Hotels may sell individual stamps; books of stamps available in many convenience stores.

→ Rates for postcards and letters to the US are $1.20, to the rest of the world $2.50.

Public Holidays

National public holidays are celebrated throughout Canada. BC, Alberta and the Yukon each observe an additional statutory holiday – often called a 'stat' – at separate times of the year. Banks, schools and government offices (including post offices) close, and transportation, museums and other services may operate on a Sunday schedule.

Many stores open on Boxing Day, but some are closed.

Holidays falling on a weekend are usually observed the following Monday. Long weekends are among the busiest on the region's roads and ferry routes.

New Year's Day January 1

Family Day second Monday in February in BC; third Monday in February Alberta

Easter (Good Friday and Easter Monday) March/April

Victoria Day Monday preceding May 25

Canada Day July 1

BC Day first Monday in August; BC only

Discovery Day third Monday in August; Yukon only

Labour Day first Monday in September

Thanksgiving second Monday in October

Remembrance Day November 11

Christmas Day December 25

Boxing Day December 26

Safe Travel

The region is relatively safe for visitors. Purse-snatching and pickpocketing occasionally occur, especially in city areas; be vigilant with your personal possessions. Theft from unattended cars is not uncommon; never leave valuables in vehicles where they can be seen.

Persistent street begging can be an issue for some visitors to Vancouver; just say 'Sorry,' and pass by if you're not interested but want to be polite. A small group of hardcore scam artists also works the city's downtown core, singling out tourists and asking for 'help to get back home.' Do not let them engage you in conversation.

Telephone

→ Always dial all 10 digits even if calling a number within the same area code. To dial long distance within this region or any other region within North America, dial ☎1, then the 10-digit number.

→ To call from outside North America, dial ☎011 followed by the country code and the 10-digit number. The country code for North America is ☎1.

→ Pay phones are increasingly rare. You'll need coins or a long-distance phonecard, available from convenience stores, post offices and gas stations. Shop around for the best deal.

→ Cell (mobile) phones use the GSM and CDMA systems, depending on the carrier.

LOCAL HOLIDAYS: WHAT THEY MEAN

Aside from the public holidays enjoyed by everyone across the region, BC, Alberta and the Yukon have their own distinctive extra days off when they spend at least a couple of hours phoning their neighbors across the country to brag about not having to go into work. On these days you can expect shops and businesses to be operating on reduced hours (or to be closed), so plan ahead. The region's three separate public holidays:

BC Day Officially called British Columbia Day, this welcome August holiday (a trigger for many locals to take a summertime long-weekend) was introduced in 1974 and was intended to recognize the pioneers that kick-started the region.

Discovery Day The Yukon's mid-August holiday marks the 1896 gold discovery in Bonanza Creek that triggered the Klondike gold rush. It starts a week-long Dawson City festival that includes historic re-creations.

Family Day This February statutory holiday was instituted in Alberta in 1990 and in BC in 2013. It does not exist (yet) in the Yukon.

Cell Phones

➜ Local SIM cards can be used in unlocked European and Australian GSM cell phones. Other phones must be set to roaming – be wary of charges.

➜ SIMs generally cost less than $50, and should include some talk minutes.

➜ Much of the backcountry has no cell-phone signal.

Time

➜ Most of BC and the Yukon operate on Pacific Time, which is eight hours behind the Greenwich Mean Time.

➜ Alberta is on Mountain Time, which is one hour ahead of Pacific Time.

➜ Clocks will be turned forward one hour on the second Sunday in March and are turned back one hour on the first Sunday in November.

➜ Canada's time zones mirror those across the border in the US.

Toilets

Public toilets can be few and far between in many towns and cities. If you are caught short, public libraries, departments stores, shopping malls and larger public parks all have washrooms.

Tourist Information

Official websites are useful for trip planning and you'll find hundreds of visitor centers across the region. Organizations in smaller regions usually operate under the umbrella of these larger bodies:

Destination British Columbia (www.hellobc.com)

Tourism Yukon (www.travel yukon.com)

Travel Alberta (www.travel alberta.com)

Travelers with Disabilities

➜ Guide dogs may legally be brought into restaurants, hotels as well as other businesses.

➜ Many public service phone numbers and some pay phones are adapted for the hearing impaired.

➜ Most public buildings are wheelchair accessible, and many parks feature trails that are likewise accessible.

➜ Many newer or renovated hotels have dedicated accessible rooms.

➜ Public transportation is increasingly accessible; for example, all buses in Vancouver are fully wheelchair accessible.

➜ Start your trip-planning at Access to Travel (www. accesstotravel.gc.ca), the Canadian federal government's dedicated website. It has information on air, bus, rail and ferry transportation.

➜ Download Lonely Planet's free Accessible Travel guide from http://lptravel.to/ AccessibleTravel

Other helpful resources:

CNIB (☏604-431-2121; www. cnib.ca) Support and services for the visually impaired.

Disability Alliance BC (☏604-875-0188; www.disability alliancebc.org) Programs and support for people with disabilities.

Western Institute for the Deaf & Hard of Hearing (☏604-736-7391; www.widhh.com) Interpreter services and resources for the hearing-impaired.

Visas

Not required for visitors from the US, the Commonwealth and most of Western Europe for stays up to 180 days. Required by those from more than 130 other countries.

Visa-exempt foreign nationals flying to Canada now require an Electronic Travel Authorization (eTA). This excludes US citizens and those who already have a valid Canadian visa. For more information on the eTA, see www.canada.ca/eta. For visa information, visit the website of **Canada Border Services Agency** (☏204-983-3500; www.cbsa.gc.ca).

Women Travelers

➜ BC, Alberta and the Yukon are generally safe places for women traveling alone, although the usual precautions apply: just use the same commonsense you would at home.

➜ In Vancouver, the Main and Hastings Sts area and Stanley Park are best avoided by solo women after dark.

➜ In more remote parts of the province, particularly in Northern BC, women traveling alone will find themselves a distinct minority, although there's no shortage of feisty locals ready to assist a sister in need, especially in the Yukon.

➜ In bars and nightclubs, solo women will probably attract a lot of male attention. If you don't want company, a firm 'No, thank you' typically does the trick. If you feel threatened in an area where there are other people, protesting loudly will usually bring others to your defense.

➜ Note that carrying mace or pepper spray is illegal throughout Canada.

➜ If you are assaulted, call the police immediately. Rape crisis hotlines include those in **Calgary** (☏403-237-5888; www.calgarycasa.com) and **Vancouver** (☏604-872-8212).

Work

→ In almost all cases, non-Canadians need a valid work permit to get a job in Canada. Obtaining one may be difficult, as employment opportunities go to Canadians first. Some jobs are exempt from the permit requirement.

→ For full details on temporary work, check with Citizenship & Immigration Canada (www.cic.gc.ca).

→ Don't try to work without a permit: if you're caught, that will be the end of your Canadian dream.

→ Short-term jobs, such as restaurant and bar work, are generally plentiful in popular tourist spots such as Whistler and Banff, where the turnover is predictably high. Resort websites often have postings.

Useful internet resources for potential job-seekers:

International Experience Canada (www.cic.gc.ca/english/work/iec)

Student Work Abroad Program (www.swap.ca)

Transportation

GETTING THERE & AWAY

British Colombia and Alberta are directly accessible from international and US destinations, while the Yukon usually requires a plane connection. Flights, cars and tours can be booked online at lonelyplanet.com/bookings.

Entering the Region

When flying into Canada, you will be expected to show your passport to an immigration officer and answer a few questions about the duration and purpose of your visit. After clearing customs, you'll be on your way.

Driving across the border from the US can be more complex. Questioning is sometimes more intense and, in some cases, your car may be searched.

Air

BC-bound travelers typically fly into Vancouver. For those heading to the Rockies, arriving in Calgary or Edmonton in Alberta is more convenient; you can then travel to BC via the Rockies before departing from Vancouver. Yukon-bound travelers generally connect to Whitehorse from BC or Alberta.

Airports & Airlines

Abbotsford International Airport (www.abbotsfordairport.ca)

Calgary international Airport (www.yyc.com)

Edmonton International Airport (www.flyeia.com)

Kamloops Airport (www.kamloopsairport.com)

Vancouver International Airport (www.yvr.ca)

Victoria International Airport (www.victoriaairport.com)

Whitehorse International Airport (www.hpw.gov.yk.ca)

Air Canada (www.aircanada.com) and **WestJet** (www.westjet.com) are the main Canadian airlines serving this region, while many international airlines from Europe, Asia and beyond also fly in.

Land

BC is well served by major driving routes, trains and long-distance bus services from across Canada and the US.

From the USA

BUS

Buses travel from the US to destinations in BC and Alberta, where you can connect with Whitehorse in the Yukon.

Vehicles stop at border crossings, and passengers typically have to get off and have passports and visas processed individually.

CLIMATE CHANGE & TRAVEL

Every form of transport that relies on carbon-based fuel generates CO_2, the main cause of human-induced climate change. Modern travel is dependent on airplanes, which might use less fuel per kilometer per person than most cars but travel much greater distances. The altitude at which aircraft emit gases (including CO_2) and particles also contributes to their climate change impact. Many websites offer 'carbon calculators' that allow people to estimate the carbon emissions generated by their journey and, for those who wish to do so, to offset the impact of the greenhouse gases emitted with contributions to portfolios of climate-friendly initiatives throughout the world. Lonely Planet offsets the carbon footprint of all staff and author travel.

The following services all have on-board wi-fi:

Bolt Bus (www.boltbus.com) Cross-border services to Vancouver from Bellingham, Seattle and Portland; bargain prices available if booked far enough in advance.

Greyhound (☑800-661-8747; www.greyhound.ca) Numerous cross-border services. Order tickets online in advance for best prices.

Quick Coach Lines (www.quickcoach.com) Quick Coach Lines Express buses between Seattle, Seattle's Sea-Tac International Airport and downtown Vancouver.

CAR & MOTORCYCLE

The US highway system connects directly with Canadian roads at numerous points along BC and Alberta borders. Gas (petrol) is generally cheaper in the US, so fill up before you head north: Vancouver has a reputation for having each of North America's highest pump prices.

Cars rented in the US can generally be driven over the Canadian border and back, but double-check your rental agreement. Extra charges often apply for each day you spend across the border. Make sure you have all your rental paperwork to hand when crossing the border.

The Blaine Peace Arch and Pacific Hwy border crossings near Vancouver are the region's busiest, especially on holiday weekends: consider the quieter Lynden or Sumas crossings instead. This can sometimes save an hour or two in travel time.

TRAIN

Amtrak (www.amtrak.com) Trundles into Vancouver from US destinations south of the border, including Bellingham, Seattle and Portland. Be aware that buses operate instead of trains on some runs; check at time of booking. You can also connect from San Francisco, Los Angeles, Chicago and beyond. Book ahead for best fares.

Rocky Mountaineer (☑604-606-7245; www.rockymountaineer.com) Luxury train operator offers some departures from Seattle to mountain hot spots north of the border.

From Canada

BUS

Greyhound (☑800-661-8747; www.greyhound.ca) Runs services into Alberta, BC and the Yukon from various points across Canada. Booking ahead and/or online delivers better (but nonrefundable) prices. Photo ID is required for ticket pick-up. Keep in mind that Greyhound services have been reduced on some routes in recent years.

TRAIN

VIA Rail (www.viarail.com) The *Canadian* service trundles into Edmonton, Jasper and Vancouver from Toronto three times a week. It's a slow but highly picturesque trip with a range of tickets, from sleeper cabins to regular seats. Book in advance for best prices.

Sea

Cruise ships arrive from south of the border on the highly popular Alaska run, typically stopping in Vancouver, Victoria or other smaller BC ports en route. Ferry services also arrive in BC from Alaska and Washington State. You'll be expected to clear Canadian customs and immigration at your first port of call here.

Alaska Marine Highway System (www.ferryalaska.com) Services arrive in Prince Rupert from Alaska.

Black Ball Ferry Line (www.cohoferry.com) Services to Victoria from Port Angeles.

Victoria Clipper (www.clippervacations.com) Services to Victoria from Seattle.

Washington State Ferries (www.wsdot.wa.gov/ferries) Services run from Anacortes to Sidney on Vancouver Island.

GETTING AROUND

Air

WestJet (www.westjet.com) and **Air Canada** (www.aircanada.com) are the dominant airlines servicing the region's towns and cities. An extensive network of smaller operators – often using propeller planes or floatplanes – also provide excellent, but not often cheap, quick-hop services. Reduced fares are typically available for advance booking.

Airlines in BC & the Canadian Rockies

Airlines with services to destinations in BC, Alberta and the Yukon include the following:

Air Canada Express (☑888-247-2262; www.aircanada.com) Regional wing of Canada's national airline, serving dozens of communities in BC, Alberta and beyond.

Air North (www.flyairnorth.com) Connecting to Vancouver and serving Yukon communities from its busy Whitehorse base.

Central Mountain Air (www.flycma.com) Serving Interior BC, northern BC and Vancouver Island.

Harbour Air (☑604-274-1277; www.harbourair.com) Floatplane services to Vancouver, Victoria and around BC.

Orca Airways (☑604-270-6722; www.flyorcaair.com) Linking Vancouver and Tofino.

Pacific Coastal Airlines (☑604-273-8666; www.pacificcoastal.com) Linking BC communities including Powell River and Port Hardy to Vancouver.

Salt Spring Air (☑250-537-9880; www.saltspringair.com) Floatplane connections between Vancouver and the Southern Gulf Islands.

WestJet (www.westjet.com) Canada's second major airline crisscrosses BC, Alberta and beyond with dozens of routes.

Bicycle

Cycling is one of the best ways to get around and immerse yourself in the region. With their ever-increasing bike route networks, cities such as Vancouver and Victoria are especially welcoming to cyclists, and Vancouver has a new public bike share scheme.

➡ Helmets are mandatory in BC (and in Alberta for under-18s).

➡ Many forms of public transportation – the BC Ferries system and Vancouver's TransLink buses, for example – enable you to bring your bike.

➡ Off-road mountain biking is highly popular, with some ski resorts transforming into bike parks in summer.

➡ Bike-hire operators are common, even in smaller towns. You'll likely need a credit card for a deposit; rental rates are typically from $30 per day.

Area resources:

Alberta Bicycle Association (www.albertabicycle.ab.ca)

British Columbia Cycling Coalition (www.bccc.bc.ca)

Cycling Association of Yukon (www.yukoncycling.com)

HUB (www.bikehub.ca)

Mountain Biking BC (www.mountainbikingbc.ca)

Boat

BC Ferries (☑888-223-3779; www.bcferries.com) runs 35 vessels on 24 routes around the province's coastal waters. Its extensive network includes frequent busy runs on giant 'superferries' between the mainland and Vancouver Island. Many other routes, with much smaller vessels, link shoreline communities and the Gulf Islands. The signature long-haul route is from Port Hardy to Prince Rupert, a day-long glide along the spectacular Inside Passage.

➡ Many of the routes are vehicle-accessible but walk-on passengers pay much lower fares.

➡ Low season fares are usually cheaper.

➡ Larger vessels are equipped with restaurants, shops and (sometimes patchy) wi-fi.

Popular routes:

Lower Mainland to Vancouver Island The two busiest routes are from Tsawwassen (an hour's drive south of Vancouver) to Swartz Bay (30 minutes north of Victoria), and from Horseshoe Bay (30 minutes north of downtown Vancouver) to Departure Bay near Nanaimo on central Vancouver Island. Vehicle reservations are recommended for summer and weekend travel.

Inside Passage Among one of the most scenic boat trips in the world. Summer service is scheduled for 15-hour daylight runs between Port Hardy and Prince Rupert, in different directions on alternate days. Sailings between October and May typically include stops in tiny Aboriginal villages and can take up to two days. Reserve ahead, especially in summer peak. Additional ferries connect to Haida Gwaii from Prince Rupert.

Bowen Island An excellent and accessible day trip from Vancouver. Hop a transit bus from downtown to West Vancouver's Horseshoe Bay terminal, slide through mountain-framed waters for 20 minutes and arrive in Snug Cove for restaurants, shops and scenic walks.

Bus

Several intercity bus services operate in this region. Transit services are most extensive in big cities such as Vancouver, Victoria, Calgary and Edmonton but are also present in many smaller communities.

Brewster Transportation (☑403-762-6700; www.brewster.ca) Runs regular services between Jasper, Banff and Lake Louise.

Greyhound Canada (☑800-661-8747; www.greyhound.ca) Covers routes in BC and Alberta, and has services into Whitehorse in the Yukon. Booking online delivers lower rates. Note some routes have reduced frequency in recent years.

Moose Travel Network (☑604-297-0255; www.moosenetwork.com) Backpacker bus routes across the region, linking Vancouver, Vancouver Island and the Rockies.

Snowbus (☑604-451-1130; www.snowbus.com) Popular winter-only ski-bus service between Vancouver and Whistler.

Tofino Bus (☑250-725-2871; www.tofinobus.com) Operates Vancouver Island services, many of them former Greyhound Canada routes.

SAILING THE INSIDE PASSAGE

Taking a **BC Ferries** (☑888-223-3779; www.bcferries.com) cruise along the stunning Inside Passage is likely to be the transportation highlight of your trip. Expect to see marine life ranging from whales to dolphins to lazy-looking seals lounging on the rocky shoreline. Look for eagles overhead and bears on the shore as you spend hours passing deserted islands and rocky coasts accented by waterfalls. On these runs, the crews are famously friendly and the captain will slow the ship when, say, a pod of orcas swims past. You'll spend most of your time basking on deck, but consider paying extra for a tiny cabin so you can really chill out.

SAMPLE GREYHOUND BUS ROUTES

ROUTE	TIME (HR)	FREQUENCY (DAILY)	ONE-WAY FARE ($)
Calgary–Edmonton	4	6	50
Kamloops–Vancouver	5	6	59
Vancouver–Whistler	2½	4	27
Edmonton–Jasper	5	1	70.50
Vancouver–Calgary	15	6	95

Car & Motorcycle

Despite the huge area covered by BC, Alberta and the Yukon, driving is the best way to get around. Highways are generally excellent.

Driving Licences

Your home driver's license is valid for up to six months in BC. If you plan to drive here for longer, you'll need an International Drivers Permit.

Fuel

Gasoline is sold in liters in Canada, and it's typically more expensive than in the US. Gas prices are usually much higher in remote areas than in the cities.

Hire

Major car-rental firms have offices at airports in BC, Alberta and Whitehorse, as well as in larger city centers. In smaller towns there may be independent firms.

➡ Clarify your insurance coverage for incidents such as gravel damage if you're going to be driving off major paved roads.

➡ Shop around for deals but watch out for offers that don't include unlimited kilometers.

➡ Never buy the rental-car company's gas, if offered when you pick up your car; it's a bad deal. Buy your own and return it full.

➡ If you are considering a one-way rental, be aware of high fees.

➡ Generally you must be over 25 to rent a car; some companies rent to those aged between 21 and 24 for an additional premium.

➡ Regular rates for an economy-sized vehicle are typically between $45 and $75 per day.

All the usual rental companies operate in the region, including the following:

Avis (☎800-230-4898; www.avis.ca)

Budget (☎800-268-8900; www.budget.ca)

Enterprise (☎800-261-7331; www.enterprise.ca)

Hertz (☎800-654-3001; www.hertz.ca)

National (☎877-222-9058; www.nationalcar.ca)

Zipcar (☎866-494-7227; www.zipcar.ca)

Recreational Vehicles

Recreational vehicles (RVs) are hugely popular in Western Canada, and rentals must be booked well in advance of the summer season. One-way rentals are possible, but you'll pay a surcharge. Also budget plenty for fuel as RVs typically get miserable mileage.

Large rental companies have offices in Vancouver, Calgary, Whitehorse and bigger BC towns. Operators include the following:

CanaDream (☎888-480-9726; www.canadream.com)

West Coast Mountain Campers (☎604-940-2171; www.wcm-campers.com)

Road Hazards

It's best to avoid driving in areas with heavy snow, but if you do, be sure your vehicle has snow tires or tire chains as well as an emergency kit of blankets etc. If you get stuck, don't stay in the car with the engine running: every year people die of carbon monoxide poisoning. A single candle burning in the car will keep it reasonably warm.

Make sure the vehicle you're driving is in good condition and carry tools, flares, water, food and a spare tire. Rural areas usually do not have cell-phone service.

Be careful on logging roads as logging trucks always have the right of way and often pay little heed to other vehicles. It's best not to drive on logging roads at all during weekday working hours.

Gravel roads – such as those in the Yukon – can take a toll on windshields and tires. Keep a good distance from the vehicle in front. When you see an oncoming vehicle (or a vehicle overtakes you), slow down and keep well to the right.

Wild animals are a potential hazard. Most run-ins with deer, moose and other critters occur at night when wildlife is active and visibility is poor. Many areas have roadside signs alerting drivers to possible animal crossings. Continuously scan both sides of the road and be prepared to stop or swerve. A vehicle's headlights will often mesmerize an animal, leaving it frozen in the middle of the road.

For updates on driving conditions around the region:

Alberta (www.amaroadreports.ca)

BC (www.drivebc.ca)

Yukon (www.511yukon.ca)

SAMPLE DRIVING DISTANCES

ROUTE	DISTANCE (KM)	TIME (HR)
Banff–Fernie	360	4
Calgary–Edmonton	300	3½
Edmonton–Jasper	365	4
Jasper–Banff	290	4
Kelowna–Banff	480	6
Prince George–Prince Rupert	705	8½
Prince Rupert–Whitehorse (via Stewart-Cassiar Hwy)	1375	19
Vancouver–Kelowna	390	4
Vancouver–Prince George	790	9
Whitehorse–Dawson City	530	7

Road Rules

North Americans drive on the right side of the road. Speed limits, which are posted in kilometers per hour in Canada, are generally 50km/h in built-up areas and 90km/h on highways. A right turn is permitted at a red light after you have come to a complete stop, as is a left turn from a one-way street onto another one-way street. U-turns are not allowed. Traffic in both directions must stop when stationary school buses have their red lights flashing – this means that children are getting off and on. In cities with pedestrian crosswalks, cars must stop to allow pedestrians to cross.

Seat belt use is compulsory in Canada. Children under the age of five must be in a restraining seat. Motorcyclists must use lights and wear helmets. The blood-alcohol limit when driving is 0.08% (about two drinks) and is strictly enforced with heavy fines, bans and jail terms.

Local Transportation

There is excellent, widespread local public transportation in Vancouver and Victoria, BC, and in Calgary and Edmonton, Alberta. Outside these areas, service can be sparse or infrequent.

Public transit in Whitehorse will suffice for getting around town but you'll have a hard time traveling further around the Yukon without a car.

Train

Passenger train services are limited in BC and virtually nonexistent in Alberta.

Via Rail

National carrier **VIA Rail** (www.viarail.com) has scant services, including just one route from Vancouver. Book ahead in all cases: advance tickets offer the best deals and there are regular specials online, especially in low season.

Vancouver to Jasper The *Canadian* departs three times a week and makes a few stops in BC before reaching Jasper, Alberta. The 18½-hour trip takes in some beautiful scenery; fares start at $220 and rise exponentially for a private sleeping cabin with gourmet meals and access to the dome car. From Jasper, connect to Prince Rupert or continue on the *Canadian* through Alberta, the Prairies and on to Toronto (3½ days from Vancouver).

Jasper to Prince Rupert A daytime-only trip with an overnight stay in Prince George, and stops in Terrace, New Hazelton, Smithers, Houston and Burns Lake. You must organize your own lodgings in Prince George. Fares start at $205. Deluxe service with observation car available in summer.

Vancouver Island recently lost its VIA Rail service between Victoria and Courtenay but there is a determined effort to restore it. For updates, visit www.islandrail.ca.

Rocky Mountaineer

A major player in region, the luxury **Rocky Mountaineer** (✆604-606-7245; www.rockymountaineer.com) runs multiday services from Vancouver through the Rocky Mountains into Alberta. Trains travel at 'Polaroid speed,' so you can get all the photos you need.

Behind the Scenes

SEND US YOUR FEEDBACK

We love to hear from travelers – your comments keep us on our toes and help make our books better. Our well-traveled team reads every word on what you loved or loathed about this book. Although we cannot reply individually to your submissions, we always guarantee that your feedback goes straight to the appropriate authors, in time for the next edition. Each person who sends us information is thanked in the next edition – the most useful submissions are rewarded with a selection of digital PDF chapters.

Visit **lonelyplanet.com/contact** to submit your updates and suggestions or to ask for help. Our award-winning website also features inspirational travel stories, news and discussions.

Note: We may edit, reproduce and incorporate your comments in Lonely Planet products such as guidebooks, websites and digital products, so let us know if you don't want your comments reproduced or your name acknowledged. For a copy of our privacy policy visit lonelyplanet.com/privacy.

OUR READERS

Many thanks to the travelers who used the last edition and wrote to us with helpful hints, useful advice and interesting anecdotes: Barry Humphries, Benjamin Steegmans, Brian Stepanek, Catherine Putz, Daniel Griffiths, Emma Blow, Greg Rose, Ilona Bicker, Jaqueline Welburn, Ronald Wilson, Wendy Bradley

WRITER THANKS

John Lee

Special thanks to Maggie for ensuring my sanity and delivering copious amounts of tea during the write-up for this project. Thanks also to our feline companion Max for grooming my beard on a regular basis. And cheers to my buddy Dominic for joining me on that elongated Vancouver Island road-trip. Sincere apologies to all my other Vancouver friends and family for being stuck to my keyboard for so long; I'm more than ready for a beer or two now.

Korina Miller

Thank-you to Alex Howard for inviting me to join this project and to the team of travel-thirsty authors who helped make it great. Thank-you to the many Albertans who shared their stories, insight and love for their province. Thanks to Kajsa Erickson for acquainting me with Calgary's wilder side during the height of Stampede; to my parents and daughters, Simone and Monique, for camping out in the Rockies with me; and to Kirk and Bing for keeping the home fires burning. And finally, thanks to my chiropractor, Dr Bob Mabee for straightening me out after driving 4500km in 10 days.

Ryan Ver Berkmoes

The number of folks to thank outnumber Kermode bears but here's a few: Ben Greensfelder, my fearless co-pilot who kept the supply of good beer flowing. In Prince Rupert, I am beyond indebted to Bruce Wishart for literally food, folks and fun. And words can't repay the car shuttle service. In Dawson, Tony and the gang almost made me forget my visit. Finally, to Alexis Ver Berkmoes, who I love even more than the giant beaver.

ACKNOWLEDGEMENTS

Climate map data adapted from Peel MC, Finlayson BL & McMahon TA (2007) 'Updated World Map of the Köppen-Geiger Climate Classification', Hydrology and Earth System Sciences, 11, 1633–44.

Cover photograph: Grizzly bears, Chilcotin, British Columbia, Claudio Bacinello/500px ©

THIS BOOK

This 7th edition of Lonely Planet's *British Columbia & the Canadian Rockies* guidebook was researched and written by John Lee, Korina Miller and Ryan Ver Berkmoes. The previous two editions were also written by John Lee, Brendan Sainsbury and Ryan Ver Berkmoes. This guidebook was produced by the following:

Destination Editor Alexander Howard

Product Editor Alison Ridgway

Senior Cartographer Corey Hutchison

Book Designer Michael Buick

Assisting Editors Imogen Bannister, Carly Hall, Ali Lemer, Kate Mathews, Kate Morgan, Jenna Myers, Kristin Odijk, Susan Paterson, Gabbi Stefanos, Saralinda Turner

Cover Researcher Naomi Parker

Thanks to Andi Jones, Katherine Marsh, Wayne Murphy, Claire Naylor, Karyn Noble, Tony Wheeler

Index

Map Legend

Sights
- Beach
- Bird Sanctuary
- Buddhist
- Castle/Palace
- Christian
- Confucian
- Hindu
- Islamic
- Jain
- Jewish
- Monument
- Museum/Gallery/Historic Building
- Ruin
- Shinto
- Sikh
- Taoist
- Winery/Vineyard
- Zoo/Wildlife Sanctuary
- Other Sight

Activities, Courses & Tours
- Bodysurfing
- Diving
- Canoeing/Kayaking
- Course/Tour
- Sento Hot Baths/Onsen
- Skiing
- Snorkeling
- Surfing
- Swimming/Pool
- Walking
- Windsurfing
- Other Activity

Sleeping
- Sleeping
- Camping

Eating
- Eating

Drinking & Nightlife
- Drinking & Nightlife
- Cafe

Entertainment
- Entertainment

Shopping
- Shopping

Information
- Bank
- Embassy/Consulate
- Hospital/Medical
- Internet
- Police
- Post Office
- Telephone
- Toilet
- Tourist Information
- Other Information

Geographic
- Beach
- Gate
- Hut/Shelter
- Lighthouse
- Lookout
- Mountain/Volcano
- Oasis
- Park
- Pass
- Picnic Area
- Waterfall

Population
- Capital (National)
- Capital (State/Province)
- City/Large Town
- Town/Village

Transport
- Airport
- BART station
- Border crossing
- Boston T station
- Bus
- Cable car/Funicular
- Cycling
- Ferry
- Metro/Muni station
- Monorail
- Parking
- Petrol station
- Subway/SkyTrain station
- Taxi
- Train station/Railway
- Tram
- Underground station
- Other Transport

Note: Not all symbols displayed above appear on the maps in this book

Routes
- Tollway
- Freeway
- Primary
- Secondary
- Tertiary
- Lane
- Unsealed road
- Road under construction
- Plaza/Mall
- Steps
- Tunnel
- Pedestrian overpass
- Walking Tour
- Walking Tour detour
- Path/Walking Trail

Boundaries
- International
- State/Province
- Disputed
- Regional/Suburb
- Marine Park
- Cliff
- Wall

Hydrography
- River, Creek
- Intermittent River
- Canal
- Water
- Dry/Salt/Intermittent Lake
- Reef

Areas
- Airport/Runway
- Beach/Desert
- Cemetery (Christian)
- Cemetery (Other)
- Glacier
- Mudflat
- Park/Forest
- Sight (Building)
- Sportsground
- Swamp/Mangrove

OUR STORY

A beat-up old car, a few dollars in the pocket and a sense of adventure. In 1972 that's all Tony and Maureen Wheeler needed for the trip of a lifetime – across Europe and Asia overland to Australia. It took several months, and at the end – broke but inspired – they sat at their kitchen table writing and stapling together their first travel guide, *Across Asia on the Cheap*. Within a week they'd sold 1500 copies. Lonely Planet was born.

Today, Lonely Planet has offices in Franklin, London, Melbourne, Oakland, Dublin, Beijing and Delhi, with more than 600 staff and writers. We share Tony's belief that 'a great guidebook should do three things: inform, educate and amuse'.

OUR WRITERS

John Lee

British Columbia, Plan, Understand, Survival Guide Originally from the UK, John moved to British Columbia to study at the University of Victoria in the 1990s. Eventually staying and moving to Vancouver, he started a freelance travel-writing career in 1999. Since then, he's been covering the region and beyond for Lonely Planet plus magazines, newspapers and online outlets around the world. Winner of numerous writing awards, he's very active on Twitter and a weekly columnist for Canada's the *Globe* and *Mail* national newspaper; catch up with him at www.johnleewriter.com.

Korina Miller

Alberta Korina grew up on Vancouver Island and has been exploring the globe independently since she was 16, visiting or living in 36 countries and picking up a degree in Communications and Canadian Studies, an MA in Migration Studies and a diploma in Visual Arts en route. As a writer and editor, Korina has worked on nearly 60 titles for Lonely Planet and has also worked with LP.com, BBC, The *Independent*, *The Guardian*, BBC5 and CBC, as well as many independent magazines, covering travel, art and culture. She has currently set up camp back in Victoria, soaking up the mountain views and the pounding surf.

Ryan Ver Berkmoes

British Columbia, Yukon Territory Ryan Ver Berkmoes has written more than 110 guidebooks for Lonely Planet. He grew up in Santa Cruz, California, which he left at age 17 for college in the Midwest, where he first discovered snow. All joy of this novelty soon wore off. Since then he has been traveling the world, both for pleasure and for work – which are often indistinguishable. He has covered everything from wars to bars. He definitely prefers the latter. Ryan calls New York City home. Read more at ryanverberkmoes.com and at @ryanvb.

Published by Lonely Planet Global Limited
CRN 554153
7th edition – April 2017
ISBN 978 1 78657 337 7
© Lonely Planet 2017   Photographs © as indicated 2017
10 9 8 7 6 5 4 3 2 1
Printed in China